Major Butler's Legacy

Major Pierce Butler, 1744–1822. (National Archives.)

MALCOLM BELL, JR.

Major Butler's Legacy

Five Generations of a Slaveholding Family

BROWN THRASHER BOOKS
The University of Georgia Press
Athens and London

Designed by Sandra Strother Hudson
Maps by James Ingram and Terri Ainley,
Cartographic Services, The University of Georgia
Set in Mergenthaler 10 on 13 Sabon
by The Composing Room of Michigan

The paper in this book meets the guidelines for permanence
and durability of the Committee on Production
Guidelines for Book Longevity of the Council
on Library Resources.

Printed in the United States of America
93 92 91 90 89   5 4 3 2 1

Library of Congress Cataloging in Publication Data
Bell, Malcolm, 1913–
    Major Butler's legacy.
    "Brown thrasher books."
    Bibliography: p.
    Includes index.
    1. Butler, Pierce, 1744–1822. 2. Butler family.
3. Plantation owners—Georgia—Biography.
4. Plantation owners—South Carolina—Biography. 5. Plantation
life—Georgia—History—19th century. 6. Plantation
life—South Carolina—History—19th century.
I. Title.
F290.B96B45 1987   975.8'03'0924 [B]   86-11353
ISBN 0-8203-0897-8
ISBN 0-8203-1177-4 (pbk.)

FOR MURIEL

Contents

vii

 *Illustrations*

ix

🦋 Acknowledgments

IN MY SEARCH for the substance that became *Major Butler's Legacy* I was assisted by many people in divers ways. None were more generous and more patient in their help than the professional staffs of two venerable institutions, the Historical Society of Pennsylvania in Philadelphia and the Georgia Historical Society in Savannah. I also found helping hands elsewhere. Following the path of Butler history led me to the Library Company of Philadelphia; the Library of Congress, the National Archives, and the Folger Shakespeare Library in Washington; the Georgia Department of Archives and History, the Lenox Library Association, the Midway Museum, the Museum of Coastal History on St. Simons Island, and the Newport Historical Society; the South Caroliniana Library and the South Carolina Department of Archives and History in Columbia; the South Carolina Historical Society in Charleston, the Southern Historical Collection of my old school, the University of North Carolina; and the Savannah Public Library.

Further afield I was well received and well rewarded by finding footprints of Major Butler and his son Thomas at London's great British Library. Again, Thomas Butler, and his bride Eliza de Mallevault, left a record at Fort de France in the Archives Departmentales de la Martinique. In Halifax, at the splendid Legislative Library and in the Public Archives of Nova Scotia there were traces of Major Butler when he served King George III, and of the 138 Butler slaves the king's navy had removed from St. Simons Island.

My gratitude is extended in full measure to the Historical Society of Pennsylvania's Linda Stanley and to their former staff member Bruce Laverty, who came to calling me "Major Butler." The same measure of gratitude is due Barbara Bennett and Anne Smith of the Georgia Historical

Society, and their former director Anthony R. Dees. Three old friends, Alexander Heard, Lawrence London, and William Shellman, eased my way into acceptance at the Folger Library. In Savannah, assistance came from historian Julia Floyd Smith; from Antoinette Goodrich; Rusty Fleetwood; neighbor Jacqueline Levine, who presented me with two old Kemble volumes; Preston Russell, M.D.; Jeanne Hunter; Hugh Stiles Golson; Gordon Smith; Harold Preble and his *Captain Hinckley;* and Clermont Lee, whose record of Major Butler's marmalade proposal was given cheerfully. Other Georgians who have helped are Jack Ladson; Mae Ruth Green; James Burke McEllinn; Burnette Vanstory, who was quick and generous in sharing with me her knowledge of Georgia's sea islands; Lewis Larson, Georgia's official archaeologist; Reed Ferguson; "Lucky" Lowe, who retrieved from St. Simon's waters the Swaim's Panacea bottle that once contained Roswell King, Jr.'s favorite cure-all for Butler slaves; Mary L. Waters, who unearthed the old map of Butler's Island; part-time Georgian and full-time historian Mary R. Bullard of Cumberland Island and South Dartmouth, Massachusetts, who pointed me in the right direction for my 1812 chapter.

Nicholas B. Wainwright's *Philadelphia Perspective;* Robert Manson Myers's *Children of Pride;* fellow "Kemblers" J. C. Furnas for his *Fanny Kemble* and John Anthony Scott for his enlightened edition of Fanny Kemble's plantation *Journal;* all have won my respect and admiration for their fine works that have enhanced *Major Butler's Legacy.*

I give special thanks to Alexander Gaudieri for his translation from Old and Modern French, to Mrs. Peter S. Elek, to James E. Bell and his Irish spouse Elizabeth for their research in her native land, to William Keating for many favors in London, to a gracious Martinican, Emile Hayot, to Nancy Gill, who somehow used a late twentieth-century machine to computerize a rough manuscript that described life in the eighteenth and nineteenth centuries.

Persistent encouragement came from Muriel Bell, to whom the book is dedicated, and from our sons Craig and Malcolm Bell III, the latter who read the work with professorial eyes and gave sound advice. The same can be said for newfound friend Eugene D. Genovese. I thank other readers of the manuscript of *Major Butler's Legacy.* First, Admiral Ben Scott Custer, who is another new friend, and then, the two readers who reviewed the work for the University of Georgia Press. These two were hardly unstinting in their praise, but should find *some* improvement in the finished work from the manuscript that often set them on edge. Malcolm L. Call and his staff at the University of Georgia Press, in particular, Debra Winter, a skilled and tolerant editor, and Sandra Hudson, the talented designer who has produced a book that is handsome to behold, all have won my respect and gratitude.

Finally, my thanks are cheerfully extended to two Butler descendants who have made my task easier, and who are, if you will, grandchildren of the crusty old soldier, three greats for each. They are Colonel Sir Thomas Butler, the twelfth baronet of Cloughrenan, and Francis Kemble Wister Stokes, author and family historian. Both share the interesting background that has given my life in retirement an agreeable and illuminating extra dimension.

The Butler Family Chart

Sir Richard Butler
1699–1771
m.
Henrietta Percy
1720?–1794

Thomas Middleton
1719–1766
m.
Mary Bull
1723–1760

PIERCE BUTLER
1744–1822
m. 1771
MARY MIDDLETON
d. 1790

Sarah
1772?–1831
m. 1800
James Mease
1771–1845

Anne Elizabeth
1774–1854

Frances
1774–1836

Harriot Percy
1775?–1815

Pierce
1777–1780

Thomas
1778–1838
m. 1812
Eliza de Mallevault
1792–183?

3d son
(d. young)

4th son
(d. young)

1. Buried as Pierce Butler, Jr.
2. Name changed from Mease to Butler, 1831.
3. Name changed from Mease to Butler, 1826.
4. Name changed from McAllister to Butler, 1862.

Pierce Butler[1]
1801–1810

Mary Middleton
1802–1884
m. 1832
Alfred L. Elwyn
1804–1884

Mary Middleton
d. 1862
m. 1858
S. Weir Mitchell
1829–1914

John K.
1860?–1917

Langdon Elwyn
1862–1935

Thomas
1803–1823

John[2]
1806–1847
m. 1827
Gabriella Morris
d. 1871

Pierce Butler
1828–1830

Elizabeth Manigault
1830–1862
m. 1848
Julian McAllister
1824–1887

John
1850–1850

Julia
1851–1930

Francis[4]
1853–1863

Gabriella
1854–1940

Margaret Elizabeth
1859–1946

Frances
1808–1880
m. 1837
George Cadwalader
1804–1879

Pierce Butler[3]
1810–1867
m. 1834
Frances Anne Kemble
1809–1893

Sarah
1835–1908
m. 1859
Owen J. Wister
1825–1896

Frances Kemble
1838–1910
m. 1871
James W. Leigh
d. 1923

Owen
1860–1938
m. 1898
Mary Channing Wister
1870–1913

Alice Dudley
1874–1965
m. 1906
Sir Richard Pierce Butler
1872–1955

Pierce Butler
1876–1876

Pierce Butler
1879–1879

Francis
1815?–1835?

Louis
1817–1890

John
1819?–188?
m.
Elizabeth

Anne
182?–1823

 *Introduction*

M Y OWN INTRODUCTION to the Butler family came in 1979 when I began preparation of a short paper on the great auction sale of "A Gang of 460 Negroes" at Savannah's Ten Broeck racecourse, an event well documented in an article written by the *New York Tribune*'s star reporter Mortimer Thomson, who was known by the pseudonym "Doesticks." The sale, in 1859, consisted of one-half of the slaves who worked the Butler plantations on Georgia's Altamaha River estuary. Many of these people had been owned by Major Pierce Butler when he died in 1822 in Philadelphia, whence he directed his capable work force that had numbered almost six hundred slaves. Their "issue and increase" had largely accounted for the expansion to more than nine hundred in the ensuing years. He had willed the plantations and the slaves to the young sons of his daughter, Sarah Butler Mease of Philadelphia. Two of the three grandsons had changed their name from Mease to Butler to qualify for Major Butler's inheritance, and one of these, a wastrel, was forced to convert his "Negro property" to cash to cover massive debts.

Research into the life and times of the Butlers both before and after the 1859 auction led me well beyond the intended short paper and into what has become a book-length study of one family's deep involvement with those whom Major Butler had called "the Wretched Affricans." I found the involvement to be highly significant, for few families can have played a role comparable to that of the Butlers in the Southern slave economy—from colonial times through emancipation in the 1860s and beyond into the difficult years of freedom.

When, in 1767, Pierce Butler first visited South Carolina, he was a major in George III's Twenty-ninth Regiment, and as a third son of an Irish baronet was denied succession to title and family fortune. He courted and wed Mary Middleton, the daughter of the aristocratic Colonel Thomas Middleton, a low-country planter, slave owner and dealer who imported slaves from Africa and the West Indies. The Butler-Middleton marriage in Charlestown in 1771 won fortune, if not title, for the young Irish officer who relished his acceptance into an important family with many influential connections. Mary Butler's inheritance of a share of her grandmother Mary Bull's vast estate brought several plantations and hundreds of black people under their immediate control. Thus began the Butler dependency on the institution of slavery.

Major Butler's turn to the Georgia plantations came just before the Revolution, when he was offered potentially valuable land on St. Simons Island at the mouth of the Altamaha River. The acceptance of the attractive offer ended his uncertainty about remaining loyal to the Crown, for he sold his commission in the British army and used the proceeds to purchase what came to be well known as Pierce Butler's Hampton plantation. This capable soldier's acceptance of the patriot's cause lacked both inspiration and enthusiasm. Not until the Butler South Carolina plantations were laid low and the long war ended did he give more than half-hearted support to his adopted country.

After serving several terms in the state legislature, Pierce Butler was appointed in 1787 as a South Carolina delegate to the Constitutional Convention in Philadelphia. Black slaves outnumbered the white inhabitants of South Carolina, and Major Butler had a considerable personal interest in the enslaved population. This fact influenced his actions at the convention, where his position on slavery was forthright and his arguments for its preservation numerous and contentious. No slave state delegate had more to do with fitting those held in bondage into the United States Constitution than did he. His intense interest in government led to his continuation as a member of the South Carolina legislature and to an appointment as his state's first United States senator. On the federal scene, he maintained his adamant advocacy of slavery but in other senatorial matters demonstrated frequent inconsistencies, belligerent obstinacy, and a persistent tendency to alienate his fellow members of the Congress.

The wastrel grandson who was forced to auction his inherited slaves was the Pierce Butler—born Pierce Butler Mease—whose volatile wife, the English actress Frances Anne Kemble, visited the Georgia plantations in 1838 and 1839. There she recorded her vivid impressions in a journal that was to be published a generation later in London and New York after the tempestuous Butler-Kemble marriage had ended in divorce, and civil war raged in America. I found that her account of the Georgia plantations, which created a furor of doubt and disbelief, is fully justified by the content of the weekly reports of Major Butler's plantation managers and by other records, including those kept by the Major's spinster daughter Frances Butler and by succeeding inheritors. The last of the family to own the Georgia lands was Major Butler's great-great-grandson, Owen Wister, the writer. The Butler saga ends in the early 1900s when he sold the final portion of the agricultural empire where Butler slaves had sustained the family through the successive generations.

The list of well-known men and women who are a part of this history is long, their roles varied and interesting. From South Carolina, the Middletons, Pinckneys, Bulls, Izards, Rutledges, Laurenses, Guerards, and Brewtons. From Philadelphia, the Fishers, Thomas Sully, Rebecca Gratz, the Doctors Rush, Deborah Norris Logan, the Cadwaladers, and the Wisters. On the national scene, George Washington, John Adams, James Monroe, Aaron Burr, once a refugee on a Butler plantation after killing Alexander Hamilton, Benjamin Franklin, General William T. Sherman, and Theodore Roosevelt. In England, where Major Butler's only living son attended school for eleven years—years well documented by a collection of letters in the British Library—there were the Kembles, their kinfolk and friends. Butler-Kemble daughters married a Philadelphia Wister and an English Leigh. Sarah Butler Wister had a "Jamesian" romance with Henry James. Frances Butler's husband James Wentworth Leigh became the dean of the cathedral at Hereford, but not before operating the plantations in Georgia where he established a church for blacks that continues today. He appears briefly, thinly disguised as the amiable vicar of Lockleigh, in Henry James's *Portrait of a Lady*, a work that also reflects much of the Rome the author and Sarah Wister knew together.

The slaves were bought and sold, punished and rewarded, and battered in three wars. In cold Nova Scotia there are now descendants of the 138 Butler slaves who were taken there by the British in the War of 1812, given the surname Butler and freed. The 1859 auction of the Pierce Butler slaves was said by them to be "a weeping time," and that it was. That some who were sold found their way back to the Altamaha plantations is evident from family records of postwar years when Major Butler's great-granddaughter Frances Butler Leigh operated the old places with free blacks and Irish immigrants as laborers. Also, their reappearance is revealed in the 1870 census that listed those who returned to familiar homes with surnames of their own choosing.

Savannah's Ten Broeck racecourse, where the auction of the Butler slaves occurred, is now lost in the maze of factory sites and industrial development that has obliterated the once-thriving economy that sprung from cotton, rice, and the labor of slaves. The Butler plantations, too, those of South Carolina and Georgia, have lost almost all identity as such. The only land once planted by the Butler family and at least "called" a plantation today is now owned by a descendant of slaves, a one-time boxer and former heavyweight champion of the world. The other plantations have become real estate developments, wildlife refuges, or are now abandoned marshes and lands returning to what Fanny Kemble called "the wild treasury of nature." Likewise, Major Butler's comfortable Philadelphia homes were long ago swept away by the growth and changes of a modern city.

Today a southbound traveler will find rare natural beauty surrounding that stretch of Interstate 95 as it cuts across Coastal Georgia just to the west of the small town of Darien, where the roadway breaks out of the high land to cross the low marshlands and islands of the strange, alluvial-rich estuary of the Altamaha River. The Scots who founded Darien to protect the young colony from the Spanish in Florida would hardly agree to the calling of any land in McIntosh County high land, but to the slaves who worked the low delta rice fields of the Butler plantation, the north bank of the Altamaha was high indeed. Interstate 95 crosses Butler's Island where Major Butler cultivated rice, sugar, occasional crops of cotton, and in his own fashion, black slaves. Hampton plantation was downstream from Butler's Island, some ten miles to the east and on the northern point of St. Simons Island. With Hampton in mind, Major Butler once wrote, "I go more largely on cotton than any other planter in America."

Hampton today, like Butler's Island, has been long abandoned as a working plantation. It is just now succumbing to a transitory development that has obliterated most traces of the planter economy that flourished in the years between the American Revolution and the Civil War, long years of slavery.

After the Revolution Pierce Butler planted these Georgia lands under laws put forth by his own hand at the Constitutional Convention of 1787. Butler's Island and Hampton were part and parcel of the institution of slavery, so bitterly attacked and so vigorously defended from colonial times until 1865, when the slaves were freed by the Thirteenth Amendment, long after Major Butler's death. His plantations witnessed the bitterness of the difficult years of reconstruction and produced their full share of the problems that boiled over from slavery's cauldron, problems that confront America even today.

That the lives of the Butlers and the transition of their lands can be traced from the mid-1700s until the present is due to the fortuitous protection of family records, their correspondence, and the correspondence of those with whom they communicated. These records include an assortment of unusual last wills and testaments, other documents that reveal details of property transfers—including slaves, inventories of blacks, records of their births and deaths, their escapes, recoveries, and punishments—and of the production of cotton, rice, sugar, and other plantation produce.

The Butler plantations were affected by the great events of history. They were raided by the British in the Revolution, many of their slaves freed in the War of 1812, and ultimately all were freed by the Union army and navy in the Civil War. Although Butler letters and documents are scattered, there are concentrations in Philadelphia, Washington, London, Charleston, Columbia, and Savannah. These, together with pertinent and peripheral material from other libraries, including Chapel Hill, Halifax, and Martinique, and with published journals, biographies, and histories, offer a remarkable documentation of the ownership of plantations through the times of slavery into the years following emancipation. My most recent research came from two of Major Butler's letterbooks acquired by the Historical Society of Pennsylvania in 1984. They had been found in France by an American soldier in World War I, taken to Beloit College in Wisconsin, and there remained through the ensuing years.

Major Butler's military and civil career is reasonably well documented in the official records of the British army and in those of the Constitutional Convention, the United States Senate and the South Carolina legislature. The prominence or notoriety of family members—in particular Major Butler, his grandson Pierce Butler and wife Fanny Kemble, and their grandson Owen Wister—made incidents in their lives worthy of notice in the press, biographies, histories, and of inclusion in many contemporary journals and diaries. The best of the latter is the Philadelphia journal of Sidney George Fisher. The most valuable of the Butler family journals were the two kept by Fanny Kemble, but the intermittent diaries of her daughter, Sarah Butler Wister, helped immensely in presenting an accurate depiction of the family's course through difficult times. Fanny Kemble's three biographical collections of her letters complement the journals and together with the published memoirs of Frances and Dean

Leigh bring the last years of slavery and the early years of freedom into sharp focus. Finally, the interesting observations of Owen Wister, and years later, those of his daughter, Mrs. Walter Stokes, whose sensitive and evocative portrayal of family history was edited and published by her as Fanny Kemble Wister, round out a remarkable spread of personal commentary over a span of generations of this unusual family and of their entanglement with the legacy of the progenitor, Major Pierce Butler. It was Mrs. Stokes, more than any other, who was responsible for the care and protection of the family papers. The Butler and Wister collections she deposited at the Historical Society of Pennsylvania and at the Library of Congress in Owen Wister's name were highly important in the research and writing of the present work.

In assembling material for *Major Butler's Legacy,* I have been aided by many able librarians who have guided me to and through the Butler family records and into the journals and collections of their contemporaries. Adding the results of all of this to commentary and items from newspapers, official records from federal, state, and county archives, has made the research that brings it all together a new and challenging experience for one whose professional field was the world of finance.

Major Butler's Legacy

Chapter 1

Carolina Gentry

The princely warrior is growing up manfully And in a manner of prowess is already fit for a spouse.

I N 1765, His Majesty's ship *Thunderer,* 74 guns, transported the colorful Twenty-ninth Regiment of Foot to King George III's distant North American outpost of Halifax, Nova Scotia. The Twenty-ninth, once called Thomas Farrington's Regiment and later known as the "Worcestershire," had come from Ireland, where successive tours of duty had imparted a distinctive Irish cast to the organization. Even more distinctive was the splendid regimental band. Ten black drummers, all former slaves captured from the French on the island of Guadeloupe, gave the band a special air. In their brilliant uniforms of scarlet pantaloons, silver-buttoned yellow jackets, Hessian boots, feathered turbans, and Persian scimitars, they won the admiration of all who saw and heard them perform. Their training as drummers had begun on Guadeloupe's sugar plantations, where they beat out "tam-tam" rhythms to incite their fellow slaves to increased efficiency as cane was planted, cut, or hauled away to the mills.[1]

On the staff of the Twenty-ninth Regiment was Pierce Butler, a twenty-one-year-old Irish officer who had already established a remarkable military record. He had received a commission in the King's army at the age of eleven, and in 1758 when only fourteen, was fighting the French in North America as a lieutenant in the famed Cheshire Regiment, the Twenty-second Foot. In the successful attack on the Fortress of Louisbourg, the young soldier was wounded. By 1762, and following duty with Marine companies in Ireland, Pierce Butler was said to be the youngest captain "without purchase in his Majesty's 29th Regiment."[2]

1

By 1767 the regiment contemplated transfer from Nova Scotia to duty in the uneasy American colonies of the eastern seaboard made fretful by Stamp Act woes, unreasonable applications of tariffs, and by the Royal government's lack of comprehension of New World problems. Pierce Butler, a major since April 1766, was sent with fellow officers to Philadelphia to determine where the regiment might best be stationed. From Philadelphia, Major Butler traveled down the coast alone. On December 11, 1767, a short news item in one of the Charlestown newspapers reported his arrival: "The hon. Daniel Blake, esq, Jacob Motte, Jun, esq, and John Izard, esq, with their ladies returned here last Saturday in the Philadelphia Packet, Captain Harrison, from Philadelphia in which vessel came likewise Major Pierce Butler of the 29th Regiment."[3]

In South Carolina, Major Butler was confronted with an unrest and anger characteristic of the other American colonies in 1767. Despite the prevailing difficulties between the South Carolinians and their government, Butler immediately found much to his liking. Charlestown was a sophisticated low country outpost in marked contrast to the cold Nova Scotia he had left. It was an attraction that gave cause to prolong his visit through all of 1768 and until April of the following year.

Pierce Butler was the third son and one of ten children of Sir Richard and Lady Henrietta Percy Butler of Garryhunden in Ireland. Sir Richard was the fifth baronet of Cloughrenan, and a member of Parliament from County Carlow. His inheritor was Thomas Butler, the oldest son, who became the sixth baronet in 1771 and who held the title until his death less than a year later. Pierce Butler was twice removed from inheritance and the army commission was for him a logical move. Moreover, the family had a tradition of military service. Butlers were said to be "conspicuous for high and independent feelings, united with a chivalric contempt for danger." From his father, Pierce Butler claimed the blood of Ormondes and from his mother, who was the granddaughter of Anthony Percy, a lord mayor of Dublin, laid claim to descent from Northumberland. This claim was first raised by her great-grandfather, James Percy, an Irish trunkmaker who persisted in petitioning the House of Lords for nearly twenty years. Although his claim had validity, the patience of the lords wore thin, and they sentenced the claimant to wear a paper in Westminster Hall declaring him a "false and impudent pretender to the Earldom of Northumberland." Even though the descent from the Ormondes came down an illegitimate line and the trunkmaker's claim was questionable, Pierce Butler wore his lineage proudly. He did so all his life.[4]

Major Pierce Butler, from miniatures given to Sarah Butler Wister by Louis Butler in Paris in 1882. (Library Company of Philadelphia.)

Pierce Butler brought to an appreciative South Carolina society an appealing mixture of color and elegance. His spirited impatience and Irish determination were quickly evident as he infiltrated their institutions and lay siege to the hearts of daughters of Carolina's gentry. In Philadelphia it was said that the youthful Major of an Irish regiment had made a vivid impression on the congregation attending communion service at Christ Church. He made the same impression at Charlestown's fashionable St. Michael's.[5]

In 1768 some of the young Major's characteristics were manifested in a notice he ran in the *Gazette,* and in an escapade reported by one of the Carolinians. The notice appeared on February 19, and again on February 26. His arrogance was apparent:

> Run away from the subscriber, on the 18th of February inst, an old French man, by name JAMES DUCLOS, about fifty years of age, five feet seven inches in his shoes, somewhat fat, had thin black hair, and a very black complexion. He went off in an old blue coat with yellow metal buttons. Whoever apprehends said villain and lodges him in the workhouse shall receive TEN POUNDS reward on applying to
>
> PIERCE BUTLER[6]

As for the escapade, Peter Manigault of Charlestown wrote Miles Brewton, telling of the "religious" Butler's involvement with fifteen-year-old Betsy Izard. Major Butler had engineered an elopement, borrowing Ben Huger's house at Goose Creek and engaging a parson; but Betsy's stepfather, John Channing, got wind of the coup and spirited the girl away. Manigault mimicked Captain Louis Valentine Fuser, who relished his fellow officer's predicament and gloated "Dis religion Cover great Epocrasee." This was an early reference to Major Butler's religious activities, of which there would be many more. It also marked his first attempt to win an heiress, for Betsy Izard had inherited land and money from her father, John Izard, who had died in 1754.[7]

The Butler-Izard affair was popular talk for quite a while. Although the aborted elopement had occurred in the early summer of 1768, Henry Middleton wrote his son Arthur on September 22:

> Miss I-D has not changed her name and she is still kept in the Country out of the way of the Major, tho' it is said that she now dislikes him, and that she has given him to understand that she will never have anything more to

say to him, but I doubt whether he thinks she is in earnest. The report now is that she is to have a young gentleman who lives with Mr. Henry Laurens, son of Governor Wright of Georgia.

If this match should take place it is thought she will not better herself by it—and that she would have done full as well had she been permitted to marry the Major; as the one is a sedate modest man, & the other a raw unexperienced lad, not yet nineteen years old.[8]

Experiencing trouble with his military pay, Major Butler returned to his regiment, now stationed in Boston. The *South Carolina Gazette and Country Journal* reported his departure from Charlestown in their issue of April 18, 1769: "This day the sloop *Sally,* Captain Hunt, sails for New York, in whom goes Major Pierce Butler." Coincidentally, or by design of the editor, the next item in the column announced: "Married—Alexander Wright, Esq. Son of His Excellency Governor of Georgia, to Miss Elizabeth Izard, with a fortune of *Thirty Thousand Pounds* Sterling." The Major had lost an important skirmish.[9]

In Boston, Major Butler found the Twenty-ninth Regiment abused and castigated by many of the townspeople. The situation was such that General Thomas Gage, who commanded the British forces in North America, sought a station where the Twenty-ninth would be "less obnoxious." Unfortunately, men of the Twenty-ninth were goaded into a retaliatory move resulting in the brawl that became known as the "Boston Massacre." It appears that Pierce Butler witnessed the event, although he was not one of the hated "lobster backs" who participated in the violent reaction that caused the first flow of American blood and gave the Twenty-ninth a new name—"the Vein Openers." The incident did prompt the removal of the Twenty-ninth to Newport, on to Providence, and then to several stations in New Jersey.[10]

While in Boston, Major Butler had sought permission from General Gage to go to England to seek redress of the problems with his pay. That mission accomplished, he returned to his regiment in New Jersey but was soon once again on the scene in South Carolina's promised land. His arrival on January 5 was noticed by the *South Carolina and American General Gazette,* one of the three Charlestown newspapers being published at the time: "Major Pierce Butler, of the 29th Regiment arrived here by Land from New York." The same newspaper, in the same column of Charlestown intelligence, reported his marriage on January 10, 1771, to

"Miss Polly Middleton," the daughter of the "deceased Colonel Thomas Middleton." Polly Middleton, whose real name was Mary, was named for her mother, Mary Bull, the first wife of Colonel Middleton.[11]

The marriage of Pierce Butler and Mary Middleton brought many changes into his way of life. For one, it led to surprising new allegiances but most of all it was the beginning of a lifelong dependency on the physical strength of hundreds of slaves. It was a financially rewarding yet burdensome legacy that would be passed on to three generations of the Butler family. If, as a soldier, Pierce Butler marched to the beat of black drummers, his marriage to Mary Middleton saw him, in a different sense, beginning to do the same for the rest of his days.

At the time of her marriage Mary Middleton was an heiress in the true sense of the word. Her father, mother, grandfather on her mother's side, and brother William were dead. Her mother, Mary Bull Middleton, had been the daughter of Captain John Bull and his second wife, also called Mary. It was from this grandmother, who died within the year of the Butler-Middleton marriage, that Pierce Butler's young wife received the bulk of her inheritance.

More of the Bull estate would come to the Butler family after Mary Butler's death, in circumstances disturbing to Major Butler. Mary Bull's will ordered the division of the plantations called the Euhaws on Broad River in Jasper Barony, St. Luke's Parish, into two tracts. The uppermost tract, together with Toogoodoo Plantation near Willtown Bluff in St. Paul's Parish, and a lot in the town of Beaufort were left in trust for her granddaughter Sarah Guerard, the sister of Mary Butler. The lowermost tract of the Euhaws, the Bulls' homeplace, described as "all the lands within the ditch" at Coosaw Island, except that she called it "Bull's Island," and a lot in Beaufort were similarly left in trust for her granddaughter Mary Butler and her husband Pierce. The dashing Irish soldier must have impressed the old lady, for he was included in the will, while Sarah's husband Benjamin Guerard was forcefully excluded. Sarah's share was to be received "independent of and free from the Intermeddling of her husband." Mary Bull also directed the sale of her Hilton Head Island plantation of 990 acres and a tract of 744 acres in St. Peter's Parish. The money from the two sales was to be added to "ready money" on hand, and to proceeds from the crops under cultivation. This, together with the "Rest, Residue and Remainder" of which the Bull slaves were the most valuable, was to be divided into four parts for her granddaughters Sarah Guerard, Mary Butler, Mary Izard Brewton, and Elizabeth Izard

Blake. These shares were also left in trust, with each of the women being instructed to make a testamentary disposition before their "decease." It was the disposition to be made by Elizabeth Blake that came to disturb Major Butler and to trigger his anger.[12]

Mary Butler's father, Colonel Thomas Middleton, left a different sort of legacy. He had led the South Carolina Regiment in the vindictive expedition against the Cherokee Indians in 1761, an expedition ordered by the commander of British forces in America, General Sir Jeffrey Amherst. It consisted of regular British army troops in addition to provincial forces. Colonel Middleton was rankled when command of the expedition was given to an officer of lesser rank, the Scottish soldier Lieutenant Colonel James Grant. His pique at the slight led to a duel between the two men in which only feelings were wounded. Lieutenant Colonel Grant did gain an advantage which he declined to take, thereby saving Colonel Middleton's life. Thomas Middleton was also a member of the Commons House of Assembly. Beyond his governmental and military career, he was known as the owner of several plantations, and more important, as a merchant who was one of the province's largest importers of and dealers in slaves.[13]

Little stigma was attached to the slave trade in South Carolina of that day. Many who had made their fortunes as merchants had abandoned their business enterprises to become plantation owners, and this new aristocratic class may have had a tendency to look down on the merchant class they had so recently cast aside. As merchants, they had marketed slaves to meet the needs of their clients. As affluent plantation owners, they supplied the demand for Africans that kept the likes of Thomas Middleton in business. A few itinerant slave traders who dealt solely in Negroes, and whose integrity was usually questionable, were scorned, but on the whole, the importation, purchase, or sale of black Africans was accepted as a matter of course. Those who on moral grounds chose not to engage in such trade were few indeed. Had they chosen to speak against the practice, they would have been looked on with disfavor and disdain.[14]

Thomas Middleton's family background was such that he was said to be among the last of the "great aristocrats" who continued in the merchant trade when his peers had turned to managing their slave-worked plantations. He would have done well to emulate that group, for disaster lay ahead.[15]

With his partner Samuel Brailsford, Thomas Middleton imported "37 parcels of slaves" between 1751 and 1760. During that period the firm paid duty amounting to 38,235 pounds sterling at an average of ten

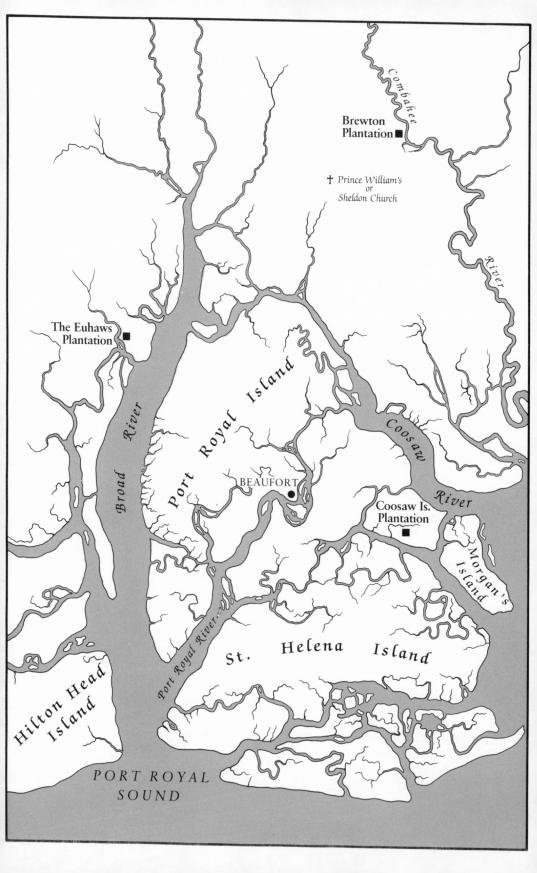

Combahee

Brewton
Plantation ■

✝ Prince William's
or
Sheldon Church

River

The Euhaws
Plantation ■

Port Royal Island

Broad
River

Coosaw

BEAUFORT ●

Coosaw Is.
Plantation
■

River

Morgan's
Island

Port Royal River

St. Helena Island

Hilton Head
Island

PORT ROYAL
SOUND

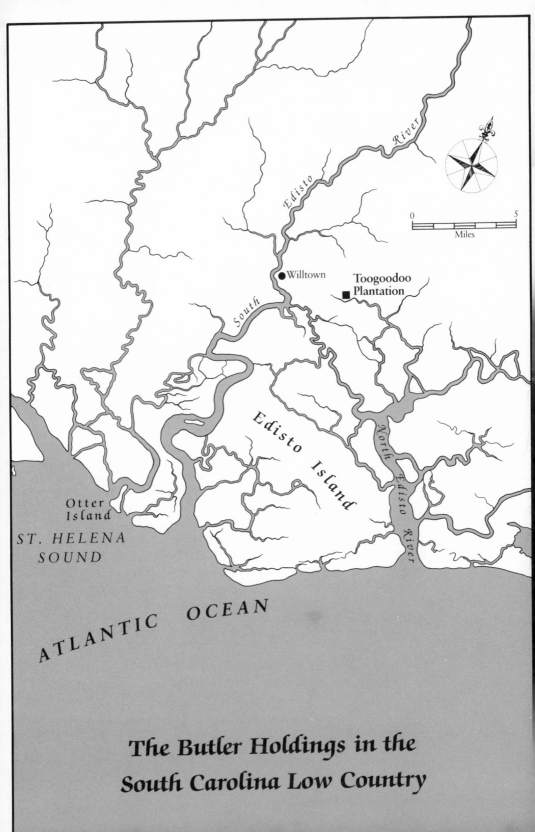

The Butler Holdings in the
South Carolina Low Country

pounds per adult slave imported. There was no duty on slaves imported for personal use, and both of the partners were in fact large slaveholders in their own right. In addition, the firm was active in the purchase and sale of slaves in the so-called domestic market. Until 1760, when the partnership was dissolved, Middleton and Brailsford vied with Miles Brewton and Henry Laurens as leaders in the South Carolina slave trade. Although Middleton and Brailsford went separate ways, each continued as dealers in Africans. Miles Brewton's successful career was terminated by his death in 1775, but Henry Laurens chose to abandon what he called "the Guinea business." He became disturbed by the cruelty of the masters of slave ships and by others who were involved in the marketing of the "wretched negroes."[16] In June 1769, he wrote a friend: "I am very much obliged to you for the preference intended to me of your African business but I have wholly retired from that branch of Trade and am endeavoring to draw all my commercial concerns within a very narrow compass."[17] More important, he was influenced by his son John, who saw slavery as an evil force. In an exchange of letters in 1776, John Laurens returned to a subject he had often discussed with his father: "I think that we Americans, at least in the Southern Colonies, cannot contend with a *good grace* for liberty, until we have enfranchised our slaves." Henry Laurens wrote John:

> You know, my Dear Son, I abhor slavery. I was born in a country where slavery had been established by British Kings and Parliaments, as well as by the laws of that Country ages before my existence. I found the Christian religion and slavery growing under the same authority and cultivation. I nevertheless disliked it. In former days there was no combatting the prejudices of men supported by interest. The day I hope is approaching when, from principles of gratitude as well as justice, every man will strive to be foremost in showing his readiness to comply with the golden rule. Not less than twenty thousand pounds Sterling would all my negroes produce if sold at auction tomorrow. I am not the man who enslaved them, they are indebted to Englishmen for that favor; nonetheless I am devising means for manumitting many of them, and for cutting off the entail of slavery.[18]

The elder Laurens struggled with his conscience and considered the financial impact of manumission on the well-being of his family. Although he bespoke his admirable sentiments, he actually did very little toward freeing his slaves. Approbation for his abandonment of the trade was scarce, and his desire to do what he thought right won no favor in his own life-

New Advertisements.

On *Wednesday* the 24th of February next, WILL BE SOLD by public *vendue*, at the *house* of Mr. Thomas Nightingale upon Charles-Town *neck*:

ABOUT

Two Hundred

VERY VALUABLE

SLAVES.

AND,

On *Friday* the 4th of March following, at the *Town* of BEAUFORT, *on* PORT-ROYAL *Island*:

A Parcel of genteel HOUS-HOLD FURNITURE, a CHARIOT, a new riding CHAIR, a TENT, a BILLIARD TABLE, a FLAT, &c.

AND,

The following Day, at the two plantations, called LAUREL-BAY and PARLEZ-VOUS, *on* the *said* Island:

ALL the STOCK on the *said* plantations; consisting of HORSES, CAT-TLE, SHEEP, HOGS, &c. and likewise the plantation tools: Being part of the personal *estate* of *Thomas Middleton*, Esq; deceased.

The conditions will be made known on the days of *sale*, by   WILLIAM MIDDLETON,
acting Executor.

N.B. *If any of the above days should prove rainy, the* SALES *will be on the first fair days following.*

ADVERTISEMENTS.

TO BE SOLD, on *Thursday* the *third* of *June* next, about *Three Hundred* and *Fifty* CHOICE *Healthy* SLAVES, Just arrived in the Ship *Benn*, Capt. *James Sherman*, directly from *Guiney*, by   *Middleton & Brailsford.*

These advertisements appeared in the South Carolina Gazette *on January 25, 1768 (left); May 29, 1756 (above); and February 2, 1765 (below). (Charleston Library Society.)*

TO BE SOLD, very reasonably, Seventeen GOLD COAST young

N E G R O E S,

Just arrived in the brigantine Alice, from Tortola, by
BREWTON & SMITH.

Who have for *sale* a handsome London-made *Horse Chair and Harness*, a few pipes of Madeira wine, and some choice old brandy.

time other than that of his son. On the contrary, he harvested the disfavor and disdain reserved for those who opposed the accepted way of life in South Carolina.[19]

In the years in which Thomas Middleton plied his trade as a slave merchant, the South Carolina market was buoyed by the demand from rice planters. Theirs was a labor-intensive crop where the needs were fulfilled by Middleton, his partners, and many competitors. Charlestown harbor was seldom without a slaver offering Negroes from diverse African regions. There were Angolas, Congos, Guineas, Whydahs, Ibos, or the broadly classified "Gold Coast Negroes." Most had come directly from Africa, but seasoned slaves were often imported from island plantations of the West Indies. In the early days of the colony, Englishmen from the Antilles brought with them their favorite Coromantees who were named for the seaboard village on the Gold Coast whence they were said to have come. The Englishman Patrick Leigh Fermor studied the descendants of the Jamaican Maroons in the late 1940s and decided that "all the Africans belonging to the Twi and Akan group of languages on the Gold Coast" came to be called "Koromantees," including the Fanti and the Ashanti. He wrote that they were "remarkable for their extraordinary strength and symmetry, their distinguished appearance and proud bearing. They were blacker and taller and handsomer than their fellow slaves; vigorous, muscular and agile, intelligent, fierce, ruthless in war, fanatically attached to the idea of liberty, and strangers to fear."[20] Many came from the Barbados as well as Jamaica, and to many a low-country planter "were the best and most faithful of our slaves." The distinguished South Carolina writer DuBose Heyward contended that the Coromantee strain "may have contributed largely to the Negro race during its period of development under slavery."[21]

In the twenty-year period of 1753–1773, there were 43,965 slaves imported into South Carolina. The frequency of newspaper notices announcing the arrival and sale of cargoes of Africans was an indication of the immensity of the traffic. Typical was an advertisement on August 20, 1753:

TO BE SOLD
On Wednesday the
22d Instant, and not
before, about *One
Hundred* as healthy

and likely grown GAMBIA
S L A V E S,
as ever were imported, just arrived in
the Ship *Molly & Sally,* Capt. *John
Wilmshurst. Middleton & Brailsford.*[22]

Among other newspaper notices were:

May 29, 1756
350 CHOICE HEALTHY
SLAVES FROM GUINEY

October 2, 1758
A CHOICE CARGO OF ABOUT 160
NEGROES DIRECTLY FROM THE RIVER GAMBIA

November 17, 1759
200 SLAVES
FROM ANGOLA

July 21, 1759
A choice Cargo of about *Three Hundred*
N E G R O E S
directly from WHIDAH, a Country greatly
preferred to any other, throughout the
West Indies, and inferior to none on the
Coast of *Africa.*

August 13, 1760
A LIKELY AND HEALTHY
CARGO OF ABOUT 200
GOLD COAST NEGROES

The last group was offered for sale at Beaufort, all of the others at Charles-town, and all by Middleton and Brailsford. On November 18, 1761, Thomas Middleton suffered a loss on his son William's True Blue planta-tion. He ran an advertisement in the *South Carolina Gazette:*

RUN away from the subscriber's plantation *True-Blue,* in *Prince-William's* parish, on the 18th *Nov.* 1761, one *Calabar* and seven *Coromantee* negro men, named DICK, ARTHUR, SMART, QUAMINO, STEPHEN, CUFFEE, and HUGHKY. They have been in the province about 15 months and speak little English; had on white negro cloth waistcoats and breeches, and took their blankets with them. A reward of forty shillings for each, and the lawful charges, will be paid to any one delivering them at the said plantation, or to the warden of the work-house.

THO. MIDDLETON[23]

Other importers were similarly active in promoting the sale of slaves from Africa and the West Indies. Typical of the newspaper notices were those of the Henry Laurens partnerships. In 1752 they offered "a parcel of Congo slaves" for sale, and in 1753 there were on one day a pair of notices for the sale of two Laurens cargoes, one from Angola, the other from Gambia.[24]

Miles Brewton, the husband of Mary Butler's cousin Mary Izard, showed the diversity of his merchandise by advertising in 1765:

TO BE SOLD, very reasonably,
Seventeen Gold Coast young
N E G R O E S
Just arrived in the brigantine
Alice, from Tortola, by
BREWTON & SMITH
Who have for sale a handsome London-made *Horse
Chair and Harness*, a few pipes of Madeira Wine,
and some choice old brandy.

A few years later one of the Brewton slaves who had developed unusual skills ran away and prompted a notice in the *Gazette:*

RUN AWAY from the Subscriber, a Mulatto young Man, named JEMMY, or JAMES, who I lately purchased at public Vendue: He is an upright, likely, arch Fellow, has a bushy Head of Hair, which he combes back; he plays on the Violin: As he pretends to be a Taylor, and a Barber, may attempt to pass for a free Man, whoever therefore harbours or employs said Mulatto Slave, may depend on being prosecuted to the utmost Rigour of the Law. Whoever will secure him in Gaol, or deliver him to me in CharlesTown, shall receive Six Pistoles Rewards; and any Person proving by whom he is harboured (either in this Province or Georgia) to the Conviction of the Offender, if a white Person, shall have Ten Pistoles, and Four Pistoles, if by a free Mulatto or Negro.

MILES BREWTON

As the above Slave, named JAMES, or JEMMY, was seen crossing the Combahee Ferry, on the 12th Instant, February, no Doubt he will endeavor to escape in some Vessel from Beaufort, or Savannah. He shews a Ticket as he passes, which he says is from me, or some other Person. All Masters of Vessels are hereby forewarned from carrying him off, as they will certainly be prosecuted for the same.[25]

When Thomas Middleton died in Beaufort in 1766 he had been a partner since 1763 with Thomas Liston and William Hope. The firm was heavily engaged in the importation of slaves. The Africans had been sold without due regard for the credit worthiness of the buyers, and as a consequence the firm was hopelessly insolvent at the time of Colonel Middleton's death.[26]

Middleton, Liston, and Hope operated from Beaufort, selling a broad range of imported goods in addition to their traffic in slaves. Beaufort, about midway between Charlestown and Savannah, and close to many of the islands spread out along the coast, became a busy marketplace for the planters of the low country. An indication of how the Middleton family lived can be gained from the advertisement that appeared on February 1, 1768. Colonel Middleton's son William, who had been named the acting executor, sold a portion of his father's belongings in an effort to meet the demands of many creditors:

On Wednesday the 24th day of February next, will be Sold by publick Vendue, at the house of Mr. Thomas Nightingall upon Charlestown Neck;
Almost   T W O   H U N D R E D   very Valuable
S L A V E S
A parcel of genteel houshold furniture, a chariot, a new riding chair, tent billiard table, a flat, &c. Likewise,

On the following day, at the two plantations called Laurel Bay, and Parlez Vous on the said island;
All the stock on the said plantations, consisting of horses, cattle, sheep, hogs, &c. and likewise, the plantation tools:
Being part of the personal estate of THOMAS MIDDLETON, esq; deceased.
The Conditions will be made known on the day of sale.
WILLIAM MIDDLETON, Acting Executor

N.B. If any of the above days should prove rainy, the sales will be on the first fair days following.[27]

At his death Thomas Middleton owned, in addition to Laurel Bay and Parlez-Vous plantations, a town house in Beaufort. There were twenty-one slaves at the Beaufort house, twenty-nine at Parlez-Vous, and fifty-eight at Laurel Bay.[28] In his will he made many specific bequests: "To the child of which my wife is now pregnant those fifty acres commonly called Cuckhold's Point and one thousand acres of land adjoining True Blue Plantation purchased by me of Mr. Thomas Shubrick." To his wife Anne Barnwell Middleton: "My two Trusty old Negroes Tom and Lymus, my Negroe Carpenter Charles and two fellows called Simon and George." To his daughter Sarah, who married Benjamin Guerard: "My Negroe Carpenter Primus." To his daughter Mary, who was to marry Pierce Butler: "My Negroe Boy Caesar." To his son William, slaves were left in three separate bequests: "My Negroe Carpenter Worster. My Negroe fellow Jack, Ship Carpenter. My new schooner called the *Betsy* with all her anchors, cables, rigging and apparel, and the Negroes belonging to her—videlict—Adam, Big Jack, Peter, Cyrus, and Boy Tom." To his daughters Sarah, Mary, Elizabeth, and the unborn child—to be divided equally: "The Rest and Residue of my Negroe Slaves."[29]

Thomas Middleton was survived by the children of his first wife, Mary Bull—namely, Mary, William, and Sarah Guerard. Also there was his wife Anne, their daughter Elizabeth, and the daughter Anne who was born the day following her father's death. Elizabeth had been given one of her father's many plantations, and Anne, the daughter, would have shared generously in the estate had the debts of Colonel Middleton not become so overwhelmingly large. Most of what he owned at death had to be sold, with notices of the sales appearing frequently in the years 1767, 1768, and on into 1769. In the wake of his financial disaster appeared advertisements liquidating properties belonging to his former partners William Hope and Thomas Liston. Those unfortunates listed for sale plantations, slaves, household furnishings, including "beds, chairs, tables, pictures, &c." Early in 1768 the Charlestown newspapers ran notices that lent further emphasis to the troubles faced by the Middleton estate:

A   T A V E R N
At the town of BEAUFORT Port Royal,
Is opened in the House lately possessed by the
deceased Col. Middleton near the Church,
at the Sign of the White Hart:
WHERE Gentlemen may depend on
the best entertainment, equal to any
in the province, from:
Their most Obedient Humble Servant,
WILLIAM TOSELAND[30]

These notices of the sale of Middleton property, particularly the one that told of the conversion of the town house to a tavern, made a lasting impression on the young and ambitious Pierce Butler.

The pressures that confronted William Middleton to meet his father's obligations were intense and contributed to his untimely death in April 1768. He died unmarried at twenty-four, and his death deeply distressed his sisters. The responsibility for liquidating Colonel Middleton's estate as well as William's was first thrust into the capable hands of Sarah Middleton Guerard's husband, Benjamin. For a time the notices of the sale of property were issued by him as administrator of both estates. A notice on January 2, 1769, listed many items, including: "A Negro Wench, who is a good seamstress, cook and washer. A clock, billiard table, a chariot, two riding chairs, a chaise, a flat, two canoes, a few swivel guns."[31] In addition, he offered the following for sale: "A new schooner, burthen about 140 barrels of rice, with her tackle and furniture, likewise five Negroes, brought up in the coasting business and now employed in her."[32] This was Thomas Middleton's *Betsy*, willed by him to his son William, with its crew of Adam, Big Jack, Peter, Cyrus, and Boy Tom.

Another notice told of the sale at public outcry of the ship *Middleton*. The ship had been a slaver and was owned by Middleton, Liston, and Hope together with George Ryall, who probably held a ship's mortgage on the vessel.[33]

Benjamin Guerard had a difficult time. The debts of the firm were enormous, and to add to his woes, Thomas Middleton had been personally liable to the firm for a large amount. A letter from Henry Laurens describes the problem: "There is not to this day Nine Pence in the pound collected. We (the Assignees) are resolved to file a bill in Chancery against Mr. Guerard next Month if he does not Account in the meantime for Six or Seven Thousand Pounds Sterling due by Mr. Middleton to the Company."[34]

In January 1771, Major Butler appeared on the family scene as Mary Middleton's husband. Soon afterward his name began to show along with that of Benjamin Guerard in legal notices pertaining to the Middleton property. On February 7, 1771, the two brothers-in-law advertised lands belonging to William Middleton's estate. To be sold were the three plantations he had inherited from his grandfather John Bull: Ashepoo of 1,020 acres, True Blue of 2,470 acres, and Harris Island of 2,185 acres. Along with Ashepoo went "25 or 30 young likely slaves" and "two Negro men and a Wind Fan."[35]

Pierce Butler had come into the Middleton family at an opportune time. His forthright manner and his ability and readiness to take command were qualities sorely needed to bring order to the chaos of the estates of Mary Butler's father and brother. This he did, and quickly began the management of the diverse properties inherited from Mary Bull.

Chapter 2

Pierce Butler, Patriot

WELL BEFORE HIS MARRIAGE to Mary Middleton, Pierce Butler, as a major in His Majesty's Twenty-ninth Regiment, had kept a weather eye on the winds of change. Despite his pride in his Irish and English background, he had developed a strong admiration for South Carolinians, particularly the planters. He was attracted to the landed gentry and their plantation society as he searched for a life that would offer potential compensation for the inheritance that he, as a third son, had been denied in Ireland. The Middleton connections had additional appeal. His wife Mary brought more than romance, land, and money to the new Butler family. Importantly, her lands were well stocked with valuable slaves. Also, there were remarkable family affiliations. The Bull family on her mother's side was well represented by Lieutenant Governor William Bull, the second of that name to hold the title, for his father had long served the Royal government from 1738 until his death in 1755. The second William Bull was a popular and fair emissary of the King who struggled mightily to quell the unrest that threatened to sweep away British rule in South Carolina. Her cousins Mary, Elizabeth, and Sarah Izard were married to Miles Brewton, Daniel Blake, and Lord William Campbell respectively. Campbell was soon to relinquish his rule of Nova Scotia to become the last of South Carolina's Royal governors, and the other two bore names to be reckoned with in the low country. Mary's sister Sarah Middleton was married to Benjamin Guerard, a young man of promise who became governor of the state in 1783. Another Sarah Middleton, a cousin, married the distinguished Charles Cotesworth Pinckney. Cousin Henrietta Middleton would marry Edward Rutledge, who later signed the Declaration of Independence, which also carried the signature of Arthur Middleton, another of Mary Butler's many cousins.[1]

Thus, wed to an heiress, surrounded by affluent and influential cousins, in-laws, and friends, it is not surprising that the young British soldier assumed the attitudes of the Carolina planters and became a colorful figure in the panorama of Charlestown. On the eve of war with Great Britain, the city was the focal point of the cultural, commercial, religious, and social activities of the Middleton-Bull connections that Pierce Butler was joining. The broad and beautiful Charlestown harbor was covered with hundreds of ships, many of them slavers from or bound to Africa or other British satellite colonies in the New World. The city's handsome public buildings were complemented by dignified churches and by many "most elegant mansion houses." A young visitor from Boston attended a concert where he found the women more richly dressed, not so florid or so healthy, but equally flirtatious as those he had known at home. The gentlemen were also richly attired with many wearing their swords. On hand were "Macaronis" from England, lending color and interest in their outlandish costumes. Social life centered around the theater and such Charlestown societies as St. Cecilia, St. Andrew's, and St. Patrick's Hibernians. The men had their Friday Night Club, their Jockey Club, and men and women managed to give their attendance at St. Michael's, St. Philip's, or the Huguenot Church an air of fashionable sociability. Not the least of the social activities were the lavish evening dinners at the mansions of the aristocracy. None were grander than those at the new home of Miles and Mary Brewton. He was certainly "a gentleman of very large fortune." His new home was described as "A most superb house said to have cost him 8000 £ Sterling, the grandest hall I ever beheld, azure blue satin window curtains, rich blue paper with gilt, mashee borders, most elegant pictures, excessive grand and costly looking glasses, etc." A Brewton dinner was a three-course affair—bolstered with knickknacks, jellies, preserves, sweetmeats, and was followed by nuts, raisins, apples, and oranges. The grand food was accompanied by the finest wines, the dining interspersed with flowerful and frequent toasts. Not every Charlestown host could boast a "very fine bird" that flew among the guests "familiarly playing over the room, under our chairs, picking up the crumbs, etc and perching on the window, sideboard and chairs: vastly pretty!" At the end of the dinner, with the departure of the ladies, the Madeiras were brought forth: "By odds the richest wine I ever tasted. Exceeds Mr. Hancocks's." More toasts—and the conversation was of politics, the British, rice, indigo, and

The Miles Brewton House in Charleston. (Drawing by Elizabeth O'Neill Verner.)

slaves. It is unlikely that Pierce Butler's advertisement on the loss of his slaves Minos and Cudjoe became a topic of the evening's conversation, or surely the young Bostonian would have noted in his journal the practice of branding slaves with the owner's initials.

R U N   A W A Y

From the Subscriber's Plantation in Prince William's *Parish,*

T W O   N E G R O   F E L L O W S

Named MINOS, and CUDJOE;—they are both strong-made Fellows. Minos appears to be near 40 Years old. Cudjoe about 26:—They are marked a little above the right Breast with the Letters PB—Whoever apprehends the said Negroes, and lodges them in the Work-House, or delivers them to my Overseer, at Coosaw, shall receive FIVE POUNDS Currency for each, on applying to Mr. JOSEPH ATKINSON, Merchant, in Charles-Town, or at Coosaw, to

PIERCE BUTLER.

And, had it happened a few months earlier, Miles Brewton might have told of Jamaica Betty, the seamstress who had run away from Mary Butler's sister, Sarah Guerard.

ABSENTED *herself about a Month ago,*
From her Mistress, Mrs. Sarah Guerard,

A   N E G R O   W E N C H,

About 35 or 40 Years of Age, bought at the sale of Mr. BERESFORD's Slaves, and called *Jamaica Betty,* she has Marks down the Side of her Face, is a good Needle Woman, and had on when she went away a striped Flannel Gown. Any Person who will take and deliver her to the Warden of the Workhouse, or give Notice so that she may be found, shall be hand-somely rewarded; or any Person who will inform of her being harboured, if by a white Person, FIFTY POUNDS shall be paid on Conviction of the Offender; and if by a black Person, TWENTY-FIVE POUNDS, to be paid by

MILES BREWTON[2]

As though unaware of the growing difficulties between the Crown and many South Carolinians, the government continued to dispense Royal grants of fallow real estate to the King's "loyal" subjects. In the years immediately following his marriage, Pierce Butler made numerous re-

RUN away from the subscriber, on the 18th of Februar inst. an old French man, by name JAMES DUCLOS, about fifty years of age, five feet seven inches in his shoes, somewhat fat, has thin black hair, and a very black complexion. He went off in an old blue coat with yellow metal buttons. Whoever apprehends said villain and lodges him in the workhouse shall receive TEN POUNDS reward on applying to   PIERCE BUTLER.

RUN AWAY,

From the Subscriber's Plantation in Prince William's Parish,

TWO NEGRO FELLOWS,

Named MINOS, and CUDJOE;—they are both strong-made Fellows. Minos appears to be near 40 Years old, Cudjoe about 26:—They are marked a little above the right Breast with the Letters PB.——Whoever apprehends the said Negroes, and lodges them in the Work-House, or delivers them to my Overseer, at Coosaw, shall receive FIVE POUNDS Currency for each, on applying to Mr. JOSEPH ATKINSON, Merchant, in Charles-Town, or at Coosaw, to
PIERCE BUTLER.

These notices appeared in the South Carolina and American General Gazette, *1768 (top), and the* South Carolina Gazette, *1772 (bottom). (Charleston Library Society.)*

quests for property and was awarded in excess of ten thousand acres, of which more than eight thousand was in the Carolina back country.[3]

South Carolina's pre-Revolutionary land policies had an indirect but important impact on the use of slaves. One basis for granting lands was the "headright," in which a family was entitled to fifty acres per settler. Major Butler, his wife Mary, and eight of their slaves, who were considered "family" and settlers, could apply for five hundred acres. Such a practice opened the doors to speculation, and while the grant books of South Carolina's archives abound with grants to Pierce Butler, many of which he planned to develop and use as the Royal government intended, much of it was obtained with an eye to profitable sales. This desire to turn land at a profit was persistent throughout his life.[4]

The young Major and his wealthy bride became an important part of Charlestown's church-oriented social structure. Within a year of his marriage his advice was sought by the vestrymen of St. Michael's as they searched for an organist. Pierce Butler "gave such flattering Accounts" of George Harland Hartley's "great Abilities" that he was readily accepted and brought to Charlestown from Barbados.[5]

Although Major Butler came to Mary Middleton with an all but empty purse, he did have one valuable asset, which was the regimental commission acquired for him so long before by his father, Sir Richard. He held firmly to it until he was sure of the course he would set in a land overcast by war clouds. His decision to convert the commission to sterling came in 1773, prompted in part to make a strategic acquisition of lands far to the south of Mary Butler's inheritance. He severed his old tie to the Royal government as his regiment was readied for a return to England. When it departed from its station in Florida, contrary winds caused the ships to put into Charlestown harbor in September, to be detained there for a time, causing Major Butler, no doubt, to reflect upon his decision. But he did not change his plans.[6]

In October 1774, using funds from the sale of his commission, Pierce Butler purchased seventeen hundred acres on St. Simons Island in coastal Georgia. The plantation, known as Hampton Point, was acquired for six thousand provincial pounds from John Graham and his wife Frances of Savannah. John Graham, staunch loyalist in a divided province, used Major Butler's funds to buy Mulberry Grove, a Savannah River plantation above the town of Savannah. Less than twenty years and a revolution later, with Mulberry Grove owned and planted by General Nathanael Greene's attractive widow, Catharine, Eli Whitney fashioned for her a small machine that separated seeds from cotton fibers. Whitney's cotton gin was to have a tremendous impact on Major Butler's Hampton plantation even as it would on the young nation that had just won its independence from Great Britain.[7]

At the time of the purchase of Hampton Point, which Major Butler usually called Hampton, he also acquired from John Graham's brother James two tracts containing additional highland, and a large expanse of marshland to the north and west of the original purchase. The Major planned to grow cotton on the highlands and to engage in an agricultural experiment by banking the hard salt marshland, to irrigate it using the great flow of fresh water coming down the Altamaha River, and there to grow additional cotton. It was a venture he was forced to defer because of the troubled times.[8]

The people of Charlestown became apprehensive on the eve of the war. Among those most uneasy were Miles and Mary Brewton, who, with their three children sailed for Philadelphia in late August 1775. With them was Mrs. Brewton's cousin—Mary Butler's sister—Sarah Guerard. Miles Brewton anticipated the impending conflict. In July he had made a hurried trip to Savannah with William Henry Drayton and had been successful in persuading the Georgians to give them five thousand pounds of gunpowder, confiscated from the British. The South Carolinians then shipped the powder on to their delegation at the Continental Congress in Philadelphia. Mary Brewton, said to be "a very nervous woman" and as though forewarned, signed her will before her departure on the ship in which Miles Brewton owned a substantial interest. Mary Brewton's fears were not centered on the British alone but encompassed the likelihood of Indian massacres and Negro insurrections. Such was her timidity that she is said to have urged her husband to have the ship's captain "hug the shore and cast anchor every night." Although it is difficult to believe that any master in his right mind would have done so, there is no doubt the ship was lost in a violent storm, and the crew and passengers were never heard from again. A news item in a Charlestown newspaper gave evidence of their fate: "We learn from North Carolina that the Damage done by the late Hurricane is incredible: the whole shore lined with wrecks. Upwards of 100 dead bodies have drifted ashore at Ocracock Island." It was a tragic break in the wide family circle that surrounded Mary and Pierce Butler.[9]

Despite his departure from the Twenty-ninth Regiment and his closeness to Middleton kinfolk who opposed the British rule, the Crown looked on Pierce Butler as a true loyalist. Former Lieutenant Governor William Bull's allegiance was firm, Mary Butler's cousin Sarah was the wife of the Royal governor, and Major Butler was quick and constant in proclaiming his British heritage. Yet, the "grace and favour" of the Crown was put aside and Pierce Butler abandoned "King and Country" to embrace the rebel cause. An early indication of his change is shown in a letter of September 16, 1775, from Dr. Charles Drayton, who told of the arming of three schooners for use against the British. He noted, "Butler's, when it returns from Philadelphia will, it is intended, be another."[10] A further, and more definite, indication came in a letter to Mary Butler's cousin, Arthur Middleton, the determined patriot who was to sign the Declaration of Independence within a few months. On March 21, 1776, Pierce Butler wrote from Coosaw Island, "Unless we have an *immediate* reinforcement from the Nor'd And a proper Military Establishment here, these Colonies are lost." The Major, who held fast to his title and who was reinforced with good military experience and intelligence, saw that voluntary soldiers would be fearful of leaving their families undefended, thereby inviting attacks from bands of Indians. "Besides," he wrote, "it is surely improper to leave Numbers of Negroes without a White Man." He called for a standing army of not less than five thousand men to protect the Carolinas and Georgia from the British and asked Arthur Middleton to prevail on the Congress to have General Charles Lee come down and take charge. The Major claimed poor health from a recent fever but added, "No Man on Earth has the *Cause* more at heart or wishes more ardently to Serve it than I do."[11]

When Pierce Butler wrote of its being "improper" to leave blacks without the protective presence of white men, he understated the true feelings of the slave owner. The fear was genuine and was widespread throughout the low country. This apprehension was expressed without equivocation by an early South Carolina historian: "No sense of patriotism, however strong, could overcome the demands of family affection and parental duty. Men would not leave their wives and children to the mercy of their slaves, incited to rapine and murder by the presence of, if not by the actual instigation of a hostile army."[12]

The anger directed at George III's Royal government as witnessed by Pierce Butler in Boston in 1770 had spread through the colonies. By June 1775, the tempers of Charlestown's growing band of patriots were as hot as the summer weather. The new Royal governor, Lord William Campbell, arrived from Nova Scotia to find no "*feu de joie*" as he would have enjoyed in a less restless time. His citizenry "presented a sullen silence," and such was the state of loyalty in this once most loyal of British outposts that the faithful attending the governor's arrival "did not exceed fifteen persons."

In November 1775, in the up-country settlement of Ninety-six, warfare came to South Carolina. By June of the following year, guns were firing in Charlestown harbor, where the British launched a futile attempt to recapture the city which was held by the patriots. Lord William Campbell had encouraged the attack in a letter to the earl of Dartmouth, the secretary of state for the colonies: "CharlesTown is the fountainhead from which all the violence flows. Stop that and the rebellion in this part of the continent will, I trust, soon be at an end."[13]

The spirited and successful defense of the fort on Sullivan's Island that protected Charlestown harbor was led by General William Moultrie, and thereafter the fort has borne his name. Among the casualties of the thwarted effort was Governor Campbell. A former naval officer, he had taken a battle station on the lower gun deck of HMS *Bristol*, was wounded, and later was transported to England, where he died.[14]

After being repulsed at Charlestown, the British then turned to more pressing matters in the North. There was relative quiet in the Carolina low country from June 1776 until their Southern campaign was opened in late 1778. Pierce Butler had time to attend to the family plantations. In December he ran the following advertisement in a Charlestown newspaper: "Wanted—an Overseer to take charge of two rice Plantations at the Euhaws, also an Overseer for an Indigo Plantation at the same place. Men properly qualified well Recommended, will meet with great Encouragement. Apply by Letter to the Subscriber at Charlestown, or in Prince William Parish. PIERCE BUTLER."[15]

Pierce Butler's decision to become a South Carolinian and to support the patriot's cause moved him headlong into a very active and decidedly varied existence. Family responsibilities called for the care of his wife Mary and their children, who appeared with some regularity in the early years of their married life. He became a justice of the peace in the Beaufort District in 1776, the first step in an enduring civil and political life. His public service was intense, often hectic, and persistently demanding. Between the politics of government and a spasmodic and unenthusiastic participation in military affairs, he found time for social activities with Mary Butler's wide circle of friends and family. He expanded his religious proclivities by increased activity as a member of St. Michael's Church. Added to these responsibilities was Pierce Butler's continuing dependence on slaves, and theirs on him. Not the least of the demands on his time was the administration of the several plantings inherited from Mary Butler's grandmother, Mary Bull. To these were added the adjoining tracts he had been granted by His Majesty's government, and occasional parcels held for other than speculative purposes. The difficult times and the magnitude of the various holdings in South Carolina put a burden on the Major's shoulders, particularly when he added to them the lands he had acquired on the Georgia coast. He knew these lands to be productive and of value only when worked by slaves.[16]

In South Carolina, and in Georgia, the pendulum of war swung back and forth—first to the Americans, then to the British, and back again. Against this backdrop divided loyalties and wavering allegiances were commonplace. For Pierce Butler, the war brought out a fundamental weakness in his character that would reappear later in his life. His embracing of the patriotic cause was awkward and uncomfortable in the years of the Revolution. It had to be troublesome to his conscience to fight the king and country he had served so short a time before. Thus, despite his training as a regimental officer and the experience gained in actual combat, he was reluctant to participate actively against his former countrymen. In his letter to Arthur Middleton of early 1776 he proclaimed his patriotism yet also wrote: "My inclination to do more is very good, but really my State of Health will not admit of it. I am just now recovering from a fever that Continued for several days. My nerves are so affected I can scarce write."[17] Pierce Butler was compromising. The letter Peter Manigault had written Miles Brewton when the Major's elopement with Betsy Izard was foiled had contained an accusal of hypocrisy. It proved to be a valid assessment of a dominant Pierce Butler characteristic.

The peace and contentment the South Carolinians had enjoyed since June 1776 changed abruptly with the return of British military forces to the Southern sector. After Savannah's fall the British began the plundering of Carolina plantations in vindictive raids of pillage and destruction. The Butler-Middleton plantations were burned and looted, and the Butlers lost many of their slaves, particularly from the Euhaw plantations near Beaufort. The impact of war moved Major Butler into a more active role in military affairs. Appointed adjutant general by Governor John Rutledge, he was a participant in a skirmish with a small force of British scouts from the Seventy-first Highlanders, a regiment the Major scorned. Three of their soldiers were captured, which must have given him some satisfaction for he considered the Seventy-first "a band of jailbirds &c," knowing the regiment had been bolstered by enrolling "culprits and convicts" from Savannah's jail.[18] While campaigning with the Americans in the vain attempt to hold off the British, Major Butler became increasingly apprehensive over the possibilities of his own capture by the army he had so recently deserted. His apprehension included his concern for the safety of his family. From a camp on the Edisto River at "Mr. Ferguson's Plantation," he expressed his fears in a letter to General Benjamin Lincoln, penned on May 3, 1779:

> Believe me Dear Sir that new terms of expression are yet to be found to make known my Distress on Account of my Family. I heard that they had set out by Water some days ago for Charles Town. They must then have either fallen into the Hands of the Enemy or in the Arms of the Deep—All my hopes and Happiness in Life centered on them. If they are gone there is no happiness left me in this world. Nothing to wish for so much as Death. I entreat you to ask Captain Morgan to go in an armed boat in Search of them.

In this letter to General Lincoln, Major Butler told of obtaining critical intelligence from one of the British prisoners who revealed the size and location of British forces under General Augustine Prevost and Lieutenant Colonel John Maitland: "This information I forced from Him with a Pistol at his Temple." Aware that his role in the war was something less than it might have been, he added, "I wish I was possessed of Powers Sufficient to enable me to be more Serviceable to a County that is Dearer to me than the one I first breathed in."

Mary Butler and her children arrived safely in Charlestown, but the Major's apprehension was to remain. In October 1779 he continued his military activities by serving as an aide to General Lachlan McIntosh in the unsuccessful attempt to dislodge the British from Savannah.[19] Back in Charlestown in November, he was confronted with the troubles brought on by the war. Needing money, he published a notice in a Charlestown newspaper: "A stock of Three Hundred Cattle, to be DISPOSED OF. Apply to John McQueen, Esq. in Charlestown, or P. Butler."[20] A few days later there was an air of desperation in a second notice:

> The Subscriber, intending shortly to depart this State for a few months for the recovery of his health—such person as may have demands on him to

apply immediately for payment—ready to appear, answer and give bail to any suit, summons or process that may be issued against him.

PIERCE BUTLER[21]

It was more a matter of "protection" of his health than its "recovery." Knowing full well what the British would do were he taken by them, Major Butler fled to North Carolina. There he became more a refugee than a soldier. He attached himself to General Gates's army, commanding a small detachment of men guarding prisoners of war at Salisbury.[22]

While Pierce Butler was in North Carolina, tragedy struck his family who had remained in Charlestown: "Sunday last a child of Pierce Butler, Esqr's was burnt by some Accident in such a manner that it expired very soon after."[23]

Major Butler's loneliness and sadness over the loss of his child was tempered by friendship and sympathy from a transplanted Englishman and fellow rebel. There began a lasting association with James Iredell, the collector of customs at Edenton, that prompted an exchange of kindnesses over a long span of years. In a letter to his friend after the war ended, Major Butler told of the loss of property to the depredations of the British: "But all of this, and more I could bear without a Sigh, were it possible to have restored to me my Favourite Son, the Promising Prop of my latter days, that they wantonly robbed me of."[24]

Since the child's death occurred in January 1780, several months before the British occupied Charlestown, it was unlikely the accusation was for a specific act on their part. Major Butler's blame of the British was probably but a continuation of his general condemnation of their recalcitrant belligerence. Whatever his meaning, his distress was evident.

Chapter 3

Spoils of War

IF THE WAR with England had played havoc with Pierce Butler's newfound world, the already uncertain existence of his and his peers' transplanted Africans was subjected to a turbulence that made his troubles pale in comparison.

In the years prior to the Revolution the low country of South Carolina, and to a lesser degree of Georgia, leaned heavily on the African slave. In both places slavery was recognized as the vital force on which the prosperity and well-being of the region depended. This was the belief of Pierce Butler, who, torn as he had been by his decision to adopt the patriot's banner, must have had a vast feeling of relief when he viewed the misfortunes of war that descended on those who remained loyal to the British government. In the early days of the war, those Loyalists who were not so fortunate to get away with the best of their slaves to the West Indies, to Bermuda, Nova Scotia, Florida, or other friendly havens, saw their properties plundered and their Negroes taken away.

The eager American military forces were fired with a strong desire for independence and also were inflamed by the alarming pronouncement of John Murray, the earl of Dunmore, who served as the last royal governor of Virginia. The proclamation was issued in Norfolk on November 7, 1775, and offered freedom to those willing to join His Majesty's forces and to take up arms against the rebels.[1]

The Dunmore proclamation spread fear throughout slave country, which was already on nervous guard against imagined uprisings of free and enslaved blacks. In August 1775, South Carolina patriots had hanged and burned Jerry, a well-known free Negro harbor pilot who they believed had armed and encouraged slaves to flee to British ships. Lord William Campbell, convinced of Jerry's innocence, told Lord Dunmore

that the patriots had "dipt their hands in blood." Within a week of the
Dunmore offer five hundred Virginia blacks had responded, and by December three hundred were wearing uniforms with the words "Liberty to
Slaves" across their chests. They were the nucleus of "Lord Dunmore's
Ethiopian Regiment." In South Carolina the hackles of slave owners were
raised and apprehension engulfed those whites living in areas where they
were outnumbered by slaves and free blacks. The Dunmore edict cast a
pall over the land.[2]

The great concerns of the South Carolinians were delineated in a letter
from Edward Rutledge to Ralph Izard, a man who had strong patriot
leanings and who was then living in England. The letter, dated December 8, 1775, was written in Philadelphia:

> You will receive by this conveyance a proclamation issued by Lord Dun-
> more—tending in my judgement, more effectively to work an eternal sepa-
> ration between Great Britain and the Colonies—than any other expedient
> which could possibly have been thought of.

> Tell me then, I beseech you (before it is too late) what are the sentiments of
> the English Nation—are the people of that Country determined to force us
> into Independence? Or do they really imagine that we are so insensitive to
> the calls of Reason—to every Injury. Do they expect that after our Towns
> have been destroyed—our Liberties repeatedly invaded—our women and
> Children driven from their Habitations—our nearest Relatives sacrificed—
> our Slaves emancipated for the express purpose of massacreing their Mas-
> ters—can they, I say after all their injuries—expect that we shall return to
> our former connection—with a forgiving and cordial Disposition?[3]

Edward Rutledge was not alone in his consternation. The Continental
Congress, where Delegate Rutledge was at work, sounded the alarm.
George Washington said of Lord Dunmore: "If, my Dear Sir, that man is
not crushed before spring he will become the most formidable enemy
America has, his strength will increase as a snowball, by rolling."[4] Newspapers in the Southern Colonies reacted excitedly, and when "two sloops
full of negroes" escaped to British men-of-war in Charlestown harbor, the
Gazette tried to downplay the importance of the act by writing that the
slaves had gone "with the foolish expectation of obtaining their Freedom." Those slaves that did heed the Dunmore proclamation were owned
mostly by patriot planters. For those unfortunates who had been the
property of Tory masters, nothing was gained. They were held closely by

their captors, and most, quite simply, became a large part of the spoils of war.[5]

In South Carolina these hapless people were put to work as military laborers in support of various American forces. Some were assigned the tasks of clearing obstructions from rivers and streams. While a few military commanders turned over their captive slaves to the commissioners for confiscated estates, who did show some restraint in disposing of the Negroes without putting families asunder, others were not so considerate. General Andrew Pickens chose to divide captured property, including slaves, among his troops. General Thomas Sumter invoked what came to be called "Sumter's Law" by offering slaves as bounty to enlistees in his patriot regiments. This was a promise that anticipated the capture of slaves and was an inducement that led to much trouble. As it turned out, his troops were unable to collect sufficient Tory slaves to fill their contracts, and so turned to filching Negroes from pro-American slaveholders, which raised a true furor.[6]

Slaves of Georgia's Loyalists fared no better than South Carolina's. In Savannah, the new government put them to work in securing military establishments against attack. Some were sent to Tybee Island to erect batteries, and others were used as specie. Slaves were given to troops in lieu of pay, to public officials as salary, and were exchanged for provisions for use by military units.[7]

To Pierce Butler, a planter's slaves were as his life's blood. He noted well the actions of his fellow patriots and their use of the Tories' slaves. These indiscretions would prompt a rather surprising act on his part when the war had ended and tempers were cooling.

Following the failure of the British to capture Charlestown in June 1776, the coastal areas of South Carolina and Georgia made good use of the quiet spell that lasted until the British flexed their muscles to capture Savannah in late 1778, although the enemy did maintain limited pressure with occasional raids by naval vessels and by the use of their psychological weapon, Lord Dunmore's proclamation. As early as March 1776, Georgia's General Lachlan McIntosh had written that the British were "encouraging our slaves to desert to them, pilfering our sea islands for provisions." In December of that year he told of an incident on Sapelo Island where a British ship had captured a guard vessel and had carried off its crew along with slaves and other valuable articles from the island.[8]

Such activity prompted a reaction from Henry Laurens. In the long letter to his son in which he expressed his views on the freeing of his slaves, he stated:

> Negroes are brought by Englishmen and sold as slaves to Americans. Bristol, Liverpool, Manchester and Birmingham, &c, live upon the slave trade. The British Parliament now employ their men-of-war to steal those negroes from the Americans to whom they have sold them pretending to set the poor wretches free, but basely trepan and sell them into tenfold worse slavery in the West Indies, where probably they become the property of Englishmen again, and some of whom sit in Parliament. What meanness! What complicated wickedness appears in this scene. O England, how Changed! How Fallen!

And Henry Laurens's outspoken son was in agreement with Lord Dunmore that the slave could be made into warrior. Colonel John Laurens had impressive military credentials that lent substance to his unpopular idea. He had fought with General Washington as his aide-de-camp. His intelligence, his fine family background, and his considerable bravery were recognized and accepted, but when he spoke his mind on the freeing of slaves, or on the wrongs of the system, a scant few accepted his message. He told his father, "We have sunk the Africans and their descendants below the standards of humanity, and almost render'd them incapable of that blessing which equal Heaven bestow'd upon us all." It was his most fervent conviction that he could arm sufficient slaves, as many as five thousand, and with a promise of freedom, bring success to a campaign against the British. In the atmosphere that prevailed in South Carolina of that troubled time such an opinion from a lesser man would not have been tolerated. Henry Laurens reacted with alarm, calling on his son to move with caution "in opposing the opinions of whole nations." He passed on a parental prayer, "My dear Son, I pray God protect you and add to your knowledge and learning, if it be necessary, discretion." But when the British came on strong, even this doubter found merit in his son's proposal. He wrote General Washington, echoing John Laurens's enthusiastic pleas, "Had we arms for three thousand such black men as I could select in South Carolina I should have no doubt of success in driving the British out of Georgia and subduing East Florida before the end of July."[9] George Washington was as cautious as Henry Laurens had been. The young Laurens persevered to present his case to the South Carolina Assembly as late as February 1782, where he won faint support. Ædanus

Burke told Arthur Middleton that fifteen members voted for the Laurens proposal, but "by all the rest, it was execrated." That General Nathanael Greene was in favor of arming the slaves, led Mr. Burke into a short dissertation on slavery:

> The northern people I have observed, regard the condition in which we hold our slaves in a light different from us. I am much deceived indeed, if they do not secretly *wish* for a general Emancipation, if the present struggle was over. A very sensible man whom you well know in Philadela once mentioned to me, that our Country wd be a fine one, if our whites & blacks intermarried—the breed wd be a hardy excellent race, he said, fit to bear our climate.[10]

In a letter to Arthur Middleton, Edward Rutledge told of the assembly's alternative to enlisting the slaves, "We have agreed to raise 2 Continental Battns at the enormous Bounty of 1 Negroe for each Year's time." But the promise of one slave for each volunteer serving one year could not be kept.[11]

Although Pierce Butler had purchased his Georgia plantation on St. Simons Island in 1774, the turbulent times prevented his planned development of the distant property. His planting interests remained in South Carolina, and when the British presence adversely affected the war for the Southerners, he began to fear for his property and for his own skin as well. The British had returned with a vengeance. Loyalists who had fled in the early days of the Revolution came back to regain their plantations and to replace their confiscated slaves with those to be taken from the likes of Pierce Butler. The patriot planters became victims of plundering bands of British soldiers and seamen. Their plantations were devastated, their homes and buildings burned after being ransacked for items of value and interest. The unfortunate slaves were once again spoils of war, gathered in by the avenging Loyalists and their military. Some became laborers for British forces; others who were not doled out to the Loyalist planters followed the surer promise of Lord Dunmore's emancipation proclamation by bearing arms against the Americans, more effectively as seamen than as soldiers. Among the former slaves who fought the Americans in South Carolina and Georgia were many who enlisted in Hessian regiments. German records made little effort to designate a soldier by color of his skin; thus, the total number of their black enlistees is not known. It is known, though, that at least forty-seven came from South Carolina, that some came from Africa and the West Indies, that most served as drummers, while others performed the menial tasks to be expected in an army. They were laborers—packhands, carters, teamsters—and rarely was one elevated to be the esteemed Hessian fighting man, a musketeer.[12]

Lieutenant Colonel Archibald Campbell, who led his Seventy-first Highlanders in the 1778 expedition against Savannah, had anticipated the pillage and plundering. In the general order to his troops prior to attacking the city, his forewarning seemed precise and determined:

> Lieutenant Colonel Campbell recommends in a particular manner not to suffer the Troops under their Orders to commit a single Act of Depredation of Plunder. In the former Instance, they will ruin a Country which is meant to be preserved; in the latter, they will injure their Reputation in point of Discipline. Marauders are the Bane and Disgrace of an Army, the stubborn Weeds of Riot and Licentiousness, and will be exterminated without mercy.
>
> The advanced Centinels and Patroles are to stop all Stragglers, whether Men or Women, Blacks or Whites, who shall attempt to pass Limits of their Post, and confine them. Such who are found with Plunder, or committing any Act of Depredation are to be sent to the Provost in Irons.[13]

The monetary value of slaves at that time was "250 Spanish Dollars," a price that played havoc with the plans of both the British and Americans. General William Moultrie lent credence to Henry Laurens's statement that the South Carolina slaves were being sent to the West Indies and sold. He wrote: "The prospects of gain, from the sale of plundered negroes, were too seducing to be resisted by the officers, privates, and followers of the British army. On their departure from Charlestown, upwards of eight hundred slaves who had been employed in the engineer department were shipped off for the West Indies." It was the general's belief that the slaves were sent by the direction of and sold for the benefit of Colonel James Moncrief, a British officer who exercised control over large numbers of blacks who had been taken from the Americans or who had come to the British seeking freedom.[14]

Throughout the course of the war South Carolina's slave population remained in constant turmoil. A contemporary historian noted the region was plundered by the British army, by patriot partisans, by the Loyalists and their militia, by lawless gangs, and by citizens of neighboring states. Add to that the slaves lost to Lord Dunmore's proclamation and the depredations become massive. American planters were not alone in losing their slaves as runaways, for their Loyalist counterparts discovered to their dismay that their own slaves harkened to the British call that promised freedom. Consequently there was a constant exodus from the low-country plantations to the British ships and military units. The fact was noted by the fearsome Lieutenant Banastre Tarleton of the British legion, the "scourge of the Carolinas":

> All the negroes, men, women and children, upon the arrival of any detachment of the King's troops, thought themselves absolved from all respect to their American masters, and entirely released from servitude.
>
> They quitted the plantations and followed the army.[15]

When the British occupied Charlestown in May 1780, they chose to banish the leaders of the patriot cause. Men were incarcerated on prison ships, many were confined at St. Augustine in Florida, and Henry Laurens was imprisoned in the Tower of London until he was exchanged for General Cornwallis after Yorktown. Following an agreement made in May 1781, the South Carolinians were exchanged for prisoners held by the Americans, and shortly thereafter, Lieutenant Colonel Nisbet Balfour, the head of His Majesty's Board of Police in Charlestown, ordered their families to depart for Philadelphia by August 1. In all, 186 men, including the St. Augustine prisoners, 120 women, and 264 children left South Carolina for Pennsylvania. Mary Butler and her six children were among the exiled. They joined Major Butler in North Carolina and together went on to Philadelphia.[16]

George Grieve, an opportunistic Briton who spent a year in America, observed the South Carolinians in Philadelphia. He enjoyed their hospitality and drank "exquisite old Port and Madeira" with young Charles Pinckney and Major Butler. Of the Carolina exiles, he wrote:

> My bosom beat high with genuine ardor in the cause for which they sacrificed every personal consideration, but I had frequently the opportunity of appreciating that sacrifice. Seeing what I saw, I want no instances of Greek or Roman virtue to stimulate my feelings, or excite my emulation; and it will ever be matter of congratulation with me, to have witnessed in the principal inhabitants of Carolina, all the blandishments of civilized society, the love of life and all its blessings, a humanity void of reproach, an hospitality not exceeded in the patriarchal ages, contrary to the paradoxes of systematic writers, blended with the inflexible virtue which distinguished

the best and purest ages of the world. From the number I shall select the brilliant examples of Major Pierce Butler, and Mr. Arthur Middleton. Wealth, honor, interest, domestic happiness, their children were nothing in the eyes of such men, though calculated to enjoy, and to communicate happiness in every sphere, when put in competition with the great objects of universal public happiness, and sacred Freedom's holy cause. How painful is it to be compelled to add, that such was the cold, selfish spirit of too many of the inhabitants of Philadelphia towards their Carolina brethren, who had every claim upon their sympathy and good offices, as to merit the indignation of every feeling mind, and to fix an indelible stain upon their character as men and citizens.[17]

If Pierce Butler suffered a Philadelphia cold shoulder, he did not show it. Yet, he was anxious to be away and back in South Carolina where many matters required his attention. He wrote his North Carolina friend James Iredell that he foresaw a quick end to the long war:

Superior by sea and land to the Enemy, we may justly, and on the best grounds, expect to put a happy issue to the contest, and very shortly be rewarded with the Blessings of Peace, Sweet Peace, Freedom and Security— those rich gifts of Heaven.

Here Trade flourishes and plenty abounds, the war is not felt here, while the Carolinas groan under the weight and miseries of it.[18]

The consternation of the American slave owner reached frantic peaks as the British first contemplated drastic measures to maintain their Southern foothold and then began planning for the ultimate evacuation of the low country. In December 1781 "John Murray, the Lord Dunmore," appeared in Charlestown hoping to find respite from the heat he had encountered in Virginia. He sought, in desperation, to arm ten thousand Negroes and turn them loose on the South Carolinians and Georgians, a scheme that surpassed his proclamation. Fortunately for the Americans, the idea was rejected by the British command. When the same command made the decision to abandon the Southern theater, a great fear swept through the American planters that there would be further and extensive reductions of their slave population.[19]

Almost immediately following the capture of Charlestown in 1780, the British had begun a widespread accumulation of blacks. Herded into makeshift camps, they suffered an appalling loss of life to inadequate care and to persistent outbreaks of smallpox. When General Charles Corn-

wallis and his army departed Charlestown toward "destiny" at Yorktown, a ragtag collection of blacks accompanied them. Ill fed, ill clothed,
ill, they stumbled toward a freedom that for all but a few was never to be.
For many of these people, their journey would end in the slave's own
freedom—death. For others, it meant a return to the South Carolina rice
fields. Following the surrender of Cornwallis, agents of the planters were
on hand to retrieve the slaves who had followed the illusive promise.
Ædanus Burke of Charlestown was there and wrote Arthur Middleton,
who was then in Philadelphia: "I Saved several Negroes for some of So
Carola friends wch the British had at York. There was one of yours, but he
went on board a vessel & cd not find him. I have one of Jno Izard's with
me."[20]

Otter Island is a small bit of sandy shoreland on St. Helena's Sound, a
few miles downstream from the Bull plantation on Coosaw Island where
Major Butler and his family lived at the beginning of the war. The sound
offered access to South Carolina plantations in the area to the east and
north of Beaufort. From their anchorage near the island the British sent
raiding parties up the Combahee and Edisto rivers to the island plantations near the sea. Their "liberation" of slaves was far greater than the
capacity of their ships. Consequently, Otter Island became one of the
marshaling points where the slaves were collected for ultimate removal in
the British evacuation. As in so many such concentrations, the means of
sustaining the men, the women, the old, the young, were just not there.
Hundreds died as fever ran through the unfortunate campsite. At the time
of departure many of the pathetic people struggled to board the longboats
to be taken to the ships at anchor. Fought off, they were left behind, either
too weak to help themselves or too frightened to return to their former
owners for fear of reprisal. In 1785 an observer wrote, "Their dead
bodies, as they lay exposed in the woods, were devoured by beasts, and
birds, and to this day the island is strewed with their bones."[21]

The number of slaves lost by the South Carolinians and the Georgians
through all the years of the Revolution is difficult to estimate. William
Moultrie wrote that between 1775 and 1783 "it has been computed by
good judges" that South Carolina lost twenty-five thousand slaves, a figure that later historians think overestimated. The generally accepted figures of blacks taken away in the final hectic evacuation at the war's end are
that 6,000 former slaves were aboard British ships when they left
Charlestown in December and that 4,000 more were transported away
from Savannah. There were 3,794 white civilians who left South Carolina

with the British fleet. In a trade-off, many British soldiers and their Hessian comrades-in-arms deserted to remain and become South Carolinians.[22]

The exodus of blacks might well have been greater except that South Carolina threatened to ignore debts due British merchants and to forgo return of confiscated estates if more slaves were taken away on their ships. Benjamin Guerard and Edward Rutledge were the Americans commissioned to work out an arrangement with the British commander General Alexander Leslie. Major Butler's good friend Roger Parker Saunders was one of the two men permitted to live in occupied Charlestown to attempt to retrieve slaves and return them to their former owners, excepting those who had made themselves "obnoxious" by attachment to British troops, and as such, "had specific promises of freedom."[23] Although their successes were limited, Major Butler was surprised to find that of the two hundred slaves taken from the Butler plantations, some were returned. In the letter to James Iredell in which he lamented the loss of his son, he also wrote: "I receiv'd more of my Negroes than I expected, but found everything else as bad as possible. All my buildings burnt, and those Settlements that were accomplished by many Years hard Industry layd entirely waste."[24]

For slaves the Revolution did mark a change in their status. For many it was only a brief cessation of turmoil and uncertainty. They returned to their prewar existence on the plantation or to their work in the town houses of their owners, regimented as before. A few won freedom, and the freedom of slaves had become an issue to be championed, or denounced. There *was* a chink in the chain that bound them.

Efforts to have the British return the slaves they had taken away met with stubborn refusal. Ralph Izard, having answered the "Public Call" and returned to America from France and England, stated the British position on the surrender of slaves in a letter to Arthur Middleton:

> I am sorry to learn that so many of your Negroes are still missing; & the more so, as I fear that it will not be an easy matter to recover them. Sir Guy Carleton has very explicitly given it as his opinion that the Negroes within the British Lines can not be claimed by virtue of the Preliminary Treaty, as property belonging to Citizens of the United States, because they have been declared free by proclamations, issued by Officers acting under the authority of the King of Great Britain. This is a most impudent evasion of the Treaty; & Yet we are not in a condition to help ourselves.[25]

The thousands of slaves carried away by the British had diverse fates. Many were returned to slavery in faraway places. Numbers of those who gained the promised freedom found that they had lost security and became disillusioned. Spread about the British Empire in the New and Old Worlds, the bewildered blacks struggled to find their way. From cold Nova Scotia, where promised land grants failed to materialize, more than a thousand returned to Africa—to Sierra Leone—in a venture beset with difficulties. On Otter Island in South Carolina, the bones of those who had found no passage on the British ships bleached in the bright sun. Perhaps the most important effect on slavery was that surrender at Yorktown established a new nation as the one in which more people were held in bondage than any other in the world.[26]

Major Butler welcomed the end of the conflict that had brought him torment, discomfort, and sadness. Despite his outward signs of allegiance to the cause of independence, his participation had been halfhearted, and he was never able to summon the fervent patriotism exhibited by many of his peers. Only when the British threatened the Butler plantations and were sure to carry away his slaves could he bring himself to have more than a perfunctory role in the waging of war. He was a soldier to whom peace would indeed be sweet.

When it did come, and while reflecting on the power and ambition of kings to wage wars with "wanton efusion of human blood," he wrote, "Thank God it is not in the powers of any One Man to involve Us in the horrors of War." Understandably, he could also write, "I have suffered so greatly by War that I shall the rest of my days pray for Peace on Earth."[27]

Chapter 4

Pierce Butler's Private Life

A S THE WAR approached a bitter end, an air of good cheer spread among the South Carolinians in Philadelphia. Some had begun the long journey home overland, knowing that travel by ship would be dangerous as Charlestown harbor was crowded with British warships and transports preparatory to their departure, deep laden with precious plunder and thousands of Carolina slaves. In early 1782 Ædanus Burke made the trip home and advised Arthur Middleton to take care on his journey. He cited the miserable conditions along the way, which Middleton found to be miserable indeed. While enroute, Arthur Middleton wrote his young friend Charles Pinckney, who had remained in Philadelphia. Middleton had met with "Stumps, Stones, craggy hills &c, and hairbreadth Scapes" and sent a message to the Butlers: "Remember me affectionately to the Major & his family. Tell him I think he will judge right in taking the other road, we have found this much more broken & disagreeable than I expected—let him know the two Horses he spared me are well." Pierce Butler was in the good graces of his fellow South Carolinians. Arthur Middleton planned a welcome for him at Middleton Place: "Acquaint the Major I shall depend upon his driving directly to the Ashley River, where we will make the best preparations for his reception the Times will admit of." Middleton sent his love to Mrs. McFunn, who boarded them on Second Street in Philadelphia, and to "miss Polly," his cousin, Mary Butler. He urged the Major to bring Mrs. McFunn along. She had provided a lantern and a "Bundle of good things," bringing forth praise. "Mrs. McF's light shines every night so that we see her good works." Indicative of his own situation, he asked Charles

Pinckney to "acquaint Mrs. Moreton (the fat housekeeper)" he would send her the first money he could "rake & scrape." Charles Cotesworth Pinckney, also home at last, sent his "love," or his "affection," to the Butler family on several occasions.

Conditions in South Carolina were in marked contrast to the peace and prosperity of Philadelphia. Ædanus Burke described the difficult conditions in January 1782:

> I wish I could give you a proper Idea of the distressed situation of this country & temper of the people; & this I assure you has undergone a great and Serious revolution since you were here. The outrage & cruelty of the British is beyond description, and the inveterate hatred and spirit of Vengeance wch they have excited in the breasts of our Citizens is such as you can form no idea of.

Governor John Mathews verified the words of Ædanus Burke: "Of all the insatiable Devils that were ever let loose to torment mankind, the British army—especially in this country—must bear away the bays."

Of interest to Major Butler would have been Charles Cotesworth Pinckney's report that it was all but impossible to provide sustenance for the American forces commanded by Nathanael Greene and Anthony Wayne. Not only had there been ruthless destruction of plantation houses and buildings, but "all the country about the Euhaws" had been "eaten up." Yet, the violation and destruction of the plantations did not weigh so heavily as did the specter of Charlestown harbor as pictured by General Pinckney. He told of the arrival of the British frigates *Assurance, Adamant,* and *Narcissus,* the sloop of war *Cormorant,* and fifty empty transports. As he put it, "Charlestown will be shortly in our Possession," but removed from their possession would be so many of those "wretched Africans" on whom their well-being depended. This was the true reason for the anger and frustration of the South Carolina plantation people.[1]

Thus, when the Butlers returned to South Carolina in the fall of 1782, the peace they found was far from sweet. Completely vanished was the easiness that prevailed between the futile attack on Sullivan's Island in 1776 and the return of the British in 1780. In its place the Butlers found despair and desolation. Those who had been loyal to the British, and those former patriots who had wavered in their allegiance to the cause of freedom when the British reappeared, were looked on with suspicion, distrust, and hatred by many who had held fast to their belief in independence. It was the worst of times.

The Butler-Middleton circle of friends and family had been shattered by the death of Daniel Blake, of the Loyalist Lord William Campbell, by the loss of the entire Miles Brewton family and of Mary Butler's sister, Sarah Guerard. Her husband, Benjamin Guerard, had been captured at the fall of Charlestown and held on board the prison ship *Pack Horse*. The Butlers had lost their first son in an unexplained accident. Henry Laurens, released from prison in the Tower of London, mourned the loss of his son. The gallant radical John Laurens was dead of wounds received in a minor skirmish on the Combahee River near the end of the war. The "Signers" Edward Rutledge and Arthur Middleton were among those who had been imprisoned at St. Augustine; the latter, having lost his fortune and two hundred slaves, was seen about Charlestown wearing "common negro cloth." This once-fashionable gentleman was hard pressed to raise enough money to pay the "fat housekeeper" he had left in Philadelphia.[2]

The South Carolinians faced increasingly difficult times. There was scant comfort in knowing their misfortunes were shared by many. The greatest bar to their recovery was the loss of their slaves, as Pierce Butler knew full well. He lost no time in setting about a strategic use of those he continued to control. While his strategy helped to recoup his losses, it was also to win some troubles for which he had not bargained. His unrestrained use of the Butler slaves was to excite the trustees of the Mary Bull estate and to bring down their wrath. His immediate need was working capital. In angling for a loan from a Philadelphia acquaintance he painted an optimistic picture of conditions in South Carolina. He said the effect of peace was evident: "The injury this country experienced from the enemy has given a new spring to industry. All ranks of men think of little else then repairing their losses. Our wharfs present a scene of bustle and activity that I have not seen for many years."[3] To raise funds he advertised the sale of a tract of 1,859 acres on the north side of the Altamaha River in Georgia, land he had acquired and owned jointly with the "heirs of Houston." At the same time he began to search in earnest for a loan, planning to use the family's lands and the remaining slaves as security for the funds he wished to borrow.[4]

In 1784, while striving to put his own house in order, he turned his considerable energies and talents to an enlarged role in public service. The new state of South Carolina needed his help, as did his church, St. Michael's of Charleston. He gave of his time to both most generously.

In that year, Pierce Butler, his oldest daughter, Sarah, and his six-year-old son, Thomas, set out for England. They were accompanied by a slave whom Major Butler called "my servant John." The Major was bent on visiting his family in Ireland, on following the orders of his fellow vestrymen at St. Michael's to find and employ an assistant minister, but more important, to find a lender to supply the capital he so desperately needed to get the Butler agricultural empire going again. The children were to be educated in English schools: Sarah at Mrs. and Miss Moreau's Boarding School for Young Ladies on Great Cumberland and Oxford streets, and Thomas at the Reverend Weeden Butler's Classical School for Boys on Cheyne Walk, Chelsea, both in London. The forty-year-old Major made a vivid impression at the Reverend Mr. Butler's when he arrived with his young son. He was described as "Enthusiastic, enterprising, gallant & resolute. Of a tall and well proportioned frame, dignified carriage & deportment, accompanied with courtesy of manners, the result of much travel and military habits." Major Butler and Weeden Butler claimed no kinship but did become friends. Their considerable correspondence documents the attitudes and personality of the Major in the years when he laid the foundation for his own fortune and assisted in charting the course for his state and nation. For eleven years the letters went back and forth between the two men. In one of the first, Major Butler left no doubt as to his feelings: "I have entrusted you with what I value more than the Wealth of the World. The Education and Principles of an *Only Son*."[5]

Having deposited his children in the most English of educational institutions, in the heart of a land he had so recently deserted and had considered his sworn enemy, Pierce Butler then set out to find some of the "Wealth of the World" he had come seeking. His mission to find the new clergyman was not successful. A side effort to find money for the new state of South Carolina was not fulfilled, although he noted the possibility of a loan on rather stringent conditions. He was successful in finding money for his own needs. He borrowed 150,000 Dutch guilders from Jan Gabriel Tegelaar of Amsterdam. A translation from Low Dutch of the resulting mortgage names twenty-two separate tracts in South Carolina and four in Georgia that were pledged as security for the loan. The Carolina lands included the working plantations at the Euhaws, the old Middleton-Bull homeplace on Coosaw Island, his Charleston real estate on the South Bay, and many tracts containing thousands of acres granted him by the Royal government when he was its "loyal" subject. The Georgia tracts included a recent acquisition, Butler's Island in the Altamaha River, and the three tracts he had purchased from the Grahams with the money gained from the sale of his army commission. His share of the land owned with the Houstons was not included, but all else was there—the property he owned individually, and Mary Butler's Middleton-Bull inheritance as well. Definitely included were: "All such slaves, who are in being employed in the service of the aforementioned Lands at the passing of the aforesaid mortgages, moresoever, those who may be purchased or acquired in their place." On the cover sheet of the substantial document Major Butler at some time had penned: "Copies of some Transactions with that dishonest Man Jan Gabriel Tegelaar of Amsterdam." It was a typical reaction, for in many instances throughout his life the Major found reason to become an adversary to parties with whom he transacted business.[6]

Letters to the Reverend Mr. Butler show that Major Butler visited his own Butlers at their family seat—"Ballin Temple—What an Irish name"—and then traveled extensively in the British Isles and on the Continent before returning to South Carolina in late 1785, where he quickly became involved in governmental affairs. Yet there was but little diminution of his interest or attention to personal matters. Before leaving England he had instructed Weeden Butler that young Thomas was to be so polished in statesmanship that upon completion of his schooling the schoolmaster would be "restoring to his Country a *Distinguished Ornament*." The Major wished Thomas to be a replica of himself, and like himself, able to attend to matters of state and his own considerable interests at the same time.[7]

Despite the difficult times, Major Butler was so impressed with the elegant atmosphere of the river plantations on the Ashley above Charleston that he used some of the borrowed money to acquire one as a homeplace for himself and his family. In May 1786 he bought 1,168 acres for three thousand pounds sterling from Stephen and Martha Baker. The land was across the Ashley from the Drayton plantations Magnolia and Drayton Hall. He gave the new place a lovely name, Mary Ville, in honor of his wife. It proved to be the family home for only a few years, and those years were interrupted by his service to state and federal governments. Notwithstanding his residence in St. Andrew's Parish, he continued to represent Prince William's in the South Carolina legislature.[8]

The difficult times were made more so by poor rice crops in successive years, 1785 and 1786. A good crop in 1787 came at a most opportune time, for Major Butler was confronted with his busiest year in public service. His appointment by the legislature to the Constitutional Convention in Philadelphia and the Confederation Congress in New York left

Charleston, Ashley River Plantations, and the Harbor Fortifications

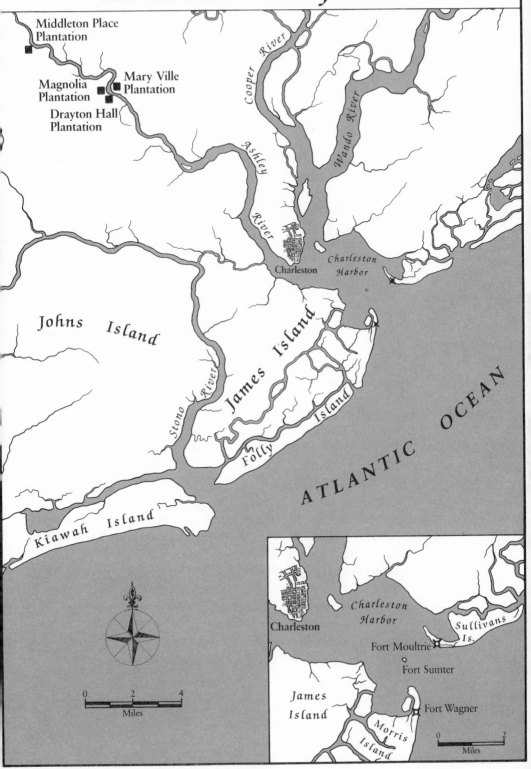

Middleton Place Plantation

Magnolia Plantation

Mary Ville Plantation

Drayton Hall Plantation

Cooper River

Wando River

Ashley River

Charleston

Charleston Harbor

Johns Island

James Island

Stono River

Folly Island

Kiawah Island

ATLANTIC OCEAN

0   2   4
Miles

Charleston

Charleston Harbor

Sullivans Is.

Fort Moultrie

Fort Sumter

James Island

Fort Wagner

Morris Island

0   2
Miles

little time to manage his agricultural empire. His attention to family business had begun to waver.[9]

The new responsibilities to the federal government called for an extended visit to Philadelphia, and later in the year, to New York. Mary Butler's health was such that her family became concerned. In August, after the delegates had recessed in Philadelphia, Pierce Butler joined her and their girls in New York, where he briefly attended the Confederation Congress already in session. He was soon back in Philadelphia, hard at the task of hammering out a constitution.

The family relished their return to Mary Ville in the fall, the Major most of all, for it gave him time to see to many problems that needed his attention. The business of government and even the business of his church had deflected him from the plantations that provided income to meet the expenses of living and to repay his debts. Despite a good rice crop in 1787 and a similar one the following year, the pressures surrounding his life put him in a testy mood. In July 1788 he exhibited his irritation in a long letter to Weeden Butler. He threatened to sell his lands, saying that were he able to do so, "you woud soon see me in England, but in a Private Station"—an inconsistent thought for an inconsistent American. In keeping with this thought he took pains to point out the evils of slavery:

> If America should be the means of opening the Eyes of the Enslaved, so as to make them cast off their Chains, I shall be better reconciled to my suffering & losses. You may naturally ask me Why, with these Sentiments, do you hold so many in Bondage. I answer You, that I woud free every one of them tomorrow if I coud do it. That is if the Legislature woud permit it. I ardently wish I never had anything to do with such property.

It was a typical Pierce Butler exaggeration. He embellished his overstatement by adding that he daily begged his slaves to find a master with whom they would be happy, but they would make no effort to find such a person—as if they could have done so. His expressed discontent with owning slaves came to be a rather commonplace reaction when difficulties were encountered on the plantations. The Major, however, was quick to recover from such extreme thoughts and to renew his usual *modus operandi* of having his agents or his managers get on with the business of buying more "likely Negroes," or moving them about from plantation to plantation as needed.[10]

Having been chosen by the South Carolina legislature to represent the state as a United States senator, Major Butler was soon back in New York with his family. He attended the first Congress to struggle with the governing of the young country under the Constitution he had helped formulate in Philadelphia. The pressures from government, from personal affairs and Mary Butler's illness were greater than ever. His senatorial career began with a steadfast belief that the federal government should not usurp the powers of the states. He argued against duties on foreign trade and against excessive federal presence in the judicial system. He became increasingly doubtful as to the worth of the Constitution as a solid foundation for government. His initial political alignment was essentially, but by no means consistently, Federalist.

In the Senate, as an in-law put it, he quickly won a reputation for being "A man of strong prejudices and feelings, with a temper somewhat more irritable than that of St. Paul. Proud by nature, given to domineering, as people would call it, which I suppose meant a determination to have his own way."[11]

President Washington, who was on hand for the meeting of Congress, eased the pressure somewhat by inviting the Butlers to social gatherings. The Major was a frequent guest and at one dinner was there with other important men, including Senator William Maclay of Pennsylvania, who noted in his diary that the president's usual poise had vanished, traded for "a settled aspect of melancholy. No cheering ray of convivial sunshine broke through the gloom of settled seriousness. At every interval of eating or drinking he played on the table with a fork or knife, like a drumstick."[12] Pierce Butler might well have joined George Washington in beating a nervous tattoo on the table, for his personal problems were legion.

After the Revolution the Butlers were visited by Major Butler's nephew Edward, a son of his oldest brother Thomas who had been the sixth baronet of Cloughrenan, and who had died in 1772. Edward, as had the Major, sold his commission in the British army and had come to seek a fortune in the Carolina low country. He came with a friend, William Payne, the son of a servant to the Irish Butlers. Edward was accepted in the family of the Carolina Butlers, and William became a clerk to the Major. Edward was given a slave, a personal servant, and both young men were made to feel very much at home. Both took undue advantage of the hospitality and generosity of the family and were soon in trouble. Butler financed the purchase of horses for his nephew who failed to repay the loan at a time when the Major desperately needed money. From New York, he wrote Edward, "Had I been in my former affluence your deficiency would have been in no merit." Major Butler noted in his letter that Edward's brother Tom, Thomas Parker Butler, in Ireland had managed to pay some of Edward's Irish debts with money promised to him, and thus he was soured on the worth of both nephews. He added, "I perceive Your loss in the early death of your Father. He would have taught both by precept & example a different sense of right, a stronger one of gratitude." Edward's behavior in Carolina prompted a letter from Major Butler to Tom: "Your brother Edward is Well in Carolina and against my repeated advice has bought some negroes injudiciously and without my knowledge. He will have occasion to repent his obstinacy." In this letter the Major admonished Tom for being inattentive to debts he had incurred in Strasbourg and for trying to obtain more funds from his family in Ireland. Major Butler sought relief from the same source. He wrote his sister Frances Butler complaining that Edward was "As unworthy and ungrateful a Young Man as I have ever seen." He also expressed his indignation over Tom's Strasbourg debts, writing, "I wish to have done with those young men." He then threw in William Payne, saying he was an Irishman "Well versed in hypocrisy and falsehood." On all three, he ended his diatribe with, "It was in the hour of my adverse fortune these unworthy men behaved ill."[13]

The problems brought on by the two nephews and William Payne were naught when compared with those resulting from Pierce Butler's endorsement of loans of Daniel Boudreaux and John McQueen, both of whom defaulted on their promises to pay, leaving a sorely strapped Pierce Butler to satisfy their obligations. Boudreaux's debt was to Hercules Daniel Bize, who was relentless in the pursuit of his money. John McQueen fled his Carolina and Georgia creditors, and his family as well, to go to Florida where he soon became Don Juan McQueen in a transformation that won the admiration of the much-harassed Major, who somehow could write, "I have never ceased to hold you as a friend."[14]

In an attempt to work out the Boudreaux-Bize loan, Major Butler's friends and agents, Alexander Gillon and Roger Parker Saunders, proposed securing Mr. Bize by giving him claim on Pierce Butler's own property. In a letter to the two men the Major approved the plan, reluctantly: "I am not without my doubts & apprehension that the painful surrender of all the property I had in my own right to Mr. Bize may be viewed in an unfavourable light by my other creditors. What will Mr. Hovy, Vanstaphorsts, Major Ladson, Mr. Russel and all my other creditors say of this partiality?" Major Butler took heart and added: "If I live I trust I shall pay them, if I die I shall make it my last request to my own children to do it."[15]

Hercules Daniel Bize demanded not only Pierce Butler's property but that of his wife and children. The Major seemed to agree to such a settlement but then withdrew the offer. Mary Butler had drawn the line and refused to permit the use of lands or slaves as security to her husband's obligations. At this time he wrote that he was a stranger to "Peace of Mind" and seriously thought of selling what he believed his most valuable property, the tidal island in the Altamaha River.[16]

As troubles mounted, Pierce Butler endeavored to collect money owed him. He threatened to sue the "McClain Estate" and Philip Minis in federal court in Savannah. He recognized Daniel Boudreaux as hopeless but kept after the eminent Don Juan McQueen:

> Let me then entreat you by the friendship you bear me & my children to timely secure me against the claims of Edward's Heirs, Phillips, Mrs. Colcock, &c. It does appear to me that it would be for your interest to make over part of your Estate to me in trust for your Creditors. Excuse my writing plain, my situation requires it. I entreat you to write me by the first opportunity what you have done. My wounded mind required not this additional distress to make me unhappy.

When Jacob Read "entered up judgement" against Major Butler for McQueen's debt to Phillips, Roger Parker Saunders was instructed to "Move all the Negroes you can from M. Ville & Euhaws to Georgia," beyond the reach of foreclosure.[17]

It was Roger Parker Saunders who finally rescued Major Butler by arranging an additional loan from Major James Ladson of Charleston, "A man of Honor and a Gentleman." Captain Saunders, a South Carolinian then living on his own Georgia plantation south of Savannah, had known Major Butler in the years of the Revolution. His considerable assistance came at a time when Pierce Butler was attending to his senatorial chores in New York and Philadelphia. Major Ladson took Hampton and Butler's Island as collateral on a loan of four thousand pounds sterling to forestall an attachment by a person unknown to Major Butler at the time. Word of the pending attachment had come to Major Butler from Edward Rutledge, causing Mary Butler "in the midst of her great indisposition" to consider a remedy in a plan of the Major's. She was to write her cousin Elizabeth Blake asking that she lend a hand by purchasing Butler's Island with funds held in trust in their Grandmother Bull's estate. The Major wanted Mrs. Blake to draw her will so that on her death the island would return to him, in trust for the Butler children. Rather than be so bold as to suggest the plan to Mrs. Blake himself, and Mary Butler being either too ill, or unwilling, the Major asked Roger Parker Saunders to convey the idea to the lady. The scheme was rejected, and as things turned out, Mary Butler's cousin had ideas of her own.[18]

In writing to thank Captain Saunders for his handling of the continuing emergency, Major Butler gave his friend complete discretion—"I give you carte-blanche"—and suggested that he convey Mary Ville to Major Ladson and sell the "back country lands" and his Charleston property on South Bay. The back-country lands had been acquired as grants, except for a large tract of twenty thousand acres in the Ninety-six District the Major had purchased at a sheriff's sale when the heirs of Joseph Salvador defaulted on a debt of thirty-seven thousand pounds sterling on a huge tract of one hundred thousand acres. Major Butler identified Salvador as "Once a distinguished Jew of London." He again urged Captain Saunders to move slaves from the Carolina plantations, suggesting that land might be rented on the Georgia side of the Savannah River. His plan was to get the valuable slaves out of South Carolina and ultimately to Hampton and Butler's Island where they would be the means of his financial recovery.[19]

As Pierce Butler struggled to protect his property and put it beyond reach of nervous creditors, his senatorial responsibilities continued. Mary Butler's lingering illness prevented her from attending President Washington's social functions, although on a few occasions the older Butler girls accompanied their father. His deep concern for Mary was expressed in his letters from New York in the early fall of 1790. He wrote Peter Spence in London: "My mind, as you well know, has been much broke in on during and since the war. It is ill prepared for such a shock." His letters to Weeden Butler and to Thomas told that she was "as helpless as an infant and reduced to a shadow." To Thomas he wrote, "She loved you almost to excess." He called her "Your Dear and Excellent Mother." To the Reverend Mr. Butler the Major became emotional:

> My Dearest Wife, the friend of my bosom, the partner of my Sufferings and Losses in a long Civil War is in that painful State as to make me, even me, almost wish the last were over—When I call to mind her many Virtues I cling to her! I fondly wish to hold her back. When I behold her Sufferings I

feel my selfishness, and am ready to wish her released from them. Great
God! How shall I bear the separation!

He was honest in saying "My Mind is on the Rack." He could well lament
the end of nineteen years of "matrimonial friendship," which as he put it,
"Has so knitted our Breasts and feelings together."[20]
Mary Butler died in New York on November 13, 1790. The major's
letter to London painted "a Picture of the Scene," with his daughters
"Clinging to me and weeping day and night." He wrote Weeden Butler,
"The Decree is Sealed—Her Eyes are Closed," and he asked to be told
how Thomas received the sad news. To friends in Ireland he called Mary
"one of the best of Wives." She had wished to be buried in Charleston and
was, near the wall of St. Michael's, close by the Butler pew. Major Butler
asked their son Thomas to be responsible for the monument over Mary
Butler's grave on his return to America: "By visiting the Tomb, and if you
please, Erecting a Monument to her Memory, the inscription which must
be written by Yourself—Qualify yourself then to do Justice to her memory, for no light performance can do it." Yet the words carved on the
gravestone appear to have come from Major Butler.

HERE LIES THE BODY OF
MARY BUTLER
WIFE OF PIERCE BUTLER
WHO DEPARTED THIS LIFE
IN THE CITY OF NEW YORK
ON THE 13TH DAY OF NOVEMBER 1790
HER REMAINS ARE INTERRED HERE
AT HER OWN DESIRE
BY HER AFFECTIONATE HUSBAND
WHO TRUSTS THAT HER SOUL
HAS FLED TO RECEIVE THE REWARD[21]

Mary Butler's death left the care of their five children in Major Butler's
hands. They were heavy hands, ill prepared to meet the emotional needs
of four young daughters and a son at school in distant London, of whom
he had written: "I want no Toney-Bumkin for my Son. Let him live surrounded with Respect and Esteem, or let Him not Live."[22]
His wife's departure released Pierce Butler from a sense of obligation to
her family and their connections in South Carolina. It had been an obliga-

tion long recognized, yet one in which he was frequently uncomfortable and often chose to ignore. Her death also removed certain limitations that had restrained him when her permission was required to convey or assign property in her name. Thus he began to move with greater freedom. In addition, he was soon relieved from the Ladson loan, which, surprisingly, was quickly repaid. Anxious to get on with the development of the Georgia lands, he severed ties to the old Middleton-Bull plantations by instructing Edward Rutledge to sell the Euhaws and Coosaw Island, saying it was his intention to divide the proceeds among his children or to put the money out at interest, neither of which he did.[23]

Pierce Butler never remarried, though not because he did not try. Among papers owned by a great-granddaughter of General Thomas Pinckney is a recounting of a tale told by his second wife, Frances Motte, who at the time was the widow of John Middleton, a cousin of Mary Butler. It told of a brief courtship.

> A company of young women were tying up jars of orange marmalade when a note was brought in with the message that a servant on horseback was waiting for an answer. The note was for Mrs. Middleton (afterward 2nd Mrs. T. P.). She opened it, read a few lines, and burst out laughing, and exclaimed "Do listen to this." It was a formal offer from Major Pierce Butler (a neighbor), who after tendering his hand and heart, added that should the lady be so cruel as to refuse to accept, then would she be kind enough to return the note. Pens, paper, and sand were called for & Mrs. M. clearing the jam pots in front of her wrote a polite answer stating she was enjoying her "freedom" too much to form another alliance, never mind how flattering. After signing herself Maj. B's humble and obliged serv't, looked around for his note—alas! It was no where to be found—Every corner was searched, the reticules of the mischievous girls emptied for fear one of them might have appropriated it in joke, but no note was forthcoming. There was nothing to do but to send the refusal without the proposal at which Maj. B. was furious & never spoke to Mrs. M. again. In Dec Mrs. M. got a letter from Mrs. M. Lowndes full of the fun that had been caused in her household over the fact that in opening a jar of marmalade on the breakfast table that morning some writing was noticed on the inner side of the paper top which proved to be part of the missing proposal which Mrs. M. might now return to Maj. B. altho she thought Mrs. M. had better preserve it as it had preserved the preserves.[24]

Indicative of a new mood, Major Butler put aside his past bitterness and acknowledged a debt to his former clerk. He paid William Payne, whom he had accused of "hypocrisy and falsehood," one thousand pounds. A few months earlier he had mended the rift that alienated his nephew, Thomas Parker Butler. A letter to him in Ireland expressed friendship and a desire to renew affection. He also gave some heartfelt advice: "Till then I exhort you to keep from Debt. He who is in Debt is not Free, and he who is not Free cannot be Happy."[25]

Mary Butler's kinfolk soon stifled Major Butler's newfound free spirit. They began to question his motives and to look askance at his actions regarding property held in trust for the Butler children. Mary Bull's estate consisted of lands and slaves held in trust for Mary, her sister Sarah Guerard, and her two Izard cousins, Elizabeth Blake and Mary Brewton. Mary Butler's share, as well as those of Sarah Guerard and Mary Brewton, supposedly continued in trust for the Butler children, but all three of the trustees named in the Bull will were dead. Even when Arthur Middleton, Daniel Blake, and Miles Brewton were living Major Butler had a tendency to ignore their trusteeship.[26] He moved the Middleton-Bull slaves about at will, sold slaves that belonged to his children, and also sold one of their plantations. This pot of trouble simmered constantly, bubbled and boiled over in 1792, when Elizabeth Blake died and her will became public knowledge and the cause of much gossip. The will had been drawn in 1782 when the Blakes were living in England. Her last will and testament was not quite that, for there were nine codicils added before her death at Newington, her Ashley River plantation where Daniel Blake had predeceased her. They had no children. A codicil dated November 24, 1790, a few days after Mary Butler's death, left the four Butler daughters English and French books, prints, and a harpsichord; but it was the codicil dated February 22, 1791, that upset Major Butler. Here she paid no heed to the Major's suggestions and left the estate she had acquired from Mary Bull not as he wished, but as she desired. It was left in trust for the five Butler children, and Mrs. Blake named a formidable battery of trustees. First was Ralph Izard, Jr., and then in the order of their military importance, General Charles Cotesworth Pinckney, Major Thomas Pinckney, who had been governor of the state, Captain Thomas Gadsden, and lastly, Captain Edward Rutledge, who had signed the Declaration of Independence. She gave the trustees the right to sell and to put the proceeds at interest for legatees. She stated, however, "It is my anxious desire" that the Negroes not be sold. Young Thomas Butler, who was a favorite cousin, was left her plantation "Izard's Number One" on the Combahee River, provided he in turn would convey his interest in lands on Lady's Island and on the Pee Dee River to Ralph Izard, Jr. Major Butler scoffed at this bequest to his son: "It is requiring a Quid pro Quo (if you will pardon my Lattin)—Value for Value," which, of course, was true.[27]

To say that Major Butler was rankled by Elizabeth Blake's will is an understatement. Charles Cotesworth Pinckney said the Major was so "very much discontented" he had "thrown off his mourning." In a letter to Mrs. David Graeme, Major Butler attempted to persuade her that Mrs. Blake had treated him unfairly: "I trust the benevolence of your Breast will not hoodwink your superior understanding into a belief that Mrs. Blake's will, or rather Mr. E. Rutledge's diction, is not highly affrontive to me."[28] A letter followed to Roger Parker Saunders, an innocent participant in Major Butler's machinations to rescue himself from financial distress in the futile attempt to persuade Mrs. Blake to purchase Butler's Island with trust funds of the Bull Estate:

> I was hurried, heated and vexed while in Carolina, the effect of which I now feel, but Nothing for a series of years hurt my feelings so much as the Gross Indelicacy practiced towards me by Mrs. Blake and Mr. Edward Rutledge in the wording of that part of the Will that relates to my Children wherein she trys to hold out to the World that it would not be safe to commit anything to my trust even to my own children. The Wording and Contrivance is Mr. E. Rutledge's, a most ungenerous Base stabb!

Only past kindnesses and friendship for Mrs. Blake's attorney had restrained Major Butler from a move that would have been to Mr. E. Rutledge "the most serious act of his Life."[29]

There was much talk in Charleston of Mrs. Blake's reasons for slighting Major Butler. He answered some of this speculation in a second letter to Mrs. Graeme, she of the "benevolent Breast":

> Oh but to justify the Act, mention is made that Major Butler sold a plantation at Toogadoo, the Property of his Children. True! But when I sold it I had broke it up from the Bad Quality of the Land. It was only expence to me & at the time I knew myself to be worth a large Estate to give my Children. Major Butler also sold some Negroes the property of his Children. True! I sold seven unruly Bad behav'd Negroes and replaced them with good ones.

Again, with dueling pistols in mind, he adds: "I never heard of any Man's robbing his Children to give it to his Creditors. But as to myself, the man that ever mentions that of me must count on more than an opposition of words."[30]

A Philadelphian who recalled Pierce Butler likened him to Sir Lucius O'Trigger, the character in Sheridan's comedy *The Rivals*. Sir Lucius was "a fortune hunting Irishman, ready to fight everyone, on any matter, at any time." It was an apt comparison, and one with which the Blake trustees could have agreed.[31]

The indignant letters to Mrs. Graeme and to Captain Saunders were written in August, September, and October 1792. By November, and for some unknown reason, the Major's anger had eased. From Philadelphia he wrote a letter to "Gen'l Pinckney and Edward Rutledge, Esq.":

> I beg you will permit me to place in your cellar at Charleville for your use, a pipe of Madeira Wine as a small token of my sense of your Kindness. It is reckoned by Connoisseurs the best batch of Madeira that had been brought into this Country these Twenty years.
>
> I am with great Respect, Dear Sirs, Yr most Obed't Serv't
>
> PIERCE BUTLER[32]

Respect, perhaps. Obedient, no. General Pinckney and Edward Rutledge were well aware that Major Butler had moved the Middleton-Bull slaves about as he chose. He was moving slaves before the furor over Mrs. Blake's will, and he continued to do so after Elizabeth Blake was laid to rest. The Major, true to his military training, deployed his slaves as a general would his troops. In September 1791 he had written Roger Parker Saunders:

> I purpose moving from your place about 15 Workers and 2 or 3 from Carolina.
>
> Let Sambo point out a Driver for Hampton. In my next letter I will send a List of the Negroes that are to move.

He had already acknowledged his misbehavior by writing Captain Saunders: "I must mention to you that those Negroes I bought from time to time myself I intended for replacing those of my Children's that I sold. If you think it better to regularly convey them, do so, in trust for such of my Children as I think proper."[33] Thereafter, Major Butler made some effort to designate the ownership of slaves working his several plantations, but it was a difficult determination. A listing of 441 slaves at Hampton in May

1793 showed 295 designated either *PB, MB,* or *SG*—Pierce Butler, Mary Butler, who had left slaves in trust for her children, but more than likely, Mary Brewton, and Sarah Guerard. The others were not designated. The *MB* and *SG* slaves belonged to the Butler children, and well into the 1800s Major Butler attempted to put the record straight as to true ownership. In his own will he recognized his failure to accomplish what should have been done.[34]

Pierce Butler still could not remove the matter of the Blake will from his thought. When the time came for the delivery of the books, the prints, and the harpsichord left to his daughters by Mrs. Blake, he wrote Ralph Izard suggesting the items be kept for the eldest Izard daughters, "As the most satisfactory disposition of them to the feelings of my Daughters and myself."[35] The Blake trustees continued to monitor Major Butler and his use of the slaves they held in trust for the Butler children. On March 9, 1795, Ralph Izard and Edward Rutledge asked the court to direct a sale of slaves and land in Charleston, the proceeds to be "let out at Interest" for Thomas Butler and his sisters. The petition to the court specifically mentioned "the Negroes now hired to the Honorable Pierce Butler."[36]

From his letters in the early 1790s it is apparent that Major Butler had decided to transfer his planting activities to Georgia, where Hampton on St. Simons Island and Butler's Island near Darien offered greater potential for profit, and to free himself from the Middleton clan and their connections. He wrote an agent in Charleston: "My sincere wish is to move 15 or 20 of my Negroes at Captain Saunders, to my place Hampton Point on Great St. Simons Island, in order to prepare for planting about 130 acres of Cotton." In this letter Major Butler indicated that as the Euhaws had not been sold he would continue to plant there for another year but that the decision had been made to abandon South Carolina and to concentrate his planting on the Georgia lands. He held onto enough Carolina property to qualify as a citizen so as to maintain his position of importance in the state and federal governments.[37]

At the same time Major Butler had become increasingly attracted to life in Philadelphia. Living there in 1782 when his family was banished from Charlestown by the British, and again living in the city during the long, hot summer of 1787 when he was a delegate to the Constitutional Convention, Major Butler had come to know and respect the Quaker conservatism of the city:

> This is a handsome, large City, eminent for its order and regularity for
> which it is indebted to that wise Government under which it was first

established, th'o there have been great emigrations to this Place, from Germany & Ireland yet the principles and Interest of the Friends most prevails, and happy for the Country that it is so, for they establish order & regularity and by their wisdom and economy give value to the land.

This was a letter to a friend in Ireland, written from a rented house. The time was early 1791, when Major Butler had not fully decided to make Philadelphia his permanent home.[38] Such a decision remained in abeyance in 1793 when the city suffered a yellow fever epidemic of tragic consequence. An apprehensive Pierce Butler wrote a short note to the family physician, Dr. Benjamin Rush:

> My Good Friend—How is it? Am I to think of any preparation for leaving town? You know I am altogether under your Guidance. Has Mrs. Rush left town? Yrs Sincerely
>
> P. BUTLER[39]

A letter to Alexander Gillon of Charleston told of the unfortunate times, and of the Butler family's evacuation from the distressed city:

> I need not state to you the most distressing situation of Philadelphia. You will hear too much of it from all Quarters. It is liker a Plague than anything else. More than one hundred are buried, or rather have been for some time past, daily. Persons can scarcely be got to bury the dead. I was assured that sixty Guineas were given on Sunday last, say the 29th of Septbr to two men to Inter Mr. Prager, the head of the House in Philadelphia of Prager & Co., a very great Dutch House of the First Credit. Mr. Powel died on Sunday. We fled to a farmer's house 12 miles from Town. More than thirty thousand Citizens have left the City.[40]

Major Butler reported the epidemic, or as he wrote, "this devouring Visitant," to the Reverend Mr. Butler in England. He believed it to have been a plague, brought by slaves from Africa to the West Indies and from there to Philadelphia. In this account he said more than forty thousand citizens had left the city, and of those who had remained, "four thousand were soon hurried to sleep with their Father."[41]

The Major comforted a fellow South Carolinian who had lost a son:

> The Lodgers in the House who survived, for he fell not alone, all say that the care and attention of Mrs. Wilson to Your Son could not be exceeded. I mention this as it may in a small degree be an alleviation to your affliction

to know that you did not lose him from a want of care or attention. It was
the lot of Hundreds to die without a person to close their eyes.[42]

When the epidemic neared its end, Dr. Rush was asked if the Butler
family could return safely. The Doctor's system of bleeding and purging
yellow fever victims brought on medical controversy, but not from Major
Butler, who was proud of the heroic behavior of his friend: "You risked
your Life, and with it the peace, and in some measure the independence of
your Family. You not only have parry'd the Lunge well, and with Vigour,
but you have disarm'd your Sniveling Adversaries of all Argumnt."[43]

There were new financial pressures. A recent debt to James Ladson
became past due and Major Butler was again threatened with a suit. This
prompted further efforts to sell the Salvador lands in the back country of
South Carolina. It was then he commissioned William Temple Franklin,
the grandson of Benjamin Franklin, to seek out buyers in England: "Sell I
will if it brings but half its value." The Major's asking price was 6 shillings
3 pence each for the twenty thousand acres.[44]

When Pierce Butler made up his mind to live in Philadelphia, he recognized his fondness for the place was seasonal. The fear of another yellow
fever epidemic, the heat and stench of the city in summer, brought a resolve to find a proper city house, and as well a country retreat offering
relief from such dangers and discomforts. In other ways Philadelphia was
an odd choice for this well-known public figure from South Carolina who
had owned vast plantations there and in Georgia, his livelihood dependent on hundreds of black slaves. Following the Revolution, the city had
become a haven for free Negroes, later described as a "well organized
and highly articulate group." Their presence in the city was evident. Major
Butler recognized this to be true but expressed it differently: "The
Negroes in this State are Intollerable, I do Assure you. They are more
luxurious and more Insolent than any person who has not witnessed it,
can credit."[45] The abolitionists prevailed, led by the selfsame Friends who
had established "order & regularity" to win Pierce Butler's approval. At
first their attitude disturbed the Major, and he sounded the alarm: "I am
apprehensive that the Folly of some idle people in America will sooner or
later give us some trouble with our negroes."[46] But, after weighing advantages against disadvantages, Pierce Butler decided to become a Philadelphian. He acquired a substantial house in the heart of the city and a
small, comfortable farm north of town on the York road.

Major Butler was inordinately proud of his fine town house on the

Major Pierce Butler's town house at Chestnut and Eighth streets, Philadelphia. (Watercolor by David J. Kennedy, 1836. Historical Society of Pennsylvania.)

northwest corner of Chestnut and Eighth streets. The house had been built in 1794 for Dr. Thomas Ruston, who lived there but three years, or until the house was sold by the sheriff to meet debts the doctor could not pay. Major William Jackson lived there until 1804, when Major Butler saw the handsome style and grand dimension to be exactly what he wanted. The four-story house was constructed of Philadelphia red brick over a basement-cellar. It occupied the equivalent of three or four generous building lots, the largest portion of which was a walled garden on the corner of the two streets, an area that extended far back to a small street, or alley, parallel to Chestnut Street. Large trees gave a woodland effect, rare in that part of the city. The centered doorway opened from a small porch, six white marble steps above the street. In order to prepare the house for occupancy by himself and four of his five grown offspring, Major Butler made some changes using pine and oak from his Georgia plantations, whence came many of the servants who saw to the comfort of the family. An unfriendly abolitionist who viewed the house under difficult circumstances shortly after the Butlers moved in found it to be filled with fine pictures and rich furniture, the walls decorated with handsome imported wallpaper, all of which he said were luxuries obtained through the enforced labor of African slaves. The abolitionist was not invited to see Major Butler's splendid wine cellar, nor were the fine Carrara marble "chimney pieces" in place at the time of his visit.[47]

The rural retreat that complemented the new town house was acquired "for the benefit of breathing purer air." In giving instructions to friends on how to find him, it was "the road forks at the Rising Sun," that being the name of a well-known tavern on the thoroughfare that was called the York Road and that gave the Butler farm its name. York Farm served the family well, even after the 1810 purchase of a greater tract across the road on which there was a handsome, double-piazza house soon to be known as Butler Place, and about which was written, "There is not a shadow of tinsel or tawdriness to be found about Butler Place, dignified repose being its predominant characteristic." The Philadelphian Joshua Francis Fisher was of a different mind. He called Butler Place "a poor seat on the York Road," but then he, who had little respect for Major Butler, called the Philadelphia residence "great and Gloomy." The three houses—the Chestnut Street mansion, York Farm, and Butler Place—were to become a part of the legacy of Pierce Butler.[48]

With a town house and country retreat in his possession, all that the Major seemed to lack was a new wife. Despite the marmalade rebuff, he

Butler Place on the Old York Road, near Germantown, Pennsylvania.
(Watercolor by David J. Kennedy, 1840. Historical Society of
Pennsylvania.)

kept a ready eye for a proper candidate. In 1806 Dr. Benjamin Rush told his wife of having had tea with Major Butler and a Chestnut Street neighbor, "Miss MacPherson," who had been saved in a dramatic rescue from the wreck of the ship *Rose in Bloom*. That Major Butler thought his neighbor worth saving was evidenced in an uncharacteristic gesture in which he offered three thousand dollars to the young man who effected the rescue. "Mr. Perry," of Boston, refused the money, and if the Major's generosity impressed the lady as he intended, no romance sprang from the incident.[49]

With the Georgia plantations beginning to produce as he had expected, life in Philadelphia put Major Butler a safe distance from the slings and arrows that came his way from his South Carolina peers and eliminated his dependence on the Bull-Middleton lands. Although his enthusiasm for the Quakers had diminished as their abolitionism proliferated, he continued to respect the orderliness they engendered. There can be no doubt he found egocentric enjoyment in his high-level participation in the federal government. He relished his contacts, including the adversary relationships, with George Washington, the Adams men, Franklin, Jefferson, Madison, Monroe, Hamilton, Burr, the doctors Rush, and others. In Philadelphia he could flaunt the Ormondes and Northumberland, could wear his London "perruques," pour his fine Madeiras with confidence and pride. Was it not a famous Butler Madeira that Daniel Webster, like the man who came to dinner, visited until he had finished a dozen bottles? Major Butler came to be a recognized authority on Madeira wines. He had a standing order with Newton Gordon, Murdoch and Company, on the island for a "pipe of our best old wine" annually. He did not hesitate to send a half pipe of his finest to Weeden Butler in London, where the drinking of Madeiras was an established art:

> There is not any equal to it for sale in London. I imported it myself. It is of the Vintage of 1781 and equal in flavor to any I have tasted.

> Englishmen, in general, do not do justice to Madeira wine in their treatment of it. We drink much better Madeira wine here than I have tasted in England.[50]

The Major's fame as a volatile, somewhat irrational politician came to be rivaled by his widespread recognition for his fine Madeiras. S. Weir Mitchell, the talented Philadelphia physician, writer, and Butler in-law, put the Major in his novels and in his small classic *A Madeira Party.*

Where the host "Hamilton" offered his guest a glass and won the response "That is a wine indeed!," the wine was a Butler Madeira. Pierce Butler enjoyed his acceptance as one who knew and served the best. Yet, such was his inconsistency, he could write the following to Weeden Butler:

> Having long and often observed the ill Consequences that attend the Use of Wine or other Liquor, it is my earnest wish that my Son could be induced to see it in the light I do, & be prevailed on to Use nothing stronger than Small Beer or Water. I would prefer His confining Himself intirely to Water
>
> Wine too often opens the Door for every Vice: It throws Us off Our Guard, discloses what ought not be disclosed, produces strife and animosities: And in short, is big with every Evil.
>
> By the advice of Medical Gentlemen I have been obliged to return to the Use of Wine.[51]

Pierce Butler had little embarrassment of his ownership of slaves in a place where the practice was abhorred by so many. He had helped to fashion the law that made slavery permissible. It stood to reason that to own plantations he must have Negroes to work the land. In Philadelphia the talk of free Negroes had come to bother him but slightly. In his circle of friends and acquaintances there were many who found no fault with his ownership of slaves. Those who disagreed usually kept their feelings to themselves.

As to the truly private life of Pierce Butler, Dr. Alfred Langdon Elwyn, who had married Major Butler's granddaughter, Mary Middleton Mease, was asked by a great-granddaughter to tell something of her ancestor's background. He answered this way: "No one knows anything of his private life or would disclose it if they did. There are matters connected with this that had better not be opened. I believe in his honor, but things were done condemned by his own children that have an unpleasant look. I will speak to you of these privately."[52]

Chapter 5

Pierce Butler's Public Life, 1776–1789

THE PUBLIC LIFE of Pierce Butler was closely entwined with the problems that arose from the Negro's presence in America. Early in 1773, the year in which Major Butler resigned his commission in the British army to become a member of South Carolina's ruling class, the young Bostonian Josiah Quincy, Jr., arrived in Charlestown bent on repairing his health, enjoying the hospitality of new friends, and observing their style of life. He arrived as a passenger on the *Bristol Packet* and reported in his journal: "The number of shipping far surpasses all I had ever seen in Boston. I was told they were then not so many as common at this season, tho' about 350 sail lay off the town." The activity of the port was slave-oriented, for many of the ships seen by the young visitor were slavers, or were ships in trade awaiting produce from the low-country plantations.

In Charlestown young Quincy met many South Carolinians, several of whom were active in the importation and marketing of slaves. Miles Brewton and his onetime partner Thomas Loughton Smith were two of these. Charles Cotesworth Pinckney, Edward Rutledge, and Thomas Lynch, all well versed in South Carolina law, gave him much of their time. When conversation turned toward the black people, as it usually did, these men spoke with authority. The Bostonian's journal recorded much of what he was told and much of what he learned by observation. He gave a graphic picture of the South Carolina society in which Pierce Butler had chosen to live, in particular as it related to the transplanted Africans who were to have so great an impact on his life.

66

Following a grand dinner at the Miles Brewtons' fine home, there was the usual round of toasts, and conversation:

> A young lawyer, Mr. Pinckney, a gentleman educated at the Temple and of eminence dined with us. From him and the rest of the company I was assured, by the provincial laws of the place any two justices and three freeholders might and very often did *Instanter* upon view or complaint try a negro for any crime, and might and did often award execution of death, issue their warrant and it was done forthwith. Two gentlemen present said they had issued such warrants several times. This law too was for *free* as well as *slave* negroes and mulattoes. They further informed me, that neither negroes or mulattoes could have a jury; that for killing a negro, ever so wantonly, as without provocation, there could be nothing but a fine; they gave a late instance of this; that (further) to *steal* a negro was death, but to *kill him* was only fineable.

The inconsistency brought forth this exchange: " 'Curious laws and policy!' I exclaimed. 'Very true,' cried the company, 'but this is the case.' " The religious attitudes of the South Carolinians also troubled Mr. Quincy:

> The state of religion here is repugnant not only to the ordinances and institutions of Jesus Christ, but to every law of sound policy. The Sabbath is a day of visiting and mirth with the rich, and of licence pastime and frolic for the negroes. The blacks I saw in great numbers playing pawpaw, huzzle cap, pitch penny, and quarreling around the doors of the Churches in service-time.

> The slaves who don't frolic on the Sabbath, do all kinds of work for themselves on hire.

He was troubled, too, that brutality prevailed in a land in which he estimated the blacks outnumbered the whites in a ratio of seven to one. He found the women to be saturated with "infamous and destructive ideas," and was disturbed to see they had taken on characteristics of their slaves in speech and behavior. He was surprised to find there was a certain openness in the acknowledgement of the use of Negro and mulatto women by Charlestown gentlemen. He wrote that on two occasions the assembled company had traced the likeness in mulattoes serving at their master's tables to the fathers who were present and to their black mothers.

There was interesting talk among the gentlemen with whom Josiah Quincy, Jr., was thrown. He found himself defending the people of his native state. One of his new friends saw Bostonians ready to assume the mantle of sovereignty over America should the British choose to withdraw—an assumption Quincy hotly denied. Another critical comment won an interesting reaction when the young visitor returned to Massachusetts. There he told the Sons of Liberty that South Carolinians believed Bostonians "better at resolving what to do than doing what they resolved." Stung by such sacrilege, the Bostonians resolved to stage a tea party in the city's harbor, and did what they resolved.

In the seven weeks of his Charlestown visit, this observant traveler chose not to rely alone on what he had been told but to examine the provincial law himself. He did so in the law office of Edward Rutledge. In Quincy's opinion the South Carolina constitution was defective in many respects and bad in others. He found slavery to be the "peculiar curse of the land," yet the thought by the South Carolinians that it was not a curse, but a blessing, prompted him to quote Milton: "So perfect in their misery / Not one perceive their foul disfigurement." Mr. Quincy believed slavery to be completely corruptive:

> From the same cause have their Legislators enacted laws touching negroes, mulattoes and masters which savor more of the policy of Pandemonium than the English constitution:—laws which will stand eternal records of the depravity and contradiction of the human character: laws which would disgrace the tribunal of Scythian, Arab, Hottentot and Barbarian are appealed to in decisions upon life, limb and liberty by those who assume the name of Englishmen, freemen and Christians: the place of trial no doubt is called a Court of Justice and equity—but the Judges have forgot a maxim of English law—*Jura naturalia sunt immutabilia*—and they would do well to remember that no laws of the (little) creature supercede the laws of the (great) creator. Can the institutions of man make void the decree of God?

Prophetically, he wrote: "These are but a small part of the mischiefs of slavery, new ones are every day arising, futurity will produce more and greater." Of the South Carolinians, Josiah Quincy, Jr., added: "There is much among this people of what the world call hospitality and politeness, it may be questioned what proportion there is of true humanity, Christian charity and love."[1] Against this backdrop, Pierce Butler played his role in public service.

It was not surprising that Major Butler should turn to politics. He was assertive, assured, impressive, and important. His British background was politically valuable both before and after the Revolution. Having so recently been a servant of the king, he believed he understood the British and thus was one to anticipate their actions, or if need be, to negotiate with them. At the time, the South Carolina government was very much under the influence of low-country aristocrats. In the eyes of most South Carolinians, Pierce Butler's credentials as an aristocrat were impeccable. He became spokesman for a large and important segment of the low country. A most important asset for breaking into the political scene was his Middleton-Bull connection with its influential network of spouses, siblings, cousins, aunts, uncles, friends, and slaves. For the most part, slaves excepted, these people were avowed patriots; but some were Loyalists—the former Lieutenant Governor William Bull, and his successor, cousin Sarah Izard's Lord William Campbell. Royal land grants, as well as some venturesome purchases, had spread Major Butler's land holdings beyond the low country, and this had given additional political strength. Finally, the confused times called for order and organization. There was no greater advocate available.[2]

In his long public career that began as a justice of the peace in 1776 and ended in Philadelphia as a director of the United States Bank, Pierce Butler made some contradictory turns. In South Carolina the low-country aristocrat struck some telling blows for back-country people, much to the chagrin of his Charlestown peers. In the United States Senate his staunch Federalism turned to avid Republicanism, and then turned away and off. Yet, there were no surprises in his representation of his state's interest when the question of slavery confronted the framers of the constitution at the Convention of 1787. Major Butler played a procrustean role in shaping the slave to fit the fabric of the new constitution. In a very long career of public service, it was his governmental work of greatest consequence and his most important involvement in legislation pertaining to blacks. More than any other reason, this firm stand on slavery enabled the low-country aristocrat who was so often at odds with his peers to retain his political strength. The South Carolina Federalists could not fault his views on slavery nor could they quarrel with the essence of his strong belief in the rights of states. Fractionated as they often were, they faded in the face of his commanding presence and the popular support that he gained for his "democratic" ideals and from his back-country endorsements.

Having resigned his commission in the British army, renounced his government, and aligned himself with the patriotic cause, he was chosen to serve as a member of the South Carolina House of Assembly and attended the second assembly in 1776. He represented no specific parish or district, but when chosen a member of the South Carolina House of Representatives, he attended as a delegate from Prince William's Parish of the Beaufort District. This was to be a long and cherished responsibility of Major Butler, one that continued until after the century turned, despite interruptions for duty on the federal scene. In 1785 the Major's services were much in demand. He was chosen to represent St. John's Colleton as well as Prince William's, though he served only the latter. In the legislature Major Butler participated in hundreds of issues, many having to do with financial matters. War had left the South Carolinians in desperate straits. He was not successful in his advocacy of a state bank but was determined in bringing relief to the debtors in the state who abounded in the wake of the war. Pierce Butler turned vindictively against the low-country aristocrats with whom he was so closely associated to vote against them in awarding broader representation to the back country and in relocating the state capital from Charleston to Columbia.[3] It was a reaction to a feeling of mutual resentment between Major Butler and the Middleton connections engendered by their mistrust of his motives in the management of his wife's inheritance. Yet he acted with compassion and leniency to Loyalists whose property had been confiscated in the bitterness so prevalent at the war's end. He told of this in a letter to his North Carolina friend James Iredell:

> Our Legislature have been sitting sometime, and as yet, have shown great liberality respecting those wretched people that went off with the enemy. Numbers have already been taken off the confiscation list. *All* are allowed to return, to try to vindicate themselves if they can, so that none may be condemned unheard. I hope we shall close the session as we began, with acts of mercy and forgiveness. As an individual, I do all in my power to instill in the minds of the back country members, that mercy and forgiveness are Godlike virtues.[4]

There was a bit of selfishness in his decision in 1787 to vote against the reopening of the door to the importation of slaves, a door the legislature had closed the year before. He was fearful that a flood of new slaves would dilute the value of those he already owned. His stated justification for this vote was that it would put the back-country farmer deeper in debt by the purchase of slaves he could not afford. There was no "humanitarian impulse" in this decision, nor did it mark any change in his advocacy of slavery. Major Butler was present when the legislature chose delegates to the Confederation Congress and to the Constitutional Convention. He was selected for both, and for the additional responsibility of serving with Andrew Pickens to work out a settlement between South Carolina and Georgia of a long-standing, ofttimes bitter, boundary dispute that involved lands on the far side of the Altamaha River, lands in which he had a substantial interest. In a letter to Weeden Butler, he told of another honor that had come his way and been refused: "As I declined the Honor my fellow citizens offered me of the Chief Magistrate, I could not refuse the last Appointment as Acting as one of their Commissioners to the Convention to be held at Philadelphia."[5]

After being offered the governorship of the state, and while a member of the legislature and privy council as well, the forty-third year of Major Butler's life proved to be his busiest. In the spring of 1787 the South Carolina–Georgia Boundary Commission met in Beaufort and came to terms on the disputed lands, including that between the Altamaha and St. Mary's rivers, claimed by South Carolina but contiguous to Georgia. The award to Georgia was a logical decision in which Major Butler concurred.[6]

While the commissioners were busy reaching for the solution to the border dispute, fugitive slaves from the plantations along the Savannah River who had been uprooted by the war were subsisting by raiding farms and plantations in the area. Governor Thomas Pinckney wrote to Colonel Thomas Hutson outlining a proposed solution:

> To take the most effectual & decisive measures to extirpate the runaway Negros who have lately committed depredations in the vicinity of Purrysburg. You will therefore, Sir, be pleased to endeavor to engage a Company of Minute-Men, not exceeding one hundred, to serve for one month certain, to whom the pay of one shilling a day.
>
> This added to the sum of ten pounds sterling for each Negro taken or killed.

A second letter was sent to another military man, one who lived nearby and was respected by the Catawba Indians of South Carolina. He was asked to organize a troop of Indians and to serve as their captain: "The Indians shall receive two blankets each for their Service & will likewise be entitled to receive Ten pounds sterling for each of the above mentioned

John Rutledge (top left), Charles Cotesworth Pinckney (top right), and Charles Pinckney (bottom), who with Pierce Butler were the four South Carolina delegates to the Constitutional Convention of 1787 in Philadelphia. (Library Company of Philadelphia.)

runaway Negros whom they shall take, or if they cannot apprehend them, the reward for each of them whom they shall kill in opposition or endeavor to escape."[7]

The Beaufort meeting followed the session of the South Carolina Legislature at Charleston, where Major Butler had joined Charles Pinckney and John Rutledge in voting to keep the door to the slave trade closed. Charles Cotesworth Pinckney had voted to open the trade, and these four were the delegates chosen by the legislature to go to Philadelphia to help form the foundation of the new nation. All were slave owners, and all would fight vigorously for federal laws to permit the continuation of the importation and marketing of slaves. There was really no contradiction with their Philadelphia position. The reasons the three voted to suspend trade in South Carolina were their own, or as one historian aptly stated, "All they needed was the right to import slaves when it suited them. It did not suit them in 1787." As it turned out the 1787 action was amended by the South Carolina legislature the very next year. The suspension of foreign and domestic trade was altered to permit domestic trade, while the ban on the importation of blacks from abroad was continued for five years.[8]

The Constitutional Convention in Philadelphia had first intended to revise the Articles of Confederation. In its stead the delegates produced a new government, working frequently in an atmosphere of confrontation between the states of the North and those of the South. Although the words *slave* or *slavery* do not appear in the Constitution that sprang from the deliberations of the delegates, the practice of traffic in humankind was often a factor in debate. George Washington was chosen to be the president of the convention, and he, a slave owner, helped to establish a tacit acceptance of slavery that prevailed through most of the session. Pierce Butler did not hesitate to speak his mind on the matter. There were two broad areas in which the slave was all important. In both of these Major Butler played a definite, but supporting role. In a third area, he led the way.[9]

The first bone of contention had to do with the method to be used in determining a state's representation in Congress. Delegate Butler, who despite his monetary miseries of the moment, advocated wealth, or power, as the only true measure. Wealth and power were synonymous to the Major. As a boy he had read Caesar's contention that had he money he would find soldiers and all else necessary to carry on a war. In the Major's mind, the fundamental purpose of the new nation should be the protection of property. Max Farrand, the historian, wrote that Major Butler was a man "of noble birth and inordinately vain of it." He added, "He was a man of fortune." Pierce Butler gave that impression for he attended the sessions in "a powdered wig, a handsome stock, gold lace on his coat." In determining the measure of wealth, John Rutledge thought it should be by the amount of tribute a state paid into the federal treasury. Major Butler held fast to wealth alone. Said he, "Money is strength, and every state ought to have its weight in the national council in proportion to the quantity it possesses."[10] Quite naturally, the question arose as to the measurement of slaves in the calculation of wealth. Pierce Butler had no doubts. A slave was property and as such was to be counted. According to the notes of James Madison, Major Butler, like Julius Caesar, "Contended strongly that property is the only just measure of representation. This was the great object of Governt, the great cause of war, the great means of carrying it on."[11] Yet wealth and taxation were put aside in favor of representation by population. Again, quite naturally, the question arose—how to count the slaves? There was a ready answer from South Carolina as reported by James Madison: "Mr. Butler and Gen'l Pinckney insisted that blacks be included in the role of Representation, *Equally* with the whites."[12] He noted again:

> Mr. Butler insisted that the labor of a slave in S. Carola was as productive & valuable as that of a freeman in Massts, that as wealth was the great means of defence and utility to the nation, they were equally valuable to it with freemen; and that consequently as equal representation ought to be allowed for them in Government which was instituted principally for the protection of property, and was itself to be supported by property.[13]

This prompted a response from the caustic, often obstinate, Elbridge Gerry of Massachusetts: "Blacks are property, and are used to the southward as horses and cattle to the northward." His question was, Why should not horses and cattle have the right of representation in the North? Delegate Gerry was a persistent irritant to the South Carolina delegation. A scrap of paper on which Major Butler expressed his reaction to Mr. Gerry demonstrated his irritation: "Guery—Are we to Enter into a Compact with Slaves—No! Are the men of Massachusetts to put their hand in Our Purses—No!"[14]

In the Confederation Congress the "three-fifths rule" had been proposed as a measure of taxation. This rule provided for a count of all whites and other free citizens, *plus* three-fifths of those in bondage. James Wilson of Pennsylvania proposed this to determine representation under the new constitution. James Madison took note once again, "Mr. Butler contended again—full number of inhabts, including the blacks." Pierce Butler persisted, but the Wilson proposal prevailed to relegate the slave to the official status of three-fifths of a human being. It was a status that would remain until the passing of the Fourteenth Amendment in 1868. The count was made solely to determine a state's representation in the lower house of Congress. Never had there been any thought of giving the slave true representation and the right to vote. The adoption of the rule was hardly repugnant to those from the slave states, for it did much to assure the continuation of slavery itself. In one sense, and considering the attitude of most of the slave-owning delegates, for a black slave to be considered three-fifths of a human being was generous indeed.[15]

The second important consideration having to do with slavery was the question of slavery as such. In a document so high and mighty as the proposed constitution, should the institution of slavery be permitted to continue? The majority of the delegates thought no. Yet there was little doubt that slavery would continue, for without such a concession to the Southern states there would have been no Union. The next question was, if slavery was to continue, for how long? The ultimate decision came from a rather strange coalition of interests. States in the upper South where there were more slaves than needed sought to close the foreign trade. South Carolina's delegates spoke vigorously to continue. Georgia was one with South Carolina, and both were supported by New England states who found the business of importing slaves profitable. The resulting compromise prolonged importation of slaves at least twenty years, or through the year 1807. No consideration was given to ending the system then, or at any time. Only the foreign trade could be terminated at that time.[16]

The third time the delegates faced up to the problem of Africans in their midst came in response to a proposal by Pierce Butler. It had long galled the owners to have no legal redress when their slaves escaped and found protection in free states. Major Butler's remedy came to be known as the Fugitive Slave Law. His resolution also demonstrated the reluctance of the delegates to call a slave a slave. His solution to the problem: "If any person bound to service or labor in any of the U. States shall escape into another State, he or she shall not be discharged from such service or labor, in consequence of any regulations subsisting in the State to which they escape, but shall be delivered up to the person justly claiming their service or labor." In James Madison's notes there was no obfuscation: "Mr. Butler and Mr. Pinckney moved to require fugitive slaves and servants to be delivered up like criminals." The Butler resolution was adopted unanimously, without debate, and appears in the United States Constitution as a second paragraph of section 2, article 4, with but little change from Pierce Butler's own version. Its language was lightly polished by Gouverneur Morris's committee charged with phrasing the document in its final form.[17]

Max Farrand, who edited the records of the convention, felt persuaded to comment:

> In 1787, slavery was not the important question, it might be said it was not the moral question that it later became.
>
> There was comparatively little said on subject in the Convention.

James Madison was moved to make a more pertinent observation: "The great danger to our general government is the great southern and northern interest of the continent being opposed to each other."[18]

Pierce Butler did not confine his role to those matters touching on slavery. He was much in evidence that very hot summer, and those who recorded the sessions noted his presence, his opinions, and his method of approach. William Pierce, one of the Georgia delegates, made notes on the business of the convention and fortunately left some deft character sketches of many of those who participated in the dramatic event. Of the South Carolina delegates:

> John Rutledge—Highly mounted at the commencement of the late revolution.
>
> Distinguished rank among the American worthies. This Gentleman is much famed in his own State as an Orator, but in my opinion he is too rapid with his public speaking to be denominated as an agreeable Orator.
>
> Charles Cotesworth Pinckney—A gentleman of Family and fortune in his own State. He has received the advantage of a Liberal education, and possesses a very extensive degree of legal knowledge. When warm in debate he sometimes speaks well, but he is generally considered an indifferent Orator.
>
> Charles Pinckney—A young Gentleman of the most promising talents. He is altho' only 24 ys of age, in possession of a very great variety of Knowledge. Government, Law, History and Phylosophy are his favorite studies.

He speaks with great neatness and perspicuity, and treats every subject as fully, without running into prolixity, as it requires.

Pierce Butler—Mr. Butler is a character much respected for the many excellent virtues which he possesses. But as a Politician or an Orator, he has no pretentions to either. He is a Gentleman of Fortune, and takes rank among the first, in South Carolina. He has been appointed to Congress, and is now a Member of the Legislature of South Carolina. Mr. Butler is about 40 years of age, an Irishman by birth.[19]

In taking note of Pierce Butler's appearance in the debates of the convention, William Pierce and James Madison left no doubt as to the Major's attitude. He was "against," was "strenuous against," or was "vehemently against." He "urged" and "urged warmly." He "contended," "contended again," "contended strenuously," and "contended warmly." He "opposed," was "decidedly opposed" and was "strenuously opposed." On one occasion he "revolted at the idea," and once it was noted he was "strenuous *for* the motion."[20]

At the beginning of the convention Major Butler advocated private sessions in order that deliberations would be free from the disturbing presence of the media of that day. He wanted no "Licentious publications of their proceedings." It was a policy endorsed by George Washington, and it made for free and open discussions of sensitive matters. Whether or not it was the secrecy rule that prompted Major Butler to speak his mind, there is no doubt that he did. His trip to Europe in 1784 and 1785, particularly the visits to Holland, gave an extra dimension to his thought, and on numerous occasions he likened a proposed move to something he had observed abroad. In opposing paper money, he proclaimed that it was "legal tender in no country in Europe." He cautioned the delegates against taking power away from the states, noting that there was "no right the people are more jealous of than suffrage," and emphasized that Holland had "thrown all power into the hands of the Senates who fill up vacancies themselves and form a rank aristocracy." The Major believed the Senate would be "the Aristocratic part of our Government," and he cautioned the delegates that senators would have to be controlled by the several states or "they will be too independent." It was almost as though he anticipated his appointment to the Senate by the South Carolina legislature, for Delegate Butler had very definite ideas about that body. Despite his precarious financial position, he joined John Rutledge in proposing that senators serve without compensation, a motion that was voted down seven states to three, with one divided. He supported the Senate's right to negotiate peace treaties on the authority of a two-thirds vote, without the president. He thought this "a necessary security against ambitious and corrupt Presidents."[21]

With his usual vigor, Pierce Butler was opposed to permitting foreigners to become members of Congress. This, a rather strange position for an Irish immigrant, was spoken to by the Major, who acknowledged: "That if he himself had been called into public life within a short time after coming to America, his foreign habits, opinions, and attachments would have rendered him an improper agent in foreign affairs."[22]

In discussing the powers of the executive branch of the government, it had been suggested that three persons should be chosen to lead the country. Major Butler was firm in calling for *one man,* "in order to promote dispatch." He reasoned that a three-man presidency would bring "delays, divisions, and dissensions" and again brought in Holland, where many councilors had played havoc. In military matters he believed the multiple executive would prove "particularly mischievous." He opposed the presidential veto and considered the "compleat negative" an abuse of executive power, asking, "Why might not a Cataline or a Cromwell arise in this country as well as others?" In a letter to Weeden Butler, he wrote that in England "the People at large have little to say, and less to do" with who becomes the "King of G.B." But in America, he countered, the president is chosen by "much more of a popular Government—the whole is Elective." He wrote at length of the systems and the merits of the two governments and spoke with pride of the way in which Americans chose their leader: "His Election, the mode of which [the Electoral College] I had the honor of proposing in the Committee, in my judgement precludes Corruption and tumult. Yet, after all, My Dear Sir, I am free to acknowledge that His powers are full great, and greater than I was disposed to make them."[23]

It was the opinion of some of the delegates that the judicial branch needed a series of inferior courts. Pierce Butler thought state courts would suffice. He said: "The people will not bear such innovations. We must follow the example of Solon who gave the Athenians not the best Gov't he could devise, but the best they wd receive."[24]

In 1786 Pierce Butler had spoken his mind when the South Carolina legislature refused to name delegates for the Annapolis Convention that was attended by representatives from only five states. He believed the delegates attending would not be conversant "in the nature and principles of the trade in America in general, of their own states in particular." He was adamant in his belief that the new federal government should not usurp the state's role in controlling trade, and most important, the business of exports. In Philadelphia he took the same stand, saying that federal control of exports would be "unjust and alarming." Firm in favor of a limited federal government, he voiced his dissatisfaction with the right of the Congress to discharge debts of the United States, to lay and collect taxes, duties, imposts, and excises, "Lest it should compel payment as well to the Blood-suckers who had speculated on the distress of others, as to those who fought and bled for their country."[25]

Pierce Butler was relieved when the difficult task ended. In a display of false modesty he wrote Weeden Butler that it would not be worth the cost of postage to send a copy of the Constitution to London. Yet he did so, and boasted that despite "clashing interests" the document was one in which "I had some small part in frameing." He added later, in response to a favorable comment from the Reverend Mr. Butler, who had read the Constitution with great interest:

> When you consider, my Dear Sir, the Great Extent of Territory, the various Climates & products, the differing manners and, as I before observed, the Contending Commercial Interests, You will agree with me that it required a pretty General Spirit of Accomodation in the members of the Convention to bring forth such a system as would be agreeable to and approved by all. In this light then are You to View this Product of Our Joint Endeavours. The Convention saw, I think justly, the Critical Situation of the United States—Slighted from abroad and totering on the brink of Confusion at home; they therefore thought it wise to bring forward such a system as bid fairest for general approbation and adoption so as to be brought soon into operation.[26]

Major Butler had told Weeden Butler that the convention delegates sought "tranquility at home and respect from abroad." It pleased him to know that at least from his London friend he had won the latter. The South Carolina delegates returned to their homeland in search of that "tranquility," and with an honest pride in what had been accomplished. Even though history would prove them wrong, they brought forth a Constitution that protected the institution they believed vital to their well-being. In the heat of a debate on a hot day in July, Pierce Butler had said: "The security the South'n States want is that their negroes not be taken away from them, which some gentlemen within or without doors, have a good mind to do." The four men had come home, their "Negro property" was intact, they could buy more slaves when needed—from Africa at least through 1807—and their runaway slaves were to be delivered up on demand. More important, the clashing interests had been reconciled, and the course of the young country had been charted at last.[27]

The Constitution addressed the problem of slavery in the United States in this manner:

> *Article 1, section 2, the beginning of the third paragraph:*
> Representatives and direct Taxes shall be apportioned among the several States which may be included within this Union, according to their respective Numbers, which shall be determined by adding to the whole Number of free Persons, including those bound to Service for a Term of Years, and excluding Indians not taxed, three fifths of all other persons.

> *Article 1, section 9, the first paragraph:*
> The Migration or Importation of such Persons as any of the States now existing shall think proper to admit, shall not be prohibited by the Congress prior to the Year one thousand eight hundred and eight, but a Tax or duty may be imposed on such Importation, not exceeding ten dollars for each Person.

> *Article 4, section 2, the third paragraph:*
> No Person held to Service or Labour in one State under the laws thereof, escaping into another, shall, in Consequence of any Law or Regulation therein, be discharged from such Service or Labour, but shall be delivered up on Claim of the Party to whom such Service or Labour be due.[28]

Back in South Carolina, Butler maintained his public service by attending the South Carolina legislature. By a close vote a ratification convention was authorized. It was held in Charleston, with the Constitution winning South Carolina's blessing by a vote of 149 to 73. Governor Thomas Pinckney expressed his approval in a letter to "Honrble John Rutledge, CC Pinckney, C Pinckney, P Butler":

> The Convention of the People of the State of So. Carolina having considered and ratified the Constitution proposed for the Government of the U.S. have desired me to return you their unanimous thanks for the Services and Conduct as Delegates from this State to the Federal Convention.

> The gratification I receive in communicating this public acknowledgement can only be exceeded by those fine feelings which must be excited in your Breasts at the consciousness of having merited the honorable testimony of your Country's approbation.

The Governor signed the letter "With every sentiment of regard & esteem."[29]

On July 4, 1788, Philadelphia celebrated the anniversary of the Declaration of Independence and "The Establishment of the CONSTITUTION, or Frame of Government proposed by the late General Convention and now solemnly adopted and ratified by Ten of those States." The festivities began when the "rising Sun was greeted by a full peal from Christ Church STEEPLE," followed by a salute from the deck guns of the *Rising Sun,* anchored off Market Street. In the oration that climaxed the three-mile march of a "Grand Procession" of dignitaries, military units, societies, and trades, James Wilson, one of the Pennsylvania delegates, warned that much remained to be done:

> A Progressive State is necessary to the *Happiness* and *Perfection* of Man. Whatever attainments are already reached, attainments still higher should be pursued. Let us therefore thrive with noble emulation. Let us suppose we have done nothing, while anything yet remains to be done. Let us with fervent goal, press forward and make *Unceasing advances* in everything that can SUPPORT, IMPROVE, DEFINE, or EMBELLISH society.

Mr. Wilson of Pennsylvania, and Pierce Butler, of South Carolina, were of differing opinions as to what, if any, higher attainments should be pursued.[30]

In 1789 the South Carolina legislature recognized Pierce Butler's ability and his service to the state by choosing him to be their first United States senator.[31]

Chapter 6

✿ Pierce Butler's Public Life, 1789–1819

S ENATOR PIERCE BUTLER wasted no time in getting the good
word to England: "The Legislature of this State elected me
in so handsome a Manner, tho absent, to represent them in the Senate of
the United States that I could not well refuse, however inconvenient to my
private affairs to go for a short time. I am willing to give my feeble aid to
get the new Government well under way. That accomplished, I purpose
returning here."[1] Pierce Butler was again on the federal scene. His fellow
senator from South Carolina was Ralph Izard, a "haughty aristocrat,"[2]
and to that degree they were a matched pair. With them from the low
country were two members of the House of Representatives, Daniel
Huger and Izard's son-in-law William Loughton Smith. The worries at
home, Mary Butler's illness, and the demands of government contributed
to the edginess that marked Major Butler's appearances as the Senate met
in New York City. Despite the relaxation afforded by the frequent social
engagements with President Washington, he was short-tempered and irritable—more so than usual. The feisty William Maclay, senator from
Pennsylvania, noted his arrival:

> But a new phenomenon had made its appearance in the House since Friday.
> Pierce Butler, from Carolina, had taken his seat and flamed like a meteor.
> He arranged the whole Impost law, and then charged (indirectly) the whole
> Congress with a design of oppressing South Carolina.
>
> We once believed that Lee was the worst of men, but I think we have a
> much worse than he in our lately arrived Mr. Butler. This is the most
> eccentric of creatures—ever and anon crying out against local views and

partial proceedings, and that the most local and partial creature I ever heard open a mouth. He has words at will, but scatters them the most at random of any man I ever heard pretend to speak.[3]

To add injury to insult, the Butler chaise overturned, wounding the Major's leg to such an extent the Senate resolved unanimously that he could speak from a sitting position, a favor he stubbornly disdained. "Butler, though lame, bounced up twice," said Senator Maclay.[4]

The accident was noted by an ailing Mary Butler in a letter to London, and by Judge Henry Wynkoop, who told of the injury to Congressman Daniel Huger: "Who riding in a Chair on Wednesday evening, the Horse took fright, ran off & shattered the Chair. Mr. Butler was much hurt. Mr. Huger has one of his legs so fractured that it must be taken off to save his Life, which it is said will be doubtful."[5] If the first session of Congress was stormy, and so it was, the biggest wind came from the transplanted Irishman of South Carolina. It was during a discussion of a plan for foreign trade, advanced by James Madison, that Senator Butler "flamed like a meteor." He was set off again, in: "A most flaming speech against the Judiciary bill. He was called to order from the Chair, and was not a little angry about it."[6] Here, as he had done in Philadelphia, he was trying to prevent what he thought was an undue invasion of the powers of states by the federal judiciary. He lost the battle, for even his fellow South Carolinian, Senator Izard, voted with the opposition. He became agitated in a discussion of the president's right to remove appointees from office, taking affront at remarks made by Senator Oliver Ellsworth of Connecticut. Having become a senator, his former ambivalence on the matter of their compensation disappeared. Senator Butler stated: "A member of the Senate should not only have a handsome income, but should spend it all." He added that it would be "scandalous" for a member of Congress to take any of his wages home, better to "give it to the poor."[7]

The second session of the First Congress began in January 1790. Pierce Butler had used the time between sessions to be with his ailing wife and their daughters in New York. At the outset of the meeting he quickly revealed he was something less than politic. President Washington had addressed both houses of Congress. His talk was referred to committee "Too hastily," according to Senator Butler, thereby arousing John Adams, the vice-president, who admonished him from the chair. Major Butler became indignant in his true "O'Trigger" fashion and was moved to write Mr. Adams he was disturbed by the "impropriety" of the pointed remarks. He added he would take no further notice, "but if ever anything of the kind takes place again I shall in justification of my own feelings, and of the situation on that floor, be under the necessity of personally resenting it."[8]

Early in 1790 the question of slavery surfaced anew to confront the Congress. Senators Butler and Izard attended sessions of the House of Representatives where Southern congressmen were doing battle with Philadelphia abolitionists over what William Loughton Smith called "these cursed negro Petitions."[9] The Society of Friends, once held in great respect by Pierce Butler, were the agitators. Friend Benjamin Franklin had published a broadside using the pseudonym *Historicus*. It was a bitter parody linking an imaginary Algerian sect to abolitionists. They prayed for the liberation of Americans captured by the Barbary pirates. Franklin's imaginary Algerians, who held the "Christian Dogs" in slavery, asked the fictitious sect the same questions posed abolitionists by the proslavery Georgian James Jackson:

> If we forbear to make slaves of their people who, in this hot climate, are to cultivate our lands? Who are to perform the common labors of our cities, and of our families? If then, we cease taking and plundering the infidel's ships and making slaves of the seamen and passengers, our lands will be of no value for want of cultivation. The rents of houses in the city will sink to one half, and the revenues of government arising from the share of prizes must be totally destroyed. And for what? To gratify the whim of a whimsical sect.[10]

The South Carolinians were bolstered by the Georgia delegation, and together they defended against "so violent an attack of the Constitution & our particular rights." Quakers "thronged" the galleries in support of their petitions denouncing slavery and called for a congressional committee to consider their stand. One of their number, Warren Mifflin, a huge man "near seven foot high," personally petitioned Congressman Smith, who sent him on to Senators Butler and Izard. The congressman then joined the two senators, and all three concentrated their attack on the outnumbered Friend. Scripture was quoted on both sides, and in the end Mifflin was forced to retreat. Senator Butler became so agitated over the Quaker petitions that he made a "personal attack on Dr. Franklin." Thus, within two months, Major Butler had chosen to take issue with two men who had already become American institutions. In May 1790 he did, in his own fashion, take note of Franklin's death: "Our Franklin is no more. We have lost a man of great mental powers."[11] After running afoul of his two senatorial confreres, Senator Maclay wrote in his journal: "Izard and Butler both manifested a most insulting spirit this day, when there was not the least occasion for it nor the smallest affront offered. These men have a most settled antipathy to Pennsylvania owing to the doctrines patronized in that state on the subject of slavery. Pride makes fools of them, or rather completes what Nature began."[12]

No doubt the slavery issue was behind much of the dissension in Congress. What Major Butler and his cohorts had worked into the Constitution had not laid to rest the persistent problem that would plague the United States for all its days. That he viewed his own role in the advocacy and practice of slavery with some inconsistency is evident in a letter to an Irish friend written at the time of his vigorous proslavery stance in Congress:

> I thank you my kind friend for your generous opinion of me respecting the treatment of the wretched Affricans. Had it pleased God to allow the beam of Civilization to reach their Country, it would not be in the power of Europe to enslave them. I am not a friend to the trafick in Human kind. Yet upon strict inquiry I much doubt if their situation in their own Country is finer or better. However this does not perhaps justify the trade. We should leave them to their own fate. I indeed wish I had never owned one.[13]

In other business of the Senate, Major Butler enthusiastically supported James Iredell in his successful bid for a seat on the Supreme Court of the United States. He worked hard to promote legislation that provided funding of the nation's debts and the assumption of $22 million of state debts. The president, probably remembering the contretemps following his January address, had Senator Butler read his Fourth of July oration to a joint session of Congress. It pleased Congressman Smith that the immigrant Senator Butler was forced to read of Washington's pride in being a *native-born* American. The Major was one of four senators to vote against a treaty of peace with the Creek Indians, and he humiliated himself and caused much confusion by changing his stand on the bill to establish a permanent site for the capital of the nation. He favored the Potomac but wavered on the choice of the temporary site, first supporting New York, and then Philadelphia. Congressman Smith commented: "his conduct has occasioned general disgust here—the New Yorkers reprobate his procedure & the Philadelphians say they made him fall into the pit he dug for them & laugh at him accordingly."[14] Mary Butler's death in November in New York had been expected and did not interrupt his senatorial responsibilities. A final session of the First Congress was held in December with Major Butler in attendance. He participated as vigorously as before, supporting Alexander Hamilton's plan to establish a Bank of the United States, although he opposed the federal government owning shares and later opined that the bank "Is establishing an aristocratick influence subversive of the spirit of our free, equal government."[15] He voted for a tax on whiskey, with plans for the proceeds to help offset the cost of assuming the debts of the states. As in the federal convention, he was his usual assertive self. Senator Maclay said he "railed," he was "irregular beyond all bearing," and he "blustered away." Overall, as one historian has written, Pierce Butler was "an erratic politician," not bound to one group or another. He had taken positions counter to those of Senator Izard and in opposition to the Federalist positions of Congressman Smith. Senator Butler was an unpredictable maverick.[16]

At the adjournment of the First Congress, a saddened Butler family returned to South Carolina to bury Mary Butler in St. Michael's churchyard in Charleston. The sadness was relieved, though, when Pierce Butler joined the Pinckneys, Rutledges, Izards, and other dignitaries in paying homage to President Washington on his much-heralded Southern journey. He was on hand at the Charleston wharf when the president arrived to the sounds of an artillery salute. The South Carolinians gave their distinguished visitor a grand welcome. The president, who had a ready eye for the ladies, must have been highly pleased, for after noting on May 2, 1791, that he had dined with "15 or 18 Gentlemen" at the governor's, his diary then recorded some particularly pleasant events:

> May 3—was visited about 2 o'clock, by a great number of the most respectable Ladies of Charleston—the first honor of the kind I ever experienced and it was as flattering as it was singular.

> May 4—in the evening went to a very elegant dancing Assembly at the Exchange—at which were 256 elegantly dressed & handsome ladies.

> May 5—in the evening went to a Concert at the Exchange at wch there were at least 400 ladies, the number & appearance of wch exceeded anything of the kind I had ever seen.

> May 6—Dined at Majr Butler's and went to a ball in the evening at the Governor's where there was a select Company of Ladies.[17]

On May 9, at daybreak, the president left Charleston for Savannah. Dignitaries dropped off along the wayside, but the president noted that "General Moultree" went on to Purysburg and that Major Butler accompanied the president all the way to "Savanna." A stop was made at Mulberry Grove plantation on the river above Savannah, where the president had a happy reunion with his old friend, the vivacious Catharine Greene. Mulberry Grove was the confiscated Tory estate that had been owned by the Loyalists John and Frances Graham and was purchased by them with money received from Pierce Butler when he sold his commission in the British army to buy their Hampton Point plantation in 1774. Mulberry Grove had been awarded to Nathanael Greene by the state of Georgia as a reward for his services in the Revolution. At the time of the visit by Washington the plantation was owned and planted by the widow Greene. The principal crop was cotton. In 1792, a year later, the young Yale graduate Eli Whitney appeared and fashioned his ingenious cotton gin.[18]

In Savannah, President Washington was given a ceremonial welcome, but the city fell short of Charleston's display of female beauty. He did attend a "dancing Assembly" where there were "about 100 well dressed and handsome ladies." When all the fanfare ceased, Major Butler turned to personal affairs that needed his attention. His Georgia visit remedied a pressing loan matter to prevent a considerable loss, and he furthered plans for the development of Hampton and Butler's Island. For a change, the dire straits of the past few years were behind him and prospects were bright. A letter written in 1791 even told of a speculation he had made in stock of the United States Bank. He justified his purchase by saying his ownership would have enabled him to help Charleston secure a branch of the bank, but as the directors were chosen and he was not among them, it was best to sell. He noted that one of the new directors was William Loughton Smith, who was no friend of his, and that the price of the stock was down from $205 to $136.[19]

In the Second Congress, which met in Philadelphia in late October, Senator Butler was given the chairmanship of two important committees. The first was assigned the task of finding the solution to the repeated seizure of American merchant ships and seamen by the Barbary pirates. The second was closely related to the first. Its assignment was to determine the cost of two frigates that were to counteract the depredations committed by the pirates, the so-called Algerines. Working through Thomas Jefferson, then the secretary of state, the Butler committee proposed direct negotiations with the dey of Algiers, an action the Senate refused to take. The other committee determined the cost of a frigate to be 37,021 pounds sterling, and an additional 1,551 pounds for the necessary sails and rigging. The Senate then became much involved in searching for a solution to the troubles the Indians were causing in the Northwest. Major Butler was at first understanding and sympathetic to the Indians, but on repeated reports of their cruelty to white settlers, ultimately took the hard line against them.[20]

Major Butler's reputation among his fellow senators notwithstanding, the South Carolina legislature looked with favor on his record. He was chosen for a new term, and as was his custom, he sent word to Weeden Butler in London. "Yesterday, I closed the period of my first Election to the Senate of the United States. So. Carolina has elected me in a Manner most flattering to my Feelings, having every vote but Eight, which were given to Governor Pinckney—My present intention is to decline Serving."[21]

While Congress was wrestling with Algerines and Indians, back home Major Butler's South Carolina legislature, to which he had been re-elected *in absentia,* devoted much of its time to the problem Josiah Quincy, Jr., had called "the peculiar curse of the land." The decision to close the slave trade in 1787, amended the following year to permit the continuation of the domestic trade, was a direct result of increased conflict between factions representing low-country and back- or up-country interests. A rapid increase in the white population in the up country created a demand for slaves and strong legislative support for opening the foreign trade and for continuing the domestic market. In 1790 low-country slaves outnumbered whites three to one, while up-country whites were four times as numerous as their black slaves. Low-country planters sought a closed market to bring a scarcity-value rise in the worth of the slaves they owned, while the up-country people wanted more to meet the needs of their expanding population.[22]

The differences between the two sections were put aside after 1792, when the specter of insurrection arose to frighten the people of the state, their apprehension heightened by knowledge of events in Santo Domingo where the French government had appealed in vain to Governor Charles Pinckney for military assistance to put down a violent revolution by blacks and mulattoes. In 1792 the South Carolina legislature, conscious of the fear of the outnumbered whites, voted a discriminatory tax on free Negroes and closed the foreign trade in slaves for an additional two years and the domestic trade "ever hereafter." It was a fear that persisted, for there were no slavery roll calls in the legislature from 1793 until 1801. Pierce Butler was aware of the situation. In a letter to Roger Parker Saunders, he acknowledged the concern of a slave owner: "From what you mention of the Negroes You cou'd not well leave your Plantation with a good mind." He continued by warning that the blacks "must at all times be crushed in the bud for if it ever gets any head we must suffer even in the Supression by the numbers that wou'd fall."[23] Again, in October 1793, he asked about the uprising of Heyward slaves on the Combahee River, where the Butler family owned a plantation inherited from the ill-fated Mary Brewton, and Elizabeth Blake. He expressed his displeasure with the agitation coming from those beyond the South: "Our Eastern & French friends will do No good to our Blacks. I wish they wou'd mind their own affairs."[24]

A planned visit to England was put aside when Major Butler was confronted with two situations that kept him in America. His manager, William Page, had given him bad news from Georgia, while at the same time nervous friends in South Carolina once again raised the alarm of insurrection. He wrote Weeden Butler in the fall of 1793:

> I much doubt of my being able to gratify myself by a visit to England next Spring: two Circumstances that have recently come to my Knowledge will throw much difficulty in my way—I have just rec'd letters from my Manager in Georgia informing that my fields of Cotton, at a time when we considered Ourselves sure of the reward of much toil and Expense, when the Cotton was nearly ready to be gathered in, a Host of Grasshoppers appeared and in three nights destroyed three hundred and fifty acres of Cotton, from which I had every reason to expect, on a very moderate Estimate, an Estimate much lower than all those who saw my fields made, from three thousand to three thousand five hundred pounds Sterling— Such is the uncertainty to which sublunary arrangements are liable. I submitt to the disappointment believing that it may ultimately be for my good. The Establishment of those Cotton Plantations was a favourite object. In prosecuting it I injured my health much. I looked to them for a much larger Income. It may be right I shou'd receive this check. The other obstacle which is a very serious One, that of a Report of a disposition in the Negroes of So. Carolina to revolt & of the truth of this I am not yet informed. I trust the foundation for the report is Slander. If there is any foundation for it I shall return to Carolina as soon as I am certified of it.[25]

Pierce Butler's avid enthusiasm for the French Revolution was shown in his letters to friends in London and Savannah. To one friend in England who shared his sentiments, he wrote a congratulatory letter:

> They are a Great and magnanimous people & merit all the blessings like to flow from their free well balanced & just Constitution. A Constitution that secures to the peasant, as well as to the Nabob those Rights that Nature & Nature's God gave alike to all the Sons of Adam.
>
> Frenchmen! Great People! I bow with Reverence before You! I revere Your Patriotism! Your Magnaminity! Your Philanthropy! Your Love of Freedom!

John Hunter, a fellow Irish-American living in Savannah, received the good word that "Our Country Ireland is progressing fast to a political and Civil change." The Major added that he hoped it would come as "Honorably and as efficaciously" as it had for the French.[26]

Of greater consequence might have been an ill-conceived plan undertaken with a French diplomat of dubious merit, Antoine Charbonnet Duplaine. Major Butler, who was in his second term as United States senator at the time, offered to assist Duplaine in a covert acquisition of a bit of United States territory—Cumberland Island on the coast of Georgia. The French Republic needed a source for pine and live oak timbers to be used in ship construction, and both were plentiful on the heavily wooded barrier island. Fortunately for the United States, and for Pierce Butler as well, the French government had the good sense to put the project aside.[27]

Pierce Butler's alignment with the French Republic was a projection of his "democratic" ideals, all a manifestation of his inconsistency. The lowcountry aristocrat found the new French government to his liking and approved of their strong anti-British sentiment. His mounting dissatisfaction with the Federalists was encouraged by the manipulations of the French as they played Americans against the British. In 1793 the agent of the French Republic in Charleston wrote his government in Paris: "Among the Deputies of South Carolina, there are Izard in the Senate and William Smith in the lower house, confirmed Monarchists. But the remainder are for us and Major Butler undertakes to cramp King Izard, Commodore Gillon (the same) for Smith."[28] Senator Izard believed democratic ideals and a slave system could not coexist in the same nation. It was a prophetic belief, for France, England, and his own country. Major Butler's differences with both Ralph Izard and William Loughton Smith only gave impetus to his pro–French Republic feelings.[29] Congressman

Smith was Senator Izard's son-in-law and shared his "Monarchist" views. To Ralph Izard the French Revolution was an unfortunate overthrow of government, and he professed his wariness at any anti-British alliance with the new France. He stated his position after the French had emancipated their colonial slaves. Once more the specter of Negro insurrection raised its fearsome head. Izard wrote Mathias Hutchinson:

> By a decree of the Convention of France, all the Slaves in their Colonies are emancipated. A joint war with France, under the present circumstances, would occasion a prodigious number of the lower order of Frenchmen to come to this Country, who would fraternise with our Democratical Clubs, & introduced the same horrid tragedies among our Negroes, which have been so fatally exhibited in the French Islands. Are the inhabitants of South Carolina ignorant of these things; or is it the will of God that the Proprietors of Negroes should themselves be the Instruments of destroying that species of property?[30]

Pierce Butler's discontent was evident at a November session of the Second Congress marked by the complete deterioration of his relations with Congressman William Loughton Smith. The Major's political sentiments had moved away from Federalism toward a Jeffersonian anti-Federalism—which was to say Republicanism—and Smith, very much of the former persuasion, had accused Major Butler of endangering his chances for re-election by circulating false and injurious reports. He wrote: "The Envy & Malignity of that Man are unbounded; he should however reflect that there are certain characters who gain nothing by spreading scandal, because nobody will believe them, the only chance they have of success is by concealing the quarter from which the Scandal originates."[31]

Major Butler's second term as senator was marked by the open break with the Federalists, both in the national government and at home. Undoubtedly a factor in his change to the democratic Republican party were the slights that had come his way from the Federalist leaders. Denied first the post of minister to the French Republic, he was then shunted as their choice for ambassador to Spain in favor of Thomas Pinckney. Surely then, thought Pierce Butler, he would be the president's appointee to represent his government as the special minister to negotiate an understanding between America and Britain on trade between the two countries and to put an end to the impressment of American seamen by the British navy. John

Jay was President Washington's choice, and when he came forth with the Jay treaty, Major Butler was outspoken in his opposition.[32]

By a rather remarkable coincidence Major Butler witnessed an act of transgression by the British navy. He had exercised a senator's prerogative and boarded the revenue cutter assigned to Georgia for a trip from Savannah to his plantation on St. Simons Island. As the cutter approached the Sound, the sloop *Sphynx*, a British man-of-war, fired a warning gun, which was ignored by the commanding officer of the cutter on the advice of Senator Butler. The British then fired additional rounds, bringing the cutter to. The vessel was boarded "in a hostile manner" by thirty-eight men, two ship's officers, and a lieutenant of marines. In a set-to with the officer who had taken possession of the cutter, Senator Butler at first "remonstrated with him to no purpose," but ultimately won the day. He told how it ended: "I then Stated to him the violation of the Rights of a Sovereign Power, and of the Law of Nations, Protesting against his Conduct. He replied 'Sir, you have so strongly Stated things to me I will quit the Vessel.' He went on deck and ordered his men into their boats, left the Cutter after having possession of Her about one hour."[33] The incident gave Major Butler fresh ammunition as he spoke his mind on the mischief he saw in the Jay treaty. A letter to Governor George Mathews of Georgia was indicative: "The evils of the late Treaty are like the sting of the Adder—the surface is whole but the poison has been taken in, is inflaming around it, and must finally break out with force." His forthright stand won grass-roots support from up-country South Carolina. Published resolutions from Edgefield and Laurens counties, and a glowing tribute from Philadelphia United Irishmen of Dublin, helped to convince him that he should be a member of the House of Representatives rather than remaining in that aristocratic body, the United States Senate. The Philadelphia Irishmen extolled:

> Dedication: To Pierce Butler, A senator of the United States of America; an enemy of Aristocracy, and a Friend of Man, who preferring virtue to titles, has the distinction conferred on the House of Ormond to promote the dignity of human nature, and the cause of equality; the following proceedings of a band of his Countrymen, who not debased by Slavery, have preserved their freedom of mind in the midst of chains, are inscribed by
> THOMAS STEPHENS.[34]

It was an ironic accolade for one whose considerable affluence was derived from the toil of hundreds of slaves.

The acceptance of his stand against the Jay treaty reinforced Major Butler's decision to leave the Senate and to seek election to the more democratic House of Representatives. As usual, he conveyed such thoughts, and others, to Weeden Butler. In September 1794 he responded to a rumor heard in England that President Washington had been attacked by a would-be assassin: "In one of your letters You ask me if an attempt was not made on the life of our President. There never was the smallest foundation for the report which has not even reached our Prints. We are a happy People free from such dark acts." In August 1796, just prior to the Major's resignation from the Senate, the Reverend Mr. Butler was told: "I have at length determined on returning to Private Life. I wait only the Meeting of the Legislature of S. Carolina to resign. There are about or near four years of the time I was elected for to run, but I shall never Enter the Doors of the Senate again as a Senator."[35] The last was not true, for Pierce Butler became a senator once again, in 1803. Nor had he abandoned the political scene.

Pierce Butler's hopes to return to public life as a Republican congressman surfaced after his resignation from the Senate, only to be dashed by the political force of an ardent young Federalist, Robert G. Harper. With his Salvador lands as a basis for qualification, Major Butler had hoped to represent the Ninety-six District, but turned aside when his anticipated support faded away. His run of bad luck continued when the Republicans considered him as a candidate for the vice-presidency on a slate headed by Thomas Jefferson. In his stead, they chose Aaron Burr. The year 1796 was not Pierce Butler's best. Nor was 1798, when he campaigned for the House of Representatives, offering from the Beaufort-Orangeburg District. The influential John F. Grimké riled Major Butler by publishing a pamphlet urging that his opponent, Grimké's nephew, be elected. Using General Charles Cotesworth Pinckney as a reluctant second, the hot-tempered Major challenged Grimké to a duel that was fortunately prevented by men with cooler heads. He was defeated by the incumbent John Rutledge, Jr., in a Federalist landslide that swept the state. Never again did he actively campaign for public office, although his strong desire for a suitable political appointment was kept alive by party support and his continued opposition to the hated Federalists. His vigorous backing of Jefferson and Burr in 1800 was matched by his vehement resistance to John Adams and Charles Cotesworth Pinckney.[36]

George Washington ended his second term as president in 1797. In Major Butler's judgment, Washington's brilliance had been severely tarnished by the Jay treaty. He said that the president had "retired with less popularity than he brought into office." Following Washington's death in 1799, further thoughts on his merit were prompted when a young friend sent pamphlets in praise of the first president. Major Butler was reminded of "an idle idolater by name Payne" who ranked Washington with Jesus Christ, a comparison that brought forth:

> No man in antient or modern times acquired exalted reputation more easy, possibly so cheap, as the deceased Gen'l Washington. That he had virtues, and amiable virtues, none will deny. But that he had all the qualities, and in a superlative degree, that base flatterers attribute to him, truth now, and in a future page of history, would blush to aver.[37]

If slaves and slavery were not among the issues Pierce Butler faced on the federal scene as the century moved toward the 1800s, such was not the case in the legislature of South Carolina. The fear of insurrection was persistent. In 1800 blacks were forbidden to hold religious meetings in the dark of night. Nonresident plantation owners who had no white overseers were subject to fines. In 1803, when most fears were somehow put aside and the slave trade reopened, there was a strict ban on the importation of slaves from the French West Indies, where revolt had been violent and destructive.[38]

An awareness that the United States Constitution permitted an end to the importation of slaves after 1807, and a desire to meet the needs of up-country cotton planters, prompted the legislature to throw caution to the trade winds. E. S. Thomas, a Charleston book dealer at the time, told of one reaction to their decision:

> In November 1803, I returned from my fourth voyage with a printed catalogue of fifty thousand volumes of books, in every branch of literature, arts and science, being by far the largest importation ever made into the United States. I had only got them opened, and arranged for sale three days, when news arrived from Columbia that the Legislature, then in session, had opened the port for importation of slaves from Africa. The news had not been five hours in the city, before two large *British Guineamen* that had been laying off and on the port for several days, expecting it, came up to the town, and from that day my business began to decline.
>
> Previous to this, the planters had large sums of money laying idle in the Banks, which they liberally expended not only for their actual, but supposed wants.

Vessels were fitted out in numbers, for the coast of Africa, and as they returned their cargoes were bought up with avidity.[39]

The year 1803 marked Pierce Butler's return to the Senate he had abandoned seven years before. He reappeared as an appointee, replacing the deceased John Ewing Calhoun. He returned in time to state his mind on the Twelfth Amendment to the Constitution, a remedy of the mode of electing the president and vice-president. Ever mindful of states' rights, in particular those of the small states, he warned against the powerful, but with a rather surprising exclusion of the large state in which he had chosen to live: "Whatever gentlemen might say on that subject he would say to the small States, with the Orator of Greece, 'Beware of Macedon!' Beware of the great States! In this, however, there was one exception, he would exclude the State of Pennsylvania, and civil liberty was better understood and practiced there than in any age or in any part of the world."[40]

Senator Butler's attention to the business of government was diverted in July 1804 when his friend Aaron Burr shot and killed Alexander Hamilton. Butler had disliked Hamilton and so assisted the vice-president in a flight to safety by offering his plantation Hampton as a refuge and by arranging his travel to the South as "R. King," using the name of Butler's plantation manager.[41]

The real Roswell King was probably a factor in the Major's discontent in his work in government, for he gave promise of being the plantation manager Pierce Butler had long sought. For the first time, Hampton and Butler's Island seemed ready to produce the crops and the money Major Butler had envisioned. In the early 1800s he was hard put to stay abreast of Roswell King, who needed more slaves, endless supplies, and the full attention of the absentee owner in Philadelphia.[42]

In 1804 Major Butler also experienced an upset by the actions of his party. Once again he was put aside and not chosen for a post he sorely wanted—ambassador to the court of St. James. His irritation was evident when he voted with the Federalists in opposing the Twelfth Amendment. There is nothing to indicate that he was one of John Randolph of Roanoke's Tertiam Quids, but he shared their mistrust of Thomas Jefferson and that same year showed his alienation from the third president when he gave refuge to Jefferson's avowed enemy, the fleeing, frightened Aaron Burr. With Jefferson seeming to stray from the Republican path, Senator

Butler decided he had other things to do. He chose to resign from the Senate a second time and did so in December of that eventful year.[43]

Between 1804 and 1822, the year of his death, Major Butler's life was devoted to the direction of his Georgia plantations and to the management of investment properties as far afield as Tennessee. His public service all but faded away, except that his friendship with James Monroe won service on the board of the new United States Bank. He knew the issuing of money to be one of "the attributes of Sovereignty," and for that reason advocated a strong bank that would strive "to even the Value of the Circulating paper in all the States." He wanted its stability to earn the confidence of Americans and of foreigners, and he worked toward that end. He was three times elected as a director by the stockholders and was twice appointed to the board by President Monroe, with the consent of the Senate. In January 1819 James Monroe wrote Major Butler to regret that rules prevented him from making a reappointment. He expressed high regard for the Major's friendship and a thought that it would "continue to animate me through life."[44]

The old Major was recognized by Philadelphia in occasional civic and social responsibilities and functions. As president of the Philadelphia Southern Society, he conducted their meeting in May 1818 and offered toasts to Southern patriots "from Captain John Smith to Thomas Jefferson." When Andrew Jackson visited Philadelphia in February 1819, Major Butler was chosen to preside at the festive dinner in the general's honor. Shortly before his death, the Major served as a commissioner to consider the feasibility of a much-needed bridge across the Delaware River.[45]

In 1821 Major Butler was named a trustee and was elected as president of Charles Willson Peale's Museum in Philadelphia. Although there is little to show that Pierce Butler's interest in natural history encompassed more than agriculture, he had been one of the original subscribers to Alexander Wilson's *American Ornithology*, the first volume of which appeared in 1808.[46]

Pierce Butler's public life showed the same inconsistencies demonstrated in his private life and in his family relationships. Easily affronted, he was quick to react and vindictive. From his self-centered world he was ever anxious to create an image of statesmanship in government, that of a firm but loving parent, of a successful planter with kindness and benevolence to "his people," and as a host renowned for generous hospitality. He *was* a successful planter. Otherwise, his true image was far from what he wished and thought it to be. At a low point in his public service he told Weeden Butler his long career had enabled him to acquire "a more intimate Knowledge of Man than I should otherwise have had." He added that he wished he could say his "respect had encreased with my Knowledge of him." Unfortunately, those he had come to know might well have said the same of Pierce Butler.[47]

Chapter 7

🌿 The Altamaha Estuary

IN 1736 Georgia's founder, James Edward Oglethorpe, visited the Scottish settlement of Darien, later called New Inverness for a short time. Darien is on the high, or "white," side of the Altamaha River. The low land across the river was called at the time the "Indian" side. Oglethorpe was properly kilted and tartaned for a review of the contingent of Highlanders stationed strategically to fend off the Spanish in Florida. The Scots were favorites of Oglethorpe, as he was of them. As a consequence, it was not surprising that they rallied to his cause when the course of the colony was threatened by malcontents led by lowland Scots who wished to introduce Negro slaves in violation of a specific prohibition laid down by the Georgia trustees.[1]

In 1739 the Scots of New Inverness signed a forthright petition to General Oglethorpe asking that he reject any thought of admitting slaves. They gave several reasons, including the potential loss of slaves to the Spanish who promised freedom; their belief that white men would be more usefully employed than blacks; the cost of slaves would drive colonists into debt; and the fear of having an enemy "in our Bosoms!" The final paragraph of their petition was fervent and prophetic:

> It's shocking to human Nature, that any Race of Mankind, and their
> Posterity, should be sentenced to perpetual Slavery; nor in Justice can we
> think otherwise of it, than that they are thrown amongst us to be our
> Scourge one Day or other for our Sins; and as Freedom to them must be as
> dear as to us, what a Scene of Horror must it bring about! And the longer
> it is unexecuted, the bloody Scene must be the greater. We therefore, for
> our own sake, our Wives and Children, and our Posterity, beg your Consid-
> eration, and intreat, that instead of introducing Slaves, you'll put us in the

way to get us some of our Countrymen, who with their Labour in time of Peace, and our Vigilance, if we are invaded, with the Help of those, will render it a difficult thing to hurt us, or that Part of the Province we possess. We will for ever pray for your Excellency, and are, with all Submission . . .

The document was signed by eighteen Scots, four of whom could only make their marks.[2]

The protest was in vain, for in 1749 the Georgia trustees relented to permit the importation of blacks. The great success of the planters of neighboring South Carolina was the motivating reason for the change, although General Oglethorpe bitterly opposed the move. He contended that the machinations of the British government brought it about.[3]

South Carolinians had long been aware of the value of the Altamaha lands. As early as 1756, Carolina planters had established a group settlement south of the river, an endeavor abandoned in 1759 in fear of the nearby Spaniards. The colony of Georgia had been carved out of lands originally granted to South Carolina, and as Georgia's southern boundary was the Altamaha River, it seemed reasonable for the Carolinians to lay claim to the land on the other side. In order to bolster their claim, South Carolina Governor Thomas Boone made grants to his people in 1763. He doled out forty tracts that averaged 1,540 acres, and these South Carolina planters were unhampered by the sentiments of the local Scots. To them the ownership of slaves was the accepted way of life. How else was the white man to convert wild lands, and plant and harvest indigo, cotton, and rice?[4]

To the South Carolinians, the grass on the far side of the Altamaha was green and luxuriant. They quickly appeared in the area with their Africans, causing the anti-slavery attitudes of the Darien Scots to waver a bit. Still, the belief persisted that slavery was an evil practice, and in 1775, when revolt from English rule was in the offing, those Scots whose convictions remained steadfast once again made their position known. Among other matters pertinent to "rights and liberties," the people of St. Andrew's Parish declared:

To show the world that we are not influenced by any contracted or interested motives, but a general philanthropy for all mankind, of whatever climate, language, or complexion, we hereby declare our disapprobation and abhorrence of the unnatural practice of Slavery in America, (however, the uncultivated state of our country, or other specious argument may plead for it,) a practice founded in injustice and cruelty, and highly dangerous to our liberties, (as well as lives,) debasing part of our fellow creatures below men, and corrupting the virtue and morals of the rest, and is laying the basis of that liberty we contend for (and which we pray the Almighty to continue to the latest posterity) upon a very wrong foundation. We therefore resolve, at all times to use our utmost endeavours for the manumission of our Slaves in this Colony, for the most safe and equitable footing for the masters and themselves.

Once again the pleas and warnings of the Scots went unheeded.[5]

South Carolina planters were inclined to scoff at their peers who owned and worked Governor Boone's land grants on the Altamaha. The Georgia holdings were called "Cracker plantations," a term that irritated Henry Laurens, who found his New Hope and Broughton Island plantations immensely profitable. Laurens managed his slaves with a light hand. His methods and his success, and the good fortune of other Carolina planters along the river, battered down the resistance of the Georgia Scots. They were influenced by an influx of people who viewed slavery in a different light; thus, it was not long before the sons and grandsons of those who had signed the anti-slavery petitions were building their own domains. Two of the Georgia planters who accepted the system as practiced by the South Carolinians, and who brought to it a paternalistic level even beyond Henry Laurens's temperate treatment, were both Scots. John Couper was a newcomer and Glasgow-born; Thomas Spalding was the great-grandson of John McIntosh Mohr, the author and signer of the New Inverness Protest of 1739.[6]

John Couper began to shape his St. Simons Island plantation in the 1790s. He reflected the earlier sentiments of the Darien Scots in the manner in which he managed his slaves. He had determined that slavery was an actuality, necessary to his way of life, and then set an exemplary pattern at Cannon's Point. This was the neighboring plantation to Pierce Butler's Hampton, both on the northern end of St. Simons, and with much the same configuration. John Couper was as different from Pierce Butler as cotton from rice. A writer who fell under his charm remarked:

A man of distinction was John Couper, Esquire, well over six feet in height, with keen blue eyes and red hair. He was cultured, charming, witty, a great raconteur and a famous host. With the sense of humor and spirit of mischief that had been his chief characteristic as a boy in Scotland, he used to claim that he had come to this country for the good of his native land.[7]

John Couper, if not a friend of Major Butler's, was a good neighbor to Hampton. Just as did Pierce Butler, Couper planted rice on an upriver plantation. This was Hopeton, owned jointly with his friend James Hamilton and purchased by them from the South Carolinians David Deas and Arthur Middleton, Mary Butler's cousin. As the Butler and Couper personalities differed, so did their thoughts on the management of Negroes. John Couper, patriarchal and benevolent, was particularly responsive to the needs of his people. His "humane feelings" were recognized by many visitors, and Cannon's Point under his direction, and as later managed by his son James Hamilton Couper, became a focal point for those bent on the observation of the institution of slavery.[8]

Sapelo Island lies across Altamaha and Doboy sounds, where the great river system pours its burden of Georgia topsoil into the Atlantic Ocean. There, on the south end, Thomas Spalding managed his plantation with considerable regard for the well-being of his slaves. A close friend of John Couper's, he too was a good neighbor to Major Butler's Hampton. Spalding was an innovative planter and as such had great respect for the agricultural successes on the Butler plantations. He had moved to Sapelo in 1802 from St. Simons, where he had worked a tract of land for his father, James Spalding. He well knew the anti-slavery sentiment of his ancestor. John McIntosh Mohr's beliefs tempered his own. Years later his grandson, Charles Spalding Wylly, wrote of Thomas Spalding: "Labor was absolutely necessary for the carrying out of his undertakings. His environment and that in which his father had lived, justified and encouraged it, every interest demanded it; he said to himself *They shall be more serfs on the land than slaves. I shall civilize them and better their condition.*" Mr. Wylly added, recognizing the truth of the Scot's protest: "but you cannot touch pitch and remain clean, and the penalty of *one day or another* was incurred, and the scourge was to fall." And so, Thomas Spalding, unaware of what was to come, and like John Couper, kept his slaves, gave them good living conditions, and shared with them some of the fruits of their labor.[9]

While the Couper, Spalding, and Butler plantations may have been the most notable of the region, they were but segments of a huge mosaic of agricultural development. The vast stretch of wetlands of the Altamaha delta, the woodlands of the Darien side, and across the river those that became the south branch plantations, the barrier islands on the sea coast—Sapelo and St. Simons—all were developed to a finite degree. Almost without exception the owners were proud, cultured, intelligent men and women who knew the success of their endeavors was dependent on the physical strength—the sweat and blood—of the thousands of Negro slaves who labored in their fields.

At first the South Carolina land-grant plantations were operated by absentee owners. This arrangement continued on the river plantations occupied by slaves and white overseers. The sea island plantings and those on the south branch of the Altamaha moved toward owners in residence, with Pierce Butler's Hampton being an exception.

Visitors to the Altamaha were usually surprised to find the resident plantations so much a mixture of culture and agriculture, with the relationship between the owners and their slaves not at all as expected. For one important reason, the visitors often were disarmed by the gracious hospitality encountered. One who chronicled St. Simons Island as it was in the early 1800s said the "hospitality was immense. Every door stood open to the stranger." John Couper's kitchen was ruled by a legendary slave, Sans Foix, unsurpassed as a cook; and his slave Johnny could entertain the guests with his fiddle or could skirl a Scottish tune on the Couper bagpipes. The English geologist Sir Charles Lyell visited the Altamaha estuary in 1845. His host was James Hamilton Couper, the son of John Couper, but a man quite different from the good-humored laird of Cannon's Point. Young Couper's hospitality was generous but was presented with dignified formality. Where the John Couper home often overflowed with family and friends, James Hamilton Couper's guests were more apt to be visitors from afar. A contemporary of both said the father chose the company that filled his house, whereas it was the company that sought and chose the son. Hopeton, a river plantation when planted by John Couper and James Hamilton, became a combined river and mainland plantation under the skillful management of James Hamilton Couper. Close by Butler's Island, Hopeton was to that plantation as Cannon's Point was to Major Butler's Hampton. Young Couper liked nothing better than displaying his thriving plantation to visitors. He was proud of his procedures for planting and harvesting rice, his efficient mills, and particularly of his slaves at work and in their quarters. The eminent Lyell cast a scientific eye on the slaves at Hopeton. After having viewed the "peasantry" of Europe, he found the Couper slaves offered "but small ground for lamentation or despondency."

> During a fortnight's stay at Hopeton, we had an opportunity of seeing how the planters live in the south, and the condition and prospects of the

negroes on a well-managed estate. The relation of the slaves to their owners resembles nothing in the northern states. There is an hereditary regard and often attachment on both sides, more like that formerly existing between lords and their retainers in the old feudal times of Europe, than to any thing now to be found in America. The slaves identify themselves with the master, and their sense of their own importance rises with his success in life. But the responsibility of the owners is felt to be great, and to manage a plantation with profit is no easy task; so much judgment is required, and such a mixture of firmness, forbearance, and kindness.[10]

Sir Charles Lyell was one of a great many who came to see the Altamaha plantations. In the early 1800s visitors were not so much interested in slavery as in the remarkable agricultural accomplishments. Those who had not seen a working plantation with slaves busy at their tasks found that spectacle of greater interest, as did Lyell, whose focus on natural history was diverted by the sight of hundreds of Africans thrust into a new environment and adapting their lives to the dictates of their owners. Before Lyell, Captain Basil Hall and his wife Margaret came from Scotland. Both sought in person and in the field what they did not wish to study at home "in the closet." On the Altamaha they quickly absorbed the panorama of slavery. At Cannon's Point, Captain Hall found the growing of cotton of secondary interest to the system of enforced labor. He saw the control of slaves as a challenge to the owner, and said he had looked "this great and established evil fairly in the face" and in doing so proved to himself "That there are few situations in life where a man of sense and feeling can exert himself to better purpose than in the management of slaves." Captain Hall contended that slavery's evils were manifold, writing that were one to catalog freedom's blessings and then invert them, he would get "a list of the curses of bondage." As did Mrs. Hall, he found James Hamilton Couper an exemplary slaveholder. She wrote that young Mr. Couper demonstrated "how much the evil which appears to be irremediable at present may be softened by proper management." It did not seem to concern her that her host shared her husband's low estimation of Southern women and that his expressed view that the "only chance a man had for a rational companion in his wife is to marry her when very young and cultivate her mind" had been put in practice by his recent marriage to a "pleasing young woman but sixteen years old." Mrs. Hall was unimpressed by John Couper's and Major Butler's St. Simons Island. "There is no beauty whatever," she complained, and found the island "as flat as the rest of the state" and covered with "swamps."[11]

Charles Lyell and the Halls were followed by Fredrika Bremer of Sweden, and a most unusual observer, the Honorable Amelia Matilda Murray, who had been a lady-in-waiting to Queen Victoria. Both succumbed to the persuasive intelligence of James Hamilton Couper. Their forays into the Altamaha country came in the 1850s, when slavery was being attacked from many sides. The two women reacted immediately to Altamaha slavery, and Miss Bremer's outspoken opposition seemed to soften a bit. She found Mr. Couper "a disciplinarian with great practical tact, and also some benevolence in the treatment of the negroes." She thought him like Waldo Emerson, possessing as much knowledge as an encyclopedia. She agreed with his thought that a worthy end result of slavery might well be the colonization of Africa by liberated slaves from America. That their enforced labor on the Altamaha was educational so that freed blacks might impart to Africans "the blessings of Christianity and civilization," she had the good sense to doubt. Miss Bremer saw the slave as "deficient in the power of abstract thought, of systemization, of pursuing strict laws of semi-civilization." Amelia Matilda Murray was converted. She wrote her abolitionist friends: "You will imagine I have fallen under some evil influence." She saw Hopeton slaves as "more comfortable" and "more devoted" than any English servants she had seen. It was her considered opinion that

> in intellect and moral character, they remain and ever will remain, inferior to the whites. I believe, and must not hesitate to confess my belief, the negro race is incapable of self-government; and I suspect its present condition in the United States is practically the best that the character of the negroes admits of.
>
> It has pleased Providence to make them barbarian, and as barbarian they must be governed, however Christian may be the principles and feelings of their master.

Later, she did write from Hopeton: "The Creator of men formed them for labor under guidance, and there is probably a providential intention of producing some good Christian men and women out of it in time."[12]

On the Altamaha, Miss Murray, like Captain Hall, Sir Charles Lyell, and Miss Bremer before her, was exposed to slavery where it was practiced with reasonable constraints and with unusual regard for the well-being of the people in bondage. They saw its better side. To them the lash was a symbol of authority—a policeman's nightstick. The chains were not visible. Miss Murray's summation of what she had seen included: "I here repeat, what probably my friends in England will be slow in believing, that, in the mass, Southern slaveowners are conscientiously fulfilling their trying and painful duties." Captain Hall and Sir Charles would have agreed. Miss Bremer, perhaps not, for she wrote: "In the darkness of slavery I have sought for the moment of freedom with faith and hope in the genius of America. It is no fault of mine that I have found the darkness so great, and the work of light as yet so feeble in the slave states." She did find a faint gleam of light on the Altamaha.[13]

Chapter 8

The Georgia Plantations

HAMPTON, PIERCE BUTLER'S PLANTATION on the north end of St. Simons Island, was his own. It was his answer to the Middletons and their kinfolk who planted South Carolina lands in the grand manner. His wish to be rid of the awkward relationship with the trustees of the Bull estate became evident in the early 1790s when he began to develop the land he had acquired from John and Frances Graham in 1774. For a time it appeared that Hampton would replace Mary Ville as the Butler family seat, but the attractions of Philadelphia overruled that possibility.

St. Simons is one of the barrier islands fronting the Atlantic Ocean along the Georgia coast. Hampton occupied a broad finger of land surrounded by salt marsh and tidal streams. It was separated from the sea by John Couper's Cannon's Point plantation on a similar finger of land, and by Little St. Simons Island, which confronts the Atlantic and Altamaha Sound with an expanse of hammock land, marsh, dunes, and sand beaches. The seventeen hundred acres purchased from the Grahams formed the nucleus of Major Butler's St. Simons properties. Of the two James Graham tracts that were also purchased in 1774, one of six hundred acres was mostly marsh land to the north and west of Hampton and became known as "Five Pound Tree," or usually "Five Pound." The second tract, of four hundred acres, enlarged Hampton to the south and west. Major Butler also purchased the highland of Little St. Simons Island, but did so piecemeal, the initial acquisition coming from the heirs of Samuel Augspourger in 1795. It was an unusual transaction, for it appears that Augspourger had received the island in 1760 as a grant from

George II. He gave it to the Society for the Relief of Widows and Orphans of the Church of England without the formality of a deed. Major Butler paid two hundred pounds sterling to the society, who in turn authorized Augspourger's grandsons, Gabriel and Joseph Manigault, to act in their behalf. On May 5, 1795, Pierce Butler paid the Manigaults a token "five shillings," for which they "made title" to the five hundred acre island as delineated in the 1760 survey by "Will DeBrahm." It was the principal piece of highland in the network of sloughs, marshes, hammocks, and beaches of Little St. Simons later acquired and that came to be "five thousand acres more or less." Included in the five thousand acres was the wild "Rainbow Hammock Land" on the Atlantic, south of Little St. Simons at the mouth of the Hampton River. Other tracts were acquired through the years to become a part of the Butler holdings in Glynn County, one notable acquisition being one thousand acres granted Harriot Percy Butler in 1802 by Georgia's Governor Josiah Tattnall, Jr. The acreage consisted of marshland between Hampton River and Buttermilk Sound, all of which "I, Henrietta P. Butler, otherwise Harriott Butler" conveyed to her father a year later for another "five shillings." This land, and a similar tract of 1,016 acres purchased from Henry Laurens McIntosh in 1809, gave Major Butler a sweep of land across the northern end of Little and Greater St. Simons islands. These tracts were combined with Five Pound to become Experiment Plantation.

The highland of Hampton was particularly adapted to the growing of long staple cotton. Surprisingly, the banked hard marsh of Experiment proved to have similar qualities. Both permitted Major Butler to "go on cotton" with great success until the influx of short staple that followed Eli Whitney's perfection of the mechanical gin. Competition from the many growers of upland cotton gradually diminished the demand for and profits from the "sea island cotton" for which the St. Simons plantations were known. At that time the banked lands of Experiment were converted from cotton to rice. By judicious use of the great flow of fresh water coming down the Altamaha River, and with a careful exclusion of salt water on the incoming flood tides, rice was brought to harvest as a profitable crop.

Experiment Plantation had yet another use. On that bare, windswept segment of the Altamaha delta called Five Pound Tree, the slave settlement there became the Botany Bay of the Butler plantations. The most isolated of all the Major's plantings, Five Pound on Experiment was the home of troublesome, unruly slaves where the scant amenities a slave might expect were scarce indeed.[1]

The lighter shaded areas represent
Butler land holdings.

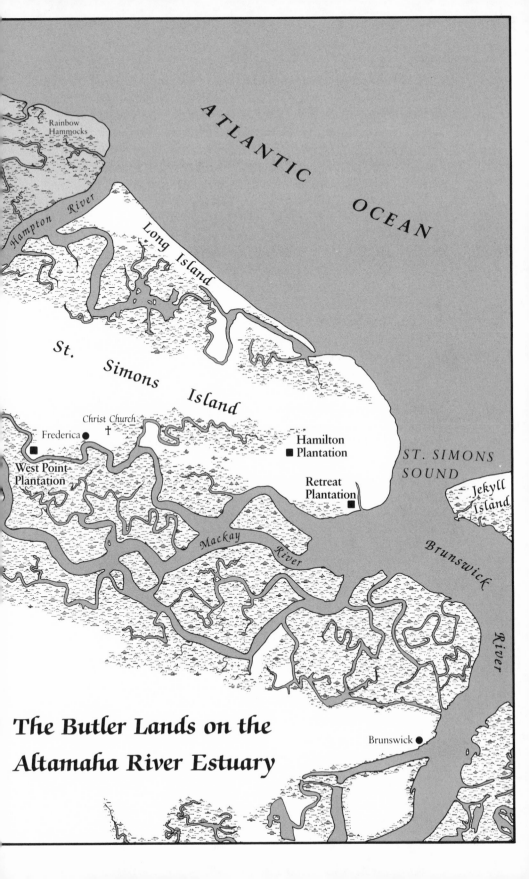

ATLANTIC OCEAN

Rainbow
Hammocks

Hampton River

Long Island

St. Simons Island

Christ Church

Frederica

West Point
Plantation

Hamilton
Plantation

Retreat
Plantation

ST. SIMONS
SOUND

Jekyll
Island

Mackay River

Brunswick River

Brunswick

The Butler Lands on the
Altamaha River Estuary

In order to improve communications and access to Hampton from the sound, Major Butler directed his slaves to dig a canal through the marsh from Hampton River. If the canal proved difficult to excavate, and it did, it also proved all but impossible to maintain at a serviceable depth. In 1824, when a similar project was being considered elsewhere on St. Simons, Major Butler's waterway was remembered in a sarcastic letter appearing in the *Darien Gazette*. The letter was directed to the "mayor" of Frederica from one of his subjects—a "Frederican," who wrote: "Your worship may remember, that under the long and elastic whip of Old Braam, the Five Pound Islanders connected the muddy waters of Buttermilk Sound with those of the serpentine creek of Hampton, by noble ditch of about three hundred yards in length, four feet wide and eight inches deep at high water to the great admiration not only of her sister marshes, but the whole of Little St. Simons." If the Five Pound cut proved impracticable, such was not always the case with similar efforts. In an area where time and tide awaited neither master nor slave, the short cut was a most useful device.[2]

In the spring of 1794, when a highly harassed Pierce Butler was attempting to begin life anew in his Philadelphia home, the directing of the Georgia plantations from his remote station proved exceedingly difficult. He had taken on a new Savannah agent and did not hesitate in putting him to the test. His letter to Thomas Young gave explicit instructions:

> It so happens in life that we have an opportunity of befriending each other. I have now to request an evidence of your Friendship. It is this, that you will go as early as you possibly can to Hampton, and do for me as you would do for yourself. I beg of you for the present, till you hear from me to take all my affairs in your hands and under your care. I give you Carte Blanche, do as you think proper. I enclose a short letter to Valley, to tell him I leave all to you. I will just mention to you a sketch of the plan I had drawn or laid down. I ordered to Hampton about 115 workers including half hands at the rate of two to one. These I wish to be divided into 3 or 4 distinct gangs, with a driver to each, to work separately. My fixed order to Valley is to plant *full 800* acres of Cotton, which he may well do, as he plants his corn among the cotton. It is altogether about seven acres to the hand, which may well be attended to. He has at present but two Drivers. I would wish a third to be appointed. I think George would be the fittest. My intention is and my order to Valley was to make four distinct settlements, 1 where Valley lives, and four others at the southern one. I intended

whenever I met with a good overseer to place one, and to give him charge
of the two Settlements, and to let Valley supervise the other two, but this I
did not communicate to Valley, not thinking it was necessary 'till I was
ready to make the arrangement. If you will order the execution of the plan
you will add to the obligation you will confer on me by an early visit to
Hampton. On my Tide Island I mean twenty workers to remain constantly
ditching. I had twenty-three there besides Cook, but I empowered Valley to
take some away in order to make up his compliment. Will you do me a
favour to take a run to the Island and see what Sambo has done. He has
been there since May. By Valley's account to me he has not done three
months work. If so I beg of you to put a sober overseer on the Island. My
orders to Sambo were not to clear any land 'till he had it first damned in,
yet I understand he has cleared a few acres. This I totally disapprove of
because it may cause some grass. Be good to write me what you think of
Sambo, and if he has been negligent. I wish the damms to be made
sloping.[3]

Hampton was long the focal point of Major Butler's Georgia plantings.
Its produce gave him strong ties to the country he had abandoned in
1773. Cotton from the St. Simons plantations brought a fat premium in
the Liverpool market, where its long staple made for superior cloth that
was much in demand by the widespread clients of the English mills. The
relationship prompted some observers to note that English demand for
slave-state cotton was a principal support of the system of slavery the
English were so quick to condemn.[4] In 1800 the Major demonstrated the
magnitude of his cotton production by chartering a ship, the brig *Anna* of
Portsmouth, to carry a cargo of Hampton-grown cotton from St. Simons
to London, or Liverpool, as the market dictated. Although most of the
Butler cotton was shipped to Savannah factors, the direct approach was
not unusual. On one occasion he chartered a ship for a long voyage to
Russia with a cargo of his fine long staple cotton, a venture made possible
by the special equipment used at Hampton.[5] Not only was there a working gin, there was a spiral screw device that was used for compressing the
cotton without damage to its long fiber. When cotton was king, it was
grown not only on Hampton's sandy fields and the banked marshland of
Experiment but on other tracts in use at varying times—Jones, Sinclair,
St. Annie's, and as a rotation crop on Butler's Island. The average allotment of land to slave was five acres, and the average yield was 150 pounds
per acre. In 1793, desirous of borrowing from twelve to fifteen thousand

pounds sterling, Major Butler wrote a London merchant offering as security "four cotton plantations in Georgia with the negroes thereon." He included Butler's Island as additional collateral:

> I will tell you, and it is strictly true, what I plant the ensuing Spring. I plant 800 acres of Cotton and about 300 of Rice. The general calculation of the Proceeds of Cotton is 150 Wt of clean Cotton to an acre of ground. Now I will go on the supposition of only 125 Wt to the Acre and 2 bbls of Rice to the Acre, and even on this estimate I am within the mark.

The "mark" was an annual repayment of five thousand pounds sterling, plus interest at 6 percent.[6]

Butler cotton was ginned by a machine made at Hampton from a design by Joseph Eve of Nassau in the Bahamas. It was horse-powered—by two horses—and manned by seven slaves. There were three boys, three girls, and one adult or "full hand," the boys and girls being considered as "quarter hands." The gin freed the cotton of most of its seed, but another step, called "moting," was required. In moting, the women picked broken seed and debris out of the cotton by hand. If necessary, the cotton was then winnowed over a fan for further cleaning. A "moter" could clean approximately fifty pounds of cotton a day, and production at the gin averaged four hundred to five hundred pounds of the clean fiber daily. The cotton was forced into three-hundred-pound bags by the compressing screw, and if sent on to Savannah or to Charleston, would be further compressed by more efficient equipment than that on the plantation. In those places the bulk was reduced to one-half of its volume, thus permitting much more cotton to be loaded aboard ship.[7]

The political career of Major Butler had brought many interesting friendships. Of these, his attachment to Aaron Burr and the subsequent escape to Hampton led to a firsthand impression of the hospitality provided a welcome guest on a Butler plantation. The Burr-Hamilton duel was a most unfortunate affair of "honor" that sparked an explosion in the American press. Burr fled south, trying to get away from:

> *Oh, Aaron Burr, what have you done?*
> *You've gone and killed great Hamilton*
> *You hid behind a great tall thistle*
> *And killed him with a big hoss pistol.*[8]

Vice-President Burr had considered taking refuge in Norfolk under a plan put forth by Charles Biddle, who was told, "my friend P.B. has

The one existing slave house at Hampton plantation in 1915. The building was constructed of tabby. (Amelia M. Watson "Kemble" Collection, Lenox Library.)

proposed another which pleases me better." The Butler plan sent the fugitive southward under the thin disguise and with the assumed name of "R. King." Passage from Philadelphia to St. Simons Island was arranged on one of the small schooners that made frequent trips between the plantation and Philadelphia and came to be known at Hampton as "the corn vessel" for its transport of a principal staple of the Butler slaves' diet. The ship departed on August 11 or 12, 1804, and arrived at Hampton on August 25. Aaron Burr again wrote Charles Biddle, "In this neighborhood I am overwhelmed with all sorts of attention and Kindness." The assumed name was ignored in Georgia, where his presence was quickly known and reported in the press. He stayed five weeks riding out the firestorm of criticism that continued elsewhere, and while there wrote several letters to his daughter, the beautiful Theodosia Burr Alston, who was living on her husband's plantation near Georgetown, South Carolina. The vice-president had no qualms on the question of slavery. He owned and had brought with him a black boy named Peter. Burr said the boy was "an intelligent, good tempered, willing fellow about fifteen; a dirty careless dog, who with the best of intentions, is always in trouble." He wrote Theodosia that his will, drawn the day before the fateful duel, left Peter to his grandson, Aaron Burr Alston. Burr lived well at Hampton:

> My establishment consists of a housekeeper, cook and chambermaid, seamstress and two footmen. There are besides two fishermen and four bargemen, always at command. The department of laundress is done abroad. The plantation affords plenty of milk, cream and butter; turkies, fowls, kids, pigs, geese and mutton; fish of course, in abundance. Of figs, peaches and mellons there are yet a few. The house affords Madeira wine, brandy and porter.

Good neighbor John Couper sent over an assortment of French wines, including "Claret, Sauterne and Champagne, all excellent." There was enough "Orange shrub" to make punch for an entire year. Mrs. Couper added "sweetmeats and pickles."9

Burr enjoyed the hospitality of some, but not all of the island planters. He was not impressed on his visit to Butler's Island, writing that "the country of course, presents no scenes for a painter." While calling on the John Coupers, he rode out a true storm, the great hurricane of September 1804 that devastated the low country and played particular havoc on the waterfronts of Savannah and Charleston. He wrote Theodosia a description of his ordeal:

When about to return in the evening, the wind had risen so that, after an ineffectual attempt, I was obliged to remain at Mr. C's. In the morning the wind was still higher. It continued to rise, and by noon blew a gale from the North, which together with the swelling of the water became alarming. From twelve to three several of the outhouses had been destroyed, most of the trees about the house were blown down. The house in which we were shook and rocked so much that Mr. C. began to express his apprehensions for our safety. Before three part of the piazza was carried away, two or three of the windows bursted in. The house was inundated with water, and presently one of the chimneys fell. Mr. C. then commanded a retreat to a storehouse about fifty yards off, and we decamped men, women and children.

The wind abated and within ten minutes all was calm. Aaron Burr "seized the moment" to return to Hampton, but before he reached the Butler mansion the storm came on again with renewed fury from the southeast. He had crossed the creek between the two plantations under the hurricane's eye. He wrote of the ruin of the buildings on the lowland, of the loss of the rice crop, and of the death of many slaves. He told Theodosia that nineteen of Major Butler's people had drowned, and a great many were lost from neighboring plantations. His letter was written while dining alone on one of the finest saltwater fish of the region—a sheepshead. He enjoyed copious champagne, drank toasts to Theodosia, to his grandson, to their friends the Sumters—"Madame" and "Mademoiselle Sumtare," and then to the one who gave him refuge—"Mais buvons 'a la sante' de mon hote et bon ami Major Butler." Burr drank to Major Butler's "zeal and animation" and to his "intrepidity and frankness." By that time he had become a bit addled. He ended by telling Theodosia that his letter would be taken to Savannah by a slave who would be forced to swim "half a dozen creeks, in one of which, *at least* it is probable he may drown," the reason being the loss of the mail boat in the hurricane. The final glass had been a bumper toast to his current lady love—his "inamorata" in Philadelphia, " 'a la sante' de Celeste." Of the nineteen slaves lost in the hurricane, sixteen died at Butler's Island, where the Altamaha rose nine feet above its usual highwater mark, far above the high bank that encircled the island plantation. Many of the buildings and "five to six hundred barrels of rice" were swept away. It was a "truly melancholy" scene.[10]

Until Hopeton was developed by James Hamilton Couper, the Butler plantations were the most important and most successful on the Altamaha estuary. During the Major's life Thomas Spalding came closest to rivaling the success of Hampton and Butler's Island. In 1809 Major Butler responded to a South Carolinian, John Potter, who had expressed an interest in purchasing his Georgia holdings. He was armed with a fresh appraisal requested of and made by William Page of St. Simons Island. Major Butler had written: "When you are at full leisure to make the estimate I shall thank you for it. I shall not advance one step in the business 'till I receive it." Mr. Page responded: "I shall confine myself first to the value of the different plantations. On Butler's Island as the one dearest, next the Experiment, next Little St. Simons, then the Hampton division, and lastly the negroes as an entire gang. I go no further of course leave out the stock of horses, mules, cattle, watercraft &c." He valued the first three at $293,000, Hampton at $42,000, and the six hundred slaves at $282,000. The total, $617,000. Major Butler's letter to Mr. Potter indicated the two differed rather widely on the value. Also, it gave a graphic view of Pierce Butler's "estate" as he saw it. His letter to Mr. Potter gives his thoughts on the accuracy of the appraisal and describes his holdings in detail:

I yesterday recd the letter you favoured me with of 21st July. From an expression in it you and myself are not so near as I concluded we were. You understand I valued the whole planting interest at from 400,000 Dollrs to 100,000 Sterling. Several Years past I was offered One Hundred Thousand pds Sterling for part of the Estate in question. I declined the offer considering it short of the Value. I then grew 400 bales of Cotton and from six to seven hundred Tierces of Rice—Of my working Negroes I keep from 40 to 50 male slaves out of the field, to wit, about 14 house carpenters, 2 mechanics, 6 ship carpenters, 12 to 15 Ditchers, 4 Tanners, Curriers and Shoemakers. I turn my own leather, make my own shoes and those of my Neighbors—my own harness, etc. 4 Blacksmiths, three masons, 2 brick makers, two painters who are also sailmakers—Should you incline to put most of these in the field you would of course much increase the income. I have always had in view the Improvement and Enlarging of my Estate more than an immediate extension of income, intending from time to time to add to the number of my Negroes. I wished to have land in order for them. I believe I have nearly doubled the quantity of River Land banked in on my River Island since I refused £100,000 Sterling. I have put up several Valuable Buildings since that time and added very considerably to the Value of my Estate in every respect. My carpenters require no White man to enable them to erect as good a House as I would desire to occupy. They glaze also. My ship carpenters have built me two Sea Vessels without any white person directing them. I make all my Cotton machinery—We never Ginn by hand.

It is my intention with God's permission to go by Water to Charleston in the latter end of October. If you wish you can accompany me to Georgia. I would not be desirous of any person in the light of a purchaser visiting my Estate in my Absence, because should the purchase not take place it would be injurious to me in the effect on the feelings of the people.

The Lands consist of Sea Island Land and an Island in the Altamaha, in the best pitch of the tide of 1,490 acres—This land is of the first quality & there are at least 700 acres banked in. I do solemnly assure you that I would not exchange that Island for any land my friend William Alston owns. I cultivate to great advantage best Cotton on my River Lands. My friend Mr. Alston can only cultivate Rice. The mail stage stops within about one mile of the Island. My residence is on a Sea Island, more healthy in my Estimation at Every Season than Charleston. I have a small box that could be added to for a family—My own people are quite competent to making the addition. The number of negroes when I last had a list, as well as my memory serves, for I am now where I cant lay my hands on the paper, amounted to 580. I have 4 settlements on my River Island, 2 on the Island of Little St. Simons which belongs wholly to me and is capable of two or three other settlements. I have three settlements on the Island of Great St. Simons where my residence is. I can go from the Sea Island to my River Island in two hours & I dont know that I can give you any other general description.

John Potter was a serious prospect. He tried again in 1815 and once more could not meet Major Butler's terms. In 1817 he bought Colerain, a Savannah River plantation owned and operated by William Mein. He paid $110,000, and Colerain became the nucleus and the first segment of a vast agricultural domain for John Potter's sons and grandsons. The purchase of Colerain was well noted by Major Butler and his manager, Roswell King. Said Mr. King in response to Pierce Butler: "Mr. Potter has purchased Rice and Society, but no Sea Island Cotton and Sugar."[11]

THE ISLAND that came to be known as Butler's Island had been one of the South Carolina land grants given by Governor Thomas Boone in 1763 in a futile attempt to retain the fertile land south of the Altamaha River as a noncontiguous part of his state.[12] As noted previously, the island had come into Pierce Butler's hand prior to 1784, for it was in-

The Butler Rice Plantation
on the Altamaha River

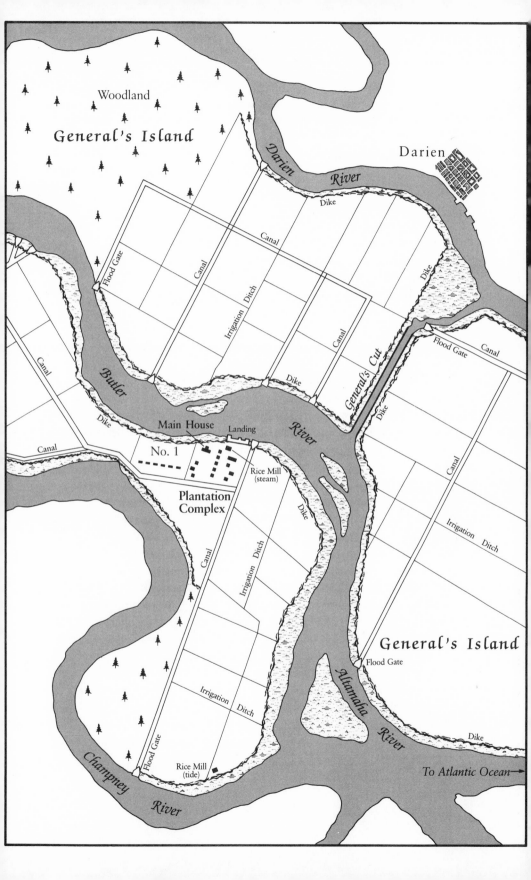

cluded in the property used to secure the loan from Jan Gabriel Tegelaar. The burning of Darien and the McIntosh County courthouse in the Civil War destroyed records of his acquisition, but it is likely to have come through William Middleton's estate. Mary Middleton's brother had received one of Governor Boone's Altamaha grants before his death in 1768. Major Butler had high expectations for the island he gave his name.[13]

As the Altamaha River approaches the sea, it breaks up into several channels that join, separate, and rejoin each other in the swamp and marshland of the river's delta. Butler's Island lies south and slightly west of the small town of Darien, and between two channels of the river. It is a good ten miles to the west, or upstream, from Hampton. When first owned by Major Butler, the island was reached from Darien by a circuitous route that was shortened considerably in 1808 by a narrow passage cut through General's Island, which lies between Butler's Island and the town. The cut was a great convenience to the rice planters of the Altamaha.[14]

Butler's Island was said to contain "1,500 acres more or less," although on occasion Major Butler would be specific and say 1,494, or 1,490, acres. Both were approximations, for the island's irregular shape made precise measurement all but impossible.[15] It had been a river swamp, as opposed to marsh, with cypress, gum, and maple trees predominating. Most of these were cut when the island was banked and then cleared for the cultivation of rice. The high bank around the perimeter was nine miles in length. For slave labor, working with hand tools, it was a massive undertaking. Most of the soil of which the bank was formed came from the island side of the bank, its removal resulting in a large ditch that became a combination aqueduct and canal. Floodgates affixed to culverts made of wood, and called trunks, were placed strategically in the high bank and were so situated that fresh water could be introduced to the areas within or, when necessary, drained back into the river. The tidal rise and fall of the river made this possible. Within the bank the heavy growth of the river swamp was gradually cleared and open areas were prepared into a vast grid of lesser banks, canals, ditches, drains, and quarter drains. On Butler's Island the highest, most accessible land was used for the overseer's house; the garden; the plantation complex, which consisted of the machine shops, the rice, and later the sugar mills; and the largest of the quarters in which the slaves were housed. The river landing, with its wharf, was much a part of this site. Major Butler mentioned four

Habersham Mungin, born a Butler slave, and his son, rowing through General's Cut enroute from Darien to Butler's Island in 1915. (Amelia M. Watson "Kemble" Collection, Lenox Library.)

Habersham Mungin at an abandoned tidal gate on Butler's Island, 1915. (Amelia M. Watson "Kemble" Collection, Lenox Library.)

settlements on Butler's Island. The other three were on the back, or southern side, along the branch of the Altamaha called the Champney River. These settlements housed only slaves and were located on the main canal behind the high bank. They were protected from flooding within the island by their own lesser banks.[16]

As early as 1793, Major Butler called his river plantation "a tide island exceeded for quality by none in the United States." He made this statement when he was offering his Georgia lands as security for a loan to enable him to purchase the Philadelphia mansion. The island was strategically located as a rice plantation. The delta soil was extremely fertile. Being in the network of freshwater streams provided ready access to the irrigation so vital to the cultivation of rice. The Major frequently and aptly said that the island was "in the best pitch of the tide." Sufficiently distant from the Atlantic Ocean, it was free of the danger of saltwater intrusion except under unusual weather and tidal conditions. Yet, at that distance, the island's location was such that the rise and fall of coastal tides assured opportunity for flooding or draining the fields. The Altamaha delta was wide enough for the periodic freshets to be spread over many miles of lowlands without a dangerous rise of water level. When such a freshet surged down the Altamaha from the Oconee and Ocmulgee rivers upstream, the plantation was well protected by the high bank on the island's perimeter. A rare combination of a freshet peaking in conjunction with a high spring tide made even higher by a strong offshore wind might have sent the Altamaha over Major Butler's high bank, or an exceptional hurricane, as in 1804 or 1824, might have done the same, but such a catastrophe would have been an unusual occurrence. At Butler's Island the Major's "pitch" was a rise of a little over seven feet from high to low water. To protect against this, the freshet, and the hurricane, the encircling high bank was a skillful engineering accomplishment. Major Butler had observed the dikes and canals of Holland and saw to it his slaves carried out similar practices on his own land. Of all the tasks put to a plantation's workmen, none was more arduous than the combined task of ditching and banking.[17]

Although Butler's Island was essentially a rice plantation as Hampton was oriented toward cotton, Major Butler practiced skilled agronomy by rotating his crops. His letter to John Potter in 1809 tells of "best Cotton" being grown there. Cotton, a dry-culture crop, needed the greatest attention when planted on land as low as that of Butler's Island. From 1806 until 1812, the British embargoed rice shipments, causing many coastal rice planters to turn to cotton in desperation. For most, it was a complete failure. The rich, moist rice-field soil prompted a flourishing early growth followed by a deterioration of the root system to doom the plant. Somehow, the Butler people were able to obtain soil conditions dry enough to sustain the cotton plant's roots. The "pitch of the tide" must have provided the drainage to permit a healthy growth. Whatever the case, Major Butler's managers were successful in their rotation of crops. Roswell King, Jr., when queried about rotation at Butler's Island, said it was necessary in order to make large crops of rice. He preferred cotton to sugar cane as it added more vegetable matter to the soil and thus was more beneficial to the following crop of rice.[18]

Thomas Spalding visited Butler's Island frequently during Major Butler's lifetime and after his death. His respect for Butler planting practices was a compliment from one skilled planter to another. He commented on the system of rotation introduced by Major Butler, "a most excellent planter." Mr. Spalding recalled a yield of two hundred pounds of cotton and three barrels of rice to the acre, which would make Major Butler's estimate to his prospective lender both conservative and fair. In 1828, Roswell King, Jr., wrote that Hampton's cotton yield was variable, from 75 to 250 pounds to the acre, and this, too, would indicate that Butler's Island cotton, although secondary to rice, was a successful crop.[19]

Thomas Spalding's most vivid impression of Butler's Island was the high bank surrounding the island. Once a rice-field bank had been formed, the usual practice was to plant small trees or shrubs on the sides of the bank so that roots would bind the soil and foliage would prevent erosion from rain. Many planters preferred *Ilex vomitoria*, the cassena or Christmas berry, that thrives on the rich delta soil and often appears as a volunteer plant. Major Butler chose to plant sour oranges on the high bank, a planting that gained him unexpected attention. The beauty of the orange trees, either in bloom or laden with fruit, often deflected the criticism of slavery by observers who visited the Altamaha estuary for a firsthand impression of Africans in bondage. Thomas Spalding had this to say in 1830:

> In the winter of 1815, the late Gen. Rutledge spent a few days with me at Sapelo Island. Anxious to interest and amuse, I took him to Maj.
> Butler's plantation, on the Alatamaha, where, for the first time, they were manufacturing sugar from cane grown on river land; but it was not the

sugar, though the crop was good, not the alternate fields of rice, and cotton, and cane, that most forcibly struck him—it was the orange hedges, of five miles in extent, which bordered the banks at the water-line upon their exterior, which most forcibly attracted his observation, and called forth his admiration—the trees were bowed down with their weight of fruit. These beautiful hedges are still bordering Maj. Butler's fields, and are still covered with fruit, for the rivers running around them, tempers the cold, while their waters secure and improve the crop. Neither the repeated hurricanes which we have had since, nor the visitations of sea-water, that have accompanied them, have been able to break down, nor destroy these hedges. Why then is not this example followed? The orange tree will grow better upon the river banks, than upon the high lands adjacent; they occupy no available space, they strengthen, and shade, and beautify the banks. Sir, it was the orange trees that formerly bordered the banks of the Mississippi, that every traveller delighted to dwell upon—they have passed away, not a remnant of them remained when I was there in 1825. Not so with us—not so with you, even as far as Charleston. Let us add, then, these beautiful orange groves to the river scenery of our country; it will cost but little care and still less labour, while it will add to the comforts of our negroes, by giving them acid after salt, the next essential sauce for every food.[20]

It would have been a bitter sauce, for sour oranges are all the name implied. Sweet oranges, with other fruit trees, were grown instead near the overseer's house at Butler's Island and in the gardens at Hampton. Major Butler was proud of his citrus trees. In Philadelphia he forsook the traditional blackthorn of the Irishman to lean upon a walking stick cut from one of his Georgia sour orange trees. The reports from his manager often mentioned the promise of fresh fruit: "The lemmon trees are nearly all alive at Tide Island & grow very well, and the sweet oranges at this place bear middling but not so well as last year, but I hope to have at least a thouson to send to your Grand Children. Do let me know how the 2 dozn oranges put up in the rice chaff did." And in 1812, William Page purchased 116 gallons of Butler orange juice for fifty-eight dollars, or fifty cents per gallon.[21]

On a rice plantation such as Butler's Island the network of banks and canals were the thoroughfares over which the people and produce moved. Until extreme winter temperatures killed the sour orange trees—contrary to what Thomas Spalding believed—the slaves moved about the plantation with some shelter from the bitter cold winds or the intense summer heat. Bermuda grass had been planted on the high bank beneath the orange trees and on the network of lesser banks. The roots of the grass helped to bind the soil, and the grass itself provided grazing for the odd assortment of livestock that existed on the plantation. With the orange trees gone, the Bermuda grass then competed with volunteer wild plants including much cassena and myrtle.[22]

Butler's Island's third crop, sugar cane, was also successful. Pierce Butler's talented manager, Roswell King, had advocated the planting of cane and the manufacture of sugar when the market for cotton began to fade. Thomas Spalding had been experimenting with sugar on Sapelo Island and noted with great interest and admiration the progress made at Butler's Island. He was impressed that 20,000 stalks of cane could grow on a single acre where 4,000 stalks of corn would be considered "thick planting." He reported that Roswell King had produced 140,000 pounds of sugar from 110 acres, and that "it will be difficult to find or difficult to grow a more beautiful field of cane in this country than that of Major Butler's." On Butler's Island sixty slaves were used in harvesting and hauling the cane to the mill, where it was crushed between rollers powered by six yokes of oxen. Spalding wrote that blacks were particularly adept at controlling the boiling of cane juice to the critical point of granulation. He observed: "In better hands it could not be placed."[23]

With Major Butler's "Tide Island" capable of producing rice, cotton, and sugar, it is not surprising that Mrs. Basil Hall should proclaim it to be the "most valuable plantation on this river." A letter from Roswell King to Major Butler gave graphic evidence of the capacity of the Butler estate. In a ten-year period from 1805 to 1815, 9,080-1/2 barrels of rice, 4,468 bales of cotton, 134-1/2 tierces of sugar, and 80 hogsheads of molasses were produced—with the sugar and molasses quantities for one year only.[24]

Chapter 9

 *The Slaves*

Which sets a price on the head of man and converts him to a beast of burden.

CAPTAIN CHARLES SPALDING WYLLY inherited the conviction of his great-great-grandfather, John McIntosh Mohr, who had participated in the New Inverness Protest of 1739. He also inherited the sensitivity of his grandfather, Thomas Spalding of Sapelo. When called on to write his memories of the plantation life he had known as a young man, he did so willingly. "I have written," he said as an old man in his mid-seventies, "Knowing well under what a light of ante-bellum semi-darkness they will be viewed by kinsman and acquaintance who may chance upon them. Be it so. I shall bare my thoughts and beliefs."

Major Pierce Butler had long been in the graveyard of Philadelphia's Christ Church when young Wylly knew the Altamaha plantations. Captain Wylly wrote that for the plantation owners who lived on the sea islands:

> Both a winter, and a summer home were possible and there was no absenteeism. The ever-present, ever-dictating, always over-ruling presence of slavery there assumed its least harmful form. In the best instances it became patriarchal in its government, and in its worst was tempered by the pride of ownership and softened by the direct personal attention of the owner.

In contrast, Captain Wylly said, the rice plantations lacked the personal touch, the civilizing amenities the "home place" plantations embodied. With the owner having delegated his authority to an overseer insensitive to the needs of his charges, there, "gradually, and certainly, what had been serfhood became slavery, and the slaves sank to but a *chattel*, having lost even the personal acquaintanceship and feudal love which once had gilded his chain."[1]

Captain Wylly put his finger on the fundamental difference between Hampton and Butler's Island in the decades before and after 1800, and as well a fundamental weakness in both places after that time. Major Butler's "home place" was Philadelphia, not Hampton, although he did visit with some frequency. The Major's slave-built residence on Hampton was a symbol of his power, and his managers were given broad authority. They lived on the plantation with their families and thus removed some of the liabilities of absentee ownership. As Major Butler grew older, his Georgia visits became few and far between—only once after 1810. During these long absences, "gradually, and certainly" the character of the two plantations changed. Order diminished when the strength of the owner's presence was no longer felt, nor his appearances anticipated.[2]

Although Captain Basil Hall visited the plantations of the Altamaha estuary several years after Major Butler's death, he, too, noticed a fundamental difference in rice and cotton plantations. On a cotton plantation such as Hampton: "The negroes are generally healthy—all the work being of a dry kind." But on the rice plantation, of which Butler's Island was a prime example, the growing of that profitable crop was:

> the most unhealthy work in which the slaves were employed, and in spite of every care, that they sank under it in great numbers. The causes of this dreadful mortality, are the constant moisture and heat of the atmosphere, together with the alternate floodings and drying of the fields, on which the negroes are perpetually at work, often ankle deep in mud, with their bare heads exposed to the fierce rays of the sun.[3]

The Butler plantations were often compared with those of John Couper and Thomas Spalding. Hampton and Butler's Island gave nothing to either in the efficient production of cotton, rice, or later, sugar. The treatment of slaves was a different story and a challenge Major Butler chose to meet in his own way. The Butler way was a strict, regimented, militaristic discipline, with the slaves virtually isolated on their plantations. This practice was more efficiently executed by his manager Roswell King in the early 1800s than by any other manager and at any other time. The large number of slaves on the Butler plantations helped to make possible the isolation encouraged by Major Butler. In their self-contained world his managers had little need for outside help. There was no socializing by Butler slaves with those of other plantations, and although John Couper's Cannon's Point was separated from Hampton by Jones Creek and a narrow belt of marshland, to most of the Butler slaves it was unknown territory.[4]

Pierce Butler was quick to realize the worth of his land was significant only when worked by slaves. He learned to put a value on each individual and was peculiarly adept at assessing the capabilities and determining the merit of his people. In 1793 Hampton was being supervised by his friend William Page, who sent Major Butler a list of 441 slaves then living on the plantation. Page classified the adults according to "Qualities and Characters." The slave September was "Very good field hand and well behaved"; Bess was "Very good worker and good Negroe"; Bob was "Lame"; Sue was "Likely and good hand." Major Butler had his own ideas. On the list he changed September from "Very good" to "Tolerable"; Bess from "Good Negroe" to "Excellent Negroe"; Bob to "Lame, but a trusty good Negroe"; and Sue was downgraded from "Likely and good hand" to "Good hand." He did not take issue with William Page's classification of Will as "Foolish boy" or of Die as "Stupid."[5]

The Page inventory of May 1793 revealed the 441 slaves to have included 141 males, 160 females, and 140 children aged twelve or under. The oldest men were April and Quacco, both fifty-five. Next oldest were David and Worcester, carpenters, both of whom were fifty-four. The oldest woman was Molly, "Dairy Woman," aged sixty-two. The next oldest was Auba, aged fifty-five, who cooked for the slaves. Beck was shown as "Old" with no designated age. Eight women were shown to be fifty, with four of them designated "cook" or "old cook." The absence of the very old may not have been entirely an indication of short life spans, but that Major Butler had chosen the youngest and strongest of the Middleton-Bull slaves in his move from South Carolina to Georgia. Pierce Butler reviewed the 1793 list again in December 1795 and noted that in the interval there had been eleven deaths, seven of which were of children under five years of age.[6]

Plantation slaves often would identify with their masters or the plantation on which they lived and worked. "I hol' my head jus' as high as my Missus. I'se a Wylly nig'ah" is typical of those slaves given good treatment.[7] Sapelo slaves were proud to be called Spalding. Such feelings were manifestations of their tribal background, and despite the fact that Pierce Butler was unknown to many of his slaves, the workers at Hampton, and

A List of Negroes taken at Hampton. May the 4th 1793.

No.	Names	Ages	Worked	Qualities and Characters.
1	Lewey M.B.	32	1	very good Cooper and Driver
2	Juba d.	27	2	good field hand.
3	Molly d.	11		
4	Phaby d.	6		
5	Abraham P.B.	40	3	4 Plowman Carter &c. and good Negroe
6	Phaby M.B.	30		1 An excellent worker & good Negroe.
7	Abraham d.	9	3	
8	Jane d.	4	4	
9	Hector d.		5	Child
10	Lydia d.	24	5	good field hand & well behaved.
11	Juba d.	5		
12	Tuckey d.	2		
13	Bock d.	33	6	good worker, and well behaved.
14	Dinah d.	14		a tollerable
15	Solomon P.B.	30	7	very good field hand and well behaved.
16	Billy M.B.	4		
17	Tuckey d.	5		
18	Sue d.	3		
19	Nanse d.	2		an Excellent
20	Bob S.G.	28	8	good Carpenter and field hand
21	Sue M.B.	24	9	good worker, and well behaved
22	Sam d.	6		
23	Nanny d.	1		very
24	Santee d.	38	10	good Gardener and Driver
25	Abigal d.	39	11	good worker and well behaved. Dead
26	Sue S.G.	7		
27	Santee d.	6		
28	March d.	3		
29	York M.B.	24	12	6 good Ship Carpenter, and field hand & well behaved
30	Mundah P.B.	91	13	7 good field hand & well behaved
31	Yankey M.B.	23	14	good Ship Carpenter and field hand, well behaved
32	Nancy d.	20	15	good hand & well behaved.
33	Primus d.	3		
34	George P.B.	34	16	8 good Shoemaker good
35	Molly M.B.	23	17	9 good field hand & well behaved
36	Mary d.	2		10
37	Jacob d.	1		11
38	Isaac d.	31	18	12 Blacksmith and good field hand
39	Dinah d.	20	19	13 good hand and well behaved
40	Syndy d.			14 Child
41	Nell d.	42		8 hand
42	Joan d.	37	20	good hand & well behaved. Brewton's
43	Abba d.	40	21	d. d. d. d.
44	Toney d.	17		d.
45	Milley d.	13		d.
46	Sarah P.B.	44	22	Wife to Manuel, well behaved d.
47	Sampson d.	92	23	good Carpenter & well behaved d.
48	Jenny d.	14	8	d. d.
49	Paris d.	40	4	d.
50	July d.	42	24	good worker & well behaved d.
51	Syndy d.	35	25	d. d. d.

William Page's 1793 list of Hampton slaves on which Major Butler had revised Page's "Qualities and Characters." (Historical Society of Pennsylvania.)

to a lesser degree at Butler's Island, possessed a generous measure of pride in their ability to do their jobs, for they realized they were part of a very efficient agricultural enterprise. Word of the proficiency of the Butler plantings brought visitors from near and far. The slaves took note of this interest and, understandably, shared the pride of their white owners and overseers. In addition, the Butler slaves had unusual respect for their distant owner, bestowing on him a mantle of importance in marked contrast to their feelings toward the Butler surrogates who executed his orders. It may have been a transference of the noticeable awe in which he was held by his managers, or it may well have been his impressive bearing so forcefully displayed on his visits. Frequently slaves were sent to Philadelphia to serve Major Butler and his family at his town house or in the country at Butler Place, where they found life very different from that at Hampton or Butler's Island. When these Negroes returned to Georgia, they told of what it was like in Major Butler's Philadelphia, and the telling helped to create an aura of importance and strength about their owner. Whatever the reasons, they did understand and acknowledge his authority.

In the development of his Georgia plantations Major Butler used Hampton as a command post. There he placed the better-trained Middleton slaves, who were put to work constructing the extensive plantation complex, including the owner's residence and the manager's house. At Hampton he located the artisans—the carpenters, boat builders, masons, blacksmiths, the skilled hands who could supply the equipment necessary to work the cotton fields and rice lands. A varied lot, the Butler slaves had been gathered together by his in-laws and by the Major himself. Many had been imported by Thomas Middleton, who had the pick of hundreds brought to South Carolina from Africa and by way of the West Indies. By the time they were to work the sandy fields of St. Simons and the wetlands of Butler's Island, their native rawness was replaced with the skill and dependability that made them extremely useful in their labor-intensive environment. Some of the Middleton slaves probably came from Africa with a knowledge of rice culture they could pass on to Major Butler's managers. South Carolina planters "who prided themselves on being connoisseurs of Negroes" were quick to purchase Guinea natives experienced in the growing of rice. In 1766 the Henry Laurens partnership advertised in Charlestown: "250 Fine Healthy NEGROES Just Arrived From the Windward & Rice Coast."[8]

Major Butler was much concerned that his slaves be given good care so they would be well and strong, and able to produce young to replace the aged and the infirm. In 1794, on word from overseer George Valley that food was needed at one of his plantations, Major Butler hurried off a letter to one of his agents, Richard Wayne, at Savannah: "I hope you have long ere this furnished him with corn. I have *relied* on you on that ground. It is no trifling thing to have near three hundred slaves reduced to want. I pray you to attend to this."9 Also, he expressed his anger to a new agent, Thomas Young, of Savannah:

> I rec'd a letter from Valley a few days ago which has made me very uneasy. He says my Negroes are starving, they have been without a grain of corn for two weeks & living entirely on Fish & Oysters. I cannot expect you to know how my mind is hurt by this information, and the inattention of Mr. Wayne to whom I had written to purchase corn and draw on either my Factors in Charleston, or myself to pay for it, yet he has let my Negroes suffer, and my work stand.10

More so than the slaves of other plantations in the area, the Butler people held fast to their African ways. This was accepted and talked about by both whites and blacks of nearby plantations. The reason, of course, was the enforced isolation that kept them away from the influence of others. There was little contact beyond their own settlements and less observation of the ways and talk of their "superiors." At Hampton, and at Butler's Island, there was a great mixture of people from many parts of Africa. The allegedly placid agrarian strain from the Congo was there, with sensitive and often despondent Ibos. Gambian Moslems were thrust among varied Africans, including the favored Coromantees from the Gold Coast. These several cultures, when mixed with the occasional native-born Africans purchased on shipboard or in the Savannah slave markets to meet specific needs, produced an entirely new environment for the Negroes. Yet these individual and cultural differences were facts of their lives either unknown to, or ignored by, their owners, who were inclined to see them all as, simply, Africans.11

The noted South Carolina writer DuBose Heyward was of a different mind on this topic. He wrote that traders and planters were very much aware of the advantages and disadvantages of the different African tribes: "as articles of commerce certain excellences become intrinsically valuable. It was natural then as plantations developed a gentry that prided themselves on the strains in their racing stables, they would be at least equally mindful of the racial traits that distinguished the accretions of their Negro yards."[12] That may well have been true in the purchase of one group of Africans as against another—Angolas versus Congos, Ibos, or Gaboons. But once in the quarters on the plantations, the owner and his overseers had little time for the preservation of a tribal strain or the protection of a tribal heritage. A case in point is Major Butler's purchase of slaves from a cargo of Ibos and Angolas imported in 1803 by Mein and Mackay of Savannah. Roswell King's report to Pierce Butler in Philadelphia told of bringing the slaves down the coast and sending them on up the Altamaha to Butler's Island, where after a long journey from Africa over a very salty sea, "There was much rejoicing when they found they could drink the water out of the river." He also noted: "They landed very cheerful and happy. You have no people that can talk with them but they are so smart your young Wenches are Speculating very high for husbands."[13] The offspring of the "Speculating" wenches and the chosen Africans would have been a mixed breed and the pure strain would have vanished. Also in point is the fact that advertisements for *seasoned* slaves paid little or no attention to tribal origins.

There is a landing on the back side of St. Simons Island said to be a place where a group of Ibos chose to walk into the waters of the creek, preferring death by drowning to life in bondage. At the time of the purchase of the slaves sent to Butler's Island, where they caught the eyes of Major's Butler's "wenches," John Couper and Thomas Spalding together bought a "cargo" of Ibos from Mein and Mackay. William Mein wrote Major Butler telling of the unfortunate ending to the Couper-Spalding joint venture. At Savannah the slaves were put aboard a small vessel and confined below deck for the trip down the coast to St. Simons. Upon approaching their destination at the island, the Ibos, who were frightened and restless, "rose" against John Couper's overseer Patterson and the two members of the vessel's crew. Fearing the Africans, the three men attempted to swim ashore and were drowned. According to Mr. Mein, the bewildered Ibos "took to the marsh," and in doing so "ten or twelve" also drowned. Of the others recovered, the owners had "an expense of $10 a head for salvage." This may well have been the incident that gave rise to the legend of "Ebo's Landing."[14]

The low-country plantations of South Carolina and Georgia tended to rather large concentrations of slaves. The dialects of the many African tribes, of necessity, were blended into a common language that enabled the slave to understand, if nothing else, the commands and directions of their owners. The "salt water brogue" or low-country Negro talk became known as *Gullah,* the word probably a corruption of Angola, whence many of the Negroes came. Those who spoke with strong and frequent Africanisms came to be known as "Gullah Negroes," oftentimes their given names being prefixed with the word "Gullah" or "Golla," as "Gullah Jack," or "Golla Tom." The Gullah dialect is an interesting mixture of the black man's version of white English and the rhythm and inflection of Africa. It is a pervasive speech that for years has quietly and subtly invaded that of many low-country whites. White coastal South Carolinians speak a dialect of their own that is a sort of refined Gullah. Many can sing spirituals with an authenticity envied by the blacks themselves. In Savannah, native whites of an older generation are accused of speaking *Geechee*—the Ogeechee River is nearby. It is a dialect not so strongly African as that of the South Carolinians, but one nonetheless that has felt the impact of African influence.[15]

In the late 1930s the Georgia Writers' Project of the Work Projects Administration undertook a study of the survival of African folkways among the coastal blacks of Georgia. At that time there were people living who had been born in slavery and who remembered the old ways on the low-country plantations. Repeated visits and gifts of food and clothing prompted a friendly response to the probing questions of the writers. Anna Miller of Savannah had lived on Butler's Island:

> Sebral uh dem hans wuz bery old people. Dey speak a funny language an none uh duh res of us coudn hahdly ununstan a wud dey say.

A persistent memory of old Shad Hall, who was born a Spalding slave and who lived on Sapelo, or Ryna Johnson, who had been a Couper slave, and several other elderly people was the legend of Butler's Island Africans who could fly. Shad Hall told of hearing of slaves who, resentful of the overseer's lash, flew back to Africa. Others spoke of Alexander, a Butler's Island root doctor who was "slim and bery black." His ability to fly was legend:

> Dey say duh boat leab fuh Savannah an Alexander he yuh. He say goodbye from yuh an tell him to go on widout im but he say he see em deah an wen duh boat git tuh Savannah, Alexander he in Savannah on duh dock to ketch duh line.[16]

The residents of Darien, who were familiar with plantation blacks who came to town to market their produce, thought the Butler's Island people were most unusual:

> These Butler negroes were a race apart. They never, until years after the war, mingled with other negroes.

> They had a particular lingo, which one had to be familiar with before one could understand it. An old Butler Island woman named Aunt Jerusalem used to sell me figs and blackberries, early English peas and chickens, the latter which she counted this way: Dish yuh one, dish yuh narra, dish yuh tray pun top uh tarra. Dish yuh make five wid he laig all tie togarra.[17]

Alexander and Jerusalem are typical of the names put upon the African slaves. The elderly were often known as "Aunt" and "Uncle"—pronounced "Ahnt" and "Onkle." The several lists of slaves on the Butler plantations show a mix of biblical and classical names, others straightforward and usual, with comparatively few holding fast to their African heritage. William Page's list of 1793 shows Caesar, Brutus, Nero, Pompey, Phoebe, Bacchus, and Hercules as classical names, with Abraham, Moses, Hagar, Dorcas, Simon, and Peter from the Bible. Others were named for places: some distant, Lisbon, York, Paris; some nearby, Santee, of which there were several, Johns Island, and Hampton. Some names from the calendar were March, July, and September—an African survival, for frequently the newborn carried the name of the day or month of his birth. The African names included Quaka, meaning a male born on Wednesday; Cudjo and Cuffee, meaning males born on Monday and Friday, respectively. Other African names on the 1793 list were Quash, Quamina, Juba, Pinder, and Mindah. There was also a scattering of unusual names— Yankee, Punch, Tubby, and Dago—but the great majority were the Joes and Sams, the Harrys and Bens, and several each of Betty, Molly, Sue, and Sally. Fifty-six years later a longer list of the 841 Butler slaves at Hampton and Butler's Island revealed but little change. Most of the 1793 names remained. The group with classical names includes about the same percentage of the whole but with some interesting additions—Neptune, Cleopatra, Cassandra, and Psyche, who was listed as "Sikey" by the manager and called "Sack" or "Sackey" by the slaves. A greater percentage of biblical names was a result of their greater awareness of religious doctrine. The 1793 names were there again, with Lazarus, Cain and Abel, Adam and Eve, Esau, Mark, Solomon, Esther, Hannah, Rebecca, Ezekiel,

*Shad Hall, born a slave at Thomas Spalding's plantation on Sapelo Island, recounted legends of Butler slaves who could fly. (*Drums and Shadows *photograph made in 1939 by Muriel and Malcolm Bell, Jr.)*

Joshua, and many others. Among the additions to place names were Philadelphia, Charleston, Trenton, Baltimore, Richmond, China, Flanders, and Glasgow. The name Worcester was common on the plantations and probably came from Major Butler's famous Worcester Regiment, the Twenty-ninth Foot. On the larger 1849 list, among the calendar names added to those of 1793 were Friday, Sunday, and June. The African names were less frequent. Quaka had become Quacco, Bina and Nija were additions. The most unusual names were more noticeable in 1849, for Rover, Dandy, Mustard, Tiger, Dimbo, Notion, Somersette, Trim, and Happy were additions to many of the names listed earlier. There was also St. Faux, derived perhaps from John Couper's famous cook, Sans Foix. The more commonplace names showed one interesting change. Equally plentiful and predominant as before, they included most members of the Butler family—Pierce, Mary, Sarah, Frances, Eliza, Harriet, Thomas, John, Sally, Fanny, Mease, Manigo, and Lizzy.

Roswell King, Jr.'s plantation accounts of 1845–1848 kept a record showing names using prefixes to identify the duplications. The two Londons were "Cooper" London and "Afric" London. There was Quash and "Crab" Quash, who caught the blue crabs in the tidal streams. "Fish" Harry was the plantation fisherman, and others were "Congo" Harry and "Driver" Harry. "Nurse" Molly served that function, "Barn" Mira worked there, but as to why John was called "Rock" John is not told. Sailing ships often used stone as ballast, discharged it before loading cargo, and may have provided John with an identifying name. The masons, carpenters, smiths, and coopers were usually identified as such, the latter being the most numerous. Coopers made the tierces (or rice barrels), wooden tubs, and the piggins that served the slave as food bowl and wash basin. Plantation records often resorted to identifying one of several with the same name by tying a husband to a wife or a child to a parent as Cornelia's Frank, September's Lydia, or Robert's Matty.[18]

Among themselves, slaves often used names other than those on the plantation records, names that were seldom known by their owners. Should a Butler slave be set free he would usually choose, or be given, a second name. He may well choose Butler, for his owner; or Hampton, for his home; or he might decide that, as he had been a cooper on the plantation, Cooper would be his name.[19] The Negro York had a son who was also given the name of an English city, Liverpool. When Liverpool was freed, he chose the surname Hazzard, despite having been born and raised a Butler slave. The truth of his claim that he gained his first name on a visit to England is unlikely.[20] In 1800 Major Butler signed an indenture agreeing to free one of his slaves or, as the document stated, to "Manumit, liberate, set free and release from all further or future bondage or servitude." A *proviso* to which the slave must agree was prepared and stated that he was to "Keep all his Master's secrets, and obey his lawful commands and shall not absent himself from such service without leave, and generally during the term aforesaid shall behave himself in all respects as a faithful, honest and diligent servant ought to do."[21] The term was ten years, and the slave who signed this unusual contract for his freedom in the distant future did so by making his marks. He was given not only a surname but also a middle initial: William S. Hamilton. What brought about this dubious act of generosity is not known. The slaves liberated by the British, first in the Revolution and later in the War of 1812, were given the names of their owners. Thus, Isaac the blacksmith would go ashore at Bermuda or Halifax as Isaac Butler, and all others liberated by the British from the Butler plantations would share the same last names.[22]

Major Butler was well aware of how John Couper managed his slaves on his plantation across the creek from Hampton, and of how Thomas Spalding trusted his Negroes on Sapelo Island. Spalding used no white overseers, giving his black drivers the extra authority they needed to manage their gangs. For the Major, there had to be strong dependence on his managers. Having more irons in his fire than the Georgia plantations, of necessity he had to look to William Page, to Roger Parker Saunders, to the Valleys and the Kings. He was conscious, too, of the advantages enjoyed by Spalding, Couper, and those other St. Simons planters who were "in residence" the year around. He countered this by making an extra effort to know the capabilities of his people and by being alert to opportunities and aware of what was happening on the plantations. The weekly reports from the elder Roswell King were usually compiled on Sunday. They give graphic testimony to Major Butler's full comprehension of the workings of this distant empire. In 1790, when the development of Butler's Island was contemplated, the Major was attending to his senatorial responsibilities in New York. He wrote Roger Parker Saunders, who was taking care of his Georgia interest, that he wanted a tanyard and a shoemaking shop at Hampton to supply the influx of slaves who would be going to the rice plantation as soon as an "understanding" was reached between the United States and the Spaniards in Florida. He had particular workers in mind, writing: "My Fellows George, John and Daniel, who are now with Hyndes could be sent. Toney, Titus and Peter are also capable of making

Negroe Shoes. Toney knows how to tan."[23] At this same time there was an interesting exchange between Major Butler and Captain Saunders regarding the Major's slave Sauney. Saunders owned Moll, Sauney's wife, who was in deep distress because they had been separated. He offered to buy Sauney for 120 pounds or to sell Moll and their male child for 100 pounds, payment to be made in either instance in rice at the prevailing market. Major Butler agreed to sell Sauney and replied: "You are heartily welcome to take Sauney, who was my Cook, Butler and Factotum, out of the field. I did put him in the field to punish Him for being insolent to his Mistress, but as I suppose he is by this time pretty well humbled I can forgive Him. He is if he pleases a real good Cook. Understands perfectly Bottling and managing Liquor. He is also a good Butcher."[24] Mary Butler was in the last stages of her long and difficult illness at the time, possibly a factor in the punishment of Sauney.

The sale, or the division, of slaves in estates of deceased owners often tore black families apart. Major Butler's movement of the family slaves from South Carolina to Georgia following the settlement of the Mary Brewton estate caused several such families to be put asunder. A few years following the Sauney-Moll reunion, he permitted another exchange of ownership that reunited slave families. An exchange was brought about when he wrote Mrs. Elizabeth Middleton Izard, the wife of another Ralph Izard:

> Your Servant Allick has been with me three times respecting his wife & children. I have every disposition to make them happy. If any exchange, purchase, or sale is agreeable to you, you have only to point out the mode and I will agree to it provided the poor Negroes are made happy. I feel that I have a moral duty to a black as well as to a white person. I submit, Madam, the modification entirely to yourself.

Mrs. Izard agreed, and appraisers were chosen to try and bring about a fair exchange. Not only were they able to reunite the Izard slave Allick (Aleck) with his wife Marian and their children Sealy, Stephen, and Nancy, all Butler slaves, but they were also able to bring together another Izard slave in South Carolina with his family from Hampton—his wife Binah, their child "at breast," their daughter Judea and son Bram. The Izards gave up two families to Butler slaves Quamina and Waley. Quamina regained his wife Miley, his child Betty "at breast," and daughter Bess. Waley was "made happy" by the return of his wife and children,

Nelly, Sealy, Hannah, and Little Waley "in arms." The value of the Butler slaves was greater—eight people against seven—and one of the Butler women offered a prospect of another, for she was said to be "in a thriving state and far Advanced." The money value of the two groups was 290 pounds, and 257 pounds 10 shillings. In order to balance the transaction the Izards paid Major Butler 32 pounds 10 shillings. The appraisers who arranged this remarkable trade were John McPherson, for Major Butler, and John North, for the Izards.[25]

A typical report from Roswell King at Hampton to Major Butler in Philadelphia would spell out the work to be done and that already accomplished. He would include bits of news from neighboring plantations, comments on the weather, on prices of cotton, rice or sugar, a few words on the condition of the slaves. He also did his best to respond to the Major's instructions and to answer his many questions:

> May 12, 1804—In my absence three of the new Negroes Ranaway for two days and was taken near Doboy in a cannoe, bound to Africa as they say. The leader was well whipped & the other two forgiven.

> June 2, 1804—I pray God it may be revealed to me how I can do everything as you may *think & Define*. Sickness favourable, no Deaths. No Runaways.

> January 17, 1807—If you had been behind the curtain last evening and heard me talk to Sambo & Worster, you would have said you could not believed there was so much deception in me to have spoke so kind, good and friendly to them—when I know they are two as *great rascals* as was ever sent to Botne Bay—but Simpaty for *Your Intriss* obliges me so to do.[26]

Major Butler and Roswell King were frequently at odds as to the merits of particular slaves, and although Major Butler personally ordained punishment, he seemed disturbed by the frequency and the severity of Mr. King's measures. Pierce Butler liked to believe that his own role in slavery was benevolent. Indeed, his reputation as one who gave his slaves good care was accepted rather generally in the plantation world. In 1801, Savannahian William Hunter, while on a trip to St. Mary's, stopped at Butler's Island, Five Pound Tree, and Hampton. He wrote Major Butler: "I was delighted with your situation at Hampton Point. In no place have I seen such comforts, or such arrangements. If ever the burthen of Slavery can be softened I must freely confess it is with you."[27]

William Page praised Major Butler's treatment of his slaves on two occasions. He was then living on and managing his Retreat Plantation at the south end of St. Simons Island. In June 1816 he wrote: "I very well know the tenderness you have ever had for your slaves. You spared no cost to lessen their labor & to add to their comforts & I well know that they possessed many valuable Comforts & that their service was lightly Exacted from them, yet what have they made for you!" Two years later, he again observed: "I had an opportunity of talking with Driver Harry from whom I learnt that your people were well satisfied. Indeed I cannot conceive they can have just cause of being otherwise. They are well clothed, well fed, and I suppose, labor, generally, lightly."[28] If Pierce Butler was convinced that he gave his slaves a good life, he was equally convinced that they, in turn, should not shortchange him in the performance of their work. In asking a Savannah agent to find a "Gang of Negroes" for the cultivation of rice, he made it clear: "I want no Cotton Negroes. I want people that can go in the ditch."[29]

Major Butler would tolerate no idleness. A story told on St. Simons had old Flora telling her owner that she was too old to work and could do so no longer. The Major agreed. He instructed Roswell King that Flora was not to work but was to be given a goose and a line and told to lead the goose to graze an hour each day. "For ten years did goose and woman pasture together at Hampton Point."[30]

On the lookout for seasoned slaves, Major Butler purchased a "gang" from Virginia. When they fell far short of expectations, he refused to pay in full, complaining the slaves were "the most Ordinary sett in Georgia. There are not ten among the seventy-odd who can do a days work even in my lightest ground. My boys and girls of 16 and 17 get out of the same work by two oclock that scarce one of the Virginia Negroes finish by Sunset." He had specified his purchase be limited to "Negroes *in families, Orderly,* and well behaved." Yet among the slaves were "Negroes without parents, some probably torn from their parents, others orphans, and the only two men from Colonel Talifero, Jeffrey and Alex, show backs with whales from neck to ham."[31]

For a long time Pierce Butler was aloof to the abolitionist sentiment abroad in Philadelphia. He was well attended by the best and brightest of his Georgia slaves, such as Sauney, his factotum. His city homes, particularly the mansion at Chestnut and Eighth streets, and his rural retreat Butler Place, near Germantown, were fully staffed with servants. He put much faith in one of his Savannah agents, François Didier Petit DeVillers, who purchased an exceptional servant, Henry, from George Jones of Savannah, and sent him north on the brig *Hetty* "under the kindness and protection" of the ship's master. DeVillers wrote Major Butler he feared Henry might be mistreated by some of the sailors. "This is a rude season," he said. Henry was a French slave, not surprising, as he had been acquired by Monsieur DeVillers. Not liking what he found in the Butler household, Henry ran away but was restored to his owner in a court proceeding that followed the Major's own Fugitive Slave Law. In court, the Major offered to surrender Henry to Quaker abolitionists for one-half the price he had paid George Jones in the original purchase. "Not one of the Society offered a shilling," complained the Major. Henry persevered and ran away again, this time successfully.[32]

An incident throwing a little light on black-white relationships in Major Butler's Philadelphia is told in an undated letter to John Barker, a city magistrate. The Major had hired a black to accompany a Butler servant to Burlington to fetch some mules, agreeing to pay one dollar for the man's time. The man refused the dollar, saying that he was due a greater sum. The Major was indignant: "I coud hardly suppose that any Magistrate in Philadelphia woud believe I shoud be induced to wrong a Negroe, or feel it necessary to write me a letter on such a Subject."[33]

Pierce Butler had encountered his own rude season in Philadelphia in 1804 when he was confronted with the abolitionism he preferred to ignore. It shattered anew his former respect for the Quakers and their conservatism. The occasion was a visit from one of the Friends who came to the mansion saying: "How art thou Pierce Butler? I have a writ of Habeas Corpus for thy Ben." Slave Ben had been told by the Major he was to be returned to Georgia after eleven years in Pennsylvania. He turned to the Quakers for help, who in turn sent Isaac T. Hopper to call on Major Butler. Friend Hopper was ushered out by an infuriated slave owner. The Quakers took Major Butler to court and freed Ben. The Major appealed, but Ben was once again given his freedom. The Major contended he did not live as a "nabob" as Mr. Hopper had testified, but that he was a "sojourner," a South Carolinian not subject to Pennsylvania's law that a slave was free after six month's residence. He claimed senatorial immunity, which was denied, and he proclaimed his benevolence. Mr. Hopper answered: "Thou benevolent! Why thou are not even just. Thee has sent back into bondage two men who were legally entitled to freedom by law. If thou had a proper sense of Justice thou wouldst bring them back and let them take the liberty that rightfully belongs to them."[34]

In later years Major Butler must have absorbed a bit of the Quaker spirit, for when contemplating the sale of the Georgia plantations, he suggested four of his slaves be freed. Roswell King objected strongly, giving his reasons:

> As for old Betty, she is free already. She does as she pleases, and you feed and cloth her. As for Jacob he certainly is a most deserving Negro. If you liberated Jacob, what will Bram say? He has earned you more than Ten Thousand Dollars. I know of no people more Jealous of their rights and privileges than Negroes—be assured if you begin you will create a great Murmur among the people. Jacob is very useful as head carpenter—his health is bad and I dont allow him to do anything but lay off work, as he has a large family of fine Children on the Estate. I think it would be better for to restrict one hundred dollars to be paid him yearly as long as he was useful would be much better for him, for freedom would force him to work hard for a living, which would soon kill him. As for Molley, you are no stranger to her long wish for freedom (when in Phila). I have no doubt she would have gone off with the British if her husband and children was with her, yet she is certainly a very deserving Woman and I wish the eve of her days comfortable, but I cannot (believe) freedom would be any blessing to her. As for Abraham, he and many more are very deserving Negroes. Abram is truly a faithful, sober honest negro I believe, and if you wish to do something for him send for him to Philada. Let him serve you seven years, he is the one that can git a good living free, and the only one in four that you mentioned. Be assured you have not 50 negroes but what it would be a curse to free them.

Mr. King had reasoned that once started, it would be a "difficult matter to find a stopping place" and give "Satisfaction" to those not liberated. As the proposed sale of the plantations was not consummated, the slaves remained in bondage.[35] Major Butler did send for Abraham, who became the body servant to the old soldier, "kept his armor bright," and was freed and pensioned when his owner died.[36]

Had the Butler slaves been freed and chosen to live in Darien they would have soon found obstacles to overcome. An ordinance passed in 1818 called for all "Negroes, Mullattoes, or Mustezos—persons of color" to pay an annual tax, or if a newcomer, a special fee. For those aged fifteen to fifty, men paid ten dollars and women paid five dollars annually. The newcomer fee of fifty dollars was to be paid in ten days. If either tax or fee was not paid, imprisonment would follow and "their persons would be exposed to public sale" to provide funds to pay the charges.[37]

Pierce Butler could show compassion and then turn around and be callous in his treatment of the black family. His kindness demonstrated in the Sauney-Moll and Izard-Butler exchanges are in marked contrast to his attitude on other occasions. He expressed indignation when the Virginia slaves were torn from their parents, yet thought little of freeing a husband to leave a wife and children in bondage. The conflict with the Quakers in Philadelphia concerning Ben's freedom was prompted by the intended separation of Ben from his family. In the great hurricane of 1804, when Aaron Burr was finding refuge at Hampton, one of the Butler drivers, Morris, showed exceptional courage and good sense by using his long whip to prevent an exodus from Little St. Simons Island at the height of the storm. He saved more than a hundred slaves and was rewarded by Major Butler for his bravery with an offer of freedom and a silver tankard, engraved:

TO MAURICE FROM P. BUTLER
FOR HIS FAITHFUL, JUDICIOUS, AND SPIRITED
CONDUCT IN THE HURRICANE ON THE 8TH
OF SEPTEMBER 1804, WHEREBY THE LIVES
OF MORE THAN ONE HUNDRED PERSONS
WERE, BY DIVINE PERMISSION, SAVED

Maurice, who was called Morris on the plantation, accepted the handsome tankard but refused the offer of freedom as it did not include his wife and children.[38]

Coastal hurricanes that caused loss of life prompted the plantation owners to take measures for the protection of their valuable slaves. The great storm of 1804 killed more than seventy of William Brailsford's slaves on Broughton Island, lying between Butler's Island and Five Pound Tree. On Little St. Simons Island, Morris had literally "driven" his fellow Negroes into the only shelter on the island strong enough to withstand the storm's fury. The Brailsford slaves had neither Driver Morris nor a structure able to stand against the high winds and rising water. In South Carolina, Thomas Pinckney had witnessed a similar tragedy and as a consequence designed a round building not unlike a Martello tower, with substantial walls and a raised floor. In May 1805 he sent Major Butler a drawing of his "hurricane House." Subsequently, a storm tower was constructed at Butler's Island, where the threat of inundation was greater than at Hampton.[39] Morris was long held in high regard. On one occasion

Roswell King considered the five drivers then on the plantations. He named Morris and Bram as "the only two good Drivers you have." He ignored Major Butler's favorite, Sambo, and the other two, George and Santee.[40]

The South Carolina planter-historian Duncan Clinch Heyward thought the word *Driver* a most unfortunate choice. He said it came into being in South Carolina when a seasoned slave was put in charge of a group of raw Africans to teach them the use of a hoe or a hand sickle. The title, abandoned after Emancipation for *Captain,* was less unfortunate than the symbol of authority the driver carried. The long whip, used judiciously by Morris, became representative of the ills of slavery. It made the "mark of degradation" that caused pangs of conscience even among those who were the outspoken advocates of slavery. The management of the Butler plantations depended greatly on the drivers, each of whom carried the lash and were permitted to strike a fellow slave six times—twelve for the head driver—should they feel it necessary. The usual lash had a short round handle of wood to which was attached a long tapered thong of cowhide, at its widest about one-half inch, and one-quarter inch thick for the entire length of six feet.[41]

In 1793, when William Page listed and classified the 441 slaves at Hampton for Major Butler, he named six drivers, the most important being Sambo, who was a "Most excellent Driver, Cooper and trusty fellow." The Major was in agreement, for he had long depended on Sambo, one of the Middleton slaves he was accused of usurping. "Let Sambo point out a Driver for Hampton. He knows better than I who will answer best." When Roswell King became manager for Pierce Butler in 1802, he found general disorder at Butler's Island and Hampton. His son said later that the disorder was brought on by the cruel practices of those in charge, the drivers included. It was then that enforced discipline and isolation began to be the hallmark of the two plantations.[42]

The driver, with his lash at his side, was a slave with authority. He usually lived in the first house in the yard or quarters. He awakened the slaves with a blast on a conch shell or by ringing a bell.[43] As instructed by the overseer or the manager, he assigned tasks to the gang of workers in his charge, and then supervised their work. Roswell King, Jr., left no doubt as to their authority: "An order from a Driver is to be as implicitly obeyed as if it came from myself."[44] Both Kings, father and son, urged restraint in the use of the lash. "I find *rum and Beef* is better than the Cowskin to git work done, tho they are all good in there place."[45] So

The silver tankard awarded driver Morris for saving more than a hundred Butler slaves in the hurricane of 1804. (Photograph by Richard A. Stevens. Owens Thomas House Museum, Savannah.)

wrote the elder King to Major Butler. The son remarked, "When I pass sentence myself, various modes of punishment are adopted, the lash least of all." He considered the lacerations from the lash to be the "marks of a rogue" and believed such scars would tend to make young blacks unruly as they grew older. Despite what they wrote, both Kings did use the lash, and if not indiscriminately, they did use it frequently and forcibly.[46]

No one understood the use of restraint better than a good driver, for his position was particularly acute. He was black and in bondage just as were the hands he supervised. He provided access to the white overseer, manager, or owner, and in return conveyed white to black communications. Much of the success of the plantation rode on the strong black shoulders of the drivers. On occasion, a driver would go astray. When this happened on a Butler plantation, it became a matter of great concern to the manager and to Major Butler, for it indicated a breakdown of order, so vital to successful operation. In 1806 Roswell King wrote Major Butler: "I suspect it will be proven to me that *Sambo* whipped several of your prime men *when drunk,* if so he shall pay for it."[47] Borrowing a practice from the British navy, Major Butler endorsed the doling out of drinks of rum before his slaves were sent into the fields on cold, wet mornings. Mr. King found no demons in strong rum. Writing as though he had put away a few shots of Nelson's blood himself, he requested the Major send some down from Philadelphia: "I forgot a *puncheon of rum,* a meterial article. To git mutch ditching done I must give them rum. If I buy new Negroes they must have rum. I find among the sick nothing finer than Hysop tea, with sugar and rum. To make a Negro contented, give thin tobacco and rum."[48] Captain, one of the drivers, drank no rum, and Mr. King noted he could be trusted to distribute it properly. But "most excellent Driver" Sambo succumbed to temptation, causing Mr. King to report: "I am so angry with Sambo I can hardly keep my temper with him. I always thought Sambo had no *head,* but now I say he has no *heart.*"[49] A month passed before the trouble subsided. When it did, Roswell King reflected: "There appears no difficulty between the Drivers and the people at this time, and it would always be the case if one could have the truth to act upon. But a *Driver* is more *Absolute* than the *Deay of Algiers.* It is very difficult to find a Negroe that dare tell upon them."[50]

The comparison was valid to Pierce Butler, for as United States senator from South Carolina he had struggled with the problem of the Algerian impressment of American seamen, which had been one of his committee assignments.[51]

While the drivers were unquestionably the most important of the Butler slaves, to the slave himself an assignment of almost equal importance and greater desirability was that of ship's crew, or boatman. For, Alexander excepted, access to the Butler plantations was by water. The remoteness of Butler's Island in the midst of the Altamaha delta and the distance between that island and the northern end of St. Simons Island where Hampton was situated lent considerable emphasis to the importance of water craft. Little St. Simons Island and Experiment Plantation's Five Pound Tree were both water-bound, and as there was a constant flow of slave labor, equipment, and produce from one point to another, transport by plantation boat was essential. Two years after the purchase of Hampton, Major Butler made a contract with the estate of Miles Brewton to purchase a schooner, the *Altamaha Packet,* for a price of 6,600 pounds. The price included a crew of four experienced Negroes at specified prices well in excess of those of the average field hand. The Major paid 700 pounds for Bridgewater, 500 pounds for Moody, 450 pounds for York, and 300 pounds for Billy.[52] The *Packet* joined an older ship built in 1773 by shipwrights George Russell and Edward Goff of Charleston and designed especially to carry 150 barrels of rice to market from his South Carolina plantations. Through the years, an integral part of the Major's agricultural empire were the Butler schooners, carrying cotton, rice, or sugar to markets in Savannah, Charleston, and other nearby ports, or bringing slaves and supplies to his several plantations. Major Butler's pride in the ability of his ship carpenters to build vessels capable of offshore sailing extended to their capability of constructing and maintaining the many small boats that served the plantations.[53] They made the crude "flats" used to move produce on the rivers and in the canals, but more important, built the efficient dugout canoes that were in constant use between the plantations. In 1791 Major Butler wrote an agent in Charleston asking that cotton seed, slaves, and tools be sent down to Hampton "in Captain Saunders' petiagur." A petiagur was a work boat made from one, or sometimes two, large cypress logs, dug out by hand with adzes and chisels. A single mast and sail provided motive power with an assist from coastal winds, and the frequently used auxiliary source was the long oars and strong arms of slaves. The petiagur and several smaller dugout boats and canoes were designed for inland waters and were seldom used offshore. They were shallow draft, open boats, with very little freeboard, particularly so when loaded with the usual cargo of people and freight. These boats ranged in size from ten oars down to a one-place boat sculled from the stern or rowed from a center thwart. Fish Harry or Crab Quash would have used one of these to keep the Butler's Islanders supplied with fresh seafood, much a part of their diet. The larger, broad-beamed boats were usually manned by eight oarsmen and the one who steered. The constant traffic between Hampton and Butler's Island, two hours apart—ten miles as the crow flies, but a good fifteen as the slave rows through the turns and twists of the rivers and creeks—called for one of this type. It was very similar to the petiagur, but without the sail.[54]

Unlike such onerous plantation tasks as ditching and banking, the work of a boatman was pleasant duty. No work on a plantation brought forth such cheerful song. Visitors who were taken to the Altamaha plantations by boat gained an immediate impression of people content with their lot in life as the Negroes sang such carefree songs as "Sandfly Bite Me" or "Zion," a Butler song with several verses, one of which was:

> *Five were wise an' five were foolish*
> *When the bridegroom come*
> *Five were wise an' five were foolish*
> *When the bridegroom come.*

When over ninety years old in 1915, Celia Davis, a former Butler slave, remembered a Hampton boat song, the chorus of which was:

> *Run from Pharoah, lemme run*
>   *We all goin' to meet some day.*
> *Run from Satan, lemme run*
>   *We all goin' to meet some day.*[55]

When Captain Basil Hall visited the Altamaha, he recorded in his journal how he had been met at Darien and taken downriver to St. Simons:

> In a canoe some thirty feet long, hollowed out of a cypress tree. The oars were pulled by five smart negroes, merry fellows, and very happy looking, as indeed are most of their race, in spite of their bondage. They accompanied their labour by a wild sort of song not very unlike that of the Canadian Voyageurs, but more nearly resembling that of the well-known Bunder-boatmen at Bombay.[56]

In his journal Sir Charles Lyell described a Couper boat crew: "The woods echo to their song. One of them taking the lead, first improvised a verse paying compliments to his master's family, and to a celebrated black beauty of the neighborhood who was compared to the "red bird." The other five joined in the chorus, always repeating the same words." The boatmen also sang a Methodist hymn in which they brought familiarity to a sacred subject, and then a "love ditty, almost profane." Sir Charles was impressed.[57]

During the Civil War, when many slaves abandoned their quarters for long-sought freedom, men of the Union forces were frequently surprised to find the low-country men complementing remarkable skill as boatmen with rare and unusual song. A Union officer was taken in a surfboat manned by eight oarsmen from Beaufort to Hilton Head. He heard what came to be known as the Negro spiritual, and wrote: "Our black soldiers sang as they rowed—not the songs of common sailors—but the hymns of praise mingled with those pathetic longings for a better world."[58]

Many of the lively boat songs were also sung at dances and shouts, the latter being a subdued form of the dance—"dancing before the Lord," it was called. The rhythm of the rowing song fit beautifully with the rhythm of the shout. Lydia Parrish worked with the blacks of St. Simons Island for a quarter century to resurrect and record their songs in a splendid research program that evokes much of the past that had all but disappeared. Her *Slave Songs of the Georgia Sea Islands,* published in 1942, stands alone as the finest work of its kind. She noted the dual use of the infectious rhythmic rowing and shouting songs and said the same tunes were favorites along the entire South Carolina and Georgia coasts. That certainly stands to reason, for many of the Altamaha estuary slaves were introduced to the New World in South Carolina. One former slave who sang for Mrs. Parrish was Liverpool Hazzard, who had pulled an oar on Butler boats. He sang as an old man, with spirit and dignity:

> *Tis well an' good I come here tonight*
> *come here tonight*
> *come here tonight*
> *well an' good I come here tonight*
> *For to do my Master's will.*

Liverpool was singing of his ultimate Master, not of his former owner.

At the time of Mrs. Parrish's work with the Negroes of St. Simons, she learned to respect the difference between them and those of the river plantations of Butler's Island and the Troup-Dent place, Broadfield. Where the

St. Simons people sang spirituals with greater "tonal refinement," they lacked the "exuberant vitality" of the Butler's Island and Broadfield groups, who were outstanding "shouters," as the performers of the religious dance were called. It followed that the Butler's Island and Broadfield groups also excelled at the "ring-play," the term given for the handed-down play-party games of early white settlers.

The isolation of the remote sea islands and the protective sensitivity of many of the older Negroes made it possible for a few of the songs in a true African dialect to survive and to come down through the years. These songs are rhythmic but without melody—African, as opposed to Afro-American. Mrs. Parrish had a difficult time ferreting out the African words just as she did in bringing back the African dance; but one brought out the other, and the "buzzard's lope" was followed by Dublin Scribben's:

> *Rockah mh moomba*
> *Cum bo-ba yondah*
> *Lil aye tambe*
> *I Rockah mh moomba.*

Most of their songs developed as did their language. Native rhythms, a few African words, a melody borrowed from here or there, and song took form as had the language. Yet there was one important difference. Their language was necessary for communication with their white owners or overseers, but the songs were their own and for themselves. True, a rowing song or a work song would be heard by the whites, but the dance songs, shouts, and songs of praise and longing were their own. It is no wonder that it required the compassion of Mrs. Parrish and a quarter century of persuasion to bring the songs to light.[59] Georgia Bryan Conrad, whose father, Thomas Bryan, planted the Brailsford rice plantation on Broughton Island, remembered the slave songs she heard as a child: "In the fields carrying their burdens, rowing or feeding the mill with rice, the Negroes were always singing. As I recall those days, it is ever with a sound of melody in my ears." She wrote before 1901, when her reminiscences were published: "Nothing is a greater contrast to that time than the quietness of the Negroes now. Truly their harps are hung on the willows."[60] With Emancipation, the freed slaves had put the old songs aside. Mrs. Parrish found that to be true, and it is to her credit she brought so much out of the dark past.

The Gullah language of the low-country slave permitted communication with their white owners and, as well, a consolidation of their several African dialects and English into a common tongue that became an acceptable means of human intercourse among themselves. It was an adaptation to life in the new world. The same forces influenced their song, and later their music, where they blended their African heritage with words and melodies of their own choosing from their white owners. Their religious faith, of which their song is a vital part, had much the same derivation—just enough of the white man's Christianity to fit their needs. Much of the slaves' early religion was spontaneous, as their jazz came to be. That Christianity was accepted at all is surprising when considered in the light of the background of the slave:

> On many slave ships, for example, the rather incongruous ritual of mass baptism occurred shortly before the Africans were packed below deck, chained one to another. Its acceptance is more understandable if we realize that religion was the one great kindness from master to slave, and that it was administered on a blessed day of rest. The wide gap between the doctrine of the white man's religion and its actual application surely must have confused the Negro, and perhaps is responsible to this day for the rather broad interpretation of Christianity's tenets by that race.[61]

Major Butler and the senior Roswell King paid but little attention to the religious education of the Butler slaves. Sunday, the "blessed day of rest," was observed by blacks and whites, and for a time Roswell King, Jr., permitted "a certain number" to go into Darien to sell their own produce or handiwork. In Darien, the Sunday gathering at the white churches offered a convenient marketplace and also gave the slave a chance to observe the whites practicing their religion and to hear their songs of praise. On other plantations the owners were more tolerant than Major Butler and the Roswell Kings. Religious services for the slaves were encouraged, praise houses were constructed for slave use, and white ministers were brought in to assist on special occasions. Not long after Roswell King became manager of Hampton and Butler's Island he found that religion was getting out of hand. He prescribed an unusual remedy:

> There is one plan I cannot forbade proposing (it is not much Expense) which is to send me a *full dozen Fiddles* that will cost from one to two dollars each. I must try to break up so much preaching as there is on your Estate. Some of your Negroes die for the Love of God and others through

feir of Him. Something must be done. I think Dancing will give the Negroes a better appetite for sleep than preaching.[62]

On the low-country plantations of the Reverend Charles Colcock Jones near Midway, Georgia, particular attention was paid to religious education of the Jones slaves. Jones prepared a *Catechism* especially for "Colored Persons." First published in 1837, the small book went through several editions and copies found their way to the low-country plantations. A section was devoted to "Duties of Masters and Servants." Among those for "Masters":

Q   Who is the first Master that is mentioned in the Bible?
A   Abraham.

Q   How many servants had he when he went to save Lot?
A   Three hundred and eighteen.

Q   What command has God given to Masters?
A   Masters give unto your Servants that which is just and equal, knowing that ye also have a Master in Heaven.

Q   Who is duty bound to give to Servants comfortable clothing, wholesome and abundant food?
A   The Master.

Q   Who is duty bound to instruct Servants in a knowledge of the Holy Scriptures, and to give them every opportunity and encouragement to seek their soul's salvation?
A   The Master.

Q   Who is the Master of us all in Heaven?
A   God.

Q   Does God show favour to the Master more than to the Servant, and just because he is a Master?
A   No.

Jones preferred not to call a slave, a slave. His questions and answers for "Servants":

Q   What are the Servants to count their Masters worthy of?
A   All honour.

Q   How are they to try to please their Masters?
A   Please them well in all things, not answering again.

Q   Is it right for a Servant when commanded to do anything to be sullen and slow, and answering his Master again?

A   No.

Q   But suppose the Master is hard to please, and threatens and punishes more than he ought, what is the Servant to do?

A   Do his best to please him.

Q   Are Servants at liberty to tell lies and deceive their Masters?

A   No.

Q   If servants will faithfully do their duty and Serve God in their stations as Servants, will they be respected of men, and blessed and honoured of God, as well as others?

A   Yes.[63]

By the time the Reverend Mr. Jones's *Catechism* reached the plantations, the religious education of slaves had become one of the answers to the strident complaints of the abolitionists. Religion offered a sense of purpose to slaves and could be used as a means of keeping them on the plantation. Later, their sense of purpose expanded to encompass a stronger desire for freedom. One abolitionist, who commanded a black regiment in the Civil War, noted that while he had "underrated the suffering produced by slavery," the "demoralization" he had expected to find did not exist. The strong religious temperament of the blacks had banished any such condition.[64]

The restrictions laid down by Major Butler and the Roswell Kings kept the Butler slaves busy at their tasks of propagating not the gospel, but cotton, rice, sugar cane, and more slaves. Their religion remained rudimentary and found its greatest expression in the ceremonies of baptism and burial. The road between the two was long and hard.

Chapter 10

 *Honored Sir*

PIERCE BUTLER long sought a "real good Manager for my Planting Interest in Georgia." In February 1794 he spelled out his requirements in a letter to Archibald Brown of South Carolina.

> As my principal object is to be saved the necessity of ever going to see my Estate & as it is my intention to vest such a Manager with full powers to do anything I could do were I present, I woud wish him to be such a character as is capable of Shipping my crops, purchasing clothing &c. I woud give to such a character as *You approve of* One Hundred and fifty, or Two Hundred pounds a year—expecting him to live on my Estate either on the Sea Coast or River Lands as he may prefer, using whatever he has occasion for, the produce of the Estate for his table. I would expect him to move there in the course of the present year, & it is necessary he shoud take a ride with me in April in order to understand my plan, and either return with me or remain as he may choose. If you can procure for me one or two Overseers to move there in April you will add to the favour. One of them I wish to understand ditching.[1]

Archibald Brown could not locate "such a character." It was not until eight years later that Pierce Butler finally found the man he wanted.

In the interim, Major Butler called on his friend William Page, who might have been the man he sought except that Page's interest in Hampton and Butler's Island was diminished by his own desire to plant long staple cotton on St. Simons Island. The place Page had in mind "to go on cotton" was the Spalding plantation at the opposite or southern end of the island from Hampton. Page, urged on and directed by Pierce Butler in Philadelphia, took over from the overseer, George Valley, and the recently deceased Roger Parker Saunders and began the development of what came to be the vast and successful Butler estate. Before William Page assumed management, Major Butler had made his move away from South Carolina and the Middleton-Bull trustees. He sold, and was selling, the family plantations and Crown grants, including Coosaw Island, the old Bull homeplace where General Oglethorpe had tarried on a trip from Charlestown better than a half century before. Cattle from Coosaw and the Euhaws had been herded to the Savannah River by old Abraham, Gabriel, and Primus, and from there had been shipped to the Altamaha in an expedition led by the boatman Sauney. Already on Hampton and Butler's Island were the Middleton-Bull, Brewton, and Butler slaves who also had come from Coosaw and the Euhaws and from the Blake inheritance, Brewton Plantation on the Combahee River. William Page, employed at an annual wage of one thousand dollars, was told to build a wharf supported by native palmetto logs and to construct a "manager's house," both at Hampton. He was also to proceed with a division of Butler's Island into four parts, each of one hundred acres "within the ditches," so that "at my death each of my daughters should have some land to cultivate." Major Butler gave explicit instructions on the banking and ditching:

> Mr. Joe Allston of noted memory who had the best dams in So Carolina required of his ditchers 600 cubic feet a day for each hand. God forbid I should work my Negroes so. My wish is that they should do a reasonable days work and no more, if that is 300 cubic feet, be it so. If that is too much for them, make it less. I would rather the island was sunk in the sea than I should cause the death on one Negroe. They are slaves but they are human beings.

He then tells Page that "The ditchers must have meat" and to fatten some hogs for them. Demonstrating his knowledge of the strengths and weaknesses of his Negroes, he warns Mr. Page "to keep a tighter rein with Jack" and to show no indulgence to "Ship Carpenter Sauney," who was not to be confused with "Honest boat Sauney." He ordered "George & John & two prentice boys" to make shoes for the people, of leather to be acquired from John Couper on a promise of more shoes for his people at Cannon's Point. The smiths were to be put to work fashioning "nails, screws, augurs, hoes, axes & spades" for use on the plantations, with the surplus hardware and shoes to be sold in Charleston. He wanted Bram to plant some Cayenne pepper, and Page to be on the lookout for a gang of "fifty to a hundred Negroes."[2]

William Page interrupted the constant flow of instructions by asking how he should assign tasks to women expecting children. He received an answer:

> You desire my instructions respecting an indulgence to breeding women; I never would put them to any straining or hard work, there is always suitable work in a cotton settlement for pregnant women. In assorting and suiting work to the persons employed, everything depends on Your own judgement. I will then only remark generally that it is not my wish to go to the stretch of powers with any of my People & still less so with breeding women.

The subject at hand moved Major Butler into a dissertation on the care of sick slaves:

> I earnestly request that *every possible* attention may be given to sick Negroes, save and except that of calling in a Doctor, which I never admit of unless for a fracture or venereal complaint. I never have employed Doctors to my Negroes, because country Doctors have not my confidence because they seldom feel for Negroes as they ought to, and therefore are light on their prescriptions. The moment any Negroe complains I wish him or her to be attended by Nany or Tenah. If the complaint is a fever and in the summer, let a vomit, unless to pregnant women, be given, after that some gruel, the next day if the fever continues let 12 ounces of blood be taken and a purge given of 5 grains Calomel and ten of Jallop, if that should not operate in three hours, let the doce be repeated till it operates 4 or 5 times, then let them have gruel, or fowl broth. If the fever continues a second bleeding must take place and after it plenty of tea or gruel, when the fever is checked let them drink plenty of decoction of wild cherry bark. In winter, bleed, purge and sweat freely with snake root for fevers. Let the general purge by Calomel & Jallop, not allowing them to drink anything cold during the operation. I have very much at heart indeed the preventing of deaths.[3]

Pierce Butler often directed his managers to be kind and considerate in their treatment of the slaves, but he believed kindness was not necessarily deserved, but was to be earned. If slaves shirked work or violated plantation rules, their disciplining was usually a downgrading of their work status and an assignment to a more menial and labor-intensive task, that is, "put in the field," which was a demeaning move for an artisan or a domestic. They might be deprived of food or clothing, assigned extra

William Page, 1764–1827, who managed Hampton plantation for Major Butler from 1796 until 1802 and then developed his own plantation, Retreat, on the southern end of St. Simons Island. (Courtesy of Mr. and Mrs. I. M. Aiken.)

work, or be restricted to quarters in their free time. If all else failed, the manager could inflict "punishment," which meant the lash. It was not unusual for Major Butler to order such from the comfort of his Philadelphia lodgings. He would not tolerate insubordination, an infraction that usually brought forth a severe whipping at once. He disciplined those who would not work, but nothing aroused his anger as did a runaway. He would go to great length to recover the "absconders," and if recovered, the punishment was extreme. In 1790, while attending his senatorial chores in New York, he was told a Butler runaway had been located in Nova Scotia: "If an opportunity offers for Charleston, or this Town, I will thank you to ship the Fellow, giving the Captain particular charge not to let him escape." A few years later, a domestic servant called Sommersett, "a Mustezo lad about 18 years old," was found in St. Croix in the Virgin Islands. He had attended the Butler daughters as a "hair dresser," and the distance from Philadelphia mattered little to Pierce Butler. He wanted the "Serv't of mine—a slave" to be returned. It was one of the few times Major Butler called a slave, a slave.[4]

In 1798 Major Butler seemed plagued by runaways. His troubles extended from the Altamaha to the Schuylkill and the Delaware. In June he returned two women who had been working as domestics in Philadelphia. They were sent by ship to St. Mary's, forty miles south of Hampton:

> This letter goes by way of St. Mary's with two of my Negroe women,
> Molly & Hannah. Molly has behav'd ill. Hannah unexceptionally well, but
> wishes to return. She is very sickly and can do little, perhaps spin or card.
> Molly you will please put in the field, she must be brought to work by
> degrees. She is a monster of ingratitude. I raised her here from the brink of
> the grave after being many days speechless and apparently without a pulse.
> Would you believe it, she has attempted to run off. My boy Sam has
> absconded, and thro' the baseness of some quakers I shall lose him.

"Old Justice and Primus" found the hard work on the Altamaha not to their liking and somehow were able to get back to the Combahee in South Carolina. Colonel John McPherson located the two men and sent them down to William Page. In July, Major Butler ordered the lash for two of his Negroes:

> On the subject of the runaways, punish Titus and Morris when you get
> them. I am fully satisfied, knowing my sentiments as you do with respect to

my Negroes that you will not suffer them to be ill treated. I am mortified that any of them should run off. Call the runaways before you and tell them how much it hurts me & how much displeased I am with their behaviour, believing as I do they had no just cause for going.

Major Butler had considered the purchase of slaves owned by the Houston family. He commented to Page: "I know there are some runaways among them. These I would not own if given to me. Next to a thief I avoid runaways." In October, with Titus unrecovered, or perhaps gone away again, Page was told: "Spare no pains to get them back. I will make examples of some of them. If you get Titus and Jack, iron them. A white man would be hung for what they did." Thus, if Titus and Jack were recovered, their punishment would have been the usual severe flogging awarded runaways, and in addition, their ankles would have been encased in iron collars joined left to right by a short length of heavy chain.[5]

In January 1799, while visiting his plantations, Pierce Butler, perhaps reflecting on the "punishment" inflicted the year before, offered his own version of a new year's resolution.

> I cannot resist recommending to you a paternal kindness to my People. They will have no persons but yourself and Mrs. Page to look up to, to mitigate their sorrows, to make the situation of slavery less burdensome, in short by tenderness in sickness, which I believe has not been wanting, by mildness in health, to draw forth that smile of content which must afford to You and Myself much comfort. Their reasonable and rational comfort—happiness I will not term it—is near and dear to me.[6]

William Page's interim appointment stretched into the new century. It finally ended in 1802 when he put Major Butler in touch with Roswell King. The introduction enabled Page to strike out on his own and get on with the development of the plantation he called Retreat. The meeting between Butler and King was agreeable. From the beginning, Roswell King appeared to be the man the Major had sought for so many years. A relationship began between the two families that would extend from 1802 into the 1850s, long after Major Butler's death.

Roswell King had come to Georgia in 1789. He settled in Darien and brought to that small river town New England enterprise and ingenuity. He was born in 1765 in Windsor, Connecticut, where his father was well known for having commanded the United States brig *Defiance* during the

Revolution. His ancestor John King, one of the "Kings of Boyle-Roscommon," came to America in 1645 and was an original settler of Northampton, Massachusetts. Roswell King claimed kinship with Noah and Daniel Webster, Governors Treat and Fitch of Connecticut, and John Fitch of steamboat fame. The Darien of that day was an interesting community with great promise for the future. Its prosperity centered on lumber, cotton, and rice, and the young New Englander proved himself adept in the marketing of such produce. In Darien he married Catherine Barrington, a gentle lady, who, not to be outdone by her husband, claimed kinship with General Oglethorpe, the Tudors, and Oliver Cromwell. The Barringtons lived at a remote spot on the Altamaha River, fifteen miles above Darien. Her parents, Jessiah and Sarah Barrington, owned San Sevilla, across the river from the colonial outpost of Fort Barrington. As had the Kings, the Barringtons emigrated from Ireland.[7]

Roswell King became well known for his proficiency in the use of tabby, a regional building material made of a mixture of lime, shells, sand and water. In Darien he constructed several houses and commercial buildings, including a hotel, and all the while continued his busy trade as a commission merchant in the blossoming little community.[8]

In assuming his duties as manager of the Butler estate, Roswell King first put aside his business ventures in Darien. By arrangement with Major Butler, he did assist Thomas Spalding by putting his knowledge of tabby to good use in the construction of the fine mansion on the south end of Sapelo Island, a project that continued over several years. At Hampton, he quickly took over the task with which William Page had struggled for ten long years. He moved his family of four into the new Page-built house on the northern point of the island, gathered in the many loose ends, and soon had the two plantations operating efficiently and profitably, much to the satisfaction of the autocratic owner in distant Philadelphia. As had been William Page, Roswell King was the recipient of a persistent stream of advice. Unlike Page, he responded willingly and quickly began to execute the myriad orders Major Butler sent down. Roswell King was a practical man whose intelligence and adaptability enabled him to bring his own ideas into play. As time passed, Major Butler learned he could trust King's judgment. He did so, and gave his manager greater leeway.[9]

Although it seems unlikely that one so versatile and successful would have put aside his own interests to become the manager of another's estate, the inducements were such that Roswell King accepted Major

Roswell King, manager of the Butler plantations in Georgia from 1802 until 1819, when he was succeeded by his son Roswell King, Jr. (Roswell Presbyterian Church History Room.)

Butler's terms and then gave him full measure in return. His relationship with Pierce Butler is well shown in the many letters that passed between them. King was impressed by the Major's importance and, although not the type to bask, found satisfaction in his association with the distinguished senator from South Carolina who was the friend of Washington and other important men of the times. He was impressed by the Major's intelligence and great wealth. Roswell King's letters reveal his own intelligence, although almost always show deference. The letters begin "Honored Sir," and despite the routine ending "I am Sir, your Faithful servant," one feels there is nothing perfunctory in its meaning. He expressed himself very well, wrote a neat, legible hand, frequently spelling words phonetically, and invariably wrote "get" as "git."[10]

In addition to deference, the "Honored Sir" letters showed esteem and even some affection for Major Butler. Mrs. King had much the same feelings and was often mentioned most favorably in the correspondence between Hampton and Philadelphia. Her ladylike qualities and her Irish background appealed to Major Butler. In 1815, during a particularly trying time, Roswell King wrote his employer: "My own interest is a mere nothing—in short your interest appears to be mine—and in truth there is no man on earth that I have so great a regard for as thyself."[11] Mr. King acknowledged, and did so frequently, Major Butler's kind references to Catherine King: "Mrs. King thanks you for your often inquiries and goodwill towards her."[12]

Mrs. King shared plantation responsibilities with her husband, as the domestic and household slaves were her charge. In January 1815 she sent Major Butler the annual report on his "poultry and feathers," advising him: "Betty raised 35 turkey, 10 ducks, 10 geese, and 13 common yard fowls." Roswell King usually called the latter "dung hill fowls." Mrs. King went on to say: "The feathers of 1814 are geese 36 pounds, down 5-1/4 pound, duck ten pounds. They are as beautiful feathers as I ever saw." Her long letter concluded with: "I hope it is not trespassing on your patience when you consider it comes from one who considers herself as your friend. Our family, I thank God, are well, a blessing I hope you enjoy, and may you live to see many happy returns of the season."[13]

The subject of Roswell King's Sunday letters to Philadelphia was principally the business of the plantations. He wrote with an interesting turn of phrase. When writing about a white workman who was doing a special job, he noted that Sherman, the "machien carpenter," was "blind as a horse block."[14] He found little preference for white workers over the

Butler slaves: "I find but little odds between White or Black—They are all Eye-Servants—wants two to watch one."[15] At times he revealed a dry sense of humor. A young scion of a nearby plantation had died of "dropsy": "Which was brot on by drinking, but that I believe may be called a Natural Death in Georgia."[16] He could reveal his state of mind as he ended his letters: "I am not fit for any kind of business—But am Your Faithful Servant."[17]

Before Roswell King had come to terms with Pierce Butler the plantations had been managed rather haphazardly. Years later, Roswell King, Jr., told how the Butler estate had become so successful and in such good condition:

> The reputed good condition of the Butler Estate has been the work of time, and a diligent attention to the interest of said Estate, and the comfort and happiness of the slaves on it.
>
> To Mr. R. King, Sen'r, more is due than to myself. In 1802, he assumed the management. The gang was a fine one, but was very disorderly which invariably is the case where there is a frequent change of managers. Rules and regulations were established (I may say laws), a few forcible examples made, after a regular trial in which every degree of justice was exhibited, was the first step. But the grand point was to suppress the brutality and licentiousness practiced by the principal men on it (say the drivers and tradesmen).[18]

Yet, "Mr. R. King Sen'r" entertained doubts that he was the man Major Butler needed for the difficult job. He responded to the abundant instructions that had come his way from Philadelphia in one of his Sunday letters: "My wish to fulfill all your wishes fairly confuse me in all my plans. Your knollege of your negroes always led me to believe all you said *Loud & Must Be Done*. Therefore I confess I am not the man capable of doing it, but remain trying faithfully." He added the usual report on the condition of his work force: "Sickness nothing dangerous, a number of small complaints to lose work, Breeding women &C. *No Deaths*."[19]

Roswell King lived with his family in the comfortable house at Hampton. He supervised the planting there and on the cattle farm at Little St. Simons on the Atlantic beyond John Couper's Cannon's Point. He developed and planted Experiment and Five Pound Tree, the remote tract where troublesome slaves did penance. He and Major Butler put into production other plantings at various times, the majority of which were cotton tracts on St. Simons Island. Butler's Island, two long, hard hours distant from Hampton, demanded the greatest attention. Under Roswell King's aggressive management it was to become the most productive. Mr. King and Major Butler worked well together, and the old military man relished the arrangement. King showed great respect for his imperious employer. He executed orders with dispatch and skill, and even though overwhelmed by those orders at times, he managed to keep the quick temper in Philadelphia under reasonable control by judicious use of the broad powers Major Butler granted him. The Major demonstrated his confidence in Roswell King by giving him the important authority to purchase slaves. Anxious to buy some Gold Coast slaves for use on Butler's Island, Major Butler wrote his Savannah dealers Mein and Mackay. William Mein responded to the instructions he had received: "Mr. King shall have an opportunity of choosing the 30 young lads you want & I hope the price wont exceed $350 or $375."[20]

Not long after feeling comfortable with his new responsibilities, Roswell King tested Major Butler's confidence by requesting credit of $2,600. The Major agreed, but asked for property to secure the indebtedness. Mr. King obliged by pledging "Twelve negroes the clear property of the said R. King of the following names, Bellah, Judey, Lucy, Will, Henry, Cyrus, Prince, Davy, Samson, Jim, Jacob and Peter." Mr. King's collateral was wholly acceptable to the former delegate to the Constitutional Convention in Philadelphia, who there had proclaimed the slave a proper asset in determining a man's wealth, on which he believed representation in Congress should have depended.[21]

Roswell King was indefatigable in his management of the Butler properties. He planned his work efficiently, planted and harvested at the proper times, and was well versed in the preparation of the plantation's produce. He saw to it that cotton was cleaned of seed, graded, and packed; that rice was hulled, graded, and contained in plantation-made tierces; that cane was ground, the juice processed into sugar, and barreled for market; and that all the produce was sold or traded on the best possible terms. Add to that the care and management of hundreds of slaves and the responsibility appears awesome. He kept accurate records of income and expense, and was particularly adept at determining the profitability of a new venture. The move into sugar is a good example of his prudent management:

> In the Sugar cane now lies my great hope. Sugar is now $24 per CWT, and
> probably it will not be less than $20. If that be true you may yet make
> $30,000 from that 100 acres of Cane. You see how I am led away with a

new thing that I am no judge of its production—but I must believe they make sugar profitable in Louisiana, and here we have advantages they never had, and can never have. We can flow or drain our lands, and can boat our cane to mills in canals.[22]

In this excerpt from one of Roswell King's weekly reports, he revealed his industry, his desire to innovate, his understanding of production and marketing. He had other strengths, not the least of which was his ability to deal firsthand with the owners of neighboring plantations. He was respected for his capability by Thomas Spalding, John Couper, and William Page, and was often asked to lend a hand by Major Butler's South Carolina friends. Charles Cotesworth Pinckney sought "candid advice" of Mr. King. He wanted to grow sugar cane, and wrote: "Previous to my gratifying the mania with which I am seized for growing that article."[23] It was advice Roswell King was well prepared to give.

If a gentle wife, intelligence, ingenuity, and hard work were the strengths of Roswell King, his underlying fault was his failure to comprehend the strengths and weaknesses of Major Butler's slaves. The Butler dictum that the Master will give what is needed, and what is not given is not to be desired, may have been a factor in his inability to fathom their needs.[24] Surely something more was behind Roswell King's repeated cruelty to the slaves. His efficiency was evident in the orderliness of the plantations, and when compared with the neighboring plantations where good care was the rule and not the exception, the Butler slaves were as well, if not better, clothed and fed, and worked no harder or longer than their counterparts of the Altamaha estuary. Roswell King knew that healthy slaves produced more work, and more slaves. Consequently, the good health of the Negroes was a constant and genuine concern. The outward evidence of healthy slaves and their orderly day-to-day routine in operating the plantations contributed to the general belief that Pierce Butler was a considerate slave owner. First on Roswell King's agenda was the profitability of the plantations. He would tolerate no infraction of rules that might jeopardize his mission to produce successful crops. What was not outwardly evident was his frequent resort to harsh punishment of slaves who obstructed this pursuit of success. Both Roswell King and Pierce Butler thought themselves humane, yet neither truly considered the black as a human being. As Roswell King had fathered a child by one of the slaves, perhaps his cruelty was some manifestation of this involvement. Whatever the reasons, his own words reveal his weakness.[25]

In the weekly reports that flowed from Hampton to Philadelphia, Roswell King was completely candid in his reaction to the misdeeds of the plantation slaves. What he wrote was an indictment of the system Major Butler had defended so vigorously at the Constitutional Convention in 1787, and he completely refuted the belief that Hampton and Butler's Island were plantations where the slaves were given good and fair treatment. "If *God* lets me live & gives me health," wrote Roswell King to Pierce Butler, "not one *CENT* of your wealth will be lost for lack of attention." It was a forthright statement of his mission as manager.[26]

Shortly before Roswell King's employment, Major Butler had purchased the "gang" of slaves from Virginia, slaves that Mr. King encountered on his arrival. He found them to be extremely poor workers and so advised Major Butler: "Virginia Negroes have no character."[27] A week later he went to Savannah to retrieve Albert, one of the Virginia slaves who had run away, been captured, and placed in jail, where he had remained for thirty-four days. He told of punishing Albert at the jail and leaving him to walk some sixty-five miles back to Darien. Albert returned "much swelled by lying in jail & none the smarter."[28]

The first full year of Roswell King's management was 1803. His enforced discipline brought unrest to the slaves, and as a consequence, several other slaves chose to run away. Nero was captured or persuaded to return by Ben and Pompey. Bacchus and Guy returned after short-lived freedom. Jeffrey was picked up near Darien after six days, and three slaves who attempted to get away in a log canoe were gathered in and returned by the mail boat.[29]

In July 1803 the Sunday letter told Major Butler how Roswell King had refrained from punishing some unruly Negroes. Mr. King reasoned: "But I had rather you be cheated out of a little work than me to have the name of Cruel and Unjust."[30] Yet when he did inflict punishment, he had no feelings of cruelty, and believed his actions to be fully justified. He told of his problems with the slave Chance: "They are healthy and cheerful, except the fellow I mentioned to you sometime past wouldnt work named *Chance*. He worked a few weeks but has since sworn off again. I gave him a little whipping, but it had no effect. I shall take him home with me this evening (I think he is my match). He is a very likely lad of about 18 yrs of age, young enough to be conquered."[31]

In 1808 Roswell King punished "Jacob's boy Sunday," who had broken into the barn and stolen a half barrel of rice and then had run away for two days: "I gave him a severe whipping and let Jacob have him. As he is but a lad, I hope we can make him good."[32] Here, Mr. King demonstrated an unfortunate reaction to a young slave's misbehavior, though not so unfortunate as was his reaction to a tragedy on a cold winter's day the same year. Five young slaves had set out for Hampton from Butler's Island, against orders. They used the "Eagle Boat," one of the dugout canoes. Mr. King began his report of the incident: "Giving you unfortunate news of five Negroes being Drowned last Sunday." He named four of the five: "Jack Carter's Moses of abo 18 yrs of age, Harry's boy Jacob abo 16 yrs, Worster's boy Tipee of abo 16 yrs, and Deanna's Judy of abo 14 yrs of age." The young people set out against the incoming tide in a strong northwest wind, which would have made for a dangerous trip in the broader reaches of the river. Mr. King continued his account: "A vessel going by the cut saw a canoe in the river turned over and a negro on it which drowned before they could git to speak. All the reply I made after hearing of this unfortunate accident was that there friends might find the bodies and bury them like dogs, for not one should have a coffin. I would sell the bodies to be Cut to Pieces by the Doctors."[33]

Roswell King did not always lack compassion. He demonstrated some when confronted by petty trouble on the part of two old people. He had been told to punish one by withholding a distribution of clothing to the miscreant but, with winter approaching, took it upon himself to give both of them shoes: "I have clothed the Negroes, except Mumm and Gardener Bram. Mumm it was your order not to be clothed. Old *Bram* I had no other way to punish the old rascal, only to stop his clothing. (I gave him and Mumm shoes.)"[34]

Mr. King routinely reported on the health of the Negroes and named the slaves lost through death:

> Sickness most favourable, *no Deaths,* nothing uncommon on the Plantations.

> 5£ Justice *died* last Saturday. I am much mystified at the loss of so many Negroes (But it is God's will not mine) I am your Faithful servant Roswell King.

> The loss of so many Negroes and making such a short Crop must give you a vast deal of unesiness. We have lost *three* more Negroes—March No. 4, Old Jimmy No. 4, & a new Negro boy.

> Mr. Miller's Jack is dead—died by the bite of a rattlesnake.

Fivepound Justice was so designated because he lived at Five Pound Tree. The designation No. 4 for March, who died in "great misery," and for Old Jimmy came from their living and working from the fourth settlement on Butler's Island. Mr. Miller's Jack was actually owned by Catharine Greene Miller, the widow of Major Butler's friend Nathanael Greene, who had married Phineas Miller in 1796. The leasing of slaves by one owner from another was a common practice at that time.[35]

The sickness and deaths of so many slaves prompted Mr. King to seek a remedy.

> I recommend that we save a small quantity of rice for sick Negroes.
>
> A very little salt or fresh meat will make a large quantity of Soup. I have spared no pains to give the *Sick* nurrishment.[36]

The illness of Nelly, one of the more dependable plantation women, moved Mr. King to ask that Dr. James Mease, Major Butler's son-in-law, prescribe a cure. He was not aware that Sarah Butler's husband was roundly disliked by her father. Poor Nelly—"so valuable a woman"— remained in a "lingering state."[37]

In early 1813, before greater trouble visited the plantations, Roswell King complained that directives coming from Philadelphia hampered his ability to manage the plantations as he believed they should be. His objections prompted a characteristically frank response—and from Pierce Butler, an uncharacteristic expression of approval: "I do not complain, but I can never relinquish the right of directing and controlling. I need scarcely say I am entirely satisfied with Your management. You enter thoroughly, and with good judgement into my views; and no man of my knowledge is more capable of executing them."[38]

The second war with England brought trouble to the plantations. It also brought to light more of the bitterness Roswell King manifested toward the Negroes in his charge. Difficulties caused by the British forces took him away from the plantations, and when away, the responsibilities of management fell on his nineteen-year-old son, Roswell King, Jr. The elder King advised Major Butler: "My son Roswell is very active and attentive, I have no doubt but all things will go on correctly."[39]

Several years later Roswell King, Jr., wrote an article for an agricultural journal in which he gave his views on the management of the estate. "Since childhood I have been on this place, and from the age of eighteen to this date (1828) I have had the actual management."[40] His statement was a little beyond the truth, for his father remained in firm control for several more years. The father did relinquish much of the more difficult work to his son, who, obviously, was being groomed for succession.

In 1815 the British navy and the Royal marines descended on St. Simons Island. Their arrival marked a turning point in the relationship between Pierce Butler and Roswell King, and one for the Butler plantations as well.

Chapter 11

🦎 The War of 1812

WAR WITH GREAT BRITAIN brought unexpected trouble to the planters of coastal Georgia, many of whom had strong family and commercial ties to the British Empire. Pierce Butler had been fearful of the British gaining control of Spanish Florida and becoming a threat to the Georgia coast. Yet, he had approved the hawkish attitude of those who led the Twelfth Congress into a declaration of war. The ensuing difficulties should have come as no surprise to one whose memory of the troubles wrought upon his family in the Revolution was so fresh and so painful. Nevertheless, he did little to convey his fears to his manager, Roswell King. No doubt the Major's Northumberland blood boiled when he read the April 2, 1814, proclamation of Vice Admiral Sir Alexander Cochrane, who commanded "His Majesty's Ships upon the North American Station." The admiral promised that unhappy settlers, meaning the slaves of the Southern states, would be welcome aboard British vessels, freed from bondage, and sent to British possessions in North America and the West Indies, "where they will meet with all due encouragement."[1]

Pierce Butler was reminded of the similar pronouncement issued by the earl of Dunmore during the Revolution. In his mind it was, once again, a dangerous emancipation proclamation that might well lead to violent insurrection and to the loss of much of his valuable "Negro property." Admiral Cochrane's proclamation was far more realistic than Lord Dunmore's. The Revolution had altered the British position in that the loss of the American colonies removed six hundred thousand slaves from the empire. In 1814, it was not Great Britain who was the greatest slaveholding nation in the world. With slavery no longer the economic force it had been, abolitionists came to the forefront in England and were better able to argue

170

their cause. Where British intentions had been good in the Revolution, fulfillment was miserable. In 1814 the offer of freedom was meaningful and gave the unfortunate slave a brighter promise for the future.[2]

At first the British raided the shorelines of Chesapeake Bay and Virginia plantations suffered greatly. Occasional raids were made on South Carolina—some prior to the Cochrane proclamation. In August 1813, Charles Cotesworth Pinckney told of the theft of Negroes from the Port Royal area by two brigs "who had for some time blockaded this port and burnt a schooner of my sister's."[3] The *Times* of London reported on June 27, 1814:

> A gentleman who is just arrived from Bermuda says, that the statement in the American papers of a Proclamation having been issued by Admiral Cochrane, addressed to Negro Slaves in Southern States, is perfectly correct. It offers personal freedom, and a settlement in British possessions to all who are disposed to place themselves under our protection. The effect of this measure has been most extensive. Upwards of 700 Negroes, who had obtained their liberty, had arrived at Bermuda. And it was rumoured that between 2 and 3,000, including women and children, who had escaped from bondage, had been conveyed to Halifax, where the men met with immediate employment, at the rate of a dollar per day.[4]

The planters along the Georgia coast were lulled into a false sense of security as the conflicts of the war continued to be remote from their plantations. The pleasant quiet ended abruptly on January 10, 1815, when an expeditionary force of Royal Colonial Marines landed on Cumberland, the southernmost of Georgia's barrier islands. Unaware that Andrew Jackson had repulsed the British at New Orleans, that the United States and Great Britain had agreed to terms of peace on Christmas eve 1814 at Ghent in Belgium, Sir George Cockburn, a strong, cocksure admiral, directed the landing in Georgia. It was he who put the torch to public buildings in Washington in the awesome attack of August 1814, and who had conducted the vindictive raids on Chesapeake Bay. Few antagonists who have confronted the United States in war have won such bitter hatred. Following the ruthless burning of Washington, a citizen of Pughstown, Virginia, offered a reward of five hundred dollars for each of Admiral Cockburn's ears—"on delivery."[5]

For the next two months Admiral Cockburn waged Gilbert and Sullivan warfare on the seas, sands, and sounds of Coastal Georgia. The occupation of the islands was first directed from his flagship HMS *Albion,* anchored off Cumberland Island, and later from "Head Quarters" on the island itself. On January thirtieth British forces extended their beachhead by capturing the settlement of Frederica, and then St. Simons Island in its entirety. Three ships—the *Regulus, Manley,* and *Canso*—put Royal Marines ashore in a rare invasion where the opposing sides were soon engaged in pleasant social interplay. The British officers were hospitably received by the islanders, who, in turn, were permitted to come and go "without hindrance." Admiral Cockburn's instructions to the commanding officers of the three ships were to "bring back with them such negroes as may be willing to join our standard," and this they did. An interested observer, George Baillie, reported the "seducing" of the slaves was done by the naval officers and not by the Royal Marines. The latter were "Gentlemen," in particular Marine Lieutenant John Fraser, who with his brother William Fraser, the distinguished surgeon to the expedition, successfully courted planters' daughters and remained in Georgia when Admiral Cockburn and his ships sailed away. Mr. Baillie told of British naval officers who were shameless in soliciting the slaves, even going so far as to tell them the queen of England was a black woman. He told of "reprehensible" acts of these men. They raided island poultry yards, and one of their number, named "Horton," broke into Major Butler's cabinets and stole his silver spoons.[6]

Major Butler's great concern was not his poultry and silver spoons but his slaves. Despite the very casual state of warfare that existed on the islands, there was genuine apprehension and considerable loss to the Americans whose slave quarters were decimated by the persuasive British. At Cannon's Point, where John Couper's treatment of his slaves was considered to be exemplary, his driver Tom did a bit of persuading on his own. Tom, a devout Mohammedan from the village of Silla on the Niger in the Foolah nation, and held in awe by his fellow slaves, could speak with authority on British treatment. He had been their slave in the West Indies and warned that life on St. Simons was preferable to anything the British might promise. He convinced half of those Couper slaves who had accepted the British offer to return to their quarters. Thomas Spalding's plantation on Sapelo was just beyond the sphere of British activity. He armed his slaves as if to dare the British to threaten his existence. Nonetheless, there was agitation among his slaves, who, as had John Couper's, received temperate care. This reaction of the slaves surprised the planters, who seemed blind to their intense desire for freedom.[7]

Admiral Cockburn passed on information to Admiral Cochrane that the occupation of St. Simons had proved to be fruitful for the captain of the *Regulus,* who led the foray: "The quantity of Merchandize found upon these islands and the numbers of Refugees who have joined him has induced him to prolong his stay."[8]

Three days before the actual landing on Cumberland, Roswell King became aware of the British presence in the vicinity of Hampton. He responded with great vigor, so much so that Catherine King was moved to tell Major Butler: "The anxiety I have for my husband's safety is very great. He is not only exposed to the enemy, but the weather also, for he moves at all hours night or day. He has an awning for his boat, and never loses sight of the schooner, but that is cold comfort, such very cold weather."[9]

Roswell King viewed the British invasion of St. Simons Island with trepidation and fear. Charged with the responsibility of protecting the Pierce Butler properties, he truly misread the signals coming from Major Butler's slaves. On January 20, 1815, he wrote to sound the alarm:

> I fear this is the last letter I shall write to you for a time, and I write this day for fear the Enemy will be here before my usual day of writing. With all my exertions I have Only got to Market 216 Tierces Rice, and all the old Crop of Cotton. The first 30 bales of new Cotton I put on board Mr. Couper's sloop *under deck,* and by stupid management it never started, and is now on board up the river as high as it can go, and I have 57 bales more in boats as high as I think will be safe and I must build a house to keep it out of the weather. The boats that was coming down with the Corn have all gone back—we must eat Rice and I expect the Enemy will take all we have pounded out, which is abo 300 tierces. I have stopped pounding Rice and Ginning Cotton, and drove the oxen back. By what I learn from Cumberland and St. Mary's we shall not have any kind of stock left that they can catch or Negro that they can persuade away, Cotton, Tobacco, or provisions that they can lay there hands on.[10]

Roswell King had just returned from Fernandina where he had marketed plantation produce and had provided Major Butler with $26,253.65— "money to support your family." While in Florida, he chanced upon Admiral Cockburn's secretary:

> Bro't on a Conversation on the subject of this unnatural war. I observed to him it was suspected the Negroes would be incouraged to rise and Massacre the Inhabitants, and that very many was moving off. He said *We have*

Admiral Sir George Cockburn. The burning of Washington is shown in the background. (Painting by J. J. Halls. National Maritime Museum, London.)

Admiral Sir Alexander Inglis Forrester Cochrane. (Engraving after a painting by Sir William Beechey. National Maritime Museum, London.)

Come to Conquer, and said they should use all means to Induce the
Negroes to join in the Conquest, but declared upon his honr that they
would take no Negro that had rather live with Master.

Mr. King assured the Major his efforts to represent so much property
"before a desperate Enemy" were taken seriously: "I shall keep myself
Cool, determined and resolute. You may depend on the best of my Judgement in going through the troubles that are near at hand. If I fail in Judgement you are a Ruined Man." Roswell King did not underestimate the
troubles. The British had landed approximately 2,500 troops near St.
Mary's. He said that 1,600 of these were black, who "behave better than
the white," and that these were being joined by those deserting from the
Georgia plantations. He ended his long letter with good words—"Your
Negroes truly behave well"—and a fervent "God Help us."[11]
    Major Butler wrote later that Roswell King's judgment *had* failed. He
had sent cotton high up the Altamaha River, had driven oxen into the
deep woods, but had done nothing to protect his most valuable property,
the Hampton slaves. Major Butler could not understand why the slaves
had not been taken upriver to some place where they would be beyond
the tempting offers that came from the British. Mr. King was mistaken in
his expressed belief that the slaves were behaving well, and Major Butler
blamed his manager with the interesting thought that Roswell King had
"confided too generally in the attachment of the Negroes to me."[12] He
was given the bad news in a short letter from a much disturbed Mr. King,
who had been held incommunicado—"a British Prisoner for Thirteen
days." On February 12, Roswell King's letter from Hampton described
what had happened on the Butler plantations: "There had been no per-
sonall ill treatment to the Inhabitants either by Officer or Soldier, but it
appears all Moveable property belongs to the King; not even Cotton in
Seed escapes. And the Negroes are all declared free that will go off with
them, and the most of yours as well as the others on this Island appear to
have a wish to try their New Master."[13]
    The presence of the British forces on the islands was viewed with alarm
in Savannah, where the effects of the war with Great Britain and the difficulty between Britain and France had already been detrimental to ocean
commerce, the lifeblood of the city. Pierce Butler certainly felt the war's
effect, for in 1811 he chartered the ship *Two Generals* to transport 550
bales of cotton from Hampton to St. Petersburg in Russia. The ship was
seized by French privateers and detained in Copenhagen, where for

months the cargo was in jeopardy. Savannahians had good reason to be apprehensive, for the British had planned to use their island beachhead to mount an attack on the city. The British leader, Admiral Cockburn, was well known as the "barbarian" marauder who had humiliated America by standing in the Speaker's chair in his muddy boots and ordering the new capitol in Washington burned. The Savannah reaction to his occupation of Georgia's sea islands was to bring in United States troops, augment the militia, organize vigilance committees, and order the residents—whites, free Negroes, and slaves—to assist in "throwing up breast works around the city." When Savannah learned the war had ended, the city council ordained a celebration by setting aside "a day for innocent recreation and amusement." Conditions on St. Simons were not conducive to such merriment.[14]

Even before the war, Roswell King had demonstrated his inability to cope with, or to understand, the actions and reactions of the slaves in his charge. The depredations of the British and the departure of the Butler slaves to the British ships at Cumberland put him in a vituperative frenzy. He wrote Major Butler:

> It is not you, and myself, but the Inhabitants generally have all been deceived in the Ethiopian race. Your son's observation is now verified, that Negroes have neither honr or Gratitude.

> God cursed the Negroe by making him Black. I Curse the Man that brot the first from Africa, and the Curse of God is still on them, to send them away to die a miserable death. I have no doubt the Negroes will be got back in time of Peace, but who can look at Negroes that have been so humanely treated as yours. I cannot write I am in too much pain. I am your friend in Distress.[15]

> It appears that I shall never be fit for much active business, I cannot git the use of my limbs, and as for my mind I can never git over the Baseness of your ungrateful Negroes. I cannot write nor do I know fairly what is best to be done. We have only Eight field Workers left on St. Simons, not a Shoemaker or Tanner left. 3 blacksmiths left, Jack, Sawney and Boy Billy (They was at Butler Island at work) 2 bricklayers left—Jimmy and Sancho. Sancho was here and his mother took all his clothes and Blankets from him and left him naked, but he would not go with his family. You have always, and I have these Twelve years past taken all means to make these ungrateful retches comfortable but it is all nonsense and folly. To treat Negroes with humanity is like giving Pearls to Swine, it is throwing away Value and giting insult and ingratitude in return.[16]

Roswell King divided his bitterness between the Negroes and the British.

> It gives me pain to think how you will react to this act of British Plunder,
> but you have one Consolation (that very many others have not) that you
> have left plenty of Bread to eat. I hope it will have no other effect than that
> you will devote the most of your time to invent ways and means to brake
> down that nation called Englishmen, for the good of posterity, for it will
> not be many years before they are at us again—they must he humbled or
> we ruined.

> But it is painful to look at such ungrateful rascals as your Negroes, when I
> know they would have gone off if they only had a chance. Two weeks more
> of War would have ruined the Sea Coast of Georgia. The British now have
> got abo Two Thousand Negroes. I can say no more—I am Your Faithful
> Servant.[17]

The Negroes he did not wish to "look at" were those at Butler's Island
who were not solicited by the British. Had they been, Major Butler's
losses would have been far greater. On March 4, Mr. King set out for
Cumberland "to see after the property the British have robed you of." His
health remained poor, his spirits low. He hoped to find and to persuade
Butler people to return:

> But how do you suppose I shall feel towards your foolish and ungrateful
> Negroes. But if you never git any of them back you have been a fortunate
> man to lose so few considering all circumstances. Those at the Rice Island
> have been very Rebelious, did but little for some weeks, some totally re-
> fused to work. I left them yesterday, they are planting Rice in very good
> order. I told Harry to be moderate with them until I could enquire into
> their conduct. I shall not plant largely to the hand for fear of consequences.
> I call myself a humane man, but if I live I will teach them good behaviour
> before the year is out.[18]

Mr. King, with all the troubles, did his best to get on with the business of
the plantations. The sugar project was much in his mind, and he had high
hopes for its success. The cane had been planted before the British came.
Had it not been: "I should have no heart to begin for my feelings are such
that I cant bare the sight of a Negro without Melancholy Irritation. Those
animals must be ruled with a rod of iron, which must be painful to yourself, as well as me. We have so long tryed to make them responsible
beings."[19]

Roswell King's agitation was aggravated on finding the British had come to the islands *after* the agreement to end the war. He was not alone, for Thomas Spalding and Captain Thomas M. Newell, on behalf of the planters, called on Admiral Cockburn at Cumberland. They were armed with a copy of the *National Intelligencer* that told of the Christmas Eve agreement for peace and of the treaty's ratification on February 17, 1815. They demanded the return of the fugitive slaves and of other confiscated property. The doughty admiral first refused to acknowledge the treaty and made the men painstakingly transcribe it in their own handwriting and then attest it to be a true copy. After this exercise in penmanship, he contended the Americans were rightfully entitled to those who defected *after* the ratification on February 17, and that property on Cumberland Island not on board British ships would be returned. Eighty-one slaves were returned to their owners, and most of those were sent to plantations on Cumberland. The admiral was insistent that those who had come to the British before eleven o'clock on the night of February 17 had gained their freedom and would not be returned.[20]

Admiral Sir Alexander Cochrane appeared on the scene on his flagship HMS *Tonnant*. The two admirals conferred; the senior officer backed Admiral Cockburn completely. He restated his order to the two Americans and emphasized that Admiral Cochrane "concurs with me in this opinion."[21] Mr. Spalding and Captain Newell were permitted to speak to those who had left and to urge their return to their owners. In a dramatic scene, "hundreds" of the fugitives were gathered on the deck of the HMS *Regulus,* and despite the pleas and promises of the planters' emissaries, only thirteen agreed to go back to their plantations and to slavery. One of these was a Butler slave from Hampton. Five belonged to John Couper, six came from Captain Alexander Wylly's Village Plantation on St. Simons, and one had been owned by a "Major Johnstone."[22]

Admiral Cockburn was firm in his direction that the people who sought refuge with the British were to be protected. He expressed his thoughts to his superior, Admiral Cochrane: "I find it stated by Blackstone, Book I, Chap 1, Page 127 (even before our laws abolishing the Slave trade) that the 'Spirit of Liberty is so deeply implanted in our very Soil that a *Slave or a Negro,* the moment he lands in England falls under the Protection of the Laws, and so becomes a Freeman.'" He was moved to ask, in view of Blackstone, should not he offer protection even after the ratification of peace?[23]

St. Simons planters followed their initial efforts on Cumberland with an additional complaint from Thomas Spalding to Admiral Cockburn that many of the slaves who went to the British after ratification had not returned to their owners, and that some who had, escaped again and "will unquestionably attempt to reach your ships."[24]

Roswell King obtained a copy of the peace treaty. On reading and re-reading, he took heart and believed the slaves would return. If and when they did reappear, he had a plan: "How it will please me to have the pleasure to git your Negroes back and pick out one husband, one wife, one fellow, one Wench and sell them—leaving there children or parents behind as it may happen to reflect on there wanton, Impudent folly. I pray God to help me do Justice between a *Good Master* and ungrateful servants."[25]

The British ships dispersed with their cargoes of "Supernumeraries," most of whom went to Bermuda with Admiral Cockburn, where Thomas Spalding, John Couper, and Roswell King pursued them. The message to Pierce Butler said: "Mr. Couper and myself have concluded for to go immediately to Bermuda before the Negroes git scattered. We are both sanguin that if we can find the Negroes most of them will be willing to return. It is said they are badly treated at Bermuda and dying very fast."[26] Thomas Spalding was the official representative. He had been sent by Thomas Pinckney, who was acting for President Madison. John Couper and Roswell King were on their own, the latter smarting from the loss of Major Butler's best workers. Mr. King was accompanied by a slave, Carpenter Abraham, who had been the principal accomplice in restraining those Butler's Island slaves who were strongly inclined to join their Hampton counterparts who defected to the "new master."[27]

The mission of Spalding, King, Couper, and Carpenter Abraham was of no avail, the long journey in vain. They were not permitted to use their persuasive powers on the few Georgia blacks then in Bermuda. Most had already been shipped on to Halifax. Admiral Cockburn was adamant in his refusal, saying he "would rather Bermuda and every man, woman and child in it were sunk under the sea than surrender one slave who had sought protection under the flag of England."[28] The admiral had noted that the refugees found an obstruction to their freedom "in consequence of the Colonial Law at Bermuda respecting People of Colour." With the door closed, they were detained at the Naval Dock Yard pending their being sent to Nova Scotia, where: "The Liberality of the Laws at Halifax do not oppose any difficulty on account of colour to People landing there and endeavouring by honest labour to earn their own maintenance."[29]

Roswell King's anger and frustration had begun to simmer down even before the Bermuda expedition. "Bricklayer Pompey has come home," he wrote Major Butler. Pompey, twenty-one years old and valued at nine hundred dollars, was the one Butler slave who changed his mind. Mr. King did sense a feeling of disappointment and dissatisfaction in Major Butler, and rightly so: "Do not think I shall be violent with your Negroes. They are more to be pittyed than blamed. It is the British policy (that God suffers to be a scurge and Curse on all Nations that know them) that is to blame."[30] Fortunately for the slaves, Mr. King directed much of this antipathy to the distant British. He defended his trip to Bermuda, but admitted he was "simple" to think the British would have permitted the Negroes to return. He believed implicitly: "There is no doubting the truth that the Negroes are in the hands of as great rascals as on Earth."[31]

In Philadelphia, Pierce Butler's irritation slowly mounted. He, too, blistered the British government in letters to his Liverpool agents Harrisons and Latham and to Roswell King. The latter was relieved that Major Butler's wrath was focused on Admiral Cockburn, and he approved of the Major's intention to sue the villain in the British courts. To his English agents, the irate Major wrote:

> The resentment—the disgust that prevails in this Country at this day to Britain is stronger and more general than after the Revolutionary War. There has been by your present Rulers of Your Country, a constant unnecessary animosity and haughtiness practiced towards the United States, that wounds the feelings of men and rouses resentment. "*Flog the damned Yankiis*" was and is the feeling of Lord Liverpool and the Cabinet.

On hearing that Bonaparte had fallen, Major Butler told his friends that England "will be obliged to be at Peace," except that, and with Admiral Cockburn in mind: "This will be considered by her Navy and some others in England as a misfortune."[32]

When the British came to Hampton, they confiscated an odd assortment of plantation tools and supplies, including tanned leather, raw hides, paint, rum, brandy, Irish whiskey, and—a telling blow to Major Butler—"abo 20 dozen of old wine." Roswell King regretted the loss of forty bales of cotton and two tierces of rice weighing 1,386 pounds. Mrs. King and her helper Betty lamented losing "16 geese, 37 turkeys, 7 ducks and 12 sheep." Except for Lieutenant Horton, who was "no Gentleman," the British behaved surprisingly well. In addition to "2 or 3 doz silver spoons," Horton stole "10 or 12 boxes soap and candles." Also, he carted away much of Major Butler's bottled spirits but, even worse, took off with a fifteen-year-old slave girl, Dido, one of those who defected. She was worth $450. Roswell King admitted that the British "might have done much worse than they did," excepting of course their removal of so many of the Butler slaves.[33]

On the plantations, Roswell King struggled to reestablish the old routine. His health improved. He did, however, turn more frequently to young Roswell, who had kept things together when his father traveled to Bermuda. Despite the reduced work force, the attending to slaves, planting, harvesting, and marketing went on as before. The building of the sugar mill, interrupted by the war, resumed. The emphasis on sugar irritated Major Butler, for he believed the real money crop was being neglected. "I have written him to put People at the Cotton," he told his Liverpool agents. The slaves at Butler's Island were "sickly." Hampton's wife Lenah died of a high fever, and Quash's Judy was in a "deep decline." Roswell King had written that while the "Savage British" were on the island he could "Hardly speak or breathe." For a change, he seemed to be doing both rather well.[34]

Pierce Butler lost 138 slaves to the British—not so many as James Hamilton, who lost 238 from his Hamilton plantation, but many more than John Couper's 60. The value of the Butler slaves was $61,450, as first calculated by Roswell King, Jr. Eleven of the slaves were over 45, fifty-seven from 18 to 45, thirty-six aged 10 to 18, and thirty-four children under 10. Three women from Five Pound Tree were among the 138. An affidavit made by Roswell King following the departure of the British at Hampton gave an explicit account of the departure of the slaves. In the midst of this recitation his anger overcame his reason:

> I tried to reason with some of the most sensible of the Negroes not to be so foolish and deluded as to leave their comfortable homes and go into a strange country where they would be separated, and probably not half live the year out. I found none of the negroes insolent to me, they appeared sorry, solemn, and often crying, they appeared to be infatuated to a degree of madness. While endeavouring to reason them out of their folly, some said they must follow their daughters, others their wives. I found my reasoning had no effect on a set of stupid negroes, half intoxicated with liquor and nothing to do but think their happy days had come. Five old negroes went off that had no work to do only for themselves for these four to fifteen years past. Many others started but were obliged to return finding

they were not able to walk to headquarters (Frederica) about 7 miles. Many went off and left their children, others carried off children from their parents and all relations, some left their wives and others their husbands.[35]

The St. Simons planters hired John McPherson Berrien, the distinguished Savannah attorney, contracting to pay two dollars for each slave returned. Roswell King thought Judge Berrien to be "a very propper man," and with John Couper and James Hamilton agreed to the arrangement.[36]

The struggle to have the British return the slaves was soon abandoned, for it was believed they had been dispersed to British possessions over much of the New World. In June 1815, Mr. King wrote Major Butler: "My present opinion is that those Negroes are going to Nova Scotia for the purpose of forcing them to bind themselves out and by that means they will be scattered all over the West Indies and a large portion of them become slaves again. All the ordinary negroes no one will have and of course must die the first winter."[37]

Admiral Cochrane took pains to deny the charges the British were selling the blacks in the West Indies. From HMS *Tonnant* in the sound below Cumberland Island, he wrote James Monroe, the American secretary of state:

> I have no hesitation in declaring, that I do not believe any negro, either free or slave, who had taken refuge on board the fleet under my command, has at any time been sent to the West Indies, the whole were either ordered to the island of Bermuda or to Halifax. I further declare that none of those persons have been kept in a state of slavery, but suffered to go wherever they thought proper. As the local laws of Bermuda did not permit their settling there, until opportunities offered of their being sent to Halifax, they and their families were maintained at the public expense, and those who performed any work were regularly paid for same.[38]

Thus, Roswell King was correct about Nova Scotia, for British records reveal that 139 of the Butler people were moved from ship to ship and ultimately discharged in that northern land. A case in point would be the Negroes George (the shoemaker), Cato, March, Abram (a ginner), and Sam—all having been given the last name of Butler. These five men were taken on board HMS *Terror* on February 15, 1815, to HMS *Erebus* on March 15, to HMS *Albion* on March 18, to the dock yard at Bermuda on March 30, and to Melville Island in Halifax harbor from HMS *Brune* on

May 3. Sam, who died while aboard *Albion*, was buried at sea. Lists of the Negroes received at Nova Scotia between April 1815 and October 1818 show a total of 139 bearing the name Butler. All together, there were 1,663 former slaves received during the two and one-half years. Of the 139 Butlers, many were young children born after the exodus from Georgia. The first of the 139 to arrive in Nova Scotia was one of the four "Joes" who defected to the British. He was Joe Bull Butler, his middle name showing this Joe Butler to have come down from the Bull inheritance of Pierce Butler's dead wife.[39]

The moving about caused much confusion, as did the listing by name. As a slave was often known among his peers by a name other than that used by his owners, the names on the British lists were at variance with those from the plantations. The blacks sometimes chose surnames of their own, being unaware, or perhaps uncaring, that the British had given them the names of their former owners. Too, a young woman from one of the Cumberland plantations might well have taken up with a "fellow" from Hampton and thus be given the name Butler. The dispersal by the British followed the pattern already set in the Revolution. There is even a chance that the Butler refugees of 1815–1818 found Middleton-Bull people, or their issue, at the black settlements on the fringes of the Nova Scotian townships of Halifax, Shelburne, and in Guysborough County. In their brief stays at Bermuda they may have found kinfolk from an earlier time.[40]

One of the arguments Roswell King had used in trying to persuade the Butler slaves to reject the British offer of freedom was that many would die aboard ship. Those who had known the horrors of the midpassage understood this point full well. The British had countered by telling the refugees that to die in bondage would send them to hell. Old Sam Butler, who died aboard the *Albion*, and William and Rose Butler, who died aboard the *Surprise*, must have taken some comfort in realizing they were dying free and thus were heaven-bound.[41]

Melville Island, the landing point in Nova Scotia of most of the Butler blacks, is a rocky projection of approximately three acres in the Northwest Arm of Halifax harbor. In 1815 it was converted from a military stockade to a receiving station for Admiral Cockburn's refugees. The former slaves from the Georgia coastal islands joined others from the Chesapeake Bay area who had immigrated earlier in the war and in much the same fashion, except that some of the Chesapeake slaves had been seized by the British sailors and marines and taken to Nova Scotia against their will. Both groups enlarged a small black population that began with the arrival of Loyalists who fled America during or following the Revolution, and who brought with them what property they could manage, including their slaves. In the Nova Scotia of 1815 were the remnants of approximately three thousand blacks promised their freedom in Lord Dunmore's proclamation of 1775, and also some few leftovers from an unusual group of five to six hundred "untamed" imports from Jamaica. Most of these so-called "Maroons," who were strongly laced with Coromantee blood, were shipped to Sierra Leone in 1800 following an initial exodus in 1792, when 1,190, or one-third, of the black population of Nova Scotia chose to migrate to Africa.[42]

The Butler people who disembarked at Melville Island were retained there for a time, some as long as fourteen months. There they were provisioned, clothed, and protected against the formidable climate. A few were among the five hundred who were immediately transhipped to St. John, in New Brunswick, and who from there helped to establish the black community in Loch Lomond. After the security of Melville Island the refugees found themselves facing bitter reality in isolated communities on the outskirts of Halifax. A few of the Butlers—Isaih, Tenah, and families included—settled at a community called Preston. The most interesting concentration occurred at the community of Hammond's Plains. There, on escheated land expressly dedicated to their use, many Butler people joined others from St. Simons Island in Georgia in what appeared to be a distant outpost of Glynn County. Among the people settling there were Kings, Hamiltons, McIntoshes, Wyllys, and Coupers—the latter two having undergone a slight change to "Wileys" and "Coopers." The Butlers were Maringo, two Williams, Sampson, Isaac, Francis, Hector, Joseph, Georgia, and Abraham. Most had wives and a child, or children. While many are difficult to identify from the list of slaves sent Major Butler by Roswell King, the names do appear with but few exceptions among the Butler "supernumeraries" transported to Nova Scotia on His Majesty's ships.[43]

Roswell King found it difficult to accept the loss of the Butler slaves. On hearing of their presence in Nova Scotia he made a final effort to bring them home. His failure was reported to Major Butler: "I got a letter from Messrs Bower & Deblais of Halifax wherein they inform me that they can find none that wish to return except some old ones that are not worth sending. They say a number have actually gone to *Boston* already, and are hunting places where they can." Mr. King told of Thomas Spalding's trip to Halifax as an emissary of James Monroe, secretary of state, a mission that also failed.[44]

Although efforts to retrieve the lost slaves were abandoned, the planters continued their pursuit of the British, hoping to obtain reparations for their loss of property. For Major Butler, there was no satisfaction during his lifetime. In the years before his death he corresponded with John Couper and William Page, and continued to berate Roswell King for his role in the loss of his people. Both Mr. Couper and Mr. King believed the planters were entitled to recover the monetary value of their slaves and other property, and in addition, believed they should be compensated for the crops lost due to the absence of those who would have planted, cultivated, and harvested. Mr. Couper contended his losses in slaves, property, and potential crops amounted to $204,000. He recommended the retention of Thomas Spalding and John McPherson Berrien as the best qualified to protect their interest, notwithstanding their failure to retrieve the lost slaves. Based on the Couper projection, the Butler claim would have exceeded $500,000. The actual claims against the British were pared down drastically. James Hamilton put in for $74,500, John Couper, $22,450, and the Butler estate, $56,470.[45]

Major Butler and John Couper kept each other informed as to their actions and opinions. In 1816 the Major expressed his irritation: "It is strange a Nation holding many millions of People in Slavery in India, should become Knight Errants in freeing black slaves not their own. We who have in Servitude some Coloured People have to contend with prejudices in our own Country. Some of our Sister States are hostile to us— the State of Pennsylvania particularly so. The Quakers are zealous in the cause where it cost them nothing." In 1817 he was candid in admitting the chances of recovery were slim: "I am not disappointed in getting nothing—few governments are just. Britain is too poor to be just—if she had the inclination."[46] In accordance with the Convention of 1818, the United States and Great Britain referred the dispute to a friendly sovereign, Alexander I, the tsar of Russia. The new American minister to St. Petersburg was Henry Middleton, a cousin of the Butler children and himself a slave owner. One of the reasons for being chosen was his ability to speak with conviction on the value of the slaves taken by the British. The tsar ruled for the planters, directing they be paid for their losses. Yet, it was not until 1826 that an amount was set. The British agreed to pay $1,204,960 in satisfaction of all claims for slaves and other property. The claimants had come from Chesapeake Bay to Cumberland Island. One was Roswell King himself, who put in for his man "Harry, healthy and active" and worth seven hundred dollars. The Butler estate finally received something in excess of seven thousand dollars, far below expectations.[47]

The loss of the Butler slaves had shattered the Major's confidence in his manager. His dissatisfaction was conveyed to Roswell King, causing the following response:

> I am discouraged in trying to manage your Estate and give Satisfaction. I am sure there never was a Man made greater exertions according to his understanding for another than I have done for you these two years past and to my great mortyfication almost all has displeased you. The Cause is Plain. I have grasped for too much. I have undertook to do more than a man can do and give Satisfaction. My great wish to do more than any one man can do had been my downfall.[48]

Major Butler's unhappiness with Mr. King caused him to be highly critical in other spheres of his work on the plantations. The Major's many suggestions and his criticism of the move into the production of sugar led Mr. King to believe that to be the source of his discontent. It was not. The Major's bitterness stemmed from the loss of almost sixty thousand dollars worth of valuable slaves, and of the crops they would have produced. He contended that the lost slaves would have cultivated four hundred acres and produced three hundred bales of cotton worth twenty pounds sterling each, an appraisal more realistic than John Couper's. He tired of Roswell King's discontent, and told him so. Their agreement when Mr. King was hired specified a method of termination: "If you are dissatisfied I would not wish you to remain. Only give me the notice the agreements require." His contention that the Hampton slaves should have been moved beyond the reach of the British was insistent. He conveyed his feelings to William Page and sought advice. Mr. Page replied:

> I frequently inquired of Mr. K. what your instructions were. He assured me that they were *not to move*.
>
> I saw Mr. K. who told me *he had no orders to move your people— therefore could not attempt it*.[49]

Mr. King, feeling put upon, asked for increased pay. Major Butler was surprised and annoyed that the request had come at such a time. In his opinion two thousand dollars was fair pay for a year's work, particularly when the amenities were considered. He recounted them to Mr. Page:

> A good house, wood, butter, milk and all my Poultry when I am not there, with a Garden.
>
> Liberty to kill a mutton and the natural advantages of Fish and Oysters— these are not to be picked up in Darien, or on the streets of Savannah.

To build his case with Mr. Page, he criticized Mrs. King, heretofore his friend:

> but the family want to be rich at once. I attribute the Sensation more to Mrs. than Mr. King. I conceive her ambition is less bounded than his—and I know her Will is Law, and everything with him. It therefore becomes necessary for me to look out for a person to succeed him.
>
> When by your advice I took him, he was poor—very poor. He has Educated his Children, raised a large family Decently, and is Comfortable. But he must be a Planter in his own right.

The Major reiterated that Mr. King should have removed the Hampton slaves: "Mr. King had my Authority to use his own Judgement as to removing all but a small number to prevent Conflagration."[50]

William Page cautioned Major Butler to move slowly, warning him that Mr. King would be difficult to replace. He suggested the Major plan a trip to Georgia to see firsthand whether or not the plantations were "illy conducted." Major Butler intended to do that, but could not then summon the energy to make the long, hard trip. And Roswell King painted a bleak picture of the plantations, hoping to keep the Major in the North. "Everything out of order. You have not a Building but wants painting, but little has been done these three years past to put your Estate in such order as you are fond of seeing it." An angry, but impotent Major Butler remained in Philadelphia: "I am disgusted with Negro property, and when I am offered the Value of what I Hold, I will take it, but nothing under the Value will I ever take." Roswell King weathered the storm.[51]

The difficulties encountered by Major Butler's "ungrateful retches" in their newfound freedom made Roswell King's troubles seem as naught. If, as historians have stated, Admiral Cockburn's blacks fared better than the Revolution's refugees, it is not surprising so many of the latter sought a better world in Sierra Leone. The War of 1812 immigrants were confronted with a stretch of bad weather that distressed seasoned Nova Scotians. The year of their arrival, 1815, was marked by a plague of rodents that overran much of the area around Halifax. It was "the year of the mice." The next year was said to be "the year without a summer" and was followed by a year that was equally grim and bitter. When discharged from Melville Island and allocated their ten-acre tracts at Preston or Hammond's Plains, they found farmland far different from that they had worked on the Altamaha delta. A scant overlayer of topsoil hardly covered a mass of broken stone that defied a shovel or a plow and could be broken only by a pickax. From their crude huts that proved inadequate to fend off the intense cold, the miserable group at Hammond's Plains turned to old skills to fashion crude brooms, baskets, shingles, or gathered wild berries to feed themselves and to sell after a fourteen-mile trek into Halifax.[52]

Nova Scotia's lieutenant governor, the earl of Dalhousie, complained to his higher authority that the refugees had become a public charge and a burden to the province: "Permit me to state plainly to Your Lordship that little hope can be entertained of settling these people so as to provide for their families and wants. They must be supported for many years. Slaves by habit & education, no longer working under the lash, their idea of freedom is idleness and they are therefore quite incapable of industry." He was then of the opinion their constitution was unequal to the climate and thought it most desirable to restore them to their masters in the United States, or to pack them off to Sierra Leone. After being unable to persuade the blacks to consider either alternative, he then suggested they accept transportation to the West Indies. This they also turned down, but later, and after a prolonged and seemingly endless cold, wet, and tortuous winter, a few seemed willing to go to Trinidad or to Tobago. Yet, not until 1821 was the Nova Scotia government successful in its attempt to promote a relocation in the British West Indies. Then, ninety-five departed for Trinidad, all of whom had lived in the desolation of Hammond's Plains. Joseph Butler, his wife, and their two children were among the twenty-eight families who at first indicated a willingness to leave Nova Scotia. Undoubtedly other former Butler slaves eventually left, for later lists of those living at Hammond's Plains showed a marked decrease in Butlers. By 1835, John Butler was the only one of that surname who remained.[53]

Following the departure in January 1821 of many former slaves for

Trinidad, which proved to be a successful venture, the lieutenant governor of Nova Scotia renewed the offer to transport additional blacks. In August of that year he was surprised to find no one willing to make the move to join their friends. He wrote his superior to explain why it was the black refugees preferred the misery of their Nova Scotia existence to a better life elsewhere, but what seemed to them a false promise: "But these people entertain so great a fear to slavery that no persuasion can induce them to remove to any place where Slavery exists."[54] Their philosophy was well expressed in a letter from Nova Scotia in the 1820s. The writer had questioned a Hammond's Plains resident:

> *How do you get along at the Plains, friend?*
> Oh, bad times now, Sir.
> *Then why do you stay here? Why not go back to your old Master in the States?*
> Oh no, that never do.
> *How so?*
> Cause, what I work for here, I gets.[55]

When confined to the government facility at Melville Island, the refugees were vaccinated to prevent an outbreak of smallpox as had descended on the earlier black immigrants. In 1827, the Hammond's Plains people were existing in their usual condition, living in their inadequate huts "with a want of clothing, bedding, nourishment and medicine." Some little nourishment had come from the few potatoes brought to harvest.[56] No wonder, then, the unfortunate community should be swept by disease—not smallpox, from which they were protected, but an epidemic of scarlet fever. No wonder, too, an observer could write:

> The negroes in this country are a degraded race. They are not allowed to eat at the same table or drink out of the same vessel; to sit on the same seat in the church or meeting house, or to be taught in the same school with white persons. They do not vote at elections, sit as jurors, or serve as militia men. Their whole treatment trains them to consider themselves as inferior beings; and in their conduct and deportment they manifest sufficient proof of their own entertainment of this position.[57]

A latter-day historian said the refugees had "unwittingly fanned the sparks of a more conscious, more organized, white racism than Nova

Scotia had known," and had done so at a time when "the last vestiges of slavery were passing." He expressed agreement with the earlier observer on the inherent and persistent feeling of inferiority: "These new arrivals clasped their freedom to them, willed themselves to do well, did not want to leave their new found land—and yet failed utterly.[58]

Chapter 12

Second Generation: The Butlers

W HEN MARY BUTLER DIED in 1790, five of their children were left in Pierce Butler's care. A letter from him to a South Carolina friend who had lost a son in Philadelphia's yellow fever epidemic mentioned other Butler children, two of whom were unknown to succeeding generations of their family:

> Out of four Sons, it has pleased God to spare me one, who is now in his sixteenth year. His name is Thomas. He has been in England for education some years. I purpose bringing him to America next year. The accounts I receive of him are favourable. I have four daughters who are with me, and great comforts they are to me. Better children no man is blest with. My eldest daughter who is also my eldest child is named Sarah. My second is Harriot, my third Frances and fourth Eliza.[1]

One of the three sons to die was the "promising prop" who succumbed to burns during the Revolution and who was a year older than Thomas. The other two do not appear in family records. Major Butler's letter puts Harriot's birth before that of Frances and Eliza, while other records show her to be the youngest daughter. He does not mention the latter two as being twins. In late 1781, well after the unfortunate death of the son, Mary Butler was banished from Charlestown by the British. She joined Major Butler in North Carolina and went on to Philadelphia with six of their children, a circumstance indicating that two of the four sons were living at the time—Thomas and a brother.[2]

Until her illness and death Mary Butler was in constant attendance to

192

the children, excepting, of course, Sarah during her English school time and Thomas, who was left with the Reverend Mr. Butler in London at the age of six and was not to see his mother again. Major Butler was often away from home and was much involved with the supervision of their far-flung plantation empire and later with the business of warfare, or refugee-ing from the British in North Carolina. His governmental responsibilities for South Carolina and on the federal scene caused long absences, as did his trip to England with Sarah and Thomas, and his subsequent visit to the Continent. Consequently, he had seen but little of his family, and when the untimely death of Mary thrust the care of the children into his unpracticed hands, he assumed a burden he knew not how to carry.

Three years before Mary's death, Major Butler had told Weeden Butler of his feelings for his children: "I live only for him and his Sisters. They are the Alpha and Omega of my Earthly Happiness."[3] The thought curiously excluded Mary Butler at a time when she was still very much alive. Yet the omission was typical of many such inconsistencies as told to Weeden Butler and to young Thomas in the letters saved by the English schoolmaster. The collection of almost two hundred letters consists of those chosen by the Reverend Mr. Butler's son and namesake: "These letters I have selected as perhaps the most valuable of a very interesting collection."[4]

Two years after Mary Butler's death, Pierce Butler again expressed his thoughts on his children in a long letter to Weeden Butler:

> I am either by Nature, habit, or something else, alive to the smallest inattentions from my Children, from those I love and regard tenderly. I know no Cold medium in friendship. In Duty and attention from my Children there can be no mediocrity if my feelings are to be attended to. I let no possible occasion slip me of promoting their future Welfare. I make great sacrifices for them. If then they wish to be Call'd my Children, there can be no Cessation of dutiful Attention.[5]

The Weeden Butler correspondence is in the Manuscript Division of the British Museum, where it was deposited in 1847 by another Thomas Butler, the grandson of the Reverend Mr. Butler and a secretary of the Museum. The letters to and from the school on Cheyne Walk in Chelsea provide a disproportionate share of information on young Thomas than that available on the other children. They also reflect the odd qualities and demanding nature of the headstrong father.[6]

After leaving the two children in their schools, Major Butler crossed the Channel in a search for a substantial loan that would fund the rejuvenation of the South Carolina plantations and the development of his Georgia lands. He wrote letters to the school in Chelsea from the Continent, then from Ireland, where he visited his family, and from Bath, where he stayed for several days.

Major Butler's principal concern was the education of his son, but in one of the early letters he expressed a parental worry over the physical well-being of Thomas: "I intended to request the favour of Mrs. Butler to get him, when the cool weather sets in, a little flannel under Vest, but in my hurry I forgot it. As he has been subject in Carolina in the Winter to Agues."[7]

Thomas was left with the bewigged schoolmaster who was known about the neighborhood as the "Bishop of Chelsea," and who was expected to be a substitute father, "Not only his principal Prop, but the Star that is to guide him through a World of Sin and Perfidy." The contract for the boy's education provided for board and tuition, including English, writing, accounts, Latin, Greek, and French, for sixty-three guineas per year. Major Butler paid an annual fee of one guinea for "pew rent" in the chapel, and a guinea each per quarter for "Dancing or Drawing." Other extras were for washing, mending, medicine; and Thomas was required to have his own bed and furniture, three blankets, two pairs of sheets, six towels, a knife, a fork, and a tablespoon. Riding lessons at the fashionable Captain James Fozzard's came later and were also extra.[8]

For a few years, beginning in 1778, the Butler School was located at 4 Cheyne Walk in Chelsea. At that time the Walk was on the bank of the Thames, close by the river and subject to occasional flooding. About the time of Thomas Butler's arrival the school was moved to number 6, into a house abandoned in 1782 by Dr. Bartholomew de Dominicetti, a Venetian nobleman who in 1765 had converted the property for his "fumigatory baths," an early-day sauna for the restoration of "infirm ladies and gentlemen of rank." There were "four spacious and lofty parlours, two dining rooms, and thirteen bedchambers." To many affluent Londoners, including Edward, the duke of York, the Italian doctor was a healing genius. To others, including Samuel Johnson, who suggested that Boswell go there to have his head steamed, Dr. Dominicetti was a quack. His bankruptcy gave Weeden Butler a fine place for expanding the school.[9]

Major Butler's great desire was that Thomas should be returned to America in his own image. How the Reverend Mr. Butler sustained eleven years of tedious direction from Pierce Butler is a tribute to his stamina. The Reverend Mr. Butler had known considerable troubles of his own, having acted as amanuensis to one of England's stranger characters, Dr. William Dodd, who was known as the "Macaroni Parson," and who was said to have "descended so low as to become the editor of a newspaper." Convicted of forgery, Dr. Dodd was hanged despite the presentation of many petitions to the king; some were written by Dr. Johnson, and one was signed by twenty-three thousand persons. While imprisoned, Dr. Dodd comforted fellow inmates and wrote many short works, typical of which was "Three Sermons on the Wisdom and Goodness of God in the Vegetable Kingdom." Weeden Butler succeeded Dr. Dodd as morning preacher at Charlotte Street Chapel, Pimlico.[10]

There can be no mystery as to the reaction of Thomas Butler to the relentless flow of admonitions from his father. They came firsthand in letters from Major Butler, and indirectly through his schoolmaster. The Major set the tone for what was to follow in his first letter written from London after leaving Thomas at the school: "I am supported in the separation by the well grounded hope of seeing him returned to me from You, not only as a Lettered Man, but strictly Virtuous, and nice in his Morals. Without Virtue and Morals Man is no better than a Sounding Brass or Tinkling Symbol—without these, of what avail is Knowledge! An enlightened Man, if he is wicked has the more to answer for."[11]

Many South Carolinians, kinfolk and friends, found their way to London. Should they choose to call on young Thomas: "I desire He may never be from you, or permitted to go out. You will therefore, with your usual politeness, decline for Him any invitations you may have."[12]

Thomas was frequently told to write letters and to do so in a proper hand. He was told with equal frequency he was expected to be an orator of merit. From Major Butler to the Reverend Mr. Butler: "Give my blessing and tender affection to my dear Thomas. As I do on some occasions, stand on etiquette. I wait to hear from Him before I write."[13] After hearing a twenty-five-year-old orator perform, Mary Butler urged her son onward. She told him she hoped to live to see Thomas "shine as he has done." Major Butler was more specific: "If in the Senate of this little Republick (meaning South Carolina) He may take a lead, or still more flattering, in the Senate of the United States, it will be some little reward to You for all your toils with Him, and for Him."[14]

In one of Thomas's letters to his family he mentioned the ensuing trial of Warren Hastings, governor of British India. In responding, Major

Butler was quick to attack the beleaguered Hastings, who in his mind was "the Wretch, the Monster in Human Shape, the Devil in the image of Man." As he often did, Major Butler quoted Scripture to impress Thomas and the Reverend Mr. Butler:

> What a disgraceful Situation has He brought himself to, to be obliged to Kneel to His fellow men. This is the consequence of Avarice, or a too great Desire for Money. Avarice is a bad Passion. Better, as Scripture tells us, is a Dinner of Herbs with an approving Mind or Conscience, than all the Riches on Earth without. What happiness can wretched Mr. Hastings derive from all his ill Gotten Wealth! None!

> I will never disgrace you my Boy by such an act. Be you equally careful not to disgrace Your Father by any mean or unjust act.

The Major ended this letter by telling Thomas to look to God:

> He will not Forsake You but will direct You in all Your Ways and be about Your bed and watch over You. To His all gracious Providence I commit You.
>
>
>
> being
> My Dearest Boy
> Yr Most Affectionate Father
> P. Butler
> [signed with a flourish]
>
>

Warren Hastings, "Monster in Human Shape," was acquitted of "high crimes and misdemeanors."[15]

As Thomas completed his fourth year in Chelsea, it became evident that he was falling short of the high expectations held by his father. An uneasy concern appeared, followed by increased anxiety and disappointment revealed in Major Butler's letters to Weeden Butler and to Thomas: "I find by every report of Him that he grows Lusty, if so, I woud wish Him to refrain from butter and the fat of meat."[16] The report of lustiness probably came from Dr. Peter Spence, a former South Carolinian who had been loyal to the British, was forced to leave following the Revolution, and experienced extremely hard times. He frequently measured the progress of Thomas for Major Butler. Such a measurement is apparent in the following letter:

> For rather, much rather woud l see Him die in Virtue than live in Vice.

On the Subject of his Education I have not one Word to say—I leave all to
Yourself. He is in Your hand. Fashion Him as you see best. Dr. Spence tells
me Thomas is not ready at the Lattin. I am free to own to You that this
information mortifies me. Yet double application must supply the want of
Capacity, for if he Lives he *must* be a Man of Letters, and I hope, an
Orator.[17]

A letter to Thomas, who was not yet ten years old:

If You had seen me, or coud have judged of my feelings when I got the
information from the Doctor, You woud have instantly said I am determined I will study day and night to prevent my poor Father from being
made so unhappy. If your Class shoud leave You behind, or if You shoud be
Last in the Class, and of course, the least inform'd, I shall wish Myself
under Ground.[18]

Major Butler's realization that Thomas was not developing into the
"shining light" he sought was apparent: "The Doctor says you are not a
bold reader. How does this happen? I woud rather see you dead than have
you Fear anything. It is better to die once than many times. The Brave
never die but once—The Coward dies daily."[19] In February 1789, a letter
in the same vein and with a bit of sad news for Thomas:

You are my Son approaching fast to your Eleventh Year. I have therefore a
right to look for some Fruits. I expect some buddings, at least, of a cultivated mind. If I am mistaken in You I shall be a miserable disappointed
Father.

Your poor little Cano is no more. She Expired some Days ago.[20]

Cano was the dog Thomas had left behind in South Carolina and often
mentioned in the family correspondence. Major Butler fed the dog himself, and had some trouble with her name—sometimes Canoe, and other
times Canno. As if Thomas did not have enough trouble with the "Lattin," and with his "Bold" reading, Major Butler brought in a true "shining light," his sister Sarah: "Your Sister Sarah has the Credit of writing a
better hand than any young (and I believe that I might add, old) Lady in
Carolina."[21] Sarah, back in America, had profited greatly in her father's
eyes from her brief English education. Major Butler followed the bit on
her handwriting by extolling her remarkable proficiencies in several fields.
He goaded Thomas on with a touch of sarcasm and, what is more,

sounded the brass and tinkled the "Symbol" as he had done five years before:

> I expect it is so long since I have seen your Writing that Your next Letter
> will be equal to Copperplate, and that I shall be informed of Your being at
> the Head of Your Class, and that you are so fond of reading and writing
> that Mr. Butler is obliged to prevent Your hurting Your Health. I woud
> rather Your health shoud suffer a little, for without Knowledge, what is
> Man—a Sounding brass or tinkling Symbol.
>
> Do you read well—Slow and Distinct, giving to each Sentence its due
> Force, and Harmonizing Your Voice to the Ear?[22]

Gentle Mary Butler asked Thomas to think of her "at least twice a day," and told him he was "never a moment from my thoughts." Yet she, too, prodded a bit after receiving a letter that showed some progress: "You see My Dear Child, how easy it is to please us when you wish and endeavor to do so. If you did know what a comfort it is to us to receive a well written letter from you no pain would be thought too great on your part to gratify us."[23]

In a letter to Weeden Butler, undated but probably written in late August 1789, Major Butler told of their recognition of their son's birthday with a gathering in his absence and honor. Lacking only "civilized society," from which he said they were "secluded," Major Butler invited Mary's Middleton relatives:

> It was determined that We must shew some mark of regard to the 15th of
> August. The Table was accordingly to feel the weight of a fond Mother's
> affection by having three times the Number of Dishes it usually supported.
> Among them were two that I much wished to transport to Cheyne Row, a
> Wild Turkey and a Haunch of Venison—the first cost One Shilling and two
> pence, the latter One Shilling—So that You See We made a great feast with
> little cost. The Cloth removed we drank in great form, the Day, and the
> Worthy Guides that are Guiding Our Boy, so that he may make His light
> shine before Men, and also Glorify His Heavenly Father.[24]

The following month, after a reasonably good report on reading and writing, Major Butler took issue with Thomas on his "Lattin" and again told of Sarah's prowess in her studies. He mentioned Harriot's skill in "Mathematicks" and warned the Reverend Mr. Butler "How mortified shall I be" should Thomas's sisters leave him behind. He did take some comfort in hearing that Thomas read well, "without singing or stammering." Anxious that Thomas be a well-rounded young gentleman, Major Butler queried the schoolmaster: "Does my Boy continue under the hands of the dancing master? I wish him to do so. As he grows up I wish, if it meets with your Approbation, that he shoud Learn to Draw, to fence and to ride."[25]

In 1790 Mary Butler's illness brought serious troubles into the lives of the family. Hoping to ease Mary's discomfort, the Butlers visited the seashore of Long Island while Major Butler attended to his senatorial chores in New York City. For a short time they were all together, and Mary seemed to improve. Leaving her with Frances, Major Butler returned to the city and found a "cool, pleasant House open to the Harbour." He relentlessly pursued the Reverend Mr. Butler and Thomas, striving always to "Have my Boy Qualified in a more than Ordinary manner for a Public Character." He told how it was in New York: "The boys here repeat from Demosthenes, Cicero, Shakespeare and other Authors as their Preceptors Direct or make Choice. I have heard two of them, one Nine years old, the other Seven, deliver the discourse between Brutus and Cassius with astonishing perfection." Major Butler seized that opportunity to tell how he was directed on short notice to read a tribute from South Carolina to President Washington. He spoke to a "brilliant" audience, including the president: "I felt awkward before I began, not having had time given me, but adopting the plan I recommended to my Boy of repeating Slowly and Distinctly I got through with some Eclat."[26] Thomas was urged to earn future "Eclat" of his own, but not before receiving a short essay on winning "love and Esteem":

> I love the Virtuous, just and good. I detest the wicked and unjust. I despise an Ignorant Man tho clothed in purple and fine Linnen. If you wish then for my love and Esteem You must read a great deal, by which Knowledge is to be Got. You must write a fine fair hand.
>
> My hopes on this Side of the Grave Center in You my Son, my only Son. When I am old and good for nothing I aim to look for Respect from being the Father of a Man who by this ability, Wisdom and Power of Elocution takes the lead in the Great families of his Country, who need only to rise to Command Silence and Attention in Order to shew his Country-Men the Road to Honour, Freedom and Greatness.

Major Butler then added to his son's discomfort by writing:

Your poor Mother fell into indisposition at not receiving any acct of You by the Packet. You must write Oftener.

Are you Victorious over all the difficulties of the Lattin? Surely You are! Write me what You are reading and exactly how You pass every hour in the day.[27]

The death of Mary Butler in November 1790 brought anguish to the Butler family. For a time, there was a cessation of directives from Pierce Butler to the schoolboy and his master in London, but not for long. A sad note was sounded in May 1792: "I find with some degree of Mortification, yet with resignation to the dispensation of Providence that Tom's parts are not bright."[28]

The Butler girls assumed some feeling of parental responsibility and freely dispensed wisdom and advice to their brother. A letter from Sarah: "I admire the noble sentiments of Caesar, that he would rather be the first Man in a miserable Village in the Alps which he passed on his march, than the second in the City of Rome. I do not mean the first in power for that is not worth a wish, but in merit and true greatness."[29] Sarah's handwriting must have made Thomas a little nervous, for it was what her father called true "copperplate." It was as though etched, or engraved— precise in its formal execution. Eliza was more considerate in her message, written in a fine, flowing hand: "Our Cousin Mrs. Blake desires me to remember Her affectionately to You and is concerned that Her constant indisposition prevents Her from writing to You."[30] Thomas had sent a drawing to his father that was passed on to the ailing Elizabeth Blake. He asked Thomas to send two more, one for Mrs. Anne Graeme and the other "for my own gratification," yet was quick to complain to the Reverend Mr. Butler that the drawing had "the masterly touch of the Teacher's": "That is not my object. I can Buy Drawings and Prints in profusion, but I want to see what *He* can do. Fencing, Riding, Drawing and Dancing I wish to go on, but they are Secondary objects and must yield, if found necessary, to more important requirements." In this letter, Major Butler took note once again that Thomas fell short of expectations. He urged increased applications, citing his Irish countryman Jonathan Swift, who studied thirteen hours a day for eight years:

I observe, tho Express'd with all that delicacy which marks and distinguishes every act and Sentiment of Yours, that my Son has no just claim to brilliance of parts—to quick, great or bold Conceptions. I will not try to

Conceal my Chagrin and disappointment. At the same time I thank You for Your Candor. I must and do submit to the Will of Him who gave the Child to me. Yet I am obliged to Adopt and make known to You a new Regulation in consequence of Your information. It is to buy what dint of Application will do.

Shall I have one Son only and he alone the Blockhead of my Family?[31]

Major Butler also noted that Thomas Pinckney and young George Izard had shown a cordial interest in seeing Thomas. Major Butler discouraged future visits: "Polite attention to a Country-Man is one thing, and Intimacy, another."[32]

In the fall of 1791 Charles Butler, a son of Weeden Butler, visited Charleston and made a most favorable impression. He followed a career at sea despite advice to the contrary from Butlers on both sides of the Atlantic. Major Butler saw to it that shoats and sheep and plenty of poultry were sent to his ship from the Butler plantation at the Euhaws. Early in 1792 Charles became seriously ill and Major Butler hurried to Charleston, much concerned over the condition of the young son of his English friend. An unexpected recovery—"the very next thing to a Resurrection"—was described in a letter to London. In midyear Charles rejoined his ship, the *Olive Branch*.[33]

Following the death of Elizabeth Blake, Major Butler mentioned to the Reverend Mr. Butler that Thomas had been left approximately two thousand pounds. He later passed on an unfounded rumor that Mrs. Blake's estate was insufficient to cover debts: "Mention this to my Son that he may know He has no other person to look to but me. I wish him to look to no other."[34]

Through the years of the correspondence between Pierce and Weeden Butler, the Major often tried the patience of his son's schoolmaster. His constant and repetitious stream of directives and suggestions, his pro-French, anti-British attitude, the frequent delinquency of his account with the school, and particularly Major Butler's dissatisfaction with the progress of his son—all contributed to a feeling of uneasiness on Weeden Butler's part. He welcomed the approaching departure of his American student.

A planned departure was delayed, and the letters from the family continued. Frances urged Thomas to emulate "Plinny" and to "Get Knowledge, search it wheresoever you can." Their father directed the schoolmaster to have Thomas write to Sarah in French and to Major Butler in

English and Spanish "when he can write Spanish." Harriot Percy wrote that Major Butler was much indisposed, "more so than for fifteen years past."[35]

In July 1795, seventeen-year-old Thomas Butler embarked for Philadelphia after an eleven-year separation from his family. He traveled attended by a servant, a man who was to continue in the Butlers' employ in the house on Chestnut Street. Major Butler had asked Weeden Butler to order and to surprise Thomas with a handsome coat of "best cloth," a silk vest, black silk culottes, six pairs of silk stockings, and a "new fashionable Hatt." The Reverend Mr. Butler was unable to fill an order for a second servant, "a good woman cook—a Motherly industrious woman."[36]

A long passage brought a reunion with his sisters in September and in the following month with his father. Thomas wrote to thank the Butlers on Cheyne Walk: "By every Tie, Dear Sir, have you attached me to you. To the last moment of my Existence, I shall feel the obligations I am under to you and Mrs. Butler."[37]

Major Butler wrote, expressing his "gratitude and thanks" for the Reverend Mr. Butler's long care of Thomas, "who I have at Length embraced." A month later, having had time to observe his son, he wrote his own evaluation to the schoolmaster:

> You will naturally expect I shoud say something of my Son to You. As far as I have seen of His disposition I have reason to be satisfied. With respect to his acquirements: In Greek he is backward. In Lattin not perfect. He reads English tolerably, he speaks French. Of his acquirements of the Spanish I am not Competent to Judge. In Mathematicks he is Young. His hand writing is not Good. And if He is not forward as my Feelings prompt me to wish, I am well satisfied He had had every parental attention from you.[38]

Major Butler then wrote that he planned to return Thomas to Chelsea for specific tutelage under the Reverend Mr. Butler's son, also called Weeden. This intelligence prompted an immediate reply. If "Publick Life" was to be the Major's goal for Thomas, the elder Weeden Butler thought he should attend college in America: "Your Son, in Sentiment, Spirit and Conduct I verily believe is morally and strictly virtuous. Where can he better so remain, or so happily secure as in the Bosom of his Country?"[39] Attached to this letter is a tart comment from James Neild, Esquire: "Melancholy, but capital letter from Rev. Weeden Butler declining a resumption of the too burdensome responsibility which he had borne with exemplary zeal from Sept 1784 to July 1795." Mr. Neild gave an evaluation of Thomas somewhat more realistic than that of his schoolmaster or of his father:

> The youth was endowed by nature with plain parts & a good disposition, but either discouragement by a father's constant importunities or deprest possibly by a severe complaint in his head—he improved slowly and his memory was not strong. But though trite the truth of the adage *Exquovis liguo non fit Mercurios* is not always perceptible by parental fondness. In the present instance the virtues of the heart amply compensated any deficiency in mental talent and book learning.[40]

James Neild, Esquire, was the Reverend Mr. Butler's friend, neighbor, and benefactor.

Weeden Butler's *finis* to the eleven-year effort to educate Thomas was a four-line verse sent to Major Butler in Philadelphia:

> *Our Passions gone, and Reason on her Throne*
> *Amaz'd we see the Mischiefs we have done*
> *After the Tempest, when the Storms are Laid*
> *The* Calm Sea *wonders at the* Wrecks *it made.*[41]

IN A RATHER EMOTIONAL LETTER to the Reverend Mr. Butler written some years before Thomas returned to America, Pierce Butler made a rare comment on his daughters as a group. His observation followed a typical request that Thomas be given "every advantage that the Heir to a Crown could have." His sisters, the Major wrote, "Distinguish themselves wherever they go, not by their Beauty, but by their manners and the Cultivation of their Minds." He added: "When I write on this interesting subject, a subject the nearest to my breast, the tear gushes from my eye."[42] Of the four girls, Sarah emerged with some individuality as a person in the correspondence of that time.

Pierce Butler signed a contract with Madame Frances Moreau to provide Sarah Butler with a classical education at her London boarding school. From a bevy of masters she was taught music, dancing, drawing, French, Italian, writing, and geography. The music instruction was on the harpsichord, the use of which called for an extra fee. Religious instruction, not well received by Sarah, also brought an extra charge. As he had done for Thomas, Major Butler directed just how his daughter was to be educated. Madame Moreau replied to his detailed instructions:

> I have read with great attention, your directions for the employing Miss Butler's time, and shall endeavour to make her comply with your orders as far as depends on me. They are so different from the rules established for the other ladies in my house I fear she will never attain the French language, for when they are learning lessons, or reading, she is otherwise employed. I think it my duty, Sir, to mention this to you, as I feel myself particularly interested in the improvement of the ladies under my care, and have had the satisfaction of meeting with the approbation of all their friends on the plan I have adopted. Miss Butler is now writing to you. As you particularly desired, Sir, that her letters should not be corrected, I shall not attempt it. According to your orders she should have written yesterday. I have no doubt but she will make a proper excuse for the delay.[43]

The formidable Madame Moreau forestalled a Butler-Moreau correspondence in the style of the Major's communications with Weeden Butler. Thus, the picture of Sarah that emerges does so from her letters to Thomas, and from her father's to her brother and to the Reverend Mr. Butler. She was her father's own child. He often praised her handwriting, and after her return home she frequently copied his letters to Weeden Butler to send them on across the Atlantic on a later ship to compensate for the erratic delivery of mail that was characteristic of the time. In her own letters to Thomas she used the Major's vigorous turn of phrase and made her points expressly and clearly. In one of Major Butler's early letters to Thomas he warned that Sally, as he often called Sarah, was a fine grammarian, "therefore take care when you write to her." Scant comfort to Thomas were Sally's skills:

> She is Mistress of Antient and Modern History—properly versed in Geography, and so good a Mathematician that I will venture to say that she can without looking at anything more than the figure, resolve the most difficult Proposition in Euclid as justly and rapidly as any Mathematician in Carolina. Now my Son I trust You will soon enable me to say as much for You. She is really a better Grammarian than her Father. She has a little knowledge of Astronomy and if it pleases the Great Giver of All Things to spare Her life, she will soon understand it much better. She reads French and is now learning Spanish.[44]

Thomas may well have wondered whether in his father's mind "the Great Giver of All Things" was God or Pierce Butler. A few months later Major Butler again cataloged Sarah's skills. He added "Plane and Spheric Trigonometry" and said she was "Mistress of the Book or the Pen." That same year Major Butler, feeling proud of how he had been something of a schoolmaster himself, revealed a touch of Sarah's character in a letter to Weeden Butler: "My Eldest Daughter, who has been more immediately my own Pupil, amply repays all my toils. Tho Her manners and disposition are perfectly feminine, Her mind is Masculine." The Major's pride in Sarah was intense, giving false promise it would be lasting: "What is the sum within my reach that I would not give to see Him as a Man what His Sister Sally is as a Female."[45]

Pierce Butler had often spoken in favor of the French Revolution. Sarah Butler, "Mistress of Modern History," shared that strong feeling and sensing that Thomas did not, took him to task in forthright letters that grew in intensity as the time neared for his return to America. Thomas had made the mistake of expressing horror and regret that Louis XVI had been guillotined. Sarah replied, "I join you in pitying the King of France and his family for though I hate Kings I know they are not exempt from human frailties."[46]

Major Butler had won no respect from Weeden Butler by asking if the British ministers were not to blame for encouraging "Civil War" in France and by putting greater value on a king's head than on the lives of "hundreds of thousands of our fellow men." Sarah sounded off to Thomas:

> If You are not a warm friend to their Revolution You will not suit the Meridion of Your own Country and need never return to be happy. She will foster no Man who is an Enemy to the French Revolution. What a disappointment it must be to Papa whose fondest wish has been to fit You for the stage of Publick Life, and by sparing no expense in Your education to render You capable of taking an active and useful part Yourself in the holy cause of Liberty and a watchful defense of the people's rights.

Sarah was not thinking of the Butler "people" on the plantations. She continued, and warned Thomas: "I conjure You then not to adopt the political principles or opinions of the English Ministry or Courtiers. They are subjects of the British King. You are a Citizen of the United States, they are educated in prejudice against America and against France."[47] Sarah

Butler may well have questioned Thomas's sentiments. He did become pro-French, but much later, and only through a warm attachment to a young French woman of the aristocracy, giving Major Butler one of several reasons for turning against his son. Appended to Sarah's letter is an apt comment by the Reverend Mr. Butler's friend and neighbor who had taken issue with the outspoken young American woman:

Observations by James Neild, Esq., on Miss S. Butler's Letter.

The Writer is in my Opinion a bold, daring, wicked Woman, who for base perfidiousness w'd have been a fit Companion for Jugurtha, or for aspiring Villainy to Oliver Cromwell. She endeavours by specious, but fallacious Argument to Traytorize the Heart of her Bro'r towards that country which her own family have made choice of, to educate him in, that Country to which by every Law, Human and Devine He ought to Venerate as having there rec'd the rudiments of education & His earliest Friendships.[48]

As the century turned, the talented Sarah Butler, who had inherited more than a touch of her father's stubbornness, chose to wed a young doctor, James Mease. Dr. Mease (pronounced Mays) was the son of a tax collector in Philadelphia who was the last man to wear a cocked hat in that changing city. The elder Mease was of dubious character, and with his son was much disliked by Major Butler. When Sarah and Dr. Mease were married in July 1800, their union received no blessing from her volatile father. A son, born within a year of their marriage, was named Pierce Butler Mease. The birth of the child, and the name given him, tempered the animosity Major Butler directed toward Sarah and her husband. Also, the Major quickly placed on the child the hopes and aspirations he had once bestowed on his son Thomas. Dr. Mease had a scientific turn of mind, and among other projects of interest to him was the advocacy of the growth of benne, or sesame, a plant whose seeds produced an excellent and palatable oil. He also promoted the development of silk culture in Pennsylvania and planted three thousand grapevines in the Mease vineyard on vacant ground along Cherry Alley in the center of the "ground plan" of Philadelphia. His agricultural and scientific bent brought an active participation in the Philadelphia Horticultural Society, which he had helped found, and in the American Philosophical Society. For nine thousand dollars, Major Butler purchased a town house for the burgeoning Mease family and, being sympathetic to Dr. Mease's interest in agriculture, permitted him to use a Butler farm near Darby and gave him money to construct a barn. When his son-in-law used the money to rescue his father the tax collector—who had collected and not remitted—and had also used another gift to purchase sheep contrary to Major Butler's expressed wishes, the animosity returned.[49]

Sarah and James Mease had a large family. The first son was followed by Mary Middleton in 1802, by Thomas in 1804, John, who was named for the tax collector, in 1806, Frances in 1808, and Pierce Butler Mease in 1810. The last child was born but two months after the untimely death of his brother, the first Pierce, one of the unfortunate "Principal Props" of his grandfather.[50] The much-loved child died in Philadelphia while Major Butler was tending to plantation business in Georgia. In a letter to Dr. Benjamin Rush before Christmas in 1809, and before the child's death, Pierce Butler showed the spirit of the season. He apologized for neglecting his overdue bill, and added: "I shall on tomorrow, alone, think as much of what Christ died and suffered for mankind, as if I were singing Hallelujahs in Westminster Abby."[51] When word of the death of the nine-year-old boy reached the plantation it brought forth an angry outburst. Writing from Hampton, the disconsolate Major Butler called on his friend, the distinguished Dr. Rush, to assist in finding a final resting place for the boy, and for himself at some future time. He told of his high expectations for his grandson:

> I looked for a Head, a Guardian, a Protector to the numerous children of a father who will do nothing for them. I looked to Him as the Shield of his Aunts, the provident Manager of their worldly concerns when I shall be no more! In a instant, all my hopes, and as I thought, well founded arrangements are blasted, and I am again in an advanced age afloat. Had the disrespectful obstinacy of his Mother yielded to the ardent wishes of Her Father, to the unceasing solicitations of her Son, we might still be happy, but No, she must be obeyed and to that obediance has fallen a Sacrifice.

> I beg of you to ask Bishop White if it is practicable to obtain by purchase space sufficient in the burying ground of Christ's Church, or St. Peter's, to place a vault to hold the remains of my Darling Child, and my own when the Supreme Being shall call me hence. I woud willingly procure a pew in the church in order to bring up the children left, in the Religion of Christ, in the Lutherine mode of Worship.[52]

A later letter from Major Butler to Dr. Rush revealed that Sarah Mease's "disrespectful obstinacy" was her refusal to permit the boy to accompany him on the trip to Georgia. Had she done so, the Major wrote, "he

woud still live." He believed the "ever lamented child" had been un-
necessarily exposed to inclement weather that "sow'd the seed or lay'd the
foundation of that disease which deprived me of him." Pierce Butler said
he was left "as miserable a Man as stands on Earth."[53]

Harriot Butler wrote Dr. Rush in fear the child's death might bring on
her father's demise:

> We have received no letter from the Southward and are deeply distressed,
> fearing the worst yet trusting to the Almighty for the best.

> My Sister Eliza is much indisposed in mind and body—suffering from the
> exertion, the too great exertion which she made at the moment when our
> darling little Pierce took his flight, his *upward* flight, if ever soul
> ascended.[54]

A Savannah friend noted the extent of Major Butler's grief in a letter to
his wife. Robert Mackay, a merchant bound for Florida from Savannah,
had planned a stop at Hampton to visit Major Butler: "The next night I
lay in the Boat near to Majr Butler's. I could not go ashore as the poor old
Man is in a state of derangement from the death of his Grandson, in
whom all his hopes & expectations were wrapt up." In April, Major
Butler dined in Savannah with Mackay, who reported that the Major
"looks much broke," meaning broken in spirit, not in purse, for Mackay
added, "He has declined selling his property & is about purchasing more
Negroes."[55]

Bishop White found space in the Christ Church yard for the boy with
ample room for the grandfather. Major Butler, who was determined his
heir apparent should carry the name Butler, buried the boy with the following inscription cut deeply into the stone above the tomb:

HERE LIES ENTOMBED THE BODY OF
PIERCE BUTLER, JUNIOR
BELOVED, LAMENTED
BELOVED FOR HIS AMIABLE DISPOSITION
LAMENTED FOR HIS EARLY PROMISE

AND HERE WITH GOD'S PERMISSION
WILL BE ENTOMBED
THE BODY OF PIERCE BUTLER SENIOR
AN ATTACHMENT STRONGER THAN THAT WHICH BLOOD GIVES
UNITED THE GRANDFATHER AND GRANDSON
JULY 7TH 1810

And Benjamin Rush penned a ten-line verse, a memorial to "Master Pierce Butler Mease":

> *Oh! Spare our son, his weeping parents cry*
> *Oh! Spare our boy, his weeping aunts reply,*
> *Think of the distant Sire with grief opprest*
> *And let his woes the deadly stroke arrest.*
> *I am not death, the fell disease replies,*
> *I bring a cherub's message from the skies.*
> *I come to bear the object of your love*
> *From earth's low follies to the World above,*
> *Nor will he die when he resigns his breath,*
> *Future Unhappiness alone is death.*[56]

Sarah Butler Mease, though very much the lady, was also a nonconformist wife and mother. She maintained her intellectual interests and was said to be querulous, a trait probably accentuated by poor health. She had no respect for religion, kept no Bible, and forbade her children to read one. She did permit the children to attend the Unitarian Church, believing the potential for harm there was minimal as so little religion was preached within its walls.[57]

Dr. James Mease was in and out of financial trouble, rescued, if not by Major Butler, by Sarah, and in later years by his children. He wrote an early guide to Philadelphia that was more a compendium of "facts," albeit one not always accepted as such. He was once beholden to Governor Thomas Mifflin for a patronage appointment as port physician, but in a political shake-up sent a malicious attack on the governor to a local printer asking that it be printed anonymously. The attack appeared in a city gazette along with the note requesting anonymity. The Doctor was embarrassed and his social acceptance was diminished.[58]

Despite the peculiarities of their forebears and their unusual upbringing, the Mease children were well accepted in Philadelphia society. The four who lived to a marriageable age made interesting, if not always happy, unions.

When Pierce Butler turned away from Sarah, who had been the daughter held up to his son Thomas as a proper and fitting offspring, he transferred his affection first to Harriot Percy, and then to Frances Butler. Both were unencumbered by any romantic ties and were quick to assist Major Butler in business matters by attending to details when he was away or indisposed. Frances remained on good terms with her brother

Thomas, who had soon become estranged from their father. This line of communication was often used between father and son and proved to be of considerable value to the two adversaries. Anne Elizabeth, or Eliza, the twin of Frances, was also unmarried. She contributed little one way or the other to her father's restless life. Beyond the family, almost the only notice taken of her was a classification in the city directory of Philadelphia: "Eliza Butler gentw Walnut bel Sch 8th."[59]

THOMAS BUTLER had returned to Philadelphia in September 1795 after his long stay in England. By November he could no longer suffer his father's criticism and had "expatriated." He deserted the comforts of the new home at Chestnut and Eighth streets. Weeden Butler heard of the difficulty from Major Butler in a letter written that month, and again from Thomas in a letter dated January 1796 but not received until March. He was in no hurry to answer, and when he did, expressed his surprise that Thomas would leave home "when so many and such respectable Objects of Curiosity surround you"—a rather oblique depiction of the Butler family. The Reverend Mr. Butler did not invite Thomas to return to Chelsea but expressed the hope that he had deserted the Butler hearth for "some worthier calls to study."[60]

On occasion Thomas returned and seemed to try to become a member of the family. In Major Butler's absence he recognized a family obligation to his father's friend, the Justice James Iredell, and invited him to dinner on Chestnut Street. Judge Iredell mentioned the occasion to his wife and his recognition of the trouble: "I am to dine today at Major Butler's with his son and daughters upon an invitation from 'Thomas Butler' to take a 'family dinner' with him. With all his democratical folly he has as much aristocratical pride as his father. He is very studious but I have had no opportunity of judging his understanding."[61]

That Thomas would come to cross purposes with his headstrong father and his equally headstrong sister Sarah was not surprising. That he chose to embark on a deliberate course of alienation from Major Butler, who held the strings to a fat family purse, is surprising, for Thomas was ill-prepared to face life on his own. It so happened that he did not have to. On a visit to a popular watering place in New York he found and was captivated by a beautiful young French woman from the island of Martinique. She was there, at Ballston Springs, with her mother, Madame de Mallevault, the widow of Capitaine Louis Charles François de Mallevault de la Varenne, a naval officer who had commanded fighting ships under

Louis XVI. Madame de Mallevault had a purse of her own and, like the Butlers, derived her considerable income from plantations that had been worked by slaves of African derivation. Urged on by her mother, the beautiful Eliza de Mallevault set her cap for Thomas, who in their eyes was to be the inheritor of Major Butler's huge fortune. The courtship of Thomas and Eliza came at a time when he might well have returned to the good graces of his father. The young son of Sarah Mease, who had replaced Thomas in Major Butler's plan of inheritance, had died. The royal affiliation of the de Mallevaults, however, gave the pro-Revolutionary Pierce Butler another reason to keep Thomas beyond the scheme of things for the future. Although Sarah Mease shared the disfavor of their father, she too saw nothing good in the alliance of Thomas and a family of the French aristocracy.[62]

Thomas Butler traveled the long distance to the French West Indies to wed his young lady, arriving at Martinique early in 1812. Eliza de Mallevault lived on the southeastern coast, the windward side of that beautiful island. Their home was near the shore where the Rivière Paquemar comes down through the hills to meet the sea at a blue-green bay, the Cul-de-sac de Paquemar, and where the most prominent object was the large four-bladed windmill that crushed great quantities of sugar cane brought in by the de Mallevault slaves. Thomas and Eliza were married in the parish church at the small village of Vauclin just north of Paquemar, where the Abbé Jean Baptiste de Bouille performed and recorded the ceremony in the parish records. On February 11, 1812, Thomas Butler of "Caroline du Sud aux États Unis de l'Amerique," who was "fils majeur en legitime marriage de Mr. Pierce Butler, habitant de Philadelphie, et de fine Dame Marie Meddleton d'une part," born August 13, 1778, was wed to Henriette Reine Louise Guillemine Luce Eliza de Mallevault, who was "fille mineure de feu Mr Louis Charles François de Mallevault de la Vareene, ancien Capitaine des vaisseaux de leurs majestes les Rois de France et d'Espagne, et de Dame Anne Magdeline Guillemine Pinel Dumanoir, habitante de cette paroisse." Eliza's birth was shown to have taken place at Port Royal, Isle Martinique, on August 14, 1792, fourteen years and a day later than that of Thomas. Those who attended and signed the parish records were de Mallevault kinfolk from the neighboring island of Guadeloupe and friends from Vauclin.[63]

The voyage to the young bride's new world began on June 14, 1812, on a brig bound for "Portsmouth, Massachusetts," which they abandoned at St. Bartholomews for another brig bound for New London. As the Butlers were accompanied by French-speaking de Mallevault servants who had been former slaves and by a "mass of effects," the transfer from one ship to the other was "attended with a degree of trouble of which you can have no idea," or so wrote Thomas to his friend John McQueen, Jr., in Savannah. McQueen was a Savannah planter and the son of Major Butler's old friend Don Juan McQueen. The Butlers arrived in New London unaware that a state of war existed between England and the United States.[64]

On Martinique the working of a slave plantation was similar to that of Georgia and South Carolina. Putting the difference of climate aside, other factors were much the same. The slaves, who had come from African tribal backgrounds, faced the same difficulties of orientation and communication. As in the American South, they used their owner's language as a basis for a dialect of their own. Instead of the low-country Gullah of the Butler slaves, black people spoke Martinican Creole, and although one was adapted from English and the other from French, the inflections, rhythms, and vocal timber were much the same. Thomas Butler, having learned French at Weeden Butler's school in Chelsea, should have had no more difficulty understanding the talk of a slave on Martinique than one on Butler's Island. Both took similar liberties with their owner's tongues to such a degree that their speech was, in truth, more a language than a dialect. Characteristic was their rejection of the sacred *r* sound of the pure French in favor of their own *w* sound. *Grande* became *gwande, apres* was *apwes,* and the language they spoke was *Cweole,* not *Creole.* As in America, the Negroes accepted their owner's religion with a few variations of their own, and their names were thrust upon them in the same manner as in America. True, a French given name often seemed a bit more incongruous on an African than those bestowed by the likes of Pierce Butler. On Martinique, slave girls could be Hyacinthe, or Pierette, and Hercule may well have been the young Negro who carried cane to the tower mill. Major Butler's *Alexander* would have been *Alexandre,* and *Gullah Jack's* Martinican equivalent, *Cweole Jacques.*[65]

At the time of the Butler–de Mallevault wedding the growing of cane and the making of sugar was an old story on Martinique. Back in Georgia on the Butler plantations, Roswell King was giving consideration to a third crop to replace the fast-fading long staple cotton. His plans for the extensive planting of cane and the construction of a sugar mill, which were interrupted by the war with England, might well have been advanced by knowledge gained by Thomas Butler on the de Mallevault plantation on Martinique, where the growing of cane and the manufacture of sugar was practiced with great skills, though the disaffection between Thomas and Pierce Butler made this impossible.

Roswell King may also have found interesting the Martinican slave owner's practice of including a drummer in each of their work gangs. In cutting or hauling cane, their discipline was enhanced by the persistent beat of a "tam-tam" or a "tam-bou-belai." The first of the black drummers in Major Butler's Twenty-ninth Regiment had come from the sugar plantations of neighboring Guadeloupe.[66]

The Emperor Napoleon's *Imperatrice Josephine* came from a Martinican plantation, just as did Thomas Butler's Eliza. It was said Josephine influenced Bonaparte to reopen the slave trade in 1802, an act that increased the overwhelming ratio of blacks to the relatively few white French who lived on the island. In 1812, at the time of the Butler wedding, Josephine had been cast aside for the new empress, Marie Louise. Napoleon and his *grande armée* were preparing to make their ill-fated move into Russia.[67]

As Thomas Butler grew older, he assumed certain unattractive characteristics of his father and developed a few that were uniquely his own. In addition to being humorless, he was overbearing, demanding, and obtuse. Handsome, but pompous and proud, he lacked his father's shrewdness and drive. Somehow the union with Eliza was maintained through the births of four children—three sons, Francis, Louis, and John, and a daughter Anne. Francis was named for Frances Butler, the only true friend Thomas had in his father's family. John's name came from a friend, while Louis and Anne were named for their French grandparents. Eliza de Mallevault Butler was said to be pretty and lively, and when in "Society" was given to courting attention by innocent flirtations. Such behavior was soon stifled by the proper Thomas, who closeted his attractive wife in the small Butler house at York Farm, across the road from Butler Place. His treatment of his own sons showed no improvement on the tempestuous father-son relationship that he had known.[68]

Pierce Butler thought Thomas to be incompetent and incapable of managing his own family. He believed his oldest daughter Sarah and her husband Dr. James Mease to be inattentive to parental duties and otherwise irresponsible. With but little confidence in either Sarah or Thomas, it followed that he would turn to the unmarried daughters for help. Harriot Percy, the initial choice, had good judgment and was one with whom he could share family confidences. One such incidence of that trust casts faint light on a Butler mystery.

In the Rush family papers of the Library Company of Philadelphia is an enigmatic letter from Harriot Percy Butler to Dr. Benjamin Rush. It was short, and as was her habit, undated:

> I return, My Dear Friend, the letter with my best thanks; and with an assurance that it has been seen by no eye, but my own. Ever yours,
>
> H. P. BUTLER

In the orderly arrangement in which the Rush papers are kept the letter is followed by what appears to have been an enclosure, also in Harriot's hand, and also undated: "Born on the twenty-fourth of July in the year one thousand seven hundred and eighty-one. Died on the fifth day of December, one thousand eight hundred and three. Aged twenty-three years, four months and eleven days." Dr. Rush follows that with an epitaph he had prepared for the Butlers:

> *Still lives the memory of departed worth*
> *The tear is holy, that bedews the sod*
> *Although the fading form is hid in earth*
> *The living mind, ascended to its God.*[69]

As to the identity of this unknown and unacknowledged young person, the Butlers are strangely silent except for the puzzling correspondence between Dr. Rush and Harriot. The answer would seem to be the sixth child taken to Philadelphia when the Butler family was banished from Charlestown in 1781—except that Major Butler's letter to John Allston in 1794 indicated God had spared only Thomas of his four sons, and never did he or Mary Butler mention other than the four daughters.[70]

The strong relationship between the Butlers and the Rush family was evident when Dr. Rush died in early 1813. Major Butler, urged on by Harriot Percy, persuaded James Monroe to appoint the Doctor's son, James Rush, M.D., to succeed his father as treasurer of the United States Mint in Philadelphia. When the appointment was made, Major Butler wrote young Dr. Rush to tell him he owed the favor to Harriot.[71]

The assistance given their father by the Misses Butler helped to win his acceptance of their spinsterhood. For Harriot Percy, even that state was unfortunately brief. She died unexpectedly in 1815. When Major Butler turned to Frances Butler for help, he was dutifully and quickly rewarded.

She attended to the personal and business affairs of a fretful, peevish old man and did so with remarkable efficiency.[72]

The Butler business ventures had spread far beyond Philadelphia, the York Road, and coastal Georgia. The capable Frances Butler kept busy with the records of a property called Twickenham Farm, near Darby; York Farm; Butler Place; town houses in Philadelphia; and the involved accounts of Hampton and Butler's Island. In good years the earnings from the plantations were tremendous. Money not needed for the upkeep of his residences and for his family was used to purchase more land and property and to invest in other ventures. The purchases of property included houses for Sarah, for Eliza, for Thomas, and land in Newport for Frances. These acquisitions were made to assuage any ill feeling his children might have engendered in view of his misappropriation of their interest in legacies from Elizabeth Blake and Sarah Guerard, matters that plagued his conscience. Well aware that the Blake, Guerard, and Brewton slaves he had moved from South Carolina to Georgia had lost their identities in a confusing maze of bloodlines, he, nonetheless, put Roswell King to the task of sorting them out. In June 1817, Mr. King sent a list of those of Mrs. Blake's slaves "as best I can make out." As to a list of those from Mrs. Guerard, he wrote, "I have been hammering at a long time with old Pompey and Dorcas to help me." Major Butler bought large tracts of land in Pennsylvania, some in Wayne County that he transferred to Thomas, other lands along the Allegheny River and Conewango Creek. Also in Pennsylvania, he owned shares in "Asylum lands." In distant Tennessee he held dubious title to ten thousand acres on Duck River. Among his other investments were shares in both United States banks, and several loans that were difficult to collect. Although he considered himself a South Carolinian and as nothing more than a "sojurner" in Pennsylvania, the once-considerable holdings of Carolina land were liquidated and the proceeds used to repay his own debts and to fund his Georgia plantations. As Major Butler was not one to keep accurate records of the true ownership of various holdings, it is likely the so-called "gifts" of property to his children were parcels he had purchased with funds rightfully theirs.[73]

Advancing old age and the loss of so many of his slaves to the British caused Major Butler to lose much of his vaunted determination and customary vigor. His persistent depression was evident in an exchange of letters in 1818 with William Page of St. Simons Island. Usually most proper in his inquiries as to the welfare of a spouse, on this occasion his comment offered scant comfort to either one of the Pages: "I regret to learn from it that Mrs. Page's health is not good—In truth, Mrs. Page and myself have held out longer than I expected." He then told Mr. Page of an unusual remedy for his current difficulty:

> You wish to know how I use the Columbus Toot. I put two ounces of the powder in a quart of best Brandy, suffer it to remain for a week, shaking it occasionally—At Breakfast I have a strong Tea or mixture of Columbus Toot made in a tea Pot. I put into a large Claret glass or tea cup about two or three teaspoons full of the tincture, and fill with the tea: This I take *on an empty stomach*, three times in twenty-four hours. As I sleep little, I rise at night and take it.[74]

When Major Butler neared the end of his days, he devised a plan for the continued operation of the Georgia plantations, the source of his wealth. He spelled out the plan in a will that was drawn but held in abeyance while a concerted effort was made to effect a reconciliation with Thomas that would have brought about a revision. When stubborn pride ran headlong into stubborn pride, reconciliation was not to be. Accordingly, Pierce Butler signed his will on February 14, 1822.[75]

Chapter 13

Second Generation: The Kings

W HEN THE ROSWELL KINGS MOVED to Hampton in 1802, but two of their four children were to enjoy the amenities Pierce Butler had promised his manager. Rufus, the oldest son who was nine years old, died that July. Catherine, the first daughter, had died two years before. The two boys, young Roswell and Barrington, aged six and four, were joined through the years that followed by Thomas, William, and Pierce Butler, who was born in August 1806 and died a year later, and by daughters Eliza and a second Catherine, born in 1810. Bram, one of the drivers at Hampton and a mulatto, was recognized to be the son of Roswell King but was not acknowledged as such by Major Butler's manager.[1]

Young Roswell King inherited much of his father's ingenuity and intelligence and while still a boy was most helpful in attending to plantation matters. He was dependable and willing, two traits that endeared him to his father and that would help Roswell King, Sr., to break his tie to the Major and the Butler slaves. The rise of young Roswell permitted his father to reach out beyond the Altamaha to fashion for himself a remarkable career that was unlike his subservient existence on the Butler plantations.

The shift of responsibility for the two plantations was gradual, so much so that Major Butler seemed surprised when he realized it had actually taken place. He was aware of young Roswell's participation but seemed to believe his role would be supportive of his father and that both were there to protect his interest. Major Butler's intense preoccupation in the plantations had waned considerably following the troubles brought on by the

217

War of 1812, and similarly his confidence in Roswell King had declined. The loss of the slaves and an uncharacteristic malaise that existed on the plantations created a condition that would not have been tolerated before the chaos of 1815: "We are poor for Negroes, poor for Oxen and poor for mules. I have bot no oxen for many years. I killed some of the old ones for Christmas beef. Some have died." The state of things caused Roswell King to react to Pierce Butler very much as had Thomas Butler. Weary of the constant criticism and the second guessing, Mr. King began to look be-- yond the Butler empire to his own present and future well-being. During his many years as Major Butler's manager he had been able to accumulate an estate of his own. He had acquired rental property in the thriving town of Darien, owned and planted a rice tract near Butler's Island, and managed his own "gang" of slaves. In addition, he invested in two commercial ventures in Darien that brought forth a comment from the sage in Philadelphia: "I think more of the Steam Saw Mill than I do of the Bank. I know how accommodating Directors are to each other. The Oconee Cotton Men will go home with their pockets full of Darien Banknotes." Roswell King owned the sawmill and was a director of the Darien Bank.[2]

When Roswell King made up his mind to turn over the reins to his son, he made frequent reference to his character and ability, and on one occasion tried to force an acknowledgment from the Major that the young man should be on the payroll. In an 1816 letter the Major was told young Roswell was "gitting impatient" and looking elsewhere for a livelihood. He urged Major Butler's approval with the word that Roswell, Jr., "follows your advice. He drinks nothing but water."[3]

Preparatory to making his break, the Sunday "Honored Sir" reports were pleasant and mindful of earlier times when peace prevailed between Philadelphia and the Altamaha. In 1817 one report told how Mr. King was forced to make amends to men with whom he had been doing some plantation business. He revealed a bit of his character in writing: "When I go to people for redress, it puts me in mind of my talk to your negroes when they complain to me. I talk smoothly to them, and behind their backs, tell their drivers to push them up."[4] In other letters he listed bountiful shipments to Philadelphia from the cornucopia that was Butler's Island. The largess included a box of candles, rush mats made from the tideland grasses, casks of sugar, and a barrel of arrowroot. Also, a half tierce of oranges, four barrels of peanuts—called "ground-nuts" by Mr. King. He could not send the promised lemons as they had not ripened, and he forgot the demijohn of honey. The shipment left Georgia aboard the ship that had brought kiln-dried corn from Philadelphia. It was planned for a pre-Christmas arrival, a bonus for Major Butler's family, whose prime interest in the plantations was not the produce, but the money the produce generated. Mr. King was aware of this and had once commented to Major Butler that the only thing "amusing to them" was the income: "What you and myself have so often amused ourselves in looking and planning good Order on you Estate is thrown away to them."[5]

As Roswell King neared the end of his career as the Butler manager, he began to show some tolerance to recalcitrant slaves. He reported a Butler's Island incident in which driver Harry figured:

> Harry had a boy by the name of Jimoney to give him the dodge, and was out a whole week in the woods. (not off the island) When I went to the Island he came in, in a few days. His excuse for going off was mere nothing, had got affronted with his driver. After talking to him as I thot sufficient I gave him his choice to loose his next clothing, or to pay up his lost time in Sundays work. As you could not be the looser & I advised him to do the work, which he had done and all accounts Settled. I am sure that is better than to have given him 100 lashes.[6]

Early in 1818 Major Butler expressed some doubts that Roswell King, Jr., had the ability to replace his father. He sought John Couper's advice after looking somewhat askance at the young man who, even with his father's assistance, had not produced crops up to expectations. He told John Couper that the best proof of young King's prowess would be better crops. Mr. Couper wrote, in response: "Roswell King, Junr stands high in my opinion as a Correct youth, full of Activity and Ambition to be a planter to please you." He did qualify his comment with an admission that young King's last two crops had been "badly managed," and the reason, he thought, was too much planted and poor supervision by the drivers. Mr. Couper's word left an aging Major Butler very much in doubt.[7]

Old John Couper was in an enviable position regarding succession. His son James Hamilton was all that Major Butler would have desired in an heir. Roswell King's description of young Couper came to a dejected Pierce Butler who lamented the inadequacy of his own son, Thomas, and who ignored the sons of Thomas. Likewise, he could put no faith in the immature sons of his alienated daughter, Sarah Mease. Mr. King recog-

nized James Hamilton Couper's inexperience but otherwise gave him high
marks:

> Mr. Couper's son James is almost 25 years of Age. He is an uncommon fine
> young man, no doubt he will be Great in anything he undertakes. He last
> year remained on St. Simons, and a few times visited the Swamp place
> Hopeton. This year he has taken the whole charge and I dare say he will do
> well. He is Company for Old Man. He knows more of most things than
> most people do at 50 years of Age. How he can take the lead as a Planter is
> a question. I will venture to say he doesnt know Grass from Rice. He
> certainly has it more in his power to be a Scientific planter than any Young
> man I know of. Since nine years of age he has been from Home at School,
> and in almost every branch has been leader of his Class.[8]

Not completely satisfied with John Couper's word on young Roswell
King, Major Butler then wrote his old friend William Page, asking that he
pay particular attention to the "State of Order" on the plantations. He
wanted to know "the appearance of the people whether cheerful or
gloomy," and then added:

> Mr. King has notified me of his intention to do for himself—Not knowing
> how to do better I think of trying his son, but before I do, I wish much of
> your opinion as the advisability of such a measure—he is young and the
> trust is considerable to be placed in so young a man. I am truly at a loss;
> and I wish to have your unreserved opinion. In giving it to me You are
> Confiding in a Man of Honor, who is incapable of divulging anything
> confidential.[9]

Although their reasons were at variance, Roswell King shared Major
Butler's apprehension over the future of the Georgia plantations. On several occasions Mr. King delineated the difficulties that were present, and
some that were probable:

> I may have too poor an opinion of Negro property, but the day is not far
> distant when that kind of property will fall in price. I have one new reason
> I am not pleased with. At Christmas I gave your Negroes a large quantity
> of Beef, plenty of Rum, sugar or Molasses, but I found they didnt dance
> but very little. I thot no more of it than there might be some difficulty
> among themselves respecting fiddlers, etc., but since, I find it was a general
> thing in the country that the Negroes made merry but very little.[10]

He had still another reason to warrant his concern. Rumors were rampant in the low country of Georgia that Indians were raiding white settlements. He wrote Major Butler that twenty people had been scalped within thirty miles of Darien, and that the Coupers had constructed a blockhouse armed with two six pounders and "20 stands of arms." Still smarting from the British depredations, he wrote:

> The whole country is in confusion. I do not fear the Indians, but White Indians might come and rob us and carry off the negroes where we could never find them. In truth a man might go from Mr. Couper's place Hopeton to the Mississippi and Never see a House, we are yet so much on the frontier. I dont say this to give you uneasiness but to let you know what a wild wicked country we are in, in every respect risky and deceptive.[11]

His apprehension reinforced, it is not surprising Major Butler directed Roswell King to appraise Butler's Island with an eye to selling it to a "Mr. Fitzsimmons" who had shown an interest. Mr. King determined a fair asking price would be $506,000, an amount that included 582 slaves at an average price of a little over $450. He made a rather pointed suggestion to the Major: "I think it probable if the Monied Men in the Eastern and Middle States knew of the purchase some of them would turn their attention this way—notwithstanding it is not fashionable in your Quarter to hold Slaves. I find they take hold of them very gredily when they come here."[12]

When Roswell King realized the two plantations might be sold separately, he devised an ingenious plan for Hampton, foreshadowing a project that would occupy him a few years later. Knowing that it had been almost three years since the once-productive cotton fields had been planted, he submitted a plan to convert Hampton to a "Summer Retreat." A drawing by young William King of his father's proposed "village" showed each homesite on a corner lot. "In a Summer Retreat it requires Air," wrote Roswell King. He had talked of his project among his neighbors so that when submitted to Major Butler he could show the interest of "several Respectable families," one of his prospects being John Couper. Major Butler could not bring himself to break up the plantation that had been so much a part of his life. He did, however, agree to an all-out effort to sell the entire Georgia property. Roswell King was told to prepare copy for an advertisement to run in the newspapers of Darien, Savannah, and Charleston.[13]

The advertisement appeared in December 1818 in the *Darien Gazette* with a notice to the *Georgian* in Savannah and the *City Gazette* in Charleston to pick up the copy and to run the advertisement once weekly for eight successive times. The number of slaves offered for sale had dropped from 582 offered with Butler's Island in January, to 535. The reason for the decrease was not mentioned in the King-Butler correspondence of that period. The advertisement:

A Large Estate For Sale.

That extensive and well known property belonging to PIERCE BUTLER, esq. situated on the waters of the Altamaha, in the counties of Glynn and McIntosh, consisting of about

15,000 ACRES OF LAND,

OF VARIOUS KINDS,

AND

535 NEGROES.

Among the negroes are about forty-five mechanics, viz: Blacksmiths, House and Ship Carpenters, Bricklayers, Coopers, &c. Of the prime land, there are about 1600 acres fit for immediate cultivation, viz:—800 acres of tide swamp on Butler's Island, one mile from Darien, suitable for rice, cotton or sugar; 300 acres of brackish marsh, and excellent cotton land, on Experiment, on Little St. Simon's, and 500 acres on Hampton, St. Simon's Island, consisting of old fields that have not been in cultivation for three years.

The estate is amply provided with buildings of every description, requisite in an extensive culture of rice, cotton and sugar.

A further description is considered unnecessary, as it is presumed no person would become a purchaser, without a previous examination of the premises.

Butler's Island, containing 1498 acres, (875 of which are banked in) is offered for sale in one lot, together with all the negroes, excepting a few families, that will be kept until the other property be disposed of.—The St. Simon's lands may be divided into several tracts to suit purchasers. The payment will be accommodating; 20 per cent only will be required to be paid in hand; and 7 per cent interest on the balance. Any person desirous of purchasing will please apply to the subscriber.

ROSWELL KING.[14]

In the last of the "Honored Sir" letters in which Roswell King acted in the official capacity of manager for the Butler plantations, he responded to Pierce Butler's constant criticism. The Major had queried Mr. King on hearing that his rental property in Darien provided an annual income of more than $4,000. The answer was no—his rents came to $2,025, an amount slightly in excess of his salary as manager of the estate. Without equivocation, Mr. King told Major Butler he was surrendering his control. In the letter from Mr. King, Major Butler read: "I have given up the management of your Estate to my son, but my mind and advice is much devoted to it as ever. As long as I live he will always have my advice and you my friendship."[15] Despite the affirmation of friendship, the cold facts of Mr. King's departure—coupled with the word that the advertisements for the sale of the splendid properties of Pierce Butler, Esq., had brought forth not one inquiry—prompted an immediate reaction from the crusty Major. He canceled the amenities Mr. King and his family had enjoyed while living at Hampton. The action was taken while Roswell King was away. He was busy promoting his Darien sawmill and was doing some investigative work for the Bank of Darien in his capacity as a director. He was shocked and surprised when he returned to what had been his home at Hampton. In his letter that followed, Mr. King put aside the customary "Honored Sir" and was vehemently indignant. After eighteen years of loyal service he felt badly mistreated:

> Mr. Butler, D. Sir—You put me in the necessity of applying to Mr. Couper for vegetables and Capt. Shaddack for milk. This day makes 18 years since I promised to take charge of your Estate, and within four days since I took charge of it. And to reflect from that day to this I have ever tried to promote your Interest, little thinking that I should be treated like the Dog in the fable, when too old to be useful, Neglected.
>
> It is truly mortifying to think after so many years exertion to git your friendship, it has all ended in smoke. It is useless to try long. I am Sir—[16]

As the second generation manager assumed control, the letters to Philadelphia became less candid than they had been the previous eighteen years. Young Roswell had a tendency to gloss over trouble. He had not his father's strong constitution and was frequently indisposed. His mother made the family house ready for the young bachelor prior to her move to the mainland, and on at least one occasion wrote the weekly report for her son. When ill, or when the need arose, young Roswell called on his brothers, William and Thomas, for assistance.

The transition from Roswell King, Sr., to his son was not an easy one. Long after the elder King had moved to Darien, a querulous Major Butler wrote young Roswell he was "mortified" to hear the river had gone over the bank near the Butler's Island rice mill and that young Morris was not attending to the cotton crop at Experiment and as a consequence production would fall far short of the year before. He complained, "I am at a loss to know who is to act for me." It galled the old man to feel it necessary once again to go through the litany of instruction as he had with William Page and young Roswell's father:

> It is requsite and essentially necessary that I should be minutely informed of what is doing—what has been done—and what you propose to succeed the work doing. It is all important to myself and children who may come after me that the estate should be directed in the most correct and perfect manner—that activity without severity should prevail in every part of it— that every individual discharge a reasonable duty. I fully rely on you being before time (not behind it) in your own work. I depend on you selling 200 tierces of rice *before* Christmas.[17]

That two hundred tierces of rice be sent to market before Christmas was all-important. When Roswell King, Jr., failed that test and then complained, "The management of the Estate is a heavy burthen—very heavy on me," the Major fired off a long letter on the proper procedure for marketing rice and reminded his young manager how it had been in 1820, with the owner on the plantation and in charge:

> I found no difficulty in the management of it last winter. If I resided constantly on the estate I would have everthing go on with the regularity of clockwork. With very little trouble, I would keep always before time, activity without pressure should always prevail everywhere. I would, I know, make good Crops when not disturbed by Hurricanes and still have many leisure hours. You are a young man. You have not yet established a Character in the Society around you. Believe me, as you manage the trust committed to you, so you will be thought of by your neighbours. If all things go on with order & unceasing industry, you will be esteemed, and respected by your Neighbours & acquire my future friendship. If any of your Neighbours make better Crops, if they evidence more System, You will be thought lightly of though it may not be expressed. The two visits I made to Mr. Couper's river place, observed that young Mr. Couper was aiming at Systematic management. I observed there was great quietness— no confusion of work.

Young King was upbraided for losing forty barrels of rice on the Butler schooner made unseaworthy for a lack of caulking of the vessel's seams.[18]

A week later, Major Butler thanked his manager for "a neat methodic statement of Births & Deaths in 1820." He said he had hoped the increase would have been greater and then harkened back to James Hamilton Couper's "Systematic management." He warned: "If you allow young Mr. Couper to overtake you I shall be very much mortified."[19]

The Christmas of 1820 was celebrated much as it had been in earlier years. For the slaves there was "Beef, rice, rum and molasses," and as before, rice on a rice plantation was considered a special treat by those who produced it. Major Butler was told the resourceful driver from Experiment was nearing the end of his days. "Old Morris is going Fast. He cannot live very long." The same may well have been said of Morris's owner. The end of the slave's Christmas had come without "any mischief among themselves." Roswell King, Jr., said they had all gone back to work cheerfully.[20]

The letters of the 1820s reflected a renewed interest by Major Butler in the present and future of the plantations. The diminished attention that had followed the British occupation and raid on Hampton was put aside, and Major Butler wrote of buying more slaves and planting more cotton. He told young King not to sell the St. Clair tract as had been contemplated, but to look for a gang of about sixty "swamp Negroes," slaves accustomed to hard work, to mix in with the entire work force, and then to pick some old hands and some new to work under Bram in developing St. Clair. His letters focused on the details of management: "Put every Man, Woman & young Negroe able to use a hoe into the field to keep down the grass, it is useless to plant if it is not kept clean." Major Butler knew grass to be an enemy of cotton. He complained: "The mules died from Neglect. If I treated the Negroes as they treated the mules, they would be justified in saying I was not a humane Master." And he sent a message to young Morris at Experiment:

> Since your poor Father has been unable to go into the field & attend to the Plantation, everything has gone behind hand. For the past three years you have not made half a crop. I will try you one year more. If you do not make a good crop I will remove you and put you to work in the field. You will deceive yourself & your Father if you think I will not do it.[21]

As Pierce Butler's life neared its end, his body weakened, but his mind remained alert and clear. The letters to the plantation were dictated to and written by his daughter Frances, and occasionally he called on his young Mease grandsons to do the same. Pierce, or Butler Mease, as he was called, was but eleven years old. His brother John was fifteen. The message to Morris was sent in a letter prepared by young Pierce. A John Mease letter told that Grandfather Butler wanted particular care taken to produce good rice for seeding purposes: "He desires that when a rick of rice if taken down for thrashing, you place 3 or 4 faithful elderly negroes (if you have such) to select the sheafs of the whitest rice for seed." The parenthetic remark was John's. One or the other of the grandsons followed with a letter telling Roswell King, Jr., that Major Butler expected a crop of 150 bales of cotton from Butler's Island, 100 from Experiment, and 135 from Bram at Hampton and the Jones tract.[22]

When Experiment fell short of the Major's expectation, a testy old man sent word that boded trouble for young Morris and his people: "Whoever manages for me must promptly and strictly comply with my Directions which are never unreasonable. I observe what you write of the men cotton pickers at Experiment. If they have not altered try what effect deprivation will have. If that will have no effect, the unpleasant alternative of punishment must be resorted to. They must be brought under."[23]

In Philadelphia, Pierce Butler pondered his plan to maintain the plantations after his death. He realized that Roswell King, Jr., was not the man his father had been, and the Major knew that his own stubbornness had played a role in driving Mr. King away. More important, he bemoaned his inability to confront a crisis as of old.

Chapter 14

The Mease Boys Change Their Names

I N THE SEVENTY-SIXTH YEAR of his life Pierce Butler told an Irish niece, "I feel I am approaching the last scene." He was. For a time he maintained his old crustiness, passing out advice to family and friend, manager and slave. In England, George IV's mad father had finally died, and the new king was embroiled in a dispute with Queen Caroline that disgusted the old soldier. He was not beyond offering a bit of international counsel. He wrote to his agents in Liverpool:

> I observe with concern the additional ferment into which your Country is thrown by the difference between a man & his wife. When Kings were first thought of they were intended as Organs for promoting the Happiness of the People. Ye in England are making the peace, the comfort—not to use the word Happiness—of great and magnanimous people subservient to the pride and passions of two Individuals who live on the Industry of the Country without doing it one solitary good. Let the high minded people of England put both King & Queen and the whole family in a Yatch & send them to Hanover. You will, as soon as you get rid of such nuisances, be tranquil.

He thought the queen a "mischievous woman" and was "gratified that the noises and nonsense" she occasioned finally subsided. In March 1821, a last trip to Georgia was aborted when the Major suffered an attack of illness in Newcastle, Delaware, and was obliged to return to Philadelphia. From his bed or sometimes from a "sopha," his last letters were dictated to daughter Frances or to his young Mease grandsons. He acknowledged that "the days of my years are nearly full," and knew that his glass was running and that many things needed his attention. Aside from his will that would chart the future course he wished his heirs to follow, there were matters of conscience. One was his ill treatment of Roswell King, Sr. Another, but only to a degree, was his ownership of slaves. Of the first, he tried to reestablish the old Butler-King relationship by writing several letters asking advice or assistance. On hearing Mr. and Mrs. King were intending to travel to Connecticut: "I hope you will take your passage for Philada, not New York. I am Your Friend." The Kings did stop in Philadelphia on their return. As to the slaves, Major Butler's letters to Georgia evidenced a changed attitude. He "indulged" a few of the older people by sending his manservant Abraham to Hampton for a visit to see his family. A ship captain was paid thirteen dollars for the passage to Savannah where an agent was asked to send "my faithful servant" on down to Darien. As Jacob and old Bram were ailing, Roswell King, Jr., was asked to send them to Philadelphia, where they would receive better care than that available on the plantations: "They are almost the only Negroes I have left of the old stock, and are truly faithful." Realizing young King needed help, Major Butler relented and authorized an overseer for Butler's Island, the annual salary to be "$400 or $500 at the most. He must be a mild considerate man who will not go from the Estate. I will have no man who is violent or who is disposed to flogging." In November, he reminded his manager to consider the approaching holiday: "Cloth the Negroes well, do not stint them. & make them as happy as you can on Christmas. Do not spare the Beef." In January 1822, less than a month before the "last scene" was enacted, Major Butler wrote Roswell King, Sr., and as if to show he was still in touch, asked a favor: "I beg you to keep in view purchasing 40 or 50 Negroes to put on Butler's Island. I will pay cash for them. The present low price of cotton would not justify more than 300 doll'rs around." Uncharacteristically he wanted them only "if they are willing to go and live on my Island." It was a consideration he had never before granted a slave.[1]

On February 15, 1822, in his grand Philadelphia mansion, Pierce Butler reluctantly came to "that place where master and man, planter and slave must all at last lie down together." The press took short notice: "*Died* on Friday morning last, in the seventy-seventh year of his age, Major PIERCE BUTLER."[2] A few days later the news reached Charleston:

Died at Philadelphia on the 15th inst. Major Pierce Butler in the 77th year of his age. Major Butler was one of the five delegates from South Carolina, who were sent to Philadelphia on the adoption of our present glorious Constitution. This honour was conferred upon him, as a feeble testimony of the greatness and high opinion of his countrymen for his Revolutionary services. He was several years a member of Congress, and his mind and influence were always devoted to his country's good. The wealth which fortune had bestowed upon him was used for purposes of beneficence, and his talents and generosity were universally acknowledged.[3]

It was the kind of notice Major Butler would have wished to have had clipped and sent to Weeden Butler in London.

In Philadelphia a friend responded to the death of "our old neighbor and acquaintance" with a passage in her diary: "He was very polite and well bred, his manners exceedingly polished indeed, but an inveterate slaveholder. It is said he has near 1,000 of those poor beings on his cotton plantation in Georgia."[4]

Major Butler's body was placed in the tomb at Christ Church, alongside those of his grandson and his daughter Harriot Percy, in a funeral service that was most unusual. At daybreak, from the back of the Chestnut Street house the body was taken to the churchyard in a mysterious move that fascinated Philadelphians. Although it was some time before they learned the contents of Major Butler's will, it also created a similar fascination.[5]

Being aware his time was nigh, Pierce Butler signed his will the day before he died. The will was introduced with morbid formality—"Seeing that it is appointed unto all men once to die," an admission he must have hated to acknowledge. Yet it was certainly no hastily prepared, last-minute document. On the contrary, the will contained an honest attempt, if in true Pierce Butler fashion, nevertheless, to make amends and try to settle some old matters that had plagued him since the death in 1792 of Mary Butler's cousin, Elizabeth Blake.[6]

To his alienated daughter Sarah Mease he left $67,667, in trust, with her brother Thomas and her sisters Frances and Eliza as trustees. This bequest was to be "free from the control and interference of her husband." More important, Major Butler recognized the accusations made against him for the usurping of land and slaves left his children by Elizabeth Blake and by Mary Butler's sister, Sarah Guerard. The legacy was to be "considered in full of any claim" by Sarah Mease "on account of a small legacy left by Mrs. Eliza. Blake, or supposed legacy left by Mrs. Sarah Guerard."

To his son Thomas, also alienated, Major Butler left $20,000 in lieu of Butler Place, originally intended for him. In addition, there were lands on Duck River in Tennessee and several valuable tracts in Pennsylvania. These, together "with what I gave him on his arriving at the age of twenty-one, and together with a valuable tract of land in Wayne County in the state of Pennsylvania given him several years past," were to be considered "in bar of any claim" as was the previous bequest to Sarah Mease.

Pierce Butler's gift to his son on becoming twenty-one years old was covered by a document dated December 18, 1800, a conveyance of sixty slaves. Major Butler recited: "From the Affection I bear to my Son I hereby Give and Convey to him the within named Negroes amounting to Sixty in Number for his sole and separate use and benefit." The list included four slaves who were bracketed as couples—"Quakoo and Cumba," and "April and Nancy." The document was signed "P. Butler," and the word "Brewton" appeared before the date. The cover sheet was headed "Conveyance of some of the People from PB to TB." As in the Blake and Guerard bequests to the Butler children, Major Butler had been accused of misappropriating the inheritance from Mary Brewton.[7]

His daughter Harriot Percy having died in 1815, he left the two remaining unmarried daughters, Frances and Eliza, "three fourths parts," or a percentage thought by Frances to be proper of the income from his planting interests in Georgia. He provided that should the income be diminished by "revolution or insurrection, or any similar calamity," other real estate be sold to meet their needs. Major Butler had known revolution and long feared insurrection, thus giving validity to that provision in his will. In leaving an equal lifetime interest in the Chestnut Street mansion to Frances and Eliza, he specifically proclaimed, "I forbid my said house being let or rented for a tavern, boardinghouse, bank or seminary." He had remembered the Beaufort, South Carolina, house of his father-in-law, Thomas Middleton, had become a tavern—"at the Sign of the White Hart." The memory of Pierce Butler was not to be so degraded.[8]

Butler Place, together with everything "animate and inanimate thereon," was also left to Frances and Eliza for their natural lives. In a true Pierce Butlerism, Frances was directed to designate by her will the "most worthy" of the three Mease grandsons, Thomas, John, or Pierce Butler, and to that one and his "eldest legitimate son, and the eldest legitimate male issue of his son aforesaid," Butler Place was to pass accordingly.

To Frances and Eliza he designated $10,000 each—not to use and enjoy, but to leave by their wills as they might choose. They were bequeathed household furniture in Philadelphia, the family plate and linen, and the Major's considerable collection of liquors, which included the very special Butler Madeiras and other fine wines. The two daughters did not share their father's appreciation for his wines, so they passed on the treasure to other members of the family. Major Butler assured the ladies of easy access to Butler Place from Philadelphia by leaving them his "different carriages and carriage horses." A small house on Eighth Street, then occupied by "Mr. Webster," was an additional bequest to the twin daughters. Thomas Butler was left the Major's books and bookcases.

The disposition of the "rest, residue and remainder" of his estate is where Pierce Butler truly used his dead hand to point the way in which he wanted his children and grandchildren to move. This, the great bulk of his large fortune, included the Georgia plantations from which Frances and Eliza were to receive three-fourths of the income. Again, Major Butler gave his favorite daughter Frances the discretion of decision. He directed that the estate "be disposed of applied and appropriated to such extent, in such proportions and manner, and at such times as she in her discretion may think best to and among my three grandsons" during her lifetime, but on her death, in parts and proportions as Frances should designate in writing. The three grandsons named in this part of the will were, again, the Mease boys. The three sons of Thomas and Eliza de Mallevault Butler, who were blessed at birth with the one requisite the Major sought, were put aside. Thomas, John, and Pierce Butler Mease could inherit only "upon the express condition that they shall as they respectively arrive at the age of sixteen years, or within twelve months after my demise cease to use the name *Mease* and respectively take, assume and use the surname *Butler*." If any one refused, the others would take his share. If all three chose to hold fast to *Mease,* the bequest would pass to the eldest son of Thomas Butler. Major Butler was not consistent in this provision. In leaving Butler Place he had directed Frances to name the "most worthy." That his own father's estate, including the baronetcy, had passed to the eldest son by tradition engendered a feeling of injustice he had harbored all of his life.

Taking his cue from the United States Constitution that he had "some small part in frameing," Pierce Butler was oblique in his reference to the most valuable segment of his estate, the slaves. In referring to the Brewton slaves he had given Thomas in 1800, he used the term "property." The blacks who were a part of Butler Place in the bequest to Frances and Eliza were "the animate thereon." By design, or by error, he neglected to mention the Middleton-Bull slaves that had been left to him by Mary Butler, in trust for their children. Only through the "in bar of any claim" bequests to Sarah Mease and to Thomas Butler did he attempt to deal with the snarl of lifelines brought on by the commingling of Butler, Blake, Brewton, and Guerard slaves who worked his plantations. All of *his* slaves were covered by the "rest, residue and remainder" clause of his will.[9]

The annual accounting of births and deaths on the Georgia plantations for 1822 showed that twenty-two slaves joined their owner in death during that year. Six of those were very old people, all of whom had been known to Pierce Butler, and he to them. Phyllis succumbed to "old age and fever" the same day her owner died in Philadelphia. She was followed in death by Toby, who was ninety; by the resourceful driver Morris, who was eighty; and then by Pompey, Nero, and old Molly, who never won the freedom she sought in life. In that same year, nineteen children were born to Butler slaves. Driver Bram, who was said to be the son of Roswell King, Sr., and his wife Venus begat a son, Joe. Pinder, the wife of Major Butler's favorite driver, Sambo, begat a daughter called Lydia. Among the others born in 1822 were Patience and Chloe, two Caesars, Gorham, Justice, and Flanders.[10]

Frances Butler was named the sole executrix of her father's will. She chose not to qualify as such until July 2, 1823, well over a year after her father's death. It was said in Philadelphia she wished to pass the estate "as an inheritance from her mother" but could not do so. That may well have been a reason for the delay and a possible solution to the objections to the will raised by Thomas Butler. Thomas was aware that his father, facing death, had sought a reconciliation that might have come about had he and his family been able to return to America from England. Although the illness of his daughter Anne prevented his return before Major Butler's death, Thomas was quick to appear in Philadelphia after receiving word of what happened on February 15. He left his family in Paris and crossed the Atlantic to confront his sisters with his rights as he saw them.[11]

In 1822, the year of Major Butler's death, his grandson Thomas Mease was eighteen years old. He refused to change his name to *Butler* and urged his younger brothers to ignore their grandfather's plan. The second grandson, John Mease, was sixteen years old in 1822. He also refused to change to *Butler* in the timely manner as specified in the will. Pierce Butler Mease was twelve when his grandfather died. As he grew older it became apparent he would not follow his brothers and that he would forsake the family name when he became sixteen. Thomas Butler, aware of that prob-

Roswell King, Jr.'s statement of the births and deaths of Butler slaves in the year 1822, when Major Butler died. (Historical Society of Pennsylvania.)

ability, remained in Philadelphia to assist his sister Frances in her new position as "Proprietor" and to make his own plans to attempt an upset of the division of the estate in accordance with the will.[12]

In Charleston, Denmark Vesey's futile attempt to break the chains that bound the slaves occurred in the year of Major Butler's death. The apprehension the Major had shared with Roswell King was certainly not theirs alone. The white man's fear of "the enemy in our bosoms" was widespread and particularly evident in expressions spread before the public in a pamphlet published by "a South Carolinian" who called for the banishment of "FREE BLACKS" in Charleston. Denmark Vesey had purchased his freedom with the proceeds of a winning lottery ticket, but most of that class came into being when slaves were freed for "extra-ordinary fidelity" or were former slaves who had purchased their own or their wives' freedom. A master's respect for, or the recognition of, his children by a black woman often gained their freedom, but these were mulattoes and in a different category. From the South Carolinian's pamphlet: "We look upon the existence of our FREE BLACKS among us, as the greatest and most deplorable evil with which we are unhappilly afflicted. They are, generally speaking, an idle, lazy, insolent set of vagabonds, who live by theft or gambling, or other means equally vicious and demoralizing." Fearing further insurrection, he continued: "We would respectively recommend to the Legislature therefor, *the expediency of removing this evil, and of rooting it out of the land.* A law, banishing them, under the penalty of death." He did not advocate the banishment of "FREE MULLATTOES," for he saw them as a barrier between the slaves and the whites and believed they would be on his side in any insurrection. He ended his diatribe: "Let it never be forgotten that our NEGROES are truly the *Jacobins* of the country, that they are the *Anarchists* and the *Domestic Enemy,* the *common enemy of civilized society* and the Barbarians who would IF THEY COULD, become the DESTROYERS *of our race.*"[13]

At Pierce Butler's death the flow of "Honored Sir" letters to Philadelphia came to an end. Roswell King, Jr., chose to address Frances Butler as "Miss Butler, Madam," and when the surrogate Thomas Butler assumed the burden of the plantation correspondence, it was "Mr. Butler, Sir." The deference commanded by their father had vanished. No longer was the owner in Philadelphia held in awe and esteem. Along with his optimistic crop reports and his inclination to remain silent on plantation troubles, young Mr. King seemed genuinely concerned with the health of the slaves. He expressed his philosophy: "Slave owners cannot be too particular to whom they intrust the health (I may say life) and morals of what may justly be termed the sinews of an estate. A master, or overseer, should be the kind friend and monitor to the slave, not the opressor." He strongly believed that *revenge* is the "predominant principle of the human race," an observation gained from a relatively brief lifetime spent entirely among a race he hardly thought human. He held an implicit belief in his own, and in his father's humane practices, but like his father before him, his words and his actions were rather far apart. Yet, believing as he did that slaves were "the sinews" of the estate, he sought to keep them strong and well. The pattern on the plantations had changed somewhat, for Butler's Island had moved into the ascendancy, and Hampton, now lumped together with Experiment and other St. Simons tracts, had become secondary. As it had ever been, exposure to long stretches of bad weather was invariably followed by much sickness. Roswell King, Jr., realized the rice plantation was unhealthy, particularly for children. He devised a system of moving the very young *en masse* to high and drier ground. At the same time he was proud of being able to feed "one hundred and fourteen little Negroes" an extra mess of "ocra Soup, with Pork, or a little Molasses or Hommony or Small Rice" at a cost of two cents each per week. So satisfied were the children there was "not a *dirt eater* among them." He repeatedly requested the Butlers send medicine and material for clothing, and had "Swaim's Panacea" been the curative he believed it to be, his people would have known no further illness.[14]

After the death of her autocratic father, Frances Butler braced herself for the difficult task ahead. Having suffered through his illness and death, she sought restoration at Saratoga Springs, where Roswell King, Jr.'s letters soon found her. The Denmark Vesey uprising in Charleston struck fear into the hearts of those who owned large numbers of slaves, prompting the Butlers to return to the restrictive measures first practiced at Hampton and Butler's Island by an authoritative Pierce Butler. It was a discipline that had gradually relaxed as the Major's intense interest waned. Despite the tensions, events on the plantations followed the usual routine, though one was most unusual.[15]

Shortly after Major Butler died Frances Butler fulfilled the promise her father had made to Abraham, his body servant. She wrote an explanation to young Mr. King in a letter sent along with the former slave:

> The vessel in which Abraham returns is sailing unexpectedly. I have but a
> few moments to say that he was given his freedom by my Father. When he

is on the Estate he is to be as much under your direction as he has always been, but he is to be at liberty to go from it and return to it when he wishes. I feel confident from his conduct while with us that he will not give you any trouble.

We have not time to give Abraham the proper evidence of his being free but it is our intention to send it on to him.

Abraham returned to Hampton to find himself in the unusual position of being a freedman on a Butler plantation.[16]

Roswell King, Jr., wrote to Philadelphia with the usual regularity. In June 1823, "Have nearly got through with the vaccination of the little negroes," which was another manifestation of his concern for their health. In August he made an unusual request of Miss Butler that he presumed would not be "offensive," would add to his "domestic comfort," and would do the "proprietor of the Estate, not the smallest injury":

> Hannah, who was once in Philada is now on the Estate as a common field hand, and by no means a first rate hand. I have endeavoured to purchase in Savh or Chasn a woman that was capable of managing the affairs of a house, but never was pleased with any of them, some bad quality, either dishonest or given to drink. Hannah knows the difference of the field and the house, and I think will not object to be owned by me; a person who is obliged to move about as much as I have, rarely a week in one place, arriving home late at night, either a cold dinner or no dinner, can be made much more comfortable by possessing such a servant as Hannah. I am disposed to give a very fair price for her and six children, say 1800$, much above the present price of negroes. The names and ages are thus Hannah 27, Mary 9, Flora 7, Sawney 6, John 4, James 2, Gorham 1/4. Have said more on the subject than I intended but hope that it may be agreeable to you to accede to my proposal.

Roswell King, Jr. signed the letter with an imposing flourish. His hand was well formed and legible. In November, Frances Butler agreed to the transaction and was then told by her manager that he would proceed if he could not do better.[17] He sent an unusual request for the slaves' Christmas. It was posted too late for a timely reply, which meant his request was more a notice of intention. He asked for a pint of rum for each man, and: "Application has been made to me by the principal musician to treat them to a violin for the amusement of the people this Christmas. One can be

Swaim's Panacea, a Philadelphia patent medicine administered to Butler slaves in great quantity. (This bottle was found in waters off St. Simons Island by scuba diver Lucky Lowe.)

had for 5 or 6$." After the slaves had celebrated, he sent word to the Butlers: "The Christmas Holidays among the Blacks are so far over without accident. They have had as much of every article as would do them good, say beef, rice, rum and molasses and I am happy to say I did not see one of them intoxicated, if such was the case they kept out of my view."[18]

During the year, Thomas, who was the oldest of the Mease boys, and who would not change his name to Butler, died in Philadelphia even before his Aunt Frances had proved Major Butler's will and qualified as executrix. In London, Thomas Butler's schoolmaster, the Reverend Weeden Butler, came to the end of his life. While in Paris, Anne, the daughter of Eliza de Mallevault and Thomas Butler, died and was buried at Père-Lachaise, bringing grief to a family already torn by sadness and strife. In Darien, Roswell King's Steam Saw Mill, the investment Major Butler had preferred to the bank, burned to the ground.[19]

In 1824 Roswell King, Jr., replied to a question asked by Frances Butler that showed a continued reaction to the Denmark Vesey affair:

> The negroes on this Estate behave very Well, though I am obliged to be very strict. Allow no intercourse with other Negroes. None allowed to go off without asking permission, and stating his business abroad, and every Negro to be home before night. By these means I prevent their committing depredations abroad, which some of them would do. Other planters negroes are punished publicly for crimes, which by regulations made and supported here, our negroes escape.[20]

The diet of the Butler slaves had long been bolstered by corn purchased in Savannah, Charleston, or in later years sent down from Philadelphia on the "corn vessel." Young Roswell King made a comment on human nature he believed peculiar to blacks. "Negroes are strange creatures," he said. When yellow corn was first sent down from Philadelphia, the slaves were accustomed to white corn and objected to what they believed to be horse food. The blacks having become accustomed to yellow corn, a shipment of white corn brought a return to earlier reaction. In April, Abraham had received his freedom papers and sent back his thanks. Roswell King, Jr., who had been ill, gave Miss Butler encouraging reports. He told of Hannah and of free Abraham:

> Hannah is the most proper person that I know of, is pretty intelligent, and naturally kind. Kindness to a sick person is as good as medicine.

Abraham gits nothing from the Estate. He was always a high minded chap—Squabbling with his wife or some other person but since his return from Philada, he has been the best behavd fellow I know.[21]

Again demonstrating his concern for the health of the slaves, he negotiated an arrangement with "Dr. Grosvenor" of Darien, paying three hundred dollars a year in return for a weekly visit to Butler's Island. He submitted the proposition to Philadelphia, and although the untimely death of Dr. Grosvenor while boarding a ship in Doboy Sound terminated the contract, a similar arrangement was continued with Dr. James I. Holmes.[22]

For a few days Roswell King, Sr., reappeared to look after the Butler estate while young Roswell was courting in Liberty County. Mr. King seized the opportunity to urge Miss Butler to continue the planting of sugar cane. Knowing that young Roswell found sugar a troublesome crop, he nonetheless wrote "We must and can make sugar."[23]

In September 1824 the Altamaha estuary was devastated by a tropical hurricane. Both Hampton and Butler's Island were battered by high winds and relentless rain. Buildings were blown down and away, with great destruction to slave quarters on both plantations. At Butler's Island one thousand bushels of rice were lost, but as Roswell King, Jr., reported, it was good that "*No* lives were lost and only 2 injuries." The storm and attendant rain were followed by a freshet the likes of which few had seen before. From the high bluff at Darien to the islands on the Atlantic was one great sheet of water that covered the broad expanse of rice fields, broken only by a scattering of trees and the tops of the few buildings that survived the storm. For the young Bank of Darien, the financial storm that followed saw planter's losses rock the institution to its foundations. In the weekly report, Roswell King, Jr., came quickly to the point: "A painful duty is devolved upon me to inform you of the almost total loss of the crop at Butler's Island."[24]

In 1825 Pierce Butler Mease continued to show every indication that he would change his name. Thomas Butler, despite the fact that Frances Butler had qualified as executrix and was administering the estate in accordance with the will, decided the time had come to make a move. Writing in his small, neat, very legible hand, Thomas penned a letter to his "Dear Sister Sarah" asking that she join him, Frances, and Eliza in putting aside their father's will in favor of a division of the income and a future partition of the estate into four equal parts. The letter, which gave several valid reasons for his request, consisted of twenty-seven pages of Thomas Butler's compact, Chelsea-taught handwriting. He wrote that his appeal was to "the justice of those who are concerned in our Father's will," and Sarah Mease was, indeed, one of those. He told Sarah how he had fallen into disfavor: "His feelings had always been irritated by the Idea of his Children being independent of him, and his exaction of a blind obedience invariable. To assert the former, or to refuse the latter, was sufficient to Excite his lasting Displeasure." Thomas noted that it was painful for their father to be in any way dependent on his children: "He kept them, as you know, entirely uninformed of every Circumstance connected with the Rights which they derived from their maternal Relations, and disposed of, transferred or exchanged all family Property with as unshakled a Will as if it had been his own." He told Sarah how Major Butler had enlisted the aid of his attorney, and he quoted a letter from Michael Hogan: "Your Father is really heartbroken to think you should go to France without consulting him. I observe your last son's name is Louis, after his maternal grandfather. I hope the next will be called after your own Father and that he will be born in this country." Despite Mr. Hogan's advice, Thomas had named his next son after a friend, John Devreux. Mr. Hogan told Thomas that he believed his mother-in-law, Madame de Mallevault, would return to America with his family and eliminate the need of their being in Paris.

Thomas Butler advised Sarah of other efforts on the part of Major Butler to bring about an understanding between the two. The Major had promised Thomas a new house and increased income, but as the gifts were not based on "natural and disinterested affection between a parent and a child," they were rejected. Then he told of the letter from Frances Butler to Thomas then in England, advising of Major Butler's illness and his desire to have Thomas return and be "at home in his house," where the children would be cared for by Frances, and that the first son, Francis, would be provided with ample means for his education. It was then Thomas wrote Frances telling of the illness of the child, Anne. "Before my letter could reach Philadelphia our Father had expired."

The most telling of the arguments for equal division of the estate was his quotation of the text of a letter from Major Butler to his children at a time of some stress. The letter, dated June 2, 1796, was written the year after the return of Thomas from Chelsea. At that time Major Butler had decided to resign from the Senate and was giving consideration to his ill-fated contest for the House of Representatives. He had broken with the

Federalists, and had been put aside for Aaron Burr as a candidate for the vice-presidency. Yet the financial seas on which he sailed seemed not so stormy as others he had weathered before. The letter was the best evidence Thomas presented his sister Sarah:

> My most tenderly beloved Children—I am impelled by a duty I owe to myself and to you, to take a step that may separate us forever; painful, truly painful Idea. Receive this then, as the advice of a departing Parent.
>
> If you should love me, unite from that Moment, more closely together. Allow not for a Moment, one Thought, one Impression, derogatory, from the most unreason'd Friendship and Affection to gain Admittance among you. It is the last Request of a fond Father, that you live in Union. Let no earthly Consideration induce a Separation while you remain single. In every sense, in every Light in which it can be view'd, it is your interest to live together, and closely united by Ties of Friendship and Affection.
>
> Of your worldly affairs, I wish I had the time to say more. My advice is that you, the Females, go to Carolina in the Autumn, not before the last of October on any Account, that you call all my creditors together, and assume all my just Debt, provided they will be patient, and wait to receive the Surplusage of the Crops, after reserving to yourself A really Comfortable living, or until Judge Wilson's bonds shall become due. If they attempt to tear the Estate to pieces, apply to General Pinckney and Mr. Pringle. Under old Mrs. Bull's, Mrs. Guerard's, your Mother's and Mrs. Blake's wills, most of the Negroes are your own Property. The lands at Combahee are Tom's & the rest of the Land in Carolina are your Common Property. The Lands in Georgia are the only Thing they can tear from You.

Major Butler, not one who was likely to have considered suicide, may have been thinking of taking refuge in Florida, as had his borrowing friend John McQueen in 1792. Such a move would have put him beyond reach of his creditors and of the trustees of those estates from which he had usurped his children's property. In any case, it was a candid admission of the deliberate mismanagement of their inheritance.

Thomas ended the long appeal to his sister Sarah by stating that their sister Frances "is quite ready to forego the provisions of the will in her behalf," and that likewise, Eliza had "expressed a desire" that such an arrangement be made. He reminded Sarah that when their father had given him lots in Beaufort, South Carolina, he had divided the proceeds with his sisters. Sarah was told that were she to return his long letter without comment, he would understand that her answer was no. She did.

Thomas then sent a second letter on May 26, 1825, in which he offered to submit the matter to their well-respected cousin, Dr. James Stewart, who had married Anne Middleton, half-sister to their mother, Mary Butler. Sarah Mease returned this letter unopened and said she would listen only to "verbal communications through Miss F. Butler."[25]

Thus both Thomas Butler's twenty-seven-page plea and his second letter were rejected by his oldest sister. The youngest son, Pierce Butler Mease, called "Butler" by his family and friends, turned sixteen on March 26, 1826, and rather than being called "Butler Butler" chose to be known as Pierce Butler, an act that would warm the cold heart in the Christ Church yard. He stood to inherit the vast estate that had been both the source of the family's well-being and of many of its troubles. That Major Butler had refrained from signing his will until the day prior to his death was good evidence he held out hope that Thomas, "my Son, my only Son," would return to the fold.[26]

When Sarah Mease refused to agree to his plan for a voluntary distribution of their father's estate, Thomas Butler sought legal redress. From James Stewart, their kinsman in South Carolina, Thomas obtained a list and valuation of the properties in the Bull, Blake, Brewton, and Guerard estates that would have been inherited by the Butler children. The total value, exclusive of hundreds of slaves, came to $261,889, or $65,472 for each of the four children. Included were the Euhaw plantations, Toogoodoo, town lots in Beaufort, the proceeds from the sale of plantations on Hilton Head and in St. Peters Parish, Coosaw Island, Izard's on the Combahee, a Lady's Island plantation, and two houses and lots in Charleston. A legal opinion from John Sergeant of Philadelphia was obtained that stated: "It appears beyond doubt that there was property in lands and negroes in the possession of Major Butler belonging to his children derived from the wills of Mrs. Bull, Mrs. Guerard, Mrs. Butler, and Mrs. Blake." He believed there was "an accountability" for property that "belongs to the children of Major Butler, in their own right, and is no part of the estate of Major Butler." But he cited obstacles, the difficulty of determining title to the slaves, and that those who had accepted "in lieu of" legacies under Pierce Butler's will could not at the same time claim the properties to which they were entitled from the other estates. So complex was Major Butler's entanglement, Thomas surrendered reluctantly. He decided he would remain in America to continue monitoring the business of the plantations for his sister Frances.

What little equilibrium Thomas Butler possessed was disturbed by a visit from his son Louis, who despite living in the same house could only communicate with his father by an exchange of written notes. If possible, Louis and his older brother Francis were greater irritants to their father than Thomas had been to Major Butler. Fortunately for Thomas, he was occupied by the demands of the plantations, which kept his mind diverted from personal unhappiness. He conducted the correspondence with Roswell King, Jr., and was also responsible for the dealings with the Butlers' agents in Liverpool, Messrs. Harrison, Lathan, and Company. In Charleston, he dealt with Taylor, Lawton and Company, and in Savannah, the venerable firm of Robert Habersham, Esq. He saw to it that justifiable requests that came from Georgia were met, be they corn, bar iron, flannel, medicinal supplies including Swaim's Panacea, and castor oil. He had no responsibility for plantation accounts, nor did he know how they were kept. Frances Butler, able businesswoman that she was, held that function unto herself.[27]

In 1825 Roswell King, Jr., sent word of a change in his status: "I shall be absent next Sunday on a *matrimonial expedition* and must beg that I be excused that days writing." At twenty-nine he was wed to seventeen-year-old Julia Rebecca Maxwell, the daughter of Audley Maxwell, a plantation owner of Liberty County, Georgia, and his wife Mary Stevens. Julia King was born and lived at the Maxwell plantation Carnichfergus. The Kings lived in the house at Hampton that Roswell King, Jr., had known most of his life. Both developed a very satisfactory relationship with Frances and Thomas Butler, who learned to trust and to depend on their manager much as Major Butler first depended on the elder Roswell King.[28]

Roswell King, Sr., when freed from the demands of Major Butler and his slaves, embarked on an exciting new career. A reason given by the King family for his departure from the Butler estate was a warning from a "faithful slave" of a pending insurrection of those in bondage at Darien and on St. Simons Island. Perhaps this was a factor, for he had good reason for apprehension should such an uprising be in the offing. The fundamental reason, however, had to be the deterioration of the Pierce Butler–Roswell King relationship and his subsequent failure to be accepted by the second generation. Fortunately for him the Bank of Darien reached out far beyond the Altamaha estuary in its business dealings and used the talented Mr. King as an emissary to distant interests. In the words of his admiring great-granddaughter, he was chosen "because of his character of the strictest integrity and fearlessness" to look after their gold mining venture in north Georgia and North Carolina. While on travels for the bank, Roswell King was attracted to the beautiful hill country north of present-day Atlanta. There, said his great-granddaughter, "he adopted General Oglethorpe's policy and made friends with the Indians and bought large tracts of land from them." Actually, he purchased most of the land from Fannin Brown who had acquired it in the Georgia land lottery of 1832. With his third son Barrington King, he used the land to establish villages much as he had wished to do for Major Butler on Hampton's exhausted cotton fields. The Kings offered inducements to friends in the low country of Georgia and South Carolina to build summer homes in what became the town of Roswell. Around the crossroads community of nearby Lebanon, a town of that name was developed by the Kings.

In Roswell, "the Kings, father and son, laid out the village with wide streets and a park, and gave building sites for an academy and two churches—Presbyterian and Methodist." The Presbyterian church had a slave gallery in the rear. Both towns were tied to what the Kings believed to be the stabilizing influence of industrial development—flour mills at Lebanon and cotton mills at Roswell.[29]

The younger Kings, well ensconced at Hampton, produced the first of their eleven children. Mary Elizabeth King was born in 1827, followed by James Audley Maxwell King in 1829. Roswell King, Jr., engineered a swap of Butler lands on St. Simons for some land contiguous to other Butler land, the acquired portion coming from James Hamilton, then living in Philadelphia. The Butlers surrendered their St. Clair tract and gained a portion of Village plantation, land once owned by Salzburgers. So confident was Frances Butler of the good judgment of her manager, the exchange was readily approved.[30]

Roswell King, Jr., the self-styled "kind friend and monitor to the slave" reported the death of a troublesome slave following punishment. When questioned by Thomas Butler, his answer the following week was not clear. It appeared that several slaves had been led astray by a slave named Sampson. Emanuel, the slave who died, was punished less severely than Mr. King's own servant, Balaam. The manager's letter stated:

> The cold bath is solely my punishment, never used by anyone else. I took Emanuel & my own servant Balaam to the Rice Mill where I found Sambo. Balaam being more gently in my opinion than the other. By way of graduating the punishment I gave him three buckets of water & Emanuel but

one. It is all a pretence. I never use the whip without giving me pains. I put it off to the very last. In fact punishment in any form from me to them is unpleasant.

The idea of having rules beneficial to master & man of 27 years forming destroyed by a few malignant ungrateful Scoundrels is not pleasant. Sampson succeeded as to get 6 others to join him & run away.

The answer seemed to satisfy Thomas Butler.[31]

During this period of Frances Butler's "proprietorship" the income from the Butler estate was shared by Frances and Eliza Butler and the new Pierce Butler, a young man who seemed more concerned with worldly pleasures than with the management of his unusual inheritance. The twin sisters chose to follow Major Butler's suggestion by dividing three-fourths of the earnings with the remaining quarter going to their nephew. In March 1830, another Pierce Butler, the one-year-old son of John and Gabriella Mease, died in Paris. He was the fourth of several given the name of Pierce Butler who were to die young. The following year Sarah Butler Mease died in Philadelphia, recognized, but unloved, by her brother and the two sisters who survived her. Her husband, two daughters, and two of her four sons were also survivors.[32]

Knowing her son Pierce was cared for by the provisions of her father's will and evidently aware of her son John's intentions, Sarah Mease provided in her will the house on Chestnut Street near Tenth and other property held under a deed of trust made by Major Butler at the time of her marriage in 1800 be divided between the two Mease daughters, Frances Mease Cadwalader and Mary Middleton Mease. The entailed property continued under the trusteeship of her sister Frances Butler. Household goods, furniture, plate, linen, and ornaments were also divided between the two daughters. Dr. Mease, who outlived Sarah by fourteen years, was not named as a beneficiary in her brief will.[33]

In December 1831, the year of his mother's death, John Mease belatedly changed his name to John Butler to share Major Butler's fortune. He did so with the permission and through the generosity of his brother Pierce. Gabriella Manigault Morris, who married a Mease, became a Butler, as did her infant daughter, Elizabeth, who was born a Mease.[34]

In September of 1832, and while occupied in his pursuit of idleness and entertainment, Pierce Butler received an enthusiastic letter from an English friend in New York City. He told of a pair of English theatrical people—father and daughter—then performing in a New York theater.

Of the daughter the message was: "you will fall in love with her, for she is right lovely to look upon." For the next twenty months the aimless life of Pierce Butler found a purposeful direction. In June 1834 the young English woman and Pierce Butler were married in Philadelphia.[35]

An ailing Thomas Butler went to Newport in 1835 in search of better health and to look into some property owned by his sister Frances. On an earlier visit he had determined that he, too, would own land there, joining other South Carolina families including Rutledges, Middletons, and Izards who had "invaded" the place following the Revolution. He purchased several lots of land, one of which adjoined land of Henry Middleton. To improve his land, he planned to plant as many as 450 balm of Gilead trees, a balsam poplar thought to have originated in Scotland. At the time of his visit a shipment of 247 of the trees had arrived from a New York botanical garden. In the fall he began assembling material for the construction of a house designed to bring relief from the misery of Philadelphia summers.[36]

With Thomas Butler in Newport, Frances Butler again took on the plantation correspondence. Roswell King, Jr., wrote that the "corn vessel" *Richard Henry* had arrived from Philadelphia. Expected medicinal supplies were not received, but other valuable material was gratefully acknowledged:

> The box containing Rag and some clothing with 4 pieces calico was also delivered. It was too slight to bear the weight of the articles but as far as I could see no trespass has been committed. As I mentioned before nothing in the shape of Rag comes amiss here, for pains in the face, neck & side we use poultices of meal & pepper or herbs, or flax seed. Nothing is better than an old stocking to contain it. The supply of Rag will last us a long time, sometimes we are quite destitute. In each bundle of Infants clothers there should be a supply of soft old Rag for bandages &c. The old flannel is of more value than you are aware of. I think I have before this saved at least 5 little negroes worth 500$ with 5$ worth of flannel. For instance a puny little fellow growing nowhere but head & stomach, a flannel jacket dipped in a decoction of Red oak bark, dried and worn next the skin, has a wonderful effect. Nothing I assure you but care will encrease a gang of negroes.

In the same letter he told of the condition of the crops, of severe hailstorms, freshets, and Sambo's sickness: "You say distribute the clothing and Calico to those who give the least trouble in doing their duty, about that I do not have much trouble. Tasks according to the strength of the individual is given, and not more than what can be accomplished." He said he would divide the calico among the women "advanced in life or feeble" who do the "moating or sorting" of cotton:

> I keep up a degree of Emulation among the cotton pickers in this way. When we have a heavy blow, all those who pick a given quantity or over, one Quart of small rice for supper, those below that, one pint, those who do not come up to the mark 5, 10, 15 & 20 steps on the Road, to clean up in the evening.

> The silk dresses shall be given to Molly and Jesse who are still alive and I think look nearly as well as they did 30 years ago except not quite so active. Molly is really active in raising her grand & great grand children, much more than paying her expense. You justly say, faithful old Jacob, he is though quite a cripple still very valuable in attending to grinding corn & giving out provisions, and in my absence from this place in looking after small matters.[37]

Having returned to Philadelphia, Thomas Butler resumed his work for his sister Frances. A letter from Roswell King, Jr., again told of the success of his strategy in moving young slaves from Butler's Island to high ground. He acknowledged that two slaves were causing trouble but said yet another was far worse. Despite an epidemic in the low country, there had been no Butler deaths for a week:

> The pinewood Gang of 58 children still clear of measles. There has been many fatal cases among the whites.

> I have your letter regarding London and Scipio, it is to be regretted that two such healthy tough men cannot be tamed, but the risk of loss in these erratick excurtions is very great. I can keep them at home and get their work, but it is attended with much trouble. Last winter 600$ could have been got for each. They cost 450$. There are some on the Estate whose example is far worse then London or Scipio. Our chief blacksmith Jack has not for 20 years give the satisfaction he ought to have done.
>
> Talking to him does no good. Last summer I had to give him a sound flogging, but that has not mended him. In 1820 when Mr. Butler was here he told him that unless he did better he would sell him.[38]

Frances Butler died on March 18, 1836, a death that revealed her meticulous attention to the directives given her by Major Butler in his will.

Gustavus Colhoun was named to succeed her as executor in a document she signed in 1827. He qualified as such the month following her death. She also took official notice of the death of Thomas Mease, that then John Mease had not changed his name to Butler, but that Butler Mease "now is called and Known by the name of Pierce Butler," thus preparing the estate to pass as her father had ordained. Her demise caused significant changes in the Butler family, as well as in the administration of Major Butler's estate. Although her death triggered the plan of inheritance in his will, in her own estate Frances chose to follow her personal dictates by ignoring the Mease boys. She attempted to make amends for her father's treatment of Thomas Butler by leaving him her entire estate, including the ten thousand dollars provided by Major Butler's will. There were no Pierce Butlerisms in Frances Butler's will. She left "All my Estate, Real and Personal, whatsoever and wheresoever" to Thomas Butler, and had he not outlived her, specified that her estate would pass first to his son Francis, and then to Louis. Her will had been prepared ten years before her death, at the time when Sarah had rejected Thomas's plea to approve a four-way division of Major Butler's estate. The third son, John, was an infant at the time the will was drawn. In specifying that all was left to Thomas, she wrote: "whether derived from the Will or Estate of my Father, from my Great Grandmother Mrs. Bull, my aunt Mrs. Guerard, from my Mother, or my Sister Miss H. P. Butler, or howsoever else." In addition, she named Thomas as her executor, an assignment he accepted in April. He lost no time in relinquishing his duties as correspondent and agent for the Pierce Butler estate. He wrote Roswell King, Jr., saying he had assisted his "overburdened" sister Frances in her duties as executrix of Major Butler's estate. His letter was most complimentary:

> The demise of Miss Frances Butler on the 18th ultimo, now terminates all connection on my part with the estate.
>
> In closing my correspondence with you as manager of the estate, I have great satisfaction in assuring you that Miss Butler and myself have always entertained the highest opinion of the good management, the zeal, and the remarkable integrity with which you have discharged your many and arduous duties.[39]

Death had also visited the immediate family of Thomas Butler. The unhappy Eliza de Mallevault Butler and her mother had died, as had Francis, the oldest son. Louis, in Paris, had inherited a "fortune" from his

grandmother, most of it represented by a share of the family sugar plantation on Martinique. Thomas was bitter over the behavior of his son Louis
and that of Francis before his death. That Thomas Butler was a true son of
his father was evident in letters sent to Louis in those eventful years:

> Relying upon the property left to you by your grandmother, and doubtless
> unaware of your legal position in society, you have for near the last two
> years disregarded parental authority and have taken your welfare and fu-
> ture destiny, so far as they are dependent upon human agency, into your
> own hands.

> You have in the pursuit of your own hapiness, and in utter disregard of his,
> now gone forth into the world, as, in all your respects, independent of him,
> you have, as it respects your father, drawn the sword and thrown away the
> scabbard. It would therefore, be an act of injustice, on his part, not to
> apprise you that you must, henceforth, depend upon your own pecuniary
> resources for maintenance and future establishment in life.

Thomas then gave Louis two full pages of advice on making his way in a
competitive world on the grounds of the competitors—either France or
Martinique—and then ends this document of filial detachment:

> This will be true wisdom, and may, perhaps, recommend itself to you as
> such, when you reflect that none of your father's property is intended for
> you, during either his lifetime, or after his demise. Edmund Burke says
> "What is Liberty without wisdom and without virtue? It is the greatest of
> all public evils, for it is folly, vice and madness, without tuition or
> restraint."
>
> T. BUTLER[40]

Thomas Butler returned to Newport, looking into his own and the
property he had inherited from his sister Frances. While there he became
ill—"a pulmonary disease," he wrote Louis. It struck fear into his being,
and worried about cold winters and hot summers, he told Louis he had
taken steps to guard against both. His letter, written in 1838, told of what
he had done in 1836 when he became aware of his illness: "I therefore
caus'd a lot to be purchased at the N.W. Corner of Walnut & 13th Streets
and a house to be erected on it which will, I believe, be dry and warm in
winter, and at least, some of the rooms in it, cool in summer without
being at all damp."[41]

Thomas Butler envisioned a house superior to his father's. Joshua Francis Fisher said that it had "double walls and roof, double sashes of plate glass, solid floors of yellow pine board." The house was designed so that there were "no rooms communicating," and consequently the "want of a draught" caused every fireplace to smoke. There were "English oil cloths and carpets for every room." The house, which is still standing, is built of a dull red brick with three stories, a dormered attic, and a basement. A small balcony below the peak of the roof on the Thirteenth Street side sends a flag staff towering over the house. Despite the peculiarities of its interior, the house has an attractive corner entrance and is generous in its width and handsome in the formality of its design—altogether an imposing structure. The building erected at Thirteenth and Walnut streets was not unlike its owner—handsome without and rather strange within.[42]

When Thomas Butler surrendered his responsibilities to his father's estate, he wrote a long memorandum to the new Pierce Butler. He mentioned several unfilled orders for supplies needed on the plantations, told of notifying the agents of the change, suggested that Hugh Colhoun be put aside as Philadelphia representative of the estate, as "age has rendered him inactive," and most interesting, wrote his own appraisal of the two Roswell Kings:

> In justice to Mr. Roswell King, Junr, the manager of the estate, I ought to say, that a correspondence with him of fourteen years has led me to entertain the highest opinion of his judgement as a planter, and a no less smaller opinion of his integrity.

> His manner of expressing himself, has occasionally been somewhat abrupt—but he never—I am persuaded, intended to be disrespectful. A supple artful knave is never abrupt, really honest men sometimes are.

Thomas continued, writing that the younger Mr. King had requested permission to leave the plantation from late June until October on a northern trip designed to restore Mrs. King's health, a venture Thomas had approved. He justified his decision: "If I were the owner of the estate, I should consider the loss of the present manager to be altogether irreparable and I feel confident that my opinion will be found to have been but too correct, if death, or any other cause, should remove him from the management of the estate." Of the elder Mr. King, it was a different story:

> As it respects Mr. Roswell King, Senr, I cannot put you too much on your guard. He once made the modest proposal to rent the whole estate, and it is not long since he earnestly recommended that it should be sold, offering

Thomas Butler's splendid Philadelphia house at Walnut and Thirteenth streets, now the Philadelphia Club.

his services to promote that object, and with the same disinterested views, no doubt, as those with which, as it now appears, he accepted the administration of the estate for the recovery of a few debts, which if recovered, he has appropriated to his own use. It is long since I denounced R. King, Senr to my Sister, as a man devoid of integrity, artful, designing, and provided he could promote his own interest regardless at whose expense it might be.[43]

Ill and irritable, Thomas Butler responded to a letter from Louis, the son he thought wayward. He noticed continued deterioration of character and more shameless conduct:

Until you should have become of age, it was my duty as your father, to direct your pursuits and to regulate your conduct, but believing your own will to be a safer guide than your father's experience, you set aside his authority. The result is that you left the United States having dishonor'd yourself and your family, and after arriving in France have continued to degrade yourself still more and to imprint a still deeper stain upon our names.

He counseled Louis not to come to America. "You will not be admitted to my house nor will I have any intercourse with you." Louis was told Aunt Eliza was ill and would not see him, that his present course of "shameless sensuality" and extravagance was leading "fast to the Interior of a gaol."[44]

In April 1838 Thomas Butler died. A letter to Louis shortly before his death was slightly reconciliatory. It was the letter in which he told of how his illness had come upon him two years before in Newport and of the building of his house on Walnut Street, the coolness or warmth of which he never enjoyed. Much of his fortune had been expended for homes he did not live to occupy. As it happened, even his occupancy of a carefully prepared tomb proved to be a snare and a delusion. He had directed that he be buried in the yard surrounding Philadelphia's Christ Church, in a tomb separate from that of his father and his nephew, the child Pierce Butler Mease who had supplanted him as heir apparent when less than nine years old, and where other members of the Butler family lay buried. Thomas had directed the construction of his tomb, which was built much as his house had been, double-walled, and was said to contain a stove to exclude dampness.[45]

Thomas Butler's will has the strangeness of its unhappy author. He could not bring himself to emulate his father and somehow was able to put aside his animosity to Louis, but first, he directed his executors to provide the necessary annuity for Christ Church to care for the tomb, keeping it "in perfect order and repair, internally and externally, and also the coffins deposited therein." Other annuities provided annual income of $500 to Daniel Ridgway Knight, the builder of the house on Walnut Street, $104 to Michael Laglors, and the same to Chloe Washington, "a coloured house servant." George Bussingher, also a servant, was left an outright bequest of $100. For his eldest son, Mr. Knight received the wearing apparel of the deceased Francis Butler, and Michael Laglors the considerable wardrobe of Thomas Butler himself. With atavistic blood-thirstiness, Thomas Butler also chose to "Direct and request my Executors to have shot my two dogs & my grey poney Dumpling & my bay horse George Washington." The "rest, residue and remainder" was left to his executors, who were also designated trustees, in trust for ten years with all of the earnings to be paid to Louis Butler, and at the end of ten years to be turned over to him outright provided he had not changed his family name. Should he do so, the entire estate was then left to "the Reverend George Butler, residing in England." This contingent beneficiary was a distinguished son of the Reverend Weeden Butler and, like his father a clergyman and an educator, was in his early thirties the headmaster at Harrow. George had attended the Butler school at Chelsea with Thomas. The executors and trustees were given broad powers, except that the new house was to be completed "according to the plan which I have delivered to Daniel Ridgway Knight," and if sold, then for not less than seventy thousand dollars. The Wayne County lands were to be sold in "one body," and his Newport property was not to be subdivided.

The will was signed March 2, 1838. Two codicils followed, one on March 6 and the second on March 9. In the first he was more explicit on the changing of Louis Butler's name:

> In addition to what I have expressed in my will respecting my son Louis Butler changing his family name, I now declare that should he have added to it, or should he at any further time, add to it the name of "de-Malleveault" then every devise and bequest whatsoever to him made under my said will shall be utterly revoked and annulled, and the same shall be vested in the Reverend George Butler, and his heirs and assigns forever.

The first codicil also directed a private funeral attended only by his two executors, his doctor, J. Rhea Barton, his builder Mr. Knight, and the clergyman. Thomas Butler ordered the two coffins within the tomb be stripped of their cloth coverings and placed in larger "strong red cedar coffins" with an inscription upon the lid of the one "lately" received from France. His own coffin was to be of the same strong red cedar. He added his unnamed cook to those in the will with a bequest of $100. The second codicil was brief. The $104 annuities to Michael Laglors and Chloe Washington were increased to $200. His son Francis, having died intestate, caused his father, as an heir at law, to share with his other sons the inheritance Francis had received from Madame de Mallevault. Thomas Butler recognized this and directed that whatever might come to him of her real and personal property on Martinique was to be divided between his sons, Louis and John. Thus John Butler, the youngest son, was mentioned for the first time in the will and codicils. Perhaps there was some reason for this exclusion, for he had also been ignored as a contingent beneficiary in the will of his aunt, Frances Butler. The executors were directed not to lease his residence on Chestnut Street or the new house on Walnut Street, and to refrain from renewing the lease on the Newport property.[46]

The executors and trustees were Colonel William Drayton, formerly of South Carolina, and the Honorable John Sergeant, both of Philadelphia. When the three witnesses testified to the validity of the will it was agreed that Thomas Butler was of "sound and disposing Mind." John Butler probably would have doubted both premises. The unnamed cook and Chloe Washington, though faring better than the dogs, the pony Dumpling, and the horse George Washington, might have qualified "disposing."[47]

That same year, 1838, Roswell King, Jr., resigned as manager of the Butler estate. His father and brother Barrington King were well along with their project of building the new towns far from the Altamaha delta that had nourished the King family for so many years. Their enthusiasm for their work, and the growing uneasiness with the new owners of the plantations, prompted his departure. Much of the uneasiness was born of the dispute between the Kings and the Butlers on a ten thousand dollar loan made Roswell King, Sr., by Frances Butler, and the fees he thought were due him for serving as a co-administrator of Major Butler's Georgia estate.

Despite the careful preparation of the tomb in the Christ Church yard, the vault filled with water, and the body of Thomas Butler fared little better than that of a slave buried in the low wetland of Butler's Island on the Altamaha River.[48]

Chapter 15

❧ Enter Fanny Kemble

THE ENGLISH ACTRESS who captivated Pierce Butler in 1832 was Frances Anne Kemble, one of the most talented performers to have appeared on the western side of the Atlantic Ocean. She came with her father, Charles Kemble, an actor whose whole world seemed to be the new Covent Garden Theatre in London. It was a world that had come apart only to be put back together by this young woman who was not yet twenty years old. The American trip was made in her twenty-third year, when she was fresh from two triumphant seasons at a revived Covent Garden and two conquering provincial tours through Scotland, Ireland, and England. In New York she appeared before enthusiastic audiences and to critical acclaim. The tour continued in Philadelphia, Baltimore, Washington, and Boston with repeat visits to New York and Philadelphia. The Kembles played *Hamlet, King John, Romeo and Juliet,* and *Much Ado About Nothing.* Also, there was Sheridan's *School for Scandal,* James Sheridan Knowles's *The Hunchback,* George Farquhar's *The Inconstant,* Thomas Otway's *Venice Preserved,* and Henry Hart Milman's *Fazio.* Always she played to crowded houses with phenomenal success.[1]

The talents of Fanny Kemble were great and varied. She had a bright, inquisitive, retentive mind that permitted her to commit a role to memory quickly and accurately, and to understand fully the interweaving of her part into the fabric of a play. Ofttimes beautiful, sometimes plain, she seemed to convey to those who saw her perform a vital beauty and dramatic excitement that left many spellbound. In London, a critic had proclaimed her "tender, graceful, energetic and occasionally sublime."[2] In

255

New York, an admirer wrote: "I have never witnessed an audience so moved, astonished and delighted. The expression of her wonderful face would have been a rich treat if her tongue had uttered no sound. I am quite satisfied that we have never seen her equal on the American stage."[3] In stage presence, appearance, and voice she was the consummate actress.

Fanny Kemble's talents went far beyond the stage. Her remarkable powers of observation were put to good use in her writing, which she preferred to acting, and be it a play, poetry, her several journals, or her thousands of letters, all benefited from her ability to record vividly what she saw and heard. True, Robert Browning thought her poems surprisingly poor, and she admitted to writing verse "much as a bird sings, with as little method, purpose, or trouble."[4] Her prose was often convoluted and something less than to the point. Yet, of all that great flow of words written about her in her lifetime and after her death, nothing is quite so good as what she wrote about herself. A clever mimic, she could speak French as though she were a Parisian. She read avidly and was a capable musician who was often called on to sing and to play the piano. She exercised vigorously and had a strong feeling for nature, a feeling that was satisfied by frequent walks or rides into the country, on lonely beaches, or mountain trails. Riding was a joy to Fanny Kemble. During her first season at Covent Garden she was taught by London's famous Captain James Fozzard at the school where young Thomas Butler had learned to ride before the turn of the century. The captain once put her through her paces by having her ride sidesaddle in the fashion of the day but without stirrup and with her arms held behind her, the horse plunging and rearing and going over the bars, to demonstrate his competence as a teacher and her skill as a rider. Looking on were the duchess of Kent and a young and prospective pupil, the Princess Victoria.[5]

Fanny Kemble's acting led her to make interesting acquaintances, many of which turned into friendship. Sir Walter Scott, the young poet Alfred Tennyson, and William Makepeace Thackeray were among the avid "Kemblers." Another, and particularly attentive, was Sir Thomas Lawrence, whose lovely pencil drawing was made in preparation for a full portrait of her as Juliet. The drawing was the last work done before his death.[6]

On her provincial tour she became firm friends with the Combe brothers of Edinburgh, Andrew and George. Andrew was a noted surgeon, and George, the well-known phrenologist who later married Fanny Kemble's cousin Cecilia Siddons. Andrew Combe was so taken with the young

Frances Anne Kemble. "She is right lovely to look upon." (From a painting by Thomas G. Appleton.)

actress that he wrote a formal document promising to meet her in Edinburgh were she to return at the age of sixty-five. Fanny was but twenty at
the time. If on her revisit, the document proclaimed, she was "still possess[ed] with the love of dancing, jumping, waltzing or racketing, I shall
then dance and execute with the said Frances Anne Kemble whatever pas
de deux, pas seul, hornpipe, jig, reel or quadrille may happen to be in
vogue at the time." If necessary, Dr. Combe promised to make his reappearance as a ghost or spirit, but would not be clad in a sheet as usually
worn by "ghosts, wraiths, spunkies and spirits," but would be wearing
his usual greatcoat. Fanny Kemble stimulated imaginations and won admiration wherever she played.[7]

The Kembles' American tour ended in June 1834, but not before the
young actress and Pierce Butler were married in Christ Church, Philadelphia.

A blind passion brought them to the grand folly of their union. Almost
immediately there was a conflict of wills, of beliefs, and a telling realization they were not for each other. He had supposed, once captured, she
would be his dutiful wife and bow to his every whim. She imagined that
he would keep his extravagant promises, that her newfound station would
offer comfort and stability—conditions foreign to actors, and particularly
to the hard-pressed Kembles. She had not expected to be denied freedom
of expression in her writing—or in the acting about which she had such
mixed emotions—and certainly not freedom of expression in thought. A
factor in their marriage had been Pierce Butler's infatuation. He was a
young man accustomed to having what he wanted, and his persistent and
thoughtful attention prompted a rewarding response from her. He had pursued her through most of the American tour, overwhelming her with flowers,
notes, and visits. He shared her love for music, having long played the
flute, often in a group with Thomas Sully, the artist. He attended her
performances with perseverance, sometimes becoming a member of the
musical ensemble accompanying the players.[8] One definite attraction she
found in him was that he seemed to enjoy riding as did she. They often
rode together. One memorable ride from Boston must have had a part in
bringing them together. Seeking relief from the tension of a successful
evening performance, and to avoid the "lumbering, rolling, rocking" of
their stagecoach, she was given permission by her father and her aunt to
ride from Boston to Dedham, having persuaded Pierce Butler to ride with
her. She described it in detail:

Pierce Butler, born a Mease in Philadelphia in 1810. He was a grandson of Major Butler and for fifteen stormy years was the husband of Frances Anne Kemble. (Historical Society of Pennsylvania.)

The therometer stood at seventeen degrees below zero; it was the middle of a Massachusetts winter and the cold intense. The moon was at the full, and the night as bright as day; not a stone but was visible on the iron-hard road, that rang under our horses hoofs. The whole country was sheeted with snow, over which the moon threw great floods of yellow light, while here and there a broken ridge in the smooth, white expanse turned a sparkling crystalline edge up to the lovely splendor. It was wonderfully beautiful and exhilarating, though so cold that my veil was frozen over my lips, and we literally hardly dared utter a word for fear of swallowing scissors and knives in the piercing air, which however was perfectly still and without the slightest breath of wind. So we rode hard and fast and silently, side by side, through the bright, profound stillness of the night, and never drew rein until we reached Dedham.

At Dedham she found protection from the cold in a candlelit workroom where two women were busy making mourning garments for a funeral. Pierce Butler stayed outside walking "to and fro," keeping himself and the horses from freezing until the coach arrived.[9]

There were other forces at play. Fanny Kemble's aunt Adelaide De Camp, her mother's sister, was a much-loved chaperon on the American tour. "Dall," as she was called, had been gravely injured when their coach overturned near Niagara Falls. Her death in Fanny's arms as the tour neared its end had a traumatic impact. Although Dall had cautioned her about Pierce Butler, Fanny may have reached to him for the love and companionship she had lost.[10] And she liked Philadelphia: "I like the town, and the little I have seen of its inhabitants, very much. I mean in private for they are intolerable audiences. There is an air of stability, of well to do, and occasionally of age, in the town, that reminds me of England."[11] Too, in the offering was Pierce Butler's inheritance of the fine Chestnut Street house, but more to her liking was the farm, Butler Place on the York Road with stables, horses, and carriages that gave promise to the satisfaction of her love of riding.

Her brother, John Mitchell Kemble, on hearing that she would soon marry Pierce Butler, wrote from Cambridge: "You will be happy, if your husband knows only how to value you." It was a gentle word of caution.[12]

Charles Kemble returned to England with most of the considerable fund earned on the American tour. Pierce and Fanny Butler had agreed to accompany her father so that she might continue the rescue of Covent Garden but at the last moment backed away from their commitment,

Charles Kemble. "Apollo might have envied his looks." (From a painting by Thomas Sully. Amelia M. Watson "Kemble" Collection, Lenox Library.)

leaving Charles Kemble greatly disappointed and believing his future in jeopardy.

In the America that Fanny had come to know on her theatrical tour the question of the rights or wrongs of slavery was often present. Outspoken abolitionists made their presence known in Philadelphia and in Boston. What to do about the Negro—the free and the slave—was a much-discussed topic in both those places, and with less compassion but equal intensity in New York and Washington. Fanny was well aware of the plight of the Negro in America, and the fact that Pierce Butler's wealth was the product of slave labor had to be known by one whose powers of observation were so acute. Yet she was to write six years later—in early 1839: "I felt the weight of an unimagined guilt upon my conscience; and yet, God knows, this feeling of self-condemnation is very gratuitous on my part, since when I married Mr. [Butler] I knew nothing of these dreadful possessions of his."[13]

In 1835, the year following her marriage, her personal record of the trip to America and the ensuing theatrical tour was published in London, Paris, and Philadelphia. The original intention had been for the publication to provide funds for Aunt Dall, whose injury and death changed this but did not negate the contract with the publishers. This "American" *Journal* (1835), not so well known as her later "Georgian" or "Plantation" *Journal* (not published until 1863) that recorded her winter at Butler's Island and Hampton in 1839, presented Fanny Butler's observations on America and Americans, done with youthful enthusiasm, and in many instances, with youthful indiscretion.

There was an interesting reaction from a Philadelphian who had received the new Mrs. Butler on a social call shortly after her marriage. Deborah Norris Logan found her "sensible and spirited," not handsome, but an "animated intelligent countenance, and a fine eye." Mrs. Logan opined that Fanny Butler's "sociability" would gain her great popularity in the neighborhood. But a few years later, when she read the American *Journal,* she commented in her diary: "I took up Fanny Butler's Journal. She seems to set herself doggedly to find fault. I imagine imperious circumstances made them come to this country to better their condition, and that she had done so admits of no doubt. She should be Easy, as the Irish would say, and not sting the foster parent that has nourished her."[14]

Mrs. Logan was not alone in that opinion. This first *Journal* brought forth a quick reaction on both sides of the Atlantic. In London, the *Literary Gazette* said: "There are also a *flippancy* and VULGARITY about it which surprises us the more, coming from such a source; a presumption, and *a lack of the finer and higher qualities which adorn the female character,* which is vexatious to contemplate in one so gifted." The *Athenaeum* reported: "It turns out to be one of the most deplorable exhibitions of *vulgar thinking and vulgar expression that it ever fell our lot to encounter.*" The *Spectator:* "In short, she exemplifies the *beau ideal* of a green room belle, whose head has been turned by flattery." A Liverpool correspondent commented: "About two thousand copies of Fanny Kemble's Journal have been sold. It excited general disgust. The authoress has unsexed herself."[15] An entry in the diary of Charles Greville showed a reaction closer to home: "May 30, 1835—The father and the mother both occupied with their daughter's book, which Kemble told me he had "never read till it appeared in print, and was full of sublime things and vulgarities," and the mother "was divided between admiration and disgust, threw it down six times, and as often picked it up."[16] In America there was annoyance and embarrassment by those who felt wounded by the Butler pen. She was ridiculed and satirized in print and on the stage. The *New York Mirror* thought the journal was "impertinent though exceedingly clever." Their critic added: "It is a remarkable work abounding with powerful passages but disfigured with a string of tittering tattlings."[17]

Fanny Butler's decision to publish had been made over Pierce Butler's objections, the issue having become an obstacle in the course of their marriage. The American *Journal* ended at Niagara following the accident in which Aunt Dall was injured. Excepting an introduction, some footnotes, and Pierce Butler—induced deletions, the journal had been written before her wedding. Although she did not dwell on black people or on slavery, she did made some pertinent comments that leave no doubt as to her convictions.

Fanny Butler's youthful *Journal* records an interesting first impression of American blacks:

> After dinner, sat looking at the blacks parading up and down; most of
> them in the height of the fashion, with every colour of the rainbow about
> them. Several of the black women I saw pass had very fine figures; (the
> women here appear to me to be remarkabley small, my own being, I should
> think, the average height) but the contrast of a bright blue or pink crape
> bonnet, with the black face, white teeth, and glaring blue whites of the
> eyes, is beyond description grotesque.[18]

A few days later, when Charles Kemble wished to reward the black cabin boy Essex, who had served them well on the packet *Pacific* crossing the Atlantic, with a gift ticket for one of their performances, he had to be limited to a seat in the gallery. Fanny Butler wrote, "I believe I turned black myself I was so indignant."[19] A more pertinent indication of her feelings was shown in an entry on September 23: "[*Ogden Hoffman*] called, and sat with us during dinner, telling us stories of the flogging of slaves, as he himself had witnessed it in the south, that forced the colour into my face, the tears into my eyes and strained every muscle in my body with positive rage and indignation: he made me perfectly sick with it."[20] She often noted the presence of blacks in the New World. Her entry on October 9, 1832, in Philadelphia told of being attended "by a fat lively Negro, by name Henry; who canters about in our behalf with great alacrity, and seems wrapt in much wonderment at many of our proceedings. By the by, the black who protected our baggage from the steamboat was yclepted *Oliver Cromwell*."[21] There can be no doubt of Pierce Butler's displeasure when he read another entry, written on November 7, 1832, in Philadelphia:

> I was horrified at *Dr. [Charles Mifflin's]* account of the negroes in the south. To teach a slave to read or write is to incur a penalty, either of fine or imprisonment. They form the larger proportion of the population, by far; and so great is the dread of insurrection on the part of the white inhabitants, that they are kept in the most brutish ignorance, and too often treated with the most brutal barbarity, in order to insure their subjection. Oh! what a breaking asunder of old manacles there will be, some of these fine days; what a fearful rising of the black flood; what a sweeping away, as by a torrent, of oppressions and tyrannies; what a fierce and horrible retaliation and revenge for wrong so long endured—so wickedly inflicted.[22]

With such feelings as those expressed in her *Journal*, all written prior to her marriage, it is difficult to understand how Fanny Kemble could become a member of a family so long dependent on slavery for its livelihood. Possibly this eminently successful young woman had confidence in her ability to direct an immature young man to her way of thought. Although some of what she wrote on first meeting Pierce Butler was deleted, this much was published in the *Journal*. It was in Philadelphia, October 13, 1832: "Came down to tea, and found a young gentleman sitting with my father; one *Mr. [Pierce Butler]*. He was a pretty-spoken *genteel* youth enough: He drank tea with us, and offered to ride with me. He is it seems, a great fortune, consequently, I suppose (in spite of his inches) a great man."[23]

The month before, Pierce Butler had received a letter from an English friend, Francis Henry Fitzhardinge Berkeley, a man some fifteen years older than he but of similar character. Henry Berkeley was said to have "loitered through life in a wholly purposeless way," and while doing so, enjoyed watching the Kembles perform. He wrote his young Philadelphia friend from New York:

> Why dont you come here and see the Kembles. I saw Alston tonight and told him I should write you & he begged me to press you to come here. Charles is the best and most finished Actor you have ever seen, and Fanny only inferior to the O'Neil. In Bianca [Fazio] she is superior to anything that can be imagined—When you see her, if we are not together remember to observe her when jealous of Fazio she says "You have seen Aldebella" the working of her fine face and the subdued and smothered voice of intense passion which she brings forth with the eye of Fire is only met with once in a man's life. In person she is pretty, rather taller and more round than Miss George, large legs and feet, large hands, large arms—never mind you will fall in love with her for she is right lovely to look upon. Her eyes when flashing with spirit vividly beautiful, when half closed with a sorrowful expression, tenderness itself. When playful they are archness itself, her mouth large with teeth of ivory, her nose straight occasionally (and too often) with a curl of contempt rather inclined upwards—her voice low soft and beautiful. Off the stage rather swarthy with her face all expression, a pleasant, agreeable, well bred Girl—worthy of the Family, a French woman able to act in the French Drama, an Italian Scholar, and a fine musician.[24]

It is no wonder that Pierce Butler appeared for tea.

Years later Fanny Kemble gave full credit to Henry Berkeley for being the means of their first acquaintance. She thought Berkeley "one of the most profligate and unprincipled men I have ever known," but that he also was "one of the most agreeable and accomplished," particularly as a musician, where he "imparted some portion of his fine taste to his disciple, Mr. Butler, among worse things."[25]

Henry Berkeley later mended his dissolute ways to join his three brothers in Parliament, where he was known for his ready wit and his steadfast efforts to bring the secret ballot to English elections.[26]

In a courtship that extended from October 1832 until June 1834, it is difficult to believe the source of her suitor's "great fortune" was not revealed to Fanny Kemble. Throughout this twenty-month period her way of thought on slavery was much in evidence; thus it is also difficult to understand why Pierce Butler was ignorant of, or chose to ignore, her strong advocation of the abolition of slavery. During this interval Fanny Kemble was much impressed by the well-known Unitarian clergyman William Ellery Channing of Boston. They became friends, she sharing his conviction that slave owners should be made to realize the error of their ways and by their own initiative free their enslaved. Pierce Butler, before or after the wedding on June 7, 1834, saw no error and certainly had no thought of freeing the slaves who were the source of his wealth. If Fanny Kemble did believe she might sway his intolerance, she was soon to find she was sorely wrong.[27]

The enthusiastic abolitionist Lydia Maria Child reported a conversation between the Butlers in the presence of Charles and Elizabeth Sedgwick:

> It seems she keeps tugging at her husband's conscience all the time, about his slaves. One day he begged her to spare him—saying "You know, Fanny, we don't feel alike on that subject. If I objected to it in my conscience, as you do, I would emancipate them all." "Pierce," exclaimed she, "look me full in the face, and say that in your conscience you think it right to hold slaves, and I will never again speak to you on the subject." He met her penetrating glance for a moment—lowered his eyes—and between a blush and a smile, said "Fanny, I cannot do it."[28]

As if the publication of the American *Journal* was not enough, the new Mrs. Butler wrote "a long and vehement treatise against negro slavery" that she had wished to publish simultaneously with the *Journal*. Pierce Butler, with his own vehemence, forbade such, warning his wife that were she to advocate the rights of blacks, their Philadelphia property might well be destroyed in retaliation. Although the treatise was not published, her friend Dr. Channing's small volume entitled *Slavery* appeared in 1835. Her reading of it prompted a response to a query from her husband, who asked if she would be willing to go to Alabama where rich lands would replace the exhausted cotton fields of Hampton in Georgia. Her reply: "I would go with delight, if we might take that opportunity of at once placing our slaves upon a more humane and Christian footing." Her plan was to give their slaves freedom in "so many years," but only those whose conduct indicated they could care for themselves. Profits from their labors would have provided a fund to enable them to begin their new existence in confidence.[29]

In May 1835, the Butlers' first child was born at Butler Place. Called Sarah, she was named for Pierce Butler's mother, Sarah Butler Mease, although the chosen name ran through Butler, Middleton, and Kemble families. Despite the demands of motherhood, Fanny Butler's energies seem fueled on her burning concern with the evils of slavery: "Oh how I wish I was a man! How I wish I owned those slaves! instead of being supported (disgracefully, it seems to me) by their unpaid labor."[30] The refrain was constant. It was not that she failed to show proper attention to the child, for there was criticism she was too attentive.

In March 1836 the death of Pierce Butler's Aunt Frances terminated the long-standing trust under which the estate of Major Butler had functioned. Except for a generous share of the income that would continue to flow to the one remaining daughter of Major Butler, Anne Eliza, title to the Georgia lands and the slaves was vested in Pierce and John Butler. The income was shared one-half to Aunt Eliza and one-fourth each to Pierce and John.

In October 1836 Fanny Butler wrote, "It is a great disappointment that I am not going to the South this winter." The reason told her by Pierce Butler was that the overseer's house on Butler's Island was not large enough to accommodate Fanny, the baby Sarah, and the nurse. "The owner will go with his brother, but without us on his expedition to Negroland," and go he did, with brother John who was just as anxious as he to keep her away from the Georgia plantations. Fanny Butler, with her child, sought a respite from the stormy marriage and sailed for England to spend a busy ten months with her family and friends.[31]

The burden of plantation matters began to occupy Pierce Butler's time. Roswell King, Jr., had resigned saying one man was incapable of managing the two plantations. Pierce Butler told John there was no quarrel over the adequacy of the annual pay of two thousand dollars, but that young King had said "he must either neglect the property if he continued on it, or kill himself." James Gowen was hired to manage Hampton, and a search was made for someone to supervise Butler's Island.[32]

Roswell King, Sr., was still demanding ten thousand dollars for his services as a co-administrator of Major Butler's estate. He wished to offset the same amount he had borrowed from Frances Butler. Mr. King was told Pierce and John Butler gained possession of the estate in 1836 and were not responsible for its operation before that time. Attorneys for the estate of Frances Butler pursued the matter of the loan to Mr. King by appointing Savannahian George J. Kollock as temporary administrator. He sued Mr. King and eventually collected $4,549.16. The Butlers contended that Mr. King had been appointed to act for Major Butler's estate only in the collection of debts, and that if any money was collected, he used it himself.[33]

In September 1837 Pierce Butler made a quick trip to England to collect his wife and child, but on their return to Butler Place the turmoil continued as before. It was interrupted for a time by his attendance at the Pennsylvania Constitutional Convention in Harrisburg in one of the few efforts of that sort he ever undertook, and by the confinement of an increasingly unhappy Fanny Butler for the birth of their second child. Frances Kemble Butler was born on her sister's third birthday, in the same room at Butler Place. Confinement and turmoil permitted the death of Pierce's uncle, Thomas Butler, to go almost unnoticed.[34]

Despite the complication of travel with young children, Fanny Butler's desire to visit the Georgia plantations remained so insistent that Pierce Butler relented and the planning was begun. She wrote of one pleasant anticipation in going was that a Georgia winter might prove beneficial to an ailing Pierce Butler, "the invalid member of our party" who was suffering from intense arthritis. "As for me," she wrote another friend:

> I am about to depart into slavery: Mr. Butler, the children and myself being bound for Georgia on the twentieth of next month. There, whether I shall die of a yellow fever or the jaundice, whether I shall be shot at from behind a tree for my Abolitionism, or swallowed horse and all by an Altamaha alligator are matters yet folded within the unopened chambers of time.[35]

Fanny Butler's preconceived ideas of the humanity she would find in Georgia put such creatures on a par with the avaricious Altamaha alligators: "The South is made up of a handful of gentleman proprietors, and a *land* full of their slaves. The intermediate classes, or rather class, is a horrible compound of ignorance and tyranny. They are generally agents, slave brokers, slave raisers, or overseers." She added: "the slave states are eaten away by that very property."[36]

On December 21, 1838, Fanny and Pierce Butler, their child Sarah, their baby Frances, their Irish nurse Margery O'Brien, with Aunt Eliza Butler, who was bound for Charleston, left Philadelphia for the Georgia plantations. By train, stage, and steamboat they traveled southward. On the steam packet *Governor Dudley* from Wilmington, North Carolina, they "bumped on the Charleston bar" on Christmas day. The *Mercury* gave a somewhat garbled report of their arrival in their issue of December 27. Eliza Butler joined her friends, but there was no noticeable recognition by the Pierce Butler family of Butler friends or relatives. Passage to Savannah was booked for an early morning departure on the steam packet *William Seabrook*. Had they arrived in Charleston a few days before Christmas they might have sailed directly to Butler's Island on the Butler schooner *Roswell King* that departed for the Altamaha on Christmas eve. Their stay in Savannah was brief, only long enough to purchase supplies and for Pierce to write his brother John:

> Of this amount you had better at once pay eight thousand dollars to Aunt Eliza and take four thousand for yourself. I have already had four thousand.
>
> When you pay any sum to Aunt Eliza be sure to take a receipt for you know who we shall have to deal with hereafter about her property.[37]

The journey down the coast of Georgia was made on the steamboat *Ocmulgee*, "a tiny, tidy little vessel." On December 30 they disembarked at Darien, where "two pretty boats" carried them across several branches of the river. Fanny Butler called them "arms." She said the Altamaha "has as many as Briareous." Finally, the landing at Butler's Island: "Which began to be crowded with Negroes, jumping, dancing, shouting, laughing, and clapping their hands (a usual expression of delight with savages and children), and using the most extravagant and ludicrous gesticulations to express their ecstasy at our arrival."[38]

Chapter 16

🖋 Negroland

When people are engaged in something they are not proud of, they do not welcome witnesses. In fact, they come to believe the witness causes the trouble.

"I PURPOSE, while I reside here, keeping a sort of a journal," wrote Fanny Butler.[1] She did, writing later that the journal was "hastily written" and received constant additional notes of things that had happened, were remembered, and added to that first written. The additions were made in an "irregular fashion," and she believed it necessary to make a second visit to Georgia with an eye to revising, correcting, and including whatever might be gained from a return journey. These later thoughts were expressed at Butler Place in the fall of 1840, but by then she had seen the last of the Altamaha plantations. Her brother-in-law John Butler said no, on the grounds that her presence in Georgia was distressing to herself, an annoyance to others, and a danger to the properties. Suffering from boredom, or as she put it, in a state of "absolute intellectual solitude," she turned to bringing some order to her Georgia journal.[2] She rejected the thought of publication, feeling it would be a breach of confidence and the violation of a trust. The journal would eventually be published, but not until her marriage was shattered and the Civil War raged in America.

In 1839 Butler's Island offered Pierce Butler and his family a comparatively primitive existence, far removed from that enjoyed by the usual low-country plantation owner and not much above that experienced by Major Butler some fifty years before when he ordered his slaves "to fix up a Log House for me against I go there which I purpose doing in March."[3] Fanny Butler described the island as:

quite the most amphibious piece of creation that I have yet had the happiness of beholding. It would be difficult to define it truly by either the name of land or water, for 'tis neither liquid nor solid but a kind of mud sponge floating on the bosom of the Altamaha.

The product of this delectable spot is rice—oranges, negroes, fleas, mosquitoes, various beautiful evergreens, sundry sort of snakes, alligators and bull rushes enough to have made cradles not for Moses alone but the whole Israelitish host besides.[4]

In 1839 rice was the money crop on the Butler plantations. Its intricate, labor-intensive cultivation no longer benefited from the skilled supervision that the Roswell Kings had provided before their departures. There was a need for experienced guidance the new owners could not provide. Fanny Butler was thus thrust into the routine of a slave plantation where life was not only relentlessly hard and cruel but desperately in need of direction. Pierce Butler's immediate concern was to bring order and profit to this strange enterprise about which he knew very little. Until his Aunt Frances's death in 1836 he had been little more than a remittance man. Although he had shown his apprehension, he seemed not to anticipate or to understand the powerful impact the plantations would have on his sensitive, volatile wife.

The Butlers were put up in their overseer's house. To attend to their needs they were given the services of a man who was "quite a tolerable cook." Jack, a young slave, was assigned to assist and protect his mistress. There was a dairy woman and her daughter Mary, who was a housemaid, and two older boys who served as footmen or waiters. The "faces, hands and naked feet" of the boys were "literally encrusted with dirt." Mary, too, was "intolerably offensive in her person," a condition understood by her mistress: "Slavery is answerable for all the evils that exhibit themselves where it exists—from lying, thieving, and adultery, to dirty houses, ragged clothes and foul smells."[5]

Wanting a horse, but denied that pleasure because of the land being "a hasty pudding of amphibious elements," the planter's lady found relaxation in one of the "gaily painted boats." She called it the *Dolphin*, often rowing alone or taking an oar with the slave Jack pulling the other. Whenever this happened, the young people gathered at the river landing giving "shrieks and yells of joy" in their "delight and amazement." Her boat was made for one or two oarsmen, had a stern seat, and was narrow enough to be called a canoe. In it she made her "walks on the water," and also used it for fishing. Several times she made trips to Darien to fetch the doctor to minister to her sick child or to ill or injured slaves.[6]

The boat landing was close by the overseer's house, with a rice mill almost adjacent and one of the four settlements of the island but a stone's throw away. Thus, their dwelling was the focal point of the plantation, offering little privacy, and cold, spartan comfort. The house was shared with the new overseer, Thomas Oden, who had come from John Couper's Cannon's Point. In Fanny Butler's eyes he had absorbed little or none of old Mr. Couper's heralded humanity. From this spare abode, sparsely equipped with rough plantation-made furniture and a few Philadelphia discards, Fanny Butler ventured forth on "one of the wildest corners of creation" to measure and assess Major Butler's legacy.[7]

To get about the island, one walked the rice field banks or rowed, paddled, or pushed one of the small boats through the network of canals within the banks, or outside them, rowed in the turgid branches of the Altamaha. The sounds of the steam engine that powered one of the three rice mills intruded on the wildness, as did a distant view over the marshes of the small river town of Darien, its buildings, steamboats, and sailing ships.

On Butler's Island, Fanny immediately became "Missis," although there was some confusion as to the function of Margery O'Brien, the children's nurse. Pierce Butler was "Massa" and was true to what they expected of their owner. But "Missis" was something special. Never had they seen or heard of a white woman with such vigor. "The negroes here, who see me row and work hard in the sun, lift heavy burthens, and make various exertions which are supposed to be their peculiar *privilege* in existence, frequently remonstrate with me, and desire me to call upon them for their services, with the remark 'What for you work, Missus! You hab niggers enough to wait upon you.' "

Celia Davis, a child in 1839, remembered "Miss Fanny Kemblin" as a "nice white lady, very rosy, clo'es always got on so rich." Celia was impressed with both quality and variety. "Ebery time she come she hab a diffrun dress. Silk, shinin' silk, so shinin'," and she added, "rich hat, look like bonnet, oh so rich."[8]

Fanny Butler's first impressions of the Butler slaves and their lot in life was surprisingly temperate. She thought them to be "sufficiently" fed and clothed, with "tolerably" good housing. She was told they were not sold to other owners, nor let out for hire to other masters. She believed them not to be "barbarously beaten," nor were families divided by moving

Celia Davis, who remembered Fanny Kemble, was born a Butler slave at Hampton plantation in the 1820s. (1915 photograph, Amelia M. Watson "Kemble" Collection, Lenox Library.)

members from plantation to plantation.⁹ But, as "Missis" moved about the island visiting the several settlements, their infirmaries, the mainland planting called Woodville, as she opened her eyes, ears, and her heart to the Negroes, she saw the place in a different light. She found the "sufficient" food came from a cookhouse, an appendage to each of the four settlements. The cooks, old women, doled out ground corn called grits and occasionally "small rice" or that unfit for market for a noon meal to be cooked and eaten in a break from work. An evening meal followed six hours later, dished out to the slaves in their small cedar piggins. Altamaha river fish, crabs, and oysters gave variety from time to time. The food was eaten without knives and forks—no tables or chairs—sometimes with an occasional iron spoon, but mostly with crude wooden ones, or as the children did, by using their fingers. It disturbed Fanny Butler to see the condition of the slaves' clothing. The annual allowance was two pairs of shoes, so many yards of flannel, and similar allotment of "plains," a rough, thick, carpetlike material inadequate in hot weather and uncomfortable the year around. Many were barefooted in January in the ever-present mud of the Altamaha delta, a condition no different from that of their African forebears. Contrary to what she thought, she learned the Negroes *were* sold for work on distant plantations and that the family was *not* sacrosanct. She interceded on behalf of Psyche, known as Sack, her children, and her husband Joe, saving first Psyche and the children, and then Joe, from being separated and sent to Roswell King, Jr.'s plantation in Alabama. As to beatings, Fanny Butler soon realized the driver's lash was no mere symbol of authority. Shortly after their arrival the slave Harriet was flogged by the overseer for having told the "Missis" the women had not time to keep their children clean. For this, and for "impudence," she was given a "good lashing." Overseer Oden gave Chloe the same treatment, also for impudence. Again, sometime later, old Teresa was flogged after complaining to her distraught "Missus." Pierce Butler justified the punishment in an angry confrontation with his wife, who reported in her journal: "I retorted, the manifest injustice of unpaid and enforced labor, the brutal inhumanity of allowing a man to strip and lash a woman, the mother of ten children; to exact from her, toil, which was to maintain in luxury idle young men, the owners of the plantation."¹⁰ To the young English woman the lash was the "hateful implement," an emblem representing all the evils of slavery. She wrote of lashings given Louisa, who told how she and others were "fastened by their wrists to a beam or a branch of a tree, their feet barely touching the ground, so as to allow them no purchase for resistance or evasion of the lash, their clothes turned over their heads, and their backs scored with a leather thong."[11] She told of Die, who was pregnant, and another woman, who were tied while:

a man with a cowhide stands and stripes them.

I, an Englishwoman, the wife of the man who owns these wretches, and I cannot *say that thing shall not be done again.*[12]

It was seven years after Fanny Butler had visited and described Butler's Island in her journal that Charles Lyell was taken there by James Hamilton Couper. Lyell wrote in his own journal: "The negro houses were neat, and white-washed, all floored with wood, each with an apartment called the hall, two sleeping rooms, and a loft for the children."[13] The brief description was in marked contrast to the bitter words of Fanny Butler:

Such of these dwellings as I visited today were filthy and wretched in the extreme, and exhibited that most deplorable consequence of ignorance and an abject condition, the inability of the inhabitants to secure and improve even such pitiful comfort as might yet be achieved by them. Instead of the order, neatness, and ingenuity which might convert even these miserable hovels into tolerable residences, there was the careless, reckless, filthy indolence which even the brutes do not exhibit in their lairs and nests, and which seemed incapable of applying to the uses of existence the few miserable means of comfort yet within their reach. Firewood and shavings lay littered about the floors, while the half-naked children were cowering round two or three smoldering cinders. The moss with which the chinks and crannies of their ill-protecting dwellings might have been stuffed was trailing in dirt and dust about the ground, while the back door of the huts, opening upon a most unsightly ditch, was left wide open for the fowls and ducks, which they are allowed to raise, to travel in and out, increasing the filth of the cabin by what they brought and left in every direction.

In the midst of the floor, or squatting round the cold hearth, would be four or five little children from four to ten years old, the latter all with babies in their arms, the care of the infants being taken from the mothers (who are driven afield as soon as they recover from child labor), and devolved upon these poor little nurses, as they are called, whose business it is to watch the infant, and carry it to its mother whenever it may require nourishment. To these hardly human little beings I addressed my remonstrances about the filth, cold, and unnecessary wretchedness of their room, bidding the older boys and girls kindle up the fire, sweep the floor, and expel the poultry. For a long time my very words seemed unintelligible to them, till, when I began to sweep and make up the fire, etc., they first fell to laughing, and then imitating me. The incrustations of dirt on their hands, feet, and faces were my next object of attack, and the stupid Negro practice (by-the-by, but a short time since nearly universal in enlightened Europe) of keeping the babies with their feet bare, and their heads, already well capped by nature with their wooly hair, wrapped in half a dozen hot, filthy coverings.

Thus I traveled down the "street," in every dwelling endeavoring to awaken a new perception, that of cleanliness, sighing, as I went, over the futility of my own exertions, for how can slaves be improved? Nathless, thought I, let what can be done; for it may be that, the two being incompatible, improvement may yet expel slavery; and so it might, and surely would, if, instead of beginning at the end, I could but begin at the beginning of my task. If the mind and soul were awakened, instead of mere physical good attempted, the physical good would result, and the great curse vanish away; but my hands are tied fast, and this corner of the work is all that I may do. Yet it cannot be but, from my words and actions, some revelations should reach these poor people; and going in and out among them perpetually, I shall teach, and they learn involuntarily a thousand things of deepest import. They must learn, and who can tell the fruit of that knowledge alone, that there are beings in the world, even with skins of a different color from their own, who have sympathy for their misfortunes, love for their virtues, and respect for their common nature—but oh! my heart is full almost to bursting as I walk among these poor creatures.[14]

If Charles Lyell's impression was based on other than a quick look from the outside, or on the words of his guide, then Fanny Butler's insistence on cleanliness and good order had borne remarkable fruit.

The excitement of moving from Butler's Island to Hampton brought a respite from the sordid life of the upriver plantation. Preparatory to moving his wife and children, Pierce Butler was taken down the river on one of the plantation boats. In 1839 steam power was coming into prominence, replacing sail in maritime commerce. Yet on the plantations, the use of small boats was unchanged from Major Butler's time. Fanny Butler watched her husband's departure for St. Simons Island and described the scene with her usual skill:

The boat he went in was a large, broad, rather heavy, though well-built craft, by no means as swift or elegant as the narrow eight-oared longboat in which he generally takes his walks on the water, but well-adapted for the traffic between the two plantations, where it serves the purpose of a sort of omnibus or stagecoach for the transfer of the people from one to the other, and of a baggage wagon or cart for the conveyance of all sorts of household goods, chattels, and necessaries. Mr. [Butler] sat in the middle of a perfect chaos of such freight; and as the boat pushed off, and the steersman took her into the stream, the men at the oars set up a chorus, which they continued to chant in unison with each other, and in time with their stroke, till the voices and oars were heard no more from the distance.[15]

When the move to St. Simons was completed, Fanny Butler frequently mentioned the great difference between the two places. It had been nineteen years since Major Butler had last visited Hampton and seventeen years since his death in Philadelphia. The island mansion was in shambles and had become the home of overseer James Gowen, his wife, and child. Gowen was struggling with the supervision of a disintegrating property that had suffered from the remote trusteeship of Frances Butler and her surrogate, Thomas Butler. The management of Roswell King, Jr., had been less than that demanded of his father by Major Butler. Scant crops of sea island cotton from Hampton's exhausted fields brought no premium in the market, causing the plantation to come on hard times. But the most striking change to Fanny Butler was finding herself high above the level of the river, or as she expressed it: "After that life in the rice swamp, where the Altamaha kept looking over the dike at me all the time as I sat in the house writing or working, it is pleasant to be on terra firma again, and to know that the river is at the conventional, not to say natural, depth below its banks, and under my feet instead of over my head."[16]

There were disappointments, too. The slaves fared no better at Hampton than at Butler's Island. True, they were dry underfoot and the land offered greater potential for a healthy life; yet the houses, while superior to the living quarters of many other St. Simons plantations, were in such a state of deterioration they were worse than those upriver. The Hampton infirmary was distressingly unclean, "a wretched abode of wretchedness."[17]

Not only did Fanny Butler detest the use of the lash and find herself ashamed of the "miserable hovels" in which the slaves lived, but she disapproved strongly of the treatment of the women, particularly those sent to work in the fields after having given birth to their children. Expectant mothers were called "lusty women" and worked together at assigned tasks in "gangs." Although their work load was lightened both before and after childbirth, they complained to Pierce Butler of overwork. He rejected their pleas, causing his wife to turn away in disgust.[18]

After a storm of protests passed on from the slaves by his wife, Pierce Butler angrily denied her the right to intervene on their behalf. She could hear their complaints but must hold them to herself. That she did, as frustration mounted and dismay increased. On a single day she recorded the visits of nine women, seven of whom came to complain. Sukey and Molly, who was Quambo's wife, came only to pay respects.

Fifty-five children had been born of these nine women, and of these, twenty-seven were dead. In addition, they had experienced twelve miscarriages. These were Hampton women, where living conditions were supposedly "more salubrious" than the miserable existence encountered on Butler's Island.[19]

Fanny Butler's revulsion at the conditions of the slave's houses was moderate when compared to what she found in the infirmaries of the two plantations:

> In the first room that I entered I found only half of the windows, of which there were six, glazed; these were almost as much obscured with dirt as the other windowless ones were darkened by the dingy shutters which the shivering inmates had closed in order to protect themselves from the cold. In the enormous chimney glimmered the powerless embers of a few chips of wood, round which as many of the sick women as had strength to approach were cowering, some on wooden settles (there was not such a thing as a chair with a back in the whole establishment), most of them on the ground, excluding those who were too ill to rise; and these poor wretches lay prostrate on the earth, without bedstead, bed, mattress, or pillow, with no covering but the clothes they had on and some filthy rags of blanket in which they endeavored to wrap themselves as they lay literally strewing the floor, so that there was hardly room to pass between them. Here, in their hour of sickness and suffering, lay those whose health and strength had given way under unrequited labor—some of them, no later than the previous day, had been urged with the lash to their accustomed tasks—and their husbands, fathers, brothers, and sons were even at that hour sweating over the earth whose increase was to procure for others all the luxuries which health can enjoy, all the comforts which can alleviate sickness. Here lay women expecting every hour the terror and agonies of childbirth, others who had just brought their doomed offspring into the world, others who were groaning under the anguish and bitter disappointment of miscarriages—here lay some burning with fever, others chilled with cold and

aching with rheumatism, upon the hard cold ground, the draughts and damp of the atmosphere increasing their sufferings, and dirt, noise, stench, and every aggravation of which sickness is capable combined in their condition. There had been among them one or two cases of prolonged and terribly hard labor; and the method adopted by the ignorant old Negress, who was the sole matron, midwife, nurse, physician, surgeon, and servant of the infirmary, to assist them in their extremity, was to tie a cloth tight round the throats of the agonized women, and by drawing it till she almost suffocated then she produced violent and spasmodic struggles, which she assured me she thought materially assisted the progress of the labor.[20]

On another day, as she came out of the infirmary at Hampton, Fanny Butler saw Friday, an old slave, die—"freed by death from bitter, bitter bondage." The sadness and futility caused her to weep uncontrollably. "Missis, you no cry; Missis, what for you cry?" came from one of the sick slaves.[21]

Across the creek was neighbor John Couper's plantation at Cannon's Point. "Dear old Mr. Couper, whose nursery and kitchen garden are a real refreshment to my spirits." Fanny Butler compared him most favorably to Major Butler, and though she did not condone his advocacy of slavery, she did note that he lived year around on his plantation, "ameliorating the condition of his slaves and his property, a benefactor to the people and the soil alike." She believed Major Butler had "left everything to ruin" with the "careless extravagance of the soldier," the fortune gleaned from slave labor enjoyed in distant Philadelphia. Nevertheless, or "nathless" as Fanny Butler would have said, she was inclined to agree with John Couper that the Butler slaves had fared better in Major Butler's day and that his death was a "great misfortune" to his "wretched Affricans."[22]

In his conversations with Fanny Butler, John Couper had few good words for the two Roswell Kings' treatment of the Butler slaves:

> of the two latter functionaries his account was terrible, and much what I had supposed any impartial account of them would be; because, let the propensity to lying of the poor wretched slaves be what it will, they could not invent, with a common consent, the things that they one and all tell me with reference to the manner in which they have been treated by the man who has just left the estate, and his father, who for the last nineteen years have been sole sovereigns of their bodies and souls.[23]

At Butler's Island, Fanny had met and talked to Roswell King, Jr. He was not at all as she had expected. He had come bearing gifts—a bag of cormorant feathers and a jug of Georgia cane syrup. She found him "a remarkable man," and aside from his attitude toward the slaves, "respected for his integrity and honorable dealings" by low-country Georgians. Their long talk was on the matter uppermost in her mind—the future of slavery—and she was surprised when he observed: "As for its being an irremediable evil—a thing not to be helped or got rid of—that's all nonsense; for, as soon as people become convinced that it is their interest to get rid of it, they will soon find the means to do so, depend upon it."[24]

Fanny Butler had long contended that slavery damned and degraded the owners. What she saw on the two Butler plantations fortified this belief. Her recognition of the kindness of John Couper, the intelligence and bravery of his son James Hamilton Couper, and the good qualities of a few of the owners of neighboring plantations was overshadowed by the true character of the two Roswell Kings who were stand-ins for the absentee owners, managing the plantations from 1802 until their resignations in 1819 and 1838. Of the elder King, she expressed the thought that "a more cruel and unscrupulous" manager would be hard to find, "even among the cruel and unscrupulous class to which he belonged."[25] At Hampton she observed a much larger proportion of mulattoes than on Butler's island. Pierce Butler told her the reason was that white men had easier access to Hampton than to the rice plantation, where the old Butler regimen was maintained and permission was required to visit. On Hampton, driver Bram, a mulatto, was the acknowledged father of a light-skinned child by one of the plantation women. In discussing the child, Fanny Butler remarked that Bram himself was "the exact image of Mr. King." Pierce Butler responded, "Very likely his brother." If the elder King did not acknowledge being the father of Bram, the younger King had been forced by Major Butler to recognize Renty, the son of Betty, as his son. Betty was the wife of Frank, the head driver at Butler's Island and one of the most intelligent and dependable of the Butler slaves. Roswell King, Jr., thought Frank possessed the principles of a white man. That was praise Fanny Butler thought to be "most equivocal." While admitting he fathered Renty, he would not acknowledge Ben and Daphne, two children of Minda who bore his likeness, but then the old Major was not in the world when they were born. Nor would he acknowledge the children of Judy and Scylla, but Mrs. King chose to recognize the kinship by having the two women removed from the infirmary following their confinement, flogged, and banished to the estate's penal colony at Five Pound Tree. Such was the state of affairs on the Butler plantations in 1839.[26]

Pierce Butler responded to his wife's story of Roswell King, Jr.'s mulatto children by Judy and Scylla by writing him at his home, South Hampton. Mr. King's reply was interesting and evasive. The Jim Valient mentioned by Butler was said to be King's son by Judy. Fanny Butler's journal recorded him as "Jem Valiant"; she wrote that his "mutinous white blood" made him an "extremely difficult subject." The King letter explains:

> Today I received yours of the 17th inst. The information you desire regarding Judy, Jim Valient, &c I will give as well as I can from recollection, some time about August 1814—see Births & Death Book, three women had mulatto children, Viz, Sophy, Judy & Sinder. As that was *contraband trade* they were sent to 5 £ and remained there until 1819 when your Grandfather visited the Estate and moved Judy and Sinder who had husbands elsewhere. Sophy thro having an husband at 5 £ has remained with that Gang—now at St. Anne—ever since. I think this punishment was at the express desire of your Grandfather. I was absent at the time the groundwork was laid, therefore cannot say anything farther on the subject, only that it was a subject of surprise that one so young and small should have a child. Since then I have known an instance—at Major Page's—when one on the day of her 12th year had a child—Why does Judy complain of her banishment to 5 £? A thing that cannot be undone, also Cassie, when I was at Butler Island complained that I whipped her when she was pregnant and when the child was born it had the whip marks on it. Jack and his *fish story* is all of a piece. Negroes invariably give their own version to their subjects; only give ear and you will have ripped up complaints of 30 years standing, even punishments that their grandfathers sustained, they impose a heavy task on you if they think you might right wrongs that they have had inflicted, for instance could they get in earshot of God, would they spare you or any of the white Race. I truly hope none of your negroes that I have managed may have worse treatment than they have had in the last 37 years.

In his letter, Roswell King, Jr., named Sinder instead of Scylla. In 1814, when "the groundwork was laid," he was eighteen years old. He asked Pierce Butler to compare Butler profits with those of other plantations and to note the increase "in numbers over deaths," a statistic he had evidently helped to produce. He then recommended camphorated oil and warmth from flannel for Mr. Butler's "Rheumatism" and sent his and Mrs. King's "respects" to Mrs. Butler.[27]

Fanny Butler's relations with the blacks at Hampton were excellent. In her journal she describes a boat trip from Butler's Island to Hampton. The boat was probably the *Water Lily*, a craft of considerable substance, broad of beam with sufficient freeboard to combat the rough seas so often encountered in the waters near Hampton. The wind was blowing a gale:

> I will tell you something curious and pleasant about my row back. The wind was so high and the river so rough when I left the rice island, that just as I was about to get into the boat I thought it might not be amiss to carry my life preserver with me, and ran back to the house to fetch it. Having taken that much care for my life, I jumped into the boat, and we pushed off. The fifteen miles' row with a furious wind, and part of the time the tide against us, and the huge broad, turbid river broken into a foaming sea of angry waves, was a pretty severe task for the men. They pulled with a will, however, but I had to forego the usual accompaniment of their voices, for the labor was tremendous, especially toward the end of our voyage, where, of course, the nearness of the sea increased the roughness of the water terribly. The men were in great spirits, however (there were eight of them rowing, and one behind was steering); one of them said something which elicited an exclamation of general assent, and I asked what it was; the steerer said they were pleased because there was not another planter's lady in all Georgia who would have gone through the storm all alone with them in a boat; i.e., without the protecting presence of a white man. "Why," said I, "my good fellows, if the boat capsized, or anything happened, I am sure I should have nine chances for my life instead of one"; at this there was one shout of "So you would, missis; true for dat, missis"; and in great mutual good humor we reached the landing at Hampton Point.[28]

Fanny Butler's ear for music was quickly attuned to the singing of the slaves. The melody of the boatmen, sung when Pierce Butler set out for Hampton from Butler's Island, reminded her of "Coming Through the Rye," although the words were something else:

> *Jenny shake her toe at me,*
> *Jenny gone away;*
> *Jenny shake her toe at me,*
> *Jenny gone away.*
> *Hurrah! Miss Susy, oh!*
> *Jenny gone away;*
> *Hurrah! Miss Susy, oh!*
> *Jenny gone away.*

She found their melodies "wild and striking" and their natural gift of music an attractive attribute. Having to make frequent trips between the two plantations, she was able to hear many of the rowing songs—songs that quickly identified a particular boat crew, or a particular Altamaha plantation. She was surprised at the number and variety of the songs. One seemed apropos to the old Major—"God makes man and man makes money." She was often brought into the songs as "Massa's Darling," or they paid tribute to her corseted "wire waist." The child Sally was a favorite for their improvisations. They likened her to roses and lilies, and sang:

> *Little Miss Sally*
> *There's a ruling lady.*

Most interesting to her was the unusual structure of their songs: "The way in which the chorus strikes in with the burden, between each phrase of the melody chanted by a single voice, is very curious and effective, especially with the rhythm of the rowlocks for accompaniment." It surprised her that most of the men had tenor voices and that only one who sang otherwise was Isaac, a man with "long thin hands, and long flat feet." He was a "basso profundo of deepest dye" who, instead of venturing a part of his own, sang with the rest in perfect unison. She wished for a talented composer who could hear and adapt the chants and choruses to "make the fortune of an opera."[29]

At Hampton, Fanny Butler enjoyed the natural beauty of her surroundings. Even at Butler's Island she found much to admire. New to her were the great blue heron, the brilliant darting cardinals, the many and different wild duck, and the large flights of rice birds that darkened the sunlight. She delighted in the "saffron brightness of morning, the blue intense brilliancy of noon, the golden splendor and rosy softness of sunset."[30] Much to her surprise, the Altamaha supplied two things dear to the English palate. When strained of Georgia topsoil and other impurities, the river water made delicious tea, the best she had ever tasted. A native fish, the "white mullet," she found delicious—"the heavenliest creature that goes upon fins" and rivaled only by the Altamaha shad, which she found delicate, and superior to the fish praised by "Northerners." Impressed by the plant life in all its variations, she wished that one thicket found when riding the mare Miss Kate could have been lifted and taken intact to England. It was "more beautiful than the most perfect arrangement of artificial planting that I ever saw in an English park." She wrote of the huge cypress trees and of the most beautiful of all, the magnolia *grandiflora* at Butler's Island. Hampton's "noble" live oaks were "like huge hoary ghosts."[31]

It had come as a pleasant surprise that the inhabitants of coastal Georgia were not all a "horrible compound of ignorance and tyranny." The hospitality and good cheer of the John Coupers, the friendliness of their daughter Ann and her husband, Captain John Fraser, were matched by her newfound friend, Dr. James Holmes of Darien. Dr. Holmes attended the Butlers and their slaves. Fanny Butler stimulated his good mind and he, hers. His disagreement with her on slavery was tempered by his recognition of its basic injustice, and he responded to her teasing with good humor.[32]

It was difficult for Fanny Butler to look upon the slaves and at the same time put aside her abiding concern for their state of bondage. After first being "confounded" by their obscuring blackness, she began to see them as individuals, with features, expressions, and personalities of their own. In some of the women she found real beauty, often found great spirit, and was particularly impressed by their good figures and erect carriage. She attributed the first to a lack of restrictive garments and the latter to having carried heavy loads atop their heads. She respected their ability to make the most of simple pleasures—to dress up for Sunday or for special occasions—and she always remembered their song. They sang at work in the fields, at the mills, or in sadness at the death of one of their kind.[33]

That Hampton offered a chance to ride again gave Fanny Butler blessed relief from the tensions of her confrontation with plantation life. She rode the paths and roadways of St. Simons and frequently paid some of the men to prepare trails through the deep woods. Of the few horses at Hampton, there were but two capable of carrying riders. Miss Kate, the brood mare, was fractious and difficult, while Montreal, a stallion turned plowhorse, gave a more exciting ride. Both were bone shakers, but to her, that she could ride again was pleasure enough—and it gave the Islanders something to talk about.[34]

The Roswell King family, who had little use for the new Mrs. Butler, handed down an impression of her dashing madly from one end of the island to the other on horseback with a black man following closely behind. What is more: "She rode a *Stallion* & it was considered *against every Law of Decency!* No lady had ever been known to ride a horse of that description—no lady could even speak of a horse of that kind, much less appear on a public road riding one."[35]

Pierce Butler was bothered not only by confrontation with his wife on the treatment of the slaves and by constant coping with plantation management, but also by persistent badgering by the King family for the ten thousand dollars in estate fees they believed was due Roswell King, Sr. On top of this, the condition for which Roswell King, Jr., had recommended camphorated oil and warm flannel had become serious and disabling. He wrote John Butler in Philadelphia that he had been on his back for five days and in such pain he had sent to Savannah for leeches in a desperate search for relief. To John he sent a cord of resin-rich pinewood, "essential for heating your bath," and asked that John consider sending some of the unusual gift over to Chestnut and Eighth streets for use by the Pierce Butlers when they returned.[36]

Fanny Butler's objections to the lack of religious training on the two plantations moved her husband to permit several of his slaves to be baptized at the Baptist church in Darien. He explained his position in two letters to churchmen, both of whom were white. The first to A. Marvin, Esq.:

> Your note of the 3rd inst was handed me by Billy whom you desire should be consulted before permission is given to any of the people on my Estate to be baptized. It would not meet my views that any one person should be set up as a spiritual censor over all the rest. Billy is an excellent old man but there are others who have imbibed the true spirit of Christ as deeply as he has. I wish it however clearly understood by the Church that I consider my permission as only the first step towards arriving at their wishes, having obtained that, I presumed that they would of course be subjected to an examination by some of the elders of the Church to ascertain if their religious preparation had been sufficient to render it proper for them to go through so solemn an order.

The second letter was written the same day, to James Smith, Esq.:

> In consequence of many of the people on my Estate receiving the benefit of religious instruction from the excellent & so much respected Pastor of the Baptist Church in Darien, I will cheerfully contribute towards his salary for the present year.
>
> My people have at all times free permission to attend divine service in Darien, but I could by no means consent to any missionary visiting the plantation.[37]

Fanny Butler's plantation journal is the product of an impassioned observer. She admittedly went south with strong bias. In April 1839, when the Butler family left Georgia to return to "Whiteland" from "Negroland," the strong bias had become true conviction.[38] For all her days she remembered the black people of Pierce Butler's plantations. She comforted them in their misery, relished their few pleasures, and taught a few to begin to read and to value cleanliness. She paid them for extra work, made clothes, gave them gifts, tended their sick, and prayed for their freedom in life and death. She read church service on Sundays and helped to bury their dead. How could she forget the slave Shadrach who died on Butler's Island? His funeral on a winter's evening was a procession down the canal bank, and the singing of a hymn "the first high wailing notes of which all sung in unison" sent a chill through her body. The service ended at the graveyard, illuminated by pinewood torches, with Pierce Butler standing as his wife and the assembled slaves knelt and wept while the coffin was lowered into a grave awash with ground water. Nor could she forget the young girls, "the half savage slips of slavery" who minded the babies of the mothers at work in the fields. It hurt her to see and hear the slaves' "unbounded insolence and tyranny" toward each other. "The worst of all tyrants is one who has been a slave."[39]

Before the Butlers departed for their home in Philadelphia, the "Missus" staged a grand ball for the people of both plantations. The Hampton slaves were conveyed to Butler's Island in a festive expedition that called for most of the plantation boats. There was good food, dance, and song, with the music led by Sawney, the "great violinist." As a special treat Fanny Butler had fashioned beribboned headdresses for each of the unmarried girls. When all the celebrating had ended and the time came for the Butlers' "residence" on the plantations to end, the slave Quash and his boatmen carried the family away on the first leg of a long journey, the short crossing over to Darien. After all had boarded the plantation boat, Quash raised the melody that all the people knew:

> *Goodbye forever,*
> *I hope the Lord will bless you*
> *Till we meet again*
> *In case I never see you anymore*
> *I hope we meet you*
> *On Canaan's happy shore.*

The women who had gathered on the river landing wept.[40]

The "sort of a journal" kept by Fanny Butler became the *Journal of a Residence on a Georgian Plantation in 1838–1839*, which was published in 1863, twenty-four long and difficult years after it was written. It bore the author's name as Frances Anne Kemble, for by that time the Georgia slaves had come between Pierce Butler and his wife. Not even after a quarter century could she forget the scene on the Altamaha:

> The Calibanish wonderment of all my visitors at the exceedingly coarse and simple furniture and rustic means of comfort of my abode is very droll. I have never inhabited any apartment so perfectly devoid of what we should consider the common decencies of life; but to them, my rude chintz-covered sofa and common pine-wood table, with its green baize cloth, seem the adornings of a palace; and often in the evening, when my bairns are asleep, and M[argery] upstairs keeping watch over them, and I sit writing this daily history for your edification, the door of the great barnlike room is opened stealthily, and one after another, men and women come trooping silently in, their naked feet falling all but inaudibly on the bare boards as they betake themselves to the hearth, where they squat down on their hams in a circle, the bright blaze from the huge pine logs, which is the only light of this half of the room, shining on their sooty limbs and faces, and making them look like a ring of ebony idols surrounding my domestic hearth. I have had as many as fourteen at a time squatting silently there for nearly half an hour, watching me writing at the other end of the room. The candles on my table give only light enough for my own occupation, the firelight illuminates the rest of the apartment; and you cannot imagine anything stranger than the effect of all these glassy whites of eyes and grinning white teeth turned towards me, and shining in the flickering light. I very often take no notice of them at all, and they seem perfectly absorbed in contemplating me. My evening dress probably excites their wonder and admiration no less than my rapid and continuous writing, for which they have sometimes expressed compassion, as if they thought it must be more laborious than hoeing; sometimes at the end of my day's journal I look up and say suddenly: "Well, what do you want?" when each black figure springs up at once, as if moved by machinery; they all answer: "Me come say ha do (how d'ye do), missis"; and then they troop out as noiselessly as they entered, like a procession of sable dreams, and I go off in search, if possible, of whiter ones..[41]

The journal that had been written in anger and frustration, in passion and compassion, was the truest measure of Major Butler's legacy.

Chapter 17

Butler vs. Butler

SHATTERED BY THE CONFLICTS encountered on the Georgia plantations, the Butler family hoped to return to an orderly existence at Butler Place, a farm as different from Hampton or Butler's Island as white from black. To Sidney George Fisher, the Philadelphia friend who made a social call with his cousins, the Joshua Francis Fishers, a few months after their return, it appeared that peace prevailed. He reported "a very pleasant visit," "animated talk, and a warm discussion on the nature of true art." Fanny Butler argued that art should be "a faithful copy of nature," with the diarist countering it should reflect the artist's own imagination. He wrote:

> She is a very gifted person, & her qualities of heart & character are as excellent as those of her intellect.
>
> Butler is extremely gentlemanlike in manner, & has I think, many excellent traits of character. Great energy & firmness, with good feeling. They are very rich and live in handsome style.[1]

The visit of the Fishers gave Fanny Butler a taste of the kind of life she wished for but could not find with Pierce Butler. So deep was the rift between them that it became impossible to repay social obligations brought on by the kindnesses of their concerned friends. Denied such intellectual stimulation, she sought respite from the turbulence of their marriage by attending to the needs of Sally and the baby, Fan, and by riding her fine horse, Forrester. All the while she could not remove the Butler slaves from her mind and conscience.

Pierce Butler, who scarcely knew the meaning of responsibility, did nonetheless for a time feel his obligation to the Georgia lands. He shared this concern with John Butler, agreeing with him that the absence of the Roswell Kings called for a show of leadership on their part. He was aware of his wife's desire to return to Georgia and was as adamant as his brother that she should be kept at a distance. It was then Fanny Butler turned to her haphazard notes and vivid memory to put her plantation journal in order. The respite of riding was noted in the Fisher diary:

> Stopped at Wakefield. Mrs. Fanny Butler there, on horse-back & alone. She is very independent & rides about constantly unattended. Had some agreeable talk & accompanied her home. Never saw her look so well. Her costume was becoming & peculiar. A green cloth riding habit, with rolling collar & open in front, under it a *man's* waistcoat with rolling collar, yellow & gilt buttons, a calico shirt collar & breast, blue striped & turned over & a black silk cravat tied sailor fashion, with a man's hat & a veil. She was mounted on a beautiful horse, highly groomed.

He also noted Butler Place was unusually attractive with its avenues of maples and hedges planted by Fanny Butler, all cared for in the manner of an English country estate. Five or six men were "employed about the grounds," a generous retinue for a Pennsylvania residence but a far cry from the attendants who had surrounded the Butlers in Georgia.[2]

In 1840 the Butler marriage was on rocky ground. Between bitter arguments there were honest efforts made by both to reconcile their persistent differences. Fanny Butler confided in her closest friends, the Sedgwick family of Lenox, Massachusetts, whom she came to know through Catharine Maria Sedgwick, a writer she admired and respected. Although Pierce Butler later turned against the Sedgwicks, he too sought their counsel when his wife refused his bed. His letters to Mrs. Charles Sedgwick told of his misery brought on by this most irrational of wives, and he asked their assistance in bringing about a change in her attitude toward him. Mrs. Sedgwick tried, urging her friend to return to rationality and her husband, saying that she believed he loved her, that her marriage contract was "pledged in the sight of heaven."[3]

In February the two brothers departed for their Georgia plantations, leaving their wives in "forlorn widowhood." John Butler returned to Philadelphia in advance of Pierce, weary of the heat and the "oppressive smell of the orange flowers." The "smell" came from the citrus grove near the river landings. Had he been on the island when the sour oranges on the main bank were in flower, he would have been overwhelmed. When Pierce

Butler returned to his family, a brief interlude of quiet occurred, soon followed by a resumption of marital warfare.[4]

In the peaceful interval Fanny Butler's cousin Cecilia Siddons, who had married George Combe, the Scottish emissary of phrenology, visited Philadelphia with her husband. He did a phrenological analysis of Pierce Butler and determined that his temperament was "Nervous, Billious, Sanguine." Those parts of the Butler head that indicated "*Combativeness*" and "*Destructiveness*" were both considered large. However, "*Benevolence*" was also large. "*Hope*" was moderate. It was to George Combe that Fanny Butler, within a year of her marriage, had written an interesting description of her husband:

> He is nothing if not mathematical, and in every subject whatsoever that comes under his contemplation, from the traditions of history, to the hypothesis of astronomical speculations, truth, reality, *fact* is the end upon which he fastens, and without a most palpable and solid body of fact there is no satisfying him. We are fortunately different in temper. He is cheerful and contented, exceedingly calm and self possessed, and has abundance of patience with my more mental construction, without, however, quite understanding it.[5]

Fanny Butler and the children joined the Sedgwicks in the Berkshires in the fall, where they found peace for a few weeks. Nearing the end of a trying year, the Butler family faced an abrupt change when word came from England that Charles Kemble was seriously ill. The Butlers arrived in London just prior to Christmas, and to Fanny's pleasure were soon joined in a rented house on Clarges Street by her shaky but recovering father.

Before the hurried trip to England, Pierce Butler had returned to the earlier ways that occupied much of his time before he had shouldered the responsibility for the Georgia plantations. He had a weakness for women in ventures beyond the bounds of holy matrimony, in which he evidently displayed a greater skill than in the pursuit of gambling, his other vice. He was often in dire financial straits from consistent losses at cards. Such was his condition as his family departed for England that it was necessary to gain help, as Fanny Butler stated, from "an elderly lady, with whom I had become connected by my marriage." This had to be Aunt Eliza, for all the other older members had found their rewards. Eliza Butler could well afford this generosity to her nephew's family, for she continued to receive

Sidney George Fisher, a friend of the Butlers and Wisters, recorded the social history of their times in his diary. (Painting by Thomas Sully. Courtesy of Mrs. Peter S. Elek.)

half of the plentiful income generated by the Butler slaves on the Altamaha River.[6]

Fanny Butler's autobiographical writings do not openly accuse Pierce Butler of infidelity. Yet she was embittered and embarrassed by his activities, and when she did put her knowledge of such behavior in writing, it was in her letters to Elizabeth and Charles Sedgwick, who purged the sensitive material later at her request. Other references to Pierce Butler's extramarital activity may have appeared in her extensive personal correspondence. Years later she took note of his infidelity in letters to Mrs. Joshua Francis Fisher.[7]

The stay in England was of longer duration than first planned. Had Fanny Butler relented in her vigorous, constant, outspoken criticism of slavery the chances for an understanding between the two would have been better, for Pierce Butler enjoyed the whirl of society in which he found himself. Such a change was not to be. His irritation with his wife continued in full and he soon turned to cards and the pursuit of the pleasures he had sought and found in America.

In London the Butlers' circle of friends and acquaintances included an English version of Sidney George Fisher. Charles C. F. Greville, a man-about-London, recorded social history in his voluminous diary. Fanny Butler thought him to be "one of the most agreeable members of our intimate society." He had known her when as nineteen-year-old Fanny Kemble she had packed the house at Covent Garden. She would have been jolted to know that he had found her "short, ill made, with large hands and feet." When he added that she gave promise of being a fine actress and that her aunt, the brilliant Sarah Siddons, at the same age was not so good, she might have been placated. In 1841, a dozen years later, she thought Charles Greville to be remarkable: "his clear good sense, excellent judgement, knowledge of the world and science of expediency combined with his good temper and ready friendliness, made him a sort of universal referee in the society to which he belonged." Of the Butlers of that time and place he expressed thoughts that would have surprised both had they seen his entry touching on their unhappy lives:

> I have been seeing lately a great deal of Mrs. Butler, whose history is a melancholy one, a domestic tragedy without any tragic events.
>
> She has discovered that she has married a weak, dawdling, ignorant, violent tempered man.

*Fanny Kemble's friend Charles C. F.
Greville of London, "one of the most
agreeable members of our intimate
society." (Full-length portrait by T. C.
Wilson, 1838. Other drawing by
A. d'Orsay, 1840. Both from the Amelia
M. Watson "Kemble" Collection, Lenox
Library.)*

With all her prodigious talents, her fine feelings, noble sentiments, and lively imaginations, she has no tact, no judgement, no discretion.

Among the most prominent causes of their disunion is her violent and undisguised detestation of slavery while he is a great slave proprietor.[8]

While the London diarist was taking note of Butler activities there, his Philadelphia counterpart was doing the same across the sea. John Butler was attending to plantation business in Georgia while his wife was far from forlorn at home. She was living in luxury in their "handsomely furnished" mansion. Of the gorgeous Gabriella Butler, Sidney George Fisher wrote:

Mrs. B. looking magnificent. The most splendid figure I ever saw. She is amiable, lively & pleasant. Apparently totally unconscious of her beauty. Tho she has no mind, she has the ease & high breeding of the southern aristocracy, a manner produced by birth, early habit & wealth. She told me Mrs. Fanny Butler has written a ballet for Fanny Elssler, founded on the story of Pocahontas, which is to be brought out in Paris, as soon as she returns.[9]

The Butlers were grist for the mills of diarists. An entry in 1842 in the diary of Charlotte Wilcocks of Philadelphia: "Ellen confided me that Mr. Butler kept a mistress, I suspected as much. I might have told her that her uncle kept two." Charlotte Wilcocks was a cousin of Gabriella Butler and attended "tea fights" at the elaborate house where lived "that stupid John."[10]

Fanny Elssler's dancing had diverted Fanny Butler from her troubles in Philadelphia. In London she did so again. A greater diversion and one more satisfying was proximity to her younger sister, Adelaide Kemble, who had come to London before singing in concert at Covent Garden. After her very successful engagement there, the Butler family held themselves together long enough to go on a concert tour of the Rhine country with Adelaide and her talented friend Franz Liszt. Back in London, the Butlers were received by Queen Victoria and Prince Albert, Mrs. Butler gaining the impression the Prince possessed the better legs. There must have been a shudder in the Philadelphia grave of Pierce Butler's mother, Sarah Mease, when he kneeled to kiss the queen's hand in the style of a British "courtier." Although he indulged himself extravagantly, Fanny Butler considered her husband parsimonious in his support of her needs.

Gabriella Manigault Morris (Mease) Butler. "The most splendid figure I ever saw," wrote Sidney George Fisher. She was married to John Butler. (Painting by George Freeman. Historical Society of Pennsylvania.)

She lamented she no longer possessed her "former convenient power of coining." The Pocahontas piece was one of several literary efforts that remedied her lack of funds.[11]

While living at London's Clarendon Hotel, a series of arguments reached a climax when Fanny Butler enraged her husband by offering the American abolitionist Lydia Maria Child a portion of her plantation journal for publication. It was the part that told of the trip from Philadelphia to the Altamaha, a travel journal that touched on slavery in general but that did not include any of her record of slave life on the Butler plantations. Pierce Butler's violent reaction shocked her and caused a withdrawal of the offer to Mrs. Child. It also prompted a physical separation that saw Fanny Butler moving in with her sister Adelaide and Pierce Butler taking up new quarters in a house on Upper Grosvenor Street. The separation ended after several days when Fanny Butler swallowed her pride, subdued her anger, and presented herself at the new house in the middle of the night. She was accepted. The reunited Butlers gave two large parties to repay many social obligations. At the second party Mrs. Butler found comfort in hearing from two distinguished Englishmen, the Lords Ashburton and Dacre, of their enthusiastic approval of her friend Dr. William Channing's antislavery views. In May 1843, the unhappy Butlers departed for America on a new Cunard paddle-wheeled steam packet.[12]

The extravagances of London had depleted the Butler exchequer to such an extent that Butler Place was leased to obtain income. Rather than inflict their troubles on the John Butlers, they occupied rooms in a Philadelphia boarding house, which provided an atmosphere in which their animosities thrived. The English governess, who Fanny Butler believed served another household function, guarded the children against their mother. Pierce Butler sold Forrester to a livery stable, causing Fanny to put together a collection of her poems, publish them, and use the sale price to repurchase her "dear and noble horse." The poems, said Sidney George Fisher, were inferior and bared her "conjugal unhappiness," which in his opinion should have been omitted. A pertinent example is the verse called "Impromptu":

> You say you're glad I write—oh say not so!
> My font of song, dear friend's a bitter well
> And when the numbers freely from it flow
> 'Tis that my heart, and eyes, o'erflow as well.[13]

Adelaide Kemble Sartoris, Fanny Kemble's sister. (Drawing by A. E. Charon, 1830. National Portrait Gallery, London.)

Fanny Butler's trials began to be revealed in her personality. An entry in the Fisher diary noted:

> Mrs. B. is an agreeble companion, but does not interest me. She is too pronounced, wants delicacy & refinement, & is the reverse of feminine in her manners & conversation. She is also guilty of the imprudence & bad taste of alluding constantly to her domestic troubles, which are brought on by her own want of tact & temper. She has talent, however, & converses well.[14]

The accusation of masculinity came from others as well. Riding alone where discreet couples chose not to ride, her forthright manner, and her open criticism of slavery contributed to this feeling in many Philadelphians. Well aware that she minced no words, she could enjoy the reaction to her directness. Sister Adelaide, she said, applied this nursery rhyme to her:

> *The Dragon of Wantley, round as a butt,*
> *Full of fire from top to toe*
> *Cock of the walk, to the village I strut,*
> *And scare them all wherever I go.*[15]

Yet Fanny Butler had her loyal supporters, too. The treatment she received from Pierce Butler was seen to be unfair and he to be callous and unusually cruel—a normal reaction, for many Philadelphians had known Pierce and John Butler to have been poor examples of manhood. Still another diarist took note. Thomas P. Cope made this observation:

> On my way to monthly meeting at West Chester, I passed R. Strode's mill pond, where Fanny Butler, late F. Kemble was with others fishing with rods & lines. She was dressed in a light frock coat, pantaloons, boots & man's hat, having every outward appearance of a male. Altho' an actress & accustomed to exposure of the person, it seemed wonderful that she should thus outrage the accustomed laws of female decorum among so plain a people. She drives her own carriage & pair around the neighborhood, with her own hands to the amusement of sober natives. She boards close by with a family of Hicksites.[16]

Beset by her own difficulties in a city torn by open warfare between rampant Protestants and belligerent Irish Catholics—"Philadelphia *flames* from river to river with the burning of Catholic churches"—she was driven to agree to extreme measures to attempt to see and be near her children. In February 1845 Pierce Butler drove a hard bargain. His wife signed an incredible agreement, "In order to remain near my children, and retain as far as possible the right of a mother over them." He saw the Charles Sedgwicks as a source of the disaffection of his wife. He could not accuse her of infidelity, for throughout the long years of their strife she gave him no cause for such an accusation. However, the Sedgwicks were written into the agreement:

> Being about to reside in Mr. Butler's house, I promise to observe the following conditions while living under his roof. I will give up all acquaintance and intercourse of whatever kind, with every member of the Sedgwick family, and hereafter I will treat them in every respect as entire strangers, and as if I had never known them. I will not keep up an acquaintance with any person of whom Mr. Butler may disapprove.
>
> I will observe an entire abstinence from all references to the past, neither will I mention to any person any circumstances which may occur in Mr. Butler's house or family.[17]

Pierce Butler saw to it that even though his wife might abide by the stringent terms, the results would not be worth her while. Harassed, insulted, ignored, unable to be with the children, she surrendered and booked passage to England. Her departure was noted by Rebecca Gratz, one of the Philadelphians who remained a true friend. Miss Gratz wrote her niece, Miriam Gratz Moses Cohen, in Savannah:

> Poor Fanny Butler, at last finds that she cannot longer sustain her painful & useless efforts to remain with her children, and leaves this city tomorrow.
>
> Mr. B. has found so many ways of thwarting her and rendering her miserable, that even her own sense of right now determines her to give up & depart. Her children have been for two months away in the country where she is not permitted to visit them so that the whole object of her residence in his house is defeated. We shall feel her loss deeply and sorrowfully, for we love her very much, and the thought of her unhappiness is even more painful than the loss of her society. She has endeared herself to us by her noble qualities, her brilliant talents, and ardent love and practice of rare virtues. Leaving her children almost breaks her heart yet in her helpless condition it would be in vain to stay pining after duties she is not permitted to perform.[18]

Both the beautiful Rebecca Gratz and Miriam Cohen had long been admirers of Fanny Kemble. Ten years before, Mrs. Cohen, then Miriam Moses, had read "Fanny Kemble's Address to a Star" that had appeared in print at the time of her marriage. Miss Moses wrote in her commonplace book of June 21, 1834, two weeks after the Butler wedding:

> *Yet strange a bride so young and fair*
> *With spirit fresh and light as air*
> *Should read in yon star that beamed so bright*
> *The lesson of a dark, dark night.*

The young Miss Moses sensed a premonition by Fanny Butler of the trouble that came so soon.[19]

In Philadelphia, Rebecca Gratz kept her eyes on the girls Fanny Butler had left behind: "Her children spent Saturday evening with us. They are very interesting little girls, but alas need their poor mother's watchful care. There is not a female in the family capable of supplying her place, or able to counteract the injurious tendency of over indulgence and the want of maternal discretion."[20]

Fanny Butler's sister Adelaide had married Edward Sartoris, an enigmatic well-to-do man who seemed to defy consistent description. An acquaintance called him a "walking pea-jacket," for he appeared almost always to have his hands pocketed in that favorite garment. Whatever he resembled, he was kind to his sister-in-law, and their invitation to her to visit them in Rome could not have come at a more opportune time. Fanny Butler, distraught and dejected, set out quickly, accompanied only by her maid. The two women traveled through France in midwinter, a journey recorded in her journal covering the Italian visit. She gave the resulting book an apt title, *A Year of Consolation.* It is a placid piece of travel writing with but few flashes of the old Kemble vitality. Despite a fascination with the Italian countryside, long walks and rides, and being engrossed in the marvelous variety of Rome, she could not shake off her desolation and the longing for her children. The day before she left, after being with the Sartoris family for almost a year, she visited the great Trevi fountain. It was "dark and gloomy and raining fast," but she drank to her return on a brighter day to a city and a land that had won a portion of her battered heart.[21]

While Fanny Butler was enroute to Rome, Pierce Butler again went to Harrisburg, this time on state business. Thomas P. Cope was there and

Sarah and Frances Butler, the daughters of Pierce Butler and Fanny Kemble. (Museum of Coastal History, St. Simons Island.)

noted what happened when Butler took issue with the formidable Thaddeus Stevens, a man with a vengeful hatred of slavery and of the South. Mr. Cope wrote: "Pierce Butler, a puerile fellow who married Fanny Kemble, the celebrated actress, was fool enough to strike a wordy blow at him, but was never again heard in that Convention. T, in his reply, said there were some insects so insignificant that if you tramp on them, they would escape under the hollow of your foot."[22]

Fanny Butler was thirty-eight when she returned to England from Italy. The Italian journal sold quickly and for a better price than she had anticipated. Free once again, but forced to exercise her "power of coining," she was understandably reluctant to try and recapture her former station. She considered herself a "stout, middle-aged, not particularly good looking woman" better suited to playing a "weightier" Lady Macbeth or Queen Katherine than a Juliet or a Julia.[23]

Putting aside her fears, she decided to return to the stage. Not in London, but in Manchester, Birmingham, Liverpool, Dublin, Bristol, Bath, Plymouth—sometimes a fortnight, sometimes a night. Her tour began in Manchester and she did play Julia in Fazio's *The Hunchback* after an interval of thirteen years. She was rather pleased, for her "self possession" had increased and her voice and delivery were as strong as when she was much younger. The many moves about the country and the demands on her time for rehearsals and for the performances were a constant strain. She wished that she could instead turn to public readings. Her father had done this very well, reading Shakespeare to appreciative audiences. Thus, she felt she could not "thrust my sickle into a field he was reaping so successfully." The demanding tour that had begun in February 1847 continued through the spring of 1848. Glasgow, Dundee, Perth, Edinburgh, Leeds, Exeter, and on, and on. When a weary Charles Kemble finally decided to give up his readings of Shakespeare, he presented his daughter with his annotated versions of the plays as he had read them. She turned eagerly to harvesting this fertile field. Her first public reading was on March 25, 1848, to an intimate gathering at Highgate. It was a great success, as was her first reading to a London audience on April 3 when she read *The Merchant of Venice*. Life had taken a turn for the better, a turn blocked very abruptly by an action of Pierce Butler in Philadelphia. On April 7, 1848, in the city's Court of Common Pleas, Pierce Butler sought a divorce and contended his wife Frances Anne had "willfully, maliciously, and without due cause, deserted him on September 11, 1845." In the midst of a burst of successful appearances, with a busy schedule of advanced bookings, Fanny Butler quickly changed course to return to America to state her case.[24]

While his wife was on her theatrical tour in England, Pierce Butler received word that his brother John had died while serving with a Philadelphia regiment in the war with Mexico. The news came in a letter from S. B. H. Vance, a friend of the Butlers who was with Captain Butler in that senseless war: "It becomes my painful duty to communicate to you intelligence of the most saddening character, our esteemed Captain Butler *is no more.* He died in the town of Meir last night at 11 oclock."

In Philadelphia it was said John Butler died of a disease "peculiar to the climate." His friend Vance said it was "dysentery in its worse form." Pierce Butler lost no time in sending Dr. Sam Wilson, who was looking after the slaves at Hampton and Butler's Island. Dr. Wilson was told to see to the return of Captain Butler's body and of his slave and manservant who had accompanied John Butler to Mexico. The favorite of his two horses, both in Mexico, was to be returned to the widow Gabriella.[25] The death was noted in the diaries of the two Fishers. Joshua Francis Fisher wrote: "News today of J. Butler's death. I feel it as he was a friend of my Boyhood—tho since I was 14 I have known little of him—nor desired to."[26] Sidney George Fisher wrote no accolade:

> He died in Mexico whither he went about a year ago as Captain of Dragoons. No man ever threw away his life more foolishly. He went to Mexico merely for amusement, for occupation & to escape the ennui of wealth & idleness at home. He saw no fighting & died of dysentery. He was, they say, a good officer, but was no loss to anyone except perhaps his wife, daughter & brother, as he was a hard, selfish, profligate fellow, totally without education or intellect. He had, however, the manners of a gentleman & exhibited great taste in dress, house & equippage.[27]

One of the Butler slaves said her owner had died in Mexico, "where money bear upon the tree. Gone there to fight for more Mexico money and Buckra kill 'im dead."[28]

Sidney George Fisher was accurate in describing John Butler as hard and selfish. His will was a remarkable document that could have come only from a man devoid of love and respect for his immediate family. He was survived by Gabriella and their seventeen-year-old daughter, Elizabeth Manigault Butler, who was known to family and friends as Lizzie.

The widow was bequeathed income for life provided she did not remarry. He stated it this way:

> And I now take occasion to declare that I am not to be understood as having any desire to forbid any Second Marriage Which My Said Wife may think proper to Contract after My decease and in annexing the Condition that She Shall not Contract Such Second Marriage to the above bequests made to her in this My last Will and Testament I merely intend to express my determination that my Estate after My deceased Shall not be enjoyed by a stranger in blood.

Before and after the above recitation he admonished his widow fourteen times to remain unmarried or suffer the consequences. As for his daughter Elizabeth, she was to share the income only by marrying a man who met the approval of her mother and her uncle, Pierce Butler. For any of Elizabeth's children to inherit the estate following her death and that of her mother's, John Butler stated his conditions coldly and interminably:

> To the first son of the body of My daughter the said Elizabeth Butler and the Heirs of Such Son forever And in case Such first Son Shall die without issue or Within the age of twenty-one years then to the Second Son of the Body of the Said Elizabeth Butler and the Heirs of Such Second Son forever. And in case Such Second Son Shall die without issue or within the age of twenty-one years, then to the third, fourth, fifth and sixth son and all and every other the Son and Sons of the Body of the said Elizabeth Butler as may be able to take under this My Last Will and Testament, Shall respectively on or before arriving at the age of twenty-one years be called and Known by and Assume and Use the Surname "Butler" and no other Surname whatever And this Condition Must not be so Construed As to enable Such Son or Sons of the Body of the Said Elizabeth Butler as shall marry have issue and die before attaining the Age of twenty-one years to transmit My said Estate to Such issue unless Such Son or Sons of the Body of the Said Elizabeth Butler shall prior to the time of his or their death be Called and Known by and Assume And Use the Surname "Butler" And No other Surname Whatever; and also upon Condition that Such Son or Sons of the Body of the Said Elizabeth Butler as may be entitled to take under this My Last Will and Testament Shall reside permanently in the United States three years being allowed for travelling in Europe or elsewhere when he or they shall have completed his or their education And attained the Age of twenty-one years.

In a rare demonstration of generosity, Gabriella Butler was left "absolutely all the furniture, plate, linen, china, stores, carriages, Horses, Wines, books, pictures and all the moveable whatsoever," after being told she could continue living in their residence on the south side of Walnut between Schuylkill Sixth and Seventh streets in Philadelphia as long as she remained unmarried. The house, according to Sidney George Fisher, was a "fine establishment built of Quincy Granite and with a porte Cocher, which I think is very convenient. It is the only house so built in town."

John Butler, he who had first refused to change his name from Mease to Butler to follow the dictates of Major Butler's will, and who shared his grandfather's estate only by favor of his brother Pierce, had the audacity to lay the condition of adopting the name "Butler" on his unborn grandson and to deny the inheritance to other children that might be born to his daughter.

The will provided for the contingency there be no "Son of the body of the said Elizabeth Butler" by leaving the estate to Pierce Butler for his natural life, meaning that he would have a life interest should Gabriella die or remarry. Otherwise, his widow would enjoy income for her lifetime. On the death of Pierce Butler under such conditions, the estate would flow to "Such son of the body of the said Pierce Butler" with the same tedious recitation of all qualifying provisions put upon the sons of Elizabeth Butler. Pierce Butler and Thomas C. James were the designated executors and trustees.

Surprisingly, John Butler directed his interest in the Georgia plantations be sold as soon as practicable following the termination of the life estate of Aunt Eliza Butler, with the proceeds to be invested in productive Pennsylvania real estate or interest-bearing securities or loans. By agreement with the trustees, Gabriella Butler qualified as administrator of the estate for the Georgia properties. In 1850 the McIntosh Superior Court ordered her to deliver the John Butler interest to his trustees, a move she was reluctant to make.[29]

Elizabeth Butler was wed to Julian McAllister, a Savannahian serving in the United States Army. The marriage in 1848, the year after her father's death, was followed in 1850 by the birth and death of their first son John, by a daughter Julia in 1851, and by a second son, called Francis, in 1853.[30]

The Philadelphia to which Fanny Butler returned was divided in its sentiment toward the contesting Butlers. Pierce Butler's friends were not confined to card players, speculators, and the social segment to which he belonged. His continuing interest in music gave an extra dimension to his circle of acquaintances. In 1847 an operatic troupe sang grand opera in Philadelphia. The fine Italian tenor Natale Perelli was persuaded by Pierce Butler to remain in Philadelphia, where he opened a studio and did much to improve the taste and to extend the quality of vocal music in his new home.[31] Although Fanny Butler welcomed the divorce action, thinking "it may prove to be the last of the strange series of persecutions" that had plagued her for so long, she was also apprehensive for fear of being branded as one who by desertion had abandoned her "most sacred duties." She was disturbed, too, that Pierce Butler seemed surrounded by good feeling and that in the eyes of many he was a "paragon of every earthly excellence," while she was a "monster of all iniquity."[32] All was not quite so dark, for her friends remained loyal. Sidney George Fisher expressed his thoughts in his diary:

> Mrs. Pierce Butler returned by the last steamer. She came in consequence of an application for a divorce on the part of her husband. He claims it on the ground of "Willful and malicious desertion." As it is quite notorious that she was driven from his house by his own barbarous treatment, I think he can hardly succeed. It is impossible to predict, however, such is often the difference between the reality and the evidence. The position is certainly a painful one. She is obliged to return to the stage for a support as Butler makes her no allowance. I shall be very glad to see her again.[33]

A similar expression came from Fanny Butler's old friend Rebecca Gratz: "My friend Mrs. Butler whose persecuting husband has forced her to this country by suing for a divorce on the pleas of her having deserted him, tho' it is well known he drove her out from her privileges of Mother & wife long before she attempted to earn a maintenance for herself in a profession she loathes." Rebecca Gratz also wrote that Fanny had received "flattering attention from all her personal friends."[34]

The Butler divorce became a public airing of the conflict that had existed between Fanny and Pierce Butler for fourteen long years. There were two basic reasons for their differences, and both were treated gingerly by the formidable batteries of attorneys representing the two adversaries. Pierce Butler had hired the best he knew, two men who were leaders of the Philadelphia bar, John Cadwalader and George Mifflin Dallas, a former mayor of Philadelphia and the vice-president of the United States. Fear of a jury trial and all that might be disclosed of his personal life prompted the nervous plaintiff to retain Daniel Webster and two stellar lawyers from New York, Charles O'Connor and John Duer, although Pierce Butler said his intentions were to prevent his wife from doing the same. He was shattered when John Cadwalader looked upon the retention of the additional lawyers as an affront and withdrew from the case. Lawyer Dallas voiced strong opposition but did not resign. Fanny Butler was well represented by William M. Meredith and Benjamin Gerhard. Associated with them was the eminent Rufus Choate of Massachusetts, and lending support were her friends Charles and Theodore Sedgwick, and Samuel Gray Ward.[35] The underlying cause of their troubles was the ownership and treatment of the Butler slaves at Hampton and Butler's Island plantations. The second basic cause for the breakup of their marriage was Pierce Butler's infidelity.

The conflict over the slaves was reason to place Pierce Butler in a disadvantageous position, for Philadelphia in 1848 was a strong center of antislavery sentiment just as it had been in Major Butler's later years. Pierce Butler's attorneys, however, were quick to brand Fanny Butler as an abolitionist, for even in Philadelphia the term carried a measure of scorn. From the material submitted to his attorneys came this statement:

> One painful subject of difference between us was that of negro slavery. Although we resided in Pennsylvania, where slavery does not exist, the greater part of my property lies in the State of Georgia, and consists of plantations and negroes. Mrs. Butler, after our marriage, not before, declared herself to be in principle an abolitionist, and her opinions were frequently expressed in a violent and offensive manner; this was grievous enough to bear; however, I seldom opposed or combatted them; but when it came to the point of publishing her sentiments, I offered the most unqualified opposition to it.

Just as Fanny Butler had written that before their marriage she "knew nothing of those dreadful possessions of his," Pierce Butler reiterated their long courtship brought forth no revelation to him of her strong and oft-expressed feelings on slavery: "Mrs. Butler's opinions and views in regard to the marriage contract and negro slavery, were either not formed or not expressed before she became my wife. A knowledge of them, or either of them, as they were afterwards exhibited, must have proved an insuperable bar to our union." The point regarding the marriage contract was that Pierce Butler saw the wife as completely subservient to the husband. In a letter to his wife he had written that reconciliation was possible "if you can consent to submit your will to mine." Fanny Butler could no more agree to such terms than she could approve of slavery. She believed marriage was a joint venture—"companionship on equal terms." In the traditional society of that day public sentiment favored Pierce Butler's interpretation of the obligations of a wife to a husband.[36]

Fanny Butler's attorneys exhibited two anonymous letters received by her that were said to be the work of Pierce Butler. The first was a bitter harassment that questioned her living with Mr. Butler and enjoying the income from, and the produce of, slaves. The letter said such action "tests the sincerity of your anxiety about the blacks." The second letter said she was a disgrace to England "and all right-minded Americans think so."[37]

As to the second underlying cause of their difficulties, Pierce Butler's infidelity, there was little said. Fanny Butler had been reticent about bringing into the open a matter to cause embarrassment to herself and her children. Prior to the trial both sides assembled information to be used in presenting their cases. Mrs. Butler's *Answer* to the charges was noted widely in American and English newspapers. Mr. Butler's *Statement*, published after the trial from material used by his attorneys, was an attempt to counter the widely known views of his wife. Fanny Butler's *Answer* did not touch on Pierce Butler's marital digressions, and while his *Statement* mentioned on three occasions events or situations where infidelity may have been at play, there was certainly no acknowledgment of such an act, rather, there was indignation expressed that such might even be thought. It may well have been that Fanny Butler's attorneys were prepared to bring the matter into the open had the case gone before a jury, which it never did. In 1844 Pierce Butler had been publicly accused of involvement in an escapade with Mrs. James Schott. The accusation told of a bedroom scene Mr. Schott was too modest to recount. He called Pierce Butler a "crafty knave" and challenged him to a duel that was staged in Maryland without casualty to either participant. Fanny Butler had written Mrs. Joshua Francis Fisher of Philadelphia, attempting to put in perspective the infidelity of Pierce Butler as a factor in their difficulties and as to the role played by her friends the Sedgwicks in counseling her. The Sedgwicks were unaware of his conduct until told by Fanny Butler, who wrote Mrs. Fisher: "and *they now,* as well as myself, possess the key to all that I have endured in the instances which have gradually and one after another been brought to light of Mr. Butler's whole career."[38] She also told Mrs. Fisher that Pierce Butler, "in a moment of unguarded exasperation," had repeatedly acknowledged to one of the Sedgwick men—an attorney—his infidelity to his wife, saying he had no fears for she had returned incriminating letters and "she knows no names."

Fanny Butler did know names. In telling the Sedgwicks of Pierce Butler's adultery she had given the name of the daughter of his doctor who had been a party to an affair at the time of Sarah's birth. Also, she had written Mrs. Fisher of the London alliance with Amelia Hall, the children's governess: "I am persuaded that almost any circumstances must be more favourable for them than the deplorable ones of their own home where the only person who has charge of them was a poor woman once my servant whom Mr. Butler seduced while we were all in England together and whom I am informed has lately taken to drinking."[39]

In Pierce Butler's *Statement* he touched on a request by Adelaide Sartoris and a friend that he dismiss Miss Hall, an act he said was an affront to the governess. He also mentioned the remarkable trip made by Fanny Butler from Butler's Island to Darien in the dead of night. She rowed her small boat, alone, hoping to find a ship that would take her away from whatever it was that motivated such a drastic escape. Fanny Kemble Wister, who has written with feeling for her great-grandmother, suggests she had discovered he had been with one of the Negro women of the plantation. But Pierce Butler blamed his wife's violent temper for this act of rashness. Again, in his *Statement,* Pierce Butler attacked the "double-dealing" confederates of his wife, the Sedgwicks, who had "spread abroad imputations against me as defamatory as they were unfounded. Not only was the slang of infidelity pertinaciously reiterated, but in their zeal to injury they did not scruple and to soil their own lips with calumnies so gross that I cannot here even allude to them." If the gross calumny was that which it appeared to be, the Sedgwick letters to and from Fanny Butler that have survived do not reveal the sordid details Pierce Butler could not mention. In the South Carolina or Georgia plantation life of Major Butler's day the slave owner–slave girl relationship was commonplace. The two Roswell Kings had fathered mulatto children on the Butler plantations, a fact of life accepted by Pierce Butler. He certainly did not wish to jeopardize his case or to endanger his imagined reputation by bringing into the open a matter his Philadelphia friends, and a jury, would see in a different light. On the other hand, his inability to face up to the "calumny" of the Sedgwicks was surely viewed by some as an admission of guilt. In considering what the Sedgwicks knew of his affairs it is not surprising he should turn against them with such vehemence. They were honorable, intelligent people completely loyal to Fanny Butler. That they followed her wishes to cut away many passages from her detailed and explicit letters, and destroyed others completely, all of which would have strengthened her position, is testimony to that loyalty.[40]

Fanny Butler had come to believe the ownership of slaves fostered personal degradation. Thus, in her mind the two underlying causes for their troubles were closely entwined. She saw Pierce Butler's philandering as an extension of that weakness, and her emotional reaction probably was of far greater import than was outwardly evident.[41]

The divorce case was prolonged and painful to both sides. It ended when the two Butlers agreed to the dissolution of their marriage, giving the mother the right to be with her children for two months every summer, and for Pierce Butler to pay her $1,500 a year in quarterly payments. His promise to pay was secured by a $60,000 mortgage on Butler Place, held by Joshua Francis Fisher as trustee for Fanny Butler. Pierce Butler also agreed to pay her the money she had earned from the publication of her American *Journal*. He sent her $2,192.19 received from Carey, Lea and Blanchard, the American publishers, and $1429.75 that had come from John Murray of London. Mr. Murray had approved of that early and controversial *Journal,* thinking it "clever, lively and original." "I hope you will continue your Journal in the same original style, throughout life, it will be a source of interesting occupation to yourself and of amusement & instruction to the world."[42]

The divorce was finally granted on September 22, 1849, at which time the Butler name was put aside as Mrs. Fanny Kemble resumed the career of Shakespearean readings begun in England in February 1847. Her American readings had begun in Boston in early 1849, when she read *The Merchant of Venice* to an enraptured audience. This reading led to many more, a profitable career that brought much-needed comfort and purpose to a strife-torn life.[43]

Chapter 18

The Weeping Time

You cannot be humane to someone you hold in bondage. The only humane act would be to set the person free. The point is not what you do with the stolen goods, but that the goods were stolen.

PUT ASUNDER by the slaves at Hampton and Butler's Island, Fanny Kemble and Pierce Butler went their separate ways. He, who had been less than magnanimous in the award to the mother of his children, continued his pre-divorce attitude by standing between her and their two girls. He interrupted a reunion in Lenox of mother and daughters by appearing unannounced. There in the Berkshires, Fanny Kemble had purchased a small cottage, using money from her well-received readings of the Shakespeare plays. Sarah and Fan were fourteen and eleven years old, and not until each became twenty-one would she feel free to be with them as she wished. She lived comfortably, for the readings brought ample funds to meet her needs. One who heard her in New York was Philip Hone, an eminently successful New York merchant. He had been maligned in the American *Journal* but had long since received Fanny's apology. He called her the "veritable Fanny Kemble" and said she had taken the city by storm. He, as did others, noted that Shakespeare was never paid for writing the plays as Fanny Kemble for reading them.[1]

Pierce Butler was sharing the income from the Georgia plantations with Gabriella Butler and his Aunt Eliza. The oldest Butler continued to receive one-half, with Pierce Butler and John's widow dividing the other half. In addition, Pierce Butler and John's estate shared the earnings from their schooner, the *Roswell King,* that carried plantation produce to market in Savannah and Charleston for their own, as well as other Altamaha plantings. When the occasion demanded, the *King* visited Philadelphia

311

and returned to Darien with corn for the slaves and other general cargo.[2] In an appraisal made for the John Butler estate, the 1849 value of the 840 slaves then working the Georgia plantations was shown at $281,125. Other plantation property, exclusive of land, brought the total to $310,742.12.[3]

Led by John Couper's erudite son James Hamilton Couper, the Altamaha plantations were undergoing a subtle change. It was as though the owners anticipated trouble and made an effort to improve the lot of their slaves. The Savannah newspapers, quick to defend slavery, took pleasure in recording any instance placing the institution in a favorable light. They did so in 1849, and told of one of the regattas that had become popular with the planters of the coastal country of Georgia and South Carolina. Their story was headed: "The Planters of the Altamaha—long may the sunshine of happiness and prosperity beam among them." The event reported was a race of plantation boats manned by enthusiastic and capable black crews. The *Georgian* said the fact that the oarsmen were slaves who took pride in their effort was "utterly inappreciable elsewhere." The Philadelphia Butlers were more interested in the sunshine of prosperity than that of happiness. The distant owners had little inclination toward such diversions. In contrast, James Hamilton Couper's slaves were active participants in boat races. They rowed sophisticated craft designed by Couper himself. His crew capped their racing careers at a large regatta in Charleston by rowing *Becky Sharp* to victory. They were led by the slave Jessie, at stroke. Their owner was the coxswain and their victory song was Jessie's favorite, "Slipper, Shoes and White Stockings."[4]

The 1850s saw Pierce Butler's life take an odd turn. Worried about his image, he joined one of Philadelphia's Episcopal churches. It was a move that startled his elderly aunt, Eliza. On hearing he had become religious she is reported to have said, "I think he must be crazy." She added for emphasis, "None of the Butlers ever had any religion."[5] At the Church of the Epiphany he was elected to the vestry, chosen to head the music committee, and increasing Aunt Eliza's amazement, taught a class of eight or nine boys "Bible and Catechism" in the church Sunday school for two successive years.[6]

Earnings from the plantations were good, but despite his religious turn, Pierce Butler continued to dissipate his income by gambling at cards and by speculating in the stock market. His life remained in turmoil, reaching a crisis in ten-year intervals. Fanny Butler had upset what little equilibrium existed by her visit to the plantations in 1839. The divorce came

Fanny Kemble's Berkshire cottage, "The Perch," at Lenox, Massachusetts. (Amelia M. Watson "Kemble" Collection, Lenox Library.)

in 1849, and deep trouble lay ahead for 1859. The ten years following the divorce were marked by other changes. Again seeking to repair his damaged image, he assembled and published the *Statement,* the compilation of material he had given his attorneys during the litigation prior to the divorce. This after-the-fact action prompted a comment from J. Francis Fisher, who wrote Fanny Kemble:

> the motive of which, at this time, I cannot imagine.

> I should be very sorry to read anything written on your subject in the spirit which I fear must activate Mr. Butler in presenting to the world his own statement after so long a time.

In a letter to a Boston friend to whom he sent a copy of the *Statement,* Pierce Butler wrote:

> The prejudice against me existed stronger and more generally in Boston, than, perhaps, in any other city, and if you can show the statement to one or two of your friends in that city it will be rendering me a service.

> I have limited its circulation to my friends, for I feared a more extended use of it might bring it before the public through the newspapers which I am particularly desirous to avoid.[7]

Bostonians had given Fanny Kemble strong support in her legal battle with Pierce Butler. Her popularity there stemmed from her several appearances on the Boston stage, the first of which was with her father, Charles Kemble, in 1832.

Change came to the Altamaha, too, for in 1850 old John Couper died. It was a year in which Major Butler's Fugitive Slave Law was strengthened in a futile effort to stem the tide of runaway Negroes. Also in 1850, the fine house at the northwest corner of Walnut and Thirteenth streets, built by Thomas Butler, was purchased by the Philadelphia Club for a total obligation of thirty thousand dollars. John Butler had been a member from 1834 until 1838, and Pierce Butler joined the year after the house was purchased. The cost of conversion from residence to clubhouse was almost eight thousand dollars, and at the grand opening celebration the membership witnessed a fellow member perform "the uncommon feat of drinking a glass of Madeira while standing on his head."[8] In 1851 Thomas Spalding of Sapelo died, and Alexander Blue became the new manager of the Butler estate in Georgia. Blue soon became embroiled in plantation problems. Glasgow, a slave who was known to Pierce Butler and who had been flogged at the time of the family visit, was again in trouble. In 1853 the slaves were owned jointly by Pierce Butler and his brother John's estate. Confronted with "the turbulent behavior of Glasgow," Pierce Butler conferred with Thomas James, his fellow trustee, and then wrote Manager Blue:

> We have come to the conclusion that the safety of others, as well as the discipline of the plantation requires that he shall be removed. We therefore authorize you to sell him away from the plantation. He has a wife and son, and if they wish to follow their father, they must be allowed the option, one or both.

> Our views are that he should be sold at such a distance from the plantation that a return to it will be out of his power.

> We also advise that no previous notice be given on the plantation as it would probably incite him to abscond, or some worse act.[9]

Glasgow, aged forty-four in 1853, was valued at $550 in the 1849 appraisal made to determine the worth of the John Butler estate's interest in the Georgia plantations. Roswell King, Jr., Alexander Blue, and Alexander Mitchell valued the 840 slaves and all of the "moveable" property. They did not attempt to evaluate the various tracts of land. Glasgow's wife, Rina, was ten years younger and valued at $425. Their son Tyrone, when ten in 1849, was appraised at $300. The lengthy appraisal gives a revealing picture of the Butler work force when it was near its peak. There were 197 family groups ranging in size from two to ten. Nineteen slaves were listed individually, some being "superannuated" who had outlived their families. There were 267 males, 252 females, and 321 children aged twelve or under. The slaves were valued individually and in their family groups. Four of the men received the highest valuation of $1,000, being drivers Frank, Angus, and Morris, and the blacksmith, John. Many women were appraised at $500, but none above that amount. The most valuable family was Frank, a "worker," his wife Clarinda, and their eight children, four of whom were under twelve. The Frank-Clarinda family was valued at $4,050. The total value of the 840 slaves was $281,125, or an average price of $334.67. In striking contrast to the William Page list of 1793, when the slave population was 441, was the longevity of the people. Of the 840 on the 1849 appraisal, fifty-five men and forty-five women were aged fifty years or older. Renty, eighty-five, was the oldest man, and Evander, seventy-five, the oldest woman. There were seven men and seven women in their seventies, fourteen men and sixteen women in their sixties, and a great many in their fifties. The value of those women in their fifties seldom exceeded $200 and averaged well below that figure.[10]

In August 1853 Pierce Butler, individually and as trustee for the estate of John Butler, purchased General's Island, a rice plantation of seven hundred acres lying between Butler's Island and Darien. At the same time and in the same manner, three tracts within and adjoining the town were bought. The Darien property consisted of forty acres of town lots, and the adjoining land included thirty acres of marsh on the Darien River and one hundred acres of pineland north of the town. The acquisition gave Pierce Butler a convenient residence on the "Ridge" that, with Hampton, served as an alternate refuge from Butler's Island in the dangerous season, and for another purpose that he had not contemplated. The total cost was thirty-six thousand dollars.[11]

Alexander Blue's management of the plantations followed Roswell King, Jr.'s second resignation. The former manager had returned to the Butler payroll in 1844, the year his father died in Roswell, Georgia, the town he had founded. The poor health that had plagued the younger King all of his adult life forced his departure this second time. He went to Woodville, on Colonel's Island, to live with his wife and children, but soon died. On July 1, 1854, his soul "passed from time to eternity." A friend said: "In a spiritual point of view Mr. King's death is a very melancholy one! He died as he lived." Which was to say, hard, and without repentance. Roswell King, Jr., left his widow Julia Rebecca Maxwell King and nine of their eleven children. At his death he owned 127 slaves, a plantation of 1,950 acres called South Hampton, 54 acres at Woodville, 50 "head of cattle," 11 oxen, 26 hogs, 5 mules, 1 colt, wagons, carts, and barrows, plus an interest in the Ogeechee Turnpike. Julia King owned 52 slaves in her own right and Georgia coastal land on Colonel's Island and at Yellow Bluff and Half Moon. She, too, owned cattle, hogs, horses, and mules. Roswell King, Jr., was buried in the cemetery of Midway Church, was said by his granddaughter to have been "worshipped" by his family, and called by them "Nature's Nobleman." Roswell King, Jr.'s will was drawn fourteen years before his death. In it, he cautioned his seven sons against a "lazy mode of life, either physic, law or gospel."[12]

In 1854 Pierce Butler sent a dilatory word to other members of the Butler family of another death, also in July. In October, his letter to Louis Butler in Paris: "We have lost the last surviving member of the older branches of our family. On Sunday, July 23, I closed the eyes in the sleep of death of our Aunt Eliza." He said that Aunt Eliza had "ever been a mother," with innumerable acts of generosity and kindness to him "throughout her whole life," which was certainly true. A similar letter was sent to Gabriella Butler.[13]

In Eliza Butler's will she dutifully passed on her father's ten thousand dollars, the earnings from which she had enjoyed since 1822. The money went to her two nieces, Frances Mease Cadwalader and Mary Middleton Mease Elwyn, with the direction to enjoy the income and to designate the ultimate distribution in their own wills. She also left to each two thousand dollars in "bonds and mortgages" in the same manner, naming their brother Pierce Butler as trustee in all instances. She wrote that he had served diligently as her agent, collecting "thousands of dollars," and was therefore not required to give bond. The original will is written in a clerk's neat hand except for that part following the clause pertaining to the disposition of "all the rest, residue and remainder." Here, in her own shaky hand, Eliza Butler penned "My nephew Pierce Butler, his heirs, executors and administrators." Eliza Butler was eighty years old. It was no wonder he could write Louis Butler of her innumerable acts of generosity and kindness.[14]

Eliza Butler's death terminated her life interest in the Georgia plantations and also brought into play the clause in John Butler's will directing his interest be sold. As long as this share was not sold, his widow and their daughter Elizabeth McAllister would have divided the considerable portion that had been paid to Eliza Butler, a fact that undoubtedly played a role in Gabriella Butler's reluctance to deliver the property to the trustees. The yield from the plantations appeared to her to be far better than what might be expected from Pennsylvania real estate or other investments available to Thomas James and Pierce Butler, the trustees of her husband's estate. On the other hand, Pierce Butler, as an individual and not as a trustee, wished to acquire his brother's interest and to own the lucrative properties himself. The inheritance from Eliza Butler made possible the purchase he contemplated.[15]

Fanny Kemble's great loss in 1854 was her father. Charles Kemble died in London with his daughter at his side. Two years later his much-loved Covent Garden Theatre was to die in flames a second time. "And now the flames had burst through the roof, and columns of fire darting through the air illuminated the surrounding neighbourhood for a distance of three miles and showed the distant Surrey hills standing out in bold relief." It was said of Charles Kemble that "Apollo might have envied his looks," and that he came on stage "with the indolent grace of a tawny lion."[16]

Sarah Butler came of age in 1856 and joined her mother for a fine and happy summer in Lenox. Fanny Kemble's life had begun to take on a semblance of order. The readings and the acclaim continued on both sides of the Atlantic. There may have been a time when, as Fanny Butler, there was a loss of confidence and an uncertain direction to her course in life. Not so in her fiftieth year. She told of a reading in Syracuse, New York:

I found an assembly of nearly two hundred young men and women, intelligent, conceited, clever, eager-looking beings, with sallow cheeks, large heads and foreheads, narrow chests and shoulders, and all the curious combination of physical characteristics that mark this most restless, ambitious, pretentious, and ignorant people, whose real desire for improvement and progress seems to me only equaled by the shallow empiricism of the cultivation they achieve. There is something at once touching and ludicrous in the extreme, in the desire exhibited at all times by the people of this country for the fine blossoms and jewels, so to speak, of civilization and education, and their neglect and ignorance of the roots and foundation of education and civilization; and so these country school-masters and mistresses earnestly desired to hear me read that they might "catch something of my style" and will elocutionize, as they call it, by the hour out of Shakespeare and Milton, and in their daily converse employ such dog English with allocutions so vulgarly ungrammatical, and an accent so vile, that Shakespeare and Milton would not know their own native tongue in their mouth. My reading (to return to that), was on this wise—

"I will read you Hamlet's soliloquy and speech to the players." Having finished them. "The air of this room is pestiferous. You have here no ventilation, and two rusty sheet-iron stoves all but red hot."

"I will now read you the lament of her brothers over the supposed dead body of Imogen." Having finished it, "You have now thrown open windows at the top and bottom, on opposite sides of the hall, producing violent draughts of cold air. Such of you as are exposed to them will get colds or the rheumatism."

"I will now read to you Mercutio's speech about dreams." Having finished it, "There is a strong escape of gas going on in this room; the screws in the gas-burners are none of them turned square; you are inhaling poison, and I am being choked."

"I will now read you Othello's defense before the Senate of Venice."

This being ended, I shut my book and asked them of what use it was for them to listen to or learn poetical declamation while they were sitting there violating every principle of health and neglecting the most necessary of all elementary knowledge, that which concerns the physical well-being of themselves and their pupils. So much for my first and last public lecture on education.[17]

Trouble and the problem of slavery followed Pierce Butler even to the Church of the Epiphany in Philadelphia. On June 29, 1856, the young minister the Reverend Dudley A. Tyng preached a sermon that he called "Our Country's Troubles." He spoke against slavery, making the point that if "great wrongs" were not challenged from the pulpit they then became accepted as not inconsistent with religion. Although he had never addressed the subject before, he thought it time to speak out, and did so. His sermon was interrupted by a church member who stood and called out that the subject was "not properly within the range of the speaker's duty." The Reverend Mr. Tyng continued his sermon, one that not surprisingly won the attention of the press. The vestry, of which Pierce Butler was a member, closed the church for a time and voted to dismiss their minister. The decision divided the church, with the congregation either violently for or opposed to the decision. None were more vehement in their support of the decision to oust the Reverend Mr. Tyng than Pierce Butler. He dismantled and removed his pew until the minister departed. The embattled Mr. Tyng did resign, "driven from that place as Paul was driven from Ephesus." He formed his own Church of the Covenant and was "honored and beloved" for his stand until his death a short time afterward.[18]

If the road through life had leveled out for Fanny Kemble, for Pierce Butler the way was steep and rocky. His losses were such in 1856 that the management of his financial affairs was taken from his hands to be placed with a triumvirate of Henry Fisher, his brother-in-law George Cadwalader, and Thomas James, his fellow trustee of John Butler's estate. Mr. James, described as a "sporting gentleman," was frequently seen about Philadelphia with Gabriella Butler, notwithstanding his seeming advocacy of Pierce Butler's desire to sever her connection with the Georgia plantations. These men did their best to quiet the many demands of creditors and to dole out to Pierce Butler an adequate income. Some of the pressure came from Fanny Kemble, for the promised annual payments of $1,500 were far in arrears. The pressure would have been greater had she not been so successful in her dramatic readings. In constant contact with her trustee, J. Francis Fisher, she took comfort in knowing she could give her children much of what they had once expected from their father. A letter to Mr. Fisher: "The miserable ruin of Mr. Butler's fortunes has of course long ago put an end to all such actions on the part of my children & I have had the great happiness of providing them not only with comfortable existences while they have been with me, but with many pleasures which they can no longer command under their father's roof." She ended this letter with "like Schiller's poor Mary Stuart, I can say with truth I have been much hated and much loved."[19]

Father's roof and all under it was soon sold. The sale was noted by Mrs. Sidney George Fisher in a letter to her husband: "Pierce Butler's town house is for sale, he asks $30,000." She added: "Mrs. John Butler's house is also for sale. She asks $40,000."[20] The Pierce Butler town house had been Major Butler's grand mansion on Chestnut and Eighth streets. In 1856 the old home had come on hard times. Disregarding his benefactor's specific wishes, Pierce Butler had permitted boarders in what he called and labeled "Butler House." In 1856 theatrical posters were plastered over the garden wall, on street trees, the steps, and the house itself. One proclaimed a Fanny Kemble play, Knowles's *The Hunchback,* with the older John Drew, and Cecile Rush playing the Kemble role. When the shabby house was demolished in 1857, Philadelphians mourned the loss of the great horse chestnut tree in the garden far more than the once proud symbol of Major Butler's worth. The trio of trustees gave thought to selling Butler Place at the time of the town house sale but were thwarted by the mortgage held by J. Francis Fisher to secure the payments long past due to Fanny Kemble. She had requested her interest be transferred to Sarah and Fan, and had Pierce Butler been able to make the transfer appear as a gift from himself rather than from their mother, it would have been done.[21]

The sale of the house in Philadelphia and the liquidation of other Butler properties fell far short of overcoming the tremendous debt. Reluctantly, the trustees began to look to the "sinews" of the Butler estate.

The year 1859 proved to be eventful. The *Southern Literary Messenger* praised Fanny Kemble after the editor saw and heard her read *Macbeth* in Baltimore. Admittedly, some old playgoers were disenchanted to see the beautiful young actress of twenty years before as the "stout and ruddy faced woman" who viewed them from the platform:

*Charles Henry Fisher, Sidney George Fisher's
brother, a friend and an inadequate financial advisor to
Pierce Butler. (Painting by Thomas Sully. Courtesy of
Mrs. Peter S. Elek.)*

Removing rather disdainfully a large bouquet of flowers that had been placed by the reading table, and announcing she had the honor of reading Macbeth to the ladies and gentlemen before her, she presently opened one of the volumes, recited in a sweet voice the *dramatis personæ* and suddenly then and there transformed into a Hecate on a blasted heath. From that moment until she completed the reading, her empery over the audience was complete. There was no need of scenic illusion to give the full effect to the wonderful drama; we were striding with Macbeth and Banquo across the desolate moor, or waiting paralyzed with horror in the silent hall of the castle while the murder was going on, or looking at the bloody apparition at the banquet, or standing in the midnight chamber as the pallid woman in her night-dress moved by in fiend-haunted slumber. Never before have we been so much impressed with the needless character of theatrical accessories to convey the meaning of the dramatist.[22]

Sarah Butler, after a false start with a young man, "Mr. Sandford of New York," to whom she was engaged in 1856, married Dr. Owen Jones Wister of Philadelphia. Near Savannah, where proslavery passions ran high, a slave trader, John Samuel Montmollin, died in such a manner as Southerners might have prescribed for an abolitionist. The boiler of a steamboat exploded, blasting him high in the air for a distance of seventy or eighty yards where he landed in a marsh, head foremost and buried to his hips. The year ended as John Brown of Osawatomie was hanged in Virginia, and Fanny Kemble was moved to write, or perhaps to copy in her own hand, a long songlike poem, a stanza from which reads:

> For now the soul of old John Brown
> From North & West comes marching down
> With wild hurrah & roll of drums
> And roar of cannon, lo it comes!
> lo it comes![23]

In 1859 the nation moved relentlessly toward conflict. The rights or wrongs of slavery were defended or argued with increasing intensity. Abolitionists had become Unionists, and in the South the proslavery advocates had become secessionists. In Savannah, two unusual events brought the issues into sharp focus. Much of the talk of the town was the ongoing story of the slave ship *Wanderer,* a venture led by the brazen secessionist Charles Augustus Lafayette Lamar. Fifty-one years after the date Major Butler and his cohorts had established that ended the importation of

Frances Anne Kemble, "stout and ruddy faced," reading Shakespeare. (Folger Shakespeare Library.)

slaves, in defiance of law, the *Wanderer* discharged 409 Africans on the beach of Georgia's Jekyll Island, where they were quickly moved inland to be sold. The pending federal case against the crew of the *Wanderer* and the flamboyant Charley Lamar was awaited with eager anticipation by the townspeople. The second topic of conversation was the auction sale of Pierce Butler's slaves that was to take place at Savannah's Ten Broeck racecourse on March 2 and 3.[24]

Savannah in 1859, as might be expected, was very much proslavery-secessionist. Not all were as adamant and as bitter as the *Daily Morning News* editor William Tappan Thompson, who fanned the fires of secession with such comments as:

> Why not stop the treasonable folly at once? Why not tell the North, once and for all, that the continuing aggression upon our rights, these continual violations of the constitution and laws, these violations of compacts and compromises, these insults and irritations—in a word, this perpetual, persistent lawless crusade against the institution of slavery must and shall end, be the consequences what they may.[25]

A few moderate voices could be heard. Charles Colcock Jones, Jr., who became Savannah's mayor in 1860, was one. He thought editor Thompson irresponsible in what he published, and when his father said Thompson "deserved a leather medal for discernment," young Jones agreed. He called Mr. Thompson a "drunken fool" for disregarding the law in the *Wanderer* case, and he called Charley Lamar a "dangerous man." The United States Supreme Court justice assigned to hear the *Wanderer* case was an unusual Savannahian. He was James Moore Wayne, a staunch Unionist. Despite his forceful charges to the jury, he saw the *Wanderer's* crew and Charley Lamar set free. This flaunting of federal law won the approval of most Savannahians.[26]

In 1859 Philadelphia was enveloped in an atmosphere equally tense. The antislavery Unionist sentiment was overwhelming, yet there was an outcropping of sympathy for the Southerners. In that year the socialites were talking about Pierce Butler and Fanny Kemble as they had been doing since the 1830s when the provocative actress first appeared in the red city. And Sidney George Fisher continued to record the gossip that enveloped the Butler family. He noted Butler Place was rented to Gabriella Butler, that Pierce Butler had squandered an inherited fortune of seven hundred thousand dollars by "sheer folly & infatuation." Talk of his affairs was an "inexhaustible subject," but Fisher gave him good marks for not wanting to sell his Negroes. He wrote in his diary: "Pierce Butler has gone to Georgia to be present at the sale of his Negroes. It is highly honorable to him that he did all he could to prevent the sale, offering to make any personal sacrifice to avoid it. But it cannot be avoided, and by the sale he will be able to keep Butler Place & have a fortune of 2 or 300,000 dollars, after paying his debts." Fisher then wrote about the slaves, reflecting a feeling prevalent among the Philadelphians who were his and Pierce Butler's friends and acquaintances:

> It is a dreadful affair, however, selling these hereditary Negroes. There are 900 of them belonging to the estate, a little community who have lived for generations on the plantation, among whom, therefore, all sorts of relations of blood & friendship are established. Butler's half, 450, to be sold at public auction & scattered over the South. Families will not be separated, that is to say, husbands & wives, parents & young children. But brothers & sisters of mature age, parents & children of mature age, all other relations & the ties of home & long association will be violently severed. It will be a hard thing for Butler to witness and it is a monstrous thing to do. Yet it is done every day in the South. It is one among the many frightful consequences of slavery and contradicts our civilization, our Christianity, our Republicanism. Can such a system endure, is it consistent with humanity, with moral progress? These are difficult questions, and still more difficult is it to say, what can be done? The Negroes of the South must be slaves or the South will be Africanized. Slavery is better for them and for us than such a result.[27]

In February 1859 Gabriella Butler was visiting her sister Margaret Ann Manigault Morris Grimball, called Meta, and her brother-in-law, the ailing John Berkley Grimball, at their plantation, the Grove, near Willtown on the Edisto River some twenty-five miles west of Charleston. She was there with her young adopted niece, Cornelia Grayson. They were attended by Mrs. Butler's French maid, Marie, in addition to the usual retinue of Grimball slaves. Gabriella Butler had just gone to her parents plantation, The Bluff, nearby, when she received an "express" urging her to be in Savannah on February 25, where her presence was "indispensable." With Marie, she boarded a train for the short trip to Charleston, and from there departed for Savannah on the steam packet.[28] In Savannah she was met by George Cadwalader and her friend Thomas James, two of the three appointed guardians of Pierce Butler's distressed fortune. George

Cadwalader was the husband of Pierce and John Butler's sister, Frances Mease. The two men were attending to the claims of Pierce Butler's creditors, and James had just returned from Butler's Island where he had seen to an equitable division of the slaves between John Butler's estate and those to be sold for his brother's account. Gabriella Butler was there to protect her interest and the future interest of her grandson, Francis Butler, the son of Elizabeth and Julian McAllister. The interested parties agreed to the division to clear the way for the slave dealer Captain Joseph Bryan to proceed with his plans for the sale he had been advertising in low- and up-country newspapers.

The division of the slaves was made as "demanded" by Pierce Butler. By a document dated February 16, 1859, Gabriella Butler, as "Administratrix with the will annexed," authorized Thomas C. James to represent her in the agreement made the following day appointing Thomas M. Foreman, James Hamilton Couper, and Thomas Pinckney Huger to appraise and divide the slaves. On February 21, the three men submitted their appraisal, showing their task had been accomplished "agreeably to Justice and Equity without favor or affection to any of the parties"—perhaps a true statement if the slaves were not considered to be one of the "parties." Although the entire work force was valued, the document listed only those slaves of "Share A," being those who were to remain on the plantations as the property of the John Butler estate.

The first two slaves on the list were Driver Frank, 61, "Bedridden & superannuated," and his wife Betty, 58, "Poultry minder." Frank had no value; Betty was worth $100. Frank had been the head driver at the time of Fanny Kemble Butler's "residence" on the plantations. Betty had birthed Renty, the son of Roswell King, Jr., long before the Butler family visit. Among those slaves not sold was Daphne, 34, "sickly," who with her twin Ben, dead in 1859, had been born of Minda by the younger Roswell King. Daphne was retained with her husband Aleck, or Alexander, 37, "good house servant," and their son Pierce Butler, 15, "good house boy, small." Another mulatto son of Roswell King, Jr., was troublesome Jim Valient, 44, son of Judy, appraised at $700 and awarded to the John Butler estate.

The most valuable man on the list was Hampton, 31, $1,800. The women given the highest value were those who were young and healthy. Jeane, 15, $950, Sinda, 15, $900, and Rhena, 26, "good house servant," $900, were topped by the highest of all, Catharine, 18, $1,000.

The appraisers used prefixes for purposes of identification. Some were familiar, others given designations difficult to fathom. There was Raccoon George, 51, $400, Crabclaw Quash, 40, $600, who was usually shown on plantation records as "Crab Quash" but on this occasion given his full name. His wife Auber, 31, "small & sickly," $600, and their son Five-pound, 15, who despite his age was a "prime plantation carpenter" and valued at $700. The reasons behind the prefixes for Bignose Isaac, 39, "rheumatic," $200, Blacksmith John, 40, $1350, and Trunk Harry, 60, "superannuated," were obvious, but as to why Jew Frank, 71, "superannuated jobber," no value, Jackstraw Abraham, and Blackfrost Adam, were so designated, is not known. Among the familiar names were Cooper London, 71, no value, who was the old barrel maker and preacher who had buried Shadrach by torchlight in the watery grave on Butler's Island twenty years before. Also, the several Abrahams, most designated as carpenters, and York, 29, $1,100, his wife Lydia, 28, $900, and their son Liverpool, 8, $400. Three old men, none of whom were given a dollar value, were shown as "superannuated Africans." They were Carpenter George, 68, Lawyer Peter, 67, and Sam, 70. Many had lost limbs, were sickly, or otherwise impaired. Common Jack, 40, $150, was deformed; Sue, 31, was deaf, but worth $700; and Trenton, 16, was a mute and valued at $400. Also listed among the "Share A" Negroes who were not auctioned was Gabriella, 6, the child of Sam and Ellen and worth $300 on her own. Other children and their values were Mease, 10, $600, Symphronia, 7, $300, and Thomas M. Oden, 1, $50, the son of Captain and Binah who bore the name of a Butler overseer. Dandy, 47, "Blacksmith & Engineer," $1,000, was retained for his value in operating the rice mills.

The appraisal was amended several times in an attempt to keep the old, or "superannuated," from being sold, or for unstated reasons when a family was moved from one share to the other. When the old were retained in "Share A," an allowance for support was given, an amount that came to a total of $3,700. After the allowance was taken into consideration, and after adjustments for other exchanges, the value of each share came to $257,900. The original valuation of all the slaves before the division, and before adjustments, was $526,100 for 919 Negroes. The average price was $572.47 per slave.[29]

Ten years before, the 1849 appraisal gave an average value of $334.67 per slave, but at that time their worth was determined with no thought of sale. In the 1859 evaluation a slave's worth was estimated at an amount they were expected to bring on the auction block. A comparison of the two appraisals of some of the slaves is shown below:

From the "Division of the Estate of John Butler, Dec'd, and Pierce Butler, in McIntosh and Glynn Counties, Georgia. Gabriella M. Butler, Admx, C.T.A. of John Butler"

Slave and age	1849	1859
Blacksmith John, 30	$1,000	$1,350
Peggy (wife), 20	500	850
John (son), 3	150	died
Peter (son), 1	100	550
Blacksmith Dandy, 37	800	1,000
Hampton, 22	550	1,800
Crabclaw Quash, 30	550	600
Auber (wife), 21	450	600
Fivepound (son), 5	125	700
Carpenter Alexander, 28	700	1,200
Daphne (wife), 24	500	800
Pierce Butler (son), 3	150	1,000

By 1859 Carpenter Alexander had become a house servant, as had his wife and child.[30]

Slave dealer Bryan was enthusiastic over prospects for a successful sale as Butler blacks were known to be well trained and were believed dependable for a full measure of work. Although his advertisement did not mention the Butler ownership, that fact was well known from news stories appearing with the notices of the sale and from the talk of many interested people. The first advertisement called for the sale of 460 slaves to be auctioned at Captain Bryan's premises, the slave pen in Savannah:

F O R S A L E
Long Cotton & Rice Negroes
A Gang of 460 Negroes

Accustomed to the culture of Rice and Provisions, among whom are a number of good mechanics and house servants, will be sold on the 2d and 3d of March next at Savannah

By Joseph Bryan
TERMS OF SALE

One-third cash, remainder by bond, bearing interest from day of sale, payable in two equal annual installments to be secured by mortgages on

the Negroes, and approved personal security; or for approved city accep-
tances on—Savannah and Charleston—purchasers pay for Papers.

The Negroes will be sold in families, and can be seen on the premises of

JOSEPH BRYAN

In Savannah, three days prior to the day of the sale, when catalogs will be
furnished.[31]

In the meantime, arrangements had been made to conduct the sale at
the Ten Broeck racecourse, three miles to the west of town on the Central
of Georgia Railroad. The slaves were housed in the stables there and were
available for inspection by prospective purchasers and by the curious. The
later advertisements took note of the change of location. Also, the number
of slaves was reduced because of the retention of some of the older slaves
among those who were to remain and because some had been sold
privately.

SALE OF

4 4 0   N E G R O E S !

PERSONS DESIRING TO INSPECT THESE

NEGROES

WILL FIND THEM AT THE

R A C E   C O U R S E,

WHERE THEY CAN BE SEEN

From 10 A.M. to 2 P.M.,

UNTIL

DAY OF SALE.

J. BRYAN,

Johnson Square.[32]

The slaves were taken to Savannah in small groups over a span of days.
Most traveled in railroad cars, with some making the trip from the islands
to Savannah by steamboat. The sale, on Wednesday and Thursday, March
2 and 3, followed the arrival of the last group by five days. In Savannah
the slaves were taken directly to the racecourse where they were placed
under the care and protection of Captain Bryan. Hard rains set in on
Monday and continued incessantly through the final day of the sale. On
the Friday following, editor Thompson of the *Daily Morning News* gave
the event scant notice. He wrote three short paragraphs under a small
heading—"Great Sale of Negroes": "The public sale of Pierce Butler's
negroes, was concluded yesterday at the Tenbroeck Race Course by
Joseph Bryan, Esq." The article told that 436 slaves were sold for a total

amount of $300,205, "Being an average of a little over $716 a head," a price well in excess of the average value of $572.47 estimated by the appraisers when the slaves were divided between Pierce Butler and his brother's estate. The editor wrote that seventeen of the slaves had been sold privately at prices not disclosed. The article ended: "The sale was largely attended by gentlemen from different portions of our state, and from South Carolina."[33]

Eleven days later, editor Thompson turned once again to the sale of Pierce Butler's slaves. Much to his surprise he had found on reading a Philadelphia newspaper that Horace Greeley's star reporter, "Doesticks," had covered the sale for the *New York Tribune* and had written a long "six column report" as he returned to New York by rail. While the Savannah editor was in the midst of preparing his story, he obtained a copy of the *Tribune* with its devastating article. After "glancing through," he reacted predictably. The fact that the real name of the *Tribune*'s reporter was Mortimer Thomson, spelled without a *p,* was quickly noted in order that readers of the *Daily Morning News* would know there are Thompsons and Thomsons. The latter was a "hiring libeler" who wrote "in a vein of native vulgarity and *flippant* insolence." His article in the *Tribune* was a "tissue of misrepresentation and falsehood": "While the article is well suited to impose on the willing credulity and excite the mawkish sentimentality of the abolition fanatics of the North, for whose edification it was written, it can induce in the minds of Southern readers only feelings of scorn and contempt."[34]

The *Savannah Republican* covered the sale with a brief story telling of large attendance from all portions of Georgia and from states adjoining. The average price the first day was $660, a figure the *Republican* thought lower than anticipated. On March 15, they told their readers of the visit of the *Tribune*'s star reporter. Doestick's comment on Georgia's "fast young men" with pantaloons tucked into their boots brought forth a quick reaction:

> Mortimer Thomson, alias Doesticks, a somewhat notorious individual, was hired as a spy by Horace Greeley of the New York *Tribune* to come to Savannah and report the details of the sale of Mr. Pierce Butler's negroes.
>
> We are sorry that our fast young men won't wear their pantaloons over their boots on a muddy day, and straighten up their caps, but when this pick of propriety comes here again as a spy he should let the fast young men know about it, and they will straighten everything except his coat tail; that task, Doesticks will perform himself.[35]

Mortimer Neal Thomson was one of the most capable and popular newsmen of his time. A favorite with editors, he was frequently quoted in papers throughout the land. His humorous work was in keeping with the popular style of the day—contrived and heavy-handed. His byline, "Q. K. Philander Doesticks, P. B.," or simply "Doesticks," somehow was enough to set a tone that delighted his readers. The humor aside, Thomson was a skilled reporter who wrote with "tense, vigorous, quick moving phrases and vivid slang." His police court sketches and feature articles, including the slave sale, helped to make the *Tribune* and Horace Greeley.[36]

It is somewhat surprising the *Tribune* sent Mortimer Thomson to Savannah to cover the Butler sale and not the case of the *Wanderer*, for the latter was an ongoing story of tremendous appeal. The Africans brought into Georgia created great excitement wherever they were seen, and the federal case against Charley Lamar and his crew received far more attention in the national press than the sale of Pierce Butler's slaves. Proslavery people in the South saw the Lamar's *Wanderer* venture as a prelude to the re-opening of the slave trade, a belief often expressed in Savannah at the time of the Doesticks visit. He noted in his article a prevailing opinion among Southerners that there should be a renewal of the importation of Africans and that in Savannah such a condition was "devoutly to be wished."

Although the reportorial style of the renowned "Doesticks" would have been ideal for a story on Charles Augustus Lafayette Lamar's *Wanderer*, and the Africans, he did very well on his Butler assignment. After his story appeared in a regular edition of the *Tribune*, the demand was such that there followed on March 11: "A Notice—In order to supply the demand for our report of the great sale of Pierce M. Butler's Slaves at auction near the city of Savannah, we shall print this morning at 10 o'clock, an extra edition of the Semi-Weekly *Tribune*, in which will be found the entire account. Price 6 cents."

Philadelphia's *Sunday Dispatch* recognized the local interest in the story and ran the entire *Tribune* article in their issue of March 13. The story was prefaced with Butler, Mease, and Kemble background, with considerable attention to Pierce Butler's role in the Dudley Tyng affair. The article remarked on the reasons for the sale:

Mr. Butler owned considerable property in Philadelphia as well as in Georgia, but a recent series of unfortunate stock speculations involved him in difficulties which resulted in enormous losses. To relieve himself from his financial reverses, a large portion of his property in and about Philadelphia has already been disposed of, and the sale reported below was effected for the same object.

The story was picked up, was condensed to four long columns, and on April 12, 1859, was run in the *Times* of London, where Pierce Butler was known as the divorced husband of the onetime London favorite, Fanny Kemble. There, too, the story was widely read, although it bespoke an attitude somewhat contrary to the editorial policy of the *Times*. That policy brought about Fanny Kemble's decision to publish her Georgia journal some four years later.

Had Doesticks been able to read the Kemble journal he would have gained a better understanding of the background of the Butler slaves he found at the Ten Broeck racecourse. As it so happened, his long *Tribune* article was republished in pamphlet form as *What Became of the Slaves on a Georgia Plantation?*, and was called a "sequel" to the Kemble *Journal*. This pamphlet appeared in 1863, when the *Journal* brought its own dramatic response to life at Butler's Island and Hampton.

The *Tribune* reporter used good judgment in appearing incognito in Savannah. Charley Lamar had publicly battered a jailer charged with custody of members of the *Wanderer* crew. It was an outrageous display of arrogance of the kind Mortimer Thomson would have encountered had he disclosed that he represented a newspaper known for its stand against slavery. Doesticks arrived in Savannah well before the sale and as he stated, "did not placard his mission." Instead, he pretended to be a potential buyer by becoming a part of the busy scene. Armed with a pencil and a catalog, he priced "likely nigger fellows" and talked to men and women who were to be sold. He mingled with buyers that he found to be "a rough breed, slangy, profane and bearish"—most of whom measured society by "revolvers and kindred delicacies." After the sale was in progress, and in order to protect his cover, the New York reporter made a few cautious bids where he felt confident he would be quickly topped.

The story in the *Tribune* told that Pierce and John Butler had inherited their father's estate worth more than a million dollars. They were, of course, grandsons. He was correct in stating the sale was to be of those slaves belonging to Pierce Butler, who was selling to cover huge debts brought on by losses in the "great crash of 1857–1858 and other exigencies of business." The story noted the sale was of great interest because Butler slaves were known to be a "choice lot," and also, the breaking up of an old estate was a matter of interest in itself. He was noticeably moved by the emotional impact on the blacks, yet had a distorted view of their lives on the "old plantation." It was in this aspect that Fanny Kemble's journal would have put him straight. His article showed his lack of understanding:

> None of the Butler slaves have ever been sold before, but have been on these two plantations since they were born. Here have they lived their humble lives, and loved their simple loves; here were they born, and here have many of them had children born unto them; here had their parents lived before them, and are now resting in quiet graves on the old plantations that these unhappy ones are to see no more forever; here they left not only the well-known scenes dear to them from very baby-hood by a thousand fond memories, and homes as much loved by them, perhaps, as brighter homes by men of brighter faces; but all the clinging ties that bound them to living hearts were torn asunder, for but one-half of each of these two happy little communities was sent to the shambles, to be scattered to the four winds, and the other half was left behind.

Sufficient emotion was packed into the racecourse stables without so false a picture of the life of a Butler slave. Had Mortimer Thomson seen Shadrach's body laid in a grave half filled with ground water, or seen Judy and Scylla strung up and lashed for birthing the plantation manager's children, or known the anguish of Jack Carter, Harry, and Worcester when their sons were lost and damned on a winter's day, he could have written without idealizing plantation life. He was wrong, too, in writing that other Butler slaves had not been sold before. Such was not the case.

When reporter Thomson remarked on the absence of "light mulattoes" with very few of the Pierce Butler slaves being "even a shade removed from the original Congo blackness," he cast light on the division process in which the many mulattoes known to have been on the plantations were purposely left behind as the property of the John Butler estate. He gave his reason, citing that pure-blooded Negroes were more readily marketable, they being "more docile and manageable" than those of mixed blood. He painted a colorful picture of the slaves:

> They were dressed in every possible variety of uncouth and fantastic garb, in every style and of every imaginable color; the texture of the garments was in all cases coarse, most of the men being clothed in the rough cloth that is made expressly for the slaves. The dresses assumed by the negro minstrels, when they give imitations of plantation character, are by no

means exaggerated; they are, instead, weak and unable to come up to the original. There was every variety of hats, with every imaginable slouch; and there was every cut and style of coat and pantaloons, made with every conceivable ingenuity of misfit, and tossed on with a general appearance of perfect looseness that is perfectly indescribable, except to say that a Southern negro always looks as if he could shake his clothes off without taking his hands out of his pockets. The women, true to the feminine instinct, had made, in almost every case, some attempt at finery. All wore gorgeous turbans, generally manufactured in an instant out of a gay-colored handkerchief by a sudden and graceful twist of the fingers; though there was occasionally a more elaborate turban, a turban complex and mysterious, got up with care, and ornamented with a few beads or bright bits of ribbon. Their dresses were mostly coarse stuff, though there were some gaudy calicos; a few had ear-rings, and one possessed the treasure of a string of yellow and blue beads. The little children were always better and more carefully dressed than the older ones, the parental pride coming out in the shape of a yellow cap pointed like a mitre, or a jacket with a strip of red broadcloth round the bottom. The children were of all sizes, the youngest being fifteen days old. The babies were generally good-natured; though when one would set up a yell, the complaint soon attacked the others, and a full chorus would be the result.

Equally colorful was the Doesticks depiction of the buyers who examined the slaves preparatory to making their bids:

> The negroes were examined with as little consideration as if they had been brutes indeed; the buyers pulling their mouths open to see their teeth, pinching their limbs to find how muscular they were, walking them up and down to detect any signs of lameness, making them stoop and bend in different ways that they might be certain there was no concealed rupture or wound; and in addition to all this treatment, asking them scores of questions relative to their qualifications and accomplishments. All these humiliations were submitted to without a murmur, and in some instances with good-natured cheerfulness—where the slave liked the appearance of the proposed buyer, and fancied that he might prove a kind "Mas'r."

The reporter's "fast young man" was said to carry a convenient knife in addition to his accessible revolver. He wore "his velvet cap jauntily dragged over to one side, his cheek full of tobacco, which he bites from a huge plug." In contrast were the silver-haired old men with their white neck cloths and gold spectacles who resembled sanctimonious church deacons from the North. These worthies were interested only in the women who were tormented with indecent questions, an ordeal withstood in "perfect decorum and self respect."

Mortimer Thomson had a few words for Joseph Bryan and his auctioneer:

> Mr. Bryan, the Negro Broker, is a dapper little man, wearing spectacles and a yachting hat, sharp and sudden in his movements, and perhaps the least bit in the world obtrusively officious—as earnest in his language as he could be without actual swearing, though acting much as if he would like to swear a little at the critical moment; Mr. Bryan did not sell the goods, he merely superintended the operation, and saw that the entry clerks did their duty properly. The auctioneer proper was a Mr. Walsh, who deserves a word of description. In personal appearance he is the very opposite of Mr. Bryan, being careless in his dress instead of scrupulous, a large man instead of a little one, a fat man instead of a lean one, and a good good-natured man instead of a fierce one. He is a rollicking old boy, with an eye ever on the look-out, and that never lets a bidding nod escape him; a hearty word for every bidder who cares for it, and plenty of jokes to let off when the business gets a little slack. Mr. Walsh has a florid complexion, not more so, perhaps, than is becoming, and possibly not more so than is natural in a whiskey country. Not only is his face red, but his skin has been taken off in spots by blisters of some sort, giving him a peely look; so that, taking his face all in all, the peeliness and the redness combined, he looks much as if he had been boiled in the same pot with a red cabbage.

In the opinion of the *Tribune* reporter, that slaves were sold in families was as much policy as kindness, for it made possible the sale of the "aged and unserviceable" who otherwise would have been difficult to sell.

The long article in the *Tribune* contained a reprint of two pages from Joseph Bryan's catalog, being Negroes Nos. 1–4, Nos. 99–122, and Nos. 341–69. The first four were George, Sue, and their two boys. They were sold for $620 each, or $2,480 for the family. Considered a "family" were Negroes 116–17. No. 116 was Rina, 18, a prime young woman experienced in rice culture; her family was Lena, No. 117, one year old. The price paid for these two was $645 each. Likewise, Dorcas, 17, No. 345, a prime cotton worker, and her son Joe, 3, No. 346, brought $1,200 each. As young children were worth about $200 on the auction block, Rina's true worth to her buyer was close to $1,000, and Dorcas to hers, $2,200. Dorcas was an exceptional young woman. From the catalog:

Catalog number	Name	Age	Remarks
1	George	27	Prime Cotton Planter
2	Sue	26	Prime Rice Planter
3	George	6	Boy Child
4	Harry	2	Boy Child

Sold for $510 each.

99	Kate's John	30	Rice, Prime Man
100	Betsey	29	Rice, Unsound
101	Kate	6	
102	Violet	3 months	

Sold for $510 each.

103	Wooster	45	Rice Hand, and Fair Mason
104	Mary	40	Cotton Hand

Sold for $300 each.

105	Commodore Bob		Rice Hand
106	Kate		Cotton
107	Linda	19	Cotton, Prime Young Woman
108	Joe	13	Rice, Prime Boy

Sold for $600 each.

109	Bob	30	Rice
110	Mary	25	Rice, Prime Woman

Sold for $1,135 each.

111	Anson	49	Rice—Ruptured, one eye
112	Violet	55	Rice Hand

Sold for $250 each.

113	Allen Jeffrey	46	Rice Hand and Sawyer in Steam Mill
114	Sikey	43	Rice Hand
115	Watty	5	Infirm Legs

Sold for $520 each.

116	Rina	18	Rice, Prime Young Woman
117	Lena	1	

Sold for $645 each.

118	Pompey	31	Rice—Lame in One Foot
119	Kitty	30	Rice, Prime Woman
120	Pompey, Jr.	10	Prime Boy

Catalog number	Name	Age	Remarks
121	John	7	
122	Noble	1	Boy

Sold for $580 each.

341	Goin	39	Rice Hand
342	Cassander	35	Cotton Hand—Has Fits
343	Emiline	19	Cotton, Prime Young Woman
344	Judy	11	Cotton, Prime Girl

Sold for $400 each.

345	Dorcas	17	Cotton, Prime Woman
346	Joe	3 months	

Sold for $1,200 each.

347	Tom	22	Cotton Hand

Sold for $1,260.

348	Judge Will	55	Rice Hand

Sold for $325.

349	Lowden	54	Cotton Hand
350	Hagar	50	Cotton Hand
351	Lowden	15	Cotton, Prime Boy
352	Silas	13	Cotton, Prime Boy
353	Lettia	11	Cotton, Prime Girl

Sold for $300 each.

354	Fielding	21	Cotton, Prime Young Man
355	Abel	19	Cotton, Prime Young Man

Sold for $1,295 each.

356	Smith's Bill	Aged	Sore Leg
357	Leah	46	Cotton Hand
358	Sally	9	

Withdrawn.

359	Adam	24	Rice, Prime Man
360	Charlotte	22	Rice, Prime Woman
361	Lesh	1	

Sold for $750 each.

362	Maria	47	Rice Hand
363	Luna	22	Rice, Prime Woman
364	Clementina	17	Rice, Prime Young Woman

Sold for $950 each.

continued

Catalog number	Name	Age	Remarks
365	Tom	48	Rice Hand
366	Harriet	41	Rice Hand
367	Wanney	19	Rice Hand, Prime Young Man
368	Deborah	6	
369	Infant	3 months	

Sold for $700 each.

Primus, a plantation carpenter, was sold with his wife Daphne and two children. Dido, the older child, was three years old, and the other was a new baby born on St. Valentine's Day. When presented to the buyers, Daphne covered herself and the new baby with a large shawl as protection against the cold rain. The buyers objected, called for the auctioneer to "pull off her rags" and asked, "Who's going to bid on that nigger if you keep her covered up?" The Primus family sold for $2,500.

Jeffrey, No. 319, was unencumbered, twenty-three years old, and was sold for $1,310. He pleaded with his new owner to purchase Dorcas, No. 278, a young woman he had planned to wed until their plans were upset by the sale. Much to his pleasure, the new owner was willing until he found that Dorcas was being sold with a family of four and could not be purchased independently. Jeffrey and Dorcas went their separate ways. No. 322, Dembo, and No. 404, Frances, were able to solve a similar problem by finding a minister among those attending the sale. Married, they became a family and were sold as such, but suffered "coarse jokes" from the auctioneer and ribald remarks from the surrounding crowd. The two made a sizable contribution to the settlement of Pierce Butler's debts for they brought $1,320 each from an Alabama cotton planter.

Pierce Butler was present at the Ten Broeck racecourse for both days of the sale. Mortimer Thomson wrote that the sale was necessary because a "gentleman" could not live on a "beggarly pittance of half a million." When the hard-pressed owner appeared among his people, he spoke to all and was recognized with "seeming pleasure":

> The men obsequiously pulled off their hats and made that indescribable sliding hitch with the foot which passes with a negro for a bow; and the women each dropped the quick curtsy, which they seldom vouchsafe to any other than their legitimate master and mistress. Occasionally, to a very old or favorite servant, Mr. Butler would extend his gloved hand, which mark

of condescension was instantly hailed with grins of delight from all the sable witnesses.

When, at last, the sale had ended, Joseph Bryan rewarded the white folk who had attended with several baskets of champagne. For those who were sold there was also a reward, from "Pierce M. Butler, of the free city of Philadelphia":

> who was solacing the wounded hearts of the people he had sold from their firesides and their homes, by doling out to them small change at the rate of a dollar a head. To every negro he had sold, who presented his claim for the paltry pittance, he gave the munificent stipend of one whole dollar, in specie; he being provided with two canvas bags of 25 cent pieces, fresh from the mint, to give an additional glitter to his generosity.

So ended a bitter chapter. It was an interval in their lives the blacks were to call "the weeping time." At the racecourse the rain stopped for the first time in four days and a "soft sunlight fell on the scene." The article in the *Tribune* ended with the trains and the steamboats leaving "that cruel city" with their burden of unhappy and apprehensive people: "But the stars shone out as brightly as if such things had never been, the blushing fruit-trees poured their fragrance on the evening air, and the scene was as calmly sweet and quiet as if Man had never marred the glorious beauties of Earth by deed of cruelty and wrong."[37] In Philadelphia, the *Argus* reported:

> "Doesticks" has examined into the wonders of Niagara, has experimented on the intoxicating qualities of beer, has tried the virtues of fortune telling and free love, and tired of all these pleasures, he has attended a slave sale in Savannah to report the particulars for the New York *Tribune*. If "Doesticks" suffers himself to get mixed up in the "nigger business" many persons will be convinced that he and "Damphool" are one and the same individual.[38]

The events in Savannah provided the Reverend George B. Cheever of New York's Church of the Puritans a text for sermons on successive Sundays. He preached against Pierce Butler one Sunday, and Charley Lamar the next. Pierce Butler was a prominent member of a Northern church, proclaimed Dr. Cheever, who when rebuked by the abolitionists, "that sainted young man, Dudley Tyng," led the outcry against him. Butler, he said, was "sick of the agitation, not of the sin." The next week it was Lamar, like Butler, an Episcopalian, who after the public sale of the *Wanderer* and the knocking down of the jailer, attended church in Savannah and heard a sermon preached by the eminent bishop of the diocese. Dr. Cheever asked a pointed question. If the New York Yacht Club felt disposed to expel the captain of the *Wanderer*, could not the Episcopal Church muster sufficient energy to discipline Mr. Butler and Mr. Lamar?[39]

As Fanny Kemble was staying in Philadelphia at the time of the sale, there is no doubt she was well aware of what to her was a tragic event. No one, the slaves excepted, realized the import as did she. Years later she responded to a friend's inquiry, writing that Pierce Butler had not "taken abolition by the forelock" to alleviate trouble with the federal government for his Southern proclivities, or in anticipation of their liberation. She said the sale of his slaves had "caused him extreme pain and mortification," conditions not evident on those days of rain at Savannah's Ten Broeck racecourse. In a letter to J. Francis Fisher, she called off any attempts to "settle" with Pierce Butler on the matter of his past due payments agreed to in the divorce settlement. She believed his financial situation was so improved that it "promises a comfortable maintenance hence forward to his daughters." She preferred not to talk of this unfortunate matter, dismissing the subject with "I knew he had met with domestic calamity."[40]

Chapter 19

The Dogs
of Civil War

FOLLOWING THE SALE of his slaves, Pierce Butler, if stronger
financially, was not so physically. He made a trip to "Southern Europe" hoping to recover good health, and on return to Philadelphia
joined a contemporary fitness club. Hlasko's Institute for Physical Education offered its members a "swimming bath," instructions in gymnastics,
and dancing. He continued his interest in music and maintained his sharp
eye for attractive young women, one of whom found this much older man
"very gentle and dignified." She knew he had "a reputation for fascination
and charm, and even *danger*," and described him as "a strange looking
man, rather short and thick set, extraordinarily pale, of an ivory tint, very
carefully though fancifully dressed, not at all handsome; but his manners
were suave and courteous, to a degree 'old school.' His voice was music
and his conversation rich and delightful." She held him in "profound respect" and added that he gave the impression of "a constant sadness. I
never saw inside his heart and I don't know whether it was temperamental
or an adopted manner, or whether the tragedy of his life left an efface-
able gloom, but I think of him as a 'bruised soul.' "[1]

Pierce Butler's financial statement revealed a comfortable net worth of
$398,534. Although massive debts had been repaid with the proceeds of
the sale of his slaves, he still owed approximately $127,000 including
$59,925 to the estate of his brother, John Butler. Among his assets were a
large loan of $87,000 of dubious merit to C. H. Fisher, and his interest in
the Georgia plantations carried at $114,067.[2]

As 1859 moved into the fateful 1860s, Pierce Butler visited the plantations preparatory to a subsequent stay there with his daughter Frances,

whom he called Fanny. The change was quickly evident. The once-thriving Hampton was all but abandoned, the total work force was reduced by
one-half, and those who remained were the property of the John Butler
estate. While in Georgia he stayed in the house at Butler's Island where he
had been with his family twenty years before. On his visit to the desolate
Hampton he traversed the length of the island to call at Retreat, the old
William Page plantation then owned by the daughter and son-in-law of
Mr. Page, the Thomas Butler Kings. There, at the time, were Mr. Page's
grandchildren, Georgia King and Henry Lord King, both good friends of
the Butler daughters. Georgia King wrote to her "own precious Father,"
Thomas Butler King, and gave a rather touching picture of Pierce Butler,
sans slaves:

> He, Mr. Butler, was out on his plantation for a few days & came over to
> Hampton Friday morning. He was kindly anxious to call to see us, and tho
> he could only find an old marsh tacky to ride, he came all the way down
> Friday evening remaining until twelve Saturday. Lordy insisted on sending
> him back in the buggy—of course. He leaves for the North tomorrow, but
> will return during the middle of January bringing Fanny with him. He
> promised to bring her to pay a visit. Mr. Butler made himself very pleas-
> ant—and he must have felt we were really glad to see him—I heard from
> Sarah by the last mail. She is very comfortably fixed in Germantown in her
> own home.[3]

Fanny Kemble faced the advent of the 1860s with great concern for the
future of America. She saw the division between North and South ever
widening, with "folly and wickedness" on both sides. She believed "a
grievous civil war" might mean the salvation of the country, and in Philadelphia and New York had seen the actual and frenzied preparation for
such a happening. In both places she gave swords and pistols to young
volunteers, soldiers she had remembered as "boys in round jackets." In
her own Lenox the patriotic spirit was muted—a faint "tap of a drum"
and the flag flying from scattered farmhouses.[4]

The persistent Philadelphia diarist, who took note of such things, recorded an important event in the Butler family:

> Dr. Wister had a son born to him yesterday morning at 5 o'clock. No one
> was in the house at the time but himself and a servant girl. All that had to
> be done was therefore done by him. Moreover, no clothing had been pro-

vided for the baby. This is a state of things inconcievable to me. There is an old saying that blacksmiths' horses and shoemakers' wives are worse shod than those of other people, but how it was that neither Sarah herself nor his mother nor any of her female friends should have the forethought to make preparation for such an event, I cannot understand. They say that Sarah was fractious and odd & would do nothing. Mother & child are, however, well.[5]

The child was the first Butler-Kemble grandchild, named Owen Wister, but called Dan to prevent being confused with his father. Grandmother Fanny Kemble was soon on hand at the Wisters'. Sidney George Fisher blew hot and cold on the former Mrs. Butler, but found her this time "a woman of genius & noble impulses & feelings." He said she was more quiet than usual and was not only cordial, but easy and pleasant. He gave Sarah Wister a good report, saying she shared her mother's character and talent. He thought the young mother looked well, but a bit pale and thin following the experience on July 14.[6]

Sarah Wister tried her own hand at keeping a diary. It was spasmodic, kept haphazardly, but for a few months in 1861 was an interesting record of a troubled time. What has come to be called her "Civil War Journal" began April 15 and ended September 8, 1861. In one entry she turned tables on the "real" diarist: "Sidney George blew & puffed himself up & was as consequential & inconsequent as usual. They think him a great man but she is the man of the two, with her head & brow, & sweet satiric smile." "She" was his wife, Elizabeth Ingersoll Fisher.[7]

In December, as South Carolina seceded from the Union, the already divided Butler family was further partitioned by different strong beliefs. Very much pro-Union were Fanny Kemble, Sarah, and Dr. Wister. Despite her Southern background, the comely widow Gabriella Butler was firmly with the North. Pierce Butler, in Philadelphia at the time, left no doubt as to his feelings, or to those of his daughter Frances. The Fisher diary revealed: "Butler is eager for secession & has just returned from Georgia, where he says there is no difference of opinion. He said he came here only to *buy arms* and intends to return immediately and join the army. He will take his daughter Fanny with him and has bought a rifle for *her,* too, for he says even the women in the South are going to fight."[8]

Although Frances Butler supported her father in his strong pro-Southern feelings, she was more aware than he of the import of current events on the national scene. Her reluctance to face the dangers of the trip to Georgia brought forth a letter from her father:

> If there was any such apprehension of danger in going to Georgia, I would not take you there. I am very sorry that you have a feeling of aversion and fear about going, but you may rely upon it that it will all vanish as soon as we reach Savannah, and you receive the warm welcome of the friends you made there. I do not believe there will be civil war, or any fighting at all. If there should be it is not probable that I would be called upon or expected to take up arms, unless the danger should happen to be near our property, which is not likely. I feel compelled to go; my sympathies are entirely with the South; all the trouble has been caused by the bad faith and bad conduct of the people of the North, who have violated their duty to the Union and the Constitution. I must be in Savannah to attend the argument before the Supreme Court, and if that decision should be in my favour it will be necessary for me to go to the Plantations at once. If anything should oblige me to leave the Plantation, I would not think of leaving you there alone. My dearest Fanny, your love, devotion and loyalty are not lost on me, and you may be sure I would not take them unnecessarily. Therefore, if I cannot comply with your wishes to postpone our going to Georgia, it is because there is a necessity for my presence there which I must not neglect, and likewise because I am certain you will not regret having accompanied me.[9]

He signed the letter "Your affectionate Father." His statement that the Constitution was being violated would have brought cheers from his grandfather, for Major Butler would have been one with his grandson that the North was at fault. The statement that he must be in Savannah to attend the argument before the Supreme Court had to do with the estate of John Butler. By agreement with the executors, Gabriella Butler had qualified as administrator of her husband's estate in Georgia and, despite the 1850 order from the Superior Court of McIntosh County and a similar order from the court in Chatham County, continued in her refusal to turn over the Georgia properties to Pierce Butler and Thomas C. James, the executors and trustees, who wished to sell the John Butler interest as directed by his will. Gabriella Butler well knew the sale the two men had in mind was from themselves as trustees to Pierce Butler individually.[10]

Frances Butler was convinced by her father's reasoning and did go to Georgia. Her sister Sarah Wister embarked on an opposite course. She mastered the sewing machine to make garments for Union soldiers but preferred doing secretarial work. An entry in her wartime journal reminded her that as a child of "six or seven" she had cried secretly after being taunted by English children for the family's dependence on slaves. And she wrote: "What fools these Southerners are to talk of courage when there's not one in hundreds has one grain of moral courage or even understands the term."[11]

Before departing for Georgia, Pierce Butler shipped nineteen cases of personal belongings. He wrote his namesake and godson Pierce Butler Holmes of Darien to be alert to their arrival, asking that he give particular attention to two quarter barrels of lager beer and to several cases containing demijohns of wine. When father and daughter left for the South, it was not before he had resigned from the nonactive roll of the Philadelphia City Troop. His resignation came at a time when Philadelphians were enthusiastically joining, not leaving, the city's military organizations. The Butlers were accompanied to Charleston by Mrs. J. Francis Fisher, her two children, Sophy and George Harrison Fisher. Mrs. Fisher was born Elizabeth Middleton, a cousin to the Butlers, but had remained a true and loyal friend of Fanny Kemble throughout the acrimonious fight with Pierce Butler. Her pro-Southern bent gave sufficient reason for her to swallow her pride and to accept his care and protection on the trip to South Carolina.[12]

The father and daughter paused briefly in Charleston, only long enough for Pierce Butler to demonstrate his open advocacy of the Confederates. In a letter dated April 11, 1861, Sarah Wister was told of his tour of Charleston's harbor fortifications with a group of Southern military men led by General P. G. T. Beauregard, the commander of South Carolina's military forces. The day after the harbor tour General Beauregard touched the match to the powder keg and orderd his forces to attack Fort Sumter. The war began.[13]

The two Butlers hurried to Savannah and then to Butler's Island, where his presence was needed. He hoped to bring order to a situation already changed by the sale of his slaves, but more so by the impact of the fearful times. The difficulty with Gabriella Butler was on his mind and was noted by Sarah Wister in her journal after hearing from her sister in Georgia. To them "Aunt Ella" was a "goose" and a "dangerous bird."[14]

The great threat to the Butler empire was the war. Whatever his sentiments, Pierce Butler knew the plantations would become unmanageable in a nation torn by conflict. He reflected his fear and apprehension in sad and "unspeakably desolate letters" to Sarah and Dr. Wister. Sarah wrote in her journal, "Poor Father, poor, poor Father." On hearing the William

Page grandchildren, Lordy King and his brother Floyd, had joined the Confederate army, Sarah Wister again turned to her journal: "I expect to hear next that my Father has joined it." A few days later, expecting Butler Place might be confiscated because of Pierce Butler's Southern proclivities, she paid a sentimental visit to gather wild violets while the tenants were away—"for who knows whether even now Father is not in the Southern army?" In Philadelphia she attended church services to pray, not for her father, but for those who were fighting the Confederates. Her journal reflected her feelings toward the South and the English who supported them: "I wish any church-going could take some of the hatred out of my heart, but I cannot wish the war to stop. I cannot but hope that some lives may be lost in battle & some on the gallows, & I cannot speak or even think of the English without almost going into spasms."[15]

Fanny Kemble felt no anguish or surprise that Pierce Butler supported the Southern cause. She did share her daughter Sarah's distress over Frances Butler's beliefs, and she long suffered the loyalty of Frances to her father and her acceptance of his endorsement and dependence on slavery. Despite their differences, Sarah Wister retained a strong family love for her sister and her father, and they for her. It was a bond that caused certain tension between Sarah and her mother. When her journal reported her fear that her father would become a Confederate soldier, her mother was visiting the Wisters and the time had come for her departure. Sarah noted that Dr. Wister "in a moment of insanity begged Mother to prolong her visit." Sarah's silence terminated the matter: "I drove down to the Kensington depot with Mother to see her off at 11-1/2. There was a row with the maid, an alarm about the luggage, a wrench at parting, & at last she was gone. I wish I could say: Peace go with her, but that it never will."[16]

In August, Pierce Butler was confronted with real trouble. He and Frances had returned from Georgia, he angry and apprehensive over the turn of events between the North and the South. He became agitated after a visit from his niece Elizabeth, her in-law Ward McAllister, and her attorney, William B. Reed. He explained his predicament in a letter to Charles Henry Fisher, one of the three men who had been chosen to manage his chaotic affairs. Pierce Butler was unaware of an order issued by the secretary of war two days before. It was an order that boded even greater trouble than that brought by the McAllisters. His letter to Henry Fisher stated:

Yesterday Cadwalader and I went over the statement of my affairs that was prepared by Mr. Hollis last December. The unpaid debts amount to one hundred and fifty-five thousand dollars. Of that, the one which presses on me is the balance of the mortgage to my brother's estate of forty thousand dollars. The non-payment of this debt will entail serious consequences. Mr. Wm. B. Reed has given me notice that he intends to apply to have the trustees dismissed on the grounds of mismanagement of the estate, and he relies chiefly on the impropriety of the loan by one trustee to another trustee without the sanction of the court, and on the present insecurity of the loan. The mortification of a dismissal as trustee would not end the difficulty; the debt would still be due, and with new trustees my estate in Georgia would be liable to execution under an immediate foreclosure of the mortgage.

Nor would this be all: the suit now pending in Georgia would undoubtedly go against me, after my dismissal here as trustee, and from the fact of my being a debtor to the estate. These consequences would be avoided by paying off the mortgage at once, for I do not see that apart from this loan they have much to build upon.

I have of course always relied on the money in your hands to pay this as well as other debts, and I have no other source to look to. I am sorry to be obligated to agitate this matter at this time, but I am placed in such a painful dilemma that I cannot avoid it. Will you therefore be so good as to write me a few lines I can show Cadwalader, to say how far I can depend on the money in your hands to pay off the mortgage.

Mr. Ward McAllister and my niece Elizabeth McAllister came in from Newport the day before yesterday to see Mr. Reed and myself, and the result of the meeting was the determination on their part to proceed at once before the auditor with the accounts, and to ask for our dismissal.

Cadwalader was George Cadwalader, Pierce Butler's brother-in-law, who with Thomas James and Henry Fisher were the managers of his financial affairs. Thomas James was also co-trustee with Pierce Butler of the John Butler estate. In the strange will left by John Butler following his death in 1847, the two trustees were named with an expression of faith in their honesty. Yet, that he felt impelled to include such an expression may have indicated a prevalent doubt. He said in his will: "I have entire Confidence in their Judgement and Integrity and I am assured that the Principal sums of Money which may thus pass through their hands will never be broken in upon."[17]

Elizabeth McAllister had produced two other children following the birth of her son Francis. Both were daughters—Gabriella and Margaret Elizabeth. Her husband, Colonel Julian McAllister, was busy preparing to wage war on the southland whence he came. Elizabeth was supported by his eccentric brother, Ward McAllister, an erstwhile attorney and the noted social arbiter of New York and Newport, where he was known as "Wardy." Elizabeth's arrival had also been noted in Sarah Wister's journal. She recorded a visit in striking contrast to Lizzie's call on her father: "She has lost the mountain of flesh with which she had been disfigured for the last ten years, her figure is slight & girlish, her face small & blooming altogether at thirty-one & the mother of five children. She looked as young as she did when she married at eighteen. She paid me a long & pleasant visit."[18]

The order from the secretary of war was prompted by Pierce Butler's outspoken criticism of the federal government and his open support of the Southern cause:

> WAR DEPARTMENT, Washington, August 15, 1861, Hon. William Millward, U. S. Marshal, Philadelphia.
> Arrest Pierce Butler, of Philadelphia, make careful examination for a commission from the Southern Confederacy. Send him at once under guard to Fort Hamilton.
>
> Simon Cameron
> Secretary of War[19]

The reaction in Philadelphia was as might have been expected. His support of the South was widely known and it was believed that he had gone to South Carolina and Georgia on the April trip "taking with him a number of secession cockades, pistols, etc., and it was claimed he had returned to the city for the purpose of aiding the Confederates."[20] Sidney George Fisher expressed the feelings of the Butler-Kemble friends and acquaintances:

> The only news of interest this morning was that yesterday Pierce Butler was arrested on a charge of treason and sent off to Fort Hamilton at New York. It is said that he had been in correspondence with the secessionists in the South, which I do not believe, unless about private business. He has expressed, however, since his return the strongest opinions in favor of the Southern cause and wishes for its success in earnest language, as he did here the other day, and in such times as these that alone is sufficient to

justify his arrest. I am sorry for him and for his daughters & sisters, and yet I think it was right to commit him. Perhaps, also it is a good thing for him, as it will keep him quiet and out of harm's way. I suppose he will be comfortable at the Fort and he will meet there a number of gentlemen from Baltimore, prisoners like himself & congenial companions.[21]

The action was also noted in Sarah Wister's journal. She had been pondering the likelihood of a Southern victory and was asking herself where in the world the Wisters, as "miserable exiles," would go, when: "Just at 10 o'clock the door bell rang & to my unutterable amazement my cousin Alfred (Elwyn) came in, came to tell me that at 4 in the afternoon Father had been arrested by the U. S. Marshall on a special order from Cameron, & taken to New York by the 6 o'clock line to be placed in Fort Hamilton."[22] She lost no time in telegraphing her sister, who was visiting their mother in Lenox. A plan to meet in New York and together to see their father at Fort Lafayette, where he was actually imprisoned, was put aside as impractical. In its stead Sarah Wister enlisted the aid of her uncle George Cadwalader and Charles Henry Fisher. Henry Fisher's letter to Secretary Cameron stretched a point in stating the prisoner's two daughters "are both strong Northern women." Sarah took it upon herself to write President Lincoln.[23]

Fanny Kemble's reaction to the event was one of mild surprise tinged with a bit of silent satisfaction. She wrote a friend after Frances Butler, who had been joined by her sister, departed for New York in the futile effort to visit their father:

> The charge against him is that he acted as an agent for the Southerners in a visit he paid this spring, having received large sums of money for the purchase and transmission of arms. Knowing Mr. B——s Southern sympathies, I think the charge very likely to be true; whether it can be proved or not is quite another question, and I think it probable, that, if it is not proved Mr. B—— will still be detained till the conclusion of the war, as he is not likely to accept any oath of allegiance tendered to him by the Government, being a determined democrat and inimical, both on public and private grounds, to Mr. Lincoln and his ministers.[24]

Pierce Butler's reaction to his own arrest was quiet, calm, self-control, except for turning "white & with slightly quivering lips & nostrils," a typical response when he was angered. That condition was constant, for

three days later Sarah Wister received a letter from her father—"as cold
& bitter a composition as I ever read."

> He speaks of his arrest, of his journey to New York & removal to Ft.
> Lafayette for it is there & not at Ft. Hamilton that he is incarcerated, I
> find; & incarcerated it is; they are six in a casemate, double locked, only
> allowed exercise at stated times, from 7 to 9 A.M. in the quadrangle of the
> fort. The whole letter is in a tone of biting sarcasm though like all the
> communications it passed under the eye of the commandant. He says that
> visits are not allowed & therefore, that neither I nor any of his friends need
> attempt to see him.[25]

Despite a troublesome feeling shared with Henry Fisher, Uncle George
Cadwalader, and Mrs. Jones, the housekeeper who witnessed the arrest,
Sarah Wister was relieved to know the federal government found nothing
incriminating among her father's papers. He was set free on an order
dated September 21 from the Department of State. Henry Fisher had gone
to Washington and brought about the release much to the satisfaction of
Sarah Wister, Frances Butler, and of the prisoner. Henry Fisher's brother
reacted otherwise:

> I think he was wrong to make the application & the government to grant
> it. It is true that no overt acts of treason were committed by Butler, nor was
> he committed for punishment or trial, but as a precaution & because his
> general conversation was seditious & tended to strengthen the influence of
> the rebellion in this part of the country. He refused to take the oath of
> allegiance and is morally as much a traitor as any man in the Confederate
> army. His arrest had a very good effect here and his release will have a bad
> effect. It will be ascribed to the influence of his position and of rich friends.
> I hope when he gets out he will either go to Georgia and stay there or go to
> Europe and am sorry that Henry has connected himself with the affair at
> all.[26]

Precedent to his release, Pierce Butler signed a statement that he would
"do no act hostile to the United States" and that he would not visit South
Carolina without a passport from the secretary of state. He would have
had greater reason to visit Georgia, but as it turned out, chose not to go to
either state until the war ended. His anger persisted for some time following the release, so much so that he sued Simon Cameron for "trespass, *vi
et armis,* assault and battery, and false imprisonment." Cameron, by that

time no longer secretary of war, and a very unpopular man, was arrested in order to answer the charges against him. The Department of State, the attorney general, and President Lincoln himself mustered sufficient support to quash the case. Pierce Butler somehow managed to hold his tongue and curb his anger so that he had no further trouble with the "Government of the U.S." He remained close to Philadelphia, holding fast to his desire for a Southern victory while his plantation world disintegrated.[27]

He might well have heeded the words of his grandfather, who, while reflecting on the havoc wrought on his properties in the Revolution, had said: "When once the Dogs of Civil War are let loose it is no easy matter to get them back."[28]

Chapter 20

Yankee Vandals in the Low Country

Following the attack on Fort Sumter, the federal government moved quickly to stifle the water-borne commerce of the South by blockading ports and by patrolling the long coastline. In mid-1861 the Atlantic Blockading Squadron was divided into two sections, the South Atlantic Squadron being charged with South Carolina, Georgia, and the east coast of Florida. In early October seven U.S. naval vessels were assigned to cover the coastline from Georgetown, South Carolina, to Fernandina, Florida. Among these was the frigate *St. Lawrence,* the first of many ships to be stationed off St. Simons Island. The appearance of the heavily armed warship struck fear into the hearts of the owners and managers of the coastal plantations.[1]

To maintain an operation as far-flung as that charged to the South Atlantic section, strategic land bases were necessary. Accordingly, on October 29, 1861, a large land-sea expedition sailed from Hampton Roads, Virginia, for Port Royal Sound, just north of Hilton Head Island in South Carolina. It was a move that came as no great surprise to the South Carolinians. That such a move had been expected was evident in a letter written from the field near Manassas on September 7, 1861. Captain Hamilton Couper sent word to his sister Maggie that trouble was on the way:

> The good people at Beaufort, S.C. will I think have the next sight of "the Hessians," "the Vandals," "the Wretches" to use the elegant language of the Virginians. Then we may look for them on St. Simons & at Brunswick so I

have written to Father, advising the removal of the Hamilton negroes on the 1st Nov. You see now why I did not wish your husband to leave Savannah.[2]

The Union naval forces were commanded by the newly appointed flag officer, Captain Samuel Francis DuPont, and the land forces by Brigadier General Thomas W. Sherman. On November 7, in a classic naval maneuver, Captain DuPont's ships reduced Forts Walker on Hilton Head and Beauregard across the sound on Bay Point. Hilton Head plantations, including the Mary Bull lands sold to provide much of Mary Butler's inheritance, were quickly occupied by Union forces, and the island became an important base throughout the war for military operations on the South Atlantic coast. One of the first was a move up the Port Royal River to Beaufort, where they found the town abandoned by its white population and being plundered by Negroes who were in "a lawless condition."[3]

General Isaac Ingalls Stevens, who commanded Union forces in Beaufort, wrote that when news of DuPont's victory at Port Royal reached that town the white residents fled in terror. They also deserted their plantations, leaving more than ten thousand of their slaves, who:

> flocked into Beaufort on the hegira of the whites, and held high carnival in the deserted mansions, smashing doors, mirrors and furniture, and appropriating all that took their fancy.

> After this sack, they remained at home upon the plantations and revelled in unwonted idleness and luxury, feasting upon the corn, cattle and turkeys of their fugitive masters.[4]

A young Union officer stationed on Hilton Head found the island sandy, but beautiful, with oranges in "ripe profusion," cotton and corn unpicked in the island's broad fields. He wrote:

> Here lived the Pinckneys, the Draytons and other high blooded Hidalgos, whose effervescing exuberance of gentlemanly spirit have done so much to cause our present troubles. Alas! Yankee hordes, ruthless invaders—the vile Hessians—infest their splendid plantations.

> Negroes crowd in swarms to our lines, happy in the thought of freedom, dancing, singing, void of care, and vainly dreaming that all toil is in future to be spared, and that henceforth they are to lead that life of lazy idleness which forms the Nigger's Paradise. I fear that before long they have passed only from the hands of one taskmaster into the hands of another.[5]

Captain DuPont, "that stately and courtly potentate, elegant as one's ideal French marquis," gave his reasons for the flight of Beaufort's white people. He reported to Gideon Welles, secretary of the navy:

> The people left their property in such a state as to show their precipitate flight was either the result of real terror or of a design to make it appear such.
>
> They have so long asserted that we carry on the war without regard to the common humanities and courtesies of modern hostilities that some persons have probably become the dupes of their own misrepresentations, some are actually deceived, while those who take the lead in promoting these opinions are driven to the necessity of acting as if they were true.
>
> A fear of slaves is no doubt one of the chief troubles and lies much deeper than even any apprehension of ourselves.
>
> The deserted city and neighboring plantations exhibit a most melancholy example of weakness and dereliction from duty, the only excuse for which must be the well founded dread of a servile insurrection.[6]

The "neighboring plantations" of Captain DuPont's report included the lands planted by Major Butler before the concentration of his efforts at Hampton and Butler's Island. The Euhaw plantations, and Coosaw Island, the old Bull-Middleton homeplace, were abandoned, and Coosaw became a haven for hundreds of slaves who gained there an initial experience at fending for themselves.[7]

Captain DuPont and his officers were confused by the abandonment of Beaufort, and more so by the problem of what to do about the blacks who had been set adrift by the consequences of the federal occupation. A naval officer was assigned the task of bringing order: "You will employ your force in suppressing any excesses on the part of the negroes, and you will take pains to assure the white inhabitants that there is no intention to disturb them in the exercise of their private rights or in the enjoyment of their private property."[8] An enigmatic notice was posted at a prominent place in the town: "Every effort has been made by us to prevent the negroes from plundering their master's houses. Had the owners remained and taken care of their property and negroes, it would not have occurred. I only trust that we will not be accused of vandalism." The notice was signed "an American Navy Officer," and evidently, one who did not subscribe to the common belief that Union forces intended to free the slaves.[9]

U.S.S. St. Lawrence, *on station in 1861 off the southern end of St. Simons Island.*

As Roswell King had stated during the War of 1812, the slaves appeared "to have a wish to try their New Master." They did so in 1861 in ever increasing numbers. On a determined but uncertain course between bondage and freedom they turned to the Union forces for direction and help. The official reception, based on orders given the leaders of the Port Royal expedition, was somewhat different. Captain DuPont was told that when faced with the problem of "persons of color commonly known as *contraband*," they should not be turned away or maintained unemployed, but when their services could be made useful they be enlisted in the naval service. Secretary Welles directed Captain DuPont: "They will be allowed, however, no higher rating than boys, at a compensation of $10 per month, and one ration a day." Secretary of War Simon Cameron instructed General Sherman to receive the refugees, but there was to be no "general arming" of the men, and even this flew in the face of federal policy of 1861 that saw the war as preserving the Union and not as an effort to free the slaves. Whatever the official reception, the blacks gained a sense of freedom in a Union army camp or on a Union ship. They spread the word about the low country and descended on their reluctant new masters in droves.[10]

The onslaught of what Captain DuPont called "our weaker brethren" continued. The able-bodied men were taken into the service as "boys" or put to work as laborers. The wives and children and the old and infirm were placed in camps on Coosaw, Edisto, or Botany Bay islands, and as the British had done in the Revolution, on little Otter Island at the entrance to St. Helena Sound. Captain DuPont addressed the problem in a confidential report to the assistant secretary of the navy in which he noted that in addition to the contrabands who had turned to the military for help, there were many without work on their plantations. A reporter for *Harper's Weekly* wrote that some slaves preferred to remain at their homes, the reasons not being based on "apprehension of the Yankees," but on "the dislike of leaving their families and the 'tings'—their little property. They have a cat-like clinging to their old quarters, and do not generally manifest any desire to quit them." Captain DuPont's report lamented the condition of the eight to ten thousand Negroes within the Union lines in February 1862:

> But the contraband question is a very intricate one, how to employ them, who is to control, what positions are they to have, what authority to be given those who work them? The various so-called agents who come down

here—more or less accredited—the collectors of cotton, collectors of negro statistics, the people of God, the best of the party who want to establish schools, do not all agree. Then we have the philanthropic newspaper correspondents whose special happiness seems to be to abuse a general, who, surrounded with extreme difficulties, is doing his best to overcome them. One thing is certain, that while the most rabid abolitionist had not exaggerated their degraded condition, the transition state has not improved it. In England (I hate to quote her now for anything) a commission would be appointed by Parliament of wise, unprejudiced, disinterested, and practical individuals to examine and report.[11]

General Sherman, on Hilton Head, had no toleration for the emissaries of the abolitionists and the federal agents. He "packed them off" to General Stevens, who wrote: "There descended on the Department of the South, like locusts in Egypt, a swarm of Treasury agents and humanitarians, male and female, all zealously bent on educating and elevating the "freedmen" as they immediately dubbed the blacks. The irreverent young officers styled these good people the 'Gideonites.' " General Stevens was said to have exerted "a decided and salutary influence" and was able to modify some of their extravagant misconceptions.[12] Savannah's *Daily Morning News* reported the Yankees at Port Royal were tired of supporting the refugees—"The pesky creatures do nothing but eat."[13]

Even before the fall of Fort Sumter, Georgia's Governor Joseph E. Brown took steps to defend Savannah and Brunswick against attack he believed to be inevitable. St. Simons Island was a strategic point offering defense of St. Simons Sound and Brunswick harbor. The island provided a bountiful larder capable of sustaining a large force, and in any federal attempt to blockade Southern ports it gave potential for a convenient base for ships that might have a try at running the gauntlet set by the U.S. Navy. On the south end of the island the Page-King plantation, Retreat, provided a perfect site for a fortification overlooking the entrance to the sound. The Georgia authorities commandeered island slaves, including some from Hampton and the Five Pound settlement on Experiment. They constructed five batteries built of earth with an overlayer of palmetto logs, iron rails, and iron shutters. Palmettos, plentiful on the island, were soft and would not splinter when struck by gunshot. They had been used successfully on fortifications in Charleston harbor during the Revolution. The five batteries mounted at least three large guns each, including Columbiads and, rare to the Confederacy, a rifled cannon. The fortifications were first manned by an artillery company from Macon. When President Lincoln directed the coast be subjected to the naval blockade, Governor Brown placed 1,500 Georgia troops on the island and braced Brunswick for an invasion. The crushing defeat of the Southern troops in the capture of Hilton Head in November 1861 brought cold reason into play. Apprehensive white planters abandoned St. Simons and moved their slaves to inland plantations at Waynesville, to a refugee colony called Tebeauville, near Waycross, or to Savannah, where Fort Pulaski promised protection from the fearsome Yankees. The managers and slaves at Butler's Island were joined by those who had remained at Hampton and Experiment, and all moved to an inland plantation for what was expected to be the duration of the war. In February 1862, General Robert E. Lee, then commanding the southern region, ordered the evacuation of the troops and the removal of the St. Simons guns to Savannah, deemed of greater importance to the Confederacy than Brunswick and Darien.[14]

The new facility on Port Royal Sound enabled the Union forces to enlarge their activities on the Georgia and Florida coasts. The Navy department recognized the importance of St. Simons and Brunswick, where: "The harbor is perfectly landlocked, large enough to float the navies of Europe; water on the bar as shown by the Coast Survey sufficient to float any naval frigate, water in harbor ample depth, harbor perfectly protected; location as healthy as any on the coast, or more so."[15] They believed it to be one of the best points on the South Atlantic coast for a military base. Accordingly, Captain DuPont ordered Commander Sylvanus W. Godon to lead a survey in his U.S.S. *Mohican*, accompanied by naval ships *Potomska* and *Pocahontas*. He was directed to reconnoiter the inland passage between Brunswick and Darien. The ships, all steampowered sailing vessels, were thought to be able to navigate the shallow waters. Commander Godon, however, chose to anchor the *Mohican* in the sound just off the unmanned and unarmed Confederate batteries on Retreat plantation. He led *Potomska* and *Pocahontas* in his launch, which was armed with a howitzer. He and his men determined Brunswick to be abandoned and enroute to Darien found the passage between Altamaha and Doboy sounds to be obstructed by pilings, which were removed by the crews of the two ships. Except for two small steamboats that beat a hasty retreat up the Altamaha River and a company of Confederate horsemen, Darien was also deserted. The Georgians had spent much time and money on the two vessels, intending to mount guns and to armor them with cotton bales preparatory to doing battle with the federal gunboats in the sounds. A state board of inquiry determined their condition was such "the ships could not bear the concussion of a single gun, their bottoms would not hold together." The horsemen at Darien had intended to burn the town if the Union force showed signs of attacking. Commander Godon kept his men on board their vessels except at St. Simons, where he led a small group on an exploratory landing. There he was surprised to find the island deserted by plantation owners and slaves, except for an unlikely trio of desolate people. The planter James Frewin, his mother, and his young grandson John Stevens were the only occupants. Commander Godon covered the island from Hampton and Cannon's Point on the north and to Retreat on the south, where a few days before Lieutenant George B. Balch, commanding the *Pocahontas,* had raised the American flag over the abandoned batteries.[16]

To the Union men, the desertion of St. Simons was motivated by the same fears that caused the South Carolinians to abandon their plantations and the town of Beaufort. Uppermost was the fear of a slave insurrection, followed closely by their apprehension of Union raids of pillage and destruction. Although the evacuation of the Georgia troops left little of value from a military point of view—for they had even destroyed the lighthouse constructed in 1811 on a foundation of tabby mined from the ruins of colonial Frederica—the planters did leave much of worth in their haste to depart. Lieutenant Balch and Commander Godon respected private property, purchased foodstuffs from Mr. Frewin, and posted notices promising safety and urging the other owners to return to their homes.[17]

The information obtained by Commander Godon's task force led to a change in blockading tactics. Since October 1861 ships had been ordered to take up their duties "off St. Simons Sound." The abandoned defenses permitted a station within the sound, a move that provided greater control and a psychological impact by showing the flag to wary natives on the mainland.[18]

The increased visibility of the Union presence prompted a flood of blacks seeking refuge from slavery. Commander Godon reported, "Contrabands continue to come to us." At first he sent them to a new Union base at Fernandina, but others needing attention were accumulated on St. Simons. The settling of the blacks at St. Simons was the beginning of a colony in which Commander Godon and Captain DuPont took pride. The St. Simons colony utilized the slave quarters at Retreat near the protecting naval vessel stationed in the sound. Forty slaves from Colonels Island, near Brunswick, were the nucleus of the settlement that Com-

mander Godon believed would reach one thousand and be self-support-
ing. He recommended to Captain DuPont that a marine battalion be
quartered on both ends of the island, at Hampton and at Retreat, and that
the waters of the north end be patrolled by a small gunboat, thereby securing Darien.[19]

The planters along the Georgia coast considered themselves to be benevolent slaveholders. Greatly disturbed by the presence of Union ships in
their waters, they were truly perturbed to find their slaves leaving home to
join the enemy. Among those expressing both surprise and dismay was the
family of the Reverend Charles Colcock Jones of Liberty County. It was he
who had written the *Catechism* for "colored persons." Of him it was said,
"Happy is that community, black or white, who has such a shepherd."
The Jones plantations, Arcadia at Midway, Montivideo on the North
Newport River, and Maybank, just inland from St. Catherines Island,
were near the home of their good friend Julia Maxwell King, the widow of
Roswell King, Jr. Mrs. King was "Aunt Julia" to the Jones children, who
were the best of friends with the flock of young Kings. The Reverend Mr.
Jones wrote his son Charles Colcock Jones, Jr., who was then serving as a
first lieutenant in the Chatham Artillery: "*Fifty-one* have already gone
from this country. Your Uncle John has lost five. Three are said to have left
from your Aunt Susan's and Cousin Laura's; one was captured, two not,
and one of these was *Joefinny!*" The Reverend Mr. Jones believed that
the runaway slaves were traitors who might "pilot an enemy into your
bedchamber!"[20]

Young Lieutenant Jones, an intelligent, compassionate man, gave an
answer uncharacteristic, but one in keeping with the troubled times:

> I deeply regret to learn that the Negroes still continue to desert to the
> enemy. Joefinny's conduct surprises me. You ask my opinion as to the
> proper disposition to be made of absconding Negroes, and also inquire
> what would be done with white men detecting in the act of giving over to
> the enemy. If a white man be apprehended under such circumstances, he
> would doubtless be hung, and in many instances, if the proof be clear, by
> an indignant and patriotic community without the intervention of either
> judge or jury. In the case of a Negro, it is hard to mete out a similar
> punishment under similar circumstances. Ignorance, credulity, pliability,
> desire for change, the absence of the political ties of allegiance, the peculiar
> status of the race—all are to be considered, and must exert their influences
> in behalf of the slave. If, however, a Negro be found digesting a matured
> plan of escape and enticing others to do the same; or if, after having once

effected his escape to the enemy, he returns with a view to induce others to accompany him, thus in fact becoming an emissary of the enemy; or if he be found under circumstances which indicate that he is a spy, it is my opinion that he should undoubtedly suffer death, both as a punishment for his grave offense and as an example to evildoers. In the case, however, of a Negro endeavoring to effect his escape to the enemy detected in the effort, my opinion is that he should not be put to death, but that he be taken to the county seat of the county in which the offense was committed and there publicly and severely punished.

On second thought, young Jones wrote his father that, "where life is at stake," white or black is entitled to a trial by jury, and the jury should be constituted in accordance with law. To act otherwise would "savor of mob law." He returned to irrationality in the same letter, proclaiming: "The main object of the gunboats now lying along our coast doubtless is to encourage the escape of negroes, and by stealing and reselling them aid in swelling personal wealth and in defraying the expense of war."[21]

Fear of even greater losses of slaves caused a general exodus from the coastal region. The Jones family purchased a distant and costly farm one hundred miles inland from Savannah. Yet the St. Simons colony of contrabands continued to grow apace. The determination of the slaves was intense. A Union soldier wrote, "The marshes, or savannahs, in this part of the country, which border the rivers are almost impassable for human beings, yet many a slave has waded through them toward the North star of Freedom."[22]

On April 10, 1862, the count stood at fifty-five; on April 18, at eighty-nine. St. Simons food supplies were bolstered by corn from the Spalding barn on Sapelo and by beef and potatoes from Jekyll Island across St. Simons Sound. The move toward self-sufficiency was slowed by the ever-increasing population. June brought forty additional refugees, with several coming from as far away as Macon, quite possibly some of the Pierce Butler slaves sold at Savannah before the war. They would have found the Oconee and Altamaha rivers a proper thoroughfare from middle Georgia to St. Simons.[23]

Captain DuPont maintained a proprietary interest in his Southern province. He sent for the *Mohican*, asking Commander Godon: "Select, if you can do so, thirty stout contrabands for work on boats and bring them with you to Port Royal. They should be single men of course." Only twenty "stout contrabands" could be mustered, and those remaining at the colony were given an indication of how it would be to be free and black. To the commanding officer of the U.S.S. *Florida*, Captain DuPont sent orders and an afterthought: "P.S.—You will please receive from Commander Parrott a certain quantity of condemned bread, which you will take to St. Simons for the contrabands."[24] A general order was transmitted to his command:

> The hot season on this coast, now approaching, renders it advisable that acclimated persons be employed on board of the ships of this squadron in such duties as involve much exposure to sun and heat, such as boat service and work in engine rooms.

> The Commanding officers are therefore authorized to enlist contrabands, with their consent, on their respective vessels, rating them as boys, at $8, $9, and $10 per month, and one ration, this privilege to be exercised with sound discretion.[25]

The colony rose to "upward of 300" by the end of May, and in August pushed up past five hundred. The contrabands' self-sufficiency overflowed to such an extent that they were permitted to sell goods and services to the Union men. An order from the commanding officer on St. Simons set the terms:

> Tariff of prices to be charged to officers' messes and sailors for articles purchased of negroes on the island of St. Simon's, Georgia.

> U.S.S. *Florida,* July 1, 1862.

		Cents
Milk	per quart	4
Corn	per doozen	5
Terrapins	each	10
Watermelons (according to size)	do	5–15
Eggs	per dozen	12
Turtle eggs	do	5
Okra	per 1/2 peck	10
Bean peas	do	5
Squash	2 for	3
Chickens	each	12
Shrimps	per 2 quarts	10
Rabbits	each	10
Cantaloupes	do	1–3
Whortleberries	per quart	5

Fish:

In bunches	per dozen	5
Large Fish	per pound	2

Washing:

Large pieces, when soap and starch are furnished	per dozen	50
Small pieces	do	25

The prices of making pantaloons or shirts shall not be over 50 cents each; coats, 75 cents each, where the materials are furnished.

The Officers are requested not to exceed these prices, and the men are forbidden to do so.

J. R. GOLDSBOROUGH,
Commander, Comdg. U.S. Naval Forces,
St. Simon's, Georgia.[26]

In June 1862, when Commander Godon relinquished his responsibility for St. Simons and the colony of contrabands to Commander John R. Goldsborough, who was commanding the U.S.S. *Florida,* he gave a final report to Captain DuPont and left his relief notes on the care and protection of the blacks. A veritable bonanza of rice had been found at Champney Island, adjoining Butler's Island, yet Commander Godon could still say "my supplies have been mostly from Pierce Butler's place." The new commanding officer was warned of the tendency of the blacks to shirk responsibilities. When work was neglected, Commander Godon had eliminated rations of beef or placed men in irons for punishment. He added: "I would also remark that idleness, improvidence, theft and a disposition to vagrancy are the besetting sins of the contraband race on the island. There are some marked exceptions, however. Your utmost efforts will be required to counteract the evil effects of the above vices in the colony."[27]

Commander Godon had suspected that one of the blacks, Henry, who was living at the Hazzard plantation, was in collaboration with raiding Confederates who visited the island bent on destruction of federal property. It proved to be a valid suspicion and resulted in the arming of the contrabands for guard duty at several of the island's landings.[28]

In August 1862 control of the island was turned over to Brigadier General Rufus Saxton, the military governor of South Carolina. He arrived with a force of black troops from the First South Carolina Regiment Volunteers. Commander Goldsborough was told to support the new command with his gunboats and to show the same interest in the contraband colony as heretofore, "which owes its origin and existence to the Navy."[29]

The mainlanders became apprehensive when former slaves returned as the armed enemy. Their sorties from St. Simons were met with faint resistance by the inadequate defenders and with considerable fear and foreboding from the civilian population. The black troops raided Butler's Island, where they gathered in eighty bushels of rice, burned the Spalding mainland plantation, and raided Mallow, the home of Roswell King's aged brother, Reuben. Hardly tested in combat, the volunteers nonetheless won praise from their white officers:

> The colored men fought with astonishing coolness and bravery. For alacrity in effective landings, and determination, and for bush fighting, I found them all I could desire—more than I hoped. They behaved bravely, gloriously, and deserve all praise.
>
> I started from St. Simons with 62 colored fighting men and returned with 156 fighting men (all colored). As soon as we took a slave from his claimant we placed a musket in his hands and he began to fight for the freedom of others.[30]

The armed contrabands and the black soldiers of the South Carolina Volunteers were enough to deter Confederate raids for a while. William Miles Hazzard, one of the raiders, said, "If you wish to know hell before your time, go to St. Simons and be hunted ten days by niggers."[31]

A skirmish between Confederate raiders and the black soldiers resulted in the death of one of the latter, by name, John Brown. He was thought to be the first black soldier to die in the war and as such was said by the members of his regiment to be the "hero of John Brown hymn," a song sung by them "as no white regiment can sing it, so full of pathos and harmony."[32]

The black troops desecrated the island to such an extent word of their actions reached the mainland. Miles Hazzard returned to find the family graveyard had been violated. He left a note for the federal command, saying that even the savage respected the home of the dead: "If it is honorable for you to disturb the dead, I shall consider it an honor, and will make it my ambition to disturb your living." The "living" that young Hazzard intended to disturb were Union sentinels at their posts, the shooting of whom his commander had always "discountenanced." In transmitting the Hazzard note to Flag Officer DuPont, by then an admiral, the naval officer on St. Simons added, "I am fearful the complaint of the writer is but too true."[33]

To the island planters the most sacred spot on St. Simons was Christ Church, a small but handsome, steepled, white frame structure not unlike the New England–style church at Midway. It, too, was violated and left in ruins, as was much of the planters' property over the entire island. In November 1862, before the destruction was irreparable, the black troops were recalled to Port Royal and orders were given to disband the contraband colony. Able-bodied men were enlisted in the federal services or used as military laborers in South Carolina. The old and infirm and the women and children went on to Hilton Head; a few stragglers were sent to Fernandina. In their first brush with freedom the blacks on St. Simons, both the contraband and the military, won scant praise from their liberators and hatred from their former owners whose properties they had violated.[34]

Early in 1863, black troops again appeared on St. Simons. A regiment had been formed on St. Helena Island, near Beaufort. While most of the men were former slaves from South Carolina, some had been taken to Port Royal after seeking their freedom with the Union forces on St. Simons. One of their first assignments was to dismantle the batteries on Retreat plantation that some of them had helped to construct at the beginning of the war. The railroad irons were removed and shipped to the "United States," and at the same time, the surgeon who accompanied the troops on their expedition to St. Simons told how he improved his hospital back on Hilton Head: "With Lieut. West, I went up to the Hon. Thomas Butler King's estate and confiscated a nice bath tub and three new windows for my hospital, which has only shutters."[35]

In June 1863 a black regiment from the North, the Fifty-fourth Massachusetts, was sent to Port Royal for duty. Troops from the Fifty-fourth were combined with a force from General David Hunter's South Carolina Volunteers, also blacks, some of whom had been stationed on St. Simons the year before. Together these groups formed a special force sent on an expedition up the Altamaha River against Darien. They paused briefly on St. Simons both before and after the Darien raid, giving Colonel Robert Gould Shaw, the young commanding officer of the Fifty-fourth, an opportunity to visit Hampton, the Butler plantation he knew through his fami-

ly's close friendship with Fanny Kemble. He told of the visit in a letter to
his family:

> Today I rode over to Mr. Butler's plantation. It is an immense place & parts
> of it are very beautiful. The house is small and badly built like almost all I
> have seen here. There are about ten of his slaves left here, all of them sixty
> or seventy years old. He sold three hundred of them about three years ago
> & I talked with some whose children & grandchildren were sold then &
> though they said that was a "weeping day" they maintained that "Massa
> Butler was a good Massa" and they would give anything to see him again.
> When I told them I had seen "Miss Fanny," they looked much pleased &
> one named "John" wanted me to tell her I had seen him. They said all the
> house servants had been taken inland at the beginning of the war & they
> asked if we couldn't get their children back to the island again. These were
> all born & bred on the place & even selling away their families wouldn't
> entirely efface their love for their Master. I couldn't help thinking of that
> summer in Sorrento—what she told you of her paying the house servants
> wages & little thought then that I should ever visit the place under such
> circumstances.

Colonel Shaw described the island with its long, oyster-shell road, the
abandoned fields, the tabby buildings. He told how the Butler slaves
thought Fanny Kemble was "a very fine lady" and how he had repaired
the desecrated chapel for a Sunday service. He visited the empty Couper
house at Cannon's Point, "the finest on the island": "A deserted home-
stead is always a sad sight, but here in the South we must look a little
deeper than the surface, and then we see that every such overgrown plantation & empty house is a harbinger of freedom to the slaves, & every
lover of his country, even if he have no feeling for the slaves themselves,
should rejoice."[36]

Colonel Robert Gould Shaw led his men in the Darien raid. It was a
disgraceful performance. Darien, abandoned and defenseless and already
battered and war torn, was pillaged and burned on the orders of Colonel
James Montgomery of the Volunteers. Colonel Shaw was shocked and
ashamed that he and his soldiers played a role in the senseless, vindictive
action. Georgians reacted understandably as reported in Savannah's
Daily Morning News:

> The accursed Yankee vandals came up yesterday with three gunboats and
> two transports and laid the city in ruins. They carried off every negro that

Augustus Saint-Gaudens's study of a black soldier for his
Boston memorial to Colonel Robert Gould Shaw and the
men of the Fifty-fourth Massachusetts Regiment.
(Photograph by Jerry L. Thompson.)

was in the place, except one old African woman named *Nancy* who told them she was from Africa and that she would not go again on the big water.

The destruction of Darien was a cowardly, wanton outrage for which the Yankee vandals have not even the excuse of plunder. The town had for a long time been nearly destroyed and there was nothing left in the place to excite even Yankee cupidity. It afforded a safe opportunity to inflict injury upon unarmed and defenseless private citizens, and it is in such enterprises that Yankee negro valor displays itself.[37]

Colonel Shaw attempted to justify his role in a letter to his mother. He gave Colonel Montgomery's reasons and in a private letter to their headquarters questioned Montgomery's authority as well. "The reasons he gave me for destroying Darien were that the Southerners must be made to feel that this is a real war, and that they were to be swept away by the hand of God like the Jews of old."[38] One day later, his letter to Lieutenant Colonel Charles G. Halpine, A.A.G., Tenth Army Corps, questioned:

Has Colonel Montgomery orders from General Hunter to burn & destroy *all* towns and dwelling houses he may capture?

On the 11th inst as you know we took the town of Darien without opposition. The place being occupied as far as we ascertained by non-combatants.

Col. Montgomery burned it to the ground, having first shelled it from the river. If he does this on his own responsibility, I shall refuse to have a share in it & take the consequences, but of course if it is an order from headquarters it is a different matter.

He ordered me, if separated from him, to burn all the planters' houses I came across. Now I am perfectly ready to burn any place which resists & gives some reason for such a proceeding but it seems to me very barbarous to turn women and children adrift in that way—and if I am only assisting Col. Montgomery in a private enterprise, it is very distasteful to me.[39]

It was ironic that Darien, whose people twice petitioned their governments to bar the introduction or use of slaves, should be destroyed by blacks seeking freedom for their race.

In Philadelphia, Pierce Butler was distressed and embittered by the dire state of affairs in coastal Georgia. The federal occupation of the islands, and the "great victory" of the black troops at Darien, was reported in the Northern press. Butler's stability was further disturbed by news of the

Colonel Robert Gould Shaw, Fanny Kemble's young friend whose Fifty-fourth Massachusetts Regiment burned defenseless Darien in 1863 and who died with many of his men in a brave but futile attack on Fort Wagner, near Charleston. (From the Augustus Saint-Gaudens memorial in Boston. Photograph by Jerry L. Thompson.)

early death of his niece Elizabeth McAllister in January 1862. Her death was a distinct surprise and coincided with the decision of the supreme court of Georgia that Gabriella Butler, as administrator of her husband's estate in Georgia, should deliver the properties to Pierce Butler and Thomas C. James, the trustees, preparatory to their sale of the John Butler interest. To protect his right to inherit the John Butler estate, Francis, the son of Elizabeth McAllister, had his name changed to Butler only to die the following year, leaving no one in the immediate family eligible to inherit. The death of nine-year-old Francis was an even greater surprise, for it brought into play the provision of John Butler's will that he must have thought an unlikely happenstance. Title to the Georgia plantations returned to Pierce Butler individually. The sale the trustees had contemplated was unnecessary, and except for the share of the income that would continue to flow to Gabriella Butler, the plantations and the slaves belonged to him. Excluded from inheritance were John and Gabriella's granddaughters, the three McAllister girls, Julia, Gabriella, and Margaret Elizabeth, called Meta. By an odd and unexpected turn of events, John Butler repaid his brother Pierce for permitting him to rectify the failure to change his name in the timely manner their grandfather had prescribed and thus share Major Butler's wealth.[40]

The campaign in June and July 1863 that culminated in the Battle of Gettysburg marked the turning point of the war. For Pierce Butler, there was a sad realization that his hopes for a Southern victory and the continuation of slavery was not to be. Following the battle he was given an intimate look at the distressing results of conflict. Among the more than twenty thousand Confederate casualties of that campaign was his godson, Lieutenant Pierce Butler Holmes, the son of Dr. James I. Holmes of Darien. It was to young Holmes that Pierce Butler had consigned his personal belongings in early 1861. His father was the friend of the Butlers, Fanny Kemble included, and had long been physician to the owners and slaves of the Butler plantations. Lieutenant Holmes was badly wounded and asked that his godfather be given permission to visit the prison hospital. The request granted, a letter to Philadelphia brought prompt and personal response in a visit to the prison by "not only Mr. Butler but by his brave daughter as well." The Butlers comforted the wounded prisoner, left him "a purse of gold," and then were given permission by the federal officers, who were aware of their pro-Southern feeling, to visit other Confederates in that part of the prison. Lieutenant Holmes recovered from his wounds and was exchanged to fight again. Wounded once more in the

Wilderness campaign, he died "like the brave soldier boy he was." Pierce Butler and Fanny Kemble both grieved over the loss of Pierce Butler Holmes.[41] They suffered other losses, too. Fanny Kemble was particularly disheartened by the death of Robert Gould Shaw, who led his Fifty-fourth Massachusetts Regiment of black soldiers in a brave but futile assault on Fort Wagner on Morris Island near Charleston. It was a tragic redemption for their actions at Darien: "But over the sanguinary field, the indomitable Shaw, ever in advance, had led the stormers then down into and through the ditch, and up the parapet of the curtain. There he stood a moment, waving his sword and shouting to his followers pressing on, and then fell dead."[42]

Colonel Shaw died with many of his men. The defenders of the fort, who also demonstrated great courage, denied they had refused the dead colonel an "honorable burial" or ordered his body to be placed in a common grave "with his niggers." An editorial in *Harper's Weekly* countered: "Where else should he be buried but with them? Of all the soil of South Carolina there is no spot so holy and prophetic as that grave."[43] Fanny Kemble also mourned the death of William Sedgwick—the son of her close friends Elizabeth and Charles Sedgwick—who, on September 17, 1862, "was struck down on the terrible field of Antietam." Fatally wounded, young Will Sedgwick wrote in his diary, "I have tried to do my duty." It was to his mother that Fanny Kemble wrote her letters of the plantation journal, and it was also to Elizabeth Sedgwick that the book was dedicated.[44]

Chapter 21

"Inevitable Sambo"

This stone (Slavery), which was rejected by the first builders, is become the chief stone of the corner in our new edifice.

To fanny kemble, the Civil War was a crusade to end slavery in America. Her attitude continued to be supported by Sarah and Dr. Wister, additionally by her Massachusetts friends, and by fellow abolitionists Charles Sumner and William Channing, the nephew of Dr. William Ellery Channing whose thoughts had influenced her in the 1830s. Also there was Frederick Law Olmsted, together, all "more or less fanatical on the slavery question." She had been accused of mistaken judgment by her English friend Henry Greville, with whom she exchanged long and forceful letters on their contrasting views of slavery and the South. She knew and was disturbed that he reflected the point of view of numerous Englishmen, many of whom were their friends. He wrote to her:

> We see nothing in this contest but a struggle for dominion on one side & independence on the other & it is needless to say that if we could feel interest in such uninteresting people our sympathy must be with the weaker party. As to abolition of slavery, it is certainly beside the question and that it has been resorted to now is merely an imaginary *help* on the conduct of the war and from no other higher motive is as plain as "pikestaff," and I dont think any abolitionist even here, has the slightest faith in any result from the meaness of the Washington Gov't.

When he wrote that her opinions were not valid because she lived in an atmosphere of fanaticism, she responded with passion and conviction:

I have not one grain of propagandism in my whole composition and do not believe in talking thoughtless people into thinking ones, or thinking ones out of the convictions they have taken the trouble of making for themselves. I have certain points of faith which are to my soul what vital air is to my lungs. Among these are belief in the ultimate triumph of truth & light for which the Lord does fight, and rejoice with all my heart that I have lived to see the beginning of the process which I should have died believing was to come of the destruction of slavery in America and the salvation of this great country from the iniquity & misery of such a system. When I used to walk on the shore of the Altamaha River three & twenty years ago—in the solitary evenings that followed days of hard & sometimes menial labour among the Butler slaves (washing and dressing with my own hands their children—making their beds & their fires & sweeping the floor of their infirmaries to teach them habits of decent order & cleanliness) I used to wonder how & when the dreadful system of human depredation in the midst of which I was living was to end.

But when I used to stand in utter despondency listening to the sea breaking on the beach at the river mouth—and watching the bright safety light that warned vessels from the dangerous bar, not seldom crying with bitter tears, "How long oh Lord, how long," I little thought to live to see the day when Northern ships would ride along that coast in spite of the extinction of the warning safety light by the Southerners—bringing freedom to the land of bondage—tho' not alms to the poor people among whom I lived and toiled for they have been scattered into a more hopeless and miserable slavery still, sold & dispersed to pay their owner's debts. To them, perhaps, the day of deliverance has not come—but one thing is certain, it has arisen all over the South and however slow its progress may be it will assuredly shine more and more until the proper day of universal freedom.[1]

When Henry Greville suggested that she had become an American, Fanny Kemble replied, "You do me wrong for I am an Englishwoman and no one alive more truly so."[2] Burdened by the knowledge of what she believed to be complete misapprehension on the part of the British, who shared Henry Greville's point of view, and with an unlikely traveling companion, considering her state of mind, Fanny Kemble and her daughter Frances left America for a trip to England. For Fan it was only a visit, but for Fanny Kemble the stay outlasted the war that raged across the Atlantic. They arrived in England in the late spring of 1862. Frances Butler was twenty-four. The year before, her sister Sarah described her as "fat & fresh," with "short curling locks, and baby mouth." In April 1864 Sidney

George Fisher found her: "a very charming person, gay, graceful, thorobred, clever, cultivated, & more than pretty. She has a good figure & an expressive face, beautiful hair & good features."[3] In the spring of 1862 the English must have seen her as something between the two versions. Fanny Kemble was determined to persuade her upper-class friends to see the struggle in America in what she believed was its true light, but for Frances, the pro-Southern sentiment was welcome and refreshing after Philadelphia, where she and her father were forced to stifle their thoughts and hopes.

In London it was not only the "ignorant and mischievous nonsense I was continually compelled to hear on the subject of slavery" from her friends, but the same sentiment so frequently proclaimed by the influential *Times* of London that brought Fanny Kemble to a decision to publish the journal of her stay on the Butler plantation through the winter of 1839.[4] The war in America brought strong beliefs into play among the English, one widely held view being that the South was entitled to "dominion." John Ruskin wrote an American friend: "If you want the slaves to be free, let their masters go free first, in God's name. If they don't like to be governed by you, let them govern themselves." He believed the Emancipation Proclamation worthless: "If I had it here—there's a fine North wind blowing and I would give it to the first boy I met to fly it at his kite's tail." With so many Englishmen, he envied the luxury that came with slaves: "As soon as I get a house, I'll ask you to send me something American—a slave perhaps. I've a great notion of a black boy in a green jacket and purple cap—in Paul Veronese's manner."[5] A petition from the "People of the United Kingdom of Great Britain and Ireland to the People of the United States of America" echoed John Ruskin's thoughts on dominion and contended the South was entitled to "set up a government of their own." The petition called for the Union to "make peace with the Southern States; we make this appeal in the name of religion, humanity, civilization and common justice."[6]

The many Englishmen of military background were inclined to support the South. Such a one was FitzGerald Ross, who spent a year with the Confederate army and kept a diary in which he often proclaimed his ardent pro-Southern and pro-slavery attitudes. He believed emancipation would be cruel to the blacks and would "in the end result in their extermination just as the Red Indian, a far nobler race, have perished before them."[7]

On the other hand, Charles Darwin thought it "dreadful" should the

South, with its "accursed slavery," triumph. When his wife suggested they give up London's eminent newspaper because of its stand, he was tempted but said: "To give up the "Bloody Old *Times*" would be to give up meat, drink and air."[8] Thomas Henry Huxley wrote his sister in America, whose fifteen-year-old son fought for the Confederacy: "It is clear to me that slavery means, for the white man, bad political economy, bad social morality, bad internal organization and a bad influence upon free labor and freedom all over the world." He wished the system ended and hoped the South had the good judgment to free the slaves "without this miserable war." Huxley said, with many thoughtful Englishmen, "My heart goes with the South, my head with the North." Thomas Carlyle expressed his own view with "astonishment and sorrow." He wrote an American friend who held anti-slavery views: "The America for which you are hoping, you will never see, and you will never see the whites and blacks in the South dwelling together as equals in peace."[9] Benjamin Disraeli gave a dire prediction to the House of Commons:

> Who ever may be young enough to live to witness the ultimate consequences of this Civil War will see, whenever the waters have subsided, a different America from that which was known to our fathers and even from that of which this generation has had so much experience. It will be an America of armies, of diplomacy, of Rival States and manoeuvering Cabinets, of frequent turbulence and probably of frequent wars.[10]

Fanny Kemble believed the truth of her journal would help to crystallize such diverse public opinion to slavery's evil presence and toward support for the North's efforts to end the system and to preserve the Union. From the journal she deleted the painful personal references of that difficult time; she wrote a brief preface saying the slaves in which she had possessed "an unfortunate interest" had been sold, which was not completely true, and the islands, meaning St. Simons and Butler's Island, were at the time "in the power of the Northern troops." She appended to the journal a long letter to Charles Greville as well as a letter to the *Times* that had never been posted, both of which stated the situation in America as she saw it. The letter intended for the *Times* was written following their comments questioning the veracity of Harriet Beecher Stowe's *Uncle Tom's Cabin*. Between the time of her decision to publish and the date the book appeared, the bitter struggle had shifted in favor of the North, and the pro-Southern sentiment so prevalent in Parliament had diminished and was fast fading away. As the published journal appeared in England at a time when feelings were changing and the defeat of the South seemed in the making, the impact of the book was not what it might have been had it been read earlier, during or before the war. Fanny Kemble's preface was written in January, with publication following in late May 1863.[11]

Among the many reviewers of the book, the *Athenaeum* of London was impressed—"A more startling and fearful narrative on a well-worn subject was never laid before readers." On the chivalry of Southern gentlemen, the graces of Southern women, the devotion of slaves to masters, and the tenderness of overseers, Mrs. Kemble's *Journal* offered a fresh point of view. The *Athenaeum* proposed, facetiously, a moral that Southern planters should not marry English ladies not reared from infancy to admire their "peculiar institutions." It was a moral with which Pierce Butler and Fanny Kemble could have agreed. Other English reviews had varied reactions. The *Spectator* thought the *Journal* good ammunition to be used against the Southern sympathizer who had become an apologist for slavery. The *Journal* was recommended for those who thought slavery preferable to laborers confronted with starvation or to an old age of abject poverty, a prevalent belief in England. The *London Review* gave Fanny Kemble credit for a graphic portrayal of slavery and for substantiating its evils. At the same time, it did not want to abandon the courage and sportsmanship of the South for the "ill-mannered Yankees." The *Saturday Review* made a point that must have shaken the author. It accused her of enjoying the sale of her book and of attacking slavery at the same time, "while she takes the English public into her confidence and informs them it was as a slave holder that she first began to entertain a dislike of her husband."[12]

As to attitudes of the English toward the war in America, the *Journal*'s immediate impact was inconsequential. Fanny Kemble did not shake the upper-class preference for the South. She was distressed to be accused by the people, "among whom I lived," of having "cooked up" the *Journal* for purposes of propaganda, and she believed such a thought might have sprung from her unwillingness to have the entire work published as written and without the meaningful personal deletions. But, as a latter-day editor of the *Journal* wrote, her work was a "dreadful indictment of a ruling class" that helped to make the English laborers aware of their own voteless position and the shortcomings of their own rulers.[13]

The American edition closely followed the *Journal*'s appearance in England. Sidney George Fisher was quick to note and comment on a review he had read in the *New York Tribune*. He wrote that the *Journal* consisted mostly of a series of letters:

> They describe plantation life there and the conditions & treatment of the Negroes and reveal the terrible secrets of the prison house. Filth, squalor, cruelty & wretchedness are painted in very strong colors, as well as the discomfort & inconvenience of Butler's own house.
>
> These letters are now printed for the first time, partly, I suppose, for the sake of annoying Butler, partly to aid the cause of abolition, & partly for the money they will bring. I am surprised at the picture they draw of the miserable condition of the Negroes, which is very discreditable to Butler.[14]

The *Tribune* review appeared in the July 6, 1863, issue that also carried a front-page spread on the "Great Victory at Gettysburg." The review was long, not unlike the attention given Mortimer Thomson's story on the sale of the slaves four years before. It was printed over parts of two pages, the equivalent of almost a full page:

> Apart from the peculiar interest which attaches to the subject, it is rich in lively and graphic descriptions, shrewd comments on the general features of Southern society, quiet touches of humor, and fine delineations of character. But the great value of the work, at this moment, consists in the faithful record which it presents of the practical influence of slavery, both on servant and master.

The review covered the *Journal* entries in some detail. Mrs. Kemble was thanked for having the courage to report the uglier aspects of slavery, "the ghastly and repulsive features" that leave impression on memory and imagination: "She has helped to produce a deeper and truer impression of the social system which its supporters have not hesitated to drench the pleasant valleys and riversides of our land in fraternal blood."[15]

Yeoman, the pseudonym for Frederick Law Olmsted, who reviewed the *Journal* for the *New York Times*, said Fanny Kemble had given validity to a series on slavery that he had once written for the *Times* and that was questioned when they appeared:

> Mrs. Kemble's observations were deep, thorough and detailed. In various instances she may possibly have been imposed upon, or self-deceived under the influence of a warm imagination, working with emotion of unusual character, but this possibility does not affect the importance of observation so constant, so detailed, and extending over so long a period.[16]

Harper's Weekly saw the *Journal* as factual: "There is nothing strained or extravagant in it. It is the plain story of the most hideous state of society that has existed anywhere in a normal Christian land."[17]

The militant abolitionist Lydia Maria Child found room for agreement: "I think it will prove one of the most powerful of the agencies now at work for the overthrow of slavery." She also found room for disagreement. Fanny Kemble had written in her *Journal* that emancipation of the slaves should be "exclusively the business and duty of their owners." Mrs. Child said that was the same as leaving "thieves and murderers to decide when and how their vocations should cease."[18]

The most positive reaction to the Kemble *Journal* was revealed in a long review by George William Curtis in *Atlantic Monthly* for August 1863. The Curtis review covered almost four full pages of the magazine.

> The dazzling phantasmagoria which life had been to the young actress was suddenly exchanged for the most practical acquaintance with its realities. She was married, left the stage, and as a wife and mother resided for a winter on the plantations of her husband upon the coast of Georgia. And now, after twenty-five years, the journal of her residence there is published. It has been wisely kept. For never could such a book speak with such power as at this moment. The tumult of the war will be forgotten, as you read, in the profound and appalled attention enforced by this remarkable revelation of the interior life of Slavery. The spirit, the character, and the purpose of the Rebellion are here laid bare. Its inevitability is equally apparent. The book is a permanent and most valuable chapter in our history; for it is the first ample, lucid, faithful, detailed account, from the actual head-quarters of a slave-plantation in this country, of the workings of the system,—its persistent, hopeless, helpless, crushing of humanity in the slave, and the more fearful moral and mental dryrot it generates in the master.

Mr. Curtis continued, saying the journal was that of "a hearty, generous, clear-sighted woman,"

> who went to the plantation, loving the master, and believing, that, though Slavery might be sad, it might also be mitigated, and the slave might be content. It is a record of a ghastly undeceiving,—of the details of a system so wantonly, brutally, damnably unjust, inhuman, and degrading, that it blights the country, paralyzes civilization, and vitiates human nature itself.

At the end, he said that such a volume could not have been written "without a solemn sense of responsibility. A sadder book the human hand never wrote."[19]

Southern criticism of the *Journal* was a return of the chill that met *Uncle Tom's Cabin,* a work on which Fanny Kemble misguidedly bestowed a garland of praise for its "accuracy."[20] It was a persistent chill that gives promise of existing through the twentieth century. In the *Journal,* in her *Records* that followed many years later, and in her letters, Fanny Kemble was to write and publish much about the Georgia plantations, and much was to be written about her. Biographers, historians, novelists, essayists, and critics have touched on almost every phase of her unusual and troubled life. The errors of judgment that abounded in her first American *Journal* were equaled in the Georgian *Journal* only in the minds of pro-Southern, pro-slavery sympathizers. There were mistakes, and in one instance she gave a firsthand account of Georgia violence as though it had happened at the time of her visit when it actually had taken place a few weeks before she appeared. It was a mistake that tends to discredit the truth of her reporting, yet her reaction to the conditions she found is completely straightforward and genuine. Her descriptions of the Butler plantations, with all the emotion of her telling of the slaves' misery, is an authentic account of the way life was lived on Hampton and Butler's Island in 1839. The factual record of Roswell King's letters to Major Butler in the early 1800s, when conditions were better, lend credence to Fanny Kemble's vivid description of what she found more than a quarter century later. True, had the *Journal* been published earlier, the impact would have been greater. Latter-day historians refute the belief that Fanny Kemble moved the British away from support to the Confederacy to hasten its downfall. Yet, the *Journal* was surely an accompanying force effecting the swing from South to North brought on by rising anti-slavery sentiment in England and the military gains of the North in America.[21]

In comparison with Fanny Kemble's intimate revelation of slavery, the words of other observers who visited the Altamaha plantations seem shallow and superficial. The Basil Halls in 1828, and Charles Lyell in 1846 were critical of the system but sympathized with the slave owners. Fredrika Bremer and Amelia Murray in the 1850s gave the woman's view, Miss Bremer's more akin to Fanny Kemble's, and Miss Murray's swamped by James Hamilton Couper's gentility and benign management theories. These people saw slavery at the Coupers', the Butlers', and at a few other

Altamaha plantations as the best or, at least, as an adequate treatment of an existing evil. Fanny Kemble saw the better side, too. Yet she looked behind the black curtain to see the existing evil as pervasive and virulent.[22]

For the slaves in Georgia, including the Butler people at their inland refuge, the labor pains of their birth as free citizens began as General William Tecumseh Sherman and his army of sixty-two thousand men commenced their march to the sea. Even before the capture of Atlanta, General Sherman gained a forewarning of what he might expect in the execution of his plan to cut and burn a swath up to sixty miles wide through central and southern Georgia to Savannah. Wherever blacks were encountered, a considerable following of slaves was attracted to the force that they believed to be their liberator. To General Sherman, who had not one scintilla of abolitionism in his intense makeup, these people encumbered the effective use of his soldiers. His foremost intention was to make the people of Georgia know the agony of war and, after Georgia was laid low, to turn his wrath to the desolation of South Carolina. He wrote: "The truth is the whole army is burning with an insatiable desire to wreak vengeance upon South Carolina. I almost tremble at her fate but feel she deserves all that seems in store for her."[23] He wanted no hindrance by hordes from the plantation country beyond Atlanta, addressed the matter personally by attempting to reason with the black followers, and instructed his officers to act accordingly. The general's field order stated: "All surplus servants, non-combatants, and refugees, should now go to the rear, and none should be encouraged to encumber us on the march. At some future time we will be able to provide for the poor whites and blacks who seek to escape the bondage under which they are now suffering."[24]

With the appearance of Sherman's army in Georgia, the apprehension of planters was conveyed to their slaves, who became restless and sometimes openly hostile. Discipline, so necessary to plantation routine, vanished. The Sherman order to his raiding parties to "forage liberally" was followed implicitly, and these groups were ruthless in their plunder of both the rich and the poor, with the scant property of black people not exempt from their voracity. The raiders, as though on a "vast holiday frolic," justly earned their designation as "Sherman's bummers." The excited blacks paid little heed to General Sherman's pleas: "The Darkies came to us from every direction. They are all looking for freedom but really dont seem to know what freedom means."[25]

Wide-ranging estimates of the number who tried to follow the federal

General William Tecumseh Sherman, who said, "But the nigger? Why, in God's name, can't sensible men let him alone?" (Engraving by William Wellstood from a photograph by Brady and Company.)

forces were as high as fifty thousand. Major General Henry W. Slocum, who commanded the left wing of the Union army—that section nearest the Savannah River and to South Carolina—reported:

> I think at least 14,000 of these people joined the two columns at different points on the march, but many of them were too old and infirm, and others too young, to endure the fatigues of the march, and therefore were left in the rear. More than one-half of the above number, however, reached the coast with us. Many of the able-bodied men were transferred to the officers of the Quartermaster and subsistence departments, and others were employed in the two corps as teamsters, cook and servants.[26]

Major General Alpheus S. Williams, who commanded the Twentieth Army Corps, one of the two columns in the left wing, told of the freedom seekers who trailed his troops:

> Negroes of all ages and of every variety of physical condition, from the infant in its mother's arms to the decrepid old man, joined the column from plantations and from cross-roads, singly and in large groups, on foot, on horseback, and in every description of vehicles. The vehicles were discarded, as obstructing the progress of our very long column. Beyond this no effect was made to drive away the fugitives. The decrepid, the aged, and the feeble were told of the long journey before them, and advised to remain behind. I estimate that at from 6,000 to 8,000 slaves, at different points in the campaign, joined the march of this corps, of whom something over 2,500 reached our camp before Savannah. About 1,700, of whom one-third were able-bodied, were, on account of scarcity of subsistence, placed in colony on the Coleraine plantation, on the Savannah River, and plentifully supplied with rice, and occasionally with beef. The able-bodied men were employed in transporting rice from the islands and in working rice mills. When communication was opened by way of the Ogeechee the whole colony was turned over to the chief quartermaster and chief commissary. Four hundred to 500, not of the colony, found employment as officer's servants and teamsters for the Government.[27]

Obstruction of the progress of Sherman's army became so great a problem that drastic measures were taken at river and creek crossings. One such instance was described by a Union officer:

> When the lower and less fruitful lands were reached, the embarrassment and military annoyance increased. This was more particularly felt in the left

wing, which was then the only one exposed to the attacks of the enemy. Losing patience at the failure of all orders and exhortations to these poor people to stay at home, General Davis (commanding the Fourteenth Corps), ordered the pontoon bridge at Ebenezer Creek to be taken up before the refugees who were following that corps had crossed, so as to leave them on the further bank of the unfordable stream and thus disembarrass the marching troops. It would be unjust to that officer to believe that the order would have been given, if the effect had been foreseen. The poor refugees had their hearts so set on liberation, and the fear of falling into the hands of the Confederate cavalry was so great, that, with wild wailings and cries, the great crowd rushed, like a stampeded drove of cattle, into the water, those who could not swim as well as those who could, and many were drowned in spite of the earnest efforts of the soldiers to help them. As soon as the character of the unthinking rush and panic was seen, all was done that could be done to save them from the water; but the loss of life was still great enough to prove that there were many ignorant, simple souls to whom it was literally preferable to die freemen rather than to live slaves.[28]

General Slocum's left wing was under constant if not serious harassment from General Joseph Wheeler's cavalry corps. The Conferate general believed his tactics caused the Union forces under General Jefferson C. Davis to abandon the blacks at Ebenezer Creek and reported that two thousand of those unfortunates were sent back to their owners.[29]

It was impossible to determine the number of blacks who followed the army. Some joined for brief intervals, became discouraged, and returned to their homes. Many found it difficult to associate freedom with the harsh measures applied by General Sherman's troops on their way to the sea. Frequently the inherent racism of many Union soldiers prevailed to give a grim preview of what the future promised. When such treatment was encountered, it caused a turning away from the jubilant march, and those who had received reasonably compassionate treatment in slavery returned to their former owners or camped gypsy-style to await an uncertain future.[30]

In a Savannah that was physically intact but desolate in spirit and desperately poor, the thousands of black refugees wandered about aimlessly, a problem for the city and for their eventual liberators. General Sherman sought help from General Rufus Saxton in Beaufort, who replied that he was already burdened with fifteen thousand contrabands and that more would cause much suffering. He reported, "Every cabin and house on the islands is filled to overflowing." He suggested the islands of St. Simons in Georgia and Edisto in South Carolina be protected by soldiers from a black regiment and used as likely refuges for the homeless people. General Sherman accepted the suggestion as meritorious, especially for women and children. He mistakenly believed that most, if not all, able-bodied men could be put to work by the quartermaster corps. Other Union officers thought that the blacks should be taken into the army and trained to be soldiers. One such advocate was General J. G. Foster at Hilton Head, who went directly to the chief of staff in Washington with his suggestion: "These men, just freed from long servitude, are of necessity, ignorant and improvident. Their idea of liberty is exemption alike from work and care. The streets of Savannah are full of them lying in the sun and waiting for bread without labor." General Foster sought permission to conscript the men into the army. "The future of the race is a matter of serious moment," he observed, believing that army life would educate the black men, make them self-reliant, and "develop their manhood." He proposed that the army camp become the "schoolhouse of this race."[31]

When substantiated stories of Union army excesses and of General Sherman's seeming callousness toward his followers reached Washington, there followed a long letter from headquarters and the appearance in Savannah of Secretary of War Edwin M. Stanton. The letter from General Henry W. Halleck:

PRIVATE AND CONFIDENTIAL.
HEADQUARTERS OF THE ARMY
Washington, D.C., December 30, 1864

Maj. Gen. W. T. SHERMAN,
Savannah:

MY DEAR GENERAL: I take the liberty of calling your attention, in this private and friendly way, to a matter which may possibly hereafter be of more importance to you than either of us may now anticipate. While almost every one is praising your great march through Georgia and the capture of Savannah, there is a certain class, having now great influence with the President, and very probably anticipating still more on a change of Cabinet, who are decidedly disposed to make a point against you—I mean in regard to "Inevitable Sambo." They say that you have manifested an almost criminal dislike to the negro, and that you are not willing to carry out the wishes of the Government in regard to him, but repulse him with contempt. They say you might have brought with you to Savannah more than 50,000 thus stripping Georgia of that number of laborers and opening a road by which as many more could have escaped from their masters; but that instead of this you drove them from your ranks, prevented them from following you by cutting the bridges in your rear, and thus caused the massacre of large numbers by Wheeler's cavalry.

To those who know you as I do such accusations will pass as the idle winds, for we presume that you discouraged the negroes from following you simply because you had not the means of supporting them and feared they might seriously embarrass your march. But there are others, and among them some in high authority, who think, or pretend to think, otherwise, and they are decidedly disposed to make a point against you.

I do not write this to induce you to conciliate this class of men by doing anything which you do not think right and proper and for the interest of the Government and the country, but simply to call your attention to certain things which are viewed here somewhat differently than from your standpoint. I will explain as briefly as possible: Some here think that, in view of the scarcity of labor in the South, and the probability that a part, at least, of the able-bodied slaves will be called into the military service of the rebels, it is of the greatest importance to open outlets by which the slaves can escape into our lines, and, they say, that the route you have passed over should be made the route of escape and Savannah the great place of refuge. These I know are the views of some of the leading men in the administration, and they now express dissatisfaction that you did not carry them out in your great raid.

Now that you are in possession of Savannah, and there can be no further fears about supplies, would it not be possible for you to reopen these avenues of escape for the negroes without interfering with your military operations? Could not such escaped slaves find, at least, a partial supply of food in the rice fields about Savannah, and occupation in the rice and cotton plantations on the coast?

I merely throw out these suggestions; I know that such a course would be approved by the Government, and I believe that a manifestation on your part of a desire to bring the slaves within our lines will do much to silence your opponents.

You will appreciate my motives in writing this private letter.

Yours, truly,

H. W. HALLECK.[32]

The beleaguered General Sherman replied with his characteristic frontal attack:

HDQRS, MILITARY DIVISION OF THE MISSISSIPPI,
In the Field, Savannah, January 12, 1865.

Major-General HALLECK:

MY DEAR FRIEND: I received yours of January 1 about the "negro." Since
Mr. Stanton got here we have talked over all matters freely, and I deeply
regret that I am threatened with that curse to all peace and comfort—
popularity; but I trust to bad luck enough in the future to cure that, for I
know enough of "the people" to feel that a single mistake made by some of
my subordinates will tumble down my fame into infamy.

But the nigger? Why, in God's name, can't sensible men let him alone?
When the people of the South tried to rule us through the negro, and
became insolent, we cast them down, and on that question we are strong
and unanimous. Neither cotton, the negro, nor any single interest or class
should govern us.

But I fear, if you be right that that power behind the throne is growing,
somebody must meet it or we are again involved in war with another class
of fanatics. Mr. Lincoln has boldly and well met the one attack, now let
him meet the other.

If it be insisted that I shall so conduct my operations that the negro
alone is consulted, of course I will be defeated, and then where will be
Sambo?

Don't military success imply the safety of Sambo and vice versa? Of
course that cock-and-bull story of my turning back negroes that Wheeler
might kill them is all humbug. I turned nobody back. Jeff C. Davis did at
Ebenezer Creek forbid certain plantation slaves—old men, women, and
children—to follow his column; but they would come along and he took
up his pontoon bridge, not because he wanted to leave them, but because
he wanted his bridge.

He and Slocum both tell me that they don't believe Wheeler killed one of
them. Slocum's column (30,000) reports 17,000 negroes. Now with 1,200
wagons and the necessary impediments of an army, overloaded with two-
thirds negroes, five-sixths of whom are helpless, and a large proportion of
them babies and small children, had I encountered an enemy of respectable
strength defeat would have been certain.

Tell the President that in such an event defeat would have cost him ten
thousand times the effort to overcome that it now will to meet this new and
growing pressure.

I know the fact that all natural emotions swing as the pendulum. These
southrons pulled Sambo's pendulum so far over that the danger is it will on
its return jump off its pivot. There are certain people who will find fault,
and they can always get the pretext; but, thank God, I am not running for

an office, and am not concerned because the rising generation will believe that I burned 500 niggers at one pop in Atlanta, or any such nonsense. I profess to be the best kind of a friend to Sambo, and think that on such a question Sambo should be consulted.

They gather round me in crowds, and I can't find out whether I am Moses or Aaron, or which of the prophets; but surely I am rated as one of the congregation, and it is hard to tell in what sense I am most appreciated by Sambo—in saving him from his master, or the new master that threatens him with a new species of slavery. I mean State recruiting agents. Poor negro—Lo, the poor Indian! Of course, sensible men understand such humbug, but some power must be invested in our Government to check these wild oscillations of public opinion.

The South deserves all she has got for her injustice to the negro, but that is no reason why we should go to the other extreme.

I do and will do the best I can for negroes, and feel sure that the problem is solving itself slowly and naturally. It needs nothing more than our fostering care. I thank you for the kind hint and will heed it so far as mere appearances go, but, not being dependent on votes, I can afford to act, as far as my influence goes, as a fly wheel instead of a mainspring.

With respect, &c., yours,

W. T. SHERMAN.[33]

The meetings with Secretary Stanton rankled General Sherman. The two men covered the same matters brought out in the letters from and to General Halleck and then completed their talks with an interview with twenty black churchmen, mostly former slaves who had become Baptist or Methodist preachers. The churchmen chose an articulate spokesman who said they agreed that freedom was "taking us from under the yoke of bondage and placing us where we could reap the fruit of our own labor and take care of ourselves." With General Sherman absent, the churchmen responded to Secretary Stanton's final question, which asked their feelings toward the general. Their answer was: "We have confidence in General Sherman and think that what concerns us could not be in better hands." One of the twenty abstained on that particular question.[34]

In reflecting on the unusual interview, General Sherman thought it passing strange that the secretary should catechize blacks concerning "The character of a General who had commanded a hundred thousand men in battle, had captured cities, conducted sixty-five thousand men across four hundred miles of hostile territory, and had brought tens of thousands of freedmen to a place of security, but because I had not loaded down my army by other hundreds of poor negroes, I was construed by others to be hostile to the black race."[35]

From the meetings with Secretary Stanton, and from the interview with the churchmen, came General Sherman's directive that all abandoned coastal plantations be turned over to the blacks. The first paragraph of Special Field Order No. 15 specified that a stretch of South Atlantic coast from Charleston to northern Florida be "reserved and set apart for the settlement of negroes now made free by the acts of war and the proclamation of the President of the United States." Former slaves, in groups of at least three, were each to "settle" not more than forty acres of tillable land, the implementation to be supervised by the Inspector of Settlements and Plantations, a new title bestowed upon General Rufus Saxton.[36]

An exasperated General Sherman, weary of the Negro problem, claimed his only objective in Georgia had been "to whip the rebels, to humble their pride, to follow them to their inmost recesses, and make them fear and dread us."[37]

To Pierce Butler in Philadelphia, the general's aim was deadly accurate. Field Order No. 15 seemed to spell the doom of all Major Butler had wrought on the Altamaha. The Butler slaves, wherever they may be, were free. Should they so choose, they could return to Hampton or to Butler's Island to settle their own forty-acre tract, grow cotton, rice, sugar cane for market or corn and sweet potatoes for themselves.

In those difficult months Pierce Butler suffered intensely as news of Northern victories was proclaimed in the Pennsylvania and New York press. His pro-Southern Philadelphians had dwindled to a scant and quiet few. Should his friends gather for meetings of their "Secession Society," he was apt to be bedeviled by his precocious grandson, Dan Wister, not yet five years old, singing "Hang Jeff Davis on a sour apple tree."[38] When Sherman's army was liberating Pierce Butler's Georgia slaves in 1864, he was taken before the mayor of Philadelphia for disturbing the peace by challenging Andrew Mehaffey to "fight at deadly weapons." The cause of this fracas was not as in the Schott affair, nor was it due to his pro-Southern attitude. The argument with Mehaffey was over their rights in a speculative venture in a Pennsylvania oil field.[39] It did show an unsettled condition. The challenge and arrest would surely have been a matter for Sidney George Fisher's diary, except that he had an attack of "rheumatic gout" and kept no record between November 1864 and April 1865. On April 15 he wrote of the "sad & terrible story" of the death of President Lincoln, and on May 5, a postscript:

Pierce Butler is living at the smaller of the two houses on his estate up the York Road near Branchtown. The house stands very near the road. The windows were not bowed because of Mr. Lincoln's death. He is known to sympathize with the South, but he is also known to be very quiet on the subject, even in private conversation. A number of laboring men, a few days ago, determined to attack his house. Mr. Morris Davis, a noted abolitionist who lives in the neighborhood, happened to hear of it. He went among them & had influence enough to keep them quiet.[40]

Throughout most of the war Pierce Butler had lived in Philadelphia, first at 424 Walnut Street, then at 2029 Walnut, and in 1864 and 1865 again at 424 Walnut until his move to York Farm. In January 1864 he purchased from Gabriella Butler the "fine establishment" at 1612 Walnut Street. He paid thirty-thousand dollars for the house she had wanted to sell for forty thousand dollars in 1856. His motive for the purchase was not stated—perhaps it was to be a fitting home for himself and his ever-loyal daughter Frances.[41]

Both daughters honored both parents with their own brand of love and respect, the strongest bond between any two of them being the relationship of Frances and her father. In 1864, when Pierce Butler's world was disintegrating, Frances was with her mother in England as she had been in 1862. For a time, and despite her closeness to her father and the conflict of their beliefs, mother and daughter got along very well. Sarah Wister's strong pro-Union support was aligned with her mother's, yet temperamentally, the relationship between the two was often strained and uncomfortable. Sarah continued her sewing for the soldiers and her secretarial work at the "Sanitary Commission." After the birth of her son Dan, she began a special journal that she called "The Early Years of a Child of Promise." Sometime later, she reflected on what had been recorded and gave an interesting picture of herself and the times:

> In looking back to that winter I wonder, as I sometimes do of the whole five years from 1860 to 65, how I did what I did & came through alive. I was not yet thirty & learning very slowly the lessons wh. came very fast; the strain of the war was such as nobody who did not live then can fancy; household matters were difficult, our mode of life monotonous yet irregular, & very hard to manage; my duties at the Sanitary Rooms continued; I kept up my social relations by a dreary semiannual round of visits, two or three hundred, generally on foot; of social pleasures outside my own house I had nearly none; I taught my child & had him a great deal with me; I

sewed constantly; I kept up my music, French, & German; I corresponded regularly with ten or twelve friends besides my weekly letter either to my Mother or my sister, who was then abroad, & I made a quantity of translations from the French, chiefly plays of Musset's, Feuillet's, & Pousard's, hoping to get them on the stage & make some money, but they were never accepted. My father took me to see James Wallack who was acting in Philadelphia that I might speak to him about them; Mr. Wallack very kindly read them, & said that with all their talent such plays, as Octave Feuillet's *L'urne* & *Le premier cheveu gris* for instance, cd. never be acted before an English speaking audience, on the ground of propriety!

There had been of course a constant coming & going of young officers at our house during those four years, the Newhalls, Scull, the Wisters, Chapman, Mitchell, & many more, & Dan told me nearly forty years afterwards that although not five at the time he had secretly admired them & thought of them as heroes.

In that Fanny Kemble–like reflection she also told of her reaction on hearing of Lincoln's death. She was with young Dan at the time: "He was present on the morning of the April when his father rushed into the room beside himself with the news of Lincoln's assassination. I fell into hysterics, a thing I had not done since I was a school girl; the little boy took it into his head that this was called fainting, & always had the notion that I had fainted on hearing it."[42] Her mother, in London, heard the same news "and burst into such passionate outcries and weeping that the poor man before me seemed terrified and shocked beyond the power of speaking."[43]

THE LONG WAR had inflicted its sorrow and tragedy on the Roswell King family also. Julia, the widow of Roswell King, Jr., was living at her home in Liberty County and saw six of her sons join the Confederate army. Julian Clarence and Bayard Hand King were captured when Sherman's soldiers swept through Georgia. William Henry King, who had attended Yale before the war to keep alive his grandfather's Connecticut heritage, was killed at Sayler's Creek in Virginia but three days before General Robert E. Lee surrendered at Appomattox. Of him it was said, "the most promising and most loved has fallen." A seventh son, John Butler King, named for John Butler and born the year after his death in Mexico in 1847, was but thirteen years old in 1861 or would have enlisted with his brothers. The town of Roswell, the true manifestation of the elder Roswell King's ingenuity, was raided by the Sherman army. Although fine homes were spared, the Roswell Manufacturing Company's cotton mill, called "the Factory," and their flour mill in nearby Lebanon were destroyed. Both mills had supplied the Confederacy and thus were destined to burn. General Sherman proclaimed, "Their utter destruction is right and meets my entire approval." In addition, he ordered the owners and more than four hundred employees, who were mostly white women, arrested for treason. When a subordinate showed some reluctance, the general reiterated: "I repeat my orders that you arrest all people, male and female, connected with those factories, no matter what the clamor, and let them foot it under guard to Marietta whence I will send them by cars to the North." He acknowledged that the poor women would probably "make a howl" over their fifteen-mile march to Marietta. And they did. The Roswell "Factory" had owned eleven slaves in its own right, but such was not noticed in the official reports.[44]

The "grievous civil war" that Fanny Kemble thought promised the "salvation" of America ended in April 1865, the country torn but the Union preserved. The slave's "day of deliverance" she had prayed for had come. Sarah Wister's hope that "some lives may be lost in battle" was fulfilled— more than 600,000, but she was thinking of Confederates. Their toll was 250,000. Young Frances Butler's fear of danger was justified. The war Pierce Butler thought would not be fought, was. The plantations he believed unlikely to be troubled, were. The produce of Hampton and Butler's Island helped to sustain black soldiers fighting for the North. The city of Savannah became a Christmas gift to President Lincoln from General Sherman. A few days later he offered much of the coast of Georgia to freed slaves—in forty-acre segments—the Butler plantations included. The slaves Pierce Butler had sold in 1859 were free, and those not sold, were free also—with more than four million others.[45]

As the war ended, Fanny Kemble wrote: "In countless thousands of lamentable graves the bitter wrong lies buried—atoned for by a four years fratricidal war: the beautiful Southern land is lifting its head from the disgrace of slavery and the agony of its defense. May its free future days surpass in prosperity (as they surely will a thousand-fold) those of its former perilous pride of privilege—of race supremacy and subjugation."[46]

Chapter 22

Why Be Free?

T HE WAR'S END and the freedom of the slaves may well have caused Fanny Kemble to ponder a day in 1839 when, as Fanny Butler, her visit to the Georgia plantations neared its end and she talked of slavery with ladies of a neighboring plantation on St. Simons Island. Faced with her vehement opposition to the slave system and to the stated beliefs that slavery was justifiable where administered with "kindness and indulgence," one neighbor, Mrs. Mary Abbot, came around to an admission that perhaps the young Mrs. Butler was right. She may have been led to Georgia "by Providence to be the means of some great change in the condition of the poor colored people."[1]

Whatever Fanny Kemble's role, the "great change" had come about. Thousands of blacks newly clad in freedom's ill-fitting cloak moved aimlessly in a search for sustenance and shelter. The desire to congregate led large numbers to cities where but few found work and but few sought labor of any kind. "Freedom" to many was freedom from toil. Women who did work were seamstresses, house servants, and washerwomen. Men found work who had been ostlers or plantation artisans—carpenters, coopers, masons, and smiths.

In a Savannah that General Sherman had refrained from burning, the white people who before the war had fed and clothed their slaves and who had employed free Negroes possessed neither the means nor the desire to meet the needs of the destitute blacks who swept into the city in the wake of the Union army. With Confederate currency worthless, their own straits were desperate. Even before the war had ended, Savannah's suffering was recognized in the North. The cities of New York, Boston, and later, Philadelphia, sent ships with generous cargoes of "breadstuffs, provisions, and other necessities of life" to a people "reduced to a dead level of poverty."[2]

The end of slavery and the prospects of operating farms and plantations with free labor were faced with despair by most planters. Some few believed emancipation relieved the white man of his responsibility for the black, that land worked by free black men would gain the value they had represented as slaves.[3] Such must have been the belief of the one referred to in an early postwar entry in the Sidney George Fisher diary:

> Pierce Butler has been offered $20,000 a year for one half of his land in Georgia, more than the whole of it with 400 Negroes ever produced before. He has been so unwise as to refuse the offer and is going, or says he is going, down to manage the estate himself, in which case, as Wister said, he will soon make ducks & drakes of it. He has an unfortunate propensity for attempting to manage business, comprised with a total incapacity for such work. Yet fortune seems to favor him. Some years before the war, having become embarrassed by stock speculation, he sold his Negroes for $400,000, enough to pay his debts. This left him a good estate, tho a small income. He had the land in Georgia & Butler Place. Some years ago, by the death of his niece, Mrs. McCallester, he got his brother's share of the estate, less Mrs. Butler's income, & now his land in the South has become more valuable than ever, because of the war.[4]

True, there was a propensity for some Northerners to believe fortunes were to be made by an infusion of capital into the destitute Southland. It was a belief then shared by Pierce Butler, who had shed his Sherman-induced despondency, and who went South with his loyal daughter Frances, then twenty-eight years old. Word had come from Georgia that many of the former slaves had returned to Butler's Island where they "were badly off, short of provisions, and would starve if something were not done for them." In March 1866 the two Butlers left Philadelphia to "look after our property in Georgia and see what could be done about it."[5]

That emancipation's "great change" reached out far beyond the South was well noted in the diary of Fisher, who often sounded the alarm: "The American people worship a villanous Mumbo Jumbo, or Boo-Ghoo-Boo, called universal suffrage. Already, in worship of this idol, they have invited the refuse pauper population of Europe to come over & govern them. Already they have bowed down before the German & the Celt, &

now they are about to place their necks under the foot of the Negro & to abdicate their rightful power over their country and its destiny." He expressed additional thoughts on the subject after dining with a young Confederate veteran in Philadelphia:

> Sam. Griffin here to dinner and to lodge. Told him that I hoped to see Negroes of the South in the position of a peasantry, working for wages & enjoying all civil rights but not the right of suffrage, but that I feared the southern people would never permit this. He said he thought they would, what did I mean by civil rights? "Why," said I, "the right to acquire property, to make contracts, to sue & be sued, to give testimony in court, to work for whom he pleased, & to go where he pleased, and the right of self-defence. Would the southern people ever permit them to exercise the last? Suppose a Negro man assaulted & struck by a white man should strike back, what would the white man do?" "Most men," he said, "would kill him." "And public opinion would justify the act?" "Certainly," he said, "more than justify, almost require it." This shows how much must be changed in the South before the Negro can become equal with the white before the law, and there is a long way from that to Negro suffrage.

Fisher believed the Republicans' condescension toward the Negro drove many from their party "into the ranks of the democracy." To get a first-hand reaction he queried one of the black workers on the Fisher farm on the Sassafras River in Maryland:

> I asked Ned what the blacks in the neighborhood thought of Negro suffrage, & his answer in my judgment tells the whole truth of the matter throughout the South. He said, "Well, Master Fisher, very few of them care anything about it or know what it means. The most of them would not vote if they could. A few talk about voting & say they have the right, but the notion has been put into their heads by white folks." He said that the gentlemen in the neighborhood were not so friendly to the Negroes as they used to be before they were free.[6]

Pierce Butler and his daughter traveled South by rail through Richmond, where Frances visited the Confederate cemetery and "found the grave I was looking for." Both were shocked to see the "ruin and desolation" that Sherman's troops had left in South Carolina. In Savannah, at Christ Church, she was saddened to find the congregation in somber mourning, so many "mere girl's faces, shaded by deep crepe veils and widow's caps." The Butlers were received in Savannah with "open arms," and Frances's room was filled with flowers. Many thanks were offered to her for "what I did for the soldiers during the war." She protested that what she had done was but little. "Oh, yes but your heart was with us."[7]

From Darien, Pierce Butler went alone to Butler's Island to reconnoiter. There he found many of the former slaves, including seven of those he had sold at the Ten Broeck racecourse eight years before. The Butler's Island blacks, less venturesome than those who chose to gather in the cities, had joined others who had been their neighbors on the Altamaha estuary plantations to make new homes in the old and familiar settings. They had returned from their upcountry refuges, walking along country roads "in twos and threes, carrying with them their belongings tied in immense bundles on their heads." Some had even drifted on rafts down the Oconee and the Ocmulgee to the Altamaha, and then on downstream to the abandoned plantations they had worked as slaves.[8]

Frances Butler wrote that her father had been received affectionately by the black people who had agreed to work on a crop-sharing basis, the owners and the workers each to receive one-half. The agreement between the Butlers and their workers was subjected to scrutiny and approval by the Freedmen's Bureau, a federal agency that gave the Butlers some trouble but also brought authority into play when owners and workers became mired in misunderstanding and disagreement. Fortunately for Pierce Butler, the difficult year of 1865 had run its course. The promise of Sherman's Special Field Order No. 15 had faded, and disappointment over the false expectation that plantations and farms were to be divided into black-owned forty-acre tracts, each with its own mule, was but a part of the disillusionment that followed their "day of jubilee." The realization that freedom's gains were limited had come with an onslaught of hunger, illness, and death. Pierce Butler found a willingness to work, or so it seemed, in the spring of 1866.[9]

The house on Butler's Island that Frances Butler had known since childhood was stripped of all its contents, the odds and ends of furnishings— caned and Windsor chairs, pine tables, featherbeds, the mahogany card table at which her mother had penned parts of her fateful journal, all gone. Pierce Butler, who was accustomed to better things, slept on the floor with a "piece of wood" for a pillow while covered with "negro blankets." Food was scarce except for the natural bounty the island offered. One of the men shot a wild turkey and presented it to Frances. Near the house magnolias and roses bloomed; the orange trees were in blossom and with fig and peach trees gave promise of abundant fruit. Also abundantly present were fleas, sandflies, and mosquitoes.[10]

So difficult had been the long years of war and the initial year of liberation there seemed a spirit of contentment among those who were living on the island. It comforted the Butlers to discover that old people who had remained on the plantations had protected and saved sheep and cows, that an old couple who at Hampton had sold chickens to a "Yankee Captain," brought in five dollars in silver coins. Frances Butler was justifiably emotional when on a Sunday morning following church in Darien nearly four hundred came to see "the Missus" and to shake her hand. She told them: "Well, you know you are free and your own masters now." Their response: "No missus, we belong to you, we be yours as long as we lib."[11]

The Butlers were confronted with the task of restructuring the plantation and its work force. They agreed to support children for a period of three years after birth, as the parents would most likely be able to take over by that time. For the very old who lived on the plantation and were beyond work, the care and protection was to be "till they die."[12]

The work force was divided into gangs as before. "Captains," not drivers, directed their tasks. At Butler's Island the crop was rice, but late planting further delayed by restorative work on banks, canals, and trunks gave promise of a poor harvest that first year. Also, Pierce Butler was discouraged to find the willingness to work was measured. Almost half the force left the fields by one o'clock and all were out by three. The order and the discipline of the prewar plantation had disappeared with the lash.

As long had been their custom, plantation owners departed from their rice plantations with the advent of hot weather. So it was with Pierce Butler and Frances. In May they moved from their sparsely furnished house on the "rice island" to a healthier and more comfortable home on the "Point" at Hampton. Pierce Butler must have been reminded of a similar move in 1839 when he and his family embarked for St. Simons on the plantation boat *Water Lily*.

> Which looked like a soldier's baggage wagon and an emigrant transport
> combined. Our crew consisted of eight men. Forward in the bow were
> miscellaneous livestock, pots, pans, household furniture, kitchen utensils,
> and an indescribable variety of heterogeneous necessaries. Enthroned upon
> beds, bedding, tables, and other chattels, sat that poor pretty chattel

The old plantation house on Butler's Island where Pierce Butler, his daughter Frances, and later her husband James Wentworth Leigh lived. (1915 photograph, Amelia M. Watson "Kemble" Collection, Lenox Library.)

The back of the house shows the improvements made by Pierce Butler for the comfort of his daughter Frances. (1915 photograph, Amelia M. Watson "Kemble" Collection, Lenox Library.)

Psyche, with her small chattel children. Midship sat the two tiny free women, and myself, and in the stern Mr. Butler steering. And "all in the blue unclouded weather" we rowed down the huge Stream, the men keeping time and tune to their oars with extemporaneous chants of adieu to the rice island and it denizens.

So wrote his wife in that "poisonous" *Journal*. One of the "tiny free women" was his daughter Frances, the other, her older sister, Sarah.[13]

The trip between the plantations was not so well organized as in 1839. Pierce Butler overslept, thwarting a tide-established departure time four hours earlier, and as a consequence caused their boats to ground on mudflats and sandbars and to be caught in drenching thunder squalls. At Hampton, and on the other St. Simons plantations, the attitude differed but slightly from that at Butler's Island. Between five and six hundred blacks were already at work, most contentedly so, for wages under contract to white planters. Those continuing to work for themselves on what the Freedmen's Bureau called "Eighteen valid land grants" were "doing indifferently." At Hampton the Butlers found fifty men and women who were respectful but quietly disappointed when Pierce Butler laid claim to the land they thought had come to them with freedom. Pressure from white planters had prompted the federal government to disallow the so-called "Sherman titles" held by the blacks. General Sherman himself attested: "I knew of course we could not convey title to land and merely provided 'possessory' titles, to be good as long as War and our Military Power lasted." Hampton blacks, through greater contact with white people before, and with military forces during the war, had "tasted the tree of knowledge," and as Frances Butler believed, had been "always the most intelligent." As they reluctantly began work under Bram, a former driver who had been one of the Hampton slaves sold in Savannah in 1859, one of the men asked, why be free "if he had to work harder than when he was a slave?" The crop was long staple sea island cotton, and Pierce Butler's hopes were high it would bring a return to the prosperous times his grandfather had so long enjoyed.[14]

In June 1866 the Butlers attended the funeral of the scholarly and versatile James Hamilton Couper. The war had been a conflict to which he was opposed and had brought death to two of his sons. His slaves had been liberated, his fortune lost. John Lord and Hamilton Couper were killed in Virginia, and both had been known to Frances and Sarah Butler. The funeral of their father was held in the vandalized church at Frederica.

It brought forth an angry outburst from Frances: "Someday justice will be done, and the Truth shall be heard above the political din of slander and lies, and the Northern people shall see things as they are, and not through the dark veil of envy, hatred and malice."[15]

A second death that eventful summer was also noted by Frances Butler and her father: Carolina, the oldest of the Butler people, had died at Hampton. He had been one of the several who had served Major Butler as a body servant. Holding to the promise to care for the old, Frances became ill herself while attending the dying man on several successive nights. Pierce Butler marked his burial place with a gravestone, unusual recognition for slave or freedman:

CAROLINA
DIED JUNE 26, 1866
AGED 100 YEARS
A long life, marked by devotion
to his Heavenly Father and
Fidelity to his Earthly Masters

The surname gained by Carolina with emancipation was not cut into the stone.[16]

In July, Frances Butler felt the effects of her illness and, with some fear for the safety and well-being of her father, left him at Hampton to return to Philadelphia. Although her fears were directed toward his physical condition, she may well have been concerned for his financial health. Her presence in Philadelphia in the following winter was noted by Sidney George Fisher:

> Went to Hollis' office & there found Miss Fanny Butler. She has left the house on the York Road & is with her sister now, but on Monday she is going to join her father on the plantation in Georgia. He is obliged to stay there, and from what Hollis has told me (he manages Butler's affairs here) Butler is again in trouble about his money matters, which is a thing of course with him & would be if he were worth a million. He undertook to manage the plantation himself last year & it did not pay expenses.[17]

"Hollis" was Peter C. Hollis, Pierce Butler's attorney who had administered the haphazard Butler finances. Indicative of the pressures surrounding Pierce Butler in his attempt to reconstitute Hampton and Butler's Island and of his constant need for money is a record of withdrawals from the John Butler estate for which he was a trustee. In the short time between July 3, 1866, and July 29, 1867, letters to Mr. Hollis authorized withdrawal of amounts totaling twenty thousand dollars, all of which was transferred to Pierce Butler's personal account. The debits to the John Butler estate followed the sale of stocks and bonds, and although the deaths of Elizabeth Butler McAllister and her son returned the estate's share of the Georgia plantations to him and left him an heir to the entire estate, John Butler's widow's income was diminished by Pierce Butler's sale and use of the proceeds of the earning assets of the estate. The confidence John Butler had expressed when he named his brother as a trustee again was proved to be faulty.[18]

The first crops were failures, just as the Butlers had feared they would be. In addition to increasing his financial woes, the inability to share earnings with the blacks further strained the tenuous relationship between Pierce Butler and those who worked his lands. The poor crops led to a change from sharing to actual wages, a system that brought greater satisfaction to the workers but one that also required even more of the capital that was in such short supply.

"Miss Fanny Butler" did return to Georgia the winter of 1866–1867, going directly to the house at Hampton, for her father had not yet made the Butler's Island residence sufficiently habitable. She found as many as three hundred people working the two places, and notwithstanding the need for constant supervision that exasperated Pierce Butler, there seemed to be a good chance for successful crops of cotton and rice. Frances shared the frustrations of her father in directing their "employees." "I generally found that if I wanted a thing done I first had to tell the Negroes to do it, then show them how, and finally do it myself."[19]

A pleasant break in the Butlers' hectic existence came when Frances and her father were visited by Sarah Wister, who was accompanied by her seven-year-old son, Dan. It was a visit noted by Sidney George Fisher. "Bet" was Mrs. Fisher:

> Dr. Wister here in the morning. Bet doing well. He had his little son they call Dan with him, a remarkably bright, intelligent boy. Dan, some weeks ago, went with his mother to pay a visit to her father at his plantation in Georgia. Before she went, Dan's father told him that the Negroes would not call him Massa now, but Bub, at which Dan was very indignant. The morning after they arrived at Savannah, Dan went out into the entry, where two clean, well dressed Negro women met him & immediately exclaimed,

"Oh what a nice young Massa, good morning young Massa." "That is the way," said Dan, "in which I always expect to be addressed." Recollecting this, I said to him this morning, "Well, Dan, I suppose you saw plenty of Negroes at the plantation." "Yes indeed." "And how did they treat you? Very politely I suppose." "They treated me very kindly," said Dan, with emphasis. I have no doubt they did, for they are the old family Negroes who have come back to work for Butler & are said to work very well. Butler is very busy on the plantation & Wister thinks will do very well, probably make a great deal of money. He likes the life & the occupation & expects to remain permanently in the South.

Many years later Owen Wister recalled the observations of one of the older plantation workers "who actually remembered Major Pierce Butler and gave a graphic description of his bad temper and his high boots." He said the former slave seemed to like the Major "in spite of his short comings."[20]

For the second consecutive year Frances Butler remained in Georgia beyond the time considered safe for a white person to be on a rice plantation. She honored this premise by living at Hampton but of necessity made many trips "to and fro" Butler's Island. Her father had no alternative. The demands at one place or the other called for his presence, and as a consequence he was hard-pressed to find respite from a regimen that had tested the stamina of two such stalwarts as Roswell King, Senior and Junior. On May 23, 1867, Frances celebrated her twenty-ninth birthday, received gifts from many of her workers, and was honored by a rousing "shout" for the occasion. Until the eve of her departure in late July she did her best to relieve Pierce Butler of the burdens that he was unable to shoulder.[21]

The rice plantation illness the white people feared was malaria, a disease then called by several names. "Autumnal" or "summer sickness," or "fever of the country," was properly laid to wet marshes and rice fields and improperly to "unwholesome vapor and miasmata" arising from those places in the heat of summer, in particular, after dark. The unrecognized scourge was the anopheles mosquito that carried the malaria parasite with devastating effect, and which did "arise" from the standing water of the marsh and the rice field. The blacks, who were certainly plagued by other rice culture-induced hazards, fortunately developed a "large degree of immunity" to the disease that caused plantation owners such apprehension. Roswell King, Jr., had believed the young did not possess that immunity and for that reason advocated the removal of children from Butler's Island to high ground, as he did in the summer of 1835. Altamaha planters shared the widespread belief that danger of infection came with nightfall and as a consequence made strenuous effort to be away from low wetlands before dark. Pierce Butler neither enjoyed the immunity of the blacks nor did he believe he could unshackle himself from planting responsibilities to avoid overnight stays on Butler's Island in the dangerous season. In mid-August 1867 he became ill and being aware of the seriousness of his trouble called on Liverpool Hazzard, a young Butler boatman, to row him across to Darien in search of help from Dr. James Holmes. He was taken to a house he owned on the Ridge on the outskirts of the war-wrecked town. There, far from family and friends, his life ended. The *Savannah Daily News and Herald* reported that "his disease was congestive chills, and his death was sudden and unexpected." His body was given a temporary burial in an "enclosure" on the Ridge near the site of his death.[22]

An ailing Sidney George Fisher read of Pierce Butler's death while taking the waters at Saratoga Springs. He wrote his wife, asking for particulars, and when back in Philadelphia in late September thought the matter of sufficient importance to record in his diary:

> Pierce Butler died at his plantation in Georgia of the country fever. He was a man of strongly marked character with some good qualities & many faults. He led a very unsatisfactory life & threw away great advantages. He was handsome, clever, most gentlemanlike in his manners, but uneducated, obstinate, prejudiced, & passionate. His daughters are in great grief. Mrs. Kemble has returned to this country, I suppose to live here with her daughters, or rather near them, for I doubt her being able to live in the same house with either. She will therefore form part of the society of the neighborhood & a person of her strongly marked character & powerful will must have considerable influence for good or ill.[23]

Fanny Kemble had indeed returned to Philadelphia. She had boarded a westbound steamship within a week of hearing that Pierce Butler had died. With her English maid she moved into the Germantown house of Sarah and Dr. Wister's, insisting on paying fifty dollars a week for board. Sarah Wister's grief and the visitation of mother and maid caused "physical & nervous shock." To Sarah, the maid was "a treacherous mischiefmaker." Sarah became ill, suffered a failure of memory, and became so agitated over the inability to be alone that she wrote her sister: "I wd gladly pass the winter in Siberia if I cd have solitude there."[24]

Fanny Kemble was always an interesting subject for the Fisher diary.

> Mrs. Kemble is at Dr. Wister's & most of her acquaintances have called to see her. She is reported as being mild & gentle & willing to be pleased. Bet confesses that she must call too, but dreads the visit as much as if she were going to have a tooth pulled. Certainly, Mrs. Kemble is a person of over-whelming vitality, & it is not easy to resist the magnetism of her presence. Nevertheless, she is a grand creature, full of intellect & passion, cultivated & accomplished, with all her faculties strengthened & trained by exercise & endowed with power which is the fruit of the combined influences of genius, culture, and performance. She is distinguished, she is famous, she has added lustre to her name by what she has done. She has written books that have been justly admired; in her youth, as an actress, she drew enthusi-astic applause, night after night for years together, from crowded houses in the best theatres of England and America, & more recently she has been able not only to win her daily bread, which was what she sought, but wealth by her readings of Shakespeare, unequalled in force & beauty by any artist before or since. What a giant is such a woman compared to ladies of ordinary experience, however clever & cultivated & elegant in person & manners. What wonder is it that they should be afraid of her. . . . And now this woman, divorced years ago by reason of her own fiery & impetuous temper & her husband's dogged & iron will, comes here as soon as he is in his grave, prosperous, victorious, & triumphant, to play the part of mother to his & her children, & to live, if she pleases, in his ancestral home—a success fairly achieved by courage, energy, & genius, making determined battle against adverse powers & finally subduing them.[25]

Fanny Kemble had little to say regarding her own feelings on Pierce Butler's death and seemed unaware of any untoward intrusion into the lives of the Wisters. There was nothing in her letters to show she recog-nized the distress of her daughters. Her mission was to lend support by being near, for there was no pretense of dispensing comfort. As with daughter Frances at the war's end, it was again a sorrow she did not wish to share.

Unlike her sister, Frances Butler was not overwhelmed with grief. Her immediate concern was to protect and to continue what she and her father had begun in postwar Georgia. The Butler agents in Savannah had sent distress signals to Philadelphia urging attention to the plantations. With energy and determination mindful of the one for whom she was named, Frances Butler responded by enlisting the aid of her brother-in-law Owen Jones Wister, and together they traveled south to put things in order. According to her mother, she had been urged not to go by family and friends. Fanny Kemble believed that whatever might be accomplished by the winter's stay of her daughter in Georgia would be jeopardized following her departure from the plantations in the late spring. She believed the contract to work would be ignored by the black people, who, in her daughter's absence, would "leave the crop to take care of itself. She has simply deferred the settlement of the question, which is most important to have speedily settled, namely whether these poor people can be made to understand that freedom means leave to labor or leave to starve."[26] She said the presence of Frances in Georgia prolonged the old feeling of dependency when the great need was to make the former slaves realize their new position as laborers. Fanny Kemble knew her daughter to be misguided in thinking there would be a return to the successes of the past. She knew also the relationship between the blacks and the whites that brought such about had vanished forever.

In a curious inversion of the traditional Butler fascination with wills, Pierce Butler died intestate, thus his estate was divided equally between his daughters. The appointed administrators were Peter C. Hollis and Dr. Wister's cousin, William Wister. They filed an inventory showing cash and investments exclusive of real estate totaling $56,221.86. In the period of their administration from September 1867 until October 1868, they settled the "decendent's" many debts and obligations, the largest being for the completion of houses under construction at Fifth and Callowhill streets, Philadelphia. There was an unusual payment to the "heir of H. R. W. Hill," a penal sum arising from a suit in the U.S. District Court in Washington, and also a settlement with John Butler's estate in which $1,975 was paid for "use, occupation, or planting" of Butler's Island, half of which came back to Pierce Butler's estate as income. Other receipts were mostly insignificant—a few small dividends from the remnants of the speculative binge that prompted the sale of his slaves in 1859, the rent and sale of church pews at Epiphany and St. Marks, and the sale of 933 shares of North Carbondale Coal Company stock to the president of the company for two dollars a share. The inventory of personal property filed with the Register of Wills consisted of the contents of the house at York Farm and that of Butler Place. There were "belongings" at his office, at the homes of his brother-in-law, Dr. Alfred Elwyn, at "Mr. Hopkin's," and at the office of Mr. Hollis. There was a preponderance of books and wine. Scattered about were 2,104 volumes of which only three were listed by name—Audubon's *Quadrupeds,* Catlin's *North American Tribes,* and Johnson's *Dictionary.* There were 250 "miscellaneous classics" in the storeroom at York Farm. Wine and its paraphernalia were also scattered about. There were 150 wine glasses, 15 decanters, 20 empty demijohns, and 200 empty bottles at York Farm where there was a ready supply of wine and rum. The total amount of wine came to 643 gallons, most in demijohns. Of this, 473 gallons was in the cellar at the office of Mr. Hollis. The wine was valued at ten dollars per gallon. None was identified, and if any of the vaunted Madeiras of Major Butler's were there, they were not mentioned. Among other personal items were one thousand small cigars, two ruby and diamond rings, one watch and gold chain, twenty dollars worth of fancy costumes, two flutes, three music stands, and thirty-seven orange and lemon trees that had been imported to Butler Place from Butler's Island by Fanny Kemble when she was a Butler.[27]

Completely apart from the administration, which was of public record, was a private agreement between Sarah and Dr. Wister, Frances Butler, Peter Hollis, and Gabriella Butler in which a deficiency of approximately $27,500 in the estate of John Butler was acknowledged. The agreement, dated October 8, 1867, recognized the obligation of the Pierce Butler estate to cover the shortage pending a determination of the exact amount.[28]

With the management of the plantations thrust upon her, Frances Butler sought advice through her friends the Pringles in Charleston. There she bought a "planting machine" as a means of alleviating some of her problems with black labor. She wrote Mr. Hollis to tell him of the purchase and related how South Carolina planters, affluent before the war, were faced with "the idle, insolent conduct of the negroes in that part of the country who will not work for any inducement." She added: "I cannot feel thankful enough for the comparative good conduct & industry of our people & the only question that bothers me is how long will it last."

In another letter Frances Butler said the South Carolinians had little time to talk of politics. They talked of one, and only one, subject. That was "rice, rice, rice"—a subject on which Frances Butler could also hold forth at great length.[29]

Chapter 23

🐚 Massa Jimmy

IN THE YEARS following the death of her father, Frances Butler
encountered difficulties never envisioned by Major Butler, the
Roswell Kings, and the others who had operated the Georgia plantations
before emancipation of the slaves. The vagaries of weather, market, river
level, crop failure, and insect infestation were magnified by the vagaries
inherent in the work force of the new era. Indicative of the "great change"
that came with the end of slavery is a comparison of the "official" 1870
census with that taken ten years before. In the last of the government's
pre-freedom counts there was a deliberate separation of the free and the
enslaved. The latter were counted on special forms for slaves. Names were
ignored, but age, sex, and color were shown. The McIntosh County census taker was unusually careful in isolating certain plantations in the
county from a general list that might have encompassed a large geograph-
ical division, as was done in Glynn County. Thus, the records of the count
for Butler's Island are distinct and available, while those for Hampton are
lost in a commingling of all inhabitants of St. Simons Island.

The 1860 census of McIntosh County gave Butler's Island a population
of 505 slaves, all of whom were shown as "black," and all of whom were
shown to have been owned by the estate of John Butler. The same census
of Glynn County shows no Butler slaves, as such. The few then living at
Hampton were either included with those of other plantations on St. Simons Island, ignored, or perhaps counted with the McIntosh County
slaves of Butler's Island.

The 1870 post-freedom census demonstrates the great change. No
longer were the blacks counted apart from white people. Color classifica-
tions were enlarged to include "White, Black, Mulatto, Chinese and In-

dian." Again, the McIntosh County official was careful to show Butler's Island as a distinct entity, and this time when listing black people, he included first and last names, occupations, age, sex, color, and birthplace. Other questions were asked in a general way to reveal interesting statistics. In June 1870 there were 216 blacks living on Butler's Island, and those who worked were under the supervision of the lone white person shown as a resident—John Nightingale, age twenty-six, the plantation manager whose occupation was shown as "farmer." The 216 Negroes were shown as 57 family groups, and often one man or one woman was the sole representative of a family. Occupations were listed as "works on farm" for most of the men—a designation that would have covered almost the entire slave population, including men, women, and older children, in the 1860 census. Most women were shown as "keeps house," and the children, "at school." Dandy, who had taken the last name Stewart, and who had been a blacksmith on the prewar plantation, retained the title given him in the 1859 sale. He held firmly to "Engineer and Blacksmith on rice farm." Sambo became Sambo Swift, "job carpenter"; and Captain became Captain James, "overseer of farm," readily taking on a designation so recently scorned. Chatham Dennis preferred to be called "foreman on farm."

Five mulattoes lived on Butler's Island, namely, Henry Frazier, Renty and Sarah Crawford and their children, James and Dorcas. Renty claimed to be the son of Roswell King, Jr., and was generally acknowledged as such. The relationship was revealed and discussed by Pierce and Fanny Butler at the time of their visit to the plantations in 1839. Renty Crawford, fifty-five years old in 1870, would have been twenty-four in 1839. All other Negroes on Butler's Island in 1870 were shown to be "black."

The newly acquired surnames were an interesting mix of the names of white planters and families throughout the low country—Wylly, Hazzard, Potts, Goulding, Gould, Lane, Cooper, Palmer, Young, Mungin, Waldburgh, Frazier, and several others. Quash and his wife Abbar (Auber) kept faith with their African heritage, except that the census taker heard their surname as "Quarker" instead of Quacco as it should have been. George and Martha could have taken the name of the distinguished slave owner at Mount Vernon but instead were listed as George and Martha Stoutenburg, after well-to-do white people in Darien. There were no Middletons and but one Bull—Diana, who was seventy-five. Six separate family groups or individuals chose to be called Butler:

Name	Age	Occupation
Katy Butler	90	At home
Mollie Butler	80	At home
Tenah Butler	50	At home
Sandy Butler	90	At home
Cudjoe	45	At home
William Butler	55	At home
Patty	65	Keeping house
Flora	40	Works on farm
Rose	8	At home
Willis	7	At home
Charles	4	At home
Judy Butler	75	At home

The last of these, Judy Butler, was shown to be blind. None of the Butler's Islanders were listed as "Deaf, Dumb, Insane, or Idiotic." The designation "At home" indicated unemployment except for the very young and those who enjoyed the "till they die" pensions. Frances Butler was offended by the unemployed. She noted that those who did no work seemed to be as healthy and well fed as those workers who were paid twelve dollars a month and received full rations.

Liverpool Hazzard, the young man who had rowed the stricken Pierce Butler from Butler's Island to Darien in August 1867, and who sang boat songs for Mrs. Lydia Parrish in the late 1930s, was listed as a "farm laborer," age eighteen.

Almost none of the blacks could read or write, most were born in Georgia, a few of the older ones in South Carolina, and twenty showed either father or mother as foreign born, meaning Africa or the West Indies.

If the most obvious difference between the census of 1860 and 1870 was the change in status as evidenced by the new surnames and the inclusion of black with white, equally significant was the number of able-bodied men and women, the "at homes," who could demonstrate new-found independence by choosing to do no work at all.[1]

Frances Butler shared something from both her mother and her father in her attitude toward the black people. As her father had firmly believed, she thought emancipation to have been a huge mistake. Her brief experience before the war when the Butler plantations were worked by slaves

Habersham Mungin and Sambo Swift, former Butler slaves who gained surnames with emancipation. (1915 photograph, Amelia M. Watson "Kemble" Collection, Lenox Library.)

and then her experience with free blacks in the peace that followed were proof enough to sustain that belief all of her days. From her mother she had somehow absorbed a generous portion of her crusading spirit and with it a desire to improve the lot of the people they had so recently owned. This trait went well beyond her father's detached selfishness. At no time did she purposely attempt to exploit the blacks, as her principal goal was to share the profits from crop production with both owners and workers. Yet, there seemed to be no end of problems in her move toward that end. The first obstacle was immediately encountered when she and Dr. Wister tried to settle accounts with the workers who had failed to produce marketable crops during that difficult first year. When, at last, some six thousand dollars was paid to the workers, the young "Missus" was disturbed to find that a few used their two hundred to three hundred dollars in earnings to purchase land of their own in Darien or the nearby pine woods. The discontent brought on by the settlement of accounts made the signing of renewal contracts more difficult. The blacks who persisted in limiting their time at work and in the fields, who refused the arduous but necessary tasks of ditching and banking, and the many "at homes" who "had a fixed notion in their minds that liberty meant idleness," tended to frustrate the intense young woman.[2]

The frustrations notwithstanding, Frances Butler set about living up to her bargain to give the people better lives. The cabins in which they lived were repaired, cleaned, and whitewashed, and one of the four-room hospitals on Butler's Island described so vividly by her mother was converted to a combination school, church, and home for aged women and a confinement place for pregnant women. The schoolmaster was a young black from Philadelphia. On a particularly difficult day she wrote her mother in Philadelphia. The letter was long and despairing. Her discontent centered on those she had been trying to help: "Last year they humbugged me completely by their expression of affection and desire to work for me, but now that the novelty has entirely worn off and they have lost their old habits of work, the effects of freedom are beginning to tell, and everywhere sullen unwillingness to work is visible, and all around us people are discussing how to get other labourers in the place of negroes."[3] Her mother's reaction came not in a letter to Frances Butler, but in one sent to a friend in Scotland:

I had a letter from F——— to-day from the plantation, written in rather a depressed state of spirits. The old leaven of personal attachment, which survived for a short while among the negroes after their emancipation, or perhaps the natural timidity of absolute ignorance which possessed and paralyzed them at first, is rapidly passing away, and they are asserting their natural and divine right to cultivate happiness (that is, idleness) instead of cotton and rice at any price; and F——, who over-estimated the strength of their old superstitions, is beginning to despond very much. For my own part, the result seems to me the only one to have been rationally expected, and I have no hope whatever that as long as one man, once a planter, and one man, once a slave, survives, any successful cultivation of the southern estates will be achieved. Indeed, it seems to me most probable that, like other regions long cursed by the evil deeds of their inhabitants, the planta-tions will be gradually restored to the wild treasury of nature, and the land "enjoy its Sabbaths" as a wilderness, peopled with snakes, for perhaps a good half century yet. I do not know why the roots of slavery should be grubbed out of the soil a day sooner. It is unlucky, no doubt, for the present holders of southern property, but then the world has laws, and I do not know that the planters of the southern states were sufficiently mer-itorious folk to have earned a miracle, especially a very immoral one, for their heirs.[4]

Frances Butler had expected no miracles, but she had put great faith in the love and respect the people had professed for her dead father. On realization that such loyalty was nonexistent, her tolerance was noticeably diminished. As if their refusal to work was not enough, she found fault with lesser things. Their "black wooly heads" became too ugly to look upon, and she urged the women to wear the "pretty, picturesque head handkerchiefs" they had worn as slaves. A greater problem was the annoy-ing proximity of the Butler's Island residence to the old "No. 1 Quarters" where many of them lived. She ordered the occupants and their cabins moved to a more distant location, "where I can neither see, hear or smell them."[5]

The head kerchiefs and the removal of the quarters were but manifesta-tions of Frances Butler's realization that her task of bringing the workers around to dependability was all but hopeless. When they refused to "go into the ditch" to repair the rice-field banks and canals, she hired a group of hungry immigrants who had come to Savannah from Ireland and to whom any work was desirable. Of the former slaves who paid no heed to the new work force in their midst, she wrote: "I confess I am utterly unable to understand them, and what God's will is concerning them, un-less He intended they should be slaves."[6]

Frances Butler said that much of her discontent with the Butler's Island work force stemmed from Tunis G. Campbell's presence in Darien. He was an unusual and vital black man whose efforts to gain for his people the equality promised by emancipation intruded on the discipline and control she believed so necessary to the successul operation of her plantation. Campbell had come from St. Catherine's Island where he established colonies of free blacks as he had on the islands of Ossabaw and Sapelo. Under General Rufus Saxton, Campbell was the "Superintendent of Islands for Georgia" and as such advocated a form of separatism, believing he could instill in black people a feeling of confidence that would enable, them to make their way independent of the whites. The low-country whites, and also his immediate superiors, looked upon his St. Catherine's colony as a "black nation," or a "kingdom," and soon caused its downfall. In prewar Darien the population of 570 had been a mix of 315 whites and 255 blacks. At the time of Campbell's arrival the population had decreased to 546, and the blacks outnumbered the whites 435 to 111. Very much a "political and spiritual overlord," Campbell preached, promised, and won voting rights for his black majority. He became a state senator and served until ousted by the white Georgia Legislature. Then, from the official position as magistrate, or justice of the peace, he wielded the power that moved the McIntosh County blacks toward the promised equality, a move that aroused antagonism in the white people of coastal Georgia. The impact was felt on Butler's Island, where the former slaves were given imagined cause to obstruct work and to flaunt their independence. Or so it seemed to Frances Butler:

> The negroes this year and the following seemed to reach the climax of
> lawless independence, and I never slept without a loaded pistol by my bed.
> Their whole manner was changed; they took to calling their former owners
> by their last name without any title before it, constantly spoke of my agent
> as old R___, dropped the pleasant term of "Mistress," took to calling me
> "Miss Fanny," walked about with guns upon their shoulders, worked just
> as much and when they pleased, and tried speaking to me with their hats
> on, or not touching them to me when they passed me on the banks. This
> last rudeness I never permitted for a moment, and always said sharply, "Take
> your hat off instantly," and was obliged to take a tone to them generally
> which I had never done before. One or two, who seemed rather more
> inclined to be insolent than the rest, I dismissed, always saying, "You are
> free to leave the place, but not to stay here and behave as you please, for I

am free too, and moreover own the place, and so have a right to give my orders on it, and have them obeyed."

The "Mistress" was greatly disturbed to find the blacks willing to follow Campbell "wherever he chose to lead them," and was additionally upset when planters in the area

> entertained the idea of seeing if they could not buy Campbell over, and induce him by heavy bribes to work for us, or rather to use his influence over our negroes to make them work for us. And this proposition was made to me, but I could not consent to such a plan. In the first place it was utterly opposed to my notions of what was right, and my pride revolted from the idea of making any such bargain with a creature like Campbell; besides which I felt sure it was bad policy, that if we bought him one day he would sell us the next. So I refused to have anything to do with the project.

Campbell's vigorous support of the McIntosh County blacks soon clashed headlong into the bitter racism that had become so rampant in the post-war South. The conflict resulted in Campbell's departure from the low country and the elimination of that particular irritative element in Frances Butler's plantation world, though it did not mean that her workers had returned to the old ways she sought. The new attitude persisted as they tested their unaccustomed freedom. Yet, all was not dismal on the Altamaha delta.[7]

The orange trees were a "miracle of beauty." Many branches were weighted down with abundant fruit, and in early 1870 there appeared in Darien a young English cleric Frances Butler had met in New York the year before. He was the Reverend James Wentworth Leigh, known to friends as "Jimbo," a name acquired at Cambridge from having performed in blackface as "Jimboli" in a school minstrel show. He was there with others from England and Philadelphia at Frances's invitation. He described his first impression of Frances: "Arrived at Darien I found some negroes, who took me across to Butler's Island, about three miles across the river. Here a fair queen resided amongst her sable subjects and entertained strangers with royal grace. Her name was Miss Fanny Butler, daughter of Mrs. Fanny Kemble, who married a Southern planter." The visit was brief, but long enough for the Reverend Mr. Leigh to preach a sermon to the blacks who gathered in the old hospital room set aside for a church. His chosen subject was St. Philip's conversion of the Ethiopian eunuch. In the late spring of the same year the fair queen deserted her realm to visit the Reverend Mr. Leigh in his family parish at Stoneleigh. She was chaperoned by her sister Sarah and, while in England, pledged her troth to the young clergyman. They were married in June of the following year at St. Thomas Church on Portman Square in London, with the Wisters and a proud Fanny Kemble in attendance and with Arthur Sullivan "at the organ." After a short honeymoon at Titsey Place, the home of the groom's twin sister, the newlyweds returned to Stoneleigh parish, where their carriage was led by a procession of school children and a drum and fife band that played the "American National Anthem."

The Reverend Mr. Leigh was a popular fellow, athletic and social, with a devotion to sports, theatricals, and conviviality. He was said to have had but little interest in intellectual matters and, his profession notwithstanding, had no "special bent for preaching or for the welfare of other people's souls." He was cheerful, but lacked humor and any semblance of subtlety. Of his wife and her trials, he wrote: "In August 1867 Mr. Butler died, having caught fever on the plantation, his daughter at this time being in the North. She went South as soon as she was able, to carry on his work and look after the negroes, who loved him so dearly and to whom he was so much attached. She had a terribly hard time of it on the plantation all by herself, until she married."[8]

In the year before her marriage, trouble that she blamed on the "overlord" Tunis G. Campbell had necessitated the removal of the white manager. Frances Butler, anxious to get on with her wedding, placed one of the black captains in command. Word reached Stoneleigh that he too was in trouble. The rice mill, all seed for the ensuing crop, and other buildings at Butler's Island had burned. The news prompted the Leighs to plan a move to Georgia and to engage in an experiment born of James Leigh's involvement with numerous unemployed English agricultural workers. Eight men were guaranteed round-trip passage to America from England in return for a promise of two years' work for wages. When the Leighs reached the plantations in August 1873, the Englishmen were there, shunned by the blacks, resented by the Irish ditchers who threatened to break in their heads, with most of them ill and "don't seem able to take a dose of castor oil unless I give it to them." Unable to cope with life on a rice plantation, two soon absconded, while others fled to the North after refusing work in Darien. One lone Englishman remained, and he a "good ploughman." But, if the hard-pressed agricultural workers found no suc-

James Wentworth Leigh, shown in minstrel blackface as "Jimboli" when an undergraduate at Cambridge, courted his "fair Queen" Frances Butler "amongst her sable subjects" on Butler's Island. (Library Company of Philadelphia.)

cor on the Altamaha, not so the Reverend James Leigh. He was as though to the plantation born. He mastered the "very peculiar and scarcely intelligible manner" in which the "sable brethren" spoke his native tongue, and then set about organizing the islanders into a proper flock of "niggers," as he, without guile, persistently called them. His cheerful demeanor and buoyant enthusiasm won them over, and "Massa Preacher," or "Massa Jimmy," became a popular figure on the plantation and in Darien. He fitted out a room in the overseer's house as a chapel where at a wedding a bridegroom, when asked "Wilt thou have this woman?," replied, "I will, Massa. I will." In Darien, then home for many of those who had worked in the rice fields of Butler's Island and for a few who continued to work there, he won the approval of white Episcopalians to establish a separate church for blacks, a task he pursued with unbounded vigor.[9]

Shortly after the Leighs' arrival they put together a grand "English harvest home on the American Thanksgiving day." A large room at the rice mill was decorated with flags, oranges, sheaves of rice, and evergreens. "Massa Jimmy" conducted a service, hymns were sung, and there was a procession to the festive room where a feast of oysters, sweet potatoes, rice, rounds of beef, ham, bacon, hominy, and coffee was enjoyed. Then followed games: "running and jumping races, a sack race, egg & spoon race, pole climbing & lastly a canoe race." As most of the men owned dugout canoes, the contest was exciting. The sports-loving Reverend Mr. Leigh was impressed. He noted, "Each nigger paddles his canoe with great dexterity." The happy occasion ended with song and dancing. "Curious but elegant," said "Massa Jimmy," who thought he detected a remnant of their African heritage. A similar celebration was enjoyed at Christmas, with a decorated tree and once again good food for all.[10]

Under James Leigh's direction, the work force at Butler's Island when at its peak consisted of eight Englishmen, seven Irish "ditchers," and from the black population, two carpenters, a trunk minder, a cow and sheep minder, an ostler, a flatman, a boatman, and about eighty laborers. Frances Leigh told her sister of another employee, an old man, Philip LeMar, who prevented woodcutters from raiding the pine forest at Hammersmith Landing. She quoted Philip's parable on a man whom he found cutting some Butler trees: "Dere was a possum and a dog. De dog hab master, de possum got none. I belong to de Butlers, I dog, I hab master. He (with scorn) possum, free nigger."[11]

The indefatigable Reverend Mr. Leigh mixed his supervision of the

The "fair Queen" herself, Frances Kemble Butler, who became
Mrs. James Wentworth Leigh in England in 1871. (Historical
Society of Pennsylvania.)

plantation with his missionary work among the black people and an active interest in Darien's white parish of St. Andrew's. At the time of his first visit to Georgia the parishioners were holding services in the McIntosh County court house while mounting a campaign to build St. Andrew's anew. Among those who contributed to the project were the mother and others in the family of the dead Colonel Robert Gould Shaw who were desirous of clearing his name with the people whose church and town had been looted and burned by the black soldiers of Colonel Shaw's Fifty-fourth Massachusetts Regiment. A contribution of $1,400 from the Shaw family helped to build the small chapel on the Ridge near Darien. It became the spiritual home of the parish until the church was built in Darien following English plans given them by James Leigh.[12]

On the plantation the Leighs confined their agricultural efforts to the cultivation of rice and oranges. Frances Leigh made the latter her own particular project and saw to it that friends and family in Philadelphia received some of the ample harvest. "Fanny sent me up from the plantation a barrel of the most magnificent oranges I ever saw," wrote Fanny Kemble. James Leigh confined the rice planting to one thousand acres on Butler's Island. The sea island cotton crop at Hampton had been abandoned after three successive failures. Planting had ended on nearby General's Island, then owned jointly among the Wisters, the Leighs, and the family of John Butler, and where the defection of black labor had prompted its lease to a neighbor. This enterprising planter sought to circumvent the labor problem by importing thirty Chinese workmen, people whom Frances Leigh believed "far more repulsive than the negroes, they have such low, cunning, ignoble countenances." She added, "Nevertheless, I should not be sorry to set about a hundred of them on this place, working, for work they will, and do." James Leigh noted that on the two islands were people from Europe, Asia, Africa, and America, followers of "Confucius, John Wesley, Roman Catholics, English Episcopalians, Baptist & I know not what else." Among the Africans in the area were forty-eight black convicts leased by Captain A. S. Barnwell to work the rice fields of Champney Island. The *Darien Timber Gazette* reported the presence of this "chain gang" and commented, "Success to the Captain and may his convict labor prove beneficial to him."[13]

Darien people were interested in the trial of Frances Butler's former antagonist, the "notorious old king of the darkies of McIntosh County," Tunis G. Campbell. Charged with an abuse of power, he was unjustly convicted, his appeal rejected, and he was finally sent away to serve his time. The judge, Henry B. Tompkins, after the case ended and ever the racist, reflected on how it had been in the first trial when the defendant was "surrounded by dusky myrmidones":

> And the streets were thronged by a dense motley crowd dark as a cloud from the plains of Africa, and the Court House was crowded, packed, jammed by the same sable-hued descendants of Africa, old men and women, middle-aged and young ones, some sitting, some dozing, some looking, all wearing a complacent expression as if around a circus ring, and yet also a look of puzzled wonder at the incomprehensive mystery of proceedings at law.

The *Gazette* had reported: "The well known Tunis G. Campbell, Sr., who has created such a fuss in this section is down in the Dade coal mines, working for the State of Georgia. The old man made a big fight but he had to succumb to justice at last. Let us hope he will be a better man when he has served out his sentence."[14]

James Leigh was mightily impressed by the unusual appearance of Hampton. On his first visit there he found the once-vital plantation abandoned except for two old people, "uncle John and Mum Peggy." Like his mother-in-law before him, he wished he could transport some of its natural beauty to England to become a "magnificent park." And the music and song impressed him, too, as it had Fanny Kemble years ago. His missionary work enabled him to hear the blacks' song in the emotional setting of their worship. The repetitious choruses were the most memorable:

> *Graveyard, O Graveyard*
> *Ring Je-ru-sa-lem*
> *Graveyard, O Graveyard*
> *Graveyard, O Graveyard*
> *Graveyard, O Graveyard*
> *Ring Je-ru-sa-lem.*

He enjoyed recalling the visit of his English friend Sir Michael Hicks-Beach and the cheerful song to him:

> *O do, Sir Michael, remember me*
> *O do, Sir Michael, remember me*
> *As the years go rolling on.*

So impressed was James Leigh with the ingenuity of their song, that he "once invited Arthur Sullivan to come down and stay with us to hear their singing and to produce an oratorio to be called *The Queen of Sheba* or some such name, with the negro choruses introduced, but he was unable to find the time." Sir Michael Hicks-Beach found that much of the South reflected Frances Leigh's sentiments in her intense bitterness toward the North. He also observed how it was with the former slaves on Butler's Island:

> The negroes live in their old houses, and except that they get wages (it is said far more than their work is worth) and can go away when they like, their position must be much the same as before. But they have a great idea of independence—and often prefer to go to the pinewoods where they can get a piece of land for next to nothing, build a hut and clear the ground, with much harder work and less comfort to working for a master on his land.[15]

To James Leigh, his greatest accomplishment in that strange Altamaha country was the church in Darien. He called it St. Cyprian's—"for the grand old African Bishop"—and was proud it had been constructed by the blacks themselves and that the interior was done to designs he had furnished. The *Timber Gazette* had watched its progress: "We note the colored Episcopalians are progressing rapidly with their new church. It will be a real neat structure." Leigh taught the children to chant and sing conventional hymns, and wrote, "Fancy a choir of small frizzle-headed little niggers in white surplices." Bishop John W. Beckwith of Savannah consecrated St. Cyprian's at "a most solemn and interesting ceremony" in a crowded church, one side of which was "filled with white citizens, the other side with coloured citizens." He confirmed nine "coloured women" and gave Holy Communion to thirty communicants and as well to six white vestrymen from St. Andrew's. A late dinner at Butler's Island caused the bishop to miss a planned carriage ride from the Darien landing to the train depot and to travel instead with the Reverend Mr. Leigh and a black friend called "Hard Times," who provided a mule-drawn, springless rice cart for a seven-mile trip through the pine woods. Also along for the ride were the Reverend Mr. Leigh's retriever Toby and a small black boy.[16]

For the Leighs, the satisfaction of his missionary work hardly compensated for the difficulties encountered on Butler's Island. The pattern of life was strenuous, the physical demands intense. Their stay on the island

James Wentworth Leigh's St. Cyprian's Church on the high bluff at Darien. (1915 photograph, Amelia M. Watson "Kemble" Collection, Lenox Library.)

began in early fall and ended with their departure at the onset of hot weather, the moves between Philadelphia and Georgia exacting a heavy toll. In June 1874, the year following their arrival in America, Alice Dudley Leigh was born at York Farm during a "furious thunderstorm." She was a bright, quiet, fragile child whose appearance on Butler's Island as "Little Missus" delighted the people as her mother's had thirty-five years before. But the presence of the delicate infant brought a new dimension to the Leighs' lives and new concerns to their minds. Fearful of the "country fever," they revived the practice of leaving the rice plantation in early May for Hampton's healthier atmosphere before departing for the North at the first of June. In the early spring of 1875, with the child less than a year old, flood waters swept down the Altamaha in a freshet that topped the rice field banks to cover the island. While Frances Leigh and her baby were confined to the isolated residence, the Reverend Leigh set about rescuing chickens, livestock, and helpless blacks. Frances wrote her sister: "Inside the house we are devoured by mosquitoes, brought by the waters, and overrun by rats and mice which have taken refuge from it."[17]

Frances Leigh responded to two letters from Dan Wister. She told of a beautiful wild horse found on Little St. Simons, given the name "Hassam" by the Leighs, but called "Horse Butler" by their friend Alex Couper who was training it for her use. Frances also told of the wedding of Quash and Nancy, of how she and Alice's governess had made bridal wreaths and a veil for the bride and had a fine cake sent from Savannah with a baked-in gold ring instead of the usual green twig to promise an early marriage for a lucky one.

The *Darien Timber Gazette* ran a short item to show that Altamaha productivity was not limited to lumber and rice:

> We take this from the *Savannah News* which shows what can be done around Darien. "We are indebted to Mr. J. W. Leigh for a box of very fine oranges and a few samples of bananas, grown on Butler's Island, near Darien. This proves that Georgia can produce as fine oranges as Florida. Nearly two hundred barrels equal to sixty thousand oranges have been shipped to Philadelphia from Butler's Island this season. Georgia is a right good place to stay at anyhow."[18]

If any one happening sealed the decision of the Leighs to leave the plantation and to abandon efforts to make it successful, it was the birth and death of their second child, Pierce Butler Leigh, in January 1876.

Sarah Wister had gone down from Philadelphia to be with her sister. It was her first visit to the plantations since being there with young Dan in 1867, nine years before. She wrote Dr. Wister: "They have the house very pretty & cozy & the yard very tidy with borders of snow drops & violets, & great trees of camellias, olives, oleanders & cape jasmines, besides the oranges. There is an arbour hidden in yellow jasmine in full flower & everything as tidy as possible." In the house, on Frances Leigh's mantel, there was a picture of Fanny Kemble wearing a cap, reading. Leaning against its gold frame was another picture, a photograph of Pierce Butler. Sarah's letter to Dr. Wister continued: "Jimmy is undoubtedly very contented & interested here & busy all the time; all day long he is out of doors, twice a week has night school, on Sunday morning Service in the little chapel he has fitted up in the old overseer's house & afternoon service at the negro church in Darien." While staying at Butler's Island, Sarah Wister was drawn to Hampton and told a friend how it had changed:

> I rode for four hours one day on St. Simons Island & met but two human beings—old negroes living each on a little patch of ground, many miles from each other. Our former neighbors there have all abandoned their plantations & emigrated to the mainland & the land has lapsed into nature's royal inheritance & become woods & wastes once again. It was overrun by the troops of both armies in the civil war but there is no more trace of them than of the French & Spanish & Indians & English who fought there in past centuries.

As for her sister's sad and trying time, Sarah told Dr. Wister that by Frances's own arrangement the nurse had not arrived until after symptoms of birth had begun, and that the aging Dr. James Holmes came only when finally sent for. He "lost his head," departed after the second day, and sent a young Dr. Kollock in his place. When all seemed desperate, James Leigh telegraphed Savannah from Darien asking for help. It arrived as "one Dr. Bullock, an elderly man," who reached the island after the emergency but stayed for two days. The greatest help came from a Mrs. Coffee, an Irish trained nurse, who "saved Fanny's life." The child lived but twenty-four hours.[19]

When the ordeal ended, Frances Leigh mended quickly and was once again her "restless & active self." James Leigh, at first "distraught with agony & anxiety," regained his equilibrium and wrote young Dan Wister, who was attending St. Paul's School in New Hampshire. He told of the "sad loss of the little boy" that made "little Alice more precious to us than ever." "I christened the little one 'Pierce' after his grandfather and he lies in the little enclosure up at the Ridge near Darien, where his grandfather's body was first laid after death." He ended his letter to Dan on a more cheerful note: "We have two Dans & may say 3 on the premises—a fine bull, a fine deer & a sharp little nigger."[20]

There were other reasons for their decision to leave the plantations. The year before the death of their baby their Savannah agent had failed, causing a loss to the Leighs of a shipment of Butler's Island rice worth a thousand pounds sterling. James Leigh's hard work had finally brought to harvest fine crops that unfortunately reached markets depressed by a huge production of Louisiana rice. Fanny Kemble, who well knew the reasons the Leighs were anxious to overcome the challenges they faced in Georgia, was nonetheless insistent in belief and persistent in comment that the former vicar of Stoneleigh should resume "his own proper position and vocation in his own country." In a letter to her friend Harriet St. Leger, she wrote:

> I do not think my dear James' liking for a Georgia plantation life so strange as it appears to you. I was fascinated by the wild singular beauty of those sea islands, and the solitary, half-savage freedom of the life on those southern rivers and sounds: and *but for the slavery,* should have enjoyed my existence there extremely. Sarah, when she came back this winter from visiting her sister, after her illness, said the place and the life and the climate were all like an enchanting dream.[21]

At first it had been their decision to sell, not to lease, the plantation with an operating agent. Frances Leigh had been adamant that she would not return to England with the property unsold, that they would "get their terms" and would be free of debt. But in that year there was a poor market for rice and for the plantations on which rice was cultivated. Indicative of conditions in Georgia was the sad state of Savannah, in 1876 a city of thirty thousand people. This figure included fourteen thousand blacks, and of these, twelve thousand were unemployed and dependent on what little charity there was in that desolate place. The city had defaulted on its public debt; its industry and trade was all but nonexistent. In August a yellow fever epidemic devastated the city and gave the Leighs good reason to stay in Pennsylvania. By the time the summer had waned their decision to return to England was unequivocal. James Leigh accepted an offer of "a living in Staffordshire." They made their plans to place Butler's

Island under an agent's management and to cross the Atlantic in early 1877.[22]

James Leigh conveyed the news of their intentions through the pages of the *Darien Timber Gazette,* but not before calling a meeting of the rice planters of the region. Names of those who attended included Pritchard, Lambright, Dent, Troup, Barnwell, Gignilliat, Couper, Akin, Nightingale, and Duncan. The purpose of the meeting was to "consider the reduction of wages now being paid to agricultural workers on the rice plantations." James Leigh said Altamaha planters paid the highest agricultural wages in America. The Association of the Planters of the Altamaha was formed, and his pending departure notwithstanding, James Leigh was chosen as president.[23]

In September, James Leigh went to Boston to negotiate a direct sale of the plantation's rice crop. He visited Washington to lobby for protective legislation on behalf of the association and was rather pleased to be referred to as a "rice bird." Not until mid-November did he believe it safe to return to the South to wind up matters at Butler's Island and to do the best he could for his flock on the island and in Darien. Savannah's epidemic was officially declared over on November 14. At its worst, 4,000 of its citizens had been stricken at one time, and 896 had died. While his wife and daughter celebrated Christmas with Fanny Kemble at York Farm, and Sarah, Dr. Wister, and Dan joined them from Butler Place across the road, James Leigh was quite alone on Butler's Island. He ordered a dugout canoe with four oarsmen who sang "their quaint songs" on a moonlit trip to Hampton. Bundled against the cold, he manned the steering oar from the stern of the boat to arrive at the abandoned plantation just at midnight. On New Year's Day the "St. Simons people came up to the house to bid me God-speed, after which I wandered in the solitary woods of the beautiful island." Back in Darien a few days later, he held a farewell service at St. Cyprian's and was touched by the congregation's affection and respect as each member shook his hand and said good-bye. When Fanny Kemble was told of his farewell visit she passed on her version to a friend:

> After performing three full church services for the people of the little town of Darien close to Butler's Island, he had rowed down, by a beautiful moonlight night to St. Simons, the island at the mouth of the Altamaha, where the cotton plantation used to be, and which, with its sea sands and noble old groups of live oaks, is a beautiful place which he delights in.[24]

As they neared the time for their departure, Frances Leigh was relieved they had not sold. She held to "her passionate preference for the place" and to the hope the venture on the Altamaha might yet prove successful. She knew James Leigh would miss the great satisfaction he found in his agricultural existence and in the fishing, boating, and hunting that had become such a happy part of his life. Most of all, she knew, he would miss the missionary work with the black people. True, she would have preferred to have lived the life Major Butler envisioned when his slaves built the big house at Hampton, or to have enjoyed the luxuries described by Aaron Burr in his letter to Theodosia. But she, too, had her own luxuries—oranges "like fruits of paradise with their royal color and delicious fragrance." And when on a Sunday, James Leigh was doing his missionary work at St. Cyprian's, did she not attend Darien's parish church in the grand manner? A parishioner thought so:

> She would come over to church in Darien in great state in a log canoe rowed by negro men. These men would wear red shirts and sailor caps one winter, the next perhaps blue shirts. There would be six of them. They would walk ahead of her to the church—two of them would go in taking a foot warmer and a rug, which they would place in her pew, then she would come in with Alice, the governess and the ward. After church the men would be lined up on each side of the steps, till she came out, quite like royalty.[25]

Chapter 24

🜚 Milestones and Gravestones

IN THE TEN YEARS that followed Pierce Butler's death Fanny Kemble's life revolved around the lives of her daughters and their families. Often the entwinement was somewhat thorny, but just as often pleasant and rewarding to all. Or, as Sarah Wister stated, "My Mother was the most stimulating companion I have ever known; she was also the most goading." Sarah gradually overcame the loss of memory and the depression that had afflicted her when her father died. Good reason for the change was: "For the first time since my marriage I had not the daily sense of being hampered as to expense. My husband had come into a good share of his parental inheritance & my father's death had given me ample means."[1]

Thus, while her sister was cultivating rice and endeavoring to persuade free blacks to be like the good slaves they had been, Sarah Wister began to write articles for magazines and to care for the unfortunate Dr. Wister, who had suffered a serious nervous breakdown brought on by family tensions and long periods of overwork during the war. Also, she did her best to guide young Owen and to record her guidance in the journal she called "The Early Years of a Child of Promise."[2]

In the same period of time there were other milestones, and some gravestones. On July 22, 1871, Sidney George Fisher penned the final entry in his diary—"Am losing ground every day." On the twenty-fifth, he died at the age of sixty-three. His wife, Elizabeth Ingersoll, she of the "sweet, satiric smile," died less than a year later. On September 7, 1871, the life of Gabriella Manigault Morris Mease Butler ended at her home, Norwood, near Philadelphia. The comely widow of John Butler was survived by three granddaughters—Julia, twenty-one; Gabriella, sixteen; Margaret McAllister, fourteen—and her adopted niece Cornelia Grayson. The McAllister girls lived with their father, Colonel Julian McAllister, in California. Peter C. Hollis, Gabriella Butler's executor, wrote one of the Morris relatives that he "was busy with the wines from early in the morning until after four o'clock. I had them all drawn off clear, measured and removed to the wine cellar in my office building where the Pierce Butler wines had been stored for many years until they were divided & sold or kept as the sisters chose." A week later he wrote Colonel McAllister, and added a postscript: "PS: the stock of wines is very small & no Butler wines among the lot." He said all had been sold for $166.91.[3]

A more cheerful event occurred in May 1874 at the White House when Nellie Grant and Algernon Sartoris were married. The groom who wed the president's beautiful daughter was the handsome son of Edward and Adelaide Kemble Sartoris. His aunt Fanny referred to the bride as "the young princess of these United States."[4]

As Fanny Kemble contemplated her new relationship with Sarah and Frances, she relinquished none of her hard-won independence. Family friend Sam Ward thought Sarah Wister to be admired for "gentle wisdom & womanly counsel," and Frances Butler, a "bel esprit & esprit fort." Fanny Kemble was in agreement with his opinion of Frances. Anxious to return to England, she earned the necessary funds for her passage by a quick "reading tour" of familiar ground—New York and New England.[5]

At her Boston reading she chose to read two emotional Civil War ballads. The first was John Greenleaf Whittier's "Barbara Frietchie":

> *"Shoot, if you must, this old gray head*
> *But spare your country's flag," she said.*

The second was her own daughter Sarah Wister's "Boat of Grass," a fairly long poem written during the war, and one in which a Georgia slave escapes:

> *The whisper spread, and lo! on high*
> *The dawn of an unhoped-for day!*
> *"Be glad: the Northern troops are nigh—*
> *The fleet is in Port Royal Bay!"*
>
> *Responsive to the words of cheer,*
> *An inner voice said, "Rise and flee!*

> *Be strong, and cast away all fear:*
> *Thou art a man, and thou art free!"*

For two nights the slave followed the "North Star," only to be captured and returned to the plantation:

> *They drag him back to stripes and shame,*
> *And bitter, unrequited toil;*
> *With red-hot chains his feet they maim,*
> *All future thought of flight to foil.*

A year passes, "His wounds were healed, / He burst his bonds, and fled again." Fashioning a "Boat of Grass," the slave and his craft "Safe floated on from dark to dawn" to find himself at sea amid the ships of the Union navy:

> *The sky grew bright, the day awoke,*
> *The sun flashed up above the sea,*
> *From countless drum and bugle broke*
> *The joyous Northern reveille.*
>
> *O white-winged warriors of the deep!*
> *No heart e'er hailed you so before:*
> *No castaway on desert steep,*
> *Nor banished man, his exile o'er.*
>
> *Nor drowning wretch lashed to a spar,*
> *So blessed your rescuing sails as he*
> *Who on them first beheld from far*
> *The morning-light of Liberty!*

For Fanny Kemble, who had no trouble with the throbbing emotion of Shakespeare's plays, "Barbara Frietchie" and Sarah's escaping slave were too much. She lost all composure and could not continue.[6]

After Boston, Fanny Kemble resumed her "reading tour" by blazing a trail into new territory—Detroit and Chicago. Her purse replenished, she then sailed for England on another of her many transatlantic voyages.[7]

For the Wister family the 1870s began poorly. Sarah Wister's depression contributed to her husband's illness. The sale of their Germantown house marked the end of a long road, "wh. had seemed to me for ten years 'the lane that had no turning,' wh. had opened with bright promise of wh. no doubt there had been some fulfillment, but in wh. we had dropped youth, health, illusions, & many hopes."[8] Dr. Wister had tried the waters at Saratoga and the fresh air and sunshine at Newport to no avail. Sarah, "broken in body & spirit," with sister Frances, her own weary husband, and eager son, sailed in May 1870 on the S.S. *Donau.* They were met at Southampton by Fanny Kemble, and on the train ride to London, Sarah's "apathy changed to delight. The look of everything, the boskiness, the boweriness, the hedgerow elms, the brimming streams, & 'lush green grasses,' the low stone bridges, thatched cottages, cathedrals, castles, the very names of the railway stations, brought before my eyes the history & romance of my life's reading. I was alive again."[9] Sarah Wister then escorted her sister to Stoneleigh, where the Reverend Mr. Leigh put into motion the plan that led to Arthur Sullivan's wedding music in June the following year. Sarah, always good on keeping in touch with family, told of a meeting with "My Aunt Mrs. Sartoris and my cousin May." May was the Sartorises' daughter:

> My cousin is a very fine, intelligent and interesting looking girl, with beautiful grey eyes, level brows, and very beautiful teeth which somehow match her brows in expression, but she has an English girl's absence of ease and adaptation and we don't make an inch of headway. My aunt is very like my mother and very unlike. I think she is exactly the author of the *Week in an French Country House,* if books were always like the people who made them.

Adelaide Sartoris, whose forte was song, was justly proud of the book she had written. The next day, Sarah and Aunt Adelaide had late breakfast together "in her curious house crowded until one can hardly turn with old glass, old china, old ivory, old ebony, old tapestry, old silver, pictures & bronzes, and marbles old & new (and all good) in short whatever can be carved or wrought of every age, size, shape & material from Venice to Japan."[10]

Young Owen, always "Dan" to his parents, was placed in a boys' school called Hofwyl, near Berne, Switzerland, while Sarah and Dr. Wister sought to regain their strength at Interlaken. Doing so, they then met Fanny Kemble for a tour of the Continent. The Wisters joined Dan for Christmas at Berne. On finding their boy "terribly dirty," there began a disenchantment with the school that first had seemed to offer so much.[11]

Frances Butler returned to her rice plantation on the Altamaha; Fanny

Kemble's road led her to Rome, where the Wisters followed in January 1871. Said Sarah, "Thus, without health, variety or society except my Mother's & husband's (wh. is not saying a little) I passed three months of perfect contentment." And she added, "It seemed as if I had been waiting for Italy all of my life."[12]

In April, on word that Dan was not well, the Wisters returned to Berne to find the child suffering from the cold weather, again "very dirty," with a noticeable facial paralysis and hands "covered with chilblains." He had studied Latin, German, French, English, music, mathematics, natural history, writing, and drawing, and a splendid report notwithstanding, was removed from the school with an admonition from the master, "Of him to whom much is given, much will be required."[13]

Next came a grand reunion at Stoneleigh for the Butler-Leigh wedding. A new school was found for Dan at Kenilworth after Sarah gave in to "incessant criticisms and complaints of his grandmother," who, in urging his enrollment at a boarding school, "drove several nails daily into my distraught brain." Although Sarah first feared Dan would learn little more than cricket, Kenilworth was successful, if for no other reason than offering access to Stoneleigh, where:

> the young American's well-cultivated imagination was stirred by the sight
> of rooms with a vaulted stone ceiling. The harvest home, the Guy Fawke's
> day, the merry Christmas, the maypole, the concert & play for the poor,
> were an initiation into the English country life so rich in customs, in
> traditions, in associations, with wh. our children have little acquaintance
> except through books, & often not that. The history & manners wh.
> underlie our own civilization & domestic life thus filtered into his mind at
> an early age & did their share towards its mellowness & power of appre-
> ciation; they made his later impressions of England clear & easily classi-
> fied. He grew familiar with English prejudices & heartiness, with different
> types, the gamekeeper, the governess, the heir & the younger son. His
> romantic soul rejoiced deeply though secretly in the beauty of Stoneleigh
> park, & in the flickering of firelight on the oaken ceiling of his bedroom at
> the Abbey. His observation of the habits of wild things, particularly of
> birds, grew keener in his half-holiday rambles, wh. he often took alone,
> apparently for the purpose of surprising their secrets. He improved his
> equitation by being regularly chucked over a hedge at a certain turn of the
> road between Kenilworth & Stoneleigh Vicarage; he was mum about these
> misadventures but the weekly return of the pony & rider independent of
> each other were significant facts to his aunt. Much as that year of separa-

tion cost me, eight unbroken months, I cd. not regret the enrichment of his life by its first associations with the meadows, the primroses, the holly, the hunt, the highdays & holydays, & the worthies of Warwickshire.[14]

In 1872 all the Wisters and Fanny Kemble were in France, and then as the year neared its end, they went to Rome to give Dan a memorable taste of the city they loved. Sarah Wister wrote in her diary that her "ambition was satisfied" in the ready acceptance by an international group of friends who responded so favorably to their invitations to musical evenings and "at homes" in their large apartment on the Via Sistina. Fanny Kemble shared the entertaining responsibilities, sometimes turning her "magnificent contralto" to baritone roles to round out the cast of impromptu operas. Among those who attended the stimulating gatherings was the American writer Henry James, then in his thirtieth year.[15]

In the presence of the good and tolerant Owen Jones Wister, there began a Jamesian romance between the dark-bearded American and the russet-haired Sarah Wister. They met at one of Sarah's "evenings," where Henry James's immediate reaction was that Fanny Kemble's "splendid handsomeness" was the best there. But, when Sarah suggested they meet the next day for a visit to the French Academy in the Villa Medici, and instead shepherded him to the Colonna Gardens, he made a note in his notebook—"an adventure which would have reconverted me to Rome if the thing were not already done." He deferred the pursuit of a James-Kemble friendship for the interest and excitement of the matter at hand. The visit to the Colonna Gardens, "where we wandered for nearly a couple of hours among mossy sarcophagi, mouldering among heaven-high vistas of ilex and orange and laurel, and lingered at the base of damp green statues and communed with the ghosts of departed Colonnas," was followed by meetings at the Villa Medici, at other Italian villas about Rome, and with picnics, rambles, and gallops through the Campagna.[16]

To a cautious Henry James, his interesting companion was ever "Mrs. Wister" or "Mrs. W." The thirty-eight-year-old Sarah was "a beautiful woman" who talked "learnedly, and even cleverly," and who had "fierce energy in a slender frame." Entries in his notebook recorded many engagements:

A drive the other day with Mrs. W. to the Villa Madama, on the side of Monte Mario; a place like a page out of Browning wonderful in its haunting memory.

Sarah Butler Wister. "A beautiful woman with fierce energy in a slender frame," wrote Henry James. (Courtesy of Fanny Kemble Wister Stokes.)

Returning, we dismounted at the gate of the Villa Medici and walked
through the twilight of the vaguely perfumed, bird-haunted alleys to H's
studio, hidden in the wood like a cottage in a fairy tale.

He duly reported his meetings with "Mrs. W" in letters to his father,
mother, sister, and brother, and received sage advice as to conduct from
each in return. Seemingly anxious to forestall loose talk, he qualified his
comments on the obvious pleasure of Sarah's company with deprecatory
bits about her personality. When he wrote his father that the handsome
lady was not "easy," in truth, the uneasiness was his own. In turn, Sarah
Wister found Henry James "a prominent figure in our circle and a friend
for life" and was careful to write little or nothing to indicate the intensity
of her fascination. For Henry James, the romantic interlude was not permitted to go beyond Rome. It lingered only in his thoughts and in his
writing, for the brief association was to appear in his *Madame de Mauves.*
Too, there is something of Sarah in his Christina Light of *Roderick Hudson;* she appears in *Transatlantic Sketches,* and much of their Rome in the
Portrait of a Lady. Sarah, who wrote short pieces for contemporary journals, examined *Roderick Hudson* for the *North American Review.* She did
not permit her presence on its pages to influence her critical judgment
though. She was "unmoved" and likened her reaction to that of a medical
student at a class in vivisection. She said all that was needed was for the
story "to have been told with more human feeling."[17]

The Wisters returned to Philadelphia in June of that year and stayed for
a time at Champlost, the home of their friend Mary Fox, while Butler
Place was being renovated for their use. Fanny Kemble returned with the
Leighs, who went on to Butler's Island. Dan Wister was then at St. Paul's
School.

As 1874 began, Fanny Kemble was living in an apartment on Philadelphia's Rittenhouse Square while the house at York Farm was made
ready. She was attended by her English maid, Ellen, who had agreed to a
stay of two years in America. Also, for a short time there was a black
servant, a former Maryland slave with a weakness for strong drink, a
habit he had gained while serving his master in the Civil War. This man
had a difficult time in postwar Philadelphia, "once the seat of enthusiastic
and self-devoted Quaker abolitionism," but now "one of the strongholds
of the most illiberal prejudice against the blacks." In Philadelphia his kind
could vote, but as people of color were denied such pleasures as attendance at theaters. Such restrictions, said Fanny Kemble, left her servant

"Good and tolerant" Owen Jones Wister, M.D. (Drawing by John Lambert, Jr. Courtesy of Fanny Kemble Wister Stokes.)

"politically, though not socially, a citizen of the United States." She answered a query as to how mulattoes fared in Philadelphia, saying they were precisely what might be expected of people either descended from slaves or themselves born in slavery. She said that they "lie and pilfer, and are dirty and lazy," but then qualified her statement by saying that they were rapidly supplanting the Irish as household servants, and:

> as a rule, they are much less addicted to drink than the white population, either native or foreign, here: they are less insolent than the Irish, and less insubordinate than the Americans, and they are (as old President Adams of Massachusetts said) the only well bred people in the country. Their manners are remarkably good, gentle, quiet, and respectful, a result, partly perhaps of slavery, and partly of their indolent Southern blood, in which there is no tendency whatever to habitual harshness, though there may be, on provocation, to sudden violence.[18]

Comfortably established in the house at York Farm, Fanny Kemble channeled her energies into the continuation of an autobiographical compilation of recollections and letters that first appeared for public edification in the *Atlantic Monthly* in August 1875. There were twenty installments of "An Old Woman's Gossip" that when published in England in 1878 became a book called *Records of a Girlhood*. Henry James called it "an overflow of conversation." Fanny Kemble's *Girlhood* ended, "I was married in Philadelphia on the 7th of June, 1834, to Mr. Pierce Butler, of that city."[19]

The basic source for *Records of a Girlhood*, and for the two volumes that followed, was the thousands of letters written to Harriet St. Leger over a half century. Old and almost blind, Miss St. Leger bundled the letters she had received and returned them to a startled but appreciative Fanny Kemble. Without hesitation she continued the assembly of what she called her "memoirs" by editing, by deleting, and by the insertion of occasional comment. She was careful to eliminate sensitive material pertaining to her turbulent life with "Mr. Pierce Butler" and was aided in the transposition of letters to manuscript by the use of a "very ingeniously contrived machine which is worked by striking keys as one plays on a piano." In preparing a typewritten letter to Dan Wister at St. Paul's, she said she used the machine with the "sudden pianos and fortes of a bad musician."[20]

Fanny Kemble and her grandson Dan Wister were kindred spirits.

Henry James, a "friend for life" of both Fanny Kemble and her daughter Sarah Wister. (Drawing by John Singer Sargent, 1886.)

When Harriet St. Leger wrote that he seemed "a precocious young man," Grandmother Kemble responded with "not at all." He was "an uncommonly clever and gifted boy." When she worried over the well-being of the "little creature Alice Leigh," she took heart in remembering Dan's "most miserable beginning of existence." "See him now," she wrote, "a tall, broad, healthy lad—*speriamo!*" In 1876 the two, one sixteen, the other sixty-seven, collaborated on the writing of an opera. Dan composed the music, and Grandmother the libretto of what she called "a pretty fairy story." Her part was produced with faculties "grown stiff with nearly seventy years' wear and tear—used, disused, and misused."[21]

In January 1877, when Fanny Kemble boarded the White Star liner *Britannic* for her eighteenth and last crossing of the Atlantic, she was well attended—the three Leighs, James, Frances, and "fragile" Alice; Ellen, the maid; an English cook; and a "young Negro servant lad" from Butler's Island. This was Dan Wing, born in 1866, raised by his grandmother Lucinda on General's Island, a mulatto descendant of the courageous Driver Morris, and the "sharp little nigger" of James Leigh's letter to Dan Wister. Dan Wing was sharp. He did his work well, was a favorite of the Leighs' English servants, but surprised all by becoming homesick and asking to be sent back to his home on the Altamaha.[22]

On Fanny Kemble's return to England the friendship with Henry James flowered. She chose Christmastime to introduce him to her second daughter, a meeting from which no romance arose. He joined the family at Stratford on the Avon, in the "divine old rambling, wainscoted, brown-chambered manor house" where, in company with the Leighs, their servants, including Dan Wing, and Fanny Kemble, they "dressed it all up with Christmas wreaths of laurel and holly." Frances Leigh gave him the full particulars of rice culture in Georgia, but it was the good weather, the picturesque old house, and Fanny Kemble, that:

> helped me through my thirty-six hours. Likewise a Christmas tree for the little girl and a tea-party for the children of the people around the place; large red-cheeked infants who kept bobbing curtseys, and pulling their forelocks. But the Leighs themselves are not interesting. J. L. is an excellent, liberal, hard-working parson, but with the intellect and manners of a boy of seven; and his wife who (except for strength of will) is inferior to both her mother and sister, is a sort of perverted Helen Perkins, hating her position in England, detesting the English, alluding to it invidiously five times a minute and rubbing it unmercifully into her good-natured husband. She has a certain charm of honesty and freshness, and her fault is in

the absurd anomaly of her position. I cannot imagine a stranger
marriage.[23]

While the decade of the 1870s neared its end, Fanny Kemble continued
the writing and assembling of material for the second volume of her
memoirs. As *Records of a Girlhood* ended with the Kemble-Butler marriage, Frances Leigh, with no faith in her mother's self-imposed cen-
sorship, envisioned the new work as one that would bare the sordid details that led to her parents' separation and to the divorce in 1849. Firmly
loyal to her father's memory, she vehemently protested the writing of the
"personal reminiscences." Her apprehension led to an unfortunate rift in
daughter-mother relations, a condition exacerbated when Fanny Kemble
refused to attend the christening of a second short-lived son because of the
name he bore. The Leighs called the child Pierce Butler as they had called
the first son who died on Butler's Island three years before. The birth and
short painful existence of the child caused a paranoid reaction in Frances
Leigh that stimulated the preparation of her own "personal reminiscences," the record of the years she spent on the Georgia plantations after
the war and following the death of her father. She seemed determined to
show Hampton and Butler's Island in a light other than that cast on the
plantations by her mother's "first Southern book, wh. nothing would ever
induce me to have in the house."[24]

On top of the bitterness of Frances Leigh, Fanny Kemble received word
of the death of Adelaide Sartoris. "Never was anybody taken to her grave
by more loving hearts, my dear friend, than your sister." The sad condition of Harriet St. Leger further depressed an aging Fanny Kemble, and
had it not been for the strong friendship and kind attention of Henry
James, her unhappiness would have been far greater. Too, she was able to
build on her love for little Alice Dudley Leigh, a love that brought about
an acceptance, if not a reconciliation, in Frances Leigh's feelings toward
her mother. However, true sustenance came from Henry James. He, in
turn, won ample reward, for he found her "the most interesting and delightful of women." He enjoyed her company—"one of the first and most
original of talkers." He said, "Her talk was everything, everything she
was," and liked best when she told of "old London," for then it became a
"gallery of portraits": "She made Count d'Orsay familiar, she made
Charles Greville present. I thought it wonderful that she could be anec-
dotic about Miss Edgeworth. She reanimated the old drawing-rooms, re-
lighted the old lamps, retuned the old pianos."[25]

Chapter 25

✣ Straight Up to God

IN 1887 Philadelphia celebrated the centennial of the United States Constitution, the document Major Pierce Butler and his colleagues had forged that summer in what he described as a "Spirit of Accommodation." The occasion, as had the one on ratification in 1788, featured a "grand procession," but this time with an innovation entitled "The Colored People's Display." Of three large floats, each drawn by four-horse teams, two were dedicated to the Negro of 1887. One float demonstrated the many trades in which the black man of the day participated, and another consisted of sixty-five boys and girls and their four teachers, with placards listing gains of the past century. Included were "Emancipation," "Enfranchisement," and several on progress in education. The third float, which led the group, was entitled "1787." It depicted a Southern plantation during slavery. A small cabin in a field of growing cotton should have been surrounded by black workers but instead was unoccupied except for the driver of the large wagon. The official report of the celebration explained that despite "the liberal offer of a pecuniary reward" no blacks could be found who were willing to go on the float as slaves.[1]

In the 1890s, Hampton Plantation was well along on its restoration to the "wild treasury of Nature," just as Fanny Kemble had predicted. Major Butler's plantation home had long since been swept away by a storm, the Roswell King house, gone too—burned in the Civil War. The few Butler people who remained on St. Simons had turned to other employment or were content to manage their own existence from their garden patches and from the natural bounty to be found in the waters and woods of the overgrown plantations. Butler's Island continued as a rice plantation, but black labor was hard to come by and the old problem of absentee ownership was magnified by the distance between the Altamaha and the Avon. Many of the former slaves who returned to the island after the war had moved to Darien, leaving a hard core of the faithful. Able-bodied men deserted the rice fields for work in Darien's vigorous timber industry. They manned sawmills or were stevedores who loaded ships with lumber cut from logs floated down the river in great rafts from the pine forests along the Oconee, the Ocmulgee, and the Ohoopee rivers that flowed into and formed the Altamaha. James Maxwell Couper, grandson of John Couper, planted Butler's Island for the Leighs. Although he had good words to say for the loyalty and skill of the old Butler people, whom he found to be "about the most intelligent, honest and industrious negroes I have ever employed," he was forced to augment the island work force with Irishmen as had been done the decade before. His 1884 work sheets show the employment of Daniel Murphy, Michael Kehoe, and three Patricks—Ivy, Riley, and Callahan. The Irish "ditchers" were paid $2 per day for the top man, $1.50 for the others. The black laborers received from 50 cents to $1.50 per day. Sambo Swift was paid $7.50 for five days' work; Levi Maxwell $4.50 for six days', Sue Wylly $2.50 for five days', and Jerusalem Blake $2.75 for four and a half days'. The 1884 work list showed thirty-five workers, a far cry from the hundreds who had worked the same fields as slaves. The promise made by Pierce Butler and his daughter to the old and infirm was kept. A few pensioners were paid from $3 to $5 per week.[2]

When Fanny Kemble's second volume of her memoirs was published in 1882 as *Records of a Later Life,* it contained nothing to alarm her youngest daughter, for her father was scarcely noticed. When it was necessary to mention Pierce Butler, he was called by such terms as "present proprietor," as "John Butler's brother," or occasionally by a long dash, "———."[3]

If relieved there was no personal attack on Pierce Butler, Frances Leigh was surely angered by her mother's oft-stated opposition to the slavery her father had endorsed and that she believed preferable to the postwar conditions she encountered on the Altamaha delta. Fanny Kemble stated that her *Records of a Later Life* omitted details on the conditions of the slaves from the letters written on the plantations in 1839, but that she had not "entirely suppressed" her strong feeling on the subject. Certainly Frances Leigh was antagonized to read those passages that did give "detail" along with "strong feeling." Such a passage telling of Butler slaves was: "They are hard worked, poorly clothed, and poorly fed; and when they are sick, cared for only enough to fit them for work again; the only calculation in the mind of an overseer being to draw from their bones and sinews money to furnish his employer's income, and secure him a continuance of his agency."[4]

Frances Leigh's *Ten Years on a Georgia Plantation Since the War* was published in London in 1883. It was less an answer to *Records of a Later Life* than to her mother's Georgian *Journal*, although in her book she did not mention either mother or *Journal*. The book contained an introduction by Owen Wister, a long poem called "Brothers Again" that was born of a visit to Savannah on Memorial Day in 1877, when at the age of seventeen he had been impressed by the conciliatory spirit of the Georgians and by an inscription on the Confederate monument in Forsyth Park.

> *Come from the four winds O Breath*
> *And breathe on these slain that they may live.*

Owen Wister recognized the healing of old wounds, a condition he believed was encouraged by the South's participation in the honest celebration of the nation's centennial the year before. The last lines of his poem read:

> *No strife, nor rancour, nothing bitter then*
> *But they shall join hands—Brothers again.*[5]

Except that Owen Wister did not address the plight of the former slaves in postwar America, his words came closer to the sentiments of Fanny Kemble than to those of her daughter. Frances Leigh's book was in keeping with her character. She showed her intensity, determination, and persistence in the attempt to justify her belief, her father's, and then her husband's that the old Butler legacy could be restored to what it had been. Her book was bolstered at the end with several long letters written by James Leigh, most of which later appeared in his own memoirs. For her part, the book ended when her Altamaha ambitions were abandoned and Butler's Island was left to a series of agents to manage in her stead and in her absence. She knew what had caused the failure and wrote at the last:

> The only two negroes on the place who can write and can add up accounts are the one we had educated at the North, and the one we had in England

for three years. And yet it is twenty years since they were freed, and have become their own masters.

What has become of their longing for better things, and what is to become of them, poor people, ignorant and degraded as they are, and, so far as one can see, becoming more and more so? As far as the masters are concerned, they are better off—relieved from the terrible load of responsibility which slavery entailed, and I have always been thankful that before the property came into my hands, the slaves were freed. But for the negroes, I cannot help thinking things are far worse than when they were disciplined and controlled by a superior race, notwithstanding the drawbacks to the system, and, in some cases, grave abuses attending it. If slavery made a Legree, it also made an Uncle Tom.[6]

If Fanny Kemble had thought Pierce Butler's death removed bitterness and embarrassment from her life, she had not reckoned with Frances Leigh's continued fidelity to her father. On his death she had assumed his role, first on the plantations, and then, protective of his memory, she added Pierce Butler attitudes to her own to disturb the already constrained relationship with her mother. Fanny Kemble wrote to Sarah:

She comes in to see me from a sense of duty and is kind and affectionately indifferent in her manner to me, but I have never been able to forget her furious outbreak of temper in Paris and am much too afraid of challenging another of the same sort to speak to her with any freedom about anything. Her servants and her clothes are the principal subjects of her conversation—when it is not the rice crop—and I say but little of what I think and feel about anything to her.

And then she added "Our intercourse is one of the tragical consequences of life—to me the most tragical."[7]

In Fanny Kemble's old age she was comforted by the continued kindness of Henry James, and much to her liking was the stimulation that came from his good mind and his ability to keep her in touch with people and events. In turn, Henry James, an old man most of his life, was comforted by her kindness and stimulated as well by her good mind. He had once likened her to an active volcano. Now, in the 1880s: "These years of rest were years of anecdote and eloquence and commentary, and of a wonderful many-hued retrospective lucidity. Her talk reflected a thousand vanished and present things."[8] On a return from a trip to southern Italy he visited his venerable friend at Lake Maggiore where she could, at least, look at the mountains she could no longer climb: "She is a very (or at least a partly) extinct volcano today, and very easy and delightful to dwell with in her aged resignation and *adoucissement.*"[9]

Keeping in touch with Fanny Kemble also kept Henry James in touch with Sarah Wister, who in a troubled time in the early 1880s spent a year and a half in Europe with Dan. Henry James saw her in France—"We had some excursions together." Fanny Kemble was there, too. Not in an amiable mood himself, James found young Dan "attractive" and "amiable," but also "light and slight, both in character and talent." It was an opinion he later modified. The fair Sarah, he said, was "so much worn, physically, I am sorry for her." As for his old friend Mrs. Kemble, she was neither "light nor slight." Some years later, when Fanny Kemble was aged and weary, Sarah Wister noted his presence at her mother's flat on Hereford Street in London: "Henry James came in & took me home, stopping for about an hour. He is very kind, the kindliest person I ever knew, or almost, but seems so dead & joyless that it is depressing to be with him." She called him a "dreary dearie." Henry James reacted otherwise. He wrote a short "tale" he called "The Solution" that was based on an incident told him by Sarah's mother. As had happened before, Sarah appeared in one of his characters. She was the charming Mrs. Rushbrook, who "had a lovely head, and her chestnut hair was of a shade I have never seen since." Like Sarah, Henry James's Mrs. Rushbrook "was natural and clever and kind, and though she was five years older . . . always struck me as the embodiment of youth, of the golden morning of life." Henry James was, indeed, Sarah Wister's friend for life.[10]

Dan Wister had gone to Europe in an attempt to find his way in life. After St. Paul's, Sarah and Dr. Wister's "child of promise" enrolled at Harvard where he majored in music, which he was determined to make his career. He was elected to the Porcellian Club, earned membership in Phi Beta Kappa, acted in campus theatricals, wrote words and music for the 1882 Hasty Pudding's *Dido and Aeneas,* and was a successful and popular student with many friends, one of whom was Theodore Roosevelt. He graduated with honors in philosophy and English composition, and with highest honors in his chosen major. The European trip was an effort to determine whether his talents in music were sufficient to offer a reasonable chance for a livelihood. Dr. Wister did not believe music to be either proper or promising and urged a career in something more fitting for an "American gentlemen." Dan Wister studied at the Paris *Conservatoire* where his teachers enthusiastically agreed music should unquestionably be his profession. He met and played an original composition for Great-Aunt Adelaide's old friend Franz Liszt, who wrote Fanny Kemble her grandson had "un talent prononcé." A stubborn Dr. Wister shattered his son's self-confidence by refusing to accept the recommendations or to honor Dan's desires. He believed Dan needed an education in the practical matters of business in order "to take care of what little he may inherit." His real fear was that Dan would take on the bad habits that had engulfed Pierce Butler, and he told Sarah, "But he can't afford to grow like your father, he is too poor. That sort of queerness requires a fortune to supply its demands."[11] He did, reluctantly and belatedly, give his permission, but by that time his son had capitulated. A dejected young man accepted a clerical position in Boston, and after a year of "hateful, sterile and unpalatable work" in a bank that brought on a physical and emotional breakdown, was sent to Wyoming by his physician and kinsman S. Weir Mitchell. There he regained his health, equilibrium, and there seeds for a new career were planted in fertile ground. He entered Harvard Law School in 1885, graduated in 1888, and the next year became a member of the Philadelphia bar and an attorney in a prestigious Chestnut Street firm. His interest in writing, however, overshadowed his interest in law, and Dan Wister became Owen Wister, writer. His first successful story, "Hank's Woman," sprang from the Wyoming he had come to love. It was written in the upstairs library of the Philadelphia Club, built as a residence in 1838 by his ill-starred great-great-uncle, Thomas Butler.[12]

S. Weir Mitchell's kinship to the Butler-Wister family came through his first marriage to Mary Middleton Elwyn, who was the daughter of Mary Middleton Mease and Dr. Alfred Langdon Elwyn. A Philadelphian, Dr. Mitchell was a skilled physician, poet, and novelist. It was he who wrote of Major Butler and his celebrated Madeira wines. Mitchell had little use for Sarah Wister's old friend Henry James, whom he met at her urging. He did, however, agree with James that Sarah had unusual charm. Mitchell said that she was "the most interesting woman" he had ever known. His fascination with the lovely Sarah ran deep—far deeper than the James-Wister attachment of Rome in the early 1870s. He also enjoyed his friendship with Sarah's mother, who was "Aunt Kemble" to his children. He once called on Fanny Kemble when she was staying at York Farm. She persuaded him not to leave, with: "No, do not go yet. I am old and lonely, and never again will you have these chances to talk with a woman who has sat at dinner alongside of Byron, who has heard Tom Moore sing, and who calls Tennyson, Alfred."[13]

As the only living grandson of Pierce Butler, had Owen Wister shown a marked interest in Hampton and Butler's Island, he would have been the logical inheritor of the Butler plantations. He did share his uncle James Leigh's love for the outdoors and, like "Massa Jimmy," got along very well with the plantation blacks. Rather than regaining his health in Wyoming, had he been sent to Hampton, perhaps a greater interest in the plantation life would have developed. As it was, his interest was casual, and he gave no indication that a life as a planter was ever considered. That he expressed no such interest may have been why Sarah Wister surrendered her share of Butler's Island to Frances Leigh, for in the last years of its existence as a Butler plantation it was owned entirely by her. What may have been an informal agreement between the sisters was documented in 1894 when an "amicable partition" was signed and recorded, giving Sarah Wister the exclusive ownership of Hampton plantation.[14]

Fanny Kemble's last years were lived in London. Not one to sit idle, she held forth as usual—reading to and reminiscing with friends. One wrote of a visit with the elderly lady:

> I myself fortunately happened to ask her some question concerning "As You Like It" which had been her sister's favourite play. Suddenly, as if by a miracle, her little room seemed transformed, there were the actors—not even actors; there stood Rosalind and Celia themselves, there stood the Duke, there was Orlando in the life and spirit. One spoke, and then another, Rosalind pleading, the stern Duke unrelenting; then we were somehow carried to the forest with its depths and delightful company. It all lasted but a few moments and there was Mrs. Kemble again sitting in her chair in her usual corner; and yet I cannot to this day realize that the whole beautiful mirage did not sweep through the little room, with color and light and emotion, and the rustling of trees, and the glitter of embroidered draperies.[15]

In early 1889 Frances Leigh returned to Philadelphia and then traveled down to Georgia to inspect her rice plantation. While there, she established herself as before in the old house on Butler's Island. Sarah Wister and young Owen paid a visit, and Sarah reported to Dr. Wister on the "hubbub" of her sister's housekeeping:

Everything Fanny has to do with is done at a different hour, by a different order & every day & the scurry & screaming before these dinners were distracting. The meals were always late but so were the guests, & when we sat down the table was well set & served & the dinner excellent & Fanny herself very lively & funny. Dan will tell you all the business side of the visit. He gets on very well with her, having tact & patience & she gets on well with him. But I find being with her a constant strain on good manners & good temper neither of wh. she has a shred of in daily intercourse under her roof. Her hospitality is active & genuine in making one physically comfortable, but there it ends.

Sarah made a special trip to Darien "to see some of the scattered old people" for whom she had genuine affection. They visited Hampton prior to returning to Philadelphia, and from there Sarah and Frances crossed to London, where they agreed their mother's infirmity called for a move from Hereford Square to the Leighs' London home at Gloucester Place on Portman Square. The transition for Fanny Kemble was eased by the presence of faithful Ellen Brianzoni, who had returned from Italy to be with her much-loved mistress. Sarah Wister's intermittent diary told of her reaction:

April 22, 1889—I found a change for wh. her letters had not in the least prepared me. I found a childish old woman.

April 25—No longer a rational being. Yet I pity her so much that I feel it easier to get on with her than ever before.

April 28—Mentally & morally she is a sort of a caricature of herself.[16]

In May, Sarah wrote Dr. Wister that her mother was as though the bronze had been removed from a casting and she the unbroken outer shell—"ready to go to pieces at a touch." She said that "the solid thing against wh. one clashed is gone." She felt pity and tenderness for "one so strongly marked, still at times so brilliant & suggesting a divine ideal wch never was." Sarah was glad young Owen would not see her again.[17]

Before returning to America, Sarah Wister visited Louis Butler in Paris in 1889, the year before his death. It was a renewal of an acquaintance with her kinsman, who had been accused by his father, Thomas Butler, of leading a life of "shameless sensuality." Sarah had sought out her Paris cousins—Louis, his brother John, and John's wife Elizabeth—in 1872 prior to her Roman winter and the romantic interlude with Henry James. John and Elizabeth then visited the Wisters in Rome, where Elizabeth played the piano for the impromptu operas while Fanny Kemble sang baritone. Sarah again met Louis in Paris in 1882 at the time Owen studied music at the *Conservatoire*. She liked Louis and liked his Paris, and they attended concerts together. It was then that Louis presented Sarah with a gift that became the subject of correspondence between Sarah and Dr. Thomas Addis Emmet, who was attempting to gather portraits of those who had participated in the Constitutional Convention of 1787 in Philadelphia. She wrote:

> I enclose copies of two miniatures of Maj. Butler wh. Mr. Louis Butler (a bachelor then over seventy years old living in Paris, France) gave me not long ago; I did not know of their existence until 1882, & never heard of any likeness of my great-grandfather, except an oil portrait wh. was last seen more than thirty years ago in a lumber room in his former house at the n.w. corner of 8th & Chestnut streets, (Phila), since pulled down.

On the occasion of their last meeting Louis Butler told Sarah that he had attempted to make necessary changes in his will so as to "provide" for his sister-in-law, Elizabeth, but found he had done so eight years before. Thus, some of Thomas Butler's inheritance did ultimately benefit, if not the son ignored in the will, the son's wife.[18]

Two Georgians who put little value on Fanny Kemble's plantation *Journal* visited London in 1890. They saw and talked to its author and many years later told of what seemed to them a softening of her views. James T. Dent, of Hofwyl, the Altamaha plantation, and a friend of the Leighs, said Mrs. Kemble had commented: "I suppose the South will never forgive me for what I wrote about slavery. I was a *young* and *passionate woman*. I have *bitterly regretted* many things that I wrote in that book. I do not mean that my attitude to slavery has changed. That is the same. But when I think of the awful results of the war to those who were dear to me, I have much to be sorry for." Mrs. Georgia Page King Wilder, whose family had planted Retreat plantation on St. Simons Island said Mrs. Kemble had taken her to Westminster Abbey and in conversation had remarked: "I wonder why my husband *had not strangled me—I was a fanatic!*" The two Georgians quoted Fanny Kemble twenty-two years after her words were spoken, in letters solicited by Caroline Couper Lovell, who was preparing copy for her book *The Golden Isles of Georgia.* Fanny Kemble, who was in her eighty-second year, made no retreat from her long-held position against slavery, but she had become more considerate and understanding toward those who had owned slaves. In responding to the Kemble opinion as expressed in the *Journal* that slavery was "horrible," Mrs. Wilder wrote: "I stand strongly against such a statement. I know personally of two generations—my parents and my own—with intimate traditions of my noble grandparents, and I knew and saw nothing horrible." Mrs. Lovell, reflective of the persistent attitudes of those whose families had owned slave plantations, asked the rhetorical question: "Which view was the truth? That of Fanny Kemble Butler, who had spent one year in the South, or that of Georgia King Wilder, who spent a lifetime?"[19]

Both Sarah Wister and Frances Leigh were in America on January 15, 1893, when their mother died. James Leigh sent word by cable and then called for help from Henry James, who hurried to the Leighs' home on Gloucester Place where Fanny Kemble's long life had ended peacefully in Ellen Brianzoni's arms. "Not a groan, not a struggle, her spirit must have flown straight up to God," said Ellen. She was buried next to her father at Kensal Green cemetery in London. Henry James attended the service with James Leigh, nineteen-year-old Alice, and Ellen, who was there "with a very white face and her hands full of flowers"—four of the six living people who loved her most. He wrote his friend "Mrs. Wister" to tell her: "I stood by your mother's grave this morning—a soft, kind, balmy day, with your brother-in-law and tall, pale, handsome Alice, and a few of those of her friends who have survived her." He said Fanny Kemble had looked, after death, extraordinarily like her sister Adelaide, that it was "like the end of some reign or the fall of some empire," and that she had left "a great image—a great memory." He had said he was conscious of a "strange bareness and a kind of evening chill."[20]

Henry James paid tribute to his friend in the essay "Frances Anne Kemble." He believed the best of her prose was the "strong, insistent, one-sided" plantation *Journal:* "The most valuable account—and as a report of strong emotion scarcely less valuable from its element of *parti-pris*—of impressions begotten of that old Southern life which we are too apt to see today as through a haze of Indian summer." He added his enthusiastic approval of *Records of a Girlhood* and *Later Life,* "copious and ever delightful." He said that together they formed "one of the most animated autobiographies in the language."[21]

In Georgia, the *Darien Timber Gazette* picked up the "London Special" and ran the story as received, replete with errors:

Miss Kemble Dead

In 1832 she came to America and played all the cities. Her last appearance was in Park Theatre in New York, in 1834—lithe, graceful, and with black hair and eyes. She possessed remarkable energy and had a voice of uncommon range and power. On June 7th of that year, she married Pierce Butler, a Southern planter and son of United States Senator Butler. She lived in Philadelphia and on Butler's Island, near Darien, Georgia.

The editor, Richard W. "Dick" Grubb, then added: "The deceased was the mother of Mrs. Frances B. Leigh, the owner of Butler's Island, just across from Darien." And that was all. He had missed an opportunity for a story the likes of which seldom crosses an editor's desk.[22]

A few weeks before Fanny Kemble's death, Julia Rebecca Maxwell King died in her seventy-fifth year at her home in Liberty County on the Georgia coast. After having outlived him thirty-eight years, she was buried at Midway by the side of Roswell King, Jr. Seven of their eleven children survived her.[23]

Chapter 26

Lady Baltimore

IN 1894, Archibald Philip Primrose, the fifth earl of Rosebery, succeeded Gladstone as Britain's prime minister. He held office but a single year, long enough to bestow a signal honor upon his friend James Leigh, who was chosen to be the dean of the great cathedral at Hereford. Lord Rosebery had visited the Leighs at Butler's Island where he was "interested and amused" by life on the Altamaha. He shot ducks and snipe and enjoyed the songs and dances of the plantation people. For the Leighs, the responsibilities of the "Deanery" put an end to any thoughts Frances Leigh entertained of a return to America and the supervision of their Georgia rice plantation. The remote management became increasingly difficult, causing the Leighs to again give thought to sale.[1]

Both families—Leighs and Wisters—maintained a loyal interest in the people of Hampton and Butler's Island. A letter in 1896 from one of the older men, Aleck Alexander, thanked Sarah Wister for a Christmas box: "My dear Mistress—With much love, I take the pleasure in writing you this letter. I have received our box in safety. Mistress I thank you Madam very much for how comfortably you have me clothes for the winter. I do just as you bid me, I gave Mr. Mann his presents and he was very glad for them." Aleck said that his wife Daphne was well, that both sent "thousands of love to you, Master Owens and Master Dan." Aleck hoped the good Lord would "spear our lives to meet once more in this life" and added that their daughter Hannah sent "thousands of howdy-do." Hannah was the second daughter of Aleck and Daphne, named for his mother, who had served Roswell King, Jr., as housekeeper and had nursed Pierce Butler through his illness in 1839. Aleck's father was Sawney, the "great violinist" who played one of the fiddles acquired by the younger King in 1823. Daphne and her twin Ben, who died young, were the children of the slave girl Minda and Roswell King, Jr., born at Hampton in 1824. Fanny Kemble wrote of Daphne and Ben in her *Journal:* "They have refined and sensitive faces as well as straight, regular features; and the expression of the girl's countenance, as well as the sound of her voice, and the sad humility of her deportment, are indescribably touching." Aleck and Daphne raised a large family. In addition to Hannah, there was Pierce Butler, who was named for their owner, and at least five others. Two were sons, and three daughters became educators. Mary married the Reverend F. M. Mann, the rector of St. Cyprian's in Darien. She founded the Mann School at St. Cyprian's with the help of Frances Leigh and Alice, who contributed more than three hundred dollars, most of which came from a benefit play in England. Alice produced the play and was its principal actress. Mary Mann's sister, Dora Jeanette, was her assistant at the school, and another sister, the formidable "Deaconess A. E. B. Alexander," founded the Good Shepherd Church at Pennick Station and taught black children in their school.[2]

For "Master Owens" the good Lord failed to "spear" his life and permit the reunion with Aleck. Dr. Owen Jones Wister died February 24, 1896, in his seventy-first year. If his devotion to his son was often misguided, he was ever true in his devotion to his unusual and difficult wife. At the time, the two were in conflict over young Owen's career in music; he had written Sarah: "You speak with sarcasm and bitterness of marriage; You forget that I am married, and not unhappily."[3]

In 1898 the wedding of his nephew Rowland Charles Frederick Leigh to Mabel Gordon of Savannah brought Dean Leigh to Georgia. He visited Darien and Butler's Island, where he was distressed to find both town and plantation severely damaged by the tropical hurricane of August 30. Butler's Island was a "perfect wreck." The rice mill, the barn, many of the people's houses, and the rice crop were destroyed. It was a bitter blow, shattering the faint hope that Major Butler's Georgia plantations would ever again provide the earnings that sustained his family through five generations. The thought of selling that had resurfaced in 1894 was revived, but the prospect of obtaining a reasonable price was disheartening.[4]

As the century turned, racial violence was prevalent through much of the South, and Darien, with a large black population, had its share. In late 1899, a Darien black, Henry Delegal, was charged with raping a white woman and lodged in the county jail. Blacks in the area who feared that Delegal would be lynched gathered in large numbers at the jail to prevent his removal to Savannah. The McIntosh County sheriff called on the

James Wentworth Leigh, dean of the great Cathedral at Hereford. (Courtesy of the Dean and Chapter of Hereford Cathedral.)

Aleck Alexander, born a Butler slave, was the son of Sawney and Hannah. (Studio photograph, Amelia M. Watson "Kemble" Collection, Lenox Library.)

Daphne Alexander, born a Butler slave and married to Aleck Alexander, was the daughter of Roswell King, Jr., and Minda. (Studio photograph, Amelia M. Watson "Kemble" Collection, Lenox Library.)

Georgia governor, who sent troops that dispersed those at the jail and then transferred the prisoner to Savannah. The trouble was exacerbated when two white men sought to remove the Delegal sons from their home near Darien. One of the white men was killed when the young men resisted. After the two Delegal sons were arrested along with the ringleaders of the occupation of the jail, the Reverend F. M. Mann, rector of St. Cyprian's, telegraphed a message of distress to Sarah Wister in Philadelphia. He followed the message with a letter.

> Dear Madam—I sent per telegraph that the Superior Court is in special session trying the colored people charged with the killing of Mr. Thownsend and those for riot. The Colored People that belonged to you who are charged with being implicated in the riot are as follows: Renty Young, the son of Isaac Young, Simon Deveraux, Jr., the son of old Simon Deveraux, Andrew Young, the grandson of old Captain Caesar Young, John & Richard Coffee, the sons of Nero Coffee, Marshall Dowsey, the son of old Amos Dowsey, William and Jack Cooper, the grandsons of old Tony Maxwell, Kitt Alexander, & old Carter Williamson. These are all that have been arrested or that warrants have been so far issued. The whole affair grew out of excitement. No one was killed or even injured in the riot, no one's property destroyed or molested. I consulted Dan Wing & others, and what these people now need is money to help pay their lawyer to defend them in Court. The White People do not seem to be anxious to injure the Colored People.[5]

Sarah Wister responded by raising a fund in the North that, when added to the little the Darien blacks were able to gather and to a small amount from Negro clergymen of Savannah, paid the attorney for a spirited defense of the accused. In March of 1900 Sarah Wister sent thirteen copies of her typewritten letter to those who responded to her call for help. She outlined the case, starting with the incidents that led to the arrests and the accusations, and told the results:

> Henry Delegal was tried in Savannah for his alleged offense, and promptly acquitted. His wife and sons were tried in Effingham County for murder, she was acquitted, the sons were found guilty, but recommended to mercy, and sentenced to imprisonment for life. More than half the Negroes arrested for riot were discharged, the rest condemned to fine or imprisonment for a year. Their Counsel, Judge Twiggs of Savannah, moved for a new trial on some technical irregularity. It was granted to one of the Delegal sons, who was acquitted, but refused to the other, and to the

Mary Mann (left) and Dora Jeanette Alexander, daughters of Aleck and Daphne Alexander. (1915 photograph, Amelia M. Watson "Kemble" Collection, Lenox Library.)

rioters. Judge Twiggs appealed to the Supreme Court of Georgia which, in January, reversed the sentence of the other Delegal, and ordered a new trial to take place in May. The sentence of the rioters, however was confirmed, and last month twenty-four of them, unable to pay the fine, were sent to an interior town to work with the chain gang.

Sarah Wister told her friends that "passion and prejudice" had played a role in the verdict, but then expressed her belief that it might have been a "salutary lesson to the negroes not to give way to excitement and impede the processes of the law." She said that "the great preponderance of their race in the black belt" made such assemblages as that at the Darien jail extremely dangerous. She told them, "the honored names of Channing, Curtis, Furness, Garrison, Higginson, Lowell, Mott and Shaw" were represented among their benefactors. In turn, she wrote the benefactors that she wished she could express the "heart-felt gratitude" of the Darien blacks in language as moving as their own.[6]

In 1901 the Butler sisters met at Darien to inspect their properties and to determine a course for the future. Frances and Alice Leigh had come up from a stay at the exclusive Jekyll Island Club, then in its heyday as a retreat for many of the nation's wealthiest families. Sarah Wister had come down from Philadelphia. At Darien she paid a call on the Charles Spalding Wyllys. Two years before, the Wyllys had been invited to dinner at Butler's Island, where Sarah found him "a very nice person, though a little deaf & a little dull." Captain Wylly remembered Sarah otherwise. In his *Memories* he wrote of women with social grace and "dignified carriage": "Mrs. Sarah Wister, calling on Mrs. Wylly, had asked for Mrs. Couper, then 80 odd years of age. On entering Mrs. Couper's room and seeing her seated, she swept the most beautiful courtesy before advancing to greet her."[7]

Faced with what seemed to them an insurmountable task of putting their property to any profitable use, the sisters decided to sell. Frances Leigh, whose need for money was greater, was the motivating force. Her decision to sell Butler's Island prompted a letter from Sarah to a Savannah agent advising that in as much as Mrs. Leigh, who wanted to sell all of her McIntosh County holdings, was a joint owner of General's Island and certain other river and mainland properties, she, too, would sell. As Sarah Wister could speak for the McAllister daughters, this meant a desire to end any Butler ownership of land in McIntosh County.[8]

Frances Leigh negotiated a contract in which all of Butler's Island was

The Mann School for black children, Darien. (1915 photograph, Amelia M. Watson "Kemble" Collection, Lenox Library.)

leased to W. H. Strain of Darien for the years 1901–1906 at an annual rental of only $125. Mr. Strain was given an option to purchase the plantation for $10,000. This was the same land Major Butler, in 1818, offered to Mr. Fitzsimmons for $506,000, though that amount did include 582 slaves at $450 each, giving an asking price of $244,100 for the plantation alone. The Strain family exercised the option by making a partial payment of $5,000 in 1903. Not until 1906 was the transaction completed, and not until 1907 was the General's Island and Darien property sold. The $1,500 received was but a small fraction of the $36,000 paid for the same land in 1853 by Pierce Butler and the estate of his brother John. Giving evidence of the depressed land values in McIntosh County was the sale of a pineland tract near Darien. In 1905 the two sisters sold 434-1/4 acres for $434.25, or one dollar per acre. If this was the "400 acres more or less" purchased in 1810 for $400 by Major Butler from the McCall family, the resulting $34.25 was the only land profit the sisters enjoyed from the sale of their McIntosh County holdings.[9]

There had been some sales of family property in Glynn County in the vicinity of Butler's Island on the far, or southern side, of the Altamaha. Considering the prices obtained, the land must have been sold for reasons other than to raise money. In 1888 the two sisters sold two tracts of pineland, a total of 1,307 acres for $653.50, or fifty cents an acre. The next year they sold the last of their holdings on that side of the upper river, a total of 1,904 acres for $1,904. The sales covered tracts purchased as long before as 1818 by Major Butler, and others bought by their father and their Uncle John.[10]

The 1894 "amicable partition" that gave Sarah Wister the 2,500 acres of Hampton Plantation, placed remote Little St. Simons Island's 5,000 acres and 800 acres of the St. Clair tract in Frances Leigh's name. St. Clair, on greater St. Simons Island, was just south of and contiguous to the Couper plantation of Cannon's Point. As Frances Leigh owned Butler's Island in McIntosh County, she held title to the greatest acreage of the old Butler holdings but not necessarily to the most valuable. The deeds effecting the division of the Butler properties were signed by each, and by their respective spouses Owen Jones Wister and James Wentworth Leigh.[11]

The usually hard-pressed Frances Leigh rounded out her holdings by buying the 500 acres of Cannon's Point, giving her a contiguous property covering all of Little St. Simons and the northeastern corner of the larger island. She offered all for sale for $30,000, or broken down to $20,000 for Little St. Simons, $6,000 for Cannon's Point, and $4,000 for the St. Clair tract. In a sales piece offering the property, she said that her sister had agreed to sell Hampton plantation, which somehow had increased to 5,000 acres from the 2,500 of the "amicable partition." Frances Leigh pointed out that the Wister and Leigh lands together, with small lots belonging to blacks and poor whites anxious to sell, would "make altogether a magnificent hunting park of about 25,000 acres."[12]

The times were not conducive to such prices. Not until 1908 were the Leigh properties sold. O. F. Chichester bought all of Little St. Simons for $12,500. F. D. M. Strachan purchased Cannon's Point for an unnamed sum and St. Clair's 790 acres for $5,000 cash. No one was ready at that time to purchase Sarah Wister's Hampton for the $25,000 she asked.[13]

While the Butler sisters were parting with their inherited plantations, Owen Wister's life had begun to follow a consistently irregular pattern that was to continue all of his life. In 1898 he married Mary Channing Wister, called Molly, his second cousin once removed. They shared a common ancestor, Daniel Wister, who was Owen's great-, and Molly's great-great-grandfather. Also, she was descended from William Ellery Channing, Fanny Kemble's old friend and mentor in matters antislavery. Molly, in her own right, was a remarkably talented young woman. Before her marriage she had been a founder of the influential Civic Club of Philadelphia, had served on a mayor's special committee to assist in the raising and expenditure of $12 million for city improvement and had introduced music into the Philadelphia public school system. A capable musician, she had long played eight-hand piano quartets with Owen and two of their friends. Following their wedding, they spent a month in Charleston—"the most appealing, the most lovely, the most wistful town in America"—and returned there for the winter of 1902 while Owen completed his first novel and best-known work, *The Virginian*. The town and its people made such a telling impression that Charleston became the locale for his second novel, *Lady Baltimore*.[14] The title came from a cake sold in the "Woman's Exchange," a tea room in the town of King's Port, the pseudonym he chose for Charleston. He later gave his reasons behind the writing of the story. On the visit in 1902 he had been reminded of the tragedy of the Civil War:

> But when I saw Charleston, it seemed to me the tragedy of all, except
> Lincoln. Whatever these people had done—and my political faith was

wholly Union—obliteration was a heavier punishment than they deserved. They had taken a splendid hand in the first making of our country, and the civilization they had produced was the most civilized in the United States.

Here it was now, fifty years after, in its dying embers—that civilization— first beaten down by a war that it had undoubtedly precipitated, and then trodden out by the infamy of reconstruction. It had been founded, true enough, on the crime of slavery, but this crime was not its own; it was part of the inheritance from England.[15]

Lady Baltimore was first published as a serial of weekly installments in the *Saturday Evening Post*. Owen Wister's treatment of the South Carolina blacks reflected his opinion and those of friends he had made during his Charleston visits. Thus, it came as a distinct surprise that he should be criticized before the serialization of the story was complete. In the introduction to the book that followed the magazine series, he commented: "Certain passages have been interpreted most surprisingly to signify a feeling against the colored race, that is by no means mine. My only wish regarding these people, to whom we owe an immeasurable responsibility, is to see the best that is in them prevail."[16]

The passages in question came mostly from the novel's narrator, a Northerner not unlike Owen Wister himself. One such excerpt is typical. It was a response to a long diatribe by a Teutonic character who has displayed to the narrator three skulls—one of an ape, the second of a Caucasian, and the third of a "South Carolina nigger." His display won the admission, "Why, in every respect that the African departed from the Caucasian, he departed in the direction of the ape!" The Teuton's diatribe ended with "They will get better results in civilization by giving votes to monkeys than teaching Henry Wadsworth Longfellow to niggers." The response:

> We need not expect a Confucius from the negro, nor yet a Chesterfield; but I am an enemy also of that blind and base hate against him, which conducts nowhere save to the de-civilizing of white and black alike. Who brought him here? Did he invite himself? Then let us make the best of it and teach him, lead him, compel him to live self-respecting, not as statesman, poet, or financier, but by the honorable toil of his hand and sweat of his brow. Because "the door of hope" was once opened too suddenly for him is no reason for slamming it now forever in his face.

Owen Wister. (Historical Society of Pennsylvania.)

Thus mentally I lectured back at the Teuton as I went through the streets of Kings Port; and after a while I turned a corner which took me abruptly, as with one magic step, out of the white man's world into the blackest Congo. Even the well-inhabited quarter of King's Port (and I had now come within this limited domain) holds narrow lanes and recesses which teem and swarm with negroes. As cracks will run through fine porcelain, so do these black rifts of Africa lurk almost invisible among the gardens and the houses. The picture that these places offered, tropic, squalid, and fecund, often caused me to walk through them and watch the basking population; the intricate, broken wooden galleries, the rickety outside staircases, the red and yellow splashes of color on the clothes lines, the agglomerate rags that stuffed holes in decaying roofs or hung nakedly on human frames, the small, choked dwellings, bursting open at doors and windows with black, round-eyed babies as an overripe melon bursts with seeds, the children playing marbles in the court, the parents playing cards in the room, the grandparents smoking pipes on the porch, and the great-grandparents upstairs gazing out at you like creatures from the Old Testament or the jungle. From the jungle we had stolen them, North and South had stolen them together, long ago, to be slaves, not to be citizens, and now here they were, the fruits of our theft; and for some reason (possibly the Teuton was the reason) that passage from the Book of Exodus came into my head: "For I the Lord thy God am a jealous God, visiting the iniquity of the fathers upon the children."[17]

In another passage the Northerner cites the reaction of the Northern people following the burning of Washington in the War of 1812 as contrasted to that of the South Carolinians after the Civil War. The comely young Eliza La Heu takes issue with his comparison:

> "In 1812, when England burned our White House down, we did not sit in the ashes; we set about rebuilding."
> And now she burst out. "That's not fair, that's perfectly inexcusable! Did England then set loose on us a pack of black savages and politicians to help us rebuild? Why, this very day I cannot walk on the other side of the river, I dare not venture off the New Bridge; and you who first beat us and then unleashed the blacks to riot in a new 'equality' that they were no more fit for than so many apes, you sat back at ease in your victory and your progress, having handed the vote to the negro as you might have handed a kerosene lamp to a child of three, and let us crushed, breathless people cope with the chaos and destruction that never came near you. Why, how can you dare _____."[18]

In a later passage, the narrator is talking to a friendly native and they find room for agreement:

> Each allowed for the other's standpoint, and both met in many views: he would have voted against the last national Democratic ticket but for the Republican upholding of negro equality, while I assured him that such stupid and criminal upholding was on the wane. He informed me that he did not believe the pure-blooded African would ever be capable of taking the intellectual side of the white man's civilization, and I informed him that we must patiently face this probability, and teach the African whatever he could profitably learn and no more; and each of us agreed with the other. I think that we were at one, save for the fact that I was, after all, a Northerner—and that is a blemish which nobody in Kings Port can quite get over.[19]

When *Lady Baltimore* was published in book form, Owen Wister sent the first copy to Dr. S. Weir Mitchell, to whom it was dedicated. The second copy was sent to his old Porcellian friend, Theodore Roosevelt, then in the White House. The president read and studied the book carefully, then responded in a fifteen-page typewritten letter. He found the novel a "sweeping indictment of the Northern people," or as he expressed himself to "Dear Dan," you "made your swine devils practically all Northerners, and your angels practically all Southerners." The "swine devils" of *Lady Baltimore* were not only Northerners, said the president, but were the "overwhelming majority of the well-to-do North, indeed of the North which leads." But it was upon the South Carolinians that President Roosevelt truly directed his artillery:

> Your particular heroes, the Charleston aristocrats, offer as melancholy an example as I know of people whose home life for generations has been warped by their own wilful perversity. In the early part of South Carolina's history there was a small federalist party and later a small and dwindling union party within the State, of which I cannot speak too highly. But the South Carolina aristocrats, the Charleston aristocrats and their kinsfolk in the up-country (let me repeat that I am of their blood, that my ancestors before they came to Georgia were members of these very South Carolina families of whom you write) have never made good their pretensions. They were no more to blame than the rest of the country for the slave trade of colonial days, but when the rest of the country woke up they shut their eyes tight to the horrors, they insisted that the slave trade should be kept, and succeeded in keeping it for a quarter of a century after the Revolutionary

war closed, they went into secession partly to reopen it. They drank and dueled and made speeches, but they contributed very, very little toward anything of which we as Americans are now proud. Their life was not as ignoble as that of the Newport people whom you rightly condemn, yet I think it was in reality an ignoble life. South Carolina and Mississippi were very much alike. Their two great men of the deified past were Calhoun and Jefferson Davis, and I confess, I am unable to see wherein any conscienceless financier of the present day is worse than these two slave owners who spent their years in trying to feed their thirst for personal power by leading their followers to the destruction of the Union. Remember that the Charleston aristocrats (under Yancey) wished to re-open the slave trade at the time of the outbreak of the Civil War. Reconstruction was a mistake as it was actually carried out, and there is very much to reprobate in what was done by Sumner and Seward and their followers. But the blame attaching to them is as nothing compared to the blame attaching to the southerners for forty years preceding the war, and for the years immediately succeeding it. There never was another war, so far as I know, where it can be honestly and truthfully said as of this war that the right was wholly on one side, and the wrong wholly on the other. Even the courage and prowess of those South Carolina aristocrats were shown only at the expense of their own country, and only in the effort to tear in sunder their country's flag.

After several pages pursuing Southerners in general and South Carolinians in particular, the president got around to Owen Wister's attitude toward black people. "Now as to the negroes! I entirely agree with you that as a race and in the mass they are altogether inferior to the whites." He told Owen Wister that while admitting the truth of much said against blacks, it was also true that a great deal said against them was untrue. He said the Wister view was that "expressed by your type of Charlestonians" and that such views were expressed only to those "who don't know the facts." He then vilified the Southern politician who (as had Major Butler) insisted blacks were unfit to cast votes but then were "equally clamorous" in insisting they be counted in the determination of congressional representation. He said that the "extra representation," which, as white men, they got by fraudulent or violent suppression of the black vote" was shameful, and that Charlestonians "lead this outcry and are the chief beneficiaries."[20] In *Lady Baltimore,* Owen Wister had written: "Yes, I was obliged to believe that the Young Kings Port African, left to freedom and the ballot, was a worse African than his slave parents."[21] The president disagreed:

I may add that my own personal belief is that the talk about the negro having become worse since the Civil War is the veriest nonsense. He has on the whole become better. Among the negroes of the South when slavery was abolished there was not one who stood as in any shape or way comparable with Booker Washington. Incidentally I may add that I do not know a white man of the South who is as good a man as Booker Washington to-day. You say you would not like to take orders from a negro yourself. If you had played football in Harvard at any time during the last fifteen years you would have had to do so, and you would not have minded it in the least; for during that time Lewis has been field captain and a coach.

He ended his criticism of *Lady Baltimore* in a paragraph beginning "Now, Dan." He cited the happenings in Indianola, Mississippi, where he denied the townspeople mail service after mob rule drove a capable and respected black woman from the office of postmistress. After his action, "the entire South, led by your friends in Charleston, screamed for months over the outrage." He told Owen Wister:

absolutely all I have been doing is to ask, not that the average negro be allowed to vote, not that ninety-five percent of the negro be allowed to vote, not that there be negro domination in any shape or form, but that these occasionally good, well-educated, intelligent and honest colored men and women be given the pitiful chance to have a little reward, a little respect, a little regard, if they can by earnest useful work succeed in winning it.

He then added: "In *Lady Baltimore* you give what strength you can to those denouncing and opposing the men who are doing their best to bring a little nearer the era of right conduct in the South." In a postscript, President Roosevelt reiterated that *Lady Baltimore* hindered rather than helped the efforts to secure a "moral regeneration." He believed it to be inaccurate "as a tract on the social life of the North, as compared with the North's past and the South's present."[22]

Owen Wister's reaction was to agree with the president's "indictment of the slaveholding minority who took the Confederacy into the Civil War." He said, "That cannot be answered," and perhaps it made him think of his grandfather, Pierce Butler. But he refused to agree with "some of his other severities about those unfortunate people." And then he added: "When I came to prepare the novel for the uniform edition of my books in 1928, a good many sentences were changed and quite a number of paragraphs were wholly omitted."[23]

Owen Wister's "uniform edition" of *Lady Baltimore* contains an informative introduction in which he noted the *Charleston News and Courier* ran an advertisement of the Woman's Exchange in which they featured the "Lady Baltimore cake that made Owen Wister famous." He told how he had met Henry James in Charleston in 1905, read the opening chapters to him, and received advice that was followed. The older writer advised the younger one not to refer to Charleston by name, but to use a pseudonym. "Charleston," he said, "this tiny cup—this so precious vessel," was not like London or Paris, "where the ocean is boundless." Thus, Charleston became "Kings Port." In his own book, *The American Scene*, Henry James also wrote of Charleston. He visited "the very Exchange" with Owen Wister and ate a piece of Lady Baltimore cake, which he found delectable. But of the town, with its charm of color, tone, and light, he found a disturbing vacancy. "How," he asked, "in a great political society can *everything* have gone?" And he asked a second question, "Had the *only* focus on life been Slavery?"[24]

Owen Wister said that the house in which Eliza La Heu and John Mayrant of his novel were married was the Miles Brewton House, that the censors who kept him straight as to Charleston attitudes and customs were Mrs. St. Julien Ravenel and Miss Susan Pringle. The new edition contained President Roosevelt's long letter, and the Roosevelt-induced deletions from the original version of *Lady Baltimore* were mostly moderations of what he called "diatribes of Augustus" as to social, political, and commercial commentary. "Augustus" was Owen Wister by another name—the narrator who told the story. He stood firm in what he had written about the black man—"the injustice we had done to *him* as well as to our own race by the Fifteenth Amendment." The passages on the black people were not among those deleted in the new edition. Later, in his book *Roosevelt: The Story of a Friendship*, he told of his reaction to Charleston, a city "of fine traditions and fierce prejudices." There, and somewhat to his surprise, he found people to be just as he was, "with feelings and thoughts and general philosophy and humor and faith and attitude towards life like my own." It was a "kinship" he felt "less and less in places like New York, Boston, and Philadelphia," as was shown so clearly in *Lady Baltimore*. [25]

A more telling criticism of the racial attitudes Owen Wister expressed in *Lady Baltimore* came from one of its readers, a Cornell University professor, Burt G. Wilder, who took strong issue with the "scientific error and politic venom that characterize the passage" on the three skulls. This accusation of racism disturbed Wister, but not so much as to make him back away from what he had written. Unable to obtain a retraction, professor Wilder persisted. Later, in an address to a national conference on the status of black people, he ridiculed Owen Wister by recounting the excerpt and declaring, "A more monstrous perversion of facts I do not remember to have seen." That Owen Wister's attitudes also persisted was evident in a 1923 talk at Harvard. He spoke against "excessive" admission of Jews and blacks. As to the latter, "There are Hampton, Tuskegee, and other colleges where Africans are taught those things for which their brains are adapted."[26]

Owen Wister thus reflected not only his inheritance of a remnant of the attitude of his slave-owning "ancestress by the name of Mary Middleton buried in the churchyard of St. Michael's," but a larger measure of the intellectual tension that enveloped Pierce Butler's and Fanny Kemble's attitudes toward those Major Butler had called "the wretched Affricans." The ambiguity of Owen Wister's views on the blacks was evident in his astonishment that first the readers of *Lady Baltimore* and then his friend Theodore Roosevelt had taken him to task for "a feeling against the colored race," a feeling that he denied he harbored. Yet, in denying that feeling, and in his rejection of the Roosevelt criticism, he showed himself to be both literally and intellectually the inheritor of his two embattled grandparents.[27]

 *Epilogue*

FOLLOWING THE PATTERN set by Owen and Molly Wister, handsome Alice Dudley Leigh wed her cousin Richard Pierce Butler in 1906 at her father's Hereford Cathedral. Major Pierce Butler's parents, Lady Henrietta and Sir Richard Butler, the fifth baronet of Cloughrenan, were their common ancestors—grandparents of both, four greats for Richard, three for Alice. The young Richard Butler was the eleventh baronet; his bride became "Lady Alice." Owen Wister, his mother, and Henry James, who had kept in touch with the Wisters and Leighs, attended the wedding. It was an occasion honored by members of St. Cyprian's Church in distant Darien on the Altamaha River. The bride's mother had sent money for a reception and a dinner for those who had known and loved "Miss Alice."

The wedding at Hereford Cathedral was the last time Henry James and Sarah Wister were to see each other, for she died in 1908 while living at Butler Place where she had been born seventy-three years before. She was remembered in her last years riding sidesaddle in Wissahickon Park "dressed entirely in dove gray with a gray bowler hat," or at home, "tall, slender and old" and wearing a white lace cap and long, flowing garments. Hampton plantation, which had not sold, was left to her son Dan.[1]

For Henry James, the death of his old friend "Mrs. Wister" found him viewing the Leighs in a new and different light. His fondness for the Dean and Frances was evident at the wedding of Sir Richard Butler and Alice Leigh, and in late 1909 a letter to Owen Wister mentioned seeing them at Hereford, where "They were most kind, the Dean dear and delightful beyond even his ancient dearness." When Frances Leigh died a year later in England, Henry James wrote Dean Leigh from Cambridge, Massachusetts: "My long friendship with her mother and her sister gave me a sense of warmth to her that grew stronger after they were gone. Now that she has followed them a wonderful chapter has been closed."

The "Venerable and Honorable Dean Leigh" believed the health of his "beloved wife" was undermined by her work in Civil War hospitals and on the plantations after her father's death. Dean Leigh was proud that "a beautiful window by Powell of Whitefriars was erected in Hereford Cathedral to her memory." The plantation people remembered Frances Leigh as well. When news of her death reached Darien, the Mann School of St. Cyprian's was draped in black and kept that way "for forty-two days & People came from all around for days & weeks to see it."[2]

A few years later, Dean Leigh told of another death. It was in the winter of 1916 when "this old and valued friend," Henry James, died in England. The Dean attended the funeral service "At the old parish church, Chelsea, which notwithstanding a heavy storm, was crowded with his numerous friends, literary and dramatic."[3]

In the first decade of the new century Owen Wister's life was marked by illness at home and by frequent periods of illness, depression, recovery, or rest away from Molly and their children. Their first child was Mary Channing Wister, Jr., born in 1899. Four other children soon followed, all born in their Philadelphia home at 913 Pine Street, where a Sully portrait of Fanny Kemble graced the front parlor. Twins Owen Jones Wister and Frances Kemble Wister were born in 1901, William Rotch Wister II, in 1904, and Charles Kemble Butler Wister, in 1908. While Owen Wister was unable to be husband, father, or author with any persistence, Molly Wister held "magnificently" to her role as wife and mother, continued her work at the Civic Club, and somehow made of their marriage, if not a happy existence, one in which strong love was present. She understood that his poor health stemmed from the physical abuse he had received as a child at winter-cold Hofwyl and that his depression arose from the misguided pressures put upon him by his father. She helped to redirect his considerable talents from the music he loved to the writing he did so well. Of his first novel, *The Virginian,* the *New York Times* had said, "Owen Wister has come pretty near to writing the American novel." It was a work of fiction that bespoke the times as truly as history. That he always held Molly's and his children's love and respect was a measure of the man. Yet, he seemed unaware of his wife's strength until after her death that followed the difficult birth in 1913 of their sixth child, a brain-damaged daughter they called Sarah Butler Wister. The birth took place at their summer home, Crowfield, in Saunderstown, Rhode Island. Molly Wister was buried at Laurel Hill in Philadelphia following a Unitarian service at Butler Place. Among the hundreds of messages sent to the Wisters was one to Owen from Theodore Roosevelt at Sagamore Hill. He wished he could help "while you tread the dark valley alone" and ended an emotional letter, "Be brave, oh gallant and highhearted friend and comrade. Face the darkness fearlessly, for whether it be light or dark you must bear yourself well in the Great Adventure."[4]

For Owen Wister, the "Great Adventure" was hardly that. His love for Molly through the years of their marriage had the same aura of detachment that had existed in his mother's relationship with his father. In the long period between Molly Wister's death and his in 1938 he found that life without her had lost most of its meaning. An entry in his diary on a summer's day in 1915:

> Lovely day—Sweet with breezes, and roses, and windows open, and waving muslin curtains. And I sit here with my solitude, up in our bed-room. It is not a fierce suffocation to-day—That will be so, often enough, and as long as I live, I suppose. The roses fill the house and bring my mother back also. Where are they, all my dead? And she who most was mine? Lowell wrote:

> *An angel stood and met my gaze,*
> *Through the low doorway of my tent;*
> *The tent is struck, the vision stays;—*
> *I only know she came and went.*

> Our fifteen years as man and wife with the years of increasing affection that preceded them, are still too close to make anything so brief as a vision— Shall I live long enough for them to recede and merge into a single memory of the soul? I think it little likely.[5]

In 1920 Owen Wister sold Major Butler's Hampton plantation to a development company on St. Simons Island. The price was $45,000 for all of the wet and dry lands, a total of 3,880 acres. The buyers made a partial payment and gave a mortgage for the balance. In 1922 they defaulted on a principal debt of $27,500, causing reacquisition of the original 1,700 acres at a sheriff's sale in which the old place was "knocked down to Owen Wister" for $5,000. The following year the Butler connec-

Sarah Butler Wister, "tall, slender and old." (Historical Society of Pennsylvania.)

tion was finally severed when the plantation was bought by John A. Metcalf for $25,000.⁶

THE NORTHWEST CORNER lot at Chestnut and Eighth streets, on which was located Major Butler's fine Philadelphia house, became successively the site of Sharpless Brothers' retail store, then several other commercial establishments, and in 1907 "a huge amusement palace where the patrons will be diverted by penny and nickel in the slot machines and other species of cheap entertainment." At present, the large lot is vacant except for a very small and somewhat battered stand-up sandwich shop called the "Mini Corner."⁷

The Philadelphia Club remains at the northwest corner of Walnut and Thirteenth streets after a century and a third in Thomas Butler's splendid house. It is unlikely that any present member could drink a glass of Butler Madeira while standing on his head.⁸

Major Butler's rural retreats, Butler Place and York Farm, were disposed of piecemeal, often to meet demands coming from the Leighs. In 1903 Sarah Wister considered subdividing the entire property, but did not do so. After her death the Owen Wisters moved in from their cramped quarters on Pine Street. Fanny Kemble, as Mrs. Pierce Butler, had left her mark. There were double rows of maple trees and spaced along the driveway were tubbed oleanders and the citrus trees brought from Butler's Island. Within the house were Kemble family portraits by Sir Thomas Lawrence and Sir Joshua Reynolds and Owen Wister's piano on which he played Hasty Pudding airs composed in his Harvard College days. York Farm, including the house where Pierce Butler stayed during the Civil War and where Fanny Kemble lived during her final visit to America, was sold first. With the farm went Pierce Butler's chapel, the "House of Prayer" in which the son-in-law he never knew held occasional services. In June 1915, Owen Wister wrote: "How beautiful this season is and how lovely does my home look in its green and its flowers! Millions of dollars could never give me what I shall part with when I have to part with Butler Place." And in June, a year later: "Butler Place still exists but doomed to be obliterated in a few years by the swiftly advancing town." It was. In 1924, after having been reduced to seventeen acres by segmental sales, the old place that had been in the family for one hundred and fourteen years was sold by Owen Wister. His daughter told of the results:

> The house at Butler Place was pulled down and all the barns and greenhouses as well, and the land was filled with row houses, which were very

The memorial window to Frances Butler Leigh in the Cathedral at Hereford. (Courtesy of the Dean and Chapter of Hereford Cathedral.)

small and ugly. There is a Kemble avenue and a Kemble Park in that neighborhood, however. We became an affluent family, owing to the million dollars from the sale of Butler Place, and so we owe our fortune to Fanny Kemble, who had demanded the mortgage from Pierce in the divorce settlement.

And to Major Butler who bought it in 1810 for sixteen thousand dollars.[9]

As Owen Wister neared the end of his life, he sought assistance from an old family friend, Florence Bayard Kane, who was "Aunt Fol" to his children. Miss Kane took on the difficult but interesting task of assembling Wister and Butler family papers that went far back to Major Butler's time on that side of the family and through Butlers, Kembles, Leighs, and Wisters of the generations that followed. Most of the vast collection was deposited with the Historical Society of Pennsylvania in Philadelphia, with a generous portion placed at the Library of Congress in Washington. Miss Kane penned pertinent information on bits of paper attached to letters and documents and on occasion made broader comment. One such observation: "Nothing related to Major Butler or his period is without interest. If material has been filed which his descendants do not care to keep themselves, they may be sure there is nothing *save in the Archives,* which they need object to giving to the Historical Society of Pennsylvania." When Miss Kane unearthed some Sartoris material it caused Owen Wister to become reflective:

> In thinking over Aunt Adelaide, I'm struck with the difference between Pierce Butler & Edward Sartoris. Both those tremendous sisters must have been very hard to live with at times—but Butler failed where Sartoris succeeded. I was brought up to revere my Grandfather, He did indeed make both his daughters adore him; that's a cardinal point in his favor when it comes to the Day of Judgement. Only since I have been past middle life have I gradually made out that on the whole he couldn't have been a good person, while Fanny Kemble, poor tempestuous spirit, swinging restlessly between dark & light, was noble & magnanimous. Butler was cold. Never forgave. That's the root of the trouble. Well. All dead & gone. The pale wraith of them that lives in me, sometimes, when I think of them, how vital and superb those sisters were, how much they exceed the average in their dimensions, glows for a moment in their light.[10]

Owen Wister's life ended in North Kingston, Rhode Island, on July 21, 1938, one week after his seventy-eighth birthday.[11]

In South Carolina, Colonel Thomas Middleton's Beaufort town house still stands but is now obscured by a storefront appendage and is not recognizable as the fine home or the tavern at the Sign of the White Hart it had been in the 1760s. Nearby, many old plantations remain intact, their present-day owners more interested in shooting than planting. Of those inherited from Mary Bull by Mary Middleton, none retain their original identity. Coosaw Island, which was called Bull's Island, is now accessible from Beaufort and Ladies Island by a bridge across Lucy Point Creek. Despite residential development, much of the island continues to resemble an African landscape. The site of the Bull-Middleton homeplace has been eroded away by northeast winds and storm tides on the Coosaw River but is revealed on the shoreline by fragments of bricks and bits of glass and china. The plantations Major Butler called the Euhaws on the Broad River on the opposite side of Beaufort from Coosaw are difficult to identify. The tidal waters of Euhaw Creek rise and fall without restraint in the abandoned rice fields. On the Combahee River, the plantation inherited by the Butler children from Mary Izard Brewton and Elizabeth Izard Blake, then called "Izard's No. 1 and No. 2," and that came to be known as "Brewton," had an interesting transition. After changing hands in transactions that altered original boundaries, the principal homesite and its 366 acres is now owned by a descendant of the slaves who once labored in the rice fields along the dark river. He is "Smokin' Joe" Frazier, the fighter and former heavyweight champion of the world.[12]

With two exceptions, the several tracts of Major Butler's old Georgia plantations are now easily accessible. A paved road takes one to Hampton at the northern end of St. Simons Island, where a network of black-topped drives covers the narrow finger of land where once the finest cotton in the New World was grown. Fragments of heavy tabby walls are all that remain of plantation structures—remnants of slave quarters and plantation buildings. Among the great live oaks the few modern houses seem an intrusion. The two principal roadways are named "Pierce Butler Drive" and "Hampton Point Drive." The shorter thoroughfares, or streets, are called "Fanny Kemble," "Mease," "Aaron Burr," "Charleston," and "Sallie"—but no "Fan," or "Frances." "Roswell King" is there, and the slaves are represented by "Driver Morris" Street. From the part of the point that fronts on the Hampton River there is a fine view over the marsh on the other side of the tidal stream. To the west, and among the inaccessible marshes of Experiment, is the site of Five Pound Tree but nothing to indicate it was ever there, except that on closer inspection by boat or by a view from the air Major Butler's cotton and rice fields are discernible by eroded but still visible canals and banks.[13]

Little St. Simons Island, where Driver Morris saved the lives of his fellow slaves during Aaron Burr's hurricane, and where "Hassam," the wild horse, swam ashore in 1874, continues remote but accessible by boat. A hospitable inn offers the island's "wild, weird, picturesque beauty" that Fanny Kemble Butler found in 1839—a low-country seashore with all of its natural magnificence.[14]

After Frances Leigh sold Butler's Island it continued as a rice plantation but was no more successful than when under her supervision or ownership. Following a series of foreclosure sales, the island enjoyed a brief period of agricultural rejuvenation after being acquired at a sheriff's sale in 1927 by Colonel Tillinghast L. Huston, an owner of the world's champion New York Yankees in the days of George Herman "Babe" Ruth. Colonel Huston brought in a fine herd of dairy cattle and installed electric milking equipment. The old rice fields were revitalized for the planting of iceberg lettuce, celery, canna lilies, and gladioli, a venture that may well have succeeded had the imaginative Colonel Huston lived to direct his enterprise through the difficult years of the depression. In the late 1940s Richard Reynolds of the North Carolina tobacco family, who also owned most of Sapelo, purchased Butler's Island and gave it a halfhearted try in the manner of Colonel Huston. The island today is a wildlife refuge owned and managed by the state of Georgia. From the Butler days, the rice, the cotton, sugar cane, oranges, and those who labored in the fields are gone. Huston's and Reynolds's dairy cattle, lettuce, celery, and acres of flowers are gone, too. Unchanged are the turgid branches of the Altamaha in which the island rests—still very much the same "mud sponge" Fanny Kemble Butler encountered in 1839. U.S. Highway 17 is built upon the roadbed of the long-abandoned Georgia Coast and Piedmont Railroad. It crosses the old plantation, as does Interstate Highway 95. The rice field banks and the tall towerlike chimney of one of the Butler rice mills are the most prominent relics of the past, but scattered over the island are other ruins, most of which are covered by deepening layers of silt or enveloped in a dense overgrowth of plantlife.[15]

For a time during the hot summer months of 1978 and 1979, a group of young people from the University of Florida worked on the island in an archaeological search for the several slave settlements and other plantation structures that existed when the Butlers were in prominence. The search was a project headed by a young woman, Teresa Singleton, who was to use her report of findings as a doctoral dissertation at the university. The young archaeologists found Butler's Island a true test, for Altamaha freshets and years of neglect of the restraining rice field banks in the early part of the century had caused silt-laden sites to be reduced to vague outlines and piles of rubble where chimneys had collapsed and crumbled. Singleton, who is a descendant of free blacks in Charleston, and her fellow students developed an appreciative understanding of her African forebears. It was a turnabout—a Butler's Island work force of whites and one Oriental supervised by a black, and a black woman, at that.[16]

A new threat confronts Roswell, the Georgia hill-country village Major Butler's manager Roswell King founded and gave his own name. The handsome houses that survived General Sherman's fiery march to the sea are now surrounded by an invasion of almost thirty thousand people who occupy a bedroom community for the city of Atlanta. To reach what was once a village of a few beautiful homes on generous parcels of land, a visitor must now run a gauntlet of fastfood franchises and roadside enterprises beyond the wildest dreams of the King family and General Sherman. Yet for now, the houses are intact. The King's Presbyterian Church is there on its hilltop, with its slave balcony, and a memorial plaque to:

Charles Pratt and John Hall
NEGRO SLAVES
Members of the Church, Educated and Freed
To Go To Africa As Missionaries[17]

Today, more than two centuries after Major Butler of His Majesty's Twenty-ninth Regiment of Foot and Mary Middleton were married in South Carolina, their Irish grandson—three greats—is the twelfth and present baronet. He, Colonel Sir Thomas Pierce Butler of Cloughrenan, C.V.O., D.S.O., O.B.E., is the distinguished only son of Sir Richard Pierce Butler, the eleventh baronet, and Lady Alice Dudley Leigh Butler.[18]

In America, the line from Mary and Major Pierce Butler continued in Mitchell grandsons of Mary Mease and Alfred Elwyn, through McAllister granddaughters of Gabriella and John Butler, and in Wister grandchildren of Sarah and Owen Jones Wister.[19]

OF THE DESCENDANTS of the Butler slaves, their latter-day progeny are widely scattered, but if there is a concentration it has to be in

Darien, the surrounding countryside, and the coastal areas of McIntosh and Glynn counties. A surprising number of the small homes the newly freed slaves acquired in or about Darien are there today. A composition, or metal roof, has replaced the cypress shingles and electric lights, the homemade candles and kerosene lamps, but no dramatic change has been achieved from the cabins in which their grandparents lived. The present-day descendants fish and farm, work for local businesses and industry, or government, teach school, along with other residents of the coastal region, with each race having a tendency to go its own way. Relations between blacks and whites appear to be natural and easy, but beneath the surface there is an undercurrent of mistrust. The Lord is still worshiped at Darien's two Episcopal churches, the white St. Andrew's and the black St. Cyprian's. At present the thirty-seven communicants of St. Cyprian's are served by the white vicar of St. Andrew's. The Mann School is gone.

The Butler workers who left the plantations for life in the larger cities of Savannah and Brunswick, and who stayed there, have been assimilated into the large black communities of those cities. For a time, those from particular areas—Sapelo, St. Catherines, the Altamaha—banded together, but that affinity gradually faded away as did the strong characteristics their insular lives had encouraged. In present-day Savannah and Brunswick, the Gullah speech, the old ways of dancing, the old spirituals, have all but vanished. Indicative of the change that has come to urban blacks is the naming of their children. Gone are the Caesars, Daphnes, Pompeys, the Glasgows, Londons, Yorks, the Rovers, Dandys, Adams, Eves, and the African names of Quacco, Quash, Minda, or Bina. All are now ignored for the new African, the Swahilian and Muslim—the Rashidas, Nadiyahs, or Shamekas. In one county birth report for a single week, the following given names appeared: Taheerah, Samiyah, Ayeasha, Je'nai, Tanesha Nicole, Jasmin Ida, Aren Daishan, Jwan Andrea, and shades of Driver Morris, Cozy Maurice.[20]

Of the one hundred and thirty-nine slaves from Hampton who were taken to Halifax, Nova Scotia, in 1815 by the British navy, not all kept the surname thrust upon them, nor did all remain in that northern land. Today, black Butlers are neither plentiful nor prominent. Hammond's Plains, the community that for a time seemed an outpost of St. Simons Island, still exists, its black residents having shown perseverance and remarkable stamina, though little progress. They are said to be more "orderly" and not so "assertive" as the black Haligonians of the capital city. The descendants of the 1815 "Refugee Negroes" have lost their identity as such and are but part of the whole—inheritors of the strengths and weaknesses of the Loyalists' slaves, the Revolution's refugees, the Maroons, and other blacks who found their way to that maritime province.

That some customs persisted is evident from the journal of a British seaman who visited Nova Scotia in 1901 aboard HMS *Ophir*. It was the royal tour of the Duke and Duchess of Cornwall and York, who later became George V and Queen Mary. While in Halifax, the seaman noted a bit of Negro culture imported from the Georgia coast:

> One thing about "Halifax" was they knew how to treat a sailor, when he happened to be partaking of a meal. I say for myself that I never had better meals and the charge was very moderate. Of course, being one of the ordinaries, I made tracks for some of the low class drinking dens and met with an agreeable surprise. The neighbourhood was infested with coloured folks, and judge to my surprise when I found them singing just the same coon songs that were so popular at home, and the same old cake walk was very popular there also. But their singing, and dancing had a certain peculiarity about it, that our professionals in the music halls could never attain to the life.[21]

The dozen fiddles Roswell King had given the Butler slaves in 1804 to encourage dancing and discourage preaching had made a lasting impact.[22]

And it may well be that Ormonde and Northumberland blood courses the veins of some descendants of slaves who worked the Altamaha plantations. If so, it would not have surprised certain members of the family who believed Major Butler and his grandson Pierce continued that proud blood in mulatto children of women they had enslaved.

THE "Accommodation" Major Butler reluctantly conceded to his fellow delegates at the Constitutional Convention was an attitude he seldom granted his family. In the yard of Christ Church, Philadelphia, the two Butler tombs, some distance apart, give silent testimony to the alienation he fostered in his own time and that continued in following generations. Thomas Butler, his young daughter Anne, his first son, Francis, and possibly his sister Frances are buried in the elaborate tomb he constructed away from the burial vault of his father's. In that tomb, in which Major Butler had interred his ten-year-old grandson, Pierce Mease, who was buried as Pierce Butler, Jr., in 1810, there are eleven or twelve others. The first to follow the boy was Major Butler's daughter, Harriot Percy Butler, in 1815. Next, in 1822, the Major himself. There followed in 1823 his grandson Thomas Mease, who preferred his own name to his grandfather's fortune. In 1831, the Major's first daughter, Sarah Butler Mease, became the fifth occupant, probably followed in 1836 by her sister, Frances Butler. Next, the Major's grandson, John Butler, who did forsake the name Mease and whose body was brought home from Mexico where he died in 1847. The infant great-great-grandson John McAllister, who died in 1850, was followed by the Major's daughter, Anne Eliza Butler, the last of her generation, in 1854. In 1862 the vault was opened again, for great-granddaughter Elizabeth Butler McAllister who was born a Mease, and she preceded her son Francis Butler, the second of the Major's great-great-grandsons, who was actually a McAllister and was buried in 1863. Then, in 1867, came Pierce Butler, the grandson and inheritor, born a Mease, from his temporary resting place on the Ridge near Darien. Finally, and to round out this incompatible gathering, there was Gabriella Manigault Morris Butler, who married a Mease, in 1871.[23]

If ever there will be "a great gittin' up morning" as many Butler slaves and their progeny sang and believed, the two Butler tombs in the Christ Church yard will bear watching. In another low-country resurrection day spiritual there is a line, "We will drink wine together on that day." For the Butlers, perhaps. Most did have an affinity for wines. But, considering their "clashing interests," such a happening would be most unlikely.[24]

If Major Pierce Butler deserves a medal, it would be for his ability to subdue his stubborn and often-misguided determination, to permit a successful adjournment of the Constitutional Convention at Philadelphia in 1787. That he, who was certainly something less than a champion of the rights of man, should have played a role in fashioning such a document as the Constitution, is difficult to contemplate. Samuel Eliot Morison called the drafting of the Constitution "a capital achievement" and "a work of genius." That the delegates were able to reconcile "unity with diversity," Morison said, was the United States' "most original contribution" to human liberty. Major Butler did share that feeling, though expressed it differently. He saw the delegates reconciling those "clashing interests" and thus being able to bring about the "Pretty General Spirit of Accommodation" that enabled the diverse interests to complete their task. In truth, his was the interest that clashed so frequently with reason and right. And it should not be forgotten that Major Pierce Butler and the other South Carolina delegates helped to make the Constitution something less than it might have been. These men put aside reason and right, and left their slaves bound and fettered to await the breaking of their chains by Abraham Lincoln and William Tecumseh Sherman.[25]

 *Personae*

The Butler Family

The First Generation

PIERCE BUTLER, 1744–1822, and his wife MARY MIDDLETON BUTLER, d. 1790. Pierce Butler was the third son and one of the ten children of Sir Richard Butler, the fifth baronet of Cloughrenan in Ireland, and Lady Henrietta Percy Butler. He was born on July 11, 1744, at Garryhunden and was commissioned in the British army when eleven years old, a duty he assumed at fifteen as a lieutenant in the famed "Cheshire" regiment, the Twenty-second Foot. He was wounded at Louisbourg in 1758 and became a captain in 1761 in the Twenty-ninth "Worcester" regiment. In 1766 he was made a major and thereafter preferred to be known by that title. In 1767 Major Butler visited Charlestown on regimental business, and there set his cap to win a South Carolina heiress, an accomplishment fulfilled in 1771 when he and Mary Middleton were married.

Mary Middleton was the second daughter and one of the three children of Colonel Thomas Middleton and his first wife, Mary Bull Middleton. She was a proper heiress, for with her sister, Sarah Guerard, and two cousins, Elizabeth Izard Blake and Mary Izard Brewton, she was to share an inheritance from their grandmother, Mary Brandford Bull. Grandmother Bull left a vast estate of several plantations, hundreds of slaves, and ample "ready money."

His bride's inheritance caused Pierce Butler to forsake his military career and his allegiance to king and country to become a low-country planter and patriot. He used the proceeds from the sale of his army commission to purchase plantations on the estuary of Georgia's Altamaha River, where there, and on his wife's Carolina plantations, commenced a Butler dependency on black slaves that was to continue until emancipation in the 1860s.

Pierce Butler's service to his state and nation was shown in a halfhearted mili-

483

tary career during the Revolution, as a South Carolina legislator over a long span of years, as a delegate to the Constitutional Convention in Philadelphia, to the Continental Congress, and as South Carolina's first United States senator. He held the latter office for one full term and parts of two others. He championed the slavery he practiced.

The Butlers lived for a time at the old Bull plantation on Coosaw Island, near Beaufort, and then in the city of Charlestown. After the Revolution they purchased and lived at Mary Ville, their plantation on the Ashley River twelve miles from Charleston. They had eight children, two of whom were unknown to succeeding generations of their family. Five of the eight lived to maturity. While Major Butler's life is well documented, and the children's in varying degrees, the life of Mary Middleton Butler remains obscure. She died in New York in 1790, and thereafter the family lived in Philadelphia and in a summer home near Germantown, on the old York Road.

Pierce Butler's headstrong approach to family and public life brought trouble and unhappiness. His death in Philadelphia in 1822 was unlamented and little noticed beyond the family and their friends.

The Second Generation

Of the eight children of Pierce and Mary Butler, their first was SARAH BUTLER, 1772?–1831, who married JAMES MEASE, M.D., 1771–1845.

Sarah Butler, called Sally when she was young, was long her father's favorite child. This advantageous position ended in 1800 when Sarah married Dr. James Mease (pronounced "Mays"), a young Philadelphian held in low regard by Major Butler. She inherited her father's alert mind, many of his peculiarities, and some developed on her own. She had little respect for her brother Thomas and, when she was superseded by her sister Frances as her father's chosen one, disdained her sister as well. Sarah Mease was accused of "disrespectful obstinacy" by her father when the first of her sons named for him died in 1810. She was bright, well educated, an avid reader except of the Bible, and was known about Philadelphia as a "free thinker." One who knew her said she was "lady-like" and in her later years, "something of an invalid." At her death in 1831 she was alienated from brother and sisters.

Dr. James Mease was regarded as a character about Philadelphia, not unlike his father, John Mease, who had crossed the Delaware with General Washington and who persistently wore his 1776 headgear and was known as the "last of the cocked hats." Dr. Mease was small and handsome and was possessed of an assortment of interests. He dabbled in agricultural science, writing, and the practice of medicine. His portrait was painted by Thomas Sully.

Sarah and James Mease had six children. Of their four sons, two died young and two chose to put aside their family name for "Butler" to enable them to inherit their grandfather's fortune. The two daughters made interesting marriages to Philadelphians.

The second and third of the children of Pierce and Mary Butler were ANNE ELIZ-ABETH BUTLER, 1774–1854, and her twin sister, FRANCES BUTLER, 1774–1836.

Anne Elizabeth and Frances Butler were born in South Carolina and lived there until the family's move to Philadelphia following their mother's death in 1790. Of the two, more is known of Frances than of Anne Elizabeth, despite Eliza, as she was called, having lived eighteen years after the death of her twin.

Frances Butler was named for her father's favorite sister. In telling the Irish Frances of her American namesake, he wrote: "She has a very good understanding—a mind as pure and chaste as innocence can make it—with vast sensibility." And he added, "She is, as indeed the four are, truly amiable." But, as a young woman she was plagued by a poor complexion causing her father to seek help from Dr. Benjamin Rush as she was inclined to "sequester herself from society." When Sarah Mease and Thomas Butler became alienated from their father, Frances became the one on whom he leaned. He relied on her good business sense in administering many properties, including the important Georgia plantations, a responsibility maintained long after his death in 1822 until her own in 1836. Frances was given generous treatment in her father's will and lived comfortably in Philadelphia on income from the "Negro Property" in Georgia. At her death the sizable estate she had accumulated on her own was bestowed upon her brother Thomas.

Eliza Butler, who lived the longest of the Butler offspring, received one-half of the plantation income following the death of Frances, some of which she spared to her wayward nephew Pierce Butler and his trouble-ridden family. She accompanied them as far as Charleston on their fateful visit to the "Georgian Plantation" in 1838. It was he who closed her eyes in death in 1854 at her Walnut Street home in Philadelphia.

Frances and Eliza Butler accepted the family's ownership of slaves without noticeable misgiving. Frances did show more than casual interest by frequent gifts of clothing and by recognition of "faithful service" in her years as executor, or as "Proprietor," of her father's estate.

The fourth child of Pierce and Mary Butler was HARRIOT PERCY BUTLER, 1775?–1815.

Although family records show Harriot Percy to have been the youngest of the four daughters, her father wrote she was born between her sister Sarah and the twins Frances and Eliza. She was named for her Irish grandmother, the wife and widow of Sir Richard Butler, the fifth baronet of Cloughrenan. As did Lady Butler, who used both names, Harriot sometimes referred to herself as "Henrietta." She appears infrequently in Butler correspondence, for a brief time in letters to and from the Doctors Rush—Benjamin and his son James—and finally when the "melancholy account" of her death at Philadelphia was duly noted by Roswell King at Hampton.

The fifth child of Pierce and Mary Butler was PIERCE BUTLER, 1777–1780.

Major Butler called this child "my Favourite Son, the Promising Prop of my latter days." The child died of accidental burns during the Revolution while the family was living in Charlestown and Major Butler was away in North Carolina. He was buried in the church yard of St. Philips.

The sixth child, and only surviving son recognized as such by Pierce and Mary Butler, was THOMAS BUTLER, 1778–1838, who married ELIZA DE MALLEVAULT, 1792–183?.

In 1784 six-year-old Thomas Butler was taken from South Carolina to England, where for eleven years he lived and studied at the classical school of the Reverend Weeden Butler in Chelsea on the bank of the Thames. An indifferent scholar, Thomas returned to America in 1795 to confront his disappointed father. He was far from being the "Man of Letters" or the "Distinguished Ornament" his father had demanded and was put aside as heir apparent to the family fortune in favor of his older sister Sarah, and later, the first of her two sons, both named Pierce Butler Mease. Thomas won additional disfavor from Major Butler when he married an attractive young French woman from an aristocratic family who owned a large sugar plantation on the island of Martinique. Henriette Reine Louise Guillemine Luce Eliza de Mallevault was born on Martinique and was fourteen years younger than Thomas. She was the daughter of Louis Charles François de Mallevault, a captain in the Royal navy, and Anne Magdeline Guillemine Pinel Dumanoir. Pompous and intolerant, Thomas Butler brought little happiness to a union that produced four children, two of whom died young in Paris where the family lived with the widowed Madame de Mallevault. The three sons suffered the same alienation Major Butler had bestowed on their father. While living in France the unhappy family was decimated by the deaths of Eliza, their oldest son, and the only daughter. Thomas Butler then returned to Philadelphia to assist his sister Frances in administering the Butler estate until her death in 1836. He lived not long enough to enjoy the wealth left him by Frances, nor did he see the completion of houses in Philadelphia and Newport. Before his death in Philadelphia in 1838 Thomas somehow brought himself to direct that his estate go to one of the two surviving sons. The other son he ignored as though not a Butler.

The seventh and eighth children of Pierce and Mary Butler were sons about whom little is known. In 1794 Major Butler wrote a friend that Thomas was the only son of four then living. In 1803, a confidential letter from Harriot Percy Butler to Dr.

Benjamin Rush told of the death of an unnamed person who had been born in 1781 and for whom Dr. Rush prepared a short memorial verse of the kind that adorn gravestones. If this young person was one of the sons, the family's desire that he not be acknowledged brings on conjecture as to their reasons.

The Third Generation

Of the six children of Sarah Butler and Dr. James Mease, the first was PIERCE BUTLER MEASE, 1801–1810.

This was the first of two of their sons to be named for Major Butler. His death in the tenth year of his life distressed Sarah Mease's father, for the boy had already replaced Thomas Butler in Major Butler's plans for the future of the Georgia plantations. "I have lost the last, the only prop of my declining years" wrote the disconsolate grandfather who blamed the boy's parents for his death. Major Butler buried the child as "Pierce Butler, Junior," assuming a control in death he did not have in life. Twelve years later the old Major shared his grandson's grave.

The second child of Sarah Butler and Dr. James Mease was MARY MIDDLETON MEASE, 1802–1884, who married DR. ALFRED LANGDON ELWYN, 1804–1884.

When Mary was thirteen, Major Butler presented her with an English piano. "She tried it this morning and is much pleased." Mary, who was named for her grandmother Butler, married Dr. Elwyn in 1832. He was said to be "respectable and intelligent," and together, the Elwyns were the most reasonable and normal of the families that came from the marriages of the Mease offspring. Dr. Elwyn's grandfather, John Langdon of New Hampshire, served at the Constitutional Convention and in the United States Senate with Major Butler. Dr. Elwyn conveyed his knowledge of older Butlers to their niece Sarah Butler Wister, the daughter of Mary's brother Pierce. On slavery, which Dr. Elwyn opposed, he told of a conversation with President Madison, who said that Elwyn would "live to see the day when a quarrel on slavery would tear this country to pieces." Said Elwyn, "I have lived to see that day." It was he who told Sarah Wister that Major Butler's private life had best remain unopened. The Elwyn daughter, also named Mary Middleton, married Dr. S. Weir Mitchell, an admirer of Sarah Butler Wister and a friend and physician to her son, Owen Wister.

The third child of Sarah Butler and Dr. James Mease was THOMAS MEASE, 1803–1823.

It was Thomas Mease, eighteen years old when his grandfather died, who refused to change his name to Butler so that he might share Major Butler's fortune. He urged his younger brothers, John and Pierce, to hold fast to their family name and perhaps would have persuaded them to do so had he not died in 1823. He was buried at Christ Church, Philadelphia, the fourth of the family to occupy the Butler tomb.

The fourth child of Sarah Butler and Dr. James Mease was JOHN (MEASE) BUTLER, 1806–1847, who married GABRIELLA MANIGAULT MORRIS, d. 1871.

John Butler, born Mease in Philadelphia in 1806, was one of the three Mease grandsons of Major Butler who were designated to inherit the Georgia plantations. He first refused to change his name from Mease to Butler, but did so in 1831 and thus shared the estate with his brother Pierce.

As John Mease he had married Gabriella Morris in 1827. She was the daughter of Colonel Lewis M. Morris, of Morrisania, New York, and Elizabeth Manigault of South Carolina. Lovely to look upon, Gabriella was an interesting mix of North and South and, although said to lack intelligence, was possessed of an independent spirit that was demonstrated in her determination to capture her and her child's right to share Major Butler's legacy. A sharp-eyed observer saw her at a Philadelphia ball in 1837: "Superb in gold turban and a dress of maroon velvet. Such a costume suits her magnificent style of beauty. She is certainly the most beautiful woman here, tho a little faded. Her manner is very gracious, and perfectly simple and unaffected. She never seems the slightest degree conscious of her appearance & has I think more sense than people generally give her credit for." The same observer took note of John Butler a few years later. Again at a ball, he was in costume: "He has a fine figure & a graceful manner & I never saw a more splendid looking fellow than he was that night."

An excellent horseman, John Butler was a captain in Philadelphia's City Troop. His death from virulent dysentery while waging war in Mexico created a problem of what to do about his slave-servant John and his two fine horses, all abandoned on that distant battleground. He was handsome, stylish, mannerly, wealthy, and inconsequential. His last will was a testament to a paucity of human spirit.

Gabriella Butler outlived her husband by twenty-four years. Of their two children, the daughter Elizabeth died unexpectedly in 1862. The firstborn, Pierce, died in Paris in his second year. John Butler was the sixth of the family to be buried in the Butler tomb at Christ Church. Gabriella was the twelfth, and last.

The fifth child of Sarah Butler and Dr. James Mease was FRANCES MEASE, 1808–1880, who married GEORGE CADWALADER, 1804–1879.

Frances, the youngest of the two Mease daughters, married George Cadwalader in Philadelphia in 1837. Her husband won a general's stars and distinction by suppressing anti-Catholic riots in Philadelphia in 1844, at Chapultepec in the Mexican War, and as a leader of Philadelphia troops in 1863. He was one of the three trustees chosen to bring order to her brother Pierce Butler's confused finances and was present at the great slave sale in Savannah in 1859. George Cadwalader was handsome, forthright, confident, intelligent, a capable lawyer, but a man with a plethora of vices. A fellow Philadelphian found him "uncultivated, unintellectual, selfish and heartless." The Cadwaladers lived in a style so lavish as to mystify most of Philadelphia. Their house had frescoed walls, fancy white-and-gold French furniture, a profusion of candelabra, the rooms "the handsomest in town." The General kept a mistress openly and, being a good provider, gave her sumptuous quarters in Philadelphia and at his place in Maryland. Should the old soldier tire of wife and mistress, he could retire to the comfort of the Philadelphia Club, which was located in Thomas Butler's Walnut Street mansion, for he had been a founder of that stalwart institution.

The Cadwaladers had no children.

The sixth child of Sarah Butler and Dr. James Mease was PIERCE (MEASE) BUTLER, 1810–1867, who married and divorced FRANCES ANNE KEMBLE, 1809–1893.

Butler Mease, as he was called, lost no time in putting aside his family name for that of his grandfather. On reaching sixteen years in 1826 he became Pierce Butler and immediately shared the earnings of the Georgia plantations with his aunts Frances and Eliza Butler. Five years later he permitted his brother John Mease to make a similar but belated change and to share the considerable income produced by nearly one thousand slaves.

In October 1832 Pierce Butler met the English actress Frances Anne Kemble, entered ardent suit, and in June 1834 the two were wed in Christ Church, Philadelphia. Their two daughters, Sarah and Frances, were born at the old family farm Butler Place, near Philadelphia, in 1835 and 1838. After a stormy life together and apart, the Butlers were divorced in 1849, their marriage rent by the infidelities of Pierce Butler and by his wife's outspoken disapproval of the family's ownership of slaves, who provided their ample means of livelihood, most of which was squandered in his dissolute life. Pierce Butler's open support of the South in 1860 and 1861 led to his arrest for treason. A brief imprisonment was followed by sullen silence until the war's end, when he and his daughter Frances, who shared his views on slavery and the South, went to Georgia in a futile attempt to restore the plantations to their prewar prosperity. Pierce Butler's life ended in 1867, when he was struck down by malarial fever induced by an overlong stay on his Altamaha rice lands. A weak and irresponsible man, he nevertheless possessed gentlemanly charm, was loved by his oldest daughter, and was loved and respected by the youngest. His attitude toward the hundreds of blacks he had inherited was almost an aloof indifference. He liked them best for what they were, or had been—slaves.

Frances Anne Kemble, known as "Fanny" all her life, was the third of five children born into the theatrical family of Charles and Marie-Therese DeCamp Kemble. Her inherited talent came down from her father, who with his sister, the splendid Sarah Siddons, was among England's preeminent performers. Fanny Kemble's own career as an actress was undertaken with some reluctance. Nevertheless, it proved to be highly successful, first in England and then in America. The American tour, begun with her father in 1832, ended following the marriage to Pierce Butler in the church where the grandfather, whose name he bore and whose fortune he enjoyed, lay buried. Until November 21, 1849, she too carried the name Butler, but thereafter was known professionally and formally as Mrs. Frances Anne Kemble.

Her life upset, Fanny Kemble returned to England to fashion an existence of theatrical readings, of writing, of new and reconstructed friendships. Her love for Sarah and Frances, even though not always returned, was true and strong. Until the death of Pierce Butler she did what she could for her children, despite the obstacles he placed in her path. After 1867 the way was easier and there were grandchildren to return her love. She lived until 1893 but was never quite able to put out of her mind the wreck of her marriage, shattered by Pierce Butler and by her advocacy of Major Butler's "wretched Affricans"—the Rentys, Psyches, Mollys, Mindas, Scyllas, Jacks, Brams, and Judys—the slaves of Hampton and Butler's Island in Georgia.

Of the four children of Thomas and Eliza de Mallevault Butler, the first was FRANCIS BUTLER, 1815?–1835?

Francis Butler was named for his father's sister Frances, the only true friend in the Butler family his father could claim. The wayward ways of Francis and his brother Louis disturbed their father, who threatened disownment. The untimely and unexplained death of Francis, about 1835, was noted in family correspondence, by his burial in the Thomas Butler tomb at Christ Church, Philadelphia, and by the disposition of his wearing apparel as directed by his father's will. Francis, having died intestate, caused the division of his share of his grandmother de Mallevault's Martinican fortune between his brothers Louis and John.

The second child of Thomas and Eliza de Mallevault Butler was LOUIS BUTLER, 1817–1890.

Louis Butler, more than his brother Francis, bore the brunt of his father's wrath for "the shameless conduct of Mr. Butler's sons" in Philadelphia and Paris. Although there was no reconciliation between father and son, Louis did inherit the Thomas Butler estate, including the new Walnut Street house that he sold to the Philadelphia Club. He found Philadelphia a cold and forbidding city and chose to live in Paris, where he shared his love for French art and music with his friend and cousin Sarah Wister on the occasion of her visits. He presented her with two miniatures that are the only known likenesses of their forebear Major Pierce Butler. Louis Butler also inherited much of the de Mallevaults' fortune, some of which he generously shared with Elizabeth Butler, the widow of his brother John who had been ignored in their father's will.

The third child of Thomas and Eliza de Mallevault Butler was JOHN BUTLER, 1819?–188?, who married ELIZABETH _____.

John Butler was ignored in the will of his aunt Frances Butler and again in the will of his father, except that he was permitted to share in that portion of the de Mallevault fortune that came to his father when his brother Francis died intestate. He lived in Paris with his wife Elizabeth, and both were known and liked by Fanny Kemble and Sarah Wister. The Butlers visited Sarah and her mother in 1872 in Rome, where Elizabeth played the piano in impromptu operas while Fanny Kemble sang baritone roles. John predeceased his brother Louis, who saw to it that Elizabeth would ultimately inherit some of their father's money by providing for her in his will.

The fourth child of Thomas and Eliza de Mallevault Butler was ANNE BUTLER, 182?–1823.

Anne Butler's illness in Paris was the reason given by Thomas Butler that he could not return to Philadelphia to attempt a reconciliation with his father. The child died the following year, was first buried at Père-Lachaise in Paris, but later was removed to the Thomas Butler tomb at Christ Church, Philadelphia.

The Fourth Generation

The daughter of Mary Middleton Mease and Alfred Langdon Elwyn was MARY MIDDLETON ELWYN, d. 1862, who was the first wife of SILAS WEIR MITCHELL, M.D., 1829–1914, and was the mother of their two sons, John and Langdon. Dr. Mitchell was an eminent Philadelphia physician, poet, and novelist. After Mary's death following the birth of Langdon, the friendship between her cousin Sarah Wister and Dr. Mitchell turned to deep devotion. They read and were critical of each other's writings, and to Dr. Mitchell, Sarah was "the most interesting woman I have ever known." Weir Mitchell was a pioneer in the use of psychology as an adjunct to the practice of medicine, and it was he who influenced a depressed Owen Wister's turn to writing by prescribing his first Wyoming trip as a remedy. From that sprang Wister's classic novel of the West, *The Virginian*. Dr. Mitchell's own historical novels were favorites of Owen Wister, who dedicated *Lady Baltimore* to him, "With the Affection and Memories of All My Life." Dr. Mitchell was an authority on fine wines. His recognition of the Butler Madeiras, frequently mentioned in his works, would have pleased Major Butler.

Of the two children of John (Mease) and Gabriella Morris Butler, the first was PIERCE BUTLER, 1828–1830.

John and Gabriella Butler's first child was born in Philadelphia and died in Paris before the family's name had been changed from Mease to Butler, yet was buried at Père-Lachaise as "Pierce Butler, Junior." He was one of several children named for Major Butler who died young.

The second child of John (Mease) and Gabriella Morris Butler was ELIZABETH MANIGAULT (MEASE) BUTLER, 1830–1862, who married JULIAN MCALLISTER, 1824–1887.

Elizabeth Butler, called "Lizzie," was born in Paris in the month following her infant brother's death. Though she was born a Mease, her name became Butler in 1831. In 1848, the year after her father's death, she married Julian McAllister of Savannah, a West Point graduate and an ordnance officer in the United States Army. While Julian McAllister was waging war on his homeland, his wife Elizabeth confronted Pierce Butler with a valid accusation of malfeasance in his role as trustee of her father's estate. She was aided by her brother-in-law Ward McAllister, who was an erstwhile lawyer as well as the social arbiter of New York and Newport. Elizabeth died unexpectedly in Newport in 1862. Equally surprising was the death of the McAllisters' son Francis the following year. He had changed his name to Butler in order to inherit the John Butler estate. Of the McAllisters' five children, John, the firstborn, died shortly after birth. The death of son Francis returned the John Butler share of Major Butler's estate to Pierce Butler, for the three daughters, all of whom lived to maturity, were barred from inheritance by their grandfather John Butler's strange will. Colonel Julian McAllister, U.S.A., died in California in 1887.

Of the two children of Pierce (Mease) Butler and Frances Anne Kemble, the first was SARAH BUTLER, 1835–1908, who married DR. OWEN JONES WISTER, 1825–1896.

Although Sarah Butler, born the year following her parents' marriage, was a bright, cheerful, healthy, and attractive girl who was much loved by both mother and father, her childhood was beset by parental strife. Born at Butler Place near Philadelphia, which was to be her home, off and on, until her death, she retained a remarkable equilibrium through the long years of the Butler-Kemble conflict that did, ultimately, leave its mark. That she was the child of her mother is evident in a descriptive bit from a friend of her mother's. Of Sally, as Sarah was sometimes called, Fredrika Bremer wrote: "A glorious girl of the New World, richly endowed in soul and body, with a spark of inspired life which is so enchanting, a girl fresh as morning dew, and who sings as I never heard anyone sing since."

In 1859 Sarah Butler married Dr. Owen Jones Wister of Germantown, a family doctor with a broad and busy practice within a thirty-mile area of his home. Dr. Wister was a kindly, gentle person with a rare sense of humor. He had an unusual tolerance and an enduring love for his emotional wife. In the trying years of the Civil War the Wisters were strongly anti-slavery, pro-Union, and thus sided with

Fanny Kemble in opposition to the equally strong proslavery, anti-Union attitudes of Pierce Butler and her sister Frances. The difference of opinion somehow did not diminish the love between the sisters, nor did it seem to affect Sarah's love for her father.

The Wisters' only child, called "Dan," was Owen Wister, whose talent and desire for a career in music was thwarted by an uncharacteristic mindset of Dr. Wister. The resulting turmoil brought unhappiness and mental anguish to the close-knit family. Travel abroad, visits to England, and to Italy in particular helped to relieve the stress and gave Sarah an opportunity to expand her good mind, to meet and know Butler and Kemble kinfolk, and to engender a lasting friendship with Henry James.

Sarah Wister shared the inheritance of the Georgia plantations with her sister Frances. Long after their productivity had vanished and the lands had returned to "the wild treasury of nature," she maintained a protective interest in the former slaves and their families.

Dr. Wister, "for whom we have such regard & in whose skill we have such confidence," died in 1896. Sarah, who was ten years younger, lived on until 1908. She died at Butler Place, where she had been born.

The second child of Pierce (Mease) Butler and Frances Anne Kemble was FRANCES KEMBLE BUTLER, 1838–1910, who married the Reverend JAMES WENTWORTH LEIGH, d. 1923.

Frances Butler was born at Butler Place on her sister Sarah's third birthday, and with her, shared the vicissitudes of childhood in a constant crossfire from parents in conflict. She inherited her mother's limitless energy but was more akin to her father in thought and attitude. Her wartime adherence to Pierce Butler's Southern proclivities continued in the peace that followed, and with him she endeavored to return the Georgia plantations to the prewar prosperity the Butler slaves had made possible. She ever believed the blacks fared better as slaves than as free people and could never understand why they would not work and obey as they had when enslaved. She helped her father rejuvenate Hampton and Butler's Island until his death in 1867, and then, against the advice of her mother and the Wisters, struggled on alone. Help appeared in 1870 when a young Englishman who was a Cambridge-educated cleric, the Reverend James Wentworth Leigh, visited Butler's Island. Smitten with the "fair Queen" amongst her "sable subjects," the Reverend Mr. Leigh entered ardent suit that brought about an 1871 wedding celebrated in England. On the plantations he quickly became the immensely popular "Massa Jimmy," or "Massa Jimbo." His hard work and Frances's kind but firm treatment of the blacks came close to making a success of a difficult venture in an unsettled postwar world. When their efforts failed, they returned to England where both wrote books that told of what it was like to live, and work free blacks, on the Altamaha River in Georgia. "Massa Jimmy" was proud of his missionary work among the black people. His St. Cyprian's Church in Darien, on which he labored, stands today. The "Vicar" of St. Cyprian's went on to a greater responsibility. He became the Very Reverend Honourable Dean Leigh of the great cathedral at Hereford.

Reluctantly, Frances Leigh disposed of her share of the Georgia plantations, selling the last tract in 1908. Two years later she died in England. Dean Leigh died in 1923.

Of the three children born to the Leighs, two sons, both named Pierce Butler, died in their infancy. Their much-loved daughter was Alice Leigh.

The Fifth Generation

The two sons of Mary Middleton Elwyn and Silas Weir Mitchell, M.D., were JOHN K. MITCHELL, M.D., 1860?–1917, who followed his father, his Mitchell grandfather for whom he was named, and his great-grandfather in the practice of medicine; and LANGDON ELWYN MITCHELL, 1862–1935, playwright and poet who also used the pseudonym John Philip Varley. Both men and their families were close friends of their cousin Owen Wister.

The five children of Elizabeth (Mease) Butler and Julian McAllister were JOHN BUTLER MCALLISTER, who was born and died in 1850; JULIA GABRIELLA MCALLISTER, 1851–1930, who died unmarried; FRANCIS (MCALLISTER) BUTLER, 1853–1863, whose name was changed so that he might inherit his grandfather's estate, and whose death in 1863 prompted the return of the Georgia plantations to his great-uncle, Pierce Butler; GABRIELLA MANIGAULT MCALLISTER, 1854–1940, who married Stanley W. Dexter; and MARGARET ELIZABETH MCALLISTER, 1859–1946, who was called "Meta" and who married John H. Janeway.

The only child of Sarah Butler and Dr. Owen Jones Wister was OWEN WISTER, 1860–1938, who married MARY CHANNING WISTER, 1870–1913.

Owen Wister was born in Germantown, and from his earliest days the free Kemble spirit that came down from his mother and her mother did battle with the straight-laced conservatism of the Quakers that engulfed Germantown and the Wisters. "Dan," as he was called, was his mother's "Child of Promise," and as such was given every opportunity to express himself, be it in conversation or music, in his reading, and later in his writing. His early years were those of wartime. Battlefield casualties brought into Philadelphia so occupied Dr. Wister's time and skill that he could pay little or no attention to his son. As a consequence, Sarah Wister became the child's guide. It was she who gave him a start in the music that revealed a rare talent, and it was she who steered him away from the cautious course Dr. Wister would have prescribed. At war's end he was taken first to a boy's school in Switzerland for the beginnings of a comprehensive, classical education, and then on to England to live with "Aunt Frances and Uncle Jimmy Leigh" at Stoneleigh, where his life was enriched by an absorption of England's traditional values. After England came school in America at St. Paul's in New Hampshire, then Harvard College, with honors in philosophy and English composition, and highest honors in music. There followed a year in Europe with a study of music composition in Paris, and then back in America, the abandonment of what he wanted most for the start of a sterile career in banking. It was a move that brought on a physical and emotional breakdown, the aftereffects of which remained with him all of his life. A cure, and a new direction, was sought in Wyoming. The latter was found to prompt a return to Harvard for the study of law. He joined the Philadelphia Bar as a member of a prestigious Chestnut Street firm but then turned to writing, where he found much of the satisfaction he had sought in music.

In 1898 Owen Wister married his good friend, fellow musician, and second cousin Mary Channing Wister. "Molly" Wister was the stronger of the two. In a quiet but determined way she had been responsible for remarkable civic improvements in Philadelphia. To their marriage she brought love and substance, as Owen Wister was unable to play his role as father in a growing family with any persistence. He was often away, resting or recovering from illnesses both real and imagined.

In the fifteen years of marriage, six children were born. In 1913, the difficult birth of the sixth child caused Molly Wister's death. Although Owen Wister lived on until 1938, much of the substance she had given his life was lost, and in those empty years he came to realize her true worth.

Owen Wister's first successful story was written in the library of the Philadelphia Club, the old Thomas Butler house on Walnut Street. His finest work, *The Virginian,* was begun in Charleston after his marriage. His fascination for the old city prompted a return, and the second novel, *Lady Baltimore,* sprang from that interest. His North-South views and his expressed thoughts on Charleston's freed blacks caused spirited criticism from his friend Theodore Roosevelt.

Owen Wister was the last of the family to own land on which the Butler slaves had produced the family's wealth. What had been Hampton plantation was sold in 1923. A year later the last seventeen acres of Butler Place was sold to developers.

The children of Owen and Mary Channing Wister were MARY CHANNING WISTER, JR., who married Andrew Dasburg; OWEN JONES WISTER II; his twin FRANCES KEMBLE WISTER, who married Walter Stokes; WILLIAM ROTCH WISTER; CHARLES KEMBLE BUTLER WISTER; and SARAH BUTLER WISTER.

Of the three children born to Frances Butler and the Reverend James Wentworth Leigh, the first was ALICE DUDLEY LEIGH, 1874–1965, who married SIR RICHARD PIERCE BUTLER, 1872–1955.

Alice Leigh was born in a thunderstorm at York Farm, across the road from Butler Place, near Philadelphia. A delicate, responsive child, she was greatly loved by her parents, was a favorite of her grandmother Kemble, and was loved and respected by the blacks who lived and worked at Butler's Island in the difficult postwar years when the Leighs struggled to revive an old way of life. Henry James called her "Handsome Alice." Her friend and cousin Owen Wister attended the ceremony in 1906 when she became Lady Alice Butler, the bride of a distant cousin, Sir Richard Pierce Butler, the eleventh baronet of Cloughrenan. Long after her mother and her aunt Sarah Wister had sold the last of their Georgia lands, Lady Alice kept in touch and helped the plantation people she had known as a child.

Three children were born to the Butlers. The first became the twelfth and present baronet, COLONEL SIR THOMAS PIERCE BUTLER. The second, JOAN BUTLER, married Robert Nigel Brunt; and the third, DOREEN FRANCES BUTLER, married Denis William Powlett Milbank.

The second and third of the children born to Frances Butler and James Wentworth Leigh were PIERCE BUTLER LEIGH, born in 1876 under trying circumstances at Butler's Island on the Altamaha River in Georgia and died the following day; and PIERCE BUTLER LEIGH, the second of that name, born at Leamington in England in 1879 and died within a year.

Notes to the Family

Basic biographical information has been derived from the following sources: *Biographical Directory of the SCHR; Dictionary of National Biography; Dictionary of American Biography;* Burke, ed., *Genealogical and Heraldic History;* the McLanahan genealogical compilation of the Butler family in the Cate Collection, Georgia Historical Society; Fisher, *Recollections;* Wainwright, *A Philadelphia Perspective;* Kemble, Georgian *Journal, Records of a Girlhood, Records of a Later Life,* and *Further Records;* Frances Butler Leigh, *Ten Years on a Georgian Plantation;* J. W. Leigh, *Other Days;* and Fanny Kemble Wister, *That I May Tell You.* Other biographical material is mostly from the collections at the Historical Society of Pennsylvania, the Library of Congress, and the South Caroliniana Library and is given in the notes to the chapters of *Major Butler's Legacy.* For this section of *Personae*, specific references and quotations originate as follows:

Pierce and Mary Middleton Butler: the will of Mary Brandford Bull, Butler Family Papers, HSP.

Sarah Butler and James Mease: PB to Benjamin Rush, February 1, 1810, SCL; Fisher, *Recollections,* p. 264; Scharf and Westcott, *History of Philadelphia,* 1: 511, 520.

Anne Elizabeth and Frances Butler: PB to Frances Butler, Ireland, February 12, 1792, Butler Letterbook, SCL; PB to Benjamin Rush, October 14, 1790, James Rush–Library Company Papers, HSP; Frances Butler to Roswell King, Jr., October 23, 1822, Pennsylvania Abolition Society, HSP.

Harriot Percy Butler: Roswell King to PB, September 17, 1815, Butler Family Papers, HSP.

Pierce Butler, 1777–1780: *Charlestown Gazette,* January 11, 1780; Higginbothan, ed., *The Papers of James Iredell,* 2:397.

Thomas and Eliza de Mallevault Butler: PB to Weeden Butler, November 16, 1788, Weeden Butler Correspondence, British Library; the Vauclin Parish records, Martinique.

The unknown sons: Harriot Percy Butler to Benjamin Rush, undated; the Benjamin Rush memorial verse, James Rush–Library Company Papers, HSP; PB to John Allston, March 25, 1794, Butler Letterbook, SCL.

Pierce Butler Mease, 1800–1810: PB to Benjamin Rush, February 1, 1810, SCL.

Mary Middleton Mease and Alfred Langdon Elwyn: PB to Harrisons and Lathan, August 17, 1815, Butler Letterbooks, HSP; ALE to Sarah Butler Wister, July 22 and 26, 1870, Wister Family Papers, HSP; Wainwright, *A Philadelphia Perspective,* p. 225.

John (Mease) and Gabriella Manigault Morris Butler: Deed of gift, PB to JB, December 1, 1831, recorded in the Philadelphia City Hall; Wainwright, *A Philadelphia Perspective,* pp. 17, 176; SBH Vance to PB, December 24, 1847, Pierce Butler Letterbook, 1843–1846, Wister Family Papers, HSP.

Frances Mease and George Cadwalader: Wainwright, *A Philadelphia Perspective,* pp. 97, 225, 270; *The Philadelphia Club.*

Pierce (Mease) and Frances Anne Kemble Butler: PB to John Leckley, February 11, 1791, Butler Letterbook, 1790–1794, SCL.

Louis Butler: Thomas Butler to LB, February 22, 1837, Wister Family Papers, HSP.

John and Elizabeth Butler: Sarah Butler Wister's diaries, March 30, 1883, and September 1, 1889, Wister Family Papers, HSP.

Elizabeth (Mease) Butler and Julian McAllister: agreement of October 8, 1867, between the heirs of Pierce Butler and Gabriella Butler, Wister Family Papers, HSP.

Sarah Butler and Owen Jones Wister: Armstrong, *Fanny Kemble,* p. 323; Wainwright, *A Philadelphia Perspective,* p. 552.

The S. Weir Mitchell family: Burr, *Weir Mitchell: His Life and Letters,* p. 283; Earnest, *S. Weir Mitchell,* pp. 73, 137, 237; Mitchell, *A Madeira Party.*

Relations

ELIZABETH IZARD BLAKE, d. 1792, and her husband, DANIEL BLAKE, 1731–1780. Major Pierce Butler first met the Blakes aboard the *Philadelphia Packet* on his initial trip to South Carolina. Elizabeth was the second Izard to marry Daniel Blake. His first wife had been her cousin, Margaret Izard. Elizabeth was also cousin to Mary Butler and Sarah Guerard and sister to Mary Brewton, and thus was one of the four granddaughters who shared the Mary Brandford Bull estate. Daniel Blake died in 1780 at his Ashley River plantation, Newington, where there and on other low-country plantations he owned more than seven hundred slaves. Pierce Butler was his executor, having been named to replace the dead Miles Brewton. Elizabeth Blake, as next of kin, inherited all undisposed real estate of Mary Brewton, who died with her husband. Elizabeth Blake died in 1792, also at Newington. Her will left Major Butler "hurried, heated and vexed." The house at Newington burned in 1817, and many years later, in 1861, deer hunters took refuge in the ruins seeking shelter from a violent rainstorm. One of the hunters uncovered a sealed closet in which he found a cache of fine Madeira wine.

Cheves, "Blake of South Carolina," p. 161; Smith, "The Ashley River," p. 165; *SCAGG*, December 4, 1767; *Biographical Directory of the SCHR*, 2:80–81; PB to John Pringle, April 22, 1807, and PB to Charles Cotesworth Pinckney, April 23, 1807, Butler Letterbooks, HSP.

MARY IZARD BREWTON, d. 1775, and her husband, MILES BREWTON, 1731–1775. The enterprising South Carolina merchant Miles Brewton was married to Mary, the daughter of Joseph and Anne Bull Izard. Mary was a sister to Elizabeth Izard Blake and first cousin to Mary Butler and Sarah Guerard. They were the four granddaughters who shared the large estate of Mary Brandford Bull. Wealthy from his successful mercantile business, his profitable slave trade, and from the operation of Brewton and Bull plantations, the Brewtons lived in their grand King Street house in Charlestown that was described so well by Josiah Quincy, Jr., in 1773 and by Owen Wister in his Charleston novel, *Lady Baltimore*. The Miles Brewton family and Sarah Guerard were lost at sea as they fled from the British in 1775. Major Pierce Butler was Miles Brewton's executor. Many years later he wrote, "On the melancholy death of Mr. Brewton, I delivered the largest estate then in Carolina to the Heirs, without charging a cent commission."

Quincy, "Journal, 1773," pp. 424–63; *SCAGG*, August 18, 1775; PB to John J. Pringle, April 22, 1807, and PB to Colonel Haynes, February 17, 1821, Butler Letterbooks, HSP; *Biographical Directory of the SCHR*, pp. 95–97.

MARY BRANDFORD BULL, 1699–1771, and her husband, JOHN BULL, 1693–1767. Mary Brandford Bull was the grandmother who left her large estate of money, land, and slaves to her four granddaughters. She married John Bull after his first wife was carried away by Indians. They lived on Bull's Island, better known as Coosaw, near Beaufort, South Carolina. Their daughter Mary and her husband Colonel Thomas Middleton were the parents of Mary Middleton Butler and Sarah Middleton Guerard. Their daughter Anne married Joseph Izard and their children were the other two granddaughters—Elizabeth Izard Blake and Mary Izard Brewton. John and Mary Brandford Bull are buried in what was the church yard of Prince William's now picturesque ruins called Sheldon Church, not far from the Combahee River plantation left to Elizabeth Blake and Mary Brewton, who passed it on to the Butlers.

The will of Mary Brandford Bull, Butler Family Papers, HSP; Cheves and Salley, "The Bull Family of South Carolina."

WILLIAM BULL, 1710–1791. Mary Butler's kinship to the popular and well-respected William Bull came through her mother, Mary Bull Middleton. In a period between 1759 and 1775 he was five times South Carolina's lieutenant governor.

Not then or later did he once waver "in his conscientious loyalty to the king." At the time of the Revolution he owned three plantations and 245 slaves. The fate of his classic Ashley Hall, near Charlestown, is indicative of how William Bull fared in those tumultuous times. In 1779 "the irregular and great swarm of negroes" that followed the British General Augustine Prevost's army ransacked the place, did away with his "bottled wines & rum," "scattered" his library. To avoid confiscation, his "princely fortune," including Ashley Hall, was assigned to Stephen Bull and never again was enjoyed by its true owner. Ill and nearly destitute, the good William Bull died in London in 1791. The old homeplace survived until 1864 when its last owner, Colonel William Izard Bull, denied General W. T. Sherman's advancing army the satisfaction of destroying his home. He did it himself by burning Ashley Hall to the ground.

Cheves and Salley, "The Bull Family of South Carolina," p. 85; Bull, "Ashley Hall Plantation," pp. 62–65; Meroney, "William Bull's First Exile," pp. 101–4; *Dictionary of American Biography; Biographical Directory of the SCHR*, vol. 2.

EDWARD BUTLER, son of Sir Thomas Butler, the sixth baronet of Cloughrenan, who visited South Carolina and the Butlers in the late 1780s. He had sold his army commission and hoped to emulate his uncle Pierce but fell on hard times before he could win a fortune. Major Butler denounced his nephew for his ill behavior and was relieved when he returned to Ireland.

Burke, ed., *Genealogical and Heraldic History;* PB to Edward Butler, February 3, 1790, and June 9, 1796, Butler Letterbook, SCL.

FRANCES BUTLER of County Carlow, Ireland. A younger sister of Major Pierce Butler, Frances was the sixth child of Sir Richard and Lady Henrietta Butler. She was her brother's principal source of family news and was the one for whom he named his daughter. Both the Irish Frances and her American namesake were unmarried.

Burke, ed., *Genealogical and Heraldic History;* PB to Frances Butler, February 12, 1792, Butler Letterbook, SCL; PB to Frances Butler, June 9, 1796, Butler Letterbooks, HSP.

SIR RICHARD BUTLER, 1699–1771, and his wife, LADY HENRIETTA PERCY, 1720?–1794. Sir Richard Butler, the fifth baronet of Cloughrenan in Ireland, gave his son Pierce a commission in the British army. He also conveyed to Pierce Butler the right to claim the blood of Ormonde, a valid claim despite having come down an illegitimate line. Lady Butler gave her son a dubious right to boast of Northumberland blood for she was a Percy, a granddaughter of Anthony Percy who had been lord mayor of Dublin. The Percys had been unable to convince Parliament of the worth of their claim to descendency from Northumberland. At Sir Richard's death in 1771 the baronetcy passed to Pierce Butler's older brother, Thomas. When Lady Butler died in 1794, Major Butler asked his sister Frances, "Pray, did she make a will?" The answer was yes. But, as the Irish Butlers knew, their American relative had married an heiress and was a successful planter. They were content to confine his inheritance to Ormonde blood, and perhaps that of Northumberland. Lady Butler was sometimes known as Harriet.

Burke, ed., *Genealogical and Heraldic History;* PB to Frances Butler, June 9, 1796, Butler Letterbooks, HSP; Thomas Butler, "The Butlers of South Carolina and County Carlow."

SIR THOMAS BUTLER, d. 1772. Sir Thomas was the older brother of Major Pierce Butler. He became the sixth baronet of Cloughrenan in 1771 and died the following year. His oldest son, Richard, became the seventh baronet. Although Major Butler professed great love for Sir Thomas, he had but little use for his sons. Sir Richard, he said, was neither "respectable nor respected." Edward and Thomas Parker Butler were "unprincipled."

Burke, ed., *Genealogical and Heraldic History;* PB to his sister "Mrs. Gordon," 1796, and PB to Edward Bayley, December 18, 1791, Butler Letterbooks, HSP.

THOMAS PARKER BUTLER. Thomas was Major Pierce Butler's Irish nephew, the son of his older brother, Sir Thomas Butler, the sixth baronet of Cloughrenan. Somehow Major Butler became involved financially with this nephew as he had with his brother Edward. Major Butler was forced to cover some of Thomas Parker Butler's indebtedness in 1789 with a shipment of rice to Amsterdam. In 1791 he effected a temporary reconciliation that ended in 1796, when he declared that both nephews were "unprincipled." Fortunately, this wayward kinsman remained on the far side of the Atlantic.

PB to Van Staphorsts, July 15, 1789, PB to Edward Bayley, December 18, 1791, and PB to his sister "Mrs. Gordon," 1796, Butler Letterbooks, HSP; PB to TPB, April 15, 1790, Butler Letterbook, SCL.

SARAH IZARD CAMPBELL and her husband, LORD WILLIAM CAMPBELL, d. 1778. The Right Honourable Lord William Campbell, fourth son of the duke of Argyle, was the commanding officer of HMS *Nightingale* when he married Sarah Izard of Charlestown in 1763. She was the very wealthy daughter of the Ralph Izards, a cousin of Mary Butler, Elizabeth Blake, and Mary Brewton, and of the Ralph Izard who served in the senate with Major Pierce Butler. Lord Campbell was "handsome, dignified, gallant and cultured," and had been the royal governor of Nova Scotia from 1766 to 1773 before becoming the last to hold that title in South Carolina. He returned to Charlestown in 1775, succeeded William Bull, and was immediately in disfavor with Carolina patriots, his wife's family included. Henry Laurens told the South Carolinians in the Continental Congress that Lord Campbell "furnished us with positive proof of his disengenuity & intention to undo us by stealth." The Governor was forced to take refuge on a British ship, while his personal belongings were confiscated to be sold. In the 1776 attack on Charlestown, Lord Campbell was wounded as he commanded a gun deck on HMS *Bristol*. He died of his wounds in England in 1778. Lady Campbell also died there, far from family and her Carolina friends.

Wallace, *The History of South Carolina*, 2:122–23; Cheves, "Blake of South Carolina," p. 160; Salley, ed., "Papers of the First Council of Safety," p. 285; Cheves, "Izard of South Carolina," p. 235.

THE REVEREND WILLIAM ELLERY CHANNING, 1780–1842. Oliver Wendell Holmes thought "Channing, with his bland superior look—Cold as a moonbeam on a frozen brook." Not so Fanny Kemble. She revered Dr. Channing and found his views on "the unspeakable evil" of slavery much as were her own. His small book *Slavery* was written, she said, "with judgement, temper and moderation." William Ellery Channing was the popular Unitarian minister of Boston's Federal Street Church. His stand against slavery was not abolitionist, for he opposed broad social reforms. He believed slaves should have been freed by their masters to prevent their harboring vindictive hatred as would result in their freedom by decree. Dr. Channing was an American pioneer in his outspoken objection to war. He was the great-grandfather of Mary Channing Wister, the wife of Owen Wister.

Burns, *The Vineyard of Liberty*, p. 479; Fanny Kemble Wister, *Fanny: The American Kemble*, pp. 118–21; Kemble, *Records of a Later Life*, p. 28.

GEORGE COMBE, 1788–1858. Combe was the Edinburgh lawyer turned phrenologist who married Fanny Kemble's cousin Cecilia, the daughter of Sarah Kemble Siddons. His analysis of Pierce Butler did little to advance the science he practiced. The Combes were fond of Fanny Kemble, and she of them. On Cecilia Siddons's death she left her friend and cousin five Kemble portraits and a pair of gloves that had been worn by William Shakespeare. The gloves had been given to Sarah Siddons by Mrs. David Garrick.

Furnas, *Fanny Kemble*, p. 123; Kemble, *Further Records*, p. 23.

ADELAIDE DE CAMP, d. 1834. Frances Anne Kemble's aunt—her mother's sister. Called "Aunt Dall," she was the devoted chaperon on Fanny Kemble's successful American tour when Pierce Butler was paying court to the young actress. It was a courtship she opposed. Her death in April 1834 followed a carriage accident on a visit to Niagara Falls. Had "Dall" lived, her objection to Pierce Butler might have prevented the marriage.

Fanny Kemble Wister, *Fanny: The American Kemble*, pp. 132–33, 139–40.

ELIZA MIDDLETON FISHER, 1815–1890, and her husband, JOSHUA FRANCIS FISHER, 1807–1873. Joshua Francis Fisher of Philadelphia was first cousin to Sidney George Fisher, the diarist. He and his South Carolina wife, Eliza Middleton, appear often in his cousin's journal that covered a span of years between 1834 and 1871. Mrs. Fisher was the daughter of Henry Middleton, 1770–1846, of Middleton Place, where the Fishers were married. Her grandfather, Arthur Middleton, signed the Declaration of Independence. Thus, Eliza was related to the Butlers through Mary Middleton Butler. The Joshua Fishers were outspoken Southern sympathizers in the 1860s. Cousin Sidney George Fisher found their attitude "treasonable nonsense" and said: "Everyone laughs at him. Times like these lift & try character & test intellect & moral worth." He thought the Joshua Francis Fishers were excessive and lived "in very lavish style, 6 horses, numerous servants, elaborate furniture & constant entertainments. There is, indeed, too much of the latter, too many dinners, too much feasting & wine drinking, too much sensuality & refined social intercourse." The Joshua Francis Fishers were strongly supportive of Fanny Kemble in the Butler-Kemble contest, but were sufficiently close to Pierce Butler for Eliza Fisher to accept his protection on a trip to Charleston just prior to the Civil War.

Wainwright, *A Philadelphia Perspective,* pp. 80, 237, 383, 468, 562.

SARAH MIDDLETON GUERARD, d. 1775, and her husband, BENJAMIN GUERARD, 1733–1789. Sarah Middleton Guerard was the daughter of Colonel Thomas Middleton and Mary Bull. With her sister Mary Middleton Butler, she was one of the four granddaughters of Mary Brandford Bull who shared that generous lady's bounty. She married Benjamin Guerard in 1766, he being the son of a Charlestown merchant, John, and Elizabeth Hill Guerard. The Guerards were among the French Huguenots who settled in South Carolina. Benjamin Guerard owned a plantation at Purysburg on the Carolina side of the Savannah River where, prior to the Revolution, he erected a school for forty indigent boys. Early in the war, when the school was in its formative stages with a tutor and upward of a dozen boys, the British raided and destroyed the entire property. Sarah Guerard was lost at sea in 1775 with her cousin Mary Brewton and the Brewton family when they attempted to flee the British threatening Charlestown. Having no children of her own, she left a life estate to Mary Butler and the principal ultimately to the Butler children. The good Benjamin Guerard was taken prisoner when the British captured Charlestown in 1780. Held aboard the prison ship *Pack Horse,* he offered his captors his entire estate as security in an effort to raise funds to assist his destitute fellow captives. The British refused. Benjamin Guerard became the third governor of South Carolina. He married a second time, to Marianne Kennan, but had no children from this union either.

SCAGG, August 25, 1775; *Biographical Directory of the SCHR,* 2:294–95; Laurens, *Papers,* 5:493n; Cheves and Salley, "The Bull Family of South Carolina," p. 86; Jervey, "Death Notices," pp. 169–70.

CHARLES KEMBLE, 1775–1854, and his wife, MARIE-THERESE DE CAMP, 1774–1838. The Kembles were the parents of Frances Anne Kemble, who became Mrs.

Pierce Butler. Charles Kemble was one of twelve children of Roger Kemble and Sally Ward, the most notable being the eldest, Sarah Siddons, the great English actress. Marie-Therese Kemble was the daughter of a French army officer and a young Swiss girl. Both Kembles were talented, Charles a fine and handsome actor, his wife an attractive actress but also a singer and a dancer. He assumed the management of London's Covent Garden Theatre from an older brother, John Philip. It was a constant struggle until October 5, 1829, when a performance of *Romeo and Juliet* with Charles as Mercutio, Marie-Therese as Lady Capulet, and, "Being her first appearance on any stage," their daughter Fanny as Juliet. Fanny Kemble's triumphant debut led to many theatrical performances with her father, to the recovery of Covent Garden, to grand tours in Great Britain and America, and to her marriage in 1834. Charles Kemble taught his versatile daughter many fine points of acting, an understanding of, love for, and the skillful reading of Shakespeare's plays. Marie-Therese died in Surrey in 1838, Charles Kemble in London in 1854. His grave in Kensal Green cemetery is also his daughter Fanny's.

Kemble, Georgian *Journal, Records of a Girlhood, Records of a Later Life,* and *Further Records;* the playbill for *Romeo and Juliet,* October 5, 1829, in Gibbs, *Affectionately Yours, Fanny,* pp. 112–13.

JOHN MITCHELL KEMBLE, 1807–1857. The oldest brother of Fanny Kemble who sent her a word of caution on hearing of her intention to marry Pierce Butler. He attended Trinity College, Cambridge, where he was a member of the elitist "Apostles" with Alfred Tennyson, and with Tennyson went to Spain to help overthrow King Ferdinand VII. John Kemble was brilliant, somewhat erratic, or as Fanny Kemble said, "He is neither tory nor whig, but a radical utilitarian—an advocate of vote by ballot, an opponent of hereditary aristocracy, the church establishment, the army and the navy, which he deems sources of unnecessary expense."

Kemble, *Records of a Girlhood,* p. 122; *Dictionary of National Biography;* JMK to FK, October 13, 1833, "Letters to and from Fanny Kemble," Folger Library, Washington.

WARD MCALLISTER, 1827–1895. The brother of Colonel Julian McAllister, U.S.A., who married Elizabeth, the daughter of John and Gabriella Butler. The McAllisters were Savannahians, and Ward, a lawyer by trade, became the eccentric and noted arbiter of New York and Newport. It was he who made society fashionable and who put "the Four Hundred" into the language of the land. He accompanied Elizabeth McAllister to Philadelphia in 1861 to confront Pierce Butler with his violation of and indebtedness to her father's estate.

McAllister, *Society As I Have Found It.*

ARTHUR MIDDLETON, 1742–1787. The first cousin of Mary Butler, Arthur Middleton was born at Middleton Place, the son of Henry and Mary Williams Middleton. He and Mary Izard, the daughter of Walter Izard, were married in 1864. He was one of the four South Carolinians to sign the Declaration of Independence, succeeded his father as a member of the Continental Congress and as the master of Middleton Place, and was in Philadelphia with the Butlers as the Revolution neared its end. The war caused him to suffer "a genuine wreck of property and fortune," including the loss of two hundred slaves, but he was quick to regain his affluence. At his death Arthur Middleton left his wife, eight children, "an untarnished name," and six hundred slaves. There were forty-eight at Middleton Place, sixteen as servants at his Charleston town house, and the others of his several plantations. Among his children was Henry Middleton, who became governor of South Carolina and minister to Russia when Tsar Alexander I was arbitrating the Anglo-American controversy over the slaves taken by the British in the War of 1812. A daughter, Emma Philadelphia, married Henry, the son of Senator Ralph Izard.

Rice, ed., *Travels by the Marquis de Chastellux*, 1:327; *Biographical Directory of the SCHR*, 2:456–58; Cheves, "Middleton of South Carolina."

HENRY MIDDLETON, 1717–1784, was the brother of Mary Butler's father, Colonel Thomas Middleton. His son Arthur signed the Declaration of Independence, as did Edward Rutledge who had married his daughter Henrietta. Another daughter, Sarah, was the wife of Charles Cotesworth Pinckney. The family plantation, Middleton Place, on the Ashley River near Charleston was close by the Butler's Mary Ville. Henry Middleton was president of the First Continental Congress, yet opposed independence, resigned, and was succeeded by his son Arthur. He proclaimed his loyalty to the Crown in 1780. The very wealthy Henry Middleton was thrice married, first to Mary Williams by whom all their twelve children were born. His second wife was Henrietta Bull, and finally, he became the fourth spouse of his third wife, Lady Mary Mackenzie. He owned many slaves.

Cheves, "Middleton of South Carolina," pp. 239–45.

HENRY MIDDLETON, 1770–1846, was the son of Arthur Middleton, "the Signer." In 1820 he was chosen by President Monroe to be minister to Russia to assist Tsar Alexander I in deciding a fair settlement of the dispute between Great Britain and the United States on the matter of the slaves taken by the British in the War of 1812, 138 of whom had been owned by Major Pierce Butler. Henry Middleton was a former governor of South Carolina, where he owned "three fine rice plantations on the Combahee & 700 negroes." He was the father of Eliza, the wife of Joshua Francis Fisher of Philadelphia, both of whom befriended Fanny Kemble Butler in her difficulties with Pierce Butler.

Berquist, "Henry Middleton and the Slave Controversy," pp. 20–31; Wainwright, *A Philadelphia Perspective*, pp. 80, 190–91; Cheves, "Middleton of South Carolina."

COLONEL THOMAS MIDDLETON, 1719–1766, and his wife, MARY BULL, 1723–1760. The Middletons were the parents of Mary Middleton Butler. They lived for a time on the old Bull homeplace on Coosaw Island, planted other low-country plantations, and owned a home in Beaufort where the Middleton firm was active in the mercantile trade and in the importation of black slaves. Many of the slaves who were to work the Butler plantations in Georgia were brought to South Carolina by Thomas Middleton and his partners. A poor businessman, his death revealed his firm to be hopelessly insolvent, a fact that negated generous bequests by will to Mary Butler, her sister Sarah Guerard, their brother William, and his second wife Anne Barnwell Middleton and their two daughters. Home, plantations, and slaves were sold but failed to satisfy the demands of creditors. Colonel Middleton, as a brother of Henry Middleton of Middleton Place, and through his daugher Mary, did leave Pierce Butler ties to the influential network of Middleton-Bull kinfolk.

Cheves, "Middleton of South Carolina," pp. 260–62; *Biographical Director of the SCHR,* 2:460–62; Laurens, Papers, 5:323n, 6:586–87.

WILLIAM MIDDLETON, 1744–1768. Mary Middleton Butler's brother was the only son of Colonel Thomas and Mary Bull Middleton. His death in 1768 was unexpected; his property, including South Carolina plantations Ashepoo, True Blue, and Harris Island with all the attendant slaves, was sold to help meet the obligations of his dead father. William Middleton died unmarried.

Cheves, "Middleton of South Carolina," p. 262; *Biographical Directory of the SCHR; SCAGG,* February 5, 1771.

SARAH MIDDLETON PINCKNEY, 1756–1784, and her husband, CHARLES COTESWORTH PINCKNEY, 1746–1825. The influential Henry Middleton family supplied Charles Cotesworth Pinckney with his wife Sarah, who was sister to Arthur Middleton and Henrietta Middleton Rutledge, and was first cousin to Mary Middleton Butler. He was educated in England and France, fought with Washington at Brandywine and Germantown, and was captured and imprisoned by the British at Charlestown in 1780. A fellow delegate with Pierce Butler to the Constitutional Convention, he was firm in his advocacy of the continued concessions that prolonged slavery. He had first owned blacks when twelve years old, left him by his father—"Slaves with their increase." Although he maintained the practice of law in Charleston, much of his interest was in the operation of two confiscated plantations owned jointly with his brother-in-law, Edward Rutledge. It was to one of these that Major Butler sent a bountiful supply of Madeira wine as a peace offering following the furor over Elizabeth Blake's will. Charles Cotesworth Pinckney was twice nominated for the presidency. He campaigned somewhat less than enthusiastically from his Pinckney's Island plantation. The Pinckneys had four children. After Sarah Pinckney's death he married a second time—to Mary Stead in 1785.

George C. Rogers, Jr., *Charleston in the Age of the Pinckneys,* pp. 116–40; Zahniser, *Charles Cotesworth Pinckney;* PB to CCP, November 12, 1792, Butler Letterbook, SCL.

HENRIETTA MIDDLETON RUTLEDGE, 1750–1792, and her husband EDWARD RUTLEDGE, 1749–1800. Edward Rutledge was one of South Carolina's signers of the Declaration of Independence. His kinship to Mary Butler came through his marriage to her first cousin, Henrietta Middleton, who brought to the marriage a dowry of seventy thousand pounds and who was a sister to his fellow "Signer," Arthur Middleton. Edward Rutledge was a member of the Continental Congress. His older brother John Rutledge served with Pierce Butler as a delegate to the Constitutional Convention in 1787. He was a capable lawyer, but as a trustee of the Mary Bull estate was unable to confine Major Butler to the restraints stipulated in the Bull will. Edward Rutledge died while serving as governor of South Carolina.

Biographical Directory of the SCHR, vol. 2; Barry, *Mr. Rutledge of South Carolina*, p. 133; PB to CCP and ER, November 12, 1792, Butler Letterbook, SCL.

ADELAIDE KEMBLE SARTORIS, 1814?–1870, and her husband, EDWARD SARTORIS, 1814–1888. Fanny Kemble's sister Adelaide shared the inherited talent that came down from their parents. She was an able actress, a competent writer, but her forte was song. In a brief career in opera she sang the title role of *Norma* in her debut at Covent Garden, and her clear soprano was particularly effective as Susannah in *The Marriage of Figaro*. Her young niece Sarah Butler was awakened to hear her song coming from a room beneath hers. "Well, how many angels have you got down there?" she asked her mother. Among Adelaide Sartoris's good friends from her world of artists, writers, and actors, were many musicians— Franz Liszt, Felix Mendelssohn, Sir Charles Halle, among others. Her career was put aside in 1842 when she and Edward Sartoris were married. He was wealthy, kind, and gave Adelaide two things she wanted most, the means to live in stylish comfort and a home in Rome. Both were attentive to Fanny Kemble as troubles with Pierce Butler mounted. Fanny Kemble's book *A Year of Consolation* that followed her stay at the Sartoris home in Italy was dedicated to Edward Sartoris— a "record of the happy year I spent in Italy." She counted him among her true friends. Others who did the same were William Makepeace Thackeray and Henry James. The Sartorises had three children. The oldest boy, Greville, died in a fall from a horse. May, who became Lady Gordon, was painted when a child in a stunning portrait by Frederic Leighton. The youngest son, Algernon, was wed to Nelly Grant, the daughter of President Ulysses S. Grant. It was an unhappy union, for he left her with their three children to return to her parents.

Kemble, *Records of a Later Life*, pp. 243, 270; Furnas, *Fanny Kemble*, p. 369; Gibbs, *Affectionately Yours, Fanny*, pp. 135, 152; painting by Frederic Leighton, cover illustration of *Smithsonian*, December 1978.

SARAH SIDDONS, 1755–1831. Born Sarah Kemble in Wales, she was the oldest of the twelve children of Roger Kemble and Sally Ward. As Charles Kemble's sister, she was Fanny Kemble's aunt, and was England's foremost actress of her day. Her husband, Henry Siddons, was an actor; their child, Cecilia, married Dr. George Combe, the Scottish phrenologist who examined Pierce Butler's head. Fanny Kemble, when on stage and at her best, was compared favorably to her aunt Sarah.

Richardson, "The Kemble Dynasty," pp. 334–41; Furnas, *Fanny Kemble,* pp. 43, 123.

THOMAS SULLY, 1783–1872. The Philadelphia artist Thomas Sully made well over twenty-five hundred paintings of which more than one thousand were portraits, and of these, as many as thirteen were said to be of Fanny Kemble. The best, she thought, was one of her as Beatrice, done from memory. She and Sully were firm friends, and he, a cousin of Pierce Butler's through their mother's Middleton blood, painted many of their family and friends. There are Sully portraits of Charles Kemble, Dr. James Mease, Sidney and Charles Fisher, Cadwaladers, Alfred Elwyn, and perhaps the best of all, of Rebecca Gratz.

Fanny Kemble Wister, *Fanny: The American Kemble,* p. 105; Armstrong, *Fanny Kemble,* p. 161; Hart, "Thomas Sully," p. 385.

Other Figures

JOHN ADAMS, 1735–1826, was the second president of the United States after serving as vice-president to George Washington. As the leader of the Senate he contended with the persistent belligerence of Pierce Butler through the years 1789–1796. He later won Major Butler's respect. The Major said of Adams, "An honester man never lived." On slavery, Adams was outspoken. He wrote that the evils of slavery "are as glaring and obvious in those countries that are cursed with its abode, as the effects of war, pestilence, or famine."

Butterfield, ed., *Letters of Benjamin Rush,* 2:1001–2; Adams, *Novangulus.*

TSAR ALEXANDER I, 1777–1825, was the "friendly sovereign" chosen by the British and American governments to arbitrate the matter of the slaves taken by the British in the War of 1812. The Russian emperor worked with Henry Middleton of South Carolina, who was specially appointed by President Monroe as American minister to St. Petersburg to represent those who had lost slaves and sought reparations. The tsar's decision that the British would pay for the blacks pleased the slave owners, who ultimately were disappointed in the amounts they received.

Berquist, "Henry Middleton and the Slave Controversy," pp. 20–31.

RICHARD D. ARNOLD, 1808–1876, was the famous Savannah physician who was a founder and the first secretary of the American Medical Association. A descendant of New England Pilgrims, an authority on fine wines, stout defender of slavery, and mayor of Savannah, it was he who surrendered his city to General Sherman in 1864 and who graciously acknowledged the generosity of New York, Boston, and Philadelphia in 1865 for gifts of food and clothing to his destitute constituents. As early as 1837, he had said slavery was so deeply rooted in his state that it would be impossible to eradicate "without upturning the foundation." He believed that "without a population of Blacks the whole Southern Country would become a desert." On the eve of conflict, he said: "We are ready for war to the knife, and the knife to the handle." On "freedom" in 1866, when thousands of blacks gathered in Savannah, Mayor Arnold repeated that they had become "nobody's niggers but their own."

Shryock, ed, *Letters of Richard D. Arnold,* pp. 14, 99, 131; *ORUCA,* series 1, vol. 47, part 2, pp. 166–69.

LIEUTENANT COLONEL NISBET BALFOUR, 1743–1823, wounded at Bunker Hill, and conspicuous for his bravery at New York and for able campaigning at Ninety-six in South Carolina, was rewarded by the British General Charles Cornwallis with an appointment in 1778 to the "difficult and invidious post of Commandant at Charleston." Balfour aroused the wrath of South Carolinians by hanging Colonel Isaac Hayne, and it was he who ordered many South Carolina patriots imprisoned in St. Augustine and their families—the Butlers included—to be banished to Philadelphia in 1781. After the Revolution he continued his military career, became a major general, and later a member of Parliament.

DNB; Wallace, *The History of South Carolina,* 2:227.

JOHN RHEA BARTON, M.D., 1794–1881. A leader in Philadelphia's medical profession in the mid-1800s, Dr. Barton attended the melancholy Thomas Butler through his last illness in 1838 and was one of the six men privileged to attend the funeral at Christ Church. In commenting on his successful career in medicine, Sidney George Fisher noted other accomplishments and shortcomings. "He has married two fine women of large fortune. His first wife was worth $150,000, his present a million. But he is a vulgar man, with talents, but a commonplace limited mind & no culture either as a gentlemen or a scholar." The wealthy second wife was Susan Ridgeway Rotch, whose sister Phoebe Ann Ridgeway was Mrs. James Rush.

Wainwright, *A Philadelphia Perspective,* p. 183.

FRANCES HENRY FITZHARDINGE BERKELEY, 1794–1870. Henry Berkeley, friend of Pierce Butler and acquaintance of Fanny Kemble, was the fourth son of Frederick Augustus, the fifth earl of Berkeley, and of Mary Cole, and was born on December

7, 1794, prior to their marriage in 1796. Talented and versatile, at sixteen he was a "first rate shot" and one of the best amateur boxers in England. His love for music was shared by Pierce Butler and respected by Fanny Kemble, who despite her antipathy, might well have found him a more suitable candidate for her hand. Henry Berkeley was responsible for Pierce Butler and Fanny Kemble meeting and knowing each other. He turned away from his easy living to join three of his brothers in Parliament. An autobiographical bit in the British Museum is rather candid: "Mr. Berkeley however has chiefly acquired his reputation as a leader of the Ballot question, his speeches in favour of which have always secured the ear of the house from their happy combination of wit and argument."

FHFB to PB September 23, 1832, Wister Family Papers, HSP; Fanny Kemble Wister, *Fanny: The American Kemble,* pp. 98–99; *DNB;* F. H. F. Berkeley, collection 28509, British Library.

JOHN MCPHERSON BERRIEN, 1781–1856, a prominent Savannah attorney who represented Major Pierce Butler and other St. Simons Island planters in their efforts, first to retrieve the Negroes taken by the British in 1815, and later to seek compensation for the hundreds of slaves who had been freed. His failure in both attempts was not indicative of his prowess as a member of the bar and as a public servant, for he became a United States senator and later attorney general under President Jackson, and was a renowned statesman and debater known as the "American Cicero." Berrien was himself a slave owner at his Savannah River plantation, Morton Hall. At his death in 1856 his will provided his plantation and slaves be kept intact until 1865, a plan upset by President Lincoln and General Sherman.

Myers, ed., *Children of Pride,* p. 1464; Granger, ed., *Savannah River Plantations,* pp. 108–10; *DAB.*

HERCULES DANIEL BIZE. In the early 1790s large loans from Bize to Daniel Boudreaux fell into default and very nearly wrecked Pierce Butler. The Major had guaranteed Boudreaux's indebtedness of forty-eight thousand pounds, an amount repaid from the proceeds of the sale of an assortment of Butler properties, including Royal land grants, speculative holdings, and trust estate lands belonging to the Butler children.

PB to Frances Butler, June 9, 1796, and PB to James Johnson, October 16, 1820, Butler Letterbooks, HSP.

DANIEL BOUDREAUX earned Pierce Butler's lasting dislike when he defaulted on large loans from Hercules Daniel Bize and forced the Major, who was his guarantor, to pay the debt in his stead. Boudreaux called Major Butler and his friends "Calumniators" for their disrespectful treatment. The Boudreaux default was a factor in Major Butler's invasion of the trust estates of his children.

PB to DB February 1, 1790, and PB to James Johnson, October 16, 1820, Butler Letterbooks, HSP.

SAMUEL BRAILSFORD, 1728–1800, was a partner with Mary Butler's father, Thomas Middleton, in the mercantile firm of Middleton and Brailsford that was said to be "large in provincial deerskin and slave trades." They imported Africans through the West Indies and directly from the continent. Brailsford had an interest in several ships active in the trade, among them the *Adventure,* the *Beaufort Packet,* and the *Charming Sukey* that were owned jointly with Thomas Middleton. The partnership ended in the early 1860s, but each continued as merchants in other firms. The "respectable" Samuel Brailsford, "an affectionate husband, a tender father and a kind master," died in 1800.

Biographical Directory of the SCHR, pp. 93–94; Register, "Marriage and Death Notices," p. 135; Olsberg, "Ship Registers in the South Carolina Archives," pp. 192, 202, 214.

FREDRIKA BREMER, 1806–1865. Miss Bremer was the Swedish writer and feminist who traveled in America and visited the Altamaha plantations in 1851. Her sensitive observations often focused on the attitudes of blacks and slaves toward religion. At the Couper plantations on St. Simons Island she gathered a group of black children about her and then recited the Lord's Prayer. "The children grinned, laughed, showed their white teeth, and evinced very plainly that none of them knew what that wonderful prayer meant nor that they had a Father in heaven." Fanny Kemble called her fellow feminist "My friend—that amiable woman." Miss Bremer made an apt comment on her friend's former husband. Of Pierce Butler: "But why then did he so absolutely endeavor to win her? He knew beforehand her temper and the anti-slavery sympathies, for she is too truthful to have concealed anything."

Bremer, *The Homes of the New World,* p. 491; Armstrong, *Fanny Kemble,* p. 222.

ELEANOR BRIANZONI, called "Ellen." Fanny Kemble's English maid was employed in the early 1870s. Her mistress called her "the bravest and least selfish creature I ever saw." Ellen's marriage to an Italian manservant, Luigi Brianzoni, was deferred for two years to permit her to accompany the aging lady to America, a favor returned by Fanny Kemble's attendance at their Italian wedding in 1877, and a year later at the christening of their first child in the northern Italian town of Stresa on Lake Maggiore. It was a saddened Ellen Brianzoni who said in 1893 that the Kemble spirit "must have flown straight up to God."

Kemble, *Further Records,* pp. 3, 28, 282; Furnas, *Fanny Kemble,* p. 439; EB to Frances Cobbe, Kemble Letters to Various People, Folger Shakespeare Library.

CAPTAIN JOSEPH BRYAN, 1812–1863, was the "dapper little man," the "Auctioneer and Negro Broker," who sold 436 of Pierce Butler's slaves in 1859 at

Savannah's Ten Broeck racecourse. He was the son of Joseph Bryan, who had read law with his good friend John Randolph of Roanoke. Before his slave dealing, Captain Bryan had been a purser in the U.S. Navy and a chief of Savannah's mounted police. The Bryan "slave pen" on Johnson Square was a busy place, for the Captain had a virtual monopoly of the coastal Georgia slave trade. In one day he offered six separate "gangs" of blacks. His commission on the Butler sale approached eight thousand dollars. At his death in 1863 the *Savannah Republican* called him a useful citizen and a rare ornament. "He was one whom a large number of the young selected as their guide and example in life."

Myers, ed., *Children of Pride,* p. 1475; Bancroft, *Slave Trading in the Old South,* pp. 233–34; *Savannah Republican,* December 18, 1863.

ÆDANUS BURKE, 1743–1802, an erstwhile Catholic priest turned Protestant who arrived in Charlestown by way of the West Indies. He was a soldier in the Revolution and an assured advocate of anti-aristocracy. His 1783 pamphlet expressing his fears that the Society of the Cincinnati would promote a privileged class bestirred a controversy. First president of Charleston's Hibernian Society, he was noted for his Irish wit and frequent blunders. A friend of the Middletons, Ædanus Burke was among the South Carolinians in Philadelphia as the war neared its end. His letters illuminate the times.

Barnwell, ed., "Correspondence of Arthur Middleton," *SCHM* 26 (1925):183–84; Bowen, ed., *The History of the Centennial,* p. 80.

AARON BURR, 1756–1836, and his daughter, THEODOSIA BURR ALSTON, 1783–1813. Aaron Burr was vice-president under Thomas Jefferson, a post coveted by his friend Pierce Butler who shared his anti-Federalist views. Major Butler had returned to the Senate in time to assist the vice-president following the unfortunate duel that ended Alexander Hamilton's life and Burr's own political career. Burr was offered Hampton plantation as a refuge and traveled south using the name of the Butler manager to divert suspicion. His letters from Hampton to his daughter Theodosia Alston reflect the life-style of the owners of St. Simons Island plantations. At the time of Burr's furtive visit, Theodosia was living with her husband Joseph and their infant son Aaron Burr Alston on their plantation near Georgetown, South Carolina. Joseph Alston, best known of the single *l* Alstons, became governor of the state in 1812, the year in which the child died, a tragedy enlarged a few months later when Theodosia was lost at sea enroute from Georgetown to meet her father returning to New York from self-imposed exile in Europe. A disconsolate John Alston died in 1816. Aaron Burr's love for Theodosia and his young grandson were manifestations of truth in an otherwise scandalous life.

Aaron Burr and the Alstons owned slaves. Burr's slave Peter, with him at Hampton, was to have been given to his grandson. Billy, a seventy-eight-year-old Burr slave, was listed in the Butler inventory of 1849. The vice-president's natural son, Jean-Pierre Burr, a mulatto, became a successful Philadelphia barber and an active participant in the underground railroad.

Van Doren, ed., *The Correspondence of Burr,* pp. 173–91; Lomansk, *Aaron Burr: From Princeton to Vice President,* pp. 187, 358–60; Webber, "Historical Notes," pp. 38–39; Ballard, *One More Day's Journey.*

CHARLES BUTLER was the seafaring son of the Reverend Weeden Butler, Thomas Butler's Chelsea schoolmaster. In 1791 young Charles visited Charleston while serving on board his ship *The Olive Branch.* He enjoyed the bounty of Butler plantations, but came so close to death from a serious illness that he caused Major Butler to hurry down from Philadelphia to see to his comfort. A remarkable recovery prompted Major Butler to write the Reverend Mr. Butler there had been a "Resurrection."

PB to WB, April 12, May 6, 1792, Weeden Butler Correspondence, British Library.

THE REVEREND GEORGE BUTLER, 1774–1853, was the second son of the Reverend Weeden Butler and fellow student at his father's classical school at Chelsea with Thomas Butler in the 1780s and 1790s. A formidable young man, George Butler became headmaster at Harrow while in his early thirties, and later the dean of Peterborough Cathedral. His oldest son, George Butler (1819–1890), followed the pattern and was himself an educator and a cleric. The second George's wife was Josephine Grey, who became an Anglican saint for her work in bettering the lot of English women. She practiced her own brand of abolitionism in helping to expose the white slave trade that saw English girls sold to European brothels. Thomas Butler named his schoolmate, the first George, as his contingent beneficiary, but when Louis Butler held fast to his name and did not change to his mother's de Mallevault, he held fast to his father's fortune, too.

The will of Thomas Butler, HSP; Burgess, "Saint Josephine, 1826–1906," pp. 68–71; Richards, "A Talk on the Family of the Reverend Weeden Butler," p. 17.

THE REVEREND WEEDEN BUTLER, 1742–1823, was for more than forty years the schoolmaster of the fashionable classical school for boys on Cheyne Walk in Chelsea, London. There young Thomas Butler lived and studied for eleven years, his attendance prompting a long and full correspondence between the Reverend Mr. Butler and the father of Thomas, Major Pierce Butler. Much of Weeden Butler's training came from his service to one of England's strangest characters, the Reverend William Dodd, for whom he acted as "amanuensis" for a period of thirteen years and whom he succeeded as the morning preacher at Charlotte Street Chapel, Pimlico. Pierce and Weeden Butler came from different branches of that family, but their letters reflect much of the former's unusual personality and his political thought at a time of great importance. The correspondence was saved, and unfortunately edited, by Weeden Butler (1773–1831), son and successor to his father both at the school and at the Chapel. It was given to another Thomas Butler, who in 1847 was a member of the British Museum's staff. Among other sons of the older schoolmaster were Charles, a seaman who was befriended by Major Butler in Charleston in 1792, and George, a brilliant scholar who attended the Chelsea school with Thomas.

Weeden Butler Correspondence, British Library; *DNB.*

JOHN CADWALADER, 1805–1879, was a leader of the Philadelphia bar, who with George Mifflin Dallas was first chosen by Pierce Butler in 1848 to represent his interest in the upcoming divorce action against Frances Anne Kemble Butler. Cadwalader abandoned the case when Butler was impelled to bring in two New York attorneys and Daniel Webster, a move that was an affront to the Philadelphia lawyer. John Cadwalader was a brother of General George Cadwalader, the husband of Pierce Butler's sister, Frances Mease.

Wainwright, ed., *A Philadelphia Perspective,* p. 151; Wainwright, *"Butler v. Butler,"* pp. 101–8.

LIEUTENANT COLONEL ARCHIBALD CAMPBELL, 1739–1791, who served in His Majesty's Twenty-ninth Regiment with Pierce Butler, was a Scotsman who led the British expedition of 1778 to recover the Province of Georgia for his government. His regiment, the Seventy-first Fraser's Highlanders, was belittled by Pierce Butler for having enlisted "culprits and convicts" from Savannah's jails, but was successful in its mission. The British gave a dubious freedom to thousands of blacks who had been slaves of planters in Georgia and South Carolina, some of whom belonged to the Pierce Butler family. Lieutenant Colonel Campbell won the approval of Savannah residents for his "benevolent and humane attentions" to the inhabitants of that distressed city. After Georgia he became a brigadier general in Jamaica, where he organized native blacks into an efficient militia that caused the French to abandon plans for an invasion. He became governor there and retired in 1784. He died in London and was buried in Westminster Abbey.

Campbell, ed., *The Journal of Colonel Archibald Campbell,* pp. ix, x, 128; Mayo, *Encyclopedia of the American Revolution.*

LYDIA MARIA CHILD, 1802–1880, the active abolitionist and feminist whose little book in 1833, *An Appeal in Favor of That Class of Americans Called Africans,* agitated the proslavery people of the North and the South. In 1842 she exacerbated the Butler-Kemble difficulties by offering to publish parts of the Georgian *Journal* (1863). Ten years later her biography of Isaac T. Hopper retold the story of Major Butler's troubles with his slave Ben. Although Fanny Kemble and Mrs.

Child shared anti-slavery sentiments, Mrs. Child thought Mrs. Kemble dead wrong in criticizing John Brown for "inciting insurrection," and again for advocating the Channing position that slaves should be freed by their masters, not by the decision of government.

DAB; Fanny Kemble Wister, *Fanny: The American Kemble,* pp. 177–81; Child, *Isaac T. Hopper: A True Life;* Meltzler and Holland, eds., *Lydia Maria Child: Selected Correspondence,* pp. 340–41, 435.

RUFUS CHOATE, 1799–1859, was one of the team of lawyers chosen to assist Fanny Kemble in the divorce action brought by Pierce Butler. He practiced in Washington and Boston, and succeeded his idol Daniel Webster as a United States senator from Massachusetts. A picturesque figure, Choate had "a profusion of wild and fantastic hair" accompanied by "a weird and exotic expression." On slavery, he once stated: "I do not believe it is the greatest good to the *slave* or the *free* that four millions of slaves should be turned loose in all their ignorance, poverty and degradation, in trust to luck for a home and a living."

Dictionary of American Biography.

ADMIRAL SIR ALEXANDER FORRESTER INGLIS COCHRANE, 1758–1832. Admiral Cochrane entered Pierce Butler's life as a figure of the War of 1812. He was appointed to command His Majesty's naval forces of the North American Station in April 1814. His proclamation offering freedom to slaves caused consternation in the coastal slave states of the South. The Cochrane proclamation was similar in content but stronger in promise than the one issued by John Murray, the earl of Dunmore, during the Revolution. Admiral Cochrane offered to transport slaves seeking freedom to His Majesty's dominions or to accept men in the British service. Much to the distress of Major Butler, 138 of his "ungrateful Negroes" accepted the offer and were transported to Halifax, a dominion far removed from the palmetto and pine of Hampton plantation. Admiral Cochrane's distinguished service had won a favorable resolution from Parliament for his role in the capture of Martinique in 1809. He later became a member of the Parliament that had honored him. He was a knight of the Bath, governor of the Leeward Islands, and was roundly disliked by Major Butler and his ilk.

DNB; Bullard, *Black Liberation;* George Cockburn Papers, Library of Congress; Mahon, *The War of 1812,* p. 247.

ADMIRAL SIR GEORGE COCKBURN, 1772–1853. Feisty Admiral Cockburn put his Royal Colonial Marines ashore on Georgia's Cumberland and St. Simons islands while unaware that his government and the Americans had agreed on terms for a cessation of hostilities. Thus, thwarted in his plan to put the torch to Savannah as he had done to Washington in 1814, he assuaged a wounded pride by sailing away with hundreds of black slaves who had sought freedom before the peace treaty was ratified on February 17, 1815. Admiral Cockburn's invasion of the Georgia islands prompted the irreparable rift between Major Pierce Butler and his manager, Roswell King, both of whom agreed with most Americans that the Admiral was a true barbarian. Admiral Cockburn returned to England a true hero, and as such was rewarded by being assigned a very special mission to convey Napoleon to St. Helena on his flagship HMS *Northumberland,* a vessel that proudly bore the name of the family whose blood Pierce Butler claimed.

George Cockburn Papers, Library of Congress; Bullard, *Black Liberation;* James, *A Full and Correct Account,* 1:336.

ANDREW COMBE, M.D., 1797–1847, was the kindly Edinburgh physician and younger brother of George Combe, who was smitten with Fanny Kemble when she visited Scotland in 1829 on her triumphant tour. He contracted to renew their visit, be he alive or dead, in 1874, when she turned sixty-five.

Bond by Doctor Andrew Combe in favor of Frances Anne Kemble, March 26, 1829, Owen Wister Papers, Library of Congress.

THOMAS P. COPE, 1758–1854, the observant Quaker who amassed a large fortune as a Philadelphia shipping merchant in the Liverpool trade. He noted in his journal interesting and odd traits of Fanny Kemble, and the insignificance of her husband, Pierce Butler. On slavery, he commented: "Man has no bowels of mercy for man. It is sufficient that a fellow being is African and black to justify the infliction of cruelty on him." Thomas Cope was long a great and generous friend to his native city. On his death in 1854 he left forty thousand dollars to the Institution of Colored Youth to found a scientific school.

Harrison, ed., *Philadelphia Merchant,* p. 9.

JAMES HAMILTON COUPER, 1794–1866. This "uncommon fine yonge man" was the learned son of John and Rebecca Maxwell Couper. His youth was spent at Cannon's Point near Major Butler's Hampton on St. Simons Island, but after returning from Yale in 1814, he managed and later owned Hopeton plantation, close by Butler's Island in the Altamaha River delta. At thirty-two, he married sixteen-year-old Caroline Georgia Wylly (1811–1897), began to "cultivate her mind," and together cultivated a large family of five sons and two daughters. Under his guidance Hopeton became the predominant Altamaha plantation, even surpassing Butler's Island. James Hamilton Couper brought a scientific approach to his planting and was careful and considerate in the employment of his slaves as had been his father before him. He survived the sinking of the steamship *Pulaski,* demonstrating great bravery to earn favorable notice in Fanny Kemble's *Journal* of her stay in Georgia. In 1859 he was one of the three appointed to appraise and divide the Butler slaves prior to the Savannah auction of Pierce Butler's share. He was a first cousin to Julia Rebecca King, the wife of Roswell King, Jr. He was opposed to secession and war but saw his sons volunteer, two of whom were killed in Virginia. He died in 1866, broken by the war he knew to be wrong. The funeral at the desecrated church on St. Simons Island was attended by Pierce Butler and his daughter Frances.

Roswell King to PB, April 2, 1818, H. E. Drayton Papers, HSP; Letter of March 13, 1828, Margaret Hall Collection, Library of Congress; Kemble, Georgian *Journal*, pp. 336–42; Cate, *Our Todays and Yesterdays*, pp. 199–206; Vanstory, *Georgia's Land of the Golden Isles*, pp. 90–96.

JOHN COUPER, 1759–1850. The cheerful Scotsman John Couper lived with his wife, Rebecca Maxwell (1775–1845), on their St. Simons Island plantation, Cannon's Point, across Jones Creek from Major Butler's Hampton. A good and dependable neighbor, John Couper well knew Pierce Butler, Roswell King, and his son, Roswell King, Jr. He won the admiration of Major Butler's grandson's young wife, Fanny Kemble, on her visit to Hampton in 1839. The Coupers' bountiful garden supplied his family's needs, with its produce often going beyond to friends and neighbors on the island. And rare and unusual produce it was—figs, lemons, oranges, pomegranates, Persian dates, olives, and vegetables in profusion. His talented black chef, Sans Foix, became an Island legend. A slave owner, John Couper set an exemplary pattern in his considerate treatment of his blacks, a design few other Island planters could match. Yet, the good care did not prevent sixty of his slaves deserting to the British in 1815, an act he found difficult to comprehend. For its owners, Cannon's Point was a happy place, with first the Couper children and later a swarm of grandchildren all beloved of their Scottish grandfather. John Couper outlived his wife by five years, dying at ninety-one at Hopeton, the home and plantation of his son James Hamilton Couper. On his gravestone in the church yard at Frederica it is said: "His long life was devoted to the duty of rendering himself most acceptable by doing the most good to his creatures."

Kemble, Georgian *Journal*, pp. 167, 237–38, 267, 283, 322; Vanstory, *Georgia's Land of the Golden Isles*, pp. 135–42; Cate, *Our Todays and Yesterdays*, pp. 130–32, 275.

GEORGE MIFFLIN DALLAS, 1792–1864, was an honor graduate of Princeton, mayor of Philadelphia, minister to Russia and to Great Britain, United States senator, and vice-president under James K. Polk. He represented Pierce Butler in his suit for divorce after fifteen years of marital warfare. A Philadelphia contemporary wrote: "He is a handsome man with very white hair, a pleasant companion, a conspicuous member of our bar—but sadly deficient in sound morals, very extravagant in his living & very poor." An advocate of the status quo, George Dallas "hated abolition and secession both."

Harrison, ed., *Philadelphia Merchant*, p. 510; *DAB*.

FRANÇOIS-JEAN, MARQUIS DE CHASTELLUX, 1734–1788. A friend of Benjamin Franklin, the Marquis de Chastellux served under Rochambeau in the French expeditionary force to America in 1780–1783, and his journal of those years was translated into English by the "agitator" George Grieve. In addition to the Marquis's formula for ending slavery in America by exporting black males and encouraging the union of black women and white men, the Marquis wrote: "It is not only the slave who is beneath his master, it is the negro who is beneath the white man. No act of enfranchisement can efface this unfortunate distinction." He believed the possession of slaves nourished "vanity and sloth" in their owners.

Rice, ed., *Travels by the Marquis de Chastellux,* 2:435, 440–41.

FRANÇOIS DIDIER PETIT DE VILLERS, 1761–1841, was a French-born aristocrat who fled Santo Domingo in fear of slave uprisings on that troubled island. He lived for a time in Philadelphia before moving to Savannah to become a commission merchant and factor. He was an occasional correspondent and agent for Major Pierce Butler. His transactions often included black slaves. Called "Petit" and also "Monsieur Petit Devil Ears," he was a good friend to many of Savannah's prominent citizens, often favoring them with produce from his garden and his own cordials, sauces, and vinegars. He once sent Major Butler a favorite blend of snuff. He is buried in Savannah's Colonial Cemetery, and as a slave owner has left the name de Villers on black families in coastal Georgia.

Hartridge, ed., *The Letters of Don Juan McQueen,* p. 276.

THE REVEREND WILLIAM DODD, 1729–1777, was the eccentric English cleric known as the "Macaroni Parson," who after being enveloped in scandals was hanged for forgery despite assistance from Dr. Samuel Johnson, who wrote petitions to George III in his behalf. The Reverend Weeden Butler, schoolmaster for Thomas Butler, had been closely associated with Dr. Dodd as "amanuensis" and as his successor as a preacher at the Charlotte Street Chapel in Pimlico.

DNB; Boswell, *The Life of Samuel Johnson,* 2:90, 110, 113.

ANTOINE CHARBONNET DUPLAINE was the French diplomat who learned from Major Pierce Butler of the vast timber reserves on Georgia's Cumberland Island and then inveigled him into a scheme to acquire the island for the new French Republic. The year was 1794, when Major Butler was in his second term as the United States senator from South Carolina. The French navy, for whom the island would have been purchased, cast doubt on the merit of Duplaine's proposal. He had been French consul at Boston and was ousted by President Washington for irregularities in the handling of prize vessels.

Hill, "A Masked Acquisition: *French Designs on Cumberland Island, 1794–1795,* pp. 306–16.

SAMUEL FRANCIS DUPONT, 1803–1865, was chosen to head the Union navy's South Atlantic Blockading Squadron in 1861. His successful reduction of Forts

Walker on Hilton Head Island and Beauregard on Bay Point won a promotion to rear admiral. As such, he prosecuted the war in the low country of South Carolina and Georgia. Admiral DuPont knew the Butlers through his friendship with the Lewis Morris family, parents of Gabriella Butler. He endorsed and supported the "contraband colony" on St. Simons Island where refugee slaves had a first taste of freedom. He called them "blackies" and fed them stale bread from naval vessels and produce from abandoned plantations, much of which came from Butler's Island. An unsuccessful attack on Charleston harbor in 1863 led to Admiral Du-Pont's resignation from the navy.

Hayes, ed., *DuPont Letters*, 1:140, 2:28n, 71; *ORUCN*, series 1, vols. 12 and 13.

FANNY ELSSLER, 1810–1884, was the Austrian ballet dancer whose eminently successful American tour in 1840–1841 cheered Fanny Kemble Butler during a trying time of her life and inspired her to write a ballet based on Pocahontas. When Elssler danced in New York in 1840, Fanny Kemble's friend Philip Hone wrote: "Fashion and taste and curiosity are all on tiptoe to see her on tiptoe."

Wainwright, ed., *A Philadelphia Perspective*, p. 113; Nevins, ed., *The Diary of Philip Hone*, p. 480.

JOSEPH EVE, 1760–1835, was born in Philadelphia, moved to the West Indies and settled in the Bahamas where he invented a machine for separating seed from cotton fiber, a forerunner of Whitney's cotton gin. Major Butler and John Couper used the Eve gin, effective on their long staple cotton. While a United States senator, Major Butler petitioned Congress for a patent on Eve's behalf. In 1810 Eve moved to Richmond County, Georgia, where he manufactured gins and other machinery. A poet, he was a friend of Benjamin Rush and Benjamin Franklin.

DAB; Legare, "Excursion into Southern Georgia," pp. 167–69, 247; Clifton, "Hopeton, Model Plantation," p. 435.

CHARLES HENRY FISHER, 1814–1862, was a younger brother of the diarist Sidney George Fisher and a leading businessman of Philadelphia in 1840–1850. He amassed a tremendous fortune in the management of property, in negotiating loans, and as a corporate agent. Henry Fisher was a loyal friend of Pierce Butler. He was one of three trustees who managed the chaotic Butler finances in the late 1850s and was successful in negotiating his release from federal prison in 1861. Much of the Fisher wealth was lost by several suspect transactions in 1859. Debts were compromised and many of the "instruments of Henry's lavish hospitality" were sold to meet demands upon his estate. At Brookwood, Henry Fisher's one-hundred-acre homeplace near Philadelphia, the "instruments" included the contents of two wine rooms and a cellar, the stock "immense & very choice, several hundred demijohns of rare & fine sherry and Madeira."

Wainwright, ed., *A Philadelphia Perspective*, pp. 405, 422–23.

SIDNEY GEORGE FISHER, 1808–1871, and his wife, ELIZABETH INGERSOLL, 1815– 1872. the Fishers were married in 1851. He had been keeping a diary since 1834 and continued to do so until shortly before his death in 1871. In 1847 he had written of another marriage: "She very rich, he very poor." And then added: "I think I shall make up my mind to follow this fashion myself one of these days. It is such an easy way to step into comfort & luxury of wealth & to get perhaps at the same time a pleasant & loving companion." In Elizabeth, who Sarah Butler Wister said was "the man of the two," he got the latter, but not the former. She brought strength to the marriage but no fat purse.

Sidney George Fisher, who believed in white supremacy, was opposed to slavery. But once, when servants were hard to come by, he wrote to Elizabeth: "I think I must stop writing against slavery and become its advocate—for it seems now that only in niggerdom is a servant possible." He gave interesting descriptions of the Butlers, the Meases, the Wisters, their friends, and of his own family who played roles in the dramatic events that engulfed Major Butler's descendants. His brother, Charles Henry Fisher, and his cousin, Joshua Francis Fisher, took strong positions in the strife between Pierce Butler and Fanny Kemble. Despite his having written "I know nothing of Pennsylvania history & care less," his diary was indeed a noteworthy literary accomplishment and a delightful social history of the times. The Fishers' only child was Sydney George Fisher, who became a well-known historian.

Wainwright, ed., *A Philadelphia Perspective*, pp. 141, 203, 562; Fanny Kemble Wister, *That I May Tell You*, p. 32; SGF to EIF, November 19, 1856, Sidney George Fisher Collection, HSP.

BENJAMIN FRANKLIN, 1706–1790. Pierce Butler first knew Benjamin Franklin at the Constitutional Convention in Philadelphia where both were delegates. He ran afoul of Franklin's strong Quaker abolitionism during his first term as United States senator and was said by Senator William Maclay to have made a "personal attack" on Dr. Franklin for backing the Quakers in their anti-slavery petitions to Congress. Franklin's grandson, William Temple Franklin, represented Major Butler in an attempt to sell a large tract of land in the back country in South Carolina.

Franklin, *Historicus*; Maclay, ed., *Journal of William Maclay*, p. 196.

WILLIAM TEMPLE FRANKLIN, 1760–1823, was born in London, the natural son of Benjamin Franklin's natural son, William. He represented Major Pierce Butler in the 1793 and 1794 attempts to sell the South Carolina back-country lands acquired at a sheriff's sale from the heirs of Joseph Salvador. The lands were sold in 1796 for twenty-five thousand pounds sterling, but whether by Franklin is not known. William Temple Franklin had been considered as secretary of the 1787 Constitutional Convention, a post he lost to Major William Jackson.

PB to WTF, August 11, 1793, Butler Letterbook, SCL; PB to WTF, August 20, 1794, and PB's letter of April 7, 1796, Butler Letterbooks, HSP.

BENJAMIN GERHARD, 1812–1864, was the Philadelphia attorney who assisted Fanny Kemble in her difficulties with Pierce Butler. At the time of his representation, Lawyer Gerhard was said to be "of excellent character" with a "good & increasing practice at the bar." A few years before, he had married Anna Sergeant, who had been jilted in a previous courtship, "putting out of order the little mind she had," but it proved a good match for the "bourgeois" Mr. Gerhard.

Fanny Kemble Wister, *Fanny: The American Kemble,* pp. 101, 104, 188; Wainwright, ed., *A Philadelphia Perspective,* pp. 147, 207.

ELBRIDGE GERRY, 1749–1814, was a signer of the Declaration of Independence from Massachusetts and a thorn in Major Pierce Butler's side at the Constitutional Convention of 1787 where both were delegates. Gerry was inconsistent in stands taken in framing the Constitution, opposed its ratification, and despite his obstinacy and his lack of interest in the common man, represented his state as governor and in the United States Congress.

DAB; Bowen, *Miracle at Philadelphia,* p. 95; PB Collection, 215-693, Library of Congress.

ALEXANDER GILLON, 1741–1794, was a Dutch-born South Carolinian who became a seafarer and a financial agent. In 1778, as commodore of the state navy of South Carolina, Gillon was sent to France to purchase warships. There he was aided by Ralph Izard and with him incurred the disfavor of Benjamin Franklin. The ship *South Carolina* was purchased, visited Cuba on the voyage to Charlestown, and engaged in an expedition with Cubans, ships from Spain, and privateers from Philadelphia to raid the Bahamas. Gillon later lost his ship to the British and after the war retired to his plantation, Gillon's Retreat, on the Congaree River where he died in 1794. Major Pierce Butler was a residuary legatee, and as a co-executor was paid his commission in black slaves which he then assigned to the widow and her children.

Rice, ed., *Travels by the Marquis de Chastellux,* p. 298; *DAB;* PB to Dr. Purcell, April 1799, PB Letterbooks, HSP.

SYLVANUS W. GODON. In October 1861, Commander Godon led his USS *Mohican* in the successful reduction of Forts Walker and Beauregard on Port Royal Sound in South Carolina. A few weeks later he commanded an exploratory survey of the waters about St. Simons Island in Georgia. More than any other Union officer, Commander Godon was responsible for the "Contraband Colony" on Retreat plantation where hundreds of freedom-seeking slaves found refuge.

ORUCN, series 1, vols. 12 and 13.

ANNE MATHEWS GRAEME of Charlestown was the widow of David Graeme (d. 1777), the district attorney for South Carolina. She was the friend of Elizabeth Blake to whom Major Butler expressed his irritation over the Blake will.

PB to Mrs. David Graeme, August 24, October 10, 1792, PB Letterbook, 1790–1794, SCL; will of Elizabeth Blake, 1792, book 24, South Carolina Department of Archives and History.

JOHN GRAHAM, c. 1718–1795, and his wife, FRANCES CROOKE. The Grahams sold Hampton Point plantation on St. Simons Island to Major Pierce Butler in 1774 and used the proceeds to purchase Mulberry Grove on the Savannah River above the town. John Graham came to Georgia from Scotland in 1753 and became a successful merchant and landowner. Loyal to the Crown, in 1776 the Grahams sought safety in England after he was given the rather hollow title of lieutenant governor of the province. John Graham returned in 1779 to assume his duties for the king but within two years was forced to leave as the war changed once more. His fine plantation, other properties, and slaves were confiscated by the new state of Georgia, and Mulberry Grove was presented to General Nathanael Greene as a reward for his role in the Revolution. Pierce Butler purchased land adjoining Hampton from John Graham's brother, James, who was then living in London.

Granger, ed., *Savannah River Plantations,* pp. 66–72; *DAB;* Graham deed, October 1, 1774, collection 1008, GHS.

REBECCA GRATZ, 1781–1869, was the seventh of the twelve children of Michael and Miriam Simon Gratz of Philadelphia. She was a beautiful, sensitive, intelligent woman who befriended Fanny Kemble when she was the young wife of Pierce Butler, and who remained loyal through the painful separation and divorce. She was said to be the role model for Sir Walter Scott's Rebecca, the heroine of *Ivanhoe.* Her portrait by Thomas Sully is one of his best.

Philipson, ed., *Letters of Rebecca Gratz,* pp. 351–52; Furnas, *Fanny Kemble,* pp. 341–42.

NATHANAEL GREENE, 1742–1786, and his wife, CATHARINE LITTLEFIELD, 1753–1814. The legislatures of South Carolina and Georgia awarded General Greene confiscated plantations for his successful harassment of the British forces under General Charles Cornwallis. He sold the Carolina plantation and used the proceeds to pay indebtedness for supplies used by his army. The Georgia award was the John Graham plantation, Mulberry Grove, on the Savannah River, enjoyed by Greene for only three years. At his death in 1786 he occupied another Graham property, the family tomb in Savannah's Colonial Cemetery, where his body was placed, soon forgotten, and not found until 1901. In 1791 Major Pierce Butler visited Mulberry Grove with George Washington, who was calling on his old friend Caty Greene, then a widow living on the plantation. The widow Greene later married Phineas Miller, who leased slaves to Major Butler on occasion. It was her slave Jack who died in 1804 from the bite of a rattlesnake.

Granger, ed., *Savannah River Plantations,* pp. 71–80; Rhode Island Assembly's *Remains of General Greene;* Stegeman and Stegeman, *Caty,* pp. 149–50, 170; Roswell King to PB, March 16, 1804, Butler Family Papers, HSP.

CHARLES CAVENDISH FULKE GREVILLE, 1794–1864, was Eton and Oxford educated, a bon vivant, and a man-about-London whose interest in the theater led to a friendship with and an admiration for the Kemble family. His diary covered a span of years from 1817 to 1860 and is a rare and interesting documentation of social history. His closeness to Fanny Kemble both before and after her marriage led to vigorous conversational exchanges, correspondence, and several pithy entries in his diary that surprised her. The two were of different minds on many subjects, one being slavery, which was the topic of a long letter to Charles Greville included in her *Journal* of the visit to the Butler plantations. But Fanny Kemble was fond of him and of his brother Henry. Charles was true to his role of "highborn, high-bred." She believed him to have better brains than Henry.

Wilson, ed., *The Greville Diary,* 2:546–47; Kemble, *Records of a Later Life,* pp. 216, 514; Kemble, Georgian *Journal,* pp. 369–83; *DNB.*

HENRY GREVILLE, 1801–1872, was, if not as smart as his older brother Charles, a truer friend of Fanny Kemble. She shared his fondness for music and drama, and his lively interest in the people who comprised the society in which they lived. She mentioned him frequently in her autobiographical records. The first time: "Henry Greville is delightful and I like him very much." Civil War in America was the subject of a spirited series of letters between the two, Fanny Kemble despairing that she seemed unable to convince him and their friends of the righteousness of the Union cause. This inability prompted the publication of her provocative *Journal* that told of her observations of slavery as practiced on the Butler plantations. The Grevilles added immeasurably to her enjoyment of life in London.

Kemble, *Records of a Girlhood,* p. 396, 471, 197; *DNB;* Letters to and from Fanny Kemble, Folger Shakespeare Library.

GEORGE GRIEVE, 1748–1809, an English opportunist whose business career gave him reasonable knowledge of France and the French language that he put to good use in an unauthorized translation of the journal of the Marquis de Chastellux's travels in America in 1780–1782. Grieve was described as an "hereditary agitator," as an adventurer, and was one who sought the company of important figures of whatever time and place he happened to be. He visited the United States in 1781–1782, stayed but a year, and met many of the South Carolina refugees making the best of a bad situation in Philadelphia. He shared an antagonism toward French aristocrats with Major Butler, who shared with Grieve "venison, moor game, the most delicious red and yellow bellied trout" and "rum and brandy of the best quality, and exquisite old Port and Madeira."

Rice, ed., *Travels by the Marquis de Chastellux*, 1:29–30, 2:649.

JOHN F. GRIMKÉ, 1752–1819. When Major Pierce Butler abandoned the United States Senate in 1796 he then offered for the more democratic House of Representatives. In 1798, his victorious young opponent was John Rutledge, Jr., the son of his fellow delegate to the Constitutional Convention. Rutledge was endorsed by his uncle, the influential Judge John F. Grimké, whose sister Elizabeth was the candidate's mother. The endorsement incensed Major Butler, who challenged the Judge to a duel. The Major's second was Charles Cotesworth Pinckney, who was then warming to an anti-dueling sentiment, and who evidently prevailed upon Major Butler to withdraw his challenge. Judge Grimké, who had fought in the Revolution, been captured at Charleston, and was well regarded there, had an interesting family. They owned slaves that his wife, Mary Smith, said she would hold unto death. Not so their daughters Sarah and Angelina and their son Thomas, three of their fourteen children. The daughters became avid, active, and outspoken abolitionists. Thomas was anti-slavery, but not so intensely as his sisters. On reading of someone named Archibald Grimké who shared their sentiments on slavery, Angelina wrote to ask how he had come by their unusual name. He replied that he was one of three sons of her brother Henry Grimké and his slave girl Nancy Weston, and therefore he was their nephew. Angelina was shocked into temporary seclusion but revived to acknowledge her new kinfolk and to continue her work. The two sisters were genteel Episcopalians who became Quakers. Angelina married Theodore Dwight Weld, also an abolitionist, and Sarah lived her life with them as house mother and as a caretaker of the Weld children. The opposition to slavery must have been ingrained into Grimkés for their aunt Elizabeth Grimké Rutledge had given up all her slaves before her death in 1793.

DAB; Lumpkin, *The Emancipation of Angelina Grimké;* Barry, *Mr. Rutledge of South Carolina,* p. 329.

CAPTAIN BASIL HALL, 1788–1844, and his wife, MARGARET HUNTER, 1799–1876. Captain Hall had been an officer in the British army. His *Travels in North America* in the years 1827–1828 took him through the Southern states, where he fulfilled his mission "to see things with my own eyes." On the low-country plantations about Charleston and Savannah, and on the Altamaha estuary, he gained firsthand knowledge of the evils of slavery, evils he knew not how to remedy. There, where the Butler family's near one thousand slaves planted cotton, rice, and sugar cane, he reluctantly concluded "that slavery is an evil in its consequences, no men that I have ever met with are more ready to grant than most American planters. That the time will come when it must cease to exist, is not, however, so general an opinion. But in the meanwhile, it is admitted by all parties to be so firmly and so extensively established, and the means of doing it away to be so completely beyond the reach of human exertions, that I consider the immediate abolition of slavery as one of the most profitless of all possible subjects of discussion."

Margaret Hunter Hall's letters, published more than a century after their trip, complemented her husband's journal by pertinent observations from another point of view: "Two days ago I heard the mocking bird for the first time, at least as far as I know for as its name denotes it mocks all other birds and therefore I may have heard it without being aware of it."

Hall, *Travels in North America,* vol. 1, preface, 2:237; letter of March 13, 1828, Margaret Hall Collection, Library of Congress.

ALEXANDER HAMILTON, 1757–1804, alone represented New York at the federal Convention of 1787 in Philadelphia, and almost alone was responsible for his state's ratification of the Constitution. He and Pierce Butler were in agreement that compromise to permit the continuation of slavery was necessary to form the Union and that the nation should be led by a single executive, but agreed on little else. Hamilton's strong Federalist position was at cross purposes with Major Butler's anti-Federalism. Hamilton offered "a melange of insolent arrogance & meaness," said Butler. The Burr-Hamilton duel that ended the life of a brilliant statesman met Pierce Butler's approval both as to method and results. He offered Aaron Burr his Georgia plantation as a refuge and helped to plan Burr's flight from public outrage that followed Hamilton's death.

Bowen, *Miracle at Philadelphia,* pp. 112, 201, 305; Schachner, *Aaron Burr,* p. 258; PB to Edmund Randolph, August 26, 1797, Butler Letterbooks, HSP.

WILLIAM MILES HAZZARD was the young Confederate soldier whose family owned St. Simons Island plantations and whose clandestine visits to the island during the federal occupation resulted in the death of a former slave, John Brown, thought to be the first black to die in armed conflict in the Civil War. It was Miles Hazzard who said, "If you wish to know hell before your time, go to St. Simons and be hunted ten days by niggers." The Hazzard family owned West Point and Pikes Bluff plantations on St. Simons Island.

Higginson, *Army Life in a Black Regiment,* pp. 212–13; ORUCN, series 1, vol. 14, pp. 150–51.

SIR MICHAEL HICKS-BEACH, 1837–1916, the ninth baronet and first earl of Aldwyn, was educated at Eton and Oxford. He was a friend of Disraeli and Lord Randolph Churchill, and served as a member of Parliament, and chancellor of the exchequer. In the late 1870s Sir Michael visited Butler's Island, where he went hunting and fishing with James Wentworth Leigh and where he observed that free blacks were not so well off as when they had been slaves.

Hicks-Beach, *Sir Michael Hicks-Beach*, 1:31–32; J. W. Leigh, *Other Days*, p. 158.

OGDEN HOFFMAN, 1793–1856, was the noted criminal lawyer from New York who told the young and impressionable Fanny Kemble of the flogging of slaves as he had witnessed it in the South. He was the district attorney for the City of New York at the time.

Kemble, American *Journal*, 1:129; Nevins, ed., *The Diary of Philip Hone*, p. 3 of dramatis personae.

PETER C. HOLLIS was a clerk in the Philadelphia office of Charles Henry Fisher and in 1862 fell heir to the problems that had come upon that unfortunate man whose death revealed a tangled web of financial difficulties. He succeeded Henry Fisher as Pierce Butler's advisor, and Thomas C. James as a trustee of the John Butler estate.

Wainwright, ed., *A Philadelphia Perspective*, pp. 421, 524.

JAMES HOLMES, M.D., 1804–1883. Born in Sunbury, Georgia, James Holmes was the son of James and Mary Kell Holmes. His mother was a granddaughter of John McIntosh Mohr, the Highland Scot who opposed the introduction of slavery in the New Inverness protest of 1739. The elder James Holmes worshipped at Midway Church where his relative Abiel, the father of Oliver Wendell Holmes, tended his flock. James Holmes studied at Yale and then graduated from the Pennsylvania Medical School in 1825. There, for a time, he was a favorite of Stephen Girard, a friendship that had an unfortunate termination. Young Dr. Holmes married Susan Oliva Clapp, a Bostonian teaching in McIntosh County. He practiced medicine at Darien and wrote with rare good humor many recollections for the *Darien Timber Gazette,* using as source material his good mind and an earlier diary that he had ceased writing when former slaves as Union soldiers burned Darien in 1863. Dr. Holmes wrote of his friendship with Pierce Butler and his wife Fanny Kemble. He attended to the medical needs of blacks and whites in the low country, including the Butlers and their slaves. His son, Lieutenant Pierce Butler Holmes, C.S.A., mortally wounded at the Wilderness in 1864, was the godson of the one whose name he bore.

Presley, ed., *Dr. Bullie's Notes*, introduction and pp. 12–22, 81, 126–27, 150–58.

LIEUTENANT PIERCE BUTLER HOLMES, d. 1864, the son of James Holmes, M.D., the Darien physician who served the Butlers and their slaves. Young Holmes was the namesake and godson of Pierce Butler (1810–1867) and was also called

"Butler." A lieutenant in the Oglethorpe Light Infantry, he was wounded at Gettysburg and while recovering in a field hospital was visited by Pierce Butler and his daughter Frances. He returned to the Southern army in an exchange of prisoners and was wounded again the following year in the Wilderness campaign. His death followed the amputation of his leg. Lieutenant Holmes was buried in Thornrose Cemetery in Staunton, Virginia. The Butlers and Fanny Kemble, who were his and his parents' friends, were saddened by the tragedy of his death.

Presley, ed., *Dr. Bullie's Notes*, pp. 125–27; Henderson, ed., *Roster of the Confederate Soldiers of Georgia, 1861–1865*, 1:928.

PHILIP HONE, 1780–1851. A shrewd and successful New York commission merchant, Philip Hone was given rude treatment in an 1832 entry in the first *Journal* (1835) of Fanny Kemble, who was then the very new Mrs. Pierce Butler. Mr. Hone and Fanny Kemble met again in 1838. He received her tearful apology. Once more he could say: "The more I see of this wonderful girl, the more I am pleased with her."

Kemble, American *Journal*, 1:103–5; Nevins, ed., *The Diary of Philip Hone*, pp. 79, 144–45, 339.

ISAAC T. HOPPER, 1771–1852, was a Philadelphia Quaker, a friend of Dr. Benjamin Rush, and an active member of the Pennsylvania Abolition Society. Said to be a "defender of the friendless and oppressed," Isaac Hopper befriended Pierce Butler's slave Ben in 1804 and took the Major to court, where Ben was given his freedom. Hopper was a worker on the underground railway and collaborated with the abolitionist Lydia Maria Child, who wrote his biography. Friend Hopper's son, daughter, and son-in-law were avid anti-slavery people.

DAB; Child, *Isaac T. Hopper: A True Life*, pp. 98–103.

DANIEL HUGER, 1741–1799, was the son of Daniel Huger and Mary Cordes, the second of his four wives. He was a member of the Continental Congress, wounded Charles Cotesworth Pinckney in a duel in 1785, and became a United States congressman at the time Major Butler served in the Senate. Both were injured in a carriage accident in Philadelphia in 1789. Daniel Huger's leg was shattered and his life endangered. Huger-Butler relations, though never close, were distanced in 1791 when Major Butler ignored Daniel Huger at his Charleston dinner for President Washington. Mrs. Huger was Sabrina Elliott. Their son, Daniel Elliott Huger, married Isabella, the daughter of Arthur Middleton and Mary Izard.

Webber, "Thomas Pinckney Family," p. 24; Mary Butler to Weeden Butler, July 15, 1789, Weeden Butler Correspondence, British Library; Beatty, ed., "Letters of Judge Henry Wynkoop," p. 57; Zahniser, *Charles Cotesworth Pinckney,* p. 245.

JAMES IREDELL, 1751–1799. Major Pierce Butler's friendship with James Iredell began in North Carolina after the British had forced his departure from Charlestown and his plantations. English-born, in the hill town of Lewes south of London, James Iredell was collector of customs at Edenton, where Major Butler had alighted as a refugee—there and at nearby Newbern. The Iredell hospitality came at a difficult time in Major Butler's life. It was a generosity he long remembered. He wrote: "I shall in prosperity or adversity, always respect with a pleasing Satisfaction, on the hours I pass'd in Your Company." Iredell was a staunch supporter of the Constitution and was largely responsible for its adoption in North Carolina. It pleased Senator Butler that he could be an important factor in the choice of Iredell for appointment to the "Supreme Federal Bench," a responsibility Mr. Justice Iredell handled very well from 1790 until his death. Major Butler thought Edenton a very unhealthy place and often urged his friend to visit him in the country north of Philadelphia.

Higginbothan, ed., *The Papers of James Iredell*, 2:349; McRee, *Life and Correspondence of James Iredell*, 2:279.

ELIZABETH IZARD, b. 1753, who became ELIZABETH IZARD WRIGHT. Major Pierce Butler's brief affair in 1768 with Betsy Izard was ended by her stepfather, John Channing. Her mother, Joanna Gibbes Izard, had married Channing on the death of Betsy's father, John Izard, in 1754. With her "Fortune of *Thirty Thousand Pounds Sterling*," Betsy soon married Alexander Wright, the son of Georgia's Royal governor, Sir James Wright. One who admired her beauty wrote: "The agreeable Mrs. Alexander Wright whose sleepy Eye Speaks the Melting Soul, all good nature, all Smiles, in short, all goodness. She could make a Saint to Sin." Alexander Wright was enough of a Loyalist to flee the Patriots with Betsy in 1776. They returned to their Savannah River plantation, Richmond and Kew, when the British captured Savannah in 1781. The Georgia plantation was confiscated and given to General Anthony Wayne for his services to Georgia in the Revolution. After the war had ended and old animosities were put aside, the Wrights returned from Charleston to become respected members of the community.

Richardson, "Letters of William Richardson, p. 15; Crouse, ed., "The Letterbook of Peter Manigault," pp. 95–96; Cheves, "Izard of South Carolina," pp. 229, 230, 233; Granger, ed., *Savannah River Plantations*, pp. 118–20.

RALPH IZARD, 1742–1804. Izard is from the French "Izod." Ralph Izard was one of many South Carolinians to be so named. At the beginning of the Revolution, he and his wife, the wealthy Alice De Lancey of West Chester, New York, were living in London, where they "enjoyed every blessing the world can afford." When England became uncomfortable for one embracing the patriot cause, the Izards moved to Paris, and there he believed he could be of greater use to the cause than he could be at home. When he did return to Charleston, he served in the Continental Congress and, with Pierce Butler, as one of South Carolina's first United States senators. An Izard daughter, Charlotte, was the wife of William Loughton Smith, who served in the House of Representatives at the time his father-in-law was in the Senate. The two had little use for Major Butler, and he for them and their Federalism. Ralph Izard suffered a stroke in 1797 but lived as an invalid until 1804. His widow Alice moved to Philadelphia, where she held forth at fashionable salons and tea parties until her death at eighty-seven. Seven of their fourteen children died young. One Izard daughter had married Gabriel Manigault; a son Henry, married Emma Philadelphia, daughter of Arthur Middleton and Mary Izard. The Izard plantations with attendant slaves—the most important of which was the Elms on Goose Creek—were left to their sons, Henry, George, and Ralph. John Singleton Copley painted the Izards in Rome. This handsome portrait is now in the Boston Museum of Fine Arts. Also, Ralph Izard was painted by the Italian Zoffani, by Benjamin West, and by John Trumbull. Alice De Lancey's portrait was painted by Thomas Gainsborough.

Izard, *Correspondence;* Cheves, "Izard of South Carolina," pp. 214–17; Rogers, *Charleston in the Age of the Pinckneys,* pp. 117–20.

MAJOR WILLIAM JACKSON, 1759–1822. Major Pierce Butler probably met Major Jackson for the first time at the siege of Savannah in 1779. Both attended the Constitutional Convention of 1787 in Philadelphia, where Jackson was chosen by ballot over William Temple Franklin to serve as secretary, a task he performed most ineffectually. Jackson, a friend of General Washington's, accompanied Colonel John Laurens on an expedition to France to obtain war material for the Patriots. He also was a secretary to Washington, accompanied the president on his Southern tour in 1791 as did Major Butler, and was living in the fine house on Chestnut Street in Philadelphia in 1804 when it was purchased by the Major and thereafter known as "the Butler mansion."

DAB; Bowen, *Miracle at Philadelphia,* pp. 30–31.

HENRY JAMES, 1843–1916, was the American expatriate novelist who was a great admirer and the last friend of Fanny Kemble. He was particularly attracted to her daughter Sarah Butler Wister when they met on a Roman holiday in 1872. Henry James turned his analytical eye on Sarah Wister to make her a character in several of his stories. He viewed with an amused eye the other Kemble daughter, Frances Butler, and her husband, the Reverend James Wentworth Leigh, the vicar of Stoneleigh. He maintained his James-Kemble connection to the Wisters in Philadelphia, by becoming fond of the Leighs in England and by offering advice to Fanny Kemble's grandson Owen Wister as late as 1905, when he was writing his second novel, *Lady Baltimore.* But, the strongest link in the James-Kemble connection was that of Henry James to the one he said was "indomitably incorruptibly superb."

James, *Essays in London and Elsewhere*, p. 117; James, *The American Scene*, pp. 416–18; Edel, ed., *The Letters of Henry James;* Owen Wister, preface to *Lady Baltimore* (1928).

THOMAS C. JAMES, 1813–1863, was a Philadelphia commission merchant, who, with Charles Henry Fisher and General George Cadwalader, was one of the three trustees chosen to bring order to Pierce Butler's confused finances. He was also a trustee of the John Butler estate and summoned Gabriella Butler to Savannah in 1859 to be present and to approve the division of the Butler slaves prior to the sale of those allotted to Pierce Butler. Until he departed for war in command of the most fashionable of Philadelphia's military organizations, the First City Troop, "Tom" James was often seen as escort to John Butler's widow. He died a colonel in the Ninth Cavalry, Ninety-second Regiment, U.S.A.

Wainwright, ed., *A Philadelphia Perspective*, p. 264.

JOHN JAY, 1745–1829, was the chief justice of the United States Supreme Court who was drafted by President Washington in 1794 to negotiate a treaty with Great Britain. The choice of Jay was an irritant to Pierce Butler, who sought the appointment for himself. The Jay Treaty fell short of what Major Butler thought necessary to protect America's sovereignty. He used his opposition to the treaty to win strength among his constituency in South Carolina. Undoubtedly a factor in his objection was Jay's failure to win compensation for the slaves lost to the British in the Revolution.

PB to Governor Mathews, October 17, 1795, PB Letterbooks, HSP; *DAB*.

THOMAS JEFFERSON, 1743–1826, was the third president of the United States. Although Jefferson was in Paris, his thoughts on the Constitution were known to Pierce Butler. Their views differed on the question of secrecy of the proceedings, favored by Major Butler; and on slavery, opposed by Thomas Jefferson. Later, in Congress, they came together as anti-Federalists, but then separated again when an inconsistent Major Butler backed away from Jefferson's policies. In 1801 he sent the new president words of advice. He urged decisiveness against the enemy (meaning the Alexander Hamilton faction) who opposed "the principles you embrace and which placed you at the Head of Govern't. Without a mark'd Decision your friends will despond and drop off." Pierce Butler was one who dropped off.

Thomas Jefferson owned as many as two hundred slaves. Yet, he believed slavery to be wrong and in his draft for the Declaration of Independence advocated its end. He saw slavery as a grave social question to be faced squarely but was unsure of how to find a remedy in emancipation. He advanced "as a suspicion only" that blacks were inferior to white, "both of mind and body." To make his point, he said: "This unfortunate difference of color, and perhaps of faculty, is a powerful obstacle to emancipation." Said Jefferson, the white slave could be freed and might then mix "without staining the blood of his master." For the blacks, Jefferson believed, freedom should put them "beyond the reach of mixture"—in a colony of their own where they could establish a free and independent society.

PB to TJ, February 26, 1801, PB Letterbooks, HSP; Malone, *Jefferson: The Virginian,* pp. 187, 266, 267.

THE REVEREND CHARLES COLCOCK JONES, 1804–1863, a retired Presbyterian minister, was born in Georgia on his family's Liberty County plantation. He owned and planted Montevideo, Maybank, and Arcadia in the Georgia low country. Of him it was said: "Happy is that community, black or white, who has such a shepherd." When religious instruction of slaves seemed one answer to the persistent criticism of slavery by Northern abolitionists, the Reverend Mr. Jones wrote and published his widely used catechism designed especially to adapt the white slave owner's Christian religion to the needs of the blacks they owned. The world of the Jones family began to come apart in the 1860s. Their travail is well documented in Robert Manson Myers's epistolary record *Children of Pride,* in which the Reverend Mr. Jones and his wife Mary Jones play the principal roles.

Myers, ed., *Children of Pride,* p. 1567; Jones, *A Catechism.*

CHARLES COLCOCK JONES, JR., 1831–1893, was the intelligent, sensitive son of the Reverend Charles Colcock and Mary Jones. He practiced law in Savannah, became the city's mayor in 1860, and volunteered in the Confederate army in 1861. Letters to and from his father and mother reflect wartime trials that confronted his family, their plantations, and their slaves as Union forces appeared on the Georgia coast. In 1862 he told his father that the emancipation proclamation of the "infamous Lincoln" would surely "subvert our entire social system, desolate our homes, and convert the quiet, ignorant, dependent black son of toil into a savage incendiary and brutal murderer." Less than a year later black troops of the Second South Carolina and Fifty-fourth Massachusetts regiments burned the undefended town of Darien to give validity to the fears expressed by the young Lieutenant Jones. After the war had ended, Charles C. Jones, Jr.'s interest in the history of his state generated several books. One was a recounting of the stories told by the Jones slaves in their own Gullah dialect. He called it *Negro Myths* and dedicated it to the memory of Montevideo plantation "and of the Family Servants whose fidelity and affection contributed so materially to its comfort and happiness."

Myers, ed., *Children of Pride,* pp. 968, 1568; Jones, *Negro Myths from the Georgia Coast.*

ROSWELL KING, 1765–1844, and his wife, CATHERINE BARRINGTON, 1776–1839. In 1802 Roswell King was employed by Pierce Butler to manage his two plantations, Hampton and Butler's Island. In 1789 he had come to Darien, Georgia, and there established himself as a successful commission broker and dealer in cotton, lumber, and rice. The son of Timothy King, who commanded the brig *Defiance* in the Revolution, and Sarah Fitch, he was born in Windsor, Connecticut, where there and in nearby Sharon the King family was well known and well connected. In 1792 he and Catherine Barrington were married in Darien. She was the daughter of Jessiah and Sarah Williams Barrington who lived high on the Altamaha River at an outpost called San Sevilla Bluff, where Catherine was born. Kinfolk of the Kings, who descended from the "Kings of Boyle Roscommon," included Governors Webster, Treat, and Fitch of Connecticut; Noah and Daniel Webster; and the John Kings of Northampton, Massachusetts. Catherine King's family background included the Tudors, Oliver Cromwell, and General James Edward Oglethorpe. The Roswell Kings produced nine children. Their second son, Roswell King, Jr., grew to manhood on the plantations and succeeded his father as manager of the Butler estate. The elder King's untiring efforts and capability as a planter did much to make Major Butler a rich man, a goal Roswell King pursued with relentless determination that warped his sense of decency in his relations with the hundreds of black slaves he controlled. His departure from the Butler estate was not friendly. Major Butler believed his manager responsible for the loss of slaves to the British during the War of 1812. Second generation Butlers believed him dishonest and self-serving. His lack of compassion in acting as a surrogate owner for Major Butler may have sprung from a subconscious reaction to the miscegenation he and his son had practiced at Hampton and Butler's Island. When Roswell King left the Butler estate, he embarked on a new career as a director of the Darien Bank. Ill-conceived ventures opened his eyes to other more promising developments. With his son Barrington, the Georgia hill towns of Roswell and Lebanon were planned and founded. Their success offered proof that Roswell King's life would have been better spent far removed from cotton and rice plantations. Had that been so, the words carved on his gravestone in Roswell might have been more to the mark as a measure of his worth: "A man of great energy, industry and perseverance, of rigid integrity, truth and justice. He early earned and long enjoyed the esteem and confidence of his fellow men." The King family owned many slaves in their own right, some of whom were taken to Roswell.

The King family register and biographical sketches by Julia King, Midway Museum; Myers, ed., *Children of Pride*, pp. 23, 1436–38, 1579; folder 416, Cate Collection, GHS.

ROSWELL KING, JR., 1796–1854, and his wife, JULIA MAXWELL, 1808–1892. Roswell King, Jr., moved to the Butler plantation Hampton when he was six years old. He was the second son of Roswell and Catherine Barrington King, and was chosen by his father to follow as manager of the Butler estate. Although he had little formal education and lacked the physical stamina and the innovative venturesome spirit of his parent, he was intelligent, energetic, and responsive—traits handed down from father to son. His letters to the Butlers were much like those of his father's—a good and legible hand, thoughts generally well stated, but without the directness that characterized the older King's reports on plantation business. As his father before him, Roswell King, Jr., was blessed with a strong, dependable wife. She was Julia Rebecca Maxwell, born of Colonel Audley and Mary Stevens Maxwell at their Carnichfergus plantation near Midway, Georgia. The Maxwell family attended Midway Church where Julia King's great-grandfather Audley Maxwell had been suspended for keeping one of his slaves in adultery. Roswell King, Jr.'s management of the Butler slaves showed an awareness of the importance of their good health, yet he demonstrated little improvement over the practices of his father. He punished with vengeance and by the time he wed Julia Maxwell had sired several mulatto children by plantation women. After she moved to Hampton, her good qualities—and there were many—were put aside when she ordered the punishment of the slaves Judy and Scylla for bringing her husband's children into a world far more difficult and miserable than her own. Roswell and Julia King had eleven children of their own—two daughters and nine sons. Two of the boys honored their Connecticut heritage by attending Yale. Seven of the nine sons survived their father's death in 1854, and of these, six fought for the Confederacy in the 1860s. Two were captured and imprisoned; William Henry, one of the Yale men, was killed at Sayler's Creek three days before Appomattox. Of him it was said, "The most promising and most loved has fallen." Julia King outlived Roswell King, Jr., by thirty-eight years. Both are buried at Midway. Of the eleven children, four had died earlier. One who survived was the third Roswell King, or "Rossie," as he was called. A favorite of his mother, he left six children who were raised by his brother Audley, and his black family with whom he lived. He too was buried at Midway.

Roswell King, Jr., owned 127 slaves at the time of his death in 1854. Julia King owned fifty-two slaves in her own name. In 1839 Roswell King, Jr., told Fanny Kemble Butler: "I hate slavery with all my heart. I consider it an absolute curse wherever it exists. It will keep those states where it does exist fifty years behind the others in improvement and prosperity."

The King family register and biographical sketches by Julia King, Midway Museum; Myers, ed., *Children of Pride*, pp. 23–25, 69, 77–78, 1437, 1585, 1586; Kemble, Georgian *Journal*, p. 111; Midway Church records, Gamble Collection, Savannah Public Library.

CHARLES AUGUSTUS LAFAYETTE LAMAR, 1824–1865, was an arrogant, impulsive, ruthless member of a distinguished Georgia family. Born of Jane Creswell and Gazaway Bugg Lamar, a man of great wealth, he was a godson of the Marquis de Lafayette who was present at his baptism in 1825. When Charles was fourteen years old, he, his father, and his Aunt Rebecca McLeod survived the sinking of the steamship *Pulaski*, a tragedy in which his mother and three younger brothers died. Active in a multitude of business ventures, Charlie Lamar was best known for his advocacy of a reopening of the African slave trade, and for his flaunting of federal law in the infamous 1858 voyage of the *Wanderer* that landed 409 of an original cargo of 487 Africans on Georgia's Jekyll Island. A persistent advocate of and a participant in duels, Lamar settled a racetrack argument by shooting and almost killing a good friend, Henry Dubignon. He was an avid secessionist, organized a state-subsidized blockade-running enterprise, formed his own military unit, "Lamar's Regiment," and was shot and killed by a nervous captor near Columbus, Georgia, seven days after General Lee had surrendered at Appomattox.

Wells, "Gentleman Slave Trader," pp. 158–68; Myers, ed., *Children of Pride*, p. 1588.

HENRY LAURENS, 1724–1792, played a major role in South Carolina's move to independence from Great Britain. His patriotism led to his presidency of the Second Continental Congress, to imprisonment in the Tower of London that ended with his exchange for General Charles Cornwallis, and though he did not serve, to his being among those chosen to be delegates to the Constitutional Convention of 1787. He was one of the first South Carolinians to plant rice on Georgia's Altamaha delta. There his plantations New Hope and Broughton Island were belittled by his Carolina peers as "Cracker Plantations," but were eminently profitable and led to a broader use of black slaves in the area. Henry Laurens had been a successful merchant whose lucrative business included the importation and marketing of slaves, a trade he abandoned in the late 1760s when he put aside the "Guinea Business." He became a reluctant slave owner and often spoke of liberation, so much so that he became known as an "emancipationist." Yet the descriptive bit was more appropriate for son than father, for John Laurens was a true advocate of emancipation, while Henry could never quite bring himself to do for his blacks what he thought should be done.

Laurens, *Papers*, 4:204n, 5:226; Wallace, *Life of Henry Laurens*, pp. 445–47; Bancroft, *Slave Trading in the Old South*, p. 3.

JOHN LAURENS, 1754–1872. Colonel John Laurens was the capable soldier son of Henry Laurens who urged his father to free the family slaves, who failed in persuading the South Carolina legislature to permit blacks to fight the British for a promise of freedom, and who lost his life in a minor skirmish as the Revolution neared its end. He had fought with Washington as aide-de-camp, was wounded at Germantown, was a special emissary to France for the Continental Congress, served at Yorktown, and won this tribute from a contemporary historian: "The warm friend of republican equality, gracious and liberal, his heart expanded with genuine philanthropy. Zealous for the rights of humanity, he contended that personal liberty was the birthright of every human being, however diversified by country, colour or capacity." John Laurens died of his wounds before receiving a letter from Alexander Hamilton: "Quit your sword, my friend; put on the toga. Come to Congress. We know each other's sentiments, our views are the same. We have fought side by side to make America free; let us hand in hand struggle to make her happy."

Laurens, *A South Carolina Protest Against Slavery;* Ramsay, *The History of the Revolution of South Carolina,* 2:374; Atherton, ed., *A Few of Hamilton's Letters,* p. 128.

SIR THOMAS LAWRENCE, 1769–1830. The last work of Sir Thomas Lawrence was his pencil drawing of Fanny Kemble done preparatory to a portrait that was never begun. Sir Thomas, who painted Kembles and Sarah Siddons, had courted both of Sarah's daughters, proposed marriage to each, and wed neither. An old flirt, he admired Fanny Kemble, attended her plays, wrote long letters of praise and criticism, and was so appealing and attentive that she felt a "dangerous fascination," despite the forty years' difference in their ages. Many years later a friend sent her a picture of the Lawrence parlor where she had been the subject of his last conversation. He talked to a friend of her performance in *Venice Preserved* shortly before his death.

Kemble, *Records of a Girlhood,* pp. 208–12; J. Hogarth to FAK, November 22, 1871, numbers 596–599, Folger Shakespeare Library; *DNB.*

FRANZ LISZT, 1811–1886. In the summer of 1841 Adelaide Sartoris and Franz Liszt gave a joint concert tour of the Rhineland. They were accompanied by Pierce and Fanny Butler and their two girls, Sarah and Frances, aged six and three. The tour was a great success as both artists performed brilliantly to "audiences who thronged to hear them." Fanny Butler thought Liszt the most celebrated pianist of her time—"first in fire, power and brilliancy of execution." Years later in the 1880s, when Franz Liszt had become the Abbé Liszt, he auditioned her grandson Owen Wister. The Abbé's judgment: "un talent prononcé."

Kemble, *Records of a Later Life,* p. 262; Fanny Kemble Wister, *That I May Tell You,* p. 110.

DEBORAH NORRIS LOGAN, 1761–1839, was the Philadelphia Quaker who knew both Major Butler and Fanny Kemble, and whose remarkable personal diary spanned the years 1815–1839 to fill seventeen volumes of social history. Her husband, Dr. George Logan, served in the United States Senate with Major Butler, who came to be their Germantown neighbor. Although not philosophically akin to Fanny Kemble's forthright feminism, an aging Mrs. Logan found much to admire in the courage and integrity of her young friend. Sidney George Fisher, himself a noteworthy diarist, said that "Aunt Logan" had lived "a long virtuous and useful life," and that the Logan home, Stenton, was rare in America and "had the prestige of time and the associations of one family attached to it."

Wainwright, ed., *A Philadelphia Perspective*, pp. 71–72, 358; Premo, "Like a Being," pp. 85–112.

SIR CHARLES LYELL, 1797–1875. Sir Charles was the much-traveled geologist who visited America on two occasions. In 1845, on the second visit, Lyell saw Charleston and noted the personal dislike between the black and white races. He believed it arose from "prejudice." Leaving Beaufort for Savannah, he reflected on the Anglo-Saxon settlers of the low country who had driven out the Indians, the Spanish, and the French but who were "doomed to share the territory with millions of negroes." On the Altamaha, he enjoyed the hospitality and the scientific intelligence of James Hamilton Couper. On his brief visit to Butler's Island he noticed the lowland behind the rice field bank and observed that the black colony there tended to be less healthful, less bright, and less prolific than that of the slaves who worked the highland plantations.

Lyell, *A Second Visit*, 1:221–22, 231, 248–49.

ROBERT MACKAY, 1772–1816, was a prominent and successful Savannah merchant whose principal contact with Major Pierce Butler came through his marriage to Eliza Anne McQueen (1778–1862), the daughter of Major Butler's good friend Don Juan McQueen. Mackay's father, for whom he was named, was a transplanted Scot and also a merchant who had settled in Augusta, Georgia. The younger Mackay was schooled in Scotland and became a partner with Scotsmen Alexander and William Mein in their Savannah firm. The Meins and Mackay imported a general mix of foreign "commodities," including black slaves and fine Madeira wine, both of particular interest to Major Butler.

Hartridge, ed., *The Letters of Robert Mackay*, pp. xxiii–xxxi.

WILLIAM MACLAY, 1734–1804, was the United States senator from Pennsylvania who viewed with alarm Senator Pierce Butler's presence at the First Congress in 1789. Maclay's personal journal is invaluable for the historical insights of lesser known congressional figures. His caustic comments on Major Butler's behavior are apt and amusing. Maclay and Butler had no common ground on slavery but did share an antagonism toward Alexander Hamilton's views, and at that time both were strong Jefferson democrats.

Maclay, ed., *Journal of William Maclay*, p. 71; *DAB*.

JAMES MADISON, 1751–1836, was the fourth president of the United States. James Madison and Major Pierce Butler met in Philadelphia where both played their roles in bringing the Constitution into being. Madison kept a record of the proceedings of the convention, notes that Thomas Jefferson proclaimed "the ablest work of this kind ever yet executed." He duly recorded the yeas and nays, the ups and downs, of South Carolina's Butler. More than from any other hand the drafting of the Constitution came from Madison. He became president in 1809, defeating Charles Cotesworth Pinckney in the electoral college. The Madison administration was marked by the political and military turmoil of the War of 1812, when Pierce Butler lost 138 of his slaves to the "savage British." Madison acknowledged "without limitation or hesitation" the evils of slavery. He saw the work of the American Colonization Society as a possible solution to "the dreadful calamity which has so long afflicted our country."

Bowen, *Miracle at Philadelphia*, p. 30; *DAB* quotes Harriet Martineau on JM.

JOHN MCQUEEN, 1751–1807, who became DON JUAN MCQUEEN in 1791. John McQueen was a land-mad friend of Major Pierce Butler. His purchase of Georgia sea islands and inland timber tracts with borrowed funds caused his precipitous flight to Florida from family, tax collector, and creditors. There he swore allegiance to His Catholic Majesty Charles II's Spanish Florida to become Don Juan McQueen. Despite the financial grief caused Major Butler by Don Juan's default on the payment of a loan, the two somehow remained friends. McQueen's daughter Eliza Anne married a young Savannah merchant, Robert Mackay, who became a partner with William and Alexander Mein in a firm that supplied the Butler plantations with an assortment of necessaries, including slaves. Don Juan died in Florida in 1807 before being able to put into practice his plan to smuggle slaves into the United States after January 1, 1808, when such an act was prohibited by the Constitution.

Hartridge, ed., *The Letters of Don Juan McQueen*, pp. xxi–xxxiv, 1–2; PB to McQueen, September 2, 1790, and December 6, 1792, PB Letterbook, 1790–1794, SCL.

WILLIAM MEIN was the Savannah merchant who became a partner of Don Juan McQueen's son-in-law, Robert Mackay. The firm of Mein and Mackay counted the Butler plantations among their better clients. It was William Mein who sold Major Butler Ibo and Angola blacks in 1803, and told of the Ibos who "rose" against the crew of the sailing vessel conveying them from Savannah to Thomas Spalding's plantation on Sapelo Island and to John Couper's Cannon's Point on St. Simons. Mein's sale in 1817 of his Savannah River plantation, Coleraine, to John Potter irritated Major Butler. Potter had long considered the purchase of Hampton and Butler's Island.

Hartridge, ed., *The Letters of Robert Mackay*, pp. xxvii, 271; WM to PB, May 24, 1803, Butler Family Papers, HSP; PB to John Potter, August 2, 1809, Wister Family Papers, HSP.

WILLIAM MEREDITH, 1799–1873, was the talented Philadelphia-born lawyer who represented Fanny Kemble in her pre-divorce trouble with Pierce Butler and at the divorce hearing in 1849. Meredith had established his reputation as a capable attorney by his work in the Stephen Girard will case. He was appointed secretary of the treasury by President Zachary Taylor at the time of the Butler divorce.

Fanny Kemble Wister, *Fanny: The American Kemble*, pp. 188, 204; *DAB*.

FRANCES MOTTE MIDDLETON, 1763–1843, who became the second wife of THOMAS PINCKNEY, 1750–1828. Frances Motte was first married to John Middleton (175?–1784), who had purchased Crowfield plantation on Goose Creek near Charleston shortly after their marriage in 1783 and before his untimely death in 1784. John Middleton, "a fine spirited, worthy little fellow," was a cousin of Mary Middleton Butler. In the early 1790s the widow Middleton received and refused Major Pierce Butler's proposal for marriage while making orange marmalade with friends. She later accepted a similar offer from General Thomas Pinckney, to whom her sister Elizabeth Motte had been married.

Smith, "Goose Creek," pp. 266–72; for the marmalade proposal, see chapter 4, "Pierce Butler's Private Life."

JOHN MCINTOSH MOHR, 1698–1761, was the leader of the Darien Scots who was responsible for the New Inverness petition of 1739 supporting General Oglethorpe's stand opposing the introduction of slavery into the colony of Georgia. He also led the large Scottish-American McIntosh family, and his descendants played a significant role in the development of Georgia. His great-grandson Thomas Spalding planted a plantation on the southern end of Sapelo Island across the Altamaha River entrance from the Butler's Hampton.

Candler and Knight, eds., *The Colonial Records of Georgia*, 3:427–28; Lewis, *They Called Their Town Darien*, pp. 15–17.

JAMES MONROE, 1758–1831, was the fifth president of the United States. James Monroe played no role in forming the Constitution and worked against its ratification in Virginia. He fought in the Revolution and served in the United States Senate, where he shared anti-Federalist views with his fellow senator Pierce Butler. Monroe made two diplomatic missions to Paris, was secretary of state, secretary of war, and governor of Virginia, and was twice elected president. As the secretary of state under President Madison, and when president, he became involved in the futile attempt to persuade the British to return the slaves taken away in the War of 1812. He appointed Henry Middleton as minister to Russia to assist Tsar Alexander I in the arbitration of the Anglo-American slave controversy. He supported the anti-slavery position that resulted in the Missouri compromise and twice appointed Major Butler to the board of the Bank of the United States.

JM to PB, January 1, 1819, Butler Family Papers, HSP; Berquist, "Henry Middleton and the Slave Controversy"; *DAB*; PB to JM, January 7, 1821, PB Letterbooks, HSP.

AMELIA MATILDA MURRAY, 1795–1884, was the English woman who had served as "Maid of Honour" of the ladies-in-waiting to Queen Victoria, and who visited the Altamaha River plantations on her tour of the United States in 1854–1855. Her zealous advocacy of the abolition of slavery was tempered by what she found on the James Hamilton Couper plantations. When forbidden to publish her observations because of her official position with the queen, Miss Murray resigned as "Maid of Honour" but was subsequently made "Extra Woman of the Bedchamber."

Murray, *Letters from the United States; DNB.*

JOHN MURRAY, THE FOURTH EARL OF DUNMORE, 1732–1809. The arrogance of Lord Dunmore, who in 1770 was the colonial governor of New York, and then of Virginia, aggravated colonists far beyond his own jurisdiction. His 1775 proclamation in which he invited slaves to desert their masters to take up British arms aroused horror and hatred in slave owners—from those who owned household servants to the plantation owners who worked hundreds—including George Washington. The great fear was insurrection. In 1781, as the war was nearing its end, Lord Dunmore again aroused the Patriots by advancing a proposal to arm ten thousand blacks and turn them loose on Georgians and South Carolinians. In 1787 Lord Dunmore acquired a new title. He became the governor of the Bahamas and served until 1796.

Quarles, *The Negro in the American Revolution*, pp. 19, 150–51; *DNB.*

JAMES EDWARD OGLETHORPE, 1696–1785, founded the colony of Georgia, where from 1733 until 1749 the Trustees forbade the introduction of black slaves. The prohibition stemmed from Oglethorpe's personal aversion to slavery. He had demonstrated this aversion in 1732, for then he was a member of the Royal African Company and learned of the sad plight of a slave from Gambia, one Job Jolla, or Job Ben Solomon, who had escaped from a Maryland plantation and revealed his high birth, his intelligence, and a knowledge of Arabic. Oglethorpe paid the necessary bond to emancipate Job and to transport him to England and thence back to Gambia.

Ettinger, *James Edward Oglethorpe*, p. 308; Harris, *Biographical Memorials of James Oglethorpe*, pp. 24–37, 102.

WILLIAM PAGE, 1764–1827. Major William Page was a South Carolinian who had been a neighbor of the Butlers in Prince Williams Parish in the Beaufort District. His title came from service with General Frances Marion in the Revolution. The Pages moved to Georgia after the war, living first at Ottassee plantation in Bryan County, and then about 1796 they moved to St. Simons, where he agreed to manage the Butler plantations on a temporary basis for one thousand dollars annually. He stayed until 1802, when he found a replacement in Roswell King. The Pages then began the development of the James Spalding plantation on the southern end of St. Simons, but a Butler-Page relationship continued until Major Butler's death. William Page frequently was called on for advice, for appraisals of property, or for assistance in plantation matters. He and his wife, Hannah Timmons, had but one child, Anne Matilda, who married Thomas Butler King. The King children were friends of Sarah Wister and Frances Leigh, the daughters of Pierce and Fanny Kemble Butler. The Page-King plantation was called Retreat and was the site of the "contraband colony" of liberated slaves in the Civil War. It is now the Sea Island Golf Club, where the tabby ruins of the old plantation structures are much in evidence.

Cate, *Our Todays and Yesterdays,* pp. 124–25; Page-Butler correspondence, William Page Papers, collection 1254, Southern Historical Collection, Chapel Hill.

WILLIAM PAYNE was the son of servants of the Irish Butlers, who migrated to Charleston in the late 1780s with Major Butler's nephew Edward Butler. He won Major Butler's disfavor by forcing payment of one thousand pounds in an unexplained transaction, and by advising the Irish Butlers in County Carlow of the Major's great wealth "got by marriage." William Payne remained in South Carolina and "married the daughter of a very Respectable Good Man," yet to Pierce Butler, was ever a "scoundrel."

PB's letter of September 8, 1794, and PB to Frances Butler, April 25, 1800, PB Letterbooks, HSP.

WILLIAM PIERCE, 1740–1789, was a Savannah businessman who served in the Revolution as aide-de-camp to General Nathanael Greene, and who became one of the delegates to the Constitutional Convention of 1787. There he was best known for his short character sketches of the delegates and for his garrulousness that threatened the secrecy rule.

DAB; Tansill, ed., *Documents of the American States,* pp. 106–7.

CHARLES PINCKNEY, 1757–1824, was the first cousin, once removed, of Charles Cotesworth Pinckney, and as did his cousin, became a British prisoner while defending Charleston in 1780. He served with his cousin and Pierce Butler in 1787 in Philadelphia, where his youthful brilliance was much in evidence. A slave owner himself, he was the only delegate to express a moral defense of slavery. In 1788 he was wed to Eleanor, the daughter of Henry Laurens. Often disliked by his own class and called "Blackguard Charlie," Pinckney was immensely popular throughout most of South Carolina. He served four terms as governor. Following the slave uprising in Santo Domingo that sent many refugees into Charleston, he was fearful of an invasion by the French from the West Indies. Charles Pinckney owned seven plantations and hundreds of black slaves. His fear of attack from afar and revolt from within was a manifestation of insular attitudes that were to prevail in a once-progressive city and state.

Rogers, *Charleston in the Age of the Pinckneys*, pp. 116–40; Wallace, *The History of South Carolina*, 2:340; Bowen, *Miracle at Philadelphia*, p. 202.

THOMAS PINCKNEY, 1750–1828. Not only did Thomas Pinckney win posts coveted by Pierce Butler—special envoy to Spain, minister to Great Britain—he won the widow Middleton, who interrupted her marmalade party to refuse Major Butler's proposal. The widow was Frances Motte Middleton, who succeeded her sister Elizabeth Motte as Thomas Pinckney's wife. He was the younger brother of Charles Cotesworth Pinckney, excelled in Greek at Oxford, and early on expressed an interest in the military. A soldier in the Revolution, he was wounded and captured by the British at Camden. As South Carolina's governor in 1787, he commended the four delegates, including his brother and Pierce Butler, for their roles in framing the Constitution and then gave valuable support for its ratification. When he was special envoy to Spain, the Pinckney Treaty opened vast lands to the spread of slavery. He first owned slaves when but eight years old. His father's will had left him "Slaves with their increase." He also owned several plantations, one of which was destroyed by the British in 1779. Thomas Pinckney abandoned the practice of law for the management of his plantations, Eldorado on the Santee River and Fairfield. His "hurricane house," a refuge for slaves in storm time, served as a model for a similar structure on Butler's Island. The Charleston town house of the Thomas Pinckneys stands today.

Rogers, *Charleston in the Age of the Pinckneys*, pp. 70, 121–24; TP to PB, May 25, 1805, Butler Family Papers, HSP.

JOSIAH QUINCY, JR., 1744–1775, was a young Bostonian who visited Charlestown in 1773 and kept a journal that recorded what he saw, whom he met, and what they talked of. An attorney by training, he paired with John Adams in a defense of the British soldiers of Pierce Butler's Twenty-ninth Regiment who, when attacked by angry citizens, reacted to cause the Boston Massacre. Quincy journeyed to England in 1774 on a secret mission. There he talked to Lords North and Dartmouth in a vain attempt to stave off impending hostilities. He died on his return trip, a week after the Battle of Lexington and a few days before his ship entered Gloucester harbor. On the Charlestown visit, Josiah Quincy, Jr., witnessed what he called "the mischiefs of slavery" and predicted that "greater mischiefs lay ahead."

Quincy, "Journal, 1773."

THEODORE ROOSEVELT, 1858–1919, was the twenty-fifth president of the United States. His mother, Martha Bulloch Roosevelt, lived in Roswell, Georgia, as a child. Following their years together at Harvard College, Theodore Roosevelt was

Owen Wister's friend for life. They shared an abiding love and respect for the American West. The president read Wister's novel of Charleston, *Lady Baltimore,* and was strongly critical. He objected to Wister's making his Northern characters "swine-devils" and his Southerners "angels." He also objected to Wister's acceptance of the Southerner's attitude toward blacks. Neither quite understood the role of blacks as citizens. The president was the more tolerant of the two; Owen Wister the kinder, and perhaps, blinder.

Owen Wister, preface to *Lady Baltimore* (1928).

BENJAMIN RUSH, M.D., 1745–1813, was the distinguished Philadelphian who signed the Declaration of Independence, and who helped in Pennsylvania's ratification of the federal Constitution. He was the family physician for the Pierce Butlers, in one sense an unlikely alignment, for Dr. Rush was a determined and outspoken opponent of slavery. In 1773 he refused a lucrative offer to practice in South Carolina, "a country where wealth had been accumulated only by the sweat and blood of negro slaves." A founder of America's first anti-slavery society, Dr. Rush was persistent in his efforts to help blacks. He charged them no fees for medical attention. In 1782 he urged General Nathanael Greene to use his good influence in South Carolina to "prohibit the future importation of slaves into your country." He did not urge emancipation, for he believed slavery had given blacks "habits of vice" that made them unfit for freedom. He thought time might unfold a method of "repairing to their posterity the injustice" done them. He advanced the theory that their blackness was the result of a great disease that had swept across Africa. The Rush-Butler ties were strong. In addition to medical care to three generations of Butlers, there was a social interchange with moral and spiritual support in times of crisis. When the Rush son James studied medicine in Scotland, Major Butler gave him a "credit" of three hundred pounds sterling a year. The unfortunate son John Rush, who lost his mind after killing a friend in a duel, once accompanied Major Butler on a trip to South Carolina. Major Butler said Dr. Rush was his "medical oracle" and was quick to support the doctor's controversial practice of bleeding yellow fever victims. Dr. Rush offered comforting verses as memorials on the death of the unknown young person in 1803 and of the Mease grandson in 1810.

Butterfield, ed., *Letters of Benjamin Rush,* 1:76, 186; Handlin, *Race and Nationality,* p. 25; Corner, ed., *The Autobiography of Benjamin Rush,* pp. 209, 280.

JAMES RUSH, M.D., 1786–1869. As was his father Benjamin, James Rush was a friend of the Butler family. Major Pierce Butler had helped fund his Scottish education. Harriot Percy Butler urged her father to assist James Rush in succeeding his father as treasurer of Philadelphia's United States Mint. He married millionairess Phoebe Ann Ridgway, who shared their father's fortune with her sister Susan, the wife of John Rhea Barton, M.D., and her brother John. Mrs. Rush was a brilliant

but eccentric leader of Philadelphia society. Her husband was just as eccentric—
"a person as wild and crazy in his way as she in hers." Phoebe Ann Rush died in
1857, Dr. Rush twelve years later, years spent "in the seclusion of his library." The
Ridgway-Rush fortune was left to the Library Company of Philadelphia.

PB to JR, April 30, 1813, James Rush Papers, vol. 21, HSP; Wainwright, ed., *A Philadelphia
Perspective*, pp. 282–84, 412, 551–52.

THOMAS RUSTON, M.D., 1742–1804, of Philadelphia built the fine house on
Chestnut and Eighth streets that became the proud home of Major Pierce Butler in
1804. The house had been sold at public outcry six years before, with the proceeds applied against debts the doctor could not pay.

Perkins Collection, vol. 8C, HSP.

JOHN RUTLEDGE, 1739–1800, was the older brother of Edward Rutledge. He was
the "highly mounted" Charlestonian who served with Pierce Butler in the Constitutional Convention of 1787. There, in his advocacy of slavery, he voiced the
sentiments of South Carolina and Georgia: "The people of those states will never
be such fools as to give up so important an interest." Yet, he was never worked
into a position where he was forced to defend slavery on moral grounds. John
Rutledge was a member of the Continental Congress and a governor of South
Carolina, and was a force in his state's ratification of the Constitution. When
appointed chief justice of the Supreme Court by President Washington, he sent
word of his acceptance to Philadelphia by one of his slaves. Before the Senate
could confirm, he made an intemperate speech on the Jay Treaty that led to his
rejection by that body. At the beginning of the Revolution, Rutledge owned sixty
slaves; at the time of the Convention, he had twenty-eight; and at his death in
1800, he owned but one. His wife, Elizabeth Grimké, of a family that became
known for its abolitionism, gave up all of her slaves prior to her death in 1793.
John Rutledge became so despondent following her death that he attempted suicide by leaping into the Ashley River from the Gibbes Bridge. He was rescued by
"a boatload of negroes." Their son John Rutledge, Jr., defeated Major Butler in
1798 after a bitter campaign for a seat in the United States House of Representatives.

Barry, *Mr. Rutledge of South Carolina*, pp. 328–29, 332; Prescott, *Drafting the Federal
Constitution*, p. 702; *Biographical Directory of the SCHR*.

JOHN RUTLEDGE, JR., 1766–1819. John Rutledge, Jr.'s father had served with
Pierce Butler as a South Carolina delegate to the Constitutional Convention of
1787. When the young Rutledge defeated Major Butler in 1798 in their contest for

a seat in the United States House of Representatives, a factor in his victory was a pamphlet prepared by his uncle, Judge J. F. Grimké, in which Rutledge was said to offer voters a better choice than Butler, who, enraged, challenged Judge Grimké to a duel. Fortunately, the challenge was withdrawn. Young Rutledge, an innocent in the Butler-Grimké affair, became a participant in an affair of honor of his own. In 1804, he shot and killed his wife's paramour, Dr. Horatio Senter of Newport. The duel, in Savannah, followed an interrupted bedroom scene at the Rutledge home in Charleston.

Stegeman and Stegeman, *Caty,* p. 183; *Biographical Directory of the SCHR.*

HARRIET ST. LEGER, 1797–1877, was the "Dearest Hal" of thousands of Fanny Kemble letters written over a span of almost fifty years. She lived near Dublin, at Ardgillan Castle, and was a tall, angular, erect, and oddly dressed woman. More than to any other person, Fanny Kemble confided in Harriet St. Leger—"a candour, a nakedness, a supreme honesty of self" is found in the Kemble side of this long correspondence. When Miss St. Leger was old and almost blind, the letters she had received were packaged and shipped to Fanny Kemble to become the basic source of her three volumes of *Records,* the first two of which Henry James said together became "one of the most animated autobiographies in the language."

Kemble, *Records of a Girlhood,* p. 91; Gibbs, *Affectionately Yours, Fanny,* p. 48; James, *Essays in London and Elsewhere,* p. 107.

ROGER PARKER SAUNDERS, d. 1795, was a South Carolinian who had been an officer in the American army during the Revolution. He served under Generals Nathanael Greene and Anthony Wayne and was said to have "caroused" with the latter. When General Wayne was awarded the Savannah River plantation Richmond and Kew, Captain Saunders assisted by purchasing forty-seven Georgia slaves for his friend. At the war's end he was one of the two Americans permitted in occupied Charleston to retrieve slaves who had deserted to the British—some for his friend Major Butler. Captain Saunders owned plantations in South Carolina and Georgia and was helpful in moving Butler slaves to Hampton and Butler's Island. In 1790 he arranged a timely loan that rescued Major Butler from imminent disaster. His wife was "the amiable Amarinthia Lowndes," so described in 1776 by the *Charleston Gazette.* In 1795, "after a short and violent illness," Captain Saunders died on his plantation in Liberty County, Georgia. Twenty-four years after Amarinthia Lowndes's first marriage, the *Gazette* gave testimony to her long-lived good nature. They reported the "amiable widow" had married John Champneys. At his death Captain Saunders owned property jointly with Major Butler in Washington County, Georgia, where he gave his name to the county seat, Saundersville (now Sandersville). He also owned an island in the Altamaha River, purchased at Major Butler's suggestion and paid for with slaves "out of a Guineaman."

Wildes, *Anthony Wayne,* pp. 291, 295, 322; *Charleston Gazette,* January 5, 1796, and September 25, 1776; PB's letter of June 1796, and PB to John Champneys, March 4, 1816, PB Letterbooks, HSP.

THE SEDGWICKS: CATHARINE MARIA SEDGWICK, 1789–1867; CHARLES SEDG-WICK, 1791–1855, and his wife, ELIZABETH DWIGHT; and THEODORE SEDGWICK, 1811–1859. Catharine and Charles Sedgwick were two of the ten children of Judge Theodore Sedgwick (1746–1813) and his second wife, Pamela Dwight. Judge Sedgwick had served in Congress at the time Pierce Butler was South Carolina's senator. Before becoming a Massachusetts Supreme Court judge, he was an attorney whose best-known case was the winning of freedom for an escaped slave. Fanny Kemble's friendship with the Sedgwick family began in Boston before her marriage when she met Catharine Maria Sedgwick, a pioneer novelist whose first work was published in 1822. In 1834, with accurate foresight, Miss Sedgwick believed the pending Butler-Kemble marriage "a dangerous experiment." In 1861 she expressed herself on the war: "I am willing to see South Carolina humbled in the dust," and added, "but beyond South Carolina I have no ill will." Fanny Kemble said Catharine Sedgwick was her first "American friend." The Kemble-Sedgwick connection continued with Charles and Elizabeth Dwight Sedgwick of Lenox, Massachusetts, where Fanny Kemble had a summer home following her separation and divorce. The Sedgwick family became a source of strength to her, and thus an anathema to Pierce Butler. It was Elizabeth Sedgwick to whom the letters that form the *Journal* of the stay on the Georgia plantations were written and to whom the book was dedicated. Their son William Sedgwick was one of the twenty-three thousand casualties on the bloody field of Antietam. Theodore Sedgwick, a nephew of Catharine and Charles, was the third to bear that name. He shared his father's and his grandfather's aversion to slavery, was an attorney as they had been, and as such supported and represented Fanny Kemble in her marital difficulties with Pierce Butler.

Sedgwick, "The Sedgwicks of Berkshire," pp. 91–106; Dewey, *Life and Letters of Catharine M. Sedgwick,* pp. 392, 393, 415; Welch, *Theodore Sedgwick, Federalist,* p. 102; *DAB.*

COLONIAL ROBERT GOULD SHAW, 1837–1863. Colonel Shaw's parents were friends of Fanny Kemble. In 1853, she and the Shaws with their young son spent several days together in Sorrento. He became the commanding officer of the Fifty-fourth Massachusetts Regiment of free blacks, who, against his will and judg-ment, participated in the burning of Darien, Georgia, in 1863. Later that year Colonel Shaw lost his life with many of his soldiers in a brave and bloody attack on Fort Wagner in Charleston harbor. His body was "thrown into a trench" with those of his soldiers. When the war had ended and the town of Darien was being rebuilt, the Shaws contributed to the construction fund for a new St. Andrew's chapel.

RGS to Sarah Shaw, June 13, 1863, Wister Family Papers, HSP; King, *Darien: The Death and Rebirth of a Southern Town*, pp. 56–59, 63–73, 95–98; Luck, *Robert Gould Shaw: Memorial*, p. 180.

GENERAL WILLIAM T. SHERMAN, 1820–1891, was the Union general who in 1864 led his army of sixty-two thousand men in a vengeful march through Georgia and South Carolina that attracted a ragtag following of thousands of former slaves. Unlike their masters, the blacks thought the general a savior from above. When taken to task by his superiors for exhibiting callousness and a lack of compassion for the blacks, General Sherman was nonplussed. His mission, he said, was "to whip the rebels" and to "make them fear and dread us." That he did.

Sherman, *Memoirs*, 2:249.

WILLIAM LOUGHTON SMITH, 1748–1812, was the husband of Charlotte Izard and thus was the son-in-law of Ralph Izard. He was in the United States House of Representatives at the time Major Pierce Butler and Ralph Izard were in the Senate. In Congress, he lamented, "We have no state to support our peculiar rights, particularly that of holding slavery, but Georgia." His dislike of Major Butler was intense. They did share common ground as proslavery politicians but otherwise were poles apart.

Rogers, *Charleston in the Age of the Pinckneys*, pp. 116–17; Rogers, "The Letters of William Loughton Smith to Edward Rutledge," p. 20.

THOMAS SPALDING, 1774–1851. James Spalding, the father of Thomas, planted what came to be known as Retreat plantation on the opposite end of St. Simons Island from Major Pierce Butler's Hampton. He was said to be a "great reader of men and of books." The latter trait he passed on to Thomas Spalding, who lived in the grand house on Sapelo Island built by his own slaves under the supervision of Roswell King. There, in a "primeval forest of lofty, out-branching oaks," the loneliness of island life was eased by his fine and extensive library but, more important, by the presence of his wife, Sarah Leake, a woman of rare accomplishments, good sense, and singular beauty. Thomas Spalding was a successful and innovative planter, one who brought renown to the Altamaha delta. He was a great-grandson of John McIntosh Mohr, the author of the New Inverness petition opposing slavery in 1739. In Spalding's favor, he was said to be "kind in all the relations of life, his slaves, of whom he had a large number, felt neither irksome toil nor disquiet under his mild and indulgent government." Yet, there was disquiet. In 1815, when Admiral Sir George Cockburn decimated the slave quarters of neighboring St. Simons Island by emancipating hundreds of blacks, the Spalding slaves surprised their owner by letting him know their toil *was* irksome, and that they, too, wanted freedom. He assisted the St. Simons planters as an emissary of President Madison and Secretary of State Monroe in voyages to Bermuda and Halifax in futile efforts to retrieve the blacks carried away by Admiral Cockburn.

White, *Historical Collections of Georgia*, pp. 634–36; Coulter, *Thomas Spalding of Sapelo*, pp. 190–94.

PETER SPENCE, M.D., a Charlestonian who was a friend of the Pierce Butlers. Peter Spence's loyalty to the Crown caused him to be classified as "Obnoxious" and brought on his banishment and the confiscation of his property. He lived almost destitute in London, where he monitored the health and scholastic progress of Thomas Butler at the Weeden Butler school in Chelsea. Somehow Dr. Spence managed to hold onto some property in America, for in 1797 there was a security interest in slaves held in his name against the estate of Major Butler's friend Roger Parker Saunders who had died in 1795.

Webber, "Josiah Smith's Diary," p. 198; Pierce Butler–Weeden Butler Correspondence, November 16, 1788, and letter 51, early 1789, British Library.

THADDEUS STEVENS, 1792–1868, was the radical Republican congressman from Pennsylvania who hated the South, slavery, secession, and masonry with a malevolent passion. In 1846, at a state meeting in Harrisburg, Stevens silenced the slave-owning Pierce Butler by likening him to an insignificant insect. He refused to own a lot in a cemetery in which blacks could not be buried. His grave, in a small integrated graveyard, was marked by a gravestone with an epitaph ending, "I have chosen this, that I might illustrate in my death the principles which I advocated through a long life—Equality of Man before his Creator."

Hodding Carter, *The Angry Scar*, pp. 100–103; Harrison, ed., *Philadelphia Merchant*, entry for February 19, 1846; *DAB*.

JAN GABRIEL TEGELAAR was the Amsterdam moneylender who loaned Major Pierce Butler 150,000 Dutch guilders in September 1785 and took as security twenty-two parcels of land, hundreds of black slaves, including land and blacks Major Butler had no legal right to pledge. When the Dutchman failed to honor several Butler drafts, he became "That knave, Tegelaar" and "that dishonest Man."

PB's letter of June 15, 1789, PB Letterbooks, HSP; the Tegelaar mortgage, September 19, 1785, Butler Family Papers, HSP.

WILLIAM TAPPAN THOMPSON, 1812–1882. An Ohio-born newspaperman, William Tappan Thompson began his career in Philadelphia where he wrote sketches, often humorous and often published as letters. He helped establish the *Savannah Daily Morning News* and was its editor for thirty-two years. A strong proponent of Southern rights, he made that position known in forceful and sarcastic comment prior to the Civil War and in coverage of the sale of the Butler slaves at Savannah in 1859. He deserted his editorial position in 1864 by joining the retreating Confederate army as a private after General Sherman had captured Savannah.

Myers, ed., *Children of Pride*, p. 1701.

MORTIMER NEAL THOMSON, 1831–1875, was the capable *New York Tribune* reporter sent by Horace Greeley to Savannah to cover the 1859 sale of Pierce Butler's blacks. Thomson used the by-line "Q. K. Philander Doesticks, P.B.," but appeared in Savannah incognito and did not reveal his presence until his return to New York. His *Tribune* article began, "The largest sale of human chattels that has been made in Star Spangled America for several years, took place on Wednesday and Thursday of last week at the Race-course near the city of Savannah, Georgia."

DAB; New York Daily Tribune, March 9, 1859.

THE REVEREND DUDLEY TYNG, 1825–1858, was the young rector of the Episcopal Church of the Epiphany of Philadelphia who in 1856 preached the sermon "Our Country's Troubles," declaring slavery to be evil and inconsistent with Christianity. Pierce Butler, a vestryman, objected and voted with others to close the church and dismiss their minister. A second reason given for Mr. Tyng's dismissal was his change in the musical program of the church without the approval of the music committee of which Pierce Butler was chairman. Epiphany reopened as the Reverend Mr. Tyng founded his own Church of the Covenant. He was killed in an accident on the family farm in 1858.

Westcott, "Scrapbooks: Biographies of Philadelphia," 2:194–95, HSP; *Philadelphia Sunday Dispatch*, March 13, 1859.

GEORGE WASHINGTON, 1732–1799. Pierce Butler and George Washington shared one common characteristic at the Constitutional Convention in Philadelphia—both were slaveholders. But then, one-third of all the delegates were owners of slaves. General Washington conducted the meetings of the convention as its presiding officer. He did so with impressive dignity. That he owned blacks undoubtedly influenced the acceptance of slavery as a fact of the present and future life of the young republic. The refusal to condemn slavery was a principal factor in what Major Butler called "a pretty General Spirit of Accommodation" that brought clashing interests together. He believed his advocacy of the secrecy rule enforced so diligently by General Washington was an important reason for the convention's success. Washington, when president, was hospitable to the Butler family, but relations between the two men were not always easy. Major Butler felt slighted when federal appointments did not come his way, and he disapproved of the Jay

Treaty. He believed the president fell far short of the superlatives "base flatterers attribute to him," and that history would judge him accordingly.

Burns, *The Vineyard of Liberty,* p. 32; PB to Governor Matthews, October 17, 1795, PB to John Sommerville, January 5, 1798, and PB to Isaac McPherson, May 25, 1800, PB Letterbooks, HSP.

JAMES MOORE WAYNE, 1790–1867, and his father, RICHARD WAYNE, 1740–1809, the Savannah agent for Major Pierce Butler for a brief time in the early 1790s. The association was terminated when Wayne failed to supply much-needed corn for hungry Butler slaves. The elder Wayne was a commission merchant, importer of slaves, and a slave owner who planted on the Back River across from Savannah. In 1835 James Moore Wayne became a justice of the Supreme Court of the United States. It was in that capacity he sat in judgment on Charles Augustus Lafayette Lamar and his fellow conspirators in the infamous case of the *Wanderer* and the 409 Africans slaves brought to Georgia's Jekyll Island in 1858. Judge Wayne, an unusual Savannahian who opposed secession, held firmly to his stand, while his son, Major Henry C. Wayne, renounced his commission in the Union army to become adjutant general of the state of Georgia. Judge Wayne, who had owned slaves as late as 1856, died in Washington in 1867. His wife and son survived him, as did a daughter, Elizabeth Isabel Clifford, who was born in 1834 to the Judge's black slave, Anna.

Lawrence, *James Moore Wayne,* pp. 161–67; Swartz, "Pauline Stoney's Story," pp. 6–7.

CHARLES SPALDING WYLLY, 1836–1923, was the son of Alexander William and Sarah Spalding Wylly. His mother was the daughter of Thomas and Sarah Leake Spalding of Sapelo, thus he was descended from John McIntosh Mohr, the author of the New Inverness petition in which Altamaha Scots opposed the introduction of slavery into colonial Georgia. Charles Spalding Wylly was blessed with a retentive memory and an interest in history. In the time in which he lived, no man knew more of the Altamaha estuary, its people, and their plantations than did he. His views on slavery were not far removed from those of his McIntosh Mohr ancestor. He was a friend of Frances Leigh and her sister, Sarah Wister, who were his contemporaries.

Wylly, *Memories* and *The Seed That Was Sown;* Vanstory, *Georgia's Land of the Golden Isles,* p. 158; Lovell, *The Golden Isles of Georgia,* pp. 208–9.

Slaves and Freedmen

ABRAHAM or ABRAM, names common on the Butler plantations.

Carpenter ABRAHAM was a trusted slave who accompanied Roswell King and Thomas Spalding to Bermuda in 1815 in a vain effort to find and persuade the

Butler slaves to return after their desertion to the British. Major Butler's desire to reward Abraham by giving him his freedom was deferred until after his death. From 1815 until 1822 Abraham served the aging Major as a manservant in Philadelphia, and after that he lived as a free black at Hampton, where Roswell King, Jr., said he was "the best behav'd Fellow I know." In 1839 Fanny Kemble Butler was told by old Abraham's grandson and namesake that the freedom had been purchased, which was not true.

Several ABRAHAMS were listed in the 1859 appraisal and division, some as carpenters. JACKSTRAW ABRAHAM was among those on the lists.

BLACKFROST ADAM, one of the slaves retained at the time of the 1859 auction.

ALECK, ALLICK, or ALEX, names found frequently on the Butler slave rolls.

The ALECK ALEXANDER family. After emancipation in 1865, Aleck and his wife Daphne chose Alexander as their surname. As free people they long kept in touch with their former owners, particularly with Frances Leigh and Sarah Wister. Daphne was born of Minda and Roswell King, Jr. Aleck's father was Sauney, "the great violinist." His mother, Hannah, nursed Pierce Butler through his illness in 1839 and was house servant for Roswell King, Jr. Both Daphne and Aleck appear in the Kemble *Journal*. Fanny Kemble taught Aleck to read as she neared the end of her visit to "this blessed purgatory." She wrote: "In that last week perhaps I may teach the boy enough to go on alone when I am gone." Aleck and Daphne's children included Pierce Butler Alexander, an able house servant; Mary, who married the Reverend F. M. Mann, the rector of St. Cyprian's in Darien; Dora Jeannette, who was the assistant at the Mann School that was founded by Mary; and Deaconess A. E. B. Alexander of the church and school at Penick Station near Darien.

ALEX, a Virginia slave purchased by Major Butler in 1802. His back showed lash scars "from neck to ham."

ALEXANDER, a Butler's Island slave, a root doctor noted for his sorcery and his ability to fly—once from Darien to Savannah.

AUBA, a popular African name, often shown as AUBER.

"Old" AUBA was fifty-five in 1793 and classified as "Negroe cook."

"Old AUBER" appears in the Kemble *Journal*. In 1839 "a stooping halting hag, came to beg for flannel and rice." This was probably the fifteen-year-old girl Auba, who was listed in 1793, making her sixty-one in 1839.

AUBER was Quash's wife and the mother of Fivepound. She was twenty-one in 1849 and valued at $450. Ten years later, although "small and sickly," she was worth $600.

BEN. After eleven years as a domestic in Philadelphia, slave Ben was told by Major Butler he was to return to work on the Georgia plantations. He sought protection from the Quakers, who won Ben's freedom in 1804 after a prolonged battle in federal courts.

BESS was listed on the 1793 inventory of Butler slaves as thirty-four years old and a "Very good worker and good Negroe." Major Butler changed the "good" to "Excellent."

BETTY was a Hampton slave who attended "Poultry and Feathers" for the Butlers under the supervision of Mrs. Roswell King. The down from plantation geese helped the Butler family to withstand cold Pennsylvania winters. The 1793 roll shows Betty, aged forty-two, as an "Excellent Negroe & Poultry & Dairy Woman." As she was a favorite of Major Butler, he wished to grant Betty her freedom in 1815 but was dissuaded by Roswell King.

BETTY, when a young woman and the wife of Frank, gave birth to a mulatto son after an enforced stay with Roswell King, Jr. In 1839, at the time of the Kemble visit, Frank had become the head driver, and Betty was described in the *Journal* as "a tidy, trim, intelligent woman with a pretty figure." Renty, or Rentee, the son, was a "lad" of ten. In the 1849 appraisal Betty, forty-seven years old, was valued at three hundred dollars. Ten years later, she had become a "poultryminder" and worth but one hundred dollars. Frank, valued at one thousand dollars in 1849, was "bedridden and superannuated" in 1859 and thus without value.

BILLY, a venerable slave in 1839, was thought by white Darien Baptist ministers to be capable of teaching his fellow slaves on the Butler plantations a proper Christianity. Pierce Butler disagreed.

JERUSALEM BLAKE returned to Butler's Island after emancipation, chose the surname of Mary Butler's cousin Elizabeth Blake, whose slaves were inherited by the Butlers in 1792. She worked as a field hand for the Leighs in the 1870s for fifty cents a day. In later years, and as "Aunt Jerusalem," she eked out a living by selling produce in Darien.

BOB, who was thirty-eight in 1793, was shown on the inventory as "Lame." Major Butler added, "But a trusty good Negroe."

Commodore BOB, a fifty-two-year-old "aged rice worker," his wife Kate, also "aged," their children Linda, nineteen, and Joe, thirteen, were sold at the Savannah auction in 1859 for six hundred dollars each. When emancipated, Kate and Bob returned to Butler's Island. Bob became their surname.

BOY BILLY, a blacksmith, was working at Butler's Island in 1815 when the British persuaded Butler slaves at Hampton to accept their offer of freedom. Of the five smiths, Boy Billy, Jack, and Sawney remained, while Isaac and young Isaac were among the 138 who deserted and ultimately found freedom in Nova Scotia, all with the surname Butler.

BRAM. Ever a popular name among the Butler slaves and one often carried by men designated as drivers. In the 1793 inventory there were five Brams, six in 1849. Occasionally spelled "Braam," and by Fanny Kemble, mistakenly, "Bran."

BRAM, fifty years old, was classified as a basket maker on the 1793 roll.

BRAM, thirty-five years old, was a gardener in 1793 and in 1794 made a special planting of cayenne pepper for Major Butler. In 1804, when forty-six years old, Bram was called an "old rascal" and denied an issue of clothing for causing "petty trouble."

BRAM, twenty-seven years old, was described as a "Very Good Driver" in 1793. He was a Hampton slave who, by 1804, was considered with Morris to be the best of the Butler drivers. Roswell King said in 1815 that Bram had earned more than ten thousand dollars for his owner. When fifty-one, "old" and ailing but "truly faithful," he was sent by Major Butler to Philadelphia for better care. In 1824 he was remembered as "Old Braam," who had led his gang in digging a canal connecting the Hampton River with Buttermilk Sound.

BRAM, the son of "Very Good Driver," succeeded his father at Hampton. In 1821 Major Butler sent word that he expected a crop of 135 bales of cotton from Bram's fields. In 1822, the year of Major Butler's death, Bram and his wife, Venus, produced a son, Joe.

BRAM, born in 1812, was the son of Roswell King and one of the slave girls. Bram and his wife, Joan, had six children, one of whom was young Bram. Bram bore a strong resemblance to his half brother, Roswell King, Jr., a fact noticed by Fanny Kemble in her *Journal*. He was a driver in 1839 and was mistakenly called "Bran" by Fanny. Sold in the slave auction in 1859, he returned to Hampton following the Civil War to work for Pierce Butler and his daughter Frances in those difficult postwar years.

JOHN BROWN. When the Union army occupied St. Simons Island in 1862, black volunteers were armed and given guard duty. In a skirmish with Confederate raiders, a black named John Brown was killed and was thought to be the first of his race to die as a soldier in the Civil War. Island blacks believed him to be the John Brown whose soul goes marching on.

DIANA BULL was the one former slave on Butler's Island shown by the 1870 census to have chosen the surname "Bull." The first of the Butler slaves had been inherited in 1771 by Mary Butler from her grandmother, Mary Bull.

BUTLER. The Butler plantations in South Carolina lost many slaves to the British in the American Revolution, but it is not known that any chose, or were given, their master's name for their own use. In 1815, when the British occupied St. Simons Island, 138 of the Butler slaves were given that last name immediately on defecting. By the time they reached Nova Scotia a few weeks after leaving Georgia, births, deaths, and man-woman alignment had changed that total to 139 of the former slaves, all of whom went ashore as Butlers. Sam, William, and Rose Butler died at sea. Joe Bull Butler, one of several Joes, was the first of the Butlers to be logged ashore. Province records show that many of the former Butler slaves settled with many St. Simons blacks at Hammond's Plains, fourteen miles from Halifax, and others at nearby Preston. A few migrated to Boston, some became a part of the colony of Loch Lomond near St. John, New Brunswick, and a scant few found a warmer climate by accepting their new government's offer of a move to Trinidad. Butlers at Hammond's Plains included Maringo, two Williams, Isaac, Sampson, Francis, Hector, Joseph, Georgia, Abraham, and their families. Joseph Butler and family agreed to move to Trinidad. In 1835 John Butler was the only one of that name living in Hammond's Plains.

Former slaves who chose the surname *Butler* when freed and were living on Butler's Island in 1870 were: Katy, 90; Mollie, 80; Tenah, 50; Sandy, 90; Cudjoe, 45; William, 55; Patty, 65; Flora, 40; Rose, 8; Willis, 7; Charles, 4; and Blind Judy, 75.

THE THOMAS BUTLER SLAVES. In 1800 Major Butler deeded sixty slaves to his son Thomas, who was their rightful owner. He had inherited them from his aunt, Mary Brewton. Among the sixty were two of the oldest couples on the Butler plantations. They were April, 62, and Nancy, 47; and Quakoo (or Quaka), 62, and Cumba, 52.

TUNIS G. CAMPBELL, 1812–1891, was the black "overlord" whose dominion over McIntosh County blacks during reconstruction alarmed Frances Butler Leigh and other planters as they struggled to bring postwar plantations to prewar prosperity. Campbell, who was born in New Jersey, won a commission in the military government and worked on the South Carolina and Georgia sea islands. As "Superintendent of Islands" for Georgia, he established island colonies where he taught free blacks to live independently and free from exploitation by whites. His fervor alarmed not only white Georgians but his own superiors, who closed down what had come to be regarded as Campbell's "black nation," or "kingdom." He then centered his activities in Darien, where he won for the former slaves of McIntosh County the right to vote, for himself election to the Georgia senate, and for all, the intense antagonism of most of the white populace. His advocacy of black rights clashed with the rampant racism so prevalent at the time and brought on his removal from the senate. As a justice of the peace in Darien he wielded such power that white law officers conspired, accused him unjustly of abuse of power, and convicted and sentenced him to imprisonment. Campbell served his time behind bars and as a leased convict laborer. He never returned to McIntosh County but continued his advocacy of black causes in Washington and in Boston, where he died in 1891.

CAPTAIN was a name often given to drivers, thus there was usually at least one Captain on the Butler slave rolls. After emancipation the term *driver* was put aside and the leader of a work detail became a "captain."

CAPTAIN, a Butler driver in the early 1800s, was a trusted black who was permitted to distribute rum to slaves who worked on wet, cold, winter mornings. He drank no rum himself and was said to be fair to all.

CAPTAIN was a former driver who returned to Butler's Island after the Civil War and was shown in the 1870 census as "Captain James, Overseer on Farm." He and his wife, Binah, named their son "Thomas M. Oden" for a Butler overseer.

CAROLINA died free in 1866, one hundred years old. He was buried at Hampton and his funeral was attended by Pierce Butler and his daughter Frances. The Butlers marked Carolina's grave with a stone that told of his long life and his "Fidelity to his Earthly Masters."

CASSIE. In 1839 Cassie complained to her sympathetic mistress, Fanny Kemble, that Roswell King, Jr.'s use of the lash when she was pregnant caused her child to be born with whip marks on its body.

CHANCE was an eighteen-year-old Butler slave who, in 1806, refused work after being lashed by Roswell King. His refusal brought about removal to the King's house, where his "obstinacy" was conquered.

CHLOE, born in 1822, the year of Major Butler's death, was flogged in 1839 by the Butler overseer, Thomas M. Oden, at the time of Fanny Kemble's visit to the plantations. Chloe, "an immense strapping lass, tall straight and extremely well made," had been impudent.

RENTY, or RENTEE, SARAH CRAWFORD, and their children, James and Dorcas, were four of the five mulattoes living on Butler's Island in 1870. Renty was the son of Roswell King, Jr., and Betty, the wife of head driver Frank.

OLIVER CROMWELL was the black man who protected the Kemble luggage in Philadelphia in 1832.

DAPHNE, wife of Primus, their three-year-old child Dido, and a newborn infant were sold in the rain at the Savannah auction in 1859. On seeing Daphne cover herself and her baby, the auctioneer was told by the buyers to "pull off her rags." The family sold for $2,500.

CELIA DAVIS, a former Butler slave, gave interesting information on the Butlers and their slaves when interviewed in Darien by Amelia M. Watson in 1915. Celia remembered "Miss Fanny Kemblin" and her clothes, "Oh so rich."

HENRY DELEGAL was a Darien black accused of raping a white girl in 1899. Fear that he would be lynched brought out a protective force of McIntosh blacks, many of whom were from Butler slave stock. Jailed in the disturbance that followed were Renty Young, Simon Devereaux, Andrew Young, John and Richard Coffee, Marshall Dowsey, and William and Jack Cooper. The Reverend F. M. Mann of St. Cyprian's church telegraphed Sarah Wister for help. She rallied the "honored names" of Channing, Curtis, Furness, Garrison, Higginson, Lowell, Mott, and Shaw, all of whom sent money for a spirited defense that won Henry Delegal's acquittal and limited chain gang sentences for the "rioters."

DEMBO, or DIMBO, was married to Frances during the Savannah auction in 1859; thus they were sold together as a family rather than separately.

CHATHAM DENNIS was a former driver who chose his new surname in 1870 and a new title, "Foreman on farm."

DIDO. At the time of the British occupation of St. Simons Island in 1815, Dido, fifteen years old, left Hampton with Lieutenant Horton, who also made off with Major Butler's silver spoons and a goodly collection of the Butler wines.

DIE was one of the Butler slaves who was flogged at the time of the Butler-Kemble visit in 1839. Die was pregnant at the time. An earlier DIE, who was twenty-two years old in 1793, was classified as "stupid."

"Old" DORCAS, who was fifty-four in 1817, helped Roswell King "sort out" slaves descended from those once owned by Sarah Guerard. She was assisted by Pompey, who was sixty-eight. In 1839 Fanny Kemble told of another "ancient" DORCAS who admired her watch and then remarked that she was "almost done with time."

DRUMMERS. Major Butler's Twenty-ninth Regiment used black drummers in their regimental band. They had been captured by the British on the island of Guadeloupe where, as slaves, they developed their skill as drummers on sugar plantations.

The *Eagle* boat slaves—Moses, son of Jack Carter; Jacob, son of Harry; Tipee, son of Worcester; and Judy, daughter of Deanna—were four of the five young slaves who appropriated the *Eagle* for a trip from Butler's Island to Hampton on a winter's day in 1808. The boat capsized in the rough waters of Buttermilk Sound and the slaves drowned. It was an act that enraged Roswell King.

EMANUEL died in 1829 from punishment administered by Roswell King, Jr. He and the Kings' slave Balaam had been "led astray" by Sampson, and all were given a "cold water" punishment that caused Emanuel's death.

ESSEX was the black cabin boy who attended Fanny Kemble, her father, and her aunt on the packet *Pacific* as they crossed the Atlantic on their trip to America in 1832. The treatment of Essex aboard ship, and ashore in New York, opened Fanny Kemble's eyes to the relations between blacks and whites in America.

FLORA was the aged slave on Hampton plantation who, because Major Butler would tolerate no idleness, grazed a goose on a line for an hour each day.

JEW FRANK was described as "superannuated" in 1849 and again in 1859. His owners considered him valueless in each appraisal.

FRIDAY was the old slave who died in a wretched Hampton infirmary as a distraught Fanny Kemble looked on.

GEORGE, a popular name on the Butler plantation.

GEORGE, in 1790, was considered by Major Butler capable of tanning leather and making shoes. The hides were acquired from John Couper's Cannon's Point plantation on St. Simons Island. In 1815 George defected to the British and was put ashore in Halifax, a free man.

In the division of slaves prior to the 1859 auction, RACCOON GEORGE, aged fifty-one, was valued at four hundred dollars. CARPENTER GEORGE, listed as "superannuated" at age sixty-eight, had no value. Both were retained. A third and fourth GEORGE, twenty-seven, and his son, six, were sold along with the wife and mother, Sue, twenty-six, and another son, Harry, two, for $620 each.

GLASGOW was flogged in 1839 at the time of the Butler-Kemble visit. He, his wife, and son were sold in 1853 for "turbulent behavior."

JOHN HALL and CHARLES PRATT were young Darien blacks given to the Reverend Nathaniel Pratt of Roswell, Georgia, in 1836. Educated and freed, the two were sent to Africa as Presbyterian missionaries. Dr. Pratt was married to Catherine Barrington King, the daughter of the elder Roswell King.

SHAD HALL of Sapelo was born a Spalding slave and remembered tales of Butler slaves who could fly.

WILLIAM S. HAMILTON was the Butler slave who was promised freedom ten years after a document was signed by Major Butler in 1800; the reason for the promise was not stated. William agreed "to keep all his Master's secrets."

HANNAH, a name that often appeared on the Butler slave rolls.

HANNAH was a Butler slave who performed domestic chores for the family in Philadelphia and was returned to Georgia in 1798 to recover from sickness in a warmer climate. She had done her work "unexceptionally well."

A later HANNAH, aged twenty-seven in 1823, became Roswell King, Jr.'s house servant when he was given permission to purchase her and her family of six children from Major Butler's estate at a total cost of $1,800. A year later he wrote, "Hannah is the most proper person I know of." She was the wife of Sauney, who played the violin, and with him the parents of Aleck, who became Aleck Alexander. In 1839 she nursed a suffering, rheumatic Pierce Butler at the time of the family visit to the plantations.

HARRIET. In 1839 Harriet was flogged by overseer Thomas M. Oden for telling her mistress, Fanny Kemble, she had no time to clean her children. Mr. Oden said that he had flogged her for impertinence.

HARRY, better known as FISH HARRY, who with those of his family who followed in his wake, caught fish in the salt and freshwater streams that surrounded Hampton and Butler's Island. The addition of seafood to the slave diet was most welcome.

When emancipation brought surnames to former slaves, the Fish Harry of that day became Bennet. Fish Harry of the 1790s, his sons, and grandsons, served the Butlers as fishermen for four generations.

A later HARRY who attended the rice field floodgates was appraised in the 1859 division of slaves as having no value. He was described as "superannuated" and identified as "Trunk Harry."

LIVERPOOL HAZZARD. Plantation records show Liverpool to be the son of York and Lydia and born in 1851. In August 1867 he rowed the mortally ill Pierce Butler from Butler's Island to Darien to seek medical aid from Dr. James Holmes. When an old man in the 1920s and 1930s, he often recited Butler slave lore to those interested and somehow became a legendary "centenarian" whose name was supposed to have originated on a visit to England after the Civil War, changed from York, or some said from Pierce Butler, to Liverpool. His only change of name in the 1860s was the addition of the surname Hazzard. In the 1930s he became a tourist attraction and for a small charge would feebly sing a boating song as he once could have done with some authority. He would then tell of his remembrances of the Butlers, Wisters, and Leighs. He died in 1936, aged eighty-five, and not over one hundred as his promoters proclaimed. Liverpool Hazzard contributed to Lydia Parrish's *Slave Songs of the Georgia Sea Islands,* a fine history of slave song and dance.

HENRY was a slave owned by the Hazzard family on St. Simons Island. He remained loyal to his owners during the Union occupation of the island and transmitted information of federal activities that proved useful to Confederate raiding parties.

The IBOS. In 1803 John Couper and Thomas Spalding purchased a "cargo" of Ibos in Savannah and shipped them to St. Simons Island, where they staged a brief mutiny that resulted in the drowning of ten or twelve slaves and three of the vessel's crew. The incident probably led to the familiar legend of the Ebo's Landing, where Ebos (Ibos) were said to have preferred drowning to lives as slaves.

ISAAC was the Butler boatman whose deep bass voice and manner of singing won the admiration of Fanny Kemble in 1839.

ISAAC. Slaves were often identified on the Butler rolls by their physical characteristics. Isaac, thirty-nine years old and valued at but two hundred dollars in 1859, was shown on the appraisal as "Bignose Isaac."

The IZARD-BUTLER exchange. In 1797 Allick, a slave owned by Elizabeth Middleton Izard at her plantation on the Combahee River in South Carolina, repeatedly petitioned Major Butler that he be reunited with his wife, Marian, a Butler slave. His request precipitated an exchange of eight Izard slaves for seven of the Butlers', with a cash difference of thirty-two pounds ten shillings. Four families, who had been separated in the distribution of Mary Brewton's estate, were brought together in this unusual transaction. The Izard slaves Allick and an unnamed black regained their wives Marian and Binah, each with three children. Butler slaves Quamina and Waley regained their Izard wives, Miley and Nelly, with two and three children respectively.

JACK, who became the chief blacksmith of the Butler plantation, was constantly in trouble. In 1797 and 1798 Major Butler disciplined Jack, ordering first a "tighter rein" and then that he be placed in leg irons. In 1815 Jack missed an opportunity for freedom by being at Butler's Island when the British persuaded Hampton slaves to desert. As late as 1835, Jack's troubles continued. He was flogged then for "insubordination."

JACK was a slave of Catharine Miller, leased to Major Butler by Phineas Miller. Jack died in 1804 from the bite of a rattlesnake. Phineas Miller had married Nathanael Greene's widow, Catharine, in 1796. He died in 1803.

JACK was a young slave assigned to guard his mistress, Fanny Kemble. He boated, fished, and rode with her, and won her friendship. From him she learned much of how it was to be a slave on a Butler plantation.

JACOB. In 1793 William Page classified twenty-two-year-old Jacob as a "Good Carpenter." Major Butler put a line through the "Good." In 1808, Jacob's boy Sunday, who was "but a lad," was given a severe whipping by Roswell King for stealing rice and for running away for two days. In 1815 Major Butler was dissuaded from freeing Jacob, but in 1821 sent for the ailing slave to give him better care in Philadelphia. Back on the plantation in 1835, Jacob, old and crippled, was said by Roswell King, Jr., to be faithful in grinding corn and attending to other "small matters."

JERRY was the free black who served Charlestown as a harbor pilot and who was hanged by Patriots who believed he was helping slaves escape to British ships in the harbor during the Revolution. Jerry's full name was Thomas Jeremiah.

JESSIE was James Hamilton Couper's slave who rowed stroke on his *Becky Sharp* to win at the Charleston regatta in 1849.

JOEFINNY was the Jones family's slave who, much to their surprise, defected to the Union forces in 1862.

JOHN. "My Servant John" was Pierce Butler's slave and manservant who accompanied the Major and his two children on the 1784 trip to England and the Continent.

JOHN, an old Butler slave, was one of the few remaining on St. Simons Island during the federal occupation in 1863. He talked to Colonel Robert Gould Shaw, the white commanding officer of the Fifty-fourth Massachusetts Regiment of free blacks, and told him of Pierce Butler, Fanny Kemble, and of the "Weeping Day" in 1859 when more than four hundred Butler slaves were sold in Savannah. When James Leigh first visited Hampton in 1873, he found "Uncle John" living there with his wife, "Mum Peggy."

JOHNNY was John Couper's talented slave at Cannon's Point who put a measure of Africa into the music he made on his Scottish master's bagpipes and on the violin. His natural propensity to adapt and to improvise was a characteristic shared with other black musicians and one that influenced the development of the Negro spiritual and much of American jazz.

JUDY was the Hampton slave who gave birth to Roswell King, Jr.'s mulatto son, Jim Valiant. Judy, with Scylla, was flogged on orders of Mrs. King. She was then banished to Five Pound, the remote settlement on Buttermilk Sound.

The KING slaves were security for a loan. In 1806 Roswell King borrowed $2,600 from Major Butler and offered as collateral property readily acceptable to his employer. The loan was secured by the King slaves Bellah, Judey, Lucy, Will, Henry, Cyrus, Prince, Davy, Samson, Jim, Jacob, and Peter.

PHILIP LEMAR was an old free black who lived on a remote timber tract near Butler's Island and protected the pine trees from poachers. He worked for the Leighs in the 1870s and likened himself to a dog, still proud of his master, as compared to a possum, free but scorned.

LONDON, the plantation cooper and part-time preacher, was seventy-one in 1859 and appraised as worthless. He conducted the service in 1839 when Shadrach was buried at night in the watery grave on Butler's Island in the presence of Pierce Butler and Fanny Kemble.

LOUISA was a Hampton slave whose graphic description of the flogging of women appears in the Kemble *Journal.*

THE REVEREND F. M. MANN was the rector of St. Cyprian's church in Darien. His wife, Mary, the daughter of Aleck and Daphne Alexander, was a granddaughter of Roswell King, Jr. In the late 1880s Mary founded the Mann School for black children, which was supported by the Leighs in England. The Delegal troubles of 1899 prompted a distress call from F. M. Mann to Sarah Wister.

MARY was the young housemaid assigned to Fanny Kemble at Butler's Island in 1839. Her lack of cleanliness made an early impression on Fanny Kemble of life on a slave plantation. Mary was "intolerably offensive in her person."

THE SLAVES OF THE THOMAS MIDDLETON WILL, 1768. Colonel Thomas Middleton made specific bequests of slaves to members of his family. To his widow, Anne Barnwell Middleton: "Trusty old Negroes Tom and Lymus, my Negroe Carpenter Charles and two fellows called Simon and George." To his daughter Sarah Guerard: Carpenter Primus. To his daughter Mary: "My Negroe Boy Caesar." To his son, William: Carpenter Worster, Ship Carpenter Jack, and the crew of his schooner *Betsy,* being Adam, Big Jack, Peter, Cyrus, and Boy Tom.

MINDA was the mother of Ben and Daphne by Roswell King, Jr.

MOLLY was a very common name on the Butler plantations, so much so that Mollys, or Molls, were often designated as "house Molly," "Toney's Molly," or "Old Moll," and so forth. One slave named MOLLY worked as a domestic in Philadelphia in the late 1790s. She surprised Major Butler by attempting to run away. In 1815 she would have departed with the British from Hampton had her family not been at Butler's Island and unable to take advantage of the British offer of freedom. Major Butler recognized her longing and suggested to Roswell King that she be set free. He objected, and Molly remained a slave until her death in 1822, the same year her owner died in Philadelphia.

Fanny Kemble noted the presence of several Mollies on the plantations in 1839. MOLLY, who was Quambo's wife, had six of her nine children living. She called on Fanny Kemble, had no complaints, only wanting to meet her new mistress.

MORRIS. Of the several Butler slaves called Morris, the best known was the Hampton driver who brought his large gang of more than one hundred slaves through the deadly hurricane of 1804 that devastated the Georgia coast at the time of Aaron Burr's visit to St. Simons as Major Butler's guest. The Major's award of a silver trophy was to "Maurice," but he was Morris on the plantation and to all of his fellow slaves. An offer of freedom was declined when it did not include his wife and children. In the 1790s William Page considered Morris, with Bram, the best of the Butler drivers. In 1820 Roswell King wrote, "Old Morris is going fast." He died in 1822, the same year his owner's life ended.

NANNY, aged fifty-two in 1793, was the plantation nurse who was assisted by Tenah, aged thirty. Major Butler called her "Nany" and gave her explicit instructions on bleeding, emetics, calomel, jallop, and gruel.

NED, a worker on Sidney George Fisher's Maryland farm, gave views on black suffrage his white employer wished to hear.

PETER was Aaron Burr's fifteen-year-old slave who accompanied the vice-president to Hampton on his flight of refuge in 1804.

PSYCHE, pronounced Sackey or Sack, was the wife of Joe. The threat of a move to Alabama put her family in jeopardy, a situation remedied by the intervention of Fanny Kemble in 1839.

QUASH, one of the most popular of the African names on the Butler plantations and often associated with boatmen or crab fishermen.

CRAB QUASH, in the 1790s, kept the Butler slaves well supplied with a favorite fare, the blue crab, which was plentiful in the saltwater rivers and creeks of St. Simons Island.

A later QUASH, full name CRABCLAW QUASH, performed the same function. He and his wife, Auber, and their son, Fivepound—who was named for the slave settlement on Buttermilk Sound—were not included among those sold in the Savannah auction of 1859. Quash and Auber were appraised at six hundred dollars each; fifteen-year-old Fivepound, a prime carpenter, at seven hundred dollars. Their chosen surname of "Quacco" was recorded as "Quarker" in the 1870 census.

QUASH, a boatman frequently mentioned in the Kemble *Journal,* lived on Little St. Simons Island. He conducted several boat trips about Hampton, including the well-recorded expedition to his own island. He led the singing of "Goodbye Forever" when the Butlers left on their return journey to Philadelphia in 1839. Ten years later, Quash, aged fifty-one, was valued at four hundred dollars. His wife, Lily, also the name of one of the plantation boats, was said to be worth three hundred dollars.

Young QUASH. In 1875, the Reverend James Leigh conducted a grand wedding ceremony at Butler's Island for young Quash and Nancy, with bridesmaids and a store-bought cake.

The RUNAWAY SLAVES. When buying slaves, Major Butler had no use for those with a tendency to run away. "Next to a thief," he said, "I avoid runaways."

Although the usual reaction of a slave owner to his runaway was one of surprise, Major Butler also responded with deep-seated anger. "They had no just cause for going away" was a typical response, as was "Spare no pains to get them back. I will make examples of some of them." Although more Butler slaves were lost to the British in two wars than by runaways during the years of this narrative, the reports of slaves breaking their bonds were frequent and persistent. The following are brief descriptions of a few of the many such efforts made by the blacks enslaved by the Butlers and some of their relatives.

Mary Butler's father, Colonel Thomas Middleton, owned True Blue plantation in South Carolina. In November 1761 eight slaves absconded and of these, one was a Calabar and six were Coromantees. They were DICK, ARTHUR, SMART, CUDJOE, QUAMINO, STEPHEN, CUFFEE, and HUGHKY.

JAMES DUCLOSS was Pierce Butler's manservant, probably a French black from Guadeloupe where the Twenty-ninth Regiment's drummers originated. He ran away from Major Butler in Charlestown in February 1768.

JEMMY, or JAMES, Miles Brewton's bushy-haired mulatto slave who played the violin, was a tailor and a barber. He ran away from Charlestown in 1771.

MINOS and CUDJOE were Pierce Butler's slaves, both branded *PB* on their chests. The two absconded from the Butlers' Coosaw plantation near Beaufort, South Carolina, in 1773.

JAMAICA BETTY, a "Negro Wench" who was a "Good Needle Woman," ran away from Sarah Guerard in 1773.

SOMERSETT was an eighteen-year-old "mustezo" slave who escaped from the Butler household in Philadelphia in 1793, only to be found at San Croix in the Virgin Islands.

In 1798, the year in which the domestic servant MOLLY attempted to run away from the Butler house in Philadelphia, several others also made their break for freedom, or for reunion with their families. SAM was successful in his effort by enlisting the aid of Philadelphia Quakers.

On the Georgia plantations, also in 1798, old JUSTICE and PRIMUS made their way across the Altamaha to the Combahee River in South Carolina, where they were recognized and returned to Major Butler's manager, William Page. Other runaways in 1798 were MORRIS, TITUS, and JACK. All were given the inevitable lashing that followed recovery. Titus and Jack were placed in leg irons to thwart further attempts to run away.

ALBERT, one of a gang of Virginia slaves purchased by Major Butler in 1803, ran away, was captured in Savannah, whipped, and made to walk back to Darien.

NERO, BACCHUS, GUY, and JEFFREY also ran away in 1803, and all were quickly found and punished.

SUNDAY, Jacob's young son who stole a half barrel of rice, ran away and was soon recovered and given a "severe whipping."

HENRY was a black from the French West Indies and was purchased by Major Butler in Savannah from François Didier Petit De Villers. He ran away from the Butler house in Philadelphia and was returned, despite intervention by Quaker abolitionists. He escaped once more and ultimately gained his freedom.

SAMBO, a favorite plantation slave of Major Butler, assisted in the move from South Carolina to Georgia. In 1793 William Page classified Sambo as a "Most Excellent driver, cooper, and trusty fellow." A year later he performed the difficult task of "ditching" Butler's Island. In 1807 Roswell King called Sambo and Worster "as *great rascals* as ever sent to Botne Bay." Sambo, drunk on plantation rum, had flogged several of his workers.

Another SAMBO and his wife, Pinder, produced a child, Lydia, in 1822.

A later SAMBO returned to Butler's Island after the Civil War. He had taken the surname SWIFT, and worked for the Leighs for $1.50 per day.

In 1829 SAMPSON was said to have been a bad influence on Balaam and Emanuel, causing the latter to lose his life following punishment administered by Roswell King, Jr. Sampson, with six others, ran away from Butler's Island.

SANS FOIX was one of John Couper's slaves at Cannon's Point plantation. He became a cook unsurpassed in the low country. The Coupers were noted for their hospitality, and Sans Foix for his many fine dishes, especially boned turkey.

SAUNEY, sometimes SAWNEY, was sold by Major Butler to Roger Parker Saunders so that he could be reunited with his wife, Moll. The trade in 1790 showed Sauney's value to be 120 British pounds, which was paid by his new owner with the equivalent value of rice.

SCYLLA, the Hampton slave who gave birth to a mulatto child by Roswell King, Jr., was flogged on orders of Mrs. King and then banished to the remote settlement of Five Pound Tree on Buttermilk Sound. Scylla may have been one and the same as SINDER.

SHADRACH was the old slave buried in a water-filled grave on Butler's Island in 1839. The evening funeral, illuminated by torchlight, was a moving entry in the Kemble *Journal*.

DANDY STEWART. As Dandy, and when thirty-seven years old in 1849, he was valued at eight hundred dollars. In the 1859 appraisal made prior to the Savannah auction, Dandy was listed as a "Blacksmith & Engineer" and valued at one thousand dollars. The surname Stewart appeared in the 1870 census in which he was described as an "Engineer & Blacksmith on Rice Farm."

TERESA was the "wretched Negress" who was punished by overseer Thomas M. Oden for complaining to Fanny Kemble "of her back being broken by hard work and child bearing." Teresa was flogged.

TOM was the Mohammedan driver on John Couper's plantation who had once been a slave of the British in the West Indies and who persuaded many of the Couper slaves to return to Cannon's Point instead of deserting to the British in the War of 1812. Tom was a Foulah native.

JIM, or JEM VALIANT, was the mulatto son of Judy by Roswell King, Jr. His "mutinous white blood" was said to have made him difficult to manage. He was among the many mulattoes retained as Butler slaves in the division that preceded the 1859 auction in Savannah. He was forty-four years old and valued at seven hundred dollars.

DENMARK VESEY was a mulatto seaman and slave who had served aboard a Charleston slaver for twenty years before winning $1,500 in a lottery, which he used to purchase his freedom. In 1821 Vesey planned and organized an insurrection of South Carolina slaves and free blacks. He used both Christian and African beliefs as justification for his cause. Blacks were solicited from "the Santee to the Euhaws" to join the fight for freedom. In May 1822 the Vesey conspiracy was uncovered through black informers. Of 131 participants, Vesey and thirty-six others were executed by hanging. Many others were banished, some were acquitted, and four involved white men were fined and imprisoned. One of the blacks set free was named Butler. Major Butler, who long feared just such an uprising, died a few months before the conspiracy was revealed, but the danger he had envisioned became more real and resulted in stricter management policies on his plantations and on other plantations throughout South Carolina and Georgia. In 1865 Charleston blacks laid a cornerstone for their new African Methodist Episcopal Church, which replaced the church that was closed following the aborted insurrection. The architect for the new building was Robert Vesey, the son of the executed leader.

CHLOE WASHINGTON, Thomas Butler's "coloured house servant," was left an annuity of two hundred dollars at his death in Philadelphia in 1838.

DAN WING, a mulatto descendant of the intrepid driver Morris, was often mentioned in the correspondence of James and Frances Leigh in the 1870s. Called "a sharp little nigger," Dan Wing was bright and resourceful. He was taken to England in 1877 and became a favorite of the English domestics at Stoneleigh. In 1899 Dan Wing, as a respected black of Darien, used his influence in subduing passions in the Henry Delegal case.

Notes to the Slaves and Freedmen

The sources most often relied upon are the "1793 List of Negroes"; the Frances Anne Kemble *Journal* (1863) of her stay on the Butler plantations; the 1849 and 1859 appraisals; the *New York Tribune* story of the 1859 slave sale in Savannah; the 1860 and 1870 census reports of McIntosh County; Frances Leigh's book *Ten Years;* and her husband James Wentworth Leigh's *Other Days.* Also, there are the many and varied plantation records that include "Births and Deaths" reports, the Sunday letters of the two Roswell Kings to the Butlers in Philadelphia, the runaway slave notices, Middleton and Butler wills, and other sources, all of which are given in the text and notes to the preceding chapters of *Major Butler's Legacy.*

✿ Abbreviations

AB	Aaron Burr
AM	Arthur Middleton
CCP	Charles Cotesworth Pinckney
DAB	*Dictionary of American Biography*
DNB	*Dictionary of National Biography*
FAK	Frances Anne Kemble
FBL	Frances Butler Leigh
FK	Fanny Kemble
FKB	Fanny Kemble Butler
GHQ	*Georgia Historical Quarterly*
GHS	Georgia Historical Society
HJ	Henry James
HL	Henry Laurens
HSP	Historical Society of Pennsylvania
JBG	John Berkley Grimball
JBS	*Journal of the Butler Society*
JMC	James M. Couper
JNH	*Journal of Negro History*
JSH	*Journal of Southern History*
JWL	James Wentworth Leigh
MHS	Massachusetts Historical Society
ORUCA	*Official Records of the Union and Confederate Armies*
ORUCN	*Official Records of the Union and Confederate Navies*
OJW	Owen Jones Wister
OW	Owen Wister
PB	Pierce Butler
PMHB	*Pennsylvania Magazine of History and Biography*
RI	Ralph Izard
RK	Roswell King

567

RK, Jr.	Roswell King, Jr.
RPS	Roger Parker Saunders
SBW	Sarah Butler Wister
SCAGG	*South Carolina and American General Gazette*
SCG	*South Carolina Gazette*
SCGCJ	*South Carolina Gazette and Country Journal*
SCHM	*South Carolina Historical Magazine*
SCHR	South Carolina House of Representatives
SCHS	South Carolina Historical Society
SCL	South Caroliniana Library
SGF	Sidney George Fisher
SHC	Southern Historical Collection
TB	Thomas Butler
WB	The Reverend Weeden Butler
WP	William Page
WTF	William Temple Franklin

 *Notes*

THE SOURCE of much of the unpublished material used in *Major Butler's Legacy* is from several collections presented to the Historical Society of Pennsylvania in the name of Major Butler's great-great-grandson, Owen Wister. The gifts were made through the good graces of his daughter, Mrs. Walter Stokes, who, as Fanny Kemble Wister, has written interesting articles and books on the history of her family. The collections include number 1855, Pierce Butler Manuscripts, which is divided into numbers 109A, Pierce Butler Estate Papers, and 109B, Pierce Butler Papers; and number 1447, Butler Papers, a large collection of some three thousand items. As none of these collections were indexed at the time of my research, I have shown all citations originating from them as "Butler Family Papers." Butler material is found in many other collections of the Society. All of these are cited specifically.

Chapter 1. *Carolina Gentry*

The lines introducing this chapter are from a tribute to an earlier and ancient Pierce Butler. Carney, ed., *Poems of the Butlers*, pp. 8, 107.

1. Everard, *Thomas Farrington's Regiment*. Hearn, *Youma*, pp. 35, 43.

2. *A List of the General and Field Officers*, 1761, p. 189; 1764, p. 82; 1765, p. 83. Doughty, ed., *Journal of Captain John Knox*, 1:121. Ford, *British Officers*. Anderson, *The Cheshire Regiment*, pp. 39, 42–49. The *London Chronicle or Universal Evening Post*, vol. 14, November 10–12, 1763, p. 457: In a list of pensions granted "on the Irish Establishment in the Reign of George III—1762, Captain Pierce Butler, or the youngest Captain without purchase in his Majesty's 29th Regiment, as long as Captain Maurice Wemys shall live, or until his Majesty shall signify to the contrary—£182.10.0."

3. Chichester and Burges-Short, *Records and Badges*, p. 417. *A List of the General and Field Officers*, 1767, p. 83. Fisher, *Recollections*, p. 261. The *Phi-*

adelphia Packet was a brigantine of sixty-five tons, built in South Carolina in 1766 (Olsberg, "Ship Registers in the South Carolina Archives," p. 189).

4. Burke, ed., *Genealogical and Heraldic History*, pp. 427–29. *DAB*, s.v. "Butler, Pierce." Playfair, *British Family Antiquity*, p. ix. Butler, "The Butlers of South Carolina and County Carlow," pp. 51–57. *DNB*, s.v. "Percy, James." Brydges, *Collins Peerage of England*, p. 356. *Collections of the Genealogical Society of Pennsylvania*, 1:129. Lady Henrietta Butler is often shown as Harriot, or Harriott. The latter is shown as the daughter of Henry Percy of Seskin in the *Abstract of Wills, 1707–1745*, p. 139. In the introduction of the Weeden Butler Correspondence in the British Library, she is Harriot. Pierce Butler's daughter, named for his mother, was Harriot Percy, frequently spelled Harriet. In a legal transfer of property to her father she wrote, "I, Henrietta P. Butler, otherwise Harriott Butler," with an extra *t* on Harriot to add to the confusion. See deed book ABEF, July 16, 1802, pp. 363–65, Glynn County, Brunswick, Ga.

5. Fisher, *Recollections*, p. 261.

6. *SCAGG*, February 12 and 26, 1768.

7. Undated letter, but between June 3 and July 25, 1768, in Crouse, ed., "The Letterbook of Peter Manigault," pp. 95–96.

8. Henry Middleton to AM, September 22, 1768, in Barnwell, ed., "Correspondence of Arthur Middleton," *SCHM* 27 (1926): 110–11.

9. *SCGCJ*, April 18, 1769. *SCG*, April 20, 1769, shows PB departing on the sloop *Jesse*.

10. Carter, ed., *The Correspondence of General Gage*, 1:249, 312. Morison, *The Oxford History of the American People*, pp. 199–200. Everard, *Thomas Farrington's Regiment*. Sikes, *The Public Life of Pierce Butler*, p. 3. Coghlan, "Senator Pierce Butler: The Aristocrat as Revolutionary," p. 465.

11. *SCAGG*, January 7, 1771.

12. Salley and Cheves, "The Bull Family of South Carolina," pp. 76–90. Cheves, "Middleton of South Carolina," pp. 228, 262. The will of Mary Bull (1699–1771) was signed on May 1, 1771; the "will" of Elizabeth Blake is actually a codicil, signed on February 22, 1791 (copies of both documents in the Butler Family Papers, HSP).

13. Wallace, *The History of South Carolina*, 2:34–35. Of the duel, James Grant wrote: "& tho he had used me worse than any Man ever did, I gave him his Life, when it was Absolutely in my Power." See Rogers, "The Papers of James Grant of Ballindalloch Castle, Scotland," p. 148. *Biographical Directory of the SCHR*, 2:460–62.

14. Wallace, *The History of South Carolina*, 2:35, 498–501.

15. Ibid., p. 35.

16. Higgins, "Factors Dealing in the External Negro Trade," p. 206, Laurens, *Papers*, 2:221n; 3:16n; 5:322, 323n. Townsend, *The Life of John Laurens*, p. 119.

17. HL to Richard Millerson, June 3, 1769, in Laurens, *Papers*, 6:587.

18. Townsend, *The Life of John Laurens,* p. 120. HL to John Laurens, August 14, 1776, in Laurens, *A South Carolina Protest Against Slavery.*

19. Wallace, *Life of Henry Laurens,* p. 456.

20. Fermor, *The Traveller's Tree,* pp. 372–74.

21. Heyward, "The Negro in the Low Country," p. 174.

22. Donnan, *Documents,* 4:463, from *SCG,* May 31, 1773. *SCG,* August 20, 1753.

23. *SCG,* May 29, 1756; October 2, 1758; July 21, 1759; November 17, 1759; August 13, 1760; November 28, 1761.

24. *SCG,* May 4, 1752; August 27, 1753.

25. *SCG,* February 2, 1765; February 28, 1771. See Windley, comp., *Runaway Slave Advertisements,* 3:296–97. A *Pistole* is a quarter Spanish doubloon, then worth about four dollars.

26. Laurens, *Papers,* 5:323n; 6:586–87.

27. *SCG,* January 25, 1768.

28. *Biographical Directory of the SCHR,* 2:460–62.

29. The will of Thomas Middleton (1719–1766) was signed on November 22, 1766, book 10B, South Carolina Department of Archives and History.

30. *SCAGG,* January 22, 1768.

31. *SCAGG,* January 2, 1769.

32. Ibid.

33. *SCAGG,* March 6, 1767.

34. HL to Robert Cathcart, October 31, 1769, in Laurens, *Papers,* 7:194.

35. *SCAGG,* February 5, 1771.

Chapter 2. *Pierce Butler, Patriot*

1. The relationship between the Middletons, Bulls, and Izards is explained in the *Personae.*

2. The young visitor from Boston was Josiah Quincy, Jr. His description of Charlestown, and the quotations, are from his "Journal, 1773," pp. 424–63. Quincy died aboard ship off Gloucester on April 26, 1775. He had been on a confidential mission to England, where he gathered information beneficial to American patriots. *SCG,* July 9, 1772; December 6, 1773. See Windley, comp., *Runaway Slave Advertisements,* 3:311–12, 332.

3. Grant books 26, 28, 30, South Carolina Department of Archives and History. *Biographical Directory of the SCHR,* 3:109.

4. Ackerman, *Land Policies,* pp. 94–95.

5. Williams, "Eighteenth-Century Organists of St. Michael's," p. 153. Hartley also played the harpsichord under contract to the St. Cecilia Society and earned a handsome income from private teaching. A Loyalist, he was removed from his

post at St. Michael's in 1776. In 1787, PB again assisted the church in a search for an organist.

6. Coghlan, "Pierce Butler, 1744–1822: First Senator from South Carolina," p. 105. Everard, *Thomas Farrington's Regiment.*

7. Deeds to PB, October 1, 1774, from John and Frances Graham, and from James Graham, collection 1008, GHS. See also recordings in deed book VV, pp. 42–51, Glynn County, Brunswick, Ga. Granger, ed., *Savannah River Plantations,* pp. 66–68.

8. The Graham deeds, GHS.

9. *SCAGG,* August 18, 1775. Ravenel, *Charleston: The Place and the People,* pp. 230–31. *SCAGG,* September 29, 1775. Drayton, *Memoirs,* 1:272.

10. Barnwell, ed., "Correspondence of Arthur Middleton," *SCHM* 27 (1926): 137.

11. PB to AM, March 21, 1776, ibid., pp. 139–41.

12. McCrady, *The History of South Carolina,* p. 297.

13. Lord Campbell to Lord Dartmouth, October 19, 1775, in Wallace, *The History of South Carolina,* 2:154–55. Drayton, *Memoirs,* 1:257–58.

14. Wallace, *The History of South Carolina,* 2:158.

15. *SCAGG,* December 12, 1776.

16. Sikes, *The Public Life of Pierce Butler,* p. 4. Coghlan, "Pierce Butler, 1744–1822: First Senator from South Carolina," p. 107.

17. Barnwell, ed., "Correspondence of Arthur Middleton," *SCHM* 27 (1926): 140–41.

18. Coghlan, "Pierce Butler, 1744–1822: First Senator from South Carolina," p. 110. *SCAGG,* May 29, 1779. Johnson, *Traditions and Reminiscences,* p. 469.

19. PB to Benjamin Lincoln, May 3, 1779, Pierce Butler Papers, Library of Congress. Coghlan, "Pierce Butler, 1744–1822: First Senator from South Carolina," p. 108.

20. *SCAGG,* November 19, 1779.

21. *SCAGG,* December 3, 1779.

22. Coghlan, "Pierce Butler, 1744–1822: First Senator from South Carolina," p. 109.

23. *SCAGG,* January 11, 1780.

24. Higginbothan, ed., *The Papers of James Iredell,* 2:397.

Chapter 3. *Spoils of War*

1. Quarles, *The Negro in the American Revolution,* p. 19.

2. Farley, "The South Carolina Negro in the American Revolution," pp. 76–77. Wright, "Red, White and Black Loyalists," p. 133.

3. Edward Rutledge to RI, December 8, 1775, in Izard, *Correspondence,*

1:164–68. RI was in England with his wife and four children, with a fifth child expected. As bitterness between England and America intensified, he sought the better political climate in France. In answer to a letter from Henry Laurens urging that he return to South Carolina, he replied, "I think I may truly say I will never neglect the Public Call. I flatter myself, I may be of more service here than I could be in America" (RI to HL, October 6, 1777).

4. Lee, *Memoir of Richard Henry Lee*, 2:9.

5. *SCAGG*, December 15, 1775.

6. Quarles, *The Negro in the American Revolution*, pp. 106–9.

7. Ibid., pp. 104, 106, 110.

8. Hawes, ed., "A Letterbook of Lachlan McIntosh," pp. 150, 260.

9. HL to John Laurens, August 14, 1776, in Laurens, *A South Carolina Protest Against Slavery.* John Laurens to HL, October 26, 1776; HL to John Laurens, February 6, 1778; HL to George Washington, March 16, 1779, in Wallace, *Life of Henry Laurens*, pp. 447–49.

10. Ædanus Burke to AM, January 25, 1782, in Barnwell, ed., "Correspondence of Arthur Middleton," *SCHM* 26 (1925): 194. One who shared the unknown Philadelphian's views on the intermarriage of blacks and whites was the Marquis de Chastellux, or perhaps he was the man to whom Burke referred. The Marquis visited Philadelphia in 1780. See note 17, this chapter.

11. Edward Rutledge to AM, February 14, 1782, in Barnwell, ed., "Correspondence of Arthur Middleton," *SCHM*, 27, 1926, p. 5.

12. Quarles, *The Negro in the American Revolution*, pp. 111–81. Jones, "The Black Hessians," pp. 287–302.

13. Campbell, ed., *The Journal of Colonel Archibald Campbell*, p. 15. Everard, *Thomas Farrington's Regiment.*

14. McCrady, *The History of South Carolina*, 1:393. Moultrie, *Memoirs of the American Revolution*, 2:351–52.

15. Ramsay, *The History of the Revolution of South Carolina*, 2:31–34. Tarleton, *Campaigns of 1780 and 1781*, quoted in Campbell, *The Journal of Archibald Campbell*, p. 120 n. 132. See also, Barnwell, "Loyalism in South Carolina."

16. Wallace, *The History of South Carolina*, 2:227. Webber, "Josiah Smith's Diary," p. 79. Smith was a South Carolina exile in Philadelphia, one of the many banished by the hated Lt. Col. Balfour. His diary is an interesting record of the Carolina exiles in Florida and Pennsylvania. In Philadelphia with his wife, five children, aged father, and four servants, he bemoaned the lack of "Washer Wench Nelly" and "Cook Wench Molly," who had refused to leave Charlestown. In May 1780, the Royalist Assembly, under Georgia's Governor James Wright, had named PB as thirtieth on a list of 151 "Georgians" as "obnoxious and guilty of high treason" (Jones, *The History of Georgia*, 2:421–23).

17. Rice, ed., *Travels by the Marquis de Chastellux*, 2:649, 593. George Grieve translated the de Chastellux journal. Grieve's stay in America was but a year long,

from late 1781 through 1782. He was described as a hereditary agitator. Grieve's pro-patriot sentiments in America and his anti-aristocracy feelings in France appealed to PB (1:29–32). The Marquis advanced an interesting plan for the elimination of slavery by exporting black men and then building on the "well-established commerce between white men and Negresses" to encourage marriage between the two. Such wholesale union, he believed, would produce a "race of quadroons, and so on, until the color would be totally changed" (2:440–41).

18. PB to James Iredell, October 6, 1781, in Higginbothan, ed., *The Papers of James Iredell*, 2:307.

19. Quarles, *The Negro in the American Revolution*, pp. 150–51.

20. Ibid., pp. 140–42. Ædanus Burke to AM, November 18, 1781, in Barnwell, ed., "Correspondence of Arthur Middleton," *SCHM* 26 (1925): 190.

21. McCrady, *The History of South Carolina*, 1:393. Ramsay, *The History of the Revolution of South Carolina*, 2:333.

22. Moultrie, *Memoirs of the American Revolution*, 2:352. Ramsay, *The History of the Revolution of South Carolina*, 2:384. Wallace, *The History of South Carolina*, 2:320. Quarles, *The Negro in the American Revolution*, p. 172.

23. McCrady, *The History of South Carolina*, 2:658–59.

24. PB to James Iredell, May 5, 1783, in Higginbothan, ed., *The Papers of James Iredell*, 2:397.

25. Ralph Izard to AM, May 30, 1783, in Barnwell, ed., "Correspondence of Arthur Middleton," *SCHM* 27 (1926): 79. Sir Guy Carleton became a Commander in the British Forces in February 1782.

26. Archibald, "The Deportation of Negroes to Sierra Leone," pp. 129–54. Glenn, "The Colonization of Sierra Leone."

27. PB to Thomas Fitzsimons, January 18, 1784, SCL. PB to WB, September 1, 1790, Weeden Butler Correspondence, British Library.

Chapter 4.
Pierce Butler's Private Life

1. Ædanus Burke to AM, November 18, 1781; AB to AM, January 25, 1782; AM to Charles Pinckney, October 20, 1782; Charles Cotesworth Pinckney to AM, June 24, 1782; CCP to AM, August 13, 1782; John Mathews to AM, August 25, 1782; CCP to AM, April 24, 1782; CCP to AM, June 24, 1782; all in Barnwell, ed., "Correspondence of Arthur Middleton," *SCHM* 26 (1925): 188–90, 192; 27 (1926): 26–27, 61, 63, 65–66, 71.

2. *Biographical Directory of the SCHR*, 2:294–95. Cheves, "Middleton of South Carolina," p. 244 n. 1.

3. PB (Charleston) to Thomas Fitzsimons, May 18, 1783, Gratz Collection, HSP, quoted in Rogers, *Evolution of a Federalist*, p. 97. Fitzsimons became a

Pennsylvania delegate to the Constitutional Convention of 1787. Charlestown became Charleston after the Revolution.

4. *Gazette of the State of Georgia,* December 18, 1783.

5. The Pierce Butler–Weeden Butler Correspondence was presented to the British Museum (British Library) in 1847 by Weeden Butler's grandson, Thomas Butler, who was a member of the museum staff. The collection consists of letters from PB to WB, from PB to his son Thomas, an occasional letter from Mary Butler to her son, from Sarah and the other girls to their brother, and a very few copies of letters from WB to PB in America. There are two letters written by Thomas from America to WB. Some sections of PB's letters have been crossed out as though of no importance. These sections contain much the same interesting revelations as do the parts unmarked. Although PB's letters originate from many places, WB remains firmly ensconced at his school on Cheyne Walk, Chelsea. The quotations in this paragraph are from PB (London) to WB, September 16, 1784; and the English Thomas Butler's January 7, 1847, introduction to the collection, Ad Mss 16.603. See also, Annie R. Butler's *Nearly a Hundred Years Ago,* a sentimental sketch of the Thomas Butler who gave the collection to the British Museum. The Moreau material is from the Butler Family Papers, HSP.

6. Sikes, *The Public Life of Pierce Butler,* pp. 12, 13. A mortgage dated September 19, 1785, from PB to Jan Gabriel Tegelaar, Butler Family Papers, HSP.

7. PB to WB, May 19, 1785; PB to WB, February 12, 1785, Butler Correspondence, British Library.

8. Smith, "The Ashley River," p. 15.

9. Sikes, *The Public Life of Pierce Butler,* p. 16. Brady, "The Slave Trade and Sectionalism in South Carolina," p. 604.

10. Sikes, *The Public Life of Pierce Butler,* p. 16. PB to WB, July 18, 1788, Butler Correspondence, British Library.

11. Alfred Langdon Elwyn to Sarah Butler Wister, July 22, 1876, Butler Family Papers, HSP.

12. Baker, "Washington After the Revolution," p. 49. Baker quotes from the *Journal* of William Maclay.

13. PB to Edward Butler, February 3, 1790; PB to Thomas Parker Butler, April 15, 1790; PB to his sister Frances Butler, April 23, 1790; PB to his niece, Dorothea Butler Fitzgerald, July 24, 1790; all in the PB Letterbook, 1790–1794, SCL. Richard, the older brother of Edward and Thomas Parker Butler, became Sir Richard, the seventh baronet, on the death of their father Sir Thomas, the sixth baronet, who held the title less than a year.

14. PB to James Seagrove, August 7, 1792; PB to Don Juan McQueen, December 6, 1792, both in the PB Letterbook, 1790–1794, SCL. Hartridge, ed., *The Letters of Don Juan McQueen,* xxvii–xxx.

15. PB to Alexander Gillon and Roger Parker Saunders, April 23, 1790, in the PB Letterbook, 1790–1794, SCL.

16. PB to Alexander Gillon, May 25, 1790; PB to John Houstoun, June 7, 1790, both in the PB Letterbook, 1790–1794, SCL.

17. PB to James Seagrove, February 4, 1790; PB to John McQueen, September 2, 1790; PB to Roger Parker Saunders, September 2, 1790; all in the PB Letterbook, 1790–1794, SCL.

18. PB to Roger Parker Saunders, August 26, 1790, PB Letterbook, 1790–1794, SCL. Indentures dated August 5 and 6, 1790, between RPS as attorney for PB, and James Ladson, as recorded in McIntosh and Glynn counties, Georgia Department of Archives and History, Atlanta. See also deed book ABEF, pp. 34–37, Glynn County, Brunswick, Ga.

19. PB to Roger Parker Saunders, August 26, 1790. Three years later PB's Ninety-six lands remained unsold. He commissioned William Temple Franklin to try for a sale in England, writing that Salvador had once considered sale to "Hollanders and Carolinians" for the purpose of establishing a Moravian settlement, asking "a Guinea an acre," PB to WTF, August 11, 1793, PB Letterbook, 1790–1794, SCL.

20. Baker, "Washington After the Revolution," p. 455. PB to Peter Spence, September 5, 1790; PB to WB, September 1, 1790; PB to Thomas Butler, October 31, 1790; PB to WB, November 4, 1790; all in the Butler Correspondence, British Library.

21. PB to WB, November 16, 1790; PB to Thomas Butler, November 13, 1791; both in the Butler Correspondence, British Library. PB to John Leckey of Bally Kealey, February 11, 1791, PB Letterbook, 1790–1794, SCL. Mary Butler's gravestone is in the churchyard of St. Michael's, Charleston. Part of the inscription appears to be covered at the base of the stone.

22. PB to WB, November 19, 1792, Butler Correspondence, British Library.

23. The satisfaction of the Ladson loan is recorded in deed book CD, December 1, 1791, Glynn County, Brunswick, Ga. PB to Edward Rutledge, October 20, 1791, PB Letterbook, 1790–1794, SCL.

24. The faint record of the marmalade proposal was copied from an earlier recounting. Mary Esther Huger, born in 1858, was the great-granddaughter of Thomas Pinckney and his first wife, Elizabeth Motte. The note was found among family papers in her house in Highlands, North Carolina, and is now owned by Clermont Lee of Savannah. "Mrs. Middleton" was Frances Motte, the sister of Thomas Pinckney's first wife and the widow of John Middleton, who died in 1784. She married General Pinckney after declining PB's hand.

25. PB to William Payne, February 18, 1792; PB to Thomas Parker Butler, November 17, 1791; both in the PB Letterbook, 1790–1794, SCL.

26. Mary Butler's grandmother, Mary Brandford Bull, died in 1771, shortly after signing her will on May 1 (Butler Family Papers, HSP).

27. Mary Butler's cousin, Elizabeth Izard Blake, died in 1792. Her will, proved in 1792, is on file in Book 24, South Carolina Department of Archives and History, Columbia.

28. Charles Cotesworth Pinckney to Thomas Pinckney, July 14, 1792, Pinckney Papers, Library of Congress, and quoted in Rogers, *Evolution of a Federalist*, p. 184. PB to Mrs. David Graeme, August 24, 1792, PB Letterbook, 1790–1794, SCL.

29. PB to Roger Parker Saunders, September 8, 1792, PB Letterbook, 1790–1794, SCL.

30. PB to Mrs. David Graeme, October 10, 1792, PB Letterbook, 1790–1794, SCL.

31. Fisher, *Recollections*, p. 262. Benét, *The Reader's Encyclopedia*, p. 807.

32. PB to Charles Cotesworth Pinckney and Edward Rutledge, November 12, 1792, PB Letterbook, 1790–1794, SCL.

33. PB to Roger Parker Saunders, September 5, 1791, and August 26, 1790, PB Letterbook, 1790–1794, SCL.

34. "A List of Negroes Taken at Hampton, May 14, 1793," by William Page, Butler Family Papers, HSP.

35. PB to Ralph Izard, January 26, 1793, PB Letterbook, 1790–1794, SCL.

36. Petition of Ralph Izard and Edward Rutledge, March 9, 1795, Mss 35–9, SCHS.

37. PB to Mr. LeMotte, October 30, 1791, PB Letterbook, 1790–1794, SCL. James LaMotte was a Charleston merchant at that time.

38. PB to John Leckey, February 11, 1791, PB Letterbook, 1790–1794, SCL.

39. PB to Dr. Benjamin Rush, no date, Library Company of Philadelphia Mss, James Rush, M.D., Papers, 7239, vol. 23, HSP.

40. PB to Commodore A. Gillon, September 26, 1793, PB Letterbook, 1790–1794, SCL.

41. PB to WB, November 5, 1793, Butler Correspondence, British Library.

42. PB to John Allston, November 16, 1793, PB Letterbook, 1790–1794, SCL.

43. PB to Dr. Benjamin Rush, October 9, 1793, Library Company of Philadelphia Mss, James Rush, M.D., Papers, 7252, vol. 36, HSP.

44. PB to James Ladson, February 18, 1794; PB to William Temple Franklin, July 23, 1793 and August 11, 1793; all in the PB Letterbook, 1790–1794, SCL. Ladson was lieutenant governor of South Carolina at the time. William Temple Franklin was the natural son of the natural son of Benjamin Franklin, or as Joshua Francis Fisher called him, "a double distilled bastard," borrowing the descriptive bit from John Brown Cutting. See Fisher, *Recollections*, p. 212.

45. Aptheker, ed., *A Documentary History of the Negro People in the United States*, 1:32. PB to John Bee Holmes, November 5, 1793, PB Letterbook, 1790–1794, SCL.

46. PB to Roger Parker Saunders, September 8, 1792, PB Letterbook, 1790–1794, SCL.

47. Wescott, *Scrapbooks: Biographies of Philadelphia*, vol. 2, part 2, p. 188, HSP. "Chestnut Street, 6th to 9th," Jane Campbell Collection, 12, HSP. "Chestnut Street, 8th to 12th," The Helen C. Perkins Collection, 8C, HSP. *The Old*

Butler Mansion, a watercolor of the Butler house in 1836 by D. J. Kennedy, HSP. Looney, *Old Philadelphia in Early Photographs,* p. 154. Simpson, *Lives of Eminent Philadelphians,* pp. 560–63. Alfred Langdon Elwyn told Sarah Butler Wister that PB had purchased the house in 1798, ALE to SBW, July 26, 1870, Wister Family Papers, HSP. He paid fifteen thousand dollars according to Charles N. Buck; see Buck, *Memoirs,* p. 104. Major William Jackson (1759–1828) was a former South Carolinian who had been appointed surveyor of customs in Philadelphia by George Washington. Also, he had been the inept secretary of the Constitutional Convention in 1787, having been chosen over William Temple Franklin. The chimney pieces were shipped to PB by Thomas Hall in 1817, who offered a statue of Venus "just got out the bath" for the bargain price of three hundred dollars but worth five hundred dollars. Hall (Leghorn) to PB, December 19, 1817, Butler Family Papers, HSP. Presley, ed., *Dr. Bullie's Notes,* p. 154.

48. PB to JI, July 31, 1782, in Higginbothan, ed., *The Papers of James Iredell,* 2:349. PB to JI, September 9, 1793, in McRee, *Life and Correspondence of James Iredell,* 2:400–401. Hotchkin, *The York Road, Old and New,* p. 56. Fisher. *Recollections,* p. 271. PB purchased "the Plantation on the Great Road leading from New York to Philadelphia" that came to be called Butler Place from Francis and Eugenia Liemon on October 22, 1810, for sixteen thousand dollars. From the original deed, Wister Family Papers, HSP.

49. BR to Mrs. R, September 9, 1806, in Butterfield, ed., *Letters of Benjamin Rush,* 1:958. "Miss MacPherson" was Elizabeth, the daughter of Colonel John MacPherson (1756–1806), who later married James R. Pringle. The dramatic rescue is memorialized in a marble bas-relief that was to have been placed in the Scot's Presbyterian Church in Charleston, but the sculptor, John Devagre, revealed so much of Miss MacPherson's anatomy, the church elders refused. All is proudly displayed in Charleston's Gibbes Art Gallery.

50. PB purchased "perruques and head dresses" for himself and daughters from A. Bowman's, 102 New Bond Street, London. The cost of his peruke and a head dress for "Miss Butler" was six pounds and six shillings each, invoice July 17, 1809, Butler Family Papers, HSP. McAllister, *Society As I Have Found It,* p. 270. Newton Gordon, Murdoch and Company (Madeira), to PB, April 18 and July 8, 1804, Butler Family Papers, HSP. PB to WB, no date, letter 27, Butler Correspondence, British Library.

51. Mitchell, *The Red City,* p. 111, and *A Madeira Party,* p. 42. PB to WB, November 19, 1792, Butler Correspondence, British Library. Mitchell's first wife was Mary Middleton Elwyn, great-granddaughter of PB.

52. Alfred Langdon Elwyn to Sarah Butler Wister, July 22, 1876, Wister Family Papers, HSP.

Chapter 5.
Pierce Butler's Public Life, 1776–1789

1. Quincy, "Journal, 1773," pp. 424–63. Wallace, *The History of South Carolina,* 1:374–75, 498, 500–501. Morison, *The Oxford History of the American People,* p. 203.

2. Grant Books 26, 28, and 30, South Carolina Department of Archives and History.

3. Coghlan, "Pierce Butler, 1744–1822: First Senator from South Carolina," p. 112. Sikes, *The Public Life of Pierce Butler,* chapter 1. The public life of PB is covered by Coghlan and Sikes.

4. PB to James Iredell, February 4, 1784, in McRee, *Life and Correspondence of James Iredell,* 2:87–88.

5. Brady, "The Slave Trade and Sectionalism in South Carolina," pp. 601, 606. Heyward, "The Negro in the Low Country," p. 177. Sikes, *The Public Life of Pierce Butler,* p. 16. Coghlan, "Pierce Butler, 1744–1822: First Senator from South Carolina," p. 113. PB to WB, August 5, 1787, Butler Correspondence, British Library.

6. Sikes, *The Public Life of Pierce Butler,* p. 16.

7. Thomas Pinckney to Colonel Thomas Hutson, March 23, 1787, Pinckney Family Papers, Library of Congress.

8. Brady, "The Slave Trade and Sectionalism in South Carolina," pp. 601–3, 608.

9. Bowen, *Miracle at Philadelphia,* p. 4. Eaton, *A History of the Old South,* pp. 141, 144.

10. Farrand, ed., *The Federal Convention of 1787,* 1:204. Bowen, *Miracle at Philadelphia,* p. 59. Farrand, *The Framing of the Constitution,* p. 31. Tansill, ed., *Documents of the American States,* p. 184.

11. Farrand, ed., *The Federal Convention of 1787,* 1:542.

12. Ibid., p. 580.

13. Tansill, ed., *Documents of the American States,* p. 354.

14. Bowen, *Miracle at Philadelphia,* p. 95. The scrap of paper, Pierce Butler Collection, 215-693, Library of Congress.

15. Bowen, *Miracle at Philadelphia,* p. 95. Farrand, ed., *The Federal Convention of 1787,* 1:592. Indentured servants were counted full value.

16. Eaton, *A History of the Old South,* pp. 143–44. Bowen, *Miracle at Philadelphia,* pp. 201–4.

17. Farrand, ed., *The Federal Convention of 1787,* 2:443, 453. On a printed proof of the Constitution as of August 6, 1787, PB penned an addition to article 15 and then offered what he had written as a resolution. The addition ultimately became a part of article 4, section 2; Pierce Butler Collection, 215-693, Library of Congress.

18. Farrand, *The Framing of the Constitution,* p. 110.

19. Tansill, ed., *Documents of the American States,* excerpts from the sketches in notes of William Pierce, pp. 106, 107.

20. Ibid., pp. 95, 149, 178, 196, 303, 346, 525, 555, 585, 686, 747. Farrand, ed., *The Federal Convention of 1787,* 1:592.

21. Sikes, *The Public Life of Pierce Butler,* p. 28. Tansill, ed., *Documents of the American States,* pp. 557, 127, 488, 814, 197, 686. On compensation of senators, PB was ambivalent. When the PB-Rutledge motion was voted down, he then proposed "adequate compensation be paid out of the Federal treasury," and a few days later he said the states should bear the cost so that they would not "lose sight of their constituents." See Prescott, *Drafting the Federal Constitution,* pp. 414, 417; White, *The Federalists,* p. 292.

22. Tansill, ed., *Documents of the American States,* pp. 505, 525. Gilpin, ed., *The Papers of James Madison,* 3:1275, 1301.

23. Tansill, ed., *Documents of the American States,* pp. 92, 93, 149, 751. PB to WB, May 5, 1788. Butler Correspondence, British Library.

24. Tansill, ed., *Documents of the American States,* p. 159.

25. PB to Thomas Fitzsimons, May 30, 1786, Gratz Collection, HSP, quoted in Rogers, *Evolution of a Federalist,* pp. 140–41. Tansill, ed., *Documents of the American States,* pp. 585, 605.

26. PB to WB, October 8, 1787; PB to WB, May 5, 1788; both in Butler Correspondence, British Library.

27. PB to WB, October 8, 1787, Butler Correspondence, British Library. Farrand, ed., *The Federal Convention of 1787,* 1:605.

28. Farrand, ed., *The Federal Convention of 1787,* 2:651–66.

29. Governor Pinckney's letter, May 24, 1788, Pinckney Family Papers, Library of Congress.

30. *Pennsylvania Gazette,* Philadelphia, July 9, 1788.

31. PB to WB, February 8, 1789, Butler Correspondence, British Library.

Chapter 6.
Pierce Butler's Public Life, 1789–1819

1. PB to WB, February 8, 1789, Butler Correspondence, British Library. Also quoted in Becker and Jensen, eds., *Documentary History of the First Federal Elections,* 1:211.

2. Wallace, *The History of South Carolina,* 2:356.

3. Maclay, ed., *Journal of William Maclay,* p. 71. "Lee" was Richard Henry Lee of Virginia.

4. Rogers, ed., "The Letters of William Loughton Smith to Edward Rutledge," p. 11. Maclay, ed., *Journal of William Maclay,* p. 104.

5. Mary Butler to WB, July 15, 1789, Butler Correspondence, British Library. Letter of June 26, 1789, in Beatty, ed., "Letters of Judge Henry Wynkoop," p. 57. Daniel Huger lost neither leg nor life, but did become alienated from PB when he was not invited to the Butler dinner party in Charleston honoring President Washington.

6. Maclay, ed., *Journal of William Maclay,* p. 74.

7. Ibid., p. 135. Sikes, *The Public Life of Pierce Butler,* pp. 61–62.

8. Maclay, ed., *Journal of William Maclay,* p. 174. PB to "His Excellency the Vice President of the United States," January 19, 1790, PB Letterbook, 1790–1794, SCL. Page Smith, *John Adams,* 2:786–87. Years later PB praised John Adams to Benjamin Rush and his good words were sent on to the former president: "An honester man than John Adams, he believes, never lived." BR to JA, April 1, 1809, in Butterfield, ed., *Letters of Benjamin Rush,* 2:1001–2.

9. Rogers, ed., "The Letters of William Loughton Smith to Edward Rutledge," pp. 103–4. Maclay, ed., *Journal of William Maclay,* p. 196. The petitions came first from the Quakers of Pennsylvania, New Jersey, Delaware, Virginia, the western parts of Maryland, and from the Pennsylvania Society for Promoting the Abolition of Slavery, Benjamin Franklin, president. See Baker, "Washington After the Revolution," p. 50.

10. Franklin, *Historicus,* March 23, 1790, in the broadside collection, HSP.

11. Rogers, ed., "The Letters of William Loughton Smith to Edward Rutledge," pp. 107–9. PB to WB, May 22, 1790, Butler Correspondence, British Library. Maclay, ed., *Journal of William Maclay,* p. 196.

12. Maclay, ed., *Journal of William Maclay,* p. 223.

13. PB to John Leckey, February 11, 1891, PB Letterbook, 1790–1794, SCL.

14. McRee, *Life and Correspondence of James Iredell,* 2:279. PB to Archibald McClean, March 3, 1790, PB Letterbook, 1790–1794, SCL. Sikes, *The Public Life of Pierce Butler,* pp. 66–67. Rogers, ed., "The Letters of William Loughton Smith to Edward Rutledge," pp. 122, 131, 137.

15. PB to General James Jackson, January 21, 1791, PB Letterbook, 1790–1794, SCL. Sikes, *The Public Life of Pierce Butler,* p. 72.

16. Coghlan, "Pierce Butler, 1744–1822: First Senator from South Carolina," pp. 117–18. Sikes, *The Public Life of Pierce Butler,* pp. 71–73. Maclay, ed., *Journal of William Maclay,* pp. 266, 298, 323.

17. Baker, "Washington After the Revolution," pp. 187, 188.

18. Ibid., p. 189. Stegeman and Stegeman, *Caty,* pp. 149–50, 156–61. Granger, ed., *Savannah River Plantations,* pp. 66, 76–78.

19. Baker, "Washington After the Revolution," p. 189. Sikes, *The Public Life of Pierce Butler,* p. 79. PB to Roger Parker Saunders, September 2, 1790; PB to Mr. LeMotte, October 30, 1791; both in the PB Letterbook, 1790–1794, SCL.

20. Memorandum on the proposed frigates, Butler Family Papers, HSP. Sikes, *The Public Life of Pierce Butler,* pp. 80–81.

21. PB to WB, March 4, 1793, Butler Correspondence, British Library.

22. Quincy, "Journal, 1773," p. 456. PB to John McPherson, November 6, 1792, PB Letterbook, 1790–1794, SCL. Brady, "The Slave Trade and Sectionalism in South Carolina," pp. 608–11.

23. Brady, "The Slave Trade and Sectionalism in South Carolina," pp. 609, 618, 610, 608. PB to Roger Parker Saunders, September 5, 1792, PB Letterbook, 1790–1794, SCL.

24. PB to Thomas Young, October 28, 1793, PB Letterbook, 1790–1794, SCL. The interest in the Combahee was understandable, for the Butlers owned and planted an old Bull plantation, inherited from Mary Brewton and Elizabeth Blake. The plantation, which came to be called Brewton, was close to the Heyward plantation.

25. PB to WB, November 5, 1793, Butler Correspondence, British Library.

26. PB to G. C. Richards, November 19, 1791; PB to John Hunter, November 22, 1791; both in the PB Letterbook, 1790–1794, SCL.

27. Hill, "A Masked Acquisition: French Designs on Cumberland Island, 1794–1795," pp. 306–16.

28. Murdoch, "Correspondence of French Consuls," p. 73.

29. Rose, *Prelude to Democracy: The Federalists in the South,* p. 110.

30. Brady, "The Slave Trade and Sectionalism in South Carolina," p. 609.

31. Rogers, ed., "The Letters of William Loughton Smith to Edward Rutledge," p. 45.

32. Sikes, *The Public Life of Pierce Butler,* pp. 85, 86–87.

33. A statement signed by PB on St. Simons Island, February 26, 1795, attested as being in agreement with the revenue cutter's log by the first mate Hendrick Fisher (Butler Family Papers, HSP).

34. PB to Governor Mathews, October 17, 1795, PB Letterbooks, HSP. Sikes, *The Public Life of Pierce Butler,* p. 87. Coghlan, "Pierce Butler, 1744 to 1822: First Senator from South Carolina," p. 117. The United Irishmen tribute, Pierce Butler Papers, SCL.

35. PB to WB, September 5, 1794; August 19, 1796, Butler Correspondence, British Library.

36. Sikes, *The Public Life of Pierce Butler,* pp. 95–97, 98. Lomansk, *Aaron Burr: From Princeton to Vice President,* p. 358. Zahniser, *Charles Cotesworth Pinckney,* p. 245 n. 30. The General was in and out of PB's good graces. PB's Republican party came to be the present-day Democrats. The Federalists are the true forerunners of today's Republicans.

37. PB to John Sommerville, January 5, 1798; PB to Isaac McPherson, May 25, 1800; both in the PB Letterbooks, HSP.

38. Brady, "The Slave Trade and Sectionalism in South Carolina," pp. 610–12.

39. Thomas, *Reminiscences,* 2:36–37.

40. Sikes, *The Public Life of Pierce Butler,* p. 100. *Annals of Congress, the Debates and Proceedings,* Eighth Congress, November–December 1803.

41. See chapter 8, "Georgia Plantations." Schachner, *Aaron Burr,* p. 258. Lomansk, *Aaron Burr: From Princeton to Vice President,* p. 187.

42. See chapter 10, "Honored Sir."

43. Sikes, *The Public Life of Pierce Butler,* pp. 103–5.

44. PB to John Couper, July 21, 1816, Butler Family Papers, HSP. In this letter that touched on several subjects, PB devoted a paragraph to his ideas for structuring a national bank. His appointment (or election) to the board was noted in Savannah newspapers. *Columbian Museum and Savannah Daily Gazette,* January 17, 1818; January 18, 1820; January 10, 1822. James Monroe to PB, January 1, 1819, Butler Family Papers, HSP. PB, not eligible to succeed himself, was, after an interval, named a director the month before his death.

45. Scharf and Westcott, *History of Philadelphia,* 1:593, 597, 601.

46. Sellers, *Mr. Peale's Museum,* pp. 239–40. Cantwell, *Alexander Wilson,* p. 282. "P. Butler" was the third signature on Mr. Peale's 1794 subscription list for the museum. His name was topped by George Washington's and John Adam's. Each paid one dollar for a year's admission (HSP).

47. PB to WB, August 19, 1796, Butler Correspondence, Add Mss 16.603, British Library. This letter was written at the time of PB's first resignation from the U.S. Senate.

Chapter 7. *The Altamaha Estuary*

1. Presley, ed., *Dr. Bullie's Notes,* p. 78. Harper, ed., *The Travels of William Bartram,* p. 58. Lewis, *They Called Their Town Darien,* p. 2. Gamble, *Scrapbooks,* 7:152. Wood, "A Note on the Georgia Malcontents," pp. 264–68. Jackson, "The Darien Anti-Slavery Petition of 1739 and the Georgia Plan," pp. 618–31.

2. Candler and Knight, eds., *The Colonial Records of Georgia,* 3:427–28.

3. Coulter, *A Short History of Georgia,* pp. 62–65. Ettinger, *James Edward Oglethorpe,* p. 308.

4. Candler and Knight, eds., *The Colonial Records of Georgia,* 7:544, 547, 548. Ackerman, *Land Policies,* p. 112. McLendon, *History of Public Domain in Georgia,* p. 19.

5. Candler, ed., *The Revolutionary Records of Georgia,* 1:41–42.

6. Laurens, *Papers,* 4:704, 5:226. Lewis, *Patriarchial Plantations of St. Simons Island,* "Cannons Point." Wylly, *Memories,* pp. 10–11, 21. Coulter, *Thomas Spalding of Sapelo,* pp. 190–94.

7. Vanstory, *Georgia's Land of the Golden Isles,* p. 135.

8. Wylly, *Memories*, p. 27. The Sanger Papers, Cate Collection, GHS.

9. Italics added. Coulter, *Thomas Spalding of Sapelo*, pp. 39–40. Wylly, *Memories*, pp. 10–12.

10. Wylly, *The Seed That Was Sown*, p. 135. Vanstory, *Georgia's Land of the Golden Isles*, p. 138. Lyell, *A Second Visit*, 1:261–62.

11. Hall, *Travels in North America*, 2:234. Margaret Hall to her sister Jane, letter begun at Mrs. Fulton's Tavern, twenty-four miles south of Savannah, and finished at Mobile, April 10, 1828, Margaret Hall Collection, 618, Library of Congress.

12. Bremer, *The Homes of the New World*, pp. 488, 489, 490. Murray, *Letters from the United States*, pp. 210, 218, 219, 225.

13. Bremer, *The Homes of the New World*, p. 492. Murray, *Letters from the United States*, p. 361.

Chapter 8. *The Georgia Plantations*

1. Copies of the Graham deeds, dated October 1, 1774, 1008, GHS. See also deed book VV, pp. 42–51, Glynn County, Brunswick, Ga. The purchase of Little St. Simons Island is recorded in deed book ABEF, pp. 366ff., in which "Gabriel" Manigault is also shown as "Gilbert" Manigault. "Will DeBraham" is JGW De-Brahm, surveyor general to the Southern Provinces. The grant to Harriott Butler, July 16, 1802, and her conveyance to PB, June 28, 1803, deed book ABEF, pp. 363–65, all Glynn County, Brunswick, Ga. The author is indebted to Burnette Vanstory, St. Simons Island, for her research on Hampton and Little St. Simons Island.

2. *Darien Gazette*, June 29, 1824. The "mayor" of Frederica was John Cole, Esq.

3. PB to Thomas Young, March 25, 1794, PB Letterbook, 1790–1794, SCL. George Valley was an overseer.

4. Hall, *Travels in North America*, 2:236.

5. On March 5, 1800, PB paid 1250 pounds to charter the *Anna*. The *Two Generals* was chartered on May 6, 1811, for a voyage to St. Petersburg, Russia (Butler Family Papers, HSP). The *Two Generals* was seized by a French privateer and detained for a time at Copenhagen. See chapter 11, "The War of 1812."

6. Legare, "Excursion into Southern Georgia," pp. 167–69, 247. Editor Legare quotes Roswell King, Jr., on procedures at Hampton. PB to Joseph Nutt, December 2, 1793, PB Letterbook, 1790–1794, SCL. The Sinclair tract was better known as St. Clair.

7. Legare, "Excursion into Southern Georgia," pp. 167–69, 247. Basil Hall said a slave could mote "twenty to thirty pounds a day." RK, Jr.'s fifty pounds might be overstated. Hall, *Travels in North America*, 2:231.

8. Atherton, ed., *A Few of Hamilton's Letters*, p. 277.

9. Schachner, *Aaron Burr*, p. 258. AB to Theodosia Burr Alston, September 6, 1804, in Van Doren, ed., *The Correspondence of Burr*, pp. 189, 175–76. Lomansk, *Aaron Burr: From Princeton to Vice President*, pp. 358, 360. Kline and Ryan, eds., *Political Correspondence and Public Papers of Aaron Burr*, 2:893–94.

10. AB to TBA, September 6 and 12, 1804, in Van Doren, ed., *The Correspondence of Burr*, pp. 181–82, 183–85. The "Sumtares" were Thomas Sumter, son of General Thomas Sumter, and his wife Natalie de L'Age, who was a friend of Theodosia Alston. Pidgin, *Theodosia*, p. 181. Lomansk, *Aaron Burr: From Princeton to Vice President*, pp. 197–98. *Darien Gazette*, October 5, 1824, comparing storm of 1804 with that of September 8, 1824.

11. PB to William Page, September 1, 1809; William Page to PB, September 13, 1809; both in William Page Papers, 1254, SHC. PB to John Potter, August 2, 1809, Wister Family Papers, HSP. Granger, ed., *Savannah River Plantations*, pp. 201, 224–44. PB to John Potter, September 24, 1815; November 24, 1815; December 16, 1815; all in the PB Letterbook, 1790–1794, SCL. Roswell King to PB, February 2, 1817, H. E. Drayton Papers, HSP.

12. McLendon, *History of Public Domain in Georgia*, pp. 24–29. Ackerman, *Land Policies*, pp. 19, 112.

13. The Telegaar mortgage, September 19, 1785, Butler Family Papers, HSP. McLendon, *History of Public Domain in Georgia*, p. 28.

14. Lewis, *They Called Their Town Darien*, p. 40.

15. The deed from PB's attorney to James Ladson, August 6, 1790, called for "1500 acres more or less," Georgia Department of Archives and History, Atlanta. The Telegaar mortgage (1484 acres) and the letter to John Potter, August 2, 1809 (1490 acres), Butler Family Papers, HSP.

16. Julia Floyd Smith, *Slavery and Rice Culture*, chapter 1, and House, *Planter Management*, introduction, give fine descriptions of rice plantations. Kemble, *Journal*, p. 57.

17. PB to Joseph Nutt, December 2, 1793, PB Letterbook, 1790–1794, SCL. PB to John Potter, August 2, 1809, Wister Family Papers, HSP.

18. Granger, ed., *Savannah River Plantations*, introduction. Washington, "Queries on the Culture of Rice," pp. 412–13 (Roswell King, Jr., answers the questions).

19. Spalding, "Brief Notes," *Southern Agriculturist* 1 (1828): 60. Legare, "Excursion into Southern Georgia," p. 169.

20. Thomas Spalding's letter to the editor, *Southern Agriculturist* 3 (1830): 73. Captain John Fraser, who married Anne, daughter of the John Coupers, acted as a guide for the Basil Halls in 1828. Captain Hall told Fraser that the orange trees at Butler's Island rivaled Niagara as a sight to see (Kemble, Georgian *Journal*, p. 113).

21. Presley, ed., *Dr. Bullie's Notes*, p. 154. Roswell King to PB, August 13, 1808, Butler Family Papers, HSP. A receipt from William Page to Roswell King, January 21, 1821, William Page Papers, SHC.

22. Kemble, Georgian *Journal,* pp. 113–14. Legare, "Excursion into Southern Georgia," p. 361n.

23. Spalding, "Brief Notes," *Southern Agriculturist* 1 (1828): 60. Coulter, *Georgia's Disputed Ruins,* pp. 235, 238–39, 241–42, 245. Coulter quotes Thomas Spalding on the cultivation of sugar cane.

24. Pope-Hennesy, ed., *The Aristocratic Journey,* p. 234. Margaret Hall to her sister, Jane, letter begun at Mrs. Fulton's tavern, twenty-four miles south of Savannah, and finished at Mobile, April 10, 1828, Margaret Hall Collection, 618, Library of Congress. Roswell King to PB, August 13, 1817, H. E. Drayton Papers, HSP.

Chapter 9. *The Slaves*

The lines introducing this chapter are from a letter addressing the slave trade between the West Indies and Africa, January 13, 1788, signed "R," *Columbian Magazine,* May 1788, Philadelphia.

1. Wylly, *The Seed That Was Sown,* pp. 13–14, 48–50, 136–37.

2. RK, Jr., to Pierce Butler (Mease), March 23, 1839, Wister Family Papers, HSP. RK, Jr., responds to an inquiry from PB as to the children of Judy and Scylla. He mentions that Major Butler had been on the plantations in 1819. Coghlan, "Senator Pierce Butler: The Aristocrat as Revolutionary," p. 471.

3. Hall, *Travels in North America,* 2:223, 214.

4. James M. Couper, grandson of John Couper, who planted Butler's Island after the slaves were freed, said he knew of no restriction on traffic between Hampton and Cannon's Point. The letters of the Kings to the Butlers show the contrary. JMC's comment in a letter to Caroline Couper Lovell, August 12, 1912, Cate Collection, GHS.

5. "A List of Negroes Taken at Hampton," May 4, 1793, by William Page, manager, Butler Family Papers, HSP.

6. Ibid.

7. Parrish, *Slave Songs,* p. 238, quoting Emma Postell Shadman on Maum Ryna, a former slave at Cannon's Point.

8. Mannix and Cowley, *Black Cargoes,* p. 168 and p. 2 of illustrations. See also Peter H. Wood, *Black Majority,* chapter 2, "Black Labor—White Rice," pp. 35–62, esp. pp. 56, 60–61. Littlefield, *Rice and Slaves,* p. 76.

9. PB to Richard Wayne, March 3, 1794, PB Letterbook, 1790–1794, SCL.

10. PB to Thomas Young, March 25, 1794, PB Letterbook, 1790–1794, SCL.

11. Many of the Butler slaves were imported by Mary Butler's father, Colonel Thomas Middleton. Purchase of certain strains were made by PB, and occasional references as to tribal origin were noted in letters and plantation records, for example, "Congo Harry."

12. Heyward, "The Negro in the Low Country," p. 173. See Herskovits, *The Myth of the Negro Past,* pp. 33–53, on tribal origins; p. 50, on Coromantees.

13. RK to PB, May 13, 1803, Butler Family Papers, HSP.

14. Work Projects Administration, *Georgia: A Guide,* p. 298. William Mein to PB, May 24, 1803, Butler Family Papers, HSP. Granger, ed., *Drums and Shadows,* p. 185.

15. Bell, "We Shall Overcome?" Andrews, *War-Time Journal,* p. 183. Turner, *Africanisms in the Gullah Dialect,* p. v.

16. Granger, ed., *Drums and Shadows,* pp. 32, 175–76, 169, 177, 184. Turner, *Africanisms in the Gullah Dialect,* p. 291, shows Shad Hall as "informant" on Gullah.

17. Hilton, *High Water on the Bar,* pp. 18–19, the quotation from Lillian F. Sinclair of Darien, "My Recollections of Darien in the Late Seventies and Eighties."

18. The names of the Butler slaves are from the William Page list of May 4, 1793, and the Inventory and Appraisement of the Estate of Captain John Butler, February 13, 1849, Butler Family Papers, HSP. See also Genovese, *Roll, Jordan, Roll,* pp. 443–450; Turner, *Africanisms in the Gullah District,* for names with African derivations; Fermor, *The Traveller's Tree,* p. 373; "The Butler Book," RK, Jr.'s plantation records, 1845–1848, Cate Collection, GHS. Among the family names, Manigo came from Manigault. John Butler's wife was Gabriella Manigault Morris; their daughter, Lizzie. Fish Harry's family ultimately gained a surname, Bennet. They served the Butler family as fishermen for four generations (Wylly, *Memories,* p. 35). PB's Wister grandchildren, three greats, owned a white Japanese "dancing mouse" named Psyche, pronounced by them "Peeshey" (Wister, *That I May Tell You,* p. 213). In the "Butler" graveyard on the Ridge Road, where many Darien blacks were buried, one grave is marked "Sackey Davis."

19. Herskovits, *The Myth of the Negro Past,* pp. 190–93.

20. See chapter 18, "The Weeping Time," and chapter 23, "Massa Jimmy."

21. Indenture between the slave William S. Hamilton, PB, and Hamilton's appointed guardian, John Cruger of New York, signed in Charleston, January 21, 1800, Butler Family Papers, HSP. The "Master's secrets" lend conjecture to the reasons for liberation.

22. Excerpts from the logs of British naval vessels, RG 76, entry 185, folder 58, National Archives, Washington. A list of the "supernumeraries" on British ships, Butler Family Papers, HSP.

23. PB to Roger Parker Saunders, August 26, 1790, PB Letterbook, 1790–1794, SCL.

24. The exchange of a letter between PB in New York and Roger Parker Saunders in Charleston occurred in 1790. The letter from Saunders is not dated, Butler

Family Papers, HSP. The response from PB, September 6, 1790, PB Letterbook, 1790–1794, SCL.

25. PB to Mrs. E. Izard, February 25, 1797; Mrs. Izard to PB, March 7, 1797; the "appraisement," made as requested by PB and Ralph Izard, March 3, 1797; all in the Butler Family Papers, HSP. The slave who regained Binah and children is not named.

26. Letters from RK to PB as of the dates shown, Butler Family Papers, HSP.

27. William Hunter (St. Marys, Ga.) to PB, August 20, 1801, Butler Family Papers, HSP.

28. William Page to PB, June 22, 1816, W. A. Couper Papers, SHC. WP to PB, June 25, 1818, Butler Family Papers, HSP.

29. PB to François Didier Petit de Villers, April 6, 1807, Mss P/2000, SCL.

30. Wylly, *The Seed That Was Sown,* p. 137.

31. PB to Colonel John Holmes, April 30, 1802, Butler Family Papers, HSP.

32. François Didier Petit de Villers to PB, February 18, 1811, Butler Family Papers, HSP. PB to John Couper, July 21, 1816, Wister Family Papers, HSP.

33. PB's short letter to the magistrate, in the Library Company of Philadelphia Mss Collection, M376, folder 48, HSP.

34. Case no. 2241, *Butler v. Hopper,* in *Federal Cases, Circuit and District Courts, 1789–1880,* book 4. Wallace, "Sketch of John Innskeep," p. 133. In reporting the Hopper remarks Wallace borrowed from the slave Ben story as told by Lydia Maria Child in her biography *Isaac T. Hopper: A True Life,* pp. 98–103. Mrs. Child had a tendency to report a conversation as though she had been there with a tape recorder. See chapter 15, "Enter Fanny Kemble." See also, Simpson, *Lives of Eminent Philadelphians,* pp. 560–63. In 1780 Pennsylvania enacted "gradual abolition," freedom for slaves at age twenty-eight, a resident of another state permitted to keep a slave no longer than six months. See Turner, *The Negro in Pennsylvania,* pp. 79–88.

35. RK to PB, January 14, 1815, Butler Family Papers, HSP.

36. Presley, ed., *Dr. Bullie's Notes,* p. 153. RK was inconsistent on the names of slaves. "Abram" became "Abraham" in the same letter. He was "Abraham, carpenter," on most plantation records. See chapter 14, "The Mease Boys Change Their Names."

37. The town of Darien's ordinance of September 14, 1818, was published in the *Darien Gazette,* November 16, 1818.

38. The bravery of Morris is an oft-told story. The tankard, fashioned from coin silver, was made in Philadelphia by Samuel Williamson. It was presented to Lady Alice Leigh Butler, great-great-granddaughter of PB, by Morris Seagrove, great-grandson of Driver Morris. The tankard is in the silver collection of Savannah's Owens-Thomas House Museum. See Cate, *Our Todays and Yesterdays,* pp. 148–151, and Leigh, *Ten Years on a Georgia Plantation,* p. 184.

39. Thomas Pinckney from his plantation El Dorado to PB, May 25, 1805,

Butler Family Papers, HSP. Bull, "Storm Towers on the Santee Delta," p. 95. Leigh, *Ten Years on a Georgia Plantation*, pp. 183–84.

40. RK to PB, October 25, 1806, H. E. Drayton Papers, HSP. For lucid descriptions of the slave driver, see Genovese, *Roll, Jordan, Roll*, "The Men Between," pp. 365–88; and Clifton, "The Rice Driver," pp. 331–53.

41. Heyward, *Seed from Madagascar*, p. 157. Parrish, *Slave Songs*, p. 202. Lyell, *A Second Visit*, 1:266.

42. The William Page list of May 4, 1793, Butler Family Papers, HSP. PB to Roger Parker Saunders, September 5, 1791, PB Letterbook, 1790–1794, SCL. RK, Jr.'s letter to the editor, *Southern Agriculturist* 1 (1828): 524.

43. Heyward, *Seed from Madagascar*, p. 179.

44. RK, Jr.'s letter to the editor, p. 524.

45. RK to PB, March 16, 1804, Butler Family Papers, HSP.

46. RK, Jr.'s letter to the editor, pp. 524, 525.

47. RK to PB, July 19, 1806, Butler Family Papers, HSP.

48. RK to PB, April 21, 1804, H. E. Drayton Papers, Butler Family Papers, HSP.

49. RK to PB, August 24, 1806, Butler Family Papers, HSP. The name "Sambo" means "to disagree, to be shameful" in a Sierra Leone dialect (Turner, *Africanisms in the Gullah Dialect*, p. 155).

50. RK to PB, August 24, 1806, Butler Family Papers, HSP.

51. Memorandum showing PB's appointment to the "Algerine" and "Frigate" committees, Butler Family Papers, HSP.

52. Memorandum showing the cost of the *Altamaha Packet* and its slave crew, purchased from the estate of Brewton, Butler Family Papers, HSP.

53. PB commissioned Russell and Goff to construct a schooner, August 6, 1773, Butler Family Papers, HSP.

54. PB to Mr. LeMotte, October 30, 1791, PB Letterbook, 1790–1794, SCL. See Fleetwood, *Tidecraft*, p. 30, on "petiagur, periaga."

55. Gordon, "The Negro Spiritual," in *Carolina Low Country*, p. 197. Parrish, *Slave Songs*, p. 158. "Zion" was sung at Melrose plantation on Daufuskie Island, South Carolina (Collection of Albert H. Stoddard, Savannah). Celia Davis of Darien was interviewed by Amelia M. Watson, "Kemble Collection," Lenox Library Associates, Lenox, Massachusetts.

56. Hall, *Travels in North America*, 2:228. The oars were pulled by four "smart negroes"; the fifth was a steersman.

57. Lyell, *A Second Visit*, 1:244.

58. Rogers, "Letters," p. 341.

59. Parrish, *Slave Songs*, pp. 130, 22. "Scribben" is a corruption of the name "Screven." See also an undated clipping from the *Atlanta Journal*, the text of a talk by Lydia Parrish at the time of the publication of *Slave Songs* in 1942 (Gamble, *Scrapbooks*, 7:169–71).

60. Conrad, "Reminiscences," p. 8.

61. Bell, "We Shall Overcome?"

62. RK, Jr.'s letter to the editor, p. 524. RK to PB, March 30, 1804, Butler Family Papers, HSP.

63. Jones, *A Catechism*, pp. 127–30.

64. Higginson, *Army Life in a Black Regiment*, p. 196.

Chapter 10. *Honored Sir*

1. PB to Archibald Brown, February 14, 1794, PB Letterbook, 1790–1794, SCL.

2. PB to Richard Wayne, August 12, 1793; PB to William Page, August 23, 1797, and November 15, 1797; all in the PB Letterbooks, HSP. PB seldom referred to his "people" as slaves.

3. PB to William Page, April 25, 1798, PB Letterbooks, HSP.

4. PB to John Coffin (Nova Scotia), June 25, 1790; PB to Henry Cooper (St. Croix), August 10, 1793; all in the PB Letterbooks, HSP.

5. PB to William Page, June 21, 1798; PB to Colonel McPherson, July 19, 1798; PB to William Page, October 10, 1798; all in the PB Letterbooks, HSP.

6. PB to William Page, January 11, 1799, PB Letterbooks, HSP.

7. Myers, ed., *Children of Pride*, p. 1584. Harden, *A History of Savannah and South Georgia*, 2:559–60. Gamble, *Scrapbooks*, 2:137. Julia R. King to Judge Sheppard, July 13, 1932; the register of the family of Roswell King and Catherine Barrington; both in the Julia King Papers, Midway Museum, Midway, Ga. The father of Catherine Barrington King is shown on the family register as "Jessiah"; elsewhere as "Josiah," or "Joseph."

8. Coulter, *Georgia's Disputed Ruins*, pp. 77–78.

9. Coulter, *Thomas Spalding of Sapelo*, pp. 43–44. Wylly, *Memories*, pp. 11–12. Cate, *Our Todays and Yesterdays*, p. 44. Hartridge, ed., *The Letters of Robert Mackay*, p. 93. The actual date of construction of the Sapelo house is not known. Coulter says, "Soon after going to Sapelo, Spalding began the construction." Coulter continues, "He was the architect, Roswell King and a gang of Negroes were the overseer and workmen." Cate says the house was built between 1800 and 1802. Mackay noted that the house was still unfinished in 1810.

10. RK's spelling of "Honored" was sometimes "Honoured," and often reduced to "Honr'd." He began words with capitals for emphasis, occasionally underlined for greater emphasis, and was inconsistent on "negro" and "Negro," frequently ending the word with an *e*.

11. RK to PB, July 23, 1815, Butler Family Papers, HSP.

12. RK to PB, August 13, 1815, Butler Family Papers.

13. Catherine King to PB, January 7, 1815, Butler Family Papers.

14. RK to PB, July 8, 1803, Butler Family Papers.

15. RK to PB, October 8, 1803, Butler Family Papers.

16. RK to PB, April 2, 1818, H. E. Drayton Papers, HSP.

17. RK to PB, January 20, 1815, Butler Family Papers, HSP.

18. RK, Jr.'s letter to the editor, pp. 67–68.

19. RK to PB, May 19, 1804, H. E. Drayton Papers, HSP.

20. William Mein to PB, May 20, 1804, Butler Family Papers, HSP.

21. The loan from PB to RK was duly recorded on March 15, 1806, in deed book ABEF, Glynn County, Brunswick, Ga.

22. RK to PB, January 20, 1815, Butler Family Papers, HSP.

23. Charles Cotesworth Pinckney to PB, January 10, 1817, Butler Family Papers, HSP.

24. Wylly, *The Seed That Was Sown,* p. 50. Captain Wylly described the Butler dictum in a comparison with procedures on the Thomas Spalding plantation on Sapelo.

25. See chapter 16, "Negroland."

26. RK to PB, October 8, 1803, Butler Family Papers, HSP.

27. RK to PB, June 17, 1803, Butler Family Papers.

28. RK to PB, June 24, 1803, Butler Family Papers.

29. RK's "Runaway Report" for 1803, H. E. Drayton Papers, HSP.

30. RK to PB, July 8, 1803, Butler Family Papers, HSP.

31. RK to PB, July 2, 1806, H. E. Drayton Papers, HSP.

32. RK to PB, July 23, 1808, Butler Family Papers, HSP.

33. RK to PB, December 31, 1805, Butler Family Papers.

34. RK to PB, November 25, 1803, Butler Family Papers.

35. RK to PB, June 17, 1803; October 29, 1803; December 3, 1803; March 16, 1804; all in the Butler Family Papers. Mary R. Bullard to the author, August 25, 1987.

36. RK to PB, November 25, 1803, Butler Family Papers.

37. RK to PB, August 9, 1806, Butler Family Papers.

38. RK to PB, March 18, 1815, Butler Family Papers.

39. PB to RK, January 21, 1813, PB Letterbooks, HSP.

40. RK, Jr.'s letter to the editor, p. 524.

Chapter 11. *The War of 1812*

1. Sikes, *The Public Life of Pierce Butler,* pp. 111–12. The Cochrane proclamation was published in many newspapers. A copy is on microfilm, box 1, GHS. See also Gamble, *City Government of Savannah,* p. 103.

2. Fogel and Engerman, *Time on the Cross,* p. 27. Drescher, *Econocide,* pp. 12–14.

3. Charles Cotesworth Pinckney to William Behr, August 26, 1813, Pinckney Family Collection, SCHS.

4. *Times*, London, June 27, 1814.

5. Bullard, *Black Liberation*, p. 47. *Niles Weekly Register*, vol. 4, August 21, 1813, p. 402.

6. George Cockburn Papers, 17576, microfilm rolls 5, 6, and 7, Library of Congress. Bullard, *Black Liberation*, chapter 6. Presley, ed., *Dr. Bullie's Notes*, pp. 131, 114, 110–16. George Baillie to William Jones, November 18, 1815, William Jones Papers, 448, GHS.

7. George White, *Statistics of Georgia*, p. 288. White said that Tom came "probably farther from the interior of Africa than any other negro in America," and that the Foolahs were "the most intelligent of the native African tribes." Lyell, *A Second Visit*, 1:266–67. Coulter, *Thomas Spalding of Sapelo*, p. 190. John Sawyer to General Blackshear, January 27, 1815, in Miller, *Memoir of General Blackshear*, pp. 455–56.

8. The British also raided Little St. Simons Island, Admiral Cockburn to Admiral Cochrane, February 11, 1815, Cockburn Papers, microfilm roll 7, Library of Congress.

9. Catherine King to PB, January 7, 1815, Butler Family Papers, HSP.

10. RK to PB, January 20, 1815, Butler Family Papers.

11. Ibid.

12. PB to William Page, May 19, 1816, W. A. Couper Papers, SHC.

13. RK to PB, February 12, 1815, Butler Family Papers, HSP.

14. PB's *Two Generals* memorandums, May 6, 1811, and March 9, 1812, Butler Family Papers. PB to Harrisons & Latham, May 6, 1815, in which PB attempted to recover from insurers by contending the ship had been boarded by Danish privateers, PB Letterbooks, HSP. Not until long after PB's death was the value of the cargo recovered. Frances Butler pursued the estate's claim against the French government, ultimately winning an award of $32,772 (Wister Family Papers, HSP). Coffin, *Building the Nation*, p. 212. Gamble, *City Government of Savannah*, pp. 103–6. Admiral Cockburn to Admiral Cochrane, January 26, 1815, and to Commodore A. F. Evans, February 10, 1815; both letters from Cumberland mention his designs on Savannah. A letter to Admiral Cochrane, February 11, 1815, stated: "Our operations in this neighbourhood have already created the greatest consternation in Georgia" (Cockburn Papers, microfilm roll 7, Library of Congress). In *A Full and Correct Account*, James states: "One of the objects in assembling troops upon this part of the coast was to assist in a combined attack upon the town of Savannah, in Georgia, a naval station of no mean importance" (1:336).

15. RK to PB, February 12, 1815, Butler Family Papers, HSP.

16. RK to PB, February 26, 1815, Butler Family Papers, HSP.

17. Ibid.

18. RK to PB, March 4, 1815, Butler Family Papers, HSP.

19. Ibid.

20. Captain Newell, often spelled Newall, was a captain in the United States Sea Fencibles. Admiral Cockburn to Newell and Thomas Spalding, March 7 and March 11, 1815, Cockburn Papers, microfilm roll 7, Library of Congress. The reports of Newell, Spalding, and Cockburn, and other papers on the British occupation of coastal Georgia are in RG 76, entry 185, folders 26, 27, 55, and 58, National Archives, Washington. See also Bullard, *Black Liberation,* p. 86. Coulter, *Thomas Spalding of Sapelo,* pp. 191–94.

21. Contained in RG 76, entry 185, folder 27, National Archives. *Niles Weekly Register,* vol. 5, September 30, 1815, pp. 80–81.

22. Bullard, *Black Liberation,* p. 91. *Niles Weekly Register,* vol. 5, September 30, 1815, p. 82.

23. Admiral Cockburn to Admiral Cochrane, February 28, 1815, Cockburn Papers, microfilm roll, 7, Library of Congress.

24. In RG 76, entry 185, folder 27, National Archives. *Niles Weekly Register,* vol. 5, September 30, 1815, p. 82.

25. RK to PB, March 4, 1815, Butler Family Papers, HSP.

26. RK to PB, March 18, 1815, Butler Family Papers, HSP.

27. Coulter, *Thomas Spalding of Sapelo,* p. 192. RK to PB, March 18, 1815, Butler Family Papers, HSP. To RK, Abraham the carpenter was often "Abram." See chapters 9, "The Slaves," and 14, "The Mease Boys."

28. Coulter, *Thomas Spalding of Sapelo,* p. 193.

29. Admiral Cockburn (HMS *Albion*) to Commodore A. F. Evans (Bermuda), December 12, 1814, Cockburn Papers, microfilm roll 7, Library of Congress.

30. RK to PB, March 18, 1815, Butler Family Papers, HSP.

31. RK to PB, June 4, 1815, Butler Family Papers, HSP.

32. PB to RK, March 31, 1815, and to Harrisons and Latham, Liverpool, June 4, 1815, PB Letterbooks, HSP.

33. PB to RK, March 31, 1815, in which RK was told to sign as "superintendent," PB believing the grander title would influence the British (PB Letterbooks, HSP). The affidavit entitled "A Narrative of the Conduct of the British Armed Forces from the 30th Jany to the 14th of Feby 1815," by Roswell King, St. Simons Island, February 14, 1815, listed the 138 slaves by name and itemized all other property removed by the British (Butler Family Papers, HSP).

34. PB to Harrisons and Latham, November 30, 1815, PB Letterbooks; RK to PB, June 4, 1815, Butler Family Papers; both HSP.

35. That PB lost 138 slaves to the British is well established by RK's "Narrative," and by a series of lists and claims in both the Butler Family Papers and the records at the National Archives. The losses of the other St. Simons planters is not so well documented. In RK to PB, March 18, 1815, the losses of James Hamilton are shown as 238; John Couper's, 60. National Archives claim, St. Mary's, May

26, 1821, shows Hamilton as 187, Couper as 65. The best measure of the losses are the actual claims shown in this chapter, but these do include other property. Among the lists of the Butler slaves are two prepared by RK, Jr., on April 28, 1815, and on September 29, 1822, the latter for Thomas Butler. Names and ages for all, identifying tasks, and quarter whence they came are shown on both lists. These two lists show the value of each slave, a total of $61,450 after deducting $900, the value of Pompey who returned from HMS *Regulus*. This figure is higher than the actual Butler claim of $56,470.

36. RK to PB, July 16, 1815, Butler Family Papers, HSP.

37. RK to PB, June 4, 1815, Butler Family Papers, HSP.

38. The Americans proved that slaves taken by the British on the "high seas" had been sold in the West Indies. "The inference is strong, if not irresistible, that slaves taken from our shores shared the same fate." So spoke the editor of the *Niles Weekly Register,* September 30, 1815, pp. 83–84. The response from Admiral Cochrane followed.

39. Excerpts from the logs of the British naval vessels show the slaves were logged as they came aboard. Their last names were those of their former owners. As claims were processed, the ship's logs were made available for purposes of verification. The movement of the Butler people can be followed from Cumberland to Halifax, as documented in RG 76, entry 185, folder 58, National Archives. PB was given a transcript showing the movement of the Butler blacks, all of whom were ultimately discharged at Melville Island, Halifax, excepting those who died at sea. See "A List of Supernumeraries borne in His Majesty's Ship *Albion*." This list includes the ships *Dragon, Surprise, Erebus, Canso, Brune,* and *Ceylon* (Butler Family Papers, HSP). Sam's death was reported in the log of *Albion*, then at anchor in the Atlantic off Cumberland: "Departed this life, Samuel Butler, a refugee negro, March 5, 1815" (Cockburn Papers, microfilm roll 5, Library of Congress).

40. Clairmont and Magill, *Nova Scotia Blacks,* p. 10.

41. The RK "Narrative," Butler Family Papers, HSP. See also the list of "Supernumeraries" mentioned above.

42. Grant, "Black Immigrants into Nova Scotia," p. 269. Martell, *Immigration to and Emigration from Nova Scotia,* p. 16. Clairmont and Magill, *Nova Scotia Blacks,* pp. 9, 112. Raddall, *Halifax, Warden of the North,* pp. 128–29, 117. See also Fermor, *The Traveller's Tree,* pp. 372–74.

43. Grant, "Black Immigrants into Nova Scotia," p. 269. Riddell, "The Slave in Canada," p. 112 n. 27. Fergusson and Harvey, *A Documentary Study,* pp. 45–46, 77, 93–94.

44. RK to PB, August 13, 1815, Butler Family Papers, HSP.

45. RK to PB, June 11, 1821; John Couper to PB, June 17, 1821; both in the Butler Family Papers, HSP. Bullard, *Black Liberation,* p. 101. PB to William Page,

April 9, 1816, and January 25, 1818; William Page to PB, June 22, 1816, and December 30, 1817; all in the W. A. Couper Papers, SHC.

46. PB to John Couper, July 21, 1816, Wister Family Papers, HSP.

47. Updyke, *The Diplomacy of the War of 1812,* p. 404. Berquist, "Henry Middleton and the Slave Controversy," pp. 20–31. RK's affidavit to the mayor of Darien on the value of his slave Harry, February 15, 1815, RG 76, entry 185, folder 26, National Archives.

48. RK to PB, July 23, 1815, Butler Family Papers, HSP.

49. William Page to PB, April 30, 1816, Butler Family Papers, HSP.

50. PB to William Page, April 9, 1816, and May 19, 1816, W. A. Couper Papers, SHC.

51. RK to PB, July 23, 1815, Butler Family Papers, HSP. PB to William Page, May 19, 1816, W. A. Couper Papers, SHC.

52. Clairmont and Magill, *Nova Scotia Blacks,* pp. 12–13. Fergusson and Harvey, *A Documentary Study,* the preface. Winks, *The Blacks in Canada,* p. 125. Moorsom, *Letters from Nova Scotia,* p. 126.

53. The Earl of Dalhousie to the Earl of Bathurst, December 29, 1816, and April 30, 1817, quoted in Fergusson and Harvey, *A Documentary Study,* pp. 28–31, 35, 52, 95, 101. Walker, *The Black Loyalists,* p. 394.

54. Lieutenant Governor James Kempt to Lord Bathurst, October 16, 1823, quoted in Fergusson and Harvey, *A Documentary Study,* p. 35.

55. Moorsom, *Letters from Nova Scotia,* p. 126.

56. Fergusson and Harvey, *A Documentary Study,* p. 52.

57. *Letters from Nova Scotia and New Brunswick,* p. 126, quoted in Chiasson, "As Others Saw Us," p. 14.

58. Winks, *The Blacks in Canada,* pp. 114, 127.

Chapter 12.
Second Generation: The Butlers

1. PB to John Allston, near Georgetown, South Carolina, March 25, 1794, PB Letterbook, 1790–1794, SCL.

2. *Charlestown Gazette,* January 11, 1780. See chapter 3, "Spoils of War." Alfred Langdon Elwyn to Sarah Butler Wister, July 26, 1870, in which Elwyn briefed his niece on the Butler family. He wrote, "Your grandmother (Sarah Butler Mease) was the eldest, then your dear aunts Frances and Elizabeth, twins, then Harriet Percy, then Thomas." Elwyn came into the Butler clan by marrying PB's granddaughter, Mary Middleton Mease (Butler Family Papers, HSP). Webber, "Josiah Smith's Diary," which lists patriot families banished to Philadelphia from South Carolina (p. 79).

3. PB to Weeden Butler, May 10, 1787, Weeden Butler Correspondence, British Library.

4. Memorandum of Weeden Butler (1773–1881), December 24, 1827. The memorandum introduced the WB Correspondence, British Library. See also chapter 4, "Pierce Butler's Private Life."

5. PB to WB, November 19, 1792, WB Correspondence, British Library.

6. Annie R. Butler, *Nearly a Hundred Years Ago.*

7. PB (Amsterdam) to WB, October 21, 1784, WB Correspondence, British Library.

8. Annie R. Butler, *Nearly a Hundred Years Ago.* PB to WB, November 30, 1786, WB Correspondence, British Library. A statement captioned "Rev'd Mr. Butler's Terms," Butler Family Papers, HSP.

9. Numbers 4 and 6 Cheyne Walk are well described in the London County Council's *Survey of London,* part 1, *Chelsea,* pp. 38–44, 45–48; and in Faulkner, *Chelsea and Its Environs,* pp. 427–28. Boswell, *The Life of Samuel Johnson,* 1:398. Dr. Johnson brought a "triumphant roar of laughter" from a motley assembly when he disagreed with Boswell's belief in the Venetian's methods: "Well, Sir, go to Dominicetti, and get thyself fumigated; but be sure the steam be directed to thy *head* for *that* is the *pecant* part."

10. *DNB,* s.v. "Butler, Weeden, 1742–1823" and "Dodd, William, 1729–1777." Boswell, *The Life of Samuel Johnson,* 2:90, 110, 113. Johnson told Boswell he wrote many of Dr. Dodd's petitions and had composed the letter Dodd sent to George III on the day prior to the execution: "The most miserable of men applies himself to your clemency." Johnson, believing Dodd would soon have an audience on high, wrote to the doomed man: "Let me beg that you make in your devotions one petition for my eternal welfare."

11. PB to WB, September 16, 1784, WB Correspondence, British Library.

12. PB to WB, November 8, 1785, WB Correspondence, British Library.

13. PB to WB, February 18, 1786, WB Correspondence, British Library.

14. Mary Butler to WB, July 4, 1787; PB to WB, March 2, 1788; both in the WB Correspondence, British Library.

15. PB to Thomas Butler, May 4, 1789; PB to WB, May 30, 1789; both in the WB Correspondence, British Library.

16. PB to WB, July 18, 1788, WB Correspondence, British Library.

17. PB to WB, November 16, 1788, WB Correspondence, British Library. Dr. Peter Spence was classified in South Carolina among the unfortunates who were "Obnoxious Persons whose Estates are Confiscated and their Persons to be Banished" (Webber, "Josiah Smith's Diary," p. 198).

18. PB to TB, November 23, 1788, WB Correspondence, British Library.

19. PB to TB in early 1789, letter 51, WB Correspondence, British Library.

20. PB to TB, February 22, 1789, WB Correspondence, British Library.

21. PB to TB, April 5, 1789, WB Correspondence, British Library.

22. PB to WB, August 12, 1789, WB Correspondence, British Library.

23. Mary Butler to TB, July 4, 1789, and August 2, 1789, WB Correspondence, British Library.

24. PB to WB, August 1789, WB Correspondence, British Library. PB missed the birthday by two days. Thomas was born August 13, 1778. The school was on Cheyne Walk, not Row.

25. PB to WB, September 20, 1789, and October 5, 1789, WB Correspondence, British Library.

26. PB to TB, July 8, 1790; PB to WB, July 6, 1790; both in the WB Correspondence, British Library.

27. PB to TB, January 4, 1790, and July 8, 1790, WB Correspondence, British Library.

28. PB to WB, May 6, 1792, WB Correspondence, British Library.

29. Sarah Butler, Newington to TB, May 17, 1792, WB Correspondence, British Library. Newington was the Daniel Blake plantation on the Ashley River, near Charleston.

30. Anne Elizabeth Butler to TB, March 4, 1792, WB Correspondence, British Library.

31. PB to TB, March 4, 1792; PB to WB, November 19, 1792; both in the WB Correspondence, British Library.

32. PB to WB, November 19, 1792, WB Correspondence, British Library.

33. PB to "Mr. LeMotte," October 20, 1791, PB Letterbook, 1790–1794, SCL. PB to WB, April 12, 1792, and May 6, 1792, WB Correspondence, British Library.

34. PB to WB, February 3, 1793, WB Correspondence, British Library.

35. PB to WB, October 27, 1794; Frances Butler to TB, February 27, 1793; PB to WB, February 3, 1793; Harriot Percy Butler to TB, March 5, 1794; all in the WB Correspondence, British Library.

36. PB to WB, September 5, 1794, and March 14, 1795, WB Correspondence, British Library.

37. PB to WB, September 1795, letter 206, WB Correspondence, British Library.

38. PB to WB, November 5, 1795, and December 13, 1795, WB Correspondence, British Library.

39. WB to PB, January 30, 1796, WB Correspondence, British Library.

40. Mr. Neild's comments are not signed or dated, but are in the same handwriting as his "observations" attached to Sarah Butler's letter of August 25, 1794, in the WB Correspondence, British Library. See this chapter, n. 48. Neild lived at 5 Cheyne Walk and sent his son and inheritor, James Camden Neild, to the Butler School with Thomas where his classical education took root and was continued at Cambridge. The elder Neild left his son a sizable fortune of property and 250,000 pounds. Young Neild became a classic example of a recluse and miser. At his

death his fortune had more than doubled, all of which he left to Queen Victoria, London County Council, *The Survey of London,* part 1, *Chelsea,* pp. 38–44.

41. WB to PB, January 30, 1796, WB Correspondence, British Library.

42. PB to WB, April 12, 1792, WB Correspondence, British Library.

43. The Moreau School was on Great Cumberland and Oxford streets in London. The bill, December 20, 1794, and Madame Moreau's letter to PB (Bath), February 17, 1785, Butler Family Papers, HSP.

44. PB to TB, April 5, 1789, WB Correspondence, British Library.

45. PB to WB, October 5, 1789, and February 3, 1793, WB Correspondence, British Library.

46. Sarah Butler to TB, April 15, 1793, WB Correspondence, British Library.

47. PB to WB, November 5, 1793; Sarah Butler to TB, August 25, 1794; both in the WB Correspondence, British Library.

48. "Observations by James Nield, Esq., on Miss S. Butler's letter," undated, WB Correspondence, British Library.

49. Fisher, *Recollections,* p. 264. *National Intelligencer,* June 11, 1812. Scharf and Westcott, *History of Philadelphia,* 1:511, 520. Buck, *Memoirs,* p. 108. Westcott, *Scrapbooks: Biographies of Philadelphia,* vol. 2, part 2, HSP.

50. The Mease family is outlined by Margaret McLanahan, great-granddaughter of John and Gabriella Butler, in a genealogical compilation for Margaret Davis Cate, Cate Collection, GHS.

51. PB ("near Darien") to Benjamin Rush, M.D., December 24, 1809, James Rush Papers, 7237, vol. 21, Library Company of Philadelphia Mss Collection, HSP. Dr. James Rush left not only family papers to the Library Company but his entire estate, almost all of which he had received on the death of his wife, Phoebe Ann Ridgway, a very wealthy Philadelphian.

52. PB ("near Darien") to Benjamin Rush, February 1, 1810, Mss P/5338, SCL.

53. PB ("near Darien") to Benjamin Rush, March 18, 1810, James Rush Papers, 7237, vol. 21, HSP. Dr. Rush had attended the child for several years. On January 28, 1803, PB had written ,"The prompt attention You gave my little G-son in Novbr, by which under Divine dispensation, You were the instrument of saving his life" (PB ["near Darien"] to Dr. Rush, citation as above). PB was actually writing from Hampton, his plantation on St. Simons Island.

54. Harriot Percy Butler to Benjamin Rush, undated letter, James Rush Papers, 7237, vol. 21, HSP. Her letter is addressed to "Dr. Rush," surely Benjamin and not James, with whom she also corresponded and for whom she showed fondness. Her letters, undated, not showing whence they came or where directed, create some uncertainty. She signs "H. P. Butler" in her large flowing hand.

55. Robert Mackay to Eliza Anne Mackay, February 13 and April 15, 1810, in Hartridge, ed., *The Letters of Robert Mackay,* pp. 206, 97. Eliza Anne Mackay was the daughter of PB's friend, Don Juan McQueen.

56. Christ Church, Philadelphia. The tomb is on the northern side of the church. Corner, ed., *The Autobiography of Benjamin Rush,* p. 287.

57. Fisher, *Recollections,* p. 264.

58. Mease, *The Picture of Philadelphia.* Fisher, *Recollections,* p. 264.

59. *The Philadelphia Directory and Register, 1840.*

60. WB to TB, May 16, 1796, WB Correspondence, British Library.

61. Letter to Mrs. Iredell, April 11, 1799, in McRee, *Life and Correspondence of James Iredell,* 2:571.

62. Fisher, *Recollections,* pp. 265–67.

63. Vauclin Parish Records, Archives Departmentales de la Martinique, Martinique, French West Indies. The author was directed to the site of the de Mallevault plantation by M. Emile Hayot, president, Societe d'Histoire de la Martinique.

64. TB to John McQueen, Jr., January 28, 1812, and August 29, 1814, Mackay Stiles Papers, SHC.

65. Fermor, *The Traveller's Tree,* pp. 95–97.

66. Hearn, *Youma,* pp. 35, 43.

67. Fermor, *The Traveller's Tree,* p. 96.

68. Fisher, *Recollections,* p. 267.

69. James Rush Papers, 7237, vol. 21, HSP.

70. See this chapter, n. 1.

71. PB to James Monroe, April 19, 1813; PB to James Rush, April 30, 1813; both in the James Rush Papers, 7237, vol. 21, HSP.

72. Roswell King to PB, September 17, 1815, in which RK acknowledges the "melancholy account" of Harriot Percy Butler's death, Butler Family Papers, HSP.

73. The many accounts maintained by Frances Butler; the lists of slaves, Guerard's at Toogoodoo, November 10, 1775, and Brewton's at Combahee, November 6, 1775; RK to PB, June 19, 1817, in which he attempts to sort out Blake and Guerard slaves; PB's will, in which is mentioned the Pennsylvania lands; all in the Butler Family Papers, HSP. For Tennessee lands, see Sikes, *Public Life of Pierce Butler,* pp. 110, 111.

74. PB to William Page, April 19, 1818, William Page Papers, 1254, SHC.

75. PB's will, Butler Family Papers, HSP.

Chapter 13.
Second Generation: The Kings

1. The register of the family of Roswell King and Catherine Barrington, Julia King Papers, Midway Museum, Midway, Ga. Kemble, Georgian *Journal,* p. 201.

2. Julia R. King to "Judge Sheppard," July 13, 1932, Julia King Papers, Midway Museum. RK to PB, October 12, 1817, and January 31, 1819, H. E. Drayton Papers, HSP. PB to John Couper, June 15, 1815, Wister Family Papers, HSP.

3. RK to PB, March 24, 1816, H. E. Drayton Papers, HSP.

4. RK to PB, June 24, 1817, H. E. Drayton Papers, HSP.

5. RK to PB, May 26, 1816; April 13, 1817; and November 16, 1817; all in the H. E. Drayton Papers, HSP. RK to PB, January 14, 1815, Butler Family Papers, HSP.

6. RK to PB, May 26, 1816, H. E. Drayton Papers, HSP.

7. PB to John Couper, January 16, 1818; John Couper to PB, February 15, 1818; both in the Wister Family Papers, HSP.

8. RK to PB, April 2, 1818, H. E. Drayton Papers, HSP.

9. PB to William Page, April 19, 1818, William Page Papers, 1254, SHC.

10. RK to PB, January 18, 1818, H. E. Drayton Papers, HSP.

11. RK to PB, April 2, 1818, H. E. Drayton Papers, HSP.

12. RK to PB, January 18, 1818, and September 22, 1818, H. E. Drayton Papers, HSP.

13. RK to PB, July 18, 1818, H. E. Drayton Papers, HSP. William King's drawing of the Hampton subdivision is not with his father's letter.

14. The advertisement is from the *Darien Gazette,* December 21, 1818, Cate Collection, GHS.

15. RK to PB, January 31, 1819, H. E. Drayton Papers, HSP.

16. RK to PB, June 4, 1820, H. E. Drayton Papers, HSP. The Bank of Darien was chartered in December 1818. RK's third son, Barrington King, was one of the original directors appointed by shareholders. RK's membership on the board came later. See Lewis, *They Called Their Town Darien,* pp. 44–45.

17. PB to RK, Jr., November 17, 1820, PB Letterbooks, HSP.

18. PB to RK, Jr., January 3, 1821, and January 16, 1821, PB Letterbooks, HSP.

19. PB to RK, Jr., January 10, 1821, PB Letterbooks, HSP.

20. RK, Jr., to PB, December 24, 1820, and December 31, 1820, H. E. Drayton Papers, HSP.

21. PB to RK, Jr., January 11, 1821; March 28, 1821; May 11 and October 1, 1821; all in the PB Letterbooks, HSP.

22. PB to RK, Jr., October 28 and November 4, 1821, PB Letterbooks, HSP.

23. PB to RK, Jr., November 10, 1821, PB Letterbooks, HSP.

Chapter 14.
The Mease Boys Change Their Names

1. PB to Fanny Palmer (near "Galloway," Ireland), May 18, 1821, PB to Harrison and Latham, September 18, 1820; February 4, May 3, and November 11, 1821, PB to Mr. McNish (Savannah), May 11, 1821; PB to RK, Jr., December 2 and November 4, 1821; PB to RK, January 13 and 18, 1822, Pierce Butler Letterbooks, HSP.

2. The quotation from Davis, *Travels in the United States,* p. 415. *American Daily Advertiser,* Philadelphia, February 18, 1822.

3. *SCG,* March 2, 1822. Henry Laurens, who did not accept the appointment, would have been one of the five delegates. See chapter 5, "PB's Public Life, 1776–1789."

4. Deborah Norris Logan Diaries, vol. 5, 1821–1822, HSP.

5. Westcott, *Scrapbooks: Biographies of Philadelphia,* vol. 2, part 2, pp. 194–95, HSP. PB's funeral cost $212.69, as recorded in Frances Butler's account book, February 15, 1822, to February 15, 1836, Loose Volumes, Wister Family Papers, HSP.

6. PB's will is on file with Philadelphia's Register of Wills. A copy is in the H. E. Drayton Collection, HSP.

7. Conveyance of slaves from PB to TB, December 18, 1800, Wister Family Papers, HSP.

8. *SCAGG,* January 22, 1768. See also chapter 1, "Carolina Gentry."

9. Mary Butler signed a testamentary document on August 16, 1790, specifying her slaves received under Mary Bull's will should be held in trust by PB for her "Dear Children" (Wister Family Papers, HSP).

10. Statement of births and deaths for the year 1822, an annual accounting, this one prepared by RK, Jr., Butler Family Papers, HSP.

11. Frances Butler's qualification is shown on the will of PB in the H. E. Drayton Collection, HSP. Fisher, *Recollections,* p. 263. TB to Sarah Butler Mease, May 25, 1825, H. E. Drayton Collection, HSP. TB to his nephew PB, April 27, 1836, Wister Family Papers, HSP.

12. The dates of birth of the Mease boys are shown in Margaret McLanahan's genealogical compilation, Cate Collection, GHS.

13. Eaton, *A History of the Old South,* p. 266. Candler and Knight, eds., *The Colonial Records of Georgia,* 3:427. Wallace, *The History of South Carolina,* 2:507. *A Refutation of the Calumnies,* by a South Carolinian, H. E. Drayton Collection, HSP.

14. RK, Jr., to William Washington, September 13, 1828, in *Southern Agriculturist* 1 (1828): 527–28. Swaim's Panacea, a patent medicine, is mentioned frequently in RK, Jr's correspondence: "His experience of its valuable properties have induced him more than once to request to have some of it sent for his own use." TB to PB, April 27, 1836, Wister Family Papers, HSP.

15. In early 1822 a few letters from RK, Jr., were forwarded from Philadelphia to Saratoga Springs.

16. The letter from Frances Butler to RK, Jr., October 23, 1822, is among the papers of the Pennsylvania Abolition Society, HSP. See also Kemble, *Georgian Journal,* pp. 190–91, in which FK mistakenly writes that Abraham had purchased his freedom. Her authority was Abraham's grandson, also called Abraham, and a carpenter at Hampton in 1839.

17. RK, Jr., to Frances Butler, June 25 and August 10, 1823, Wister Family Papers, HSP. Although FB approved the transaction in a letter to RK, Jr., November 3, 1823, Hannah and her family remained on the plantation rolls as property of the Butler estate. An 1849 list shows Hannah, aged 53, Sawney 32, Gorham 26, John 30, and five new children born to her in the interim. The letter is in the Wister Family Papers, and the 1849 list is the "Appraisement" for John Butler's estate in the Butler Family Papers, HSP.

18. RK, Jr., to Frances Butler, December 15 and December 28, 1823, Wister Family Papers, HSP.

19. The death of Thomas Mease is noted in many family papers, including the McLanahan compilation, Cate Collection, GHS. Invoices for Anne Butler's funeral are among the Butler Family Papers, HSP. In late 1837 or early 1838 her body was brought to Philadelphia from Paris and placed in the Thomas Butler tomb in the Christ Church yard. *DNB*, s.v. "Butler, Weeden." The sawmill, *Darien Gazette*, June ?, 1823.

20. RK, Jr., to Frances Butler, February 8, 1824, H. E. Drayton Collection, HSP.

21. RK, Jr., to Frances Butler, March 7 and May 16, 1824, Wister Family Papers, HSP. As did his father, RK, Jr., spells it "gits."

22. RK, Jr., to Frances Butler, May 30, 1824, Wister Family Papers, HSP. Presley, ed., *Dr. Bullie's Notes*, pp. 36, 150. RK, Jr., had mixed opinions on the value of physicians on slave plantations (Furnas, *Fanny Kemble*, p. 460 n. 27).

23. RK to Frances Butler, July 11, 1824, Wister Family Papers, HSP.

24. RK, Jr., to Thomas Butler, September 15 and 19, 1824, Wister Family Papers, HSP.

25. TB's letters to his sister Sarah, May 25 and 26, 1825, H. E. Drayton Collection, HSP. PB's letter to his children, June 2, 1796, Wister Family Papers, HSP. For John McQueen's refuge in Florida, see Hartridge, ed., *The Letters of Don Juan McQueen*, pp. xxvii–xxx.

26. The document showing the change of name is dated February 13, 1826, and was witnessed by Charles Ingersoll, H. D. Gilpin, and *John Mease*, who had not changed to Butler (Butler Family Papers, HSP). See chapter 12, "Second Generation: The Butlers."

27. The Stewart list and appraisal, February 4, 1829; the Sergeant legal opinion; TB to his nephew PB, April 27, 1836; Louis Butler notes; all in the Wister Family Papers, HSP.

28. RK, Jr., to TB, October 16, 1825, Wister Family Papers, HSP. The Julia King Papers, Midway Museum, Midway, Ga. Myers, ed., *Children of Pride*, pp. 1582, 1583.

29. An undated clipping from the *Savannah Morning News* reprinting an article, circa 1924, from the *Atlanta Constitution*, in Gamble, *Scrapbooks* 1:57, SPL. Julia King Papers, Midway Museum, Midway, Ga. Myers, ed., *Children of Pride*,

p. 1579. WPA, *Georgia: A Guide*, pp. 386–88. Martin, *The Presbyterian Church of Roswell*, pp. 16–17.

30. King Family Register, Julia King Papers, Midway Museum, Midway, Ga. Indenture of June 2, 1828, between James Hamilton and the PB estate, Cate Collection, GHS. See also deed book H, June 2, 1828, p. 112, Glynn County, Brunswick, Ga.

31. RK, Jr., to TB, March 8, 1829, Wister Family Papers, HSP.

32. The McLanahan compilation, Cate Collection, GHS. PB's first namesake, who died of burns in the Revolution, the grandson PB Mease, and PB King, the son of RK. Although John Mease had not changed his name to Butler, his son was buried at Pere LaChaise as "Pierce Butler, Junior." See LeRoy, "Americans Buried in Pere LaChaise, Paris," p. 251.

33. Sarah Mease's will is on file with Philadelphia's Register of Wills, 154, book 10, p. 155.

34. PB deeded to his brother John a one-half interest in all that he had received from his grandfather's estate. The deed, dated December 1, 1831, is recorded in Philadelphia's City Hall. It is described in a 1833 outline of a contemplated will by PB (Wister Family Papers, HSP).

35. Francis Henry Fitzhardinge Berkeley (New York) to PB, September 23, 1832, Wister Family Papers, HSP. Kemble, *Records of a Girlhood*, p. 590.

36. TB purchased land from A. M. McGregor, William C. Gibbs, and David King, agreed to an exchange of a small strip of land with Henry Middleton, and also acquired land from Henry Schroeder, Jr., who represented him in the planting of trees and the construction of the contemplated house. It was Schroeder who said the Balm of Gileads originated in Scotland. They were purchased from William Prince and Son, Linnaean Botanic Garden and Nurseries, Flushing, New York (H. E. Drayton Collection, HSP).

37. RK, Jr., to Frances Butler, May 17, 1835, Wister Family Papers, HSP. Cotton fields experience a "heavy blow" when many bolls open at once.

38. RK, Jr., to Frances Butler, August 9, 1835, Wister Family Papers, HSP.

39. Frances Butler chose Gustavus Colhoun to succeed her as executor of PB's estate in a document of January 28, 1827. He qualified, following her death, on April 2, 1836. She officially noted the change of name from "Butler Mease" to "Pierce Butler" on February 13, 1826, in a document of August 19, 1833. Her will was signed August 25, 1826. TB qualified as her executor on April 18, 1836. All in the H. E. Drayton Collection, HSP. The complimentary letter from TB to RK, Jr., April 9, 1838, was saved by the King family in the Julia King Papers, Midway Museum, Midway, Ga.

40. The deaths of Eliza de Mallevault Butler, of Francis Butler, and of Madame Louis de Mallevault are noted in letters of TB to his son Louis in Paris, March 30, 1836, and others cited hereafter.

41. TB to Louis Butler (Paris), January 19, 1838, Wister Family Papers, HSP.

42. Thomas Butler's house on Walnut and Thirteenth streets became the Philadelphia Club in 1850. It is described in Fisher, *Recollections,* pp. 267–69. See also chapter 18, "The Weeping Time."

43. Thomas Butler's memorandum of Butler estate procedures and unfinished business, with its appraisal of the merits of the two Roswell Kings, is in his hand, dated April 27, 1836, but is unsigned, and though intended for the new Pierce Butler, is not so addressed. It covers five legal-sized pages (Wister Family Papers, HSP).

44. TB to Louis Butler (Paris), February 27, 1837, Wister Family Papers, HSP. In the margin of the letter, which is the original and not a retained copy, some-one—Louis?—has penned, "What damned Humbug!"

45. TB to Louis Butler (Paris), January 19, 1838, Wister Family Papers, HSP. On May 15, 1837, TB applied to the Vestry of Christ Church for the purchase of ground in the church yard for a burial vault. The Vestry offered a square of twelve feet for two thousand dollars, an offer declined by TB, who asked to be charged a lower price in accordance with church by-laws. He was. Minutes of Christ Church Vestry, May 15 and 19, 1837, Christ Church, Philadelphia. Fisher recounts the story of the stove, surely used only for drying the tomb after construction (*Recollections,* p. 265).

46. Thomas Butler's will and codicils are on record with the Register of Wills, Philadelphia. A copy is on file in Newport County Probate Records, book 12, pp. 51–57, at the Newport Historical Society. George Butler and other Butlers before and after are told of in Lord Dunboyne's report, (*JBS* 2, no. 1). Sidney George Fisher, the Philadelphia diarist, said TB's doctor, John Rhea Barton, was "a vulgar man, with talents, but a commonplace, limited mind & no culture either as a gentlemen or a scholar." SGF noted with some envy that Dr. Barton's first wife had been worth $150,000; his second, "a million." The second wife was Susan Ridgway, the widow of Thomas Rotch and the sister of Mrs. James Rush. See Wainwright, ed., *A Philadelphia Perspective,* p. 183. The microfilm records of Christ Church, November 22, 1838, show the arrangement made for the care of the tomb, the annuity paying sixty dollars annually. Later, Louis Butler paid the church one thousand dollars for perpetual care in lieu of the annuity (Wister Family Papers, HSP). Thomas Butler's Chestnut Street house was his residence, number 309, above 10th Street. John Butler was treated as though he were a son of someone other than Thomas.

47. The usual attestation by witnesses is attached to the copy of TB's will on file in Newport County.

48. PB to John Butler, March 27, 1837, the 1837 Letterbook, Butler Family Papers, HSP; and the same source for the several documents pertaining to the dispute between the Kings and the estate of Frances Butler. George J. Kollock of

Savannah represented the estate. See chapter 15, "Enter Fanny Kemble." Fisher tells of the vault filling with water (*Recollections*, p. 265).

Chapter 15. *Enter Fanny Kemble*

1. Gibbs, *Affectionately Yours, Fanny*, p. 123.
2. Ibid., p. 65; the *Athenaeum* critic was writing of FK's Juliet.
3. Nevins, ed., *The Diary of Philip Hone*, p. 27. Hone, after being kind to FK, became a victim of her indiscretion in the American *Journal*. As FK wrote favorable words on Hone's beautiful daughter, he was forgiving and some years later received apologies from FKB. See his *Diary*, pp. 144–45, 340.
4. Fanny Kemble Wister, *Fanny: The American Kemble*, p. 124.
5. Thomas Butler to Weeden Butler, September 29, 1796, WB Correspondence, British Library. "If anyone steps into Mr. Fozzard's riding school, they will have the goodness to remember me to him" (Kemble, *Records of a Girlhood*, pp. 232–33).
6. J. C. Furnas, the author of *Fanny Kemble*, is a latter-day "Kembler," so-called by a Scottish friend (JCF to MB, Jr., February 14, 1982).
7. A "Bond by Doctor Andrew Combe in Favor of Frances Anne Kemble, March 26, 1829," Owen Wister Papers, Library of Congress. See also Fanny Kemble Wister, *Fanny: The American Kemble*, p. 30.
8. Furnas, *Fanny Kemble*, pp. 456–57 n. 45.
9. Kemble, *Records of a Girlhood*, p. 231.
10. Fanny Kemble Wister, *Fanny: The American Kemble*, pp. 139–40.
11. Kemble, American *Journal*, 1:241, November 5, 1832.
12. John Mitchell Kemble to FK, October 13, 1833, "Letters to and from Fanny Kemble," Folger Library, WB 596–599.
13. Kemble, Georgian *Journal*, p. 138.
14. Deborah Norris Logan Diaries, vol. 15, 1834–1836, and vol. 17, 1838–1839, HSP.
15. *Niles Weekly Register*, August 1, 1835, p. 379, and August 8, 1835, p. 395.
16. Wilson, ed., *The Greville Diary*, 2:546.
17. The *Mirror* criticism, June 1835, is from Amelia M. Watson's "Kemble Collection," Lenox Library, Lenox, Massachusetts.
18. Kemble, American *Journal*, 1:74.
19. Ibid., 1:120.
20. Ibid., 1:129.
21. Ibid., 1:177.
22. Ibid., 2:136.
23. Ibid., 1:192.

24. F. H. F. Berkeley to PB, September 23, 1832, Wister Family Papers, HSP. "The O'Neil" was the Irish actress Eliza O'Neill, who retired from the stage on becoming Lady Eliza Becher, wife of William Wrixon Becher, Irish member of Parliament for Mallow.

25. A handwritten addition to Fanny Kemble's American *Journal* in the Brander Matthews Dramatic Museum, Columbia University, in which she has filled in names for the spaces left blank in the published editions. See Fanny Kemble Wister, *Fanny: The American Kemble,* pp. 98–99.

26. *DNB,* s.v. Berkeley, Francis Henry Fitzhardinge.

27. Fanny Kemble Wister, *Fanny: The American Kemble,* pp. 118–21. Dr. Channing believed that should the slave "feel that liberty has been wrung from an unwilling master who would replace the chain, and jealousy, vindictiveness and hatred would spring up" (*Slavery,* p. 129).

28. LMC to Ellis Gray and Louisa Loring, December 5, 1838, in Meltzer and Holland, eds., *Lydia Maria Child: Selected Correspondence,* pp. 95–96.

29. Kemble, *Records of a Later Life,* pp. 21–22, 29–31. Fifty years later, when *Later Life* was published, FK reflected on what she had written in the 1830s: "Those (Ideas and expectations) in the state of Alabama were not only ridiculously impossible, but would speedily have found their only result in the ruin, danger, and very probably death of all concerned in the endeavor." She added that to the Butler family she must have appeared a "mischievous mad-woman."

30. Ibid., pp. 21, 42.

31. Ibid., p. 41.

32. PB to John Butler, March 27, 1837, the 1837 Letterbook, Butler Family Papers, HSP.

33. PB to RK, July 25, 1838: "We therefore decline your request regarding the ten thousand dollars"; PB to Ralph King, March 10, 1839; both in the Wister Family Papers, HSP. The Kollock-King accounts were recorded in Chatham County, Savannah, and are also in the Butler Family Papers, HSP. The money received from the Kings was paid to William Drayton, Trustee for Louis Butler, son of Thomas Butler, the inheritor of Frances Butler, H. E. Drayton Collection, HSP.

34. PB represented the Philadelphia Unitarian Society at the Harrisburg convention, where he voted for the proposal to require all electors to be "white." He was opposed to the Unitarians becoming involved with abolitionists. See Geffen, "William Henry Furness, Philadelphia Antislavery Preacher," pp. 269, 271–72. FKB to Harriet St. Leger (near Dublin), November 14, 1837, in Kemble, *Records of a Later Life,* p. 71. FK to Arthur Malkin, whose home, Glen Falloch, in the Scottish highlands, appealed to her, August 30, 1868, in Kemble, *Further Records,* p. 346: "I am writing to you now in the room where my children were born—*my room,* as it is once more called."

35. Kemble, *Records of a Later Life,* p. 103. FKB to Mrs. Henry Cleveland, May 28, 1838, in Fanny Kemble Wister, *Fanny: The American Kemble,* p. 158.

36. Fanny Kemball Wister, *Fanny: The American Kemble,* p. 151.

37. Kemble, Georgian *Journal,* pp. 36, 42. *Charleston Mercury,* December 25 and 27, 1838. PB to John Butler, December 29, 1838, Wister Family Papers, HSP.

38. Kemble, Georgian *Journal,* p. 46. Kemble, *Records of a Later Life,* p. 132.

Chapter 16. *Negroland*

The lines introducing this chapter are from John Steinbeck's *Travels with Charley,* p. 245.

1. Kemble, Georgian *Journal,* p. 53.

2. Kemble, *Records of a Later Life,* pp. 203–5.

3. PB to Roger Parker Saunders, September 5, 1791, PB Letterbook, 1790–1794, SCL.

4. FKB to Mrs. Henry Cleveland, January 15, 1839, in Fanny Kemble Wister, *Fanny: The American Kemble,* p. 164.

5. Kemble, Georgian *Journal,* pp. 60–63, 84–85.

6. Ibid., pp. 87, 90, 144. Kemble, *Records of a Later Life,* pp. 134–35.

7. Kemble, *Records of a Later Life,* p. 134.

8. Two of the rice mills were some distance from the river landing. One was powered by horses, and a larger mill by water impounded on the flood tide, then released on the ebb. Kemble, *Records of a Later Life,* p. 137. Amelia M. Watson's "Kemble Collection," Lenox Library, Lenox, Massachusetts.

9. Kemble, *Records of a Later Life,* p. 137.

10. FKB used both "Missus" and "Missis" in the *Journal* and elsewhere. Kemble, Georgian *Journal,* pp. 99–100, 160–61.

11. Ibid., pp. 112, 215.

12. Ibid., p. 241.

13. Lyell, *A Second Visit,* 1:249.

14. Kemble, Georgian *Journal,* pp. 68–69.

15. Ibid., p. 162.

16. Ibid., p. 200.

17. Ibid., p. 256.

18. Ibid., pp. 68, 179, 114.

19. Ibid., pp. 229–31.

20. Ibid., pp. 363–64. The letter used as an appendix to the Georgian *Journal* was not submitted to the editor of the *Times.*

21. Ibid., pp. 287–88.

22. Ibid., pp. 283, 274.

23. Ibid., p. 266.

24. PB to RK, Jr., January 27, 1839, Wister Family Papers, HSP. Kemble, Georgian *Journal,* pp. 109, 112.

25. Kemble, Georgian *Journal,* p. 207.

26. Ibid., pp. 201, 176, 249–50, 113, 273–74, 269. None were more disturbed by FK's plantation *Journal* than the family of the Roswell Kings. The revelation of the mulatto children of the two Kings and FK's designation of both as "overseers" caused the underlying hatred of FK shown in the many letters in the Julia King Papers at the Midway Museum and the GHS.

27. RK, Jr., to PB, March 23, 1839, Wister Family Papers, HSP.

28. Kemble, Georgian *Journal,* p. 212. To FKB the *Water Lily* was usually the *Lily.* The dramatic boat trip brought a late reaction from RK, Jr.'s granddaughter: "& another thing she did to shock the white population was to go on long distances, alone and unprotected with 9 negro men in a boat for 15 miles" (Julia King to Vara Majette, November 10, 1930, Julia King Papers, 1070, GHS).

29. Kemble, Georgian *Journal,* pp. 163, 260, 141–42, 259, 260.

30. Ibid., p. 87.

31. Ibid., pp. 89, 189, 252–53, 56, 241.

32. Fanny Kemble Wister, *Fanny: The American Kemble,* p. 151. Kemble, Georgian *Journal,* pp. 91–92, 396, 220–21, 285. Presley, ed., *Dr. Bullie's Notes,* pp. 150–54.

33. Kemble, Georgian *Journal,* pp. 78, 79, 93–94, 219–20, 141, 146–49, 162–64, 259–61.

34. Ibid., pp. 275, 246, 209–10, 278, 218, 268.

35. Julia King to Vara Majette, November 10, 1930, Julia King Papers, 1070, GHS.

36. PB to Ralph King, March 10, 1839; PB to John Butler, March 12, 1839; both in the Wister Family Papers, HSP.

37. PB to A. Marvin, Esq., and to James Smith, Esq., both letters March 19, 1839, Wister Family Papers, HSP.

38. Kemble, *Records of a Later Life,* p. 40.

39. Kemble, Georgian *Journal,* pp. 146–49, 359, 281, 124.

40. Mary Mann and Dora Jeanette Alexander of Darien to Amelia M. Watson, "Kemble Collection," Lenox Library, Lenox, Massachusetts.

41. Kemble, Georgian *Journal,* pp. 216–17.

Chapter 17. *Butler vs. Butler*

1. Wainwright, ed., *A Philadelphia Perspective,* p. 86.

2. Ibid., p. 100. Butler Place is described in Fanny Kemble Wister, *That I May Tell You,* pp. 205–14; Fanny Kemble Wister, *Owen Wister Out West,* pp. xi–xiii;

Fanny Kemble Wister, *Fanny: The American Kemble,* pp. 147–48; and Hotchkin, *The York Road, Old and New,* p. 56.

3. Pierce Butler, *Mr. Butler's Statement,* pp. 2, 40.

4. Kemble, *Records of a Later Life,* pp. 172–88.

5. The phrenological analysis is from the Combe Papers, National Library of Scotland, and was sent to the author by J. C. Furnas. See his *Fanny Kemble,* p. 123, FK to George Combe, March 20, 1835, in Fanny Kemble Wister, *Fanny: The American Kemble,* p. 150.

6. Kemble, *Records of a Later Life,* p. 205.

7. Fanny Kemble Wister, *Fanny: The American Kemble,* pp. 191–93. Constance Wright, *Fanny Kemble and the Lovely Land,* p. 153. FKB to Mrs. Joshua Francis Fisher, August 18, 1848, Joshua Francis Fisher Correspondence, Cadwalader Collection, 1454, HSP.

8. Kemble, *Records of a Later Life,* p. 216. Wilson, ed., *The Greville Diary,* 2:546–47.

9. Wainwright, ed., *A Philadelphia Perspective,* pp. 112–13.

10. The diary of Charlotte Wilcocks, September 14, 1842, 1853, HSP. Charlotte Wilcocks became Mrs. Harry McCall. "Ellen" was Ellen Kuhn. "Mr. Butler" could have been Pierce or John, although she often referred to the latter by his first name. See also Burt, *The Perennial Philadelphians,* p. 16.

11. Kemble, *Records of a Later Life,* pp. 191, 193–94, 248–69, 320–21, 325, 330. See chapter 12, "Second Generation Butlers."

12. Pierce Butler, *Mr. Butler's Statement,* pp. 15, 79. Fanny Kemble Wister, *Fanny: The American Kemble,* pp. 177–81. Kemble, *Records of a Later Life,* pp. 375, 379–83. FK did not use the travel portion in the published *Journal.*

13. Kemble, *Records of a Later Life,* pp. 372, 385, 417. Furnas, *Fanny Kemble,* pp. 276–83. Wainwright, ed., *A Philadelphia Perspective,* p. 168. Frances Anne Butler, *Poems.*

14. Wainwright, ed., *A Philadelphia Perspective,* p. 168.

15. Kemble, *Further Records,* p. 298.

16. Harrison, ed., *Philadelphia Merchant,* p. 400.

17. Kemble, *Records of a Later Life,* p. 416. *Pierce Butler vs. Frances Anne Butler,* Rare Book Room, Library of Congress.

18. Rebecca Gratz to Miriam Gratz Moses Cohen, September 13, 1845, Miriam Gratz Moses Papers, SHC.

19. Miriam Gratz Moses Commonplace book, June 21, 1834, Moses Papers, SHC. Miss Moses had read the poem that later appeared in the American *Journal* (1:33), lines from which read: "Oh night, and slumber, be ye visionless / Dark as the grave, deep as forgetfulness." The poem was inspired by FK's view of Venus, "the star of love," from shipboard enroute to America.

20. Rebecca Gratz to Miriam Cohen, February 24, 1846, dated 1845 in error, Moses Papers, SHC.

21. Ransome, ed., *The Terrific Kemble*, p. 170, the quotation from Erskine, ed., *Letters and Friendships: Anna Jameson*, p. 200. Kemble, *A Year of Consolation*, p. 170.

22. Harrison, ed., *Philadelphia Merchant*, "Pennsylvania Correspondent," HSP. Newsletter, September 1982.

23. Kemble, *Records of a Later Life*, pp. 330, 474.

24. Ibid., pp. 488–89, 490, 474, 519, 653, 657. The Highgate reading was to intimate friends. Fanny Kemble Wister, *Fanny: The American Kemble*, p. 200. Gibbs, *Affectionately Yours, Fanny*, p. 170. Kemble, *Further Records*, p. 287. *Butler vs. Butler*, Library of Congress.

25. S. B. H. Vance to PB, December 24, 1847, the 1843–1846 Letterbook of PB, Wister Family Papers, HSP.

26. Entry for January 18, 1848, diary of Joshua Francis Fisher, Collection 1664, HSP.

27. Wainwright, ed., *A Philadelphia Perspective*, p. 204.

28. The former slave was Celia Davis of Darien, then over ninety years old. She was interviewed by Amelia M. Watson, "Kemble Collection," Lenox Library.

29. Wainwright, ed., *A Philadelphia Perspective*, pp. 112–13. The will of John Butler and documents pertaining to his estate are on file in Chatham County, Savannah, file 257. The will is twenty-four pages, capitalized and punctuated haphazardly. It was signed in Philadelphia on November 23, 1842.

30. The McLanahan genealogical compilation, Cate Collection, GHS. The McAllister volume, Gamble, *Scrapbooks*, Savannah Public Library.

31. Curtis, "A Century of Grand Opera in Philadelphia," p. 45.

32. FKB to Mrs. Charles Sedgwick, May 8, 1848; FKB to Samuel Gray Ward, undated; both letters in Fanny Kemble Wister, *Fanny: The American Kemble*, pp. 200–201, 204.

33. Wainwright, ed., *A Philadelphia Perspective*, p. 210.

34. Rebecca Gratz to Ann Boswell Gratz, September 15, 1848, in Philipson, ed., *Letters of Rebecca Gratz*, pp. 351–52.

35. Wainwright, "*Butler v. Butler*: A Divorce Case Incident," pp. 101–8. Bobbe, *Fanny Kemble*, pp. 240–41. Driver, *Fanny Kemble*, p. 132. Constance Wright, *Fanny Kemble and the Lovely Land*, p. 132. Fanny Kemble Wister, *Fanny: The American Kemble*, pp. 203–4.

36. Pierce Butler, *Mr. Butler's Statement*, pp. 13, 18.

37. *Butler vs. Butler*, Library of Congress.

38. Ibid. Pierce Butler, *Mr. Butler's Statement*. For the Schott affair, see Furnas, *Fanny Kemble*, pp. 274–75; Fanny Kemble Wister, *Fanny: The American Kemble*, pp. 190–91; Wainwright, ed., *A Philadelphia Perspective*, pp. 161–62.

39. Fanny Kemble Wister, *Fanny: The American Kemble*, pp. 191–93. FKB to Mrs. Joshua Francis Fisher, August 18, 1848, Fisher Correspondence, Cadwalader Collection, 1454, HSP.

40. Pierce Butler, *Mr. Butler's Statement*. Fanny Kemble Wister, *Fanny: The American Kemble*, pp. 166–67, 187, 206.

41. See Quincy, "Journal, 1773," in chapter 5, "Pierce Butler's Public Life, 1776–1789," and Genovese, *Roll, Jordan, Roll*, pp. 67, 426–27, showing Mary Boykin Chesnut to have tied ownership of slaves to immorality in *A Diary from Dixie*, pp. 21–22, 44, 122.

42. The agreement to pay FKB fifteen hundred dollars and the attendant mortgage on Butler Place, Butler Family Papers, HSP. The payments for the American *Journal*, Frances Anne Kemble Papers, 79-28423, Library of Congress. John Murray to FKB, May 16, 1835, "Letters to and from Fanny Kemble," WB 596-599, Folger Library, Washington.

43. Gibbs, *Affectionately Yours, Fanny*, p. 175.

Chapter 18. *The Weeping Time*

The lines introducing this chapter are from Geraldine Provence's letter to the editor, March 6, 1977, *Savannah Morning News*, in which she took issue with a reader's belief that many slave owners treated slaves in a humane fashion.

1. Nevins, ed., *Diary of Philip Hone*, pp. 144–47, 339–41, 871–72.

2. Butler Family Papers, HSP.

3. Inventory and Appraisement, Estate of Captain John Butler, Butler Family Papers, HSP.

4. *The Georgian*, Savannah, April 23, 1849, Couper Collection, box 171, GHS.

5. Fisher, *Recollections*, p. 265.

6. Wister Family Papers, HSP.

7. J. Francis Fisher to FK, July 21, 1851, Frances Anne Kemble Papers, Library of Congress. *Mr. Butler's Statement* was privately printed in Philadelphia in 1850. In the bound copy in the Butler Family Papers, HSP, is a notation in Sarah Butler Wister's hand, "Seen & read by me for the first time September 25, 1890—PB's ob. Aug 16/67—'Let them rave.'" There were no further notations. PB to Alleyne Otis, Boston, October 18, 1851, Boston *Athenaeum*.

8. The Philadelphia Club was founded in 1834. In 1934 the club published a commemorative volume in honor of the first century. Called *The Philadelphia Club*, the volume recounted club history and listed members. Other than PB and JB, members included Julian McAllister (1850–1858), Owen Jones Wister (1873–1876), and Owen Wister, long a member, president in 1933, and responsible for the anniversary volume. George Chapman performed the "uncommon feat." The club continues at Walnut and Thirteenth streets in the Thomas Butler house.

9. PB to Alexander Blue, September 5, 1853, Wister Family Papers, HSP. The

reason for Glasgow's "unusually severe punishment" in 1839 was unknown to FKB (Kemble, Georgian *Journal*, p. 275).

10. Inventory and Appraisement, Estate of Captain John Butler, Butler Family Papers, HSP.

11. Indenture of August 24, 1853, John Stoddard and Francis S. Bartow, Executors William Henry Mongin to Pierce Butler individually, and to Butler and James as Trustees for Gabriella M. Butler and Elizabeth McAllister, McIntosh County, Darien, Georgia, deed book A, pp. 454–57.

12. Myers, ed., *Children of Pride*, pp. 69–70, 83, 1582–1583, 1584. The estates of Roswell King, Jr., and Mrs. King, Julia King Papers, Midway Museum.

13. PB to Louis Butler, October 6, 1854, Wister Family Papers, HSP.

14. Eliza Anne Butler's will, Register of Wills, Philadelphia, book 34, 367, 1855.

15. John Butler's will, Chatham County, Savannah, 257.

16. Gibbs, *Affectionately Yours, Fanny*, pp. 32, 177.

17. Kemble, *Further Records*, p. 323.

18. Westcott, *Scrapbooks: Biographies of Philadelphia*, vol 2, part 2, pp. 194–95, HSP. *Philadelphia Sunday Dispatch*, March 13, 1859, an account of the sale of PB's slaves in Savannah that gave background information on their owner. Tyng, *Our Country's Troubles*. Tyng, *A Statement to the Congregation*. Cuyler's discourse, *New York Evening Post*, April 27, 1856.

19. Wainwright, ed., *A Philadelphia Perspective*, p. 264. The "sporting gentleman" is from Wainwright's Fisher Diary in *PMHB* 86 (1962): 461 n. 9. FK to J. Francis Fisher, December 12, 1858, Frances Anne Kemble Papers, 79-28453, Library of Congress.

20. Elizabeth Ingersoll Fisher to SGF, November 17, 1856, Sidney George Fisher Collection, 2026, HSP.

21. "Chestnut Street, 6th to 9th," Jane Campbell Collection, 12, HSP. Photograph in Looney, *Old Philadelphia in Early Photographs*, p. 132. *Philadelphia Bulletin*, August 22, 1922, showing photograph with theatrical posters. January 1859 correspondence between FK and J. Francis Fisher showing PB's dereliction and the thought of transferring the mortgage on Butler Place, Frances Anne Kemble Papers, 79-28423, Library of Congress.

22. *Southern Literary Messenger* 28 (January 1859): 74–75.

23. Rebecca Gratz to Benjamin Gratz, March 25, 1856, Philipson, ed., *Letters of Rebecca Gratz*, p. 400. Sarah Butler and Dr. Wister were married October 1, 1859. Montmollin lost his life when the boiler of the *John G. Lawton* exploded (Myers, ed., *Children of Pride*, p. 1627). The John Brown poem is from the Owen Wister Papers in the Library of Congress. Lydia Maria Child wrote that FK was critical of John Brown for "inciting insurrection." See Meltzer and Holland, eds., *Lydia Maria Child: Selected Correspondence*, pp. 340–41.

24. Lawrence, *James Moore Wayne*, pp. 161–67.

25. *Savannah Daily Morning News,* February 5, 1859.

26. Myers, ed., *Children of Pride,* pp. 1701, 1588. Lawrence, *James Moore Wayne,* pp. 161–67.

27. Wainwright, ed., *A Philadelphia Perspective,* pp. 278, 310, 317. Gabriella Butler paid PB six hundred dollars on January 1, 1858, and one thousand dollars on January 1 in 1859 and 1860, the annual rent for Butler Place.

28. Entry for February 23, 1859, John Berkley Grimball Diary, 3. Cornelia Grayson (JBG spells it Gracen) had two sisters adopted by Mrs. Heyward Manigault, entry for January 7, 1859, in the Grimball Diary. See also "Diary of John Berkley Grimball," *SCHM* 56 (1955).

29. The documents pertaining to the division of slaves are recorded in Superior Court, Chatham County, Savannah, deed book 3-S, pp. 247–55; and in Glynn County, Brunswick, deed book N, pp. 52–71. See also the abbreviated copy, Wister Family Papers, HSP. Kemble, Georgian *Journal,* pp. 176 n. 249–50, 238.

30. Inventory and Appraisement, Estate of Captain John Butler, Butler Family Papers, HSP. The 1859 appraisal, deed book 3-S, pp. 247–55, Superior Court, Chatham County, Savannah. As the 1859 appraisal does not include the values of slaves allotted to Pierce Butler, a comparison of estimated values and actual sales prices is not available. See chapter 26, "Lady Baltimore," on Alexander and Daphne. Quash's name "Crabclaw" may have come from a belief in sorcery, for the claw of a crab is often used as a charm. See DuBose Heyward on Denmark Vesey's Gullah Jack "going to his death clutching to the last the charmed crabclaw which was supposed to render him invulnerable to the hostile magic of the white man" ("The Negro in the Low Country," pp. 181–82).

31. *Savannah Republican,* February 26, 1859. *Savannah Daily Morning News,* February 24, 1859.

32. *Savannah Daily Morning News,* February 26, 1859.

33. Ibid., March 4, 1859. The correct average price was $688.54.

34. Ibid., March 15, 1859.

35. *Savannah Republican,* March 3 and 15, 1859. The *Republican* put a *p* in Thomson.

36. *DNB,* s.v. "Thomson, Mortimer Neal."

37. The "Doesticks" article first appeared in the *New York Daily Tribune* on March 9, 1859, and was reprinted in the *New York Semi-Weekly Tribune* on March 11, 1859. The *Times* of London ran a shortened version on April 12, 1859. In 1863 FK's Georgian *Journal* again focused attention on the Butler plantations, prompting a reappearance of the article in pamphlet form as *What Became of the Slaves on a Georgia Plantation?* This pamphlet was called "A Sequel to Mrs. Kemble's Journal." The racecourse in Savannah was named for Richard Ten Broeck of Albany, New York, who owned the great Kentucky horse "Lexington." To Savannahians, the racecourse was usually "Tenbroeck." Wright, *Fanny Kemble and the Lovely Land,* quotes Colonel Robert Gould Shaw, who

visited Hampton while his regiment was on St. Simons Island during the Civil War. Old Butler blacks spoke of the Savannah sale as the "weeping time" (p. 169). Shaw wrote his mother from St. Simons on June 13, 1863, and referred to the sale as a "weeping day" (Wister Family Papers, HSP).

38. The short piece from the *Argus* of Philadelphia was carried in the *Charleston Mercury* on March 24, 1859. The *Mercury* also reprinted stories on the sale of the slaves from the *Daily Morning News.*

39. Cheever's sermons were reported in the *New York Daily News* on March 21 and 29, 1859.

40. FK may have been in New York on March 9, 1859, although she was living in Philadelphia at 1113 Walnut Street, a boarding house (Kemble, *Further Records,* pp. 326, 366). The "domestic calamity" quotation is from an undated letter from FK to J. Francis Fisher, Frances Anne Kemble Collection, 79-28423, Library of Congress.

Chapter 19.
The Dogs of Civil War

1. The "Southern Europe" quotation appeared in an undated letter from FK to J. Francis Fisher, Frances Anne Kemble Collection, 79-28423, Library of Congress. In 1860 PB purchased five certificates at fifteen dollars each for admission to Hlasko's Institute. The unnamed music student was "a handsome, clever girl" who wrote her recollection of PB nearly fifty years after she had known him. Her unsigned letter of May 26, 1908, to Georgina Schuyler was sent on to Owen Wister, Butler Family Papers, HSP.

2. PB's financial statement, August 11, 1860, Butler Family Papers, HSP. The debt to the John Butler estate was secured by a mortgage on PB's interest in Butler's Island, Hampton, General's Island, and other properties, and was recorded in deed book N, p. 144, Glynn County, Brunswick.

3. Georgia King to Thomas Butler King, December 11, 1859, Thomas Butler King Collection, 1252A, SHC. The Pierce Butler family and the Thomas Butler Kings claimed no kinship, nor did the Roswell King family.

4. FK to Arthur Malkin, May 8, 1860, in Kemble, *Further Records,* p. 331.

5. Wainwright, ed., *A Philadelphia Perspective,* p. 356. Sarah Wister wanted the boy named for his father. Dr. Wister preferred he be named for his great-grandfather Daniel Wister (Fanny Kemble Wister, *That I May Tell You,* p. 71 n. 2).

6. Wainwright, ed., *A Philadelphia Perspective,* p. 360.

7. "Sarah Butler Wister's Civil War Diary" was first published in *PMHB* 52 (1978), by her granddaughter, Fanny Kemble Wister (Mrs. Walter Stokes). It was also published as "Sarah B. Wister's Civil War Journal" in Fanny Kemble Wister,

That I May Tell You; see p. 32, April 24, 1861. Both published versions have a few omissions from the original journal in the Wister Family Papers, HSP.

8. Wainwright, ed., *A Philadelphia Perspective,* p. 375.

9. PB to Miss Frances Anne Butler (Fanny or Fan), January 7, 1861, Wister Family Papers, HSP.

10. "Butler vs. James and Butler," *Supreme Court of Georgia,* Savannah, January term 1862, pp. 148–52.

11. Fanny Kemble Wister, *That I May Tell You,* pp. 70–71, 39. In 1889 Sarah Wister annotated her original Civil War journal with explanatory notes penned in the margins. The reference to the English children was such an annotation.

12. PB to Pierce Butler Holmes, January 1, 1861, Owen Wister Papers, Library of Congress. Wainwright, ed., *A Philadelphia Perspective,* p. 400 n. 29. Joshua Francis Fisher was a first cousin of Sidney George Fisher. His wife, Elizabeth Middleton, was related to the Butlers through PB's grandmother, Mary Middleton Butler.

13. Fanny Kemble Wister, *That I May Tell You,* p. 24.

14. Ibid., p. 35.

15. Ibid., pp. 25, 28, 38, 47. Henry Lord Page King (Lordy) was killed at Fredericksburg on December 13, 1862. "He fell pierced by five balls"; his body was retrieved from the battlefield and returned to St. Simons by his servant and slave, Neptune. See Cate, *Our Todays and Yesterdays,* pp. 156, 277.

16. Fanny Kemble Wister, *That I May Tell You,* p. 34.

17. PB to Charles Henry Fisher, August 17, 1861, Wister Family Papers, HSP. See chapter 17, "Butler vs. Butler."

18. The McLanahan Genealogical Compilation, Cate Collection, GHS. Ward McAllister's social presence was much in evidence in the 1860s. For "Wardy," see Elliott, *This Was My Newport,* p. 42. The entry in Sarah Wister's journal is from the original, Wister Family Papers, HSP.

19. *ORUCA,* series 2, vol. 2, p. 505.

20. Scharf and Westcott, *History of Philadelphia,* 1:777.

21. Wainwright, ed., *A Philadelphia Perspective,* p. 400.

22. Fanny Kemble Wister, *That I May Tell You,* pp. 62–63.

23. Ibid., pp. 63, 64. *ORUCA,* series 2, vol. 2, pp. 505–6. Henry Fisher, like his client PB, had financial troubles. Sarah Wister told of his failure: "Stocks fell to 0, his notes have come due, & he is broken" (Fanny Kemble Wister, *That I May Tell You,* p. 38). SGF wrote at length of his brother's financial affairs, but said the estate would "turn out $400,000" after compromising obligations of $500,000 (Wainwright, ed., *A Philadelphia Perspective,* pp. 419–26). Henry Fisher died on March 10, 1862.

24. Kemble, *Further Records,* p. 335.

25. Fanny Kemble Wister, *That I May Tell You,* pp. 62–63, 64.

26. *ORUCA*, series 2, vol. 2, p. 506. Wainwright, ed., *A Philadelphia Perspective*, p. 405, September 23, 1861.

27. *ORUCA*, series 2, vol. 2, pp. 506–9.

28. Major Pierce Butler to Weeden Butler, May 30, 1789, WB Correspondence, British Library.

Chapter 20.
Yankee Vandals in the Low Country

1. *ORUCN*, series 1, vol. 6, pp. 313–14, 280–81.

2. *ORUCN*, series 1, vol. 12, pp. 220–21, 230–31. Captain Hamilton Couper, CSA, to Margaret Couper Stiles, September 7, 1861, the Couper Collection, Museum of Coastal History, St. Simons Island. Captain Couper was killed at Manassas on November 8, 1861. He is buried in the cemetery of Christ Church, Frederica, on St. Simons. His marker bears the inscription "Literary by taste and culture he became a soldier from sense of duty." Cate, *Our Todays and Yesterdays*, p. 276. Hamilton plantation is near the southern end of St. Simons, on the river side of the island. It is now "Epworth By the Sea."

3. *ORUCN*, series 1, vol. 12, pp. 221, 262–65, 336.

4. Lusk, *War Letters*, pp. 107–8, 129. The Lusk volume contains excerpts from Stevens, *The Life of Isaac Ingalls Stevens*, p. 353.

5. Ibid., pp. 97, 101, Captain William Thompson Lusk to his mother, from Hilton Head, November 9 and 13, 1861.

6. Higginson, *Army Life in a Black Regiment*, p. 52. *ORUCN*, I, 12, pp. 349–50.

7. *ORUCN*, series 1, vol. 12, pp. 293, 388. Quarles, *The Negro in the Civil War*, p. 70.

8. *ORUCN*, series 1, vol. 12, p. 338.

9. Ibid., p. 339.

10. Roswell King to Major Pierce Butler, February 12, 1815, Butler Family Papers, HSP. *ORUCN*, series 1, vol. 12, pp. 210, 221. Litwack, *Been in the Storm So Long*, p. 52.

11. *ORUCN*, series 1, vol. 12, pp. 388, 536, 542. *Harper's Weekly*, December 21, 1861, p. 801.

12. Lusk, *War Letters*, p. 129, an excerpt from Stevens, *The Life of Isaac Ingalls Stevens*, p. 369.

13. *Savannah Daily Morning News*, April 23, 1862.

14. Heard, "St. Simons Island During the War Between the States," pp. 249–72. *ORUCN*, series 1, vol. 12, p. 487. Leigh, *Other Days*, p. 144.

15. *ORUCN*, series 1, vol. 12, p. 345.

16. Ibid., pp. 581, 613–15, 590. Heard, "St. Simons Island During the War Between the States," pp. 253, 255. An undated letter prior to October 21, 1861, from Hugh Fraser Grant, in House, *Planter Management*, p. 291.

17. *ORUCN*, series 1, vol. 12, pp. 606, 614. Legare, "Excursion into Southern Georgia," p. 167.

18. *ORUCN*, series 1, vol. 12, p. 214.

19. Ibid., pp. 633–44. Heard, "St. Simons Island During the War Between the States," pp. 255–56.

20. Myers, ed., *Children of Pride*, pp. 1582–83, 1567, 928–30.

21. Ibid., pp. 934–35, 939–40.

22. Ibid., pp. 976, 978. *ORUCN*, series 1, vol. 12, p. 727. Heard, "St. Simons Island During the War Between the States," p. 258. Seth Rogers, "Letters," p. 354.

23. *ORUCN*, series 1, vol. 12, pp. 727, 756; vol. 13, pp. 20–21.

24. *ORUCN*, series 1, vol. 13, pp. 92, 143, 110.

25. Ibid., p. 5.

26. Ibid., pp. 21, 159.

27. Ibid., pp. 142–45. Commander Godon referred to Champney Island as "Barret's Island." Captain DuPont had visited the "contrabands" at their colony the month before. He called them "the blackies," and in his letter of May 22, 1862, to his wife said, "Pierce Butler has the credit of sending clothes longer than anybody else," indicating there must have been Butler people in the colony, or perhaps the clothes were part of the supplies mentioned by Commander Godon. See Hayes, ed., *DuPont Letters*, 2:71.

28. *ORUCN*, series 1, vol. 13, p. 144.

29. Ibid., pp. 244–45.

30. King, *Darien: The Death and Rebirth of a Southern Town*, p. 37. *ORUCN*, series 1, vol. 13, p. 439.

31. Higginson, *Army Life in a Black Regiment*, p. 213.

32. Seth Rogers, "Letters," pp. 394, 345.

33. *ORUCN*, series 1, vol. 14, pp. 150–51.

34. Ibid., p. 150. Heard, "St. Simons Island During the War Between the States," pp. 265–66. Leigh, *Ten Years on a Georgia Plantation*, p. 46.

35. Heard, "St. Simons Island During the War Between the States," p. 263. Higginson, *Army Life in a Black Regiment*, p. 53. Seth Rogers, "Letters," p. 348. *ORUCN*, series 1, vol. 13, p. 144.

36. Cornish, *The Sable Arm*, pp. 86, 148–56. A copy of an excerpt from a letter of Robert Gould Shaw to his mother, Sarah Shaw, from St. Simons, June 13, 1863, Wister Family Papers, HSP. Shaw and his parents visited the Sartoris family and FK in Italy in 1853.

37. *ORUCN*, series 1, vol. 14, pp. 318–19. *Savannah Daily Morning News*, June 16, 1863, excerpts of letters from Darien to Savannahians. Quarles, *The Negro in the Civil War*, p. 12.

38. Robert Gould Shaw to Sarah Shaw, June 13, 1863, from a copy, Wister Family Papers, HSP. See also, *Harper's Weekly,* September 3, 1870.

39. Robert Gould Shaw to Colonel Halpine, June 14, 1863, from a copy, Wister Family Papers, HSP.

40. Elizabeth Butler McAllister died in Newport on January 29, 1862. Her son Francis McAllister Butler died in 1863 (McLanahan genealogical compilation, Cate Collection, GHS). PB outlined the legal proceedings of the suit against Gabriella Butler, administratrix, in a letter of July 31, 1866, from Darien to P. C. Hollis, Wister Family Papers, HSP.

41. Presley, ed., *Dr. Bullie's Notes,* pp. 125–26. Actual casualties at Gettysburg were: Federal killed and wounded, 17,684; Confederate, 22,638 (Livermore, *Numbers and Losses,* pp. 102–3).

42. Cornish, *The Sable Arm,* pp. 148–56. Emilio, *The Assault on Fort Wagner,* microfilm, pages unnumbered, Library of Congress. Emilio was a captain in Shaw's regiment. He said Colonel Shaw's bearing throughout the attack was "composed and graceful." See also Higginson, *Army Life in a Black Regiment,* p. 176, and Quarles, *The Negro in the Civil War,* pp. 13–19. In 1876, when Massachusetts celebrated the centenary of 1776, Confederate veterans returned the battle flag of the Fifty-fourth Massachusetts, lost in the assault on Fort Wagner. It was an indication that one painful wound was healing (Hodding Carter, *Angry Scar,* p. 345).

43. *Harper's Weekly,* August 15, 1863. Burchard, *One Gallant Rush,* p. 142.

44. Wright, *Fanny Kemble and the Lovely Land,* p. 170. Dewey, *Life and Letters of Catharine M. Sedgwick,* pp. 393n, 396.

Chapter 21. *"Inevitable Sambo"*

The lines introducing this chapter are from the title page of Fanny Kemble's *Journal* of her stay on the Butler plantations. They were spoken on March 21, 1861, by Alexander Stephens, vice-president of the Confederate States of America.

1. Correspondence between Henry Greville and FK, letters 277-305, seldom dated, "Letters to and from Fanny Kemble, 1829–1890," manuscript, 4 vols., WB 596-599, Folger Library, Washington. Those quoted are early 1862 before FK left America to spend the war years in England. The "safety light" seen from the Hampton shore was the lighthouse on Sapelo Island across the Altamaha River entrance.

2. FK to Henry Greville, undated, ibid.

3. Fanny Kemble Wister, *That I May Tell You,* pp. 37, 44. Wainwright, ed., *A Philadelphia Perspective,* p. 470.

4. Kemble, *Records of a Later Life,* p. 205.

5. John Ruskin to Charles Eliot Norton, February 10, 1863, in Sideman and Friedman, eds., *Europe Looks at the Civil War,* pp. 217–18.

6. Diplomatic correspondence, 1864, ibid., pp. 254–56.

7. FitzGerald Ross diary, Charleston, September 1863, ibid., pp. 246–47.

8. Charles Darwin to Asa Gray, February 23, 1863, ibid., p. 224.

9. Thomas Henry Huxley to his sister, "Mrs Scott," May 5, 1864, ibid., pp. 258–59. Thomas Carlyle to David Conway, 1863–1864, ibid., p. 254.

10. Benjamin Disraeli to House of Commons, 1863, ibid., p. 233.

11. Kemble, Georgian *Journal,* pp. lxvii, 347–48, 369–83.

12. Lombard, "Contemporary Opinions of Mrs. Kemble's *Journal,*" pp. 335–43.

13. Kemble, *Records of a Later Life,* pp. 159–60. Kemble, Georgian *Journal,* p. lii.

14. Wainwright, ed., *A Philadelphia Perspective,* p. 456.

15. *New York Daily Tribune,* July 6, 1863.

16. *New York Times,* August 8, 1863. Roper, *FLO,* p. 115.

17. *Harper's Weekly,* July 18, 1863.

18. LMC to Oliver Johnson, before August 1863, in Meltzer and Holland, eds., *Lydia Maria Child: Selected Correspondence,* p. 435.

19. The Curtis review of FK's Georgian *Journal,* pp. 260–63.

20. Kemble, Georgian *Journal,* pp. 348–52.

21. In her Georgian *Journal,* pp. 292, 325–27, 332, FK tells of a conflict between Dr. Thomas Hazzard and John Wylly, both of St. Simons. Hazzard shot and killed Wylly in December 1838 before the Butlers arrived from Philadelphia. See Cate, "Mistakes in Fanny Kemble's Georgia Journal," in which Mrs. Cate casts doubt on the entire *Journal* because of this mistake and a lesser one. See also John Anthony Scott's comments in Kemble's Georgian *Journal,* p. lvi; Scott, "On the Authenticity of FK's Journal," *JNH* (October 1961); and Furnas, *Fanny Kemble,* pp. 398–99.

22. For the Hall, Lyell, Bremer, and Murray visits to the Altamaha plantations, see chapter 7, "The Altamaha Estuary."

23. Sherman, *Memoirs,* 2:227–28. Quarles, *The Negro in the Civil War,* p. 316.

24. Field order 119, November 8, 1864, in Sherman, *Memoirs,* 2:174.

25. Field order 120, November 9, 1864, ibid., 2:175. Gray, "The March to the Sea," p. 119. Winther, ed., *Theodore Upson: With Sherman to the Sea,* p. 136.

26. Quarles, *The Negro in the Civil War,* p. 317. *ORUCA,* series 1, vol. 44, p. 159, 836.

27. *ORUCA,* series 1, vol. 44, pp. 211–12.

28. Cox, *March to the Sea,* pp. 37–38.

29. "Report of General Joseph Wheeler, CSA," *ORUCA,* series 1, vol. 44, p. 410. Dodson, ed., *Campaigns of Wheeler,* p. 301.

30. Genovese, *Roll Jordan, Roll,* p. 154. Litwack, *Been in the Storm So Long,* p. 125.

31. *ORUCA,* series 1, vol. 44, pp. 787, 819. *ORUCA,* series 1, vol. 47, part 2, p. 210.

32. *ORUCA,* series 1, vol. 44, pp. 836–37.

33. *ORUCA,* series 1, vol. 47, part 2, pp. 36–37.

34. Ibid., pp. 37–41. Sherman, *Memoirs,* 2:244.

35. Sherman, *Memoirs,* 2:247.

36. Special field order 15, January 16, 1865. Ibid., pp. 250–52.

37. Ibid., p. 249.

38. Fanny Kemble Wister, *That I May Tell You,* p. 73.

39. Butler Family Papers, HSP. Furnas, *Fanny Kemble,* p. 470 n. 10.

40. Wainwright, ed., *A Philadelphia Perspective,* pp. 490, 492–93, 497.

41. Philadelphia City Directories. Wister Family Papers, HSP.

42. Fanny Kemble Wister, *That I May Tell You,* pp. 72–73.

43. A quotation from FK's letter to Harriet St. Leger, in the Morgan Library, New York, quoted in Furnas, *Fanny Kemble,* p. 407.

44. Myers, ed., *Children of Pride,* pp. 1580–83, 1586. Temple, *The First Hundred Years,* pp. 115, 332–34, 534. The town of Roswell, originally in Cobb County, is now in Fulton County. The slaves were owned by Barrington King, as agent for the Roswell Manufacturing Company. *ORUCA,* series 1, vol. 38, part 5, pp. 60, 68, 76–77. The mill at Roswell had flown the French flag in a futile effort to save it from Sherman's torches.

45. For FK's "grievous" quotation see chapter 19, "The Dogs of Civil War," and for "day of deliverance," see her letter to Henry Greville at the beginning of this chapter. Chapter 19 also shows Sarah Wister's "hope" and the expressed thoughts of Frances Butler and her father. *ORUCA,* series 1, vol. 44, pp. 783, 809. Sherman, *Memoirs,* 2:250–52. Casualty statistics from Beard and Beard, *The Rise of American Civilization,* 2:98. Litwack, *Been in the Storm So Long,* p. 3.

46. Kemble, *Records of a Later Life,* p. 160 n. 1.

Chapter 22. *Why Be Free?*

1. Kemble, Georgian *Journal,* pp. 330–32.

2. Gamble, *City Government of Savannah,* pp. 263–64. Mayor Richard D. Arnold's response to the generosity of New York and Boston at a public meeting, Savannah, January 25, 1865, in *ORUCA,* series 1, vol. 47, part 2, pp. 166–69.

3. Thompson, *Reconstruction in Georgia,* p. 43.

4. Wainwright, ed., *A Philadelphia Perspective,* p. 509. SGF misspells McAllister.

5. Frances Butler Leigh, *Ten Years on a Georgia Plantation*, pp. 1, 14.

6. Wainwright, ed., *A Philadelphia Perspective*, pp. 510, 515.

7. Frances Butler Leigh, *Ten Years on a Georgia Plantation*, pp. 5–6, 12–13. Frances Butler did not name the soldier whose grave she visited.

8. Conrad, *Reminiscences*, p. 25.

9. Frances Butler Leigh, *Ten Years on a Georgia Plantation*, pp. 66–69.

10. Inventory and Appraisement, Estate of Captain John Butler, Butler Family Papers, HSP. Frances Butler Leigh, *Ten Years on a Georgia Plantation*, p. 15.

11. Frances Butler Leigh, *Ten Years on a Georgia Plantation*, p. 21.

12. Ibid., p. 24.

13. Kemble, Georgian *Journal*, pp. 194–95.

14. *Savannah Daily News Herald*, June 1 and 15, 1866. Frances Butler Leigh, *Ten Years on a Georgia Plantation*, pp. 55, 33. Westwood, "Sherman Marched," p. 46.

15. Frances Butler Leigh, *Ten Years on a Georgia Plantation*, p. 45.

16. Ibid., pp. 71–72.

17. Wainwright, ed., *A Philadelphia Perspective*, p. 524. When Thomas C. James served as a captain in the Union army, P. C. Hollis replaced him as a trustee of the John Butler estate.

18. Butler Family Papers, HSP.

19. Frances Butler Leigh, *Ten Years on a Georgia Plantation*, p. 57.

20. Wainwright, ed., *A Philadelphia Perspective*, pp. 527–28. Owen Wister to Amelia M. Watson, February 7, 1922, Amelia M. Watson "Kemble Collection," Lenox Library.

21. Frances Butler Leigh, *Ten Years on a Georgia Plantation*, pp. 59–60.

22. House, *Planter Management*, p. 10. Gamble, *City Government of Savannah*, p. 114. See chapter 14, "The Mease Boys Change Their Names," on Negro children. *Savannah Daily News Herald*, August 22, 1867.

23. SGF to Elizabeth Ingersoll Fisher, August 22, 1867, Sidney George Fisher Collection, HSP. Wainwright, ed., *A Philadelphia Perspective*, p. 531.

24. Fanny Kemble Wister, *That I May Tell You*, pp. 76, 75.

25. Wainwright, ed., *A Philadelphia Perspective*, pp. 533–34.

26. Frances Butler Leigh, *Ten Years on a Georgia Plantation*, p. 73. FK to Arthur Malkin, April 29, 1865 (misdated, should be 1868), in Kemble, *Further Records*, p. 341.

27. The accounting of the administration and the inventory of PB's estate is recorded in the Register of Wills, Philadelphia, 562, 1867.

28. The agreement between the heirs of PB and Gabriella Butler, October 8, 1867, Wister Family Papers, HSP.

29. Frances Butler to P. C. Hollis, March 1868, Wister Family Papers, HSP. Frances Butler Leigh, *Ten Years on a Georgia Plantation*, p. 153.

Chapter 23. *Massa Jimmy*

1. The census of 1860 and that of 1870 for both McIntosh and Glynn counties are on microfilm, Savannah Public Library. Kemble, Georgian *Journal,* pp. 249–50. Leigh, *Ten Years on a Georgia Plantation,* p. 124. Parrish, *Slave Songs,* pp. 130, 239. There is much confusion surrounding Liverpool Hazzard, who became a Darien tourist attraction in the 1930s and died in 1936. An article by Bessie Lewis of the *McIntosh County News* (August 27, 1942) refuted Hal Steed's Liverpool as having been born "Pierce Butler." See Steed, *Georgia, Unfinished State,* p. 71. Miss Lewis said Liverpool was born York and became Liverpool on a visit to that city after the Civil War. However, the division of slaves between PB and the estate of John Butler, February 21, 1859, shows Liverpool, aged eight, to be the son of York, twenty-nine and Lydia, twenty-eight. Thus he was eighty-five when he died and not the centenarian his promoters claimed. Cate, *Our Todays and Yesterdays,* pp. 149–51, and Wright, *Fanny Kemble and the Lovely Land,* p. 215, have more on York and Liverpool.

2. Frances Butler Leigh, *Ten Years on a Georgia Plantation,* p. 79.

3. Ibid., pp. 92, 128.

4. Kemble, *Further Records,* pp. 349–50.

5. Frances Butler Leigh, *Ten Years on a Georgia Plantation,* pp. 94, 117.

6. Kemble, *Further Records,* pp. 349–50. Frances Butler Leigh, *Ten Years on a Georgia Plantation,* pp. 127, 147.

7. Coulter, "Tunis G. Campbell," *GHQ* 52 (March 1968): 16–52. Frances Butler Leigh, *Ten Years on a Georgia Plantation,* pp. 133–38. Duncan, *Freedom's Shore.*

8. J. W. Leigh, *Other Days,* pp. 90, 114, 115, 119, 127, 129. The description of JWL is from Owen Wister's preface to *Other Days.* Burnand, *Records and Reminiscences,* 2:343–45.

9. Ibid., pp. 127, 128–29. Frances Butler Leigh, *Ten Years on a Georgia Plantation,* pp. 199, 200, 202, 206, 268. Kemble, *Further Records,* pp. 37, 47.

10. J. W. Leigh, *Other Days,* pp. 129–30. Frances Butler Leigh, *Ten Years on a Georgia Plantation,* pp. 249–50. Frances Butler Leigh to Owen Wister, November 26, 1873, Owen Wister Papers, Library of Congress.

11. Frances Butler Leigh, *Ten Years on a Georgia Plantation,* p. 268. FBL to Sarah Wister, undated, Wister Family Papers, HSP.

12. J. W. Leigh, *Other Days,* p. 115. King, *Darien: The Death and Rebirth of a Southern Town,* pp. 94–99.

13. Kemble, *Further Records,* pp. 5–6, 16–17, 22, 71. Leigh, *Other Days,* pp. 135, 128–29. Frances Butler Leigh, *Ten Years on a Georgia Plantation,* pp. 151, 269. *Darien Timber Gazette,* December 10, 1875.

14. *Darien Timber Gazette,* January 14 and 21, 1876; February 4, 1876. Campbell was sentenced to two years at hard labor for the false imprisonment of

the master of a British ship loading lumber at Darien. He did not serve his time in a coal mine but as a farm worker in Washington County (Coulter, "Tunis G. Campbell," pp. 43–45).

15. J. W. Leigh, *Other Days*, pp. 139, 158, 156. Low-country tradition holds that blacks are buried in graveyards and white people in cemeteries. Hicks Beach, *Life of Sir Michael Hicks Beach,* 1:31–32. The Leighs chose to hyphenate Hicks-Beach.

16. J. W. Leigh, *Other Days*, pp. 158–60. *Darien Timber Gazette,* March 24, 1876. Frances Butler Leigh, *Ten Years on a Georgia Plantation,* p. 246.

17. Kemble, *Further Records,* pp. 37, 42, 83–84.

18. FBL to Owen Wister, March 8, (1875), Owen Wister Papers, Library of Congress.

19. Sarah Wister to Owen Jones Wister, February 14, 1876, Wister Family Papers, HSP. Mary Mann to Amelia M. Watson, 1915, in Watson "Kemble Collection," Lenox Library. Sarah Wister to George Marsh, April 30, 1876, Wister Family Papers, HSP.

20. Sarah Wister to Owen Jones Wister, February 14, 1876, Wister Family Papers, HSP. James W. Leigh to Owen Wister, January 28, 1876, Owen Wister Papers, Library of Congress. Dan Wing was the third Dan; see chapter 24, "Milestones and Gravestones."

21. Kemble, *Further Records,* pp. 88, 166, 105, 198.

22. Sarah Wister to Owen Jones Wister, February 14, 1876, Wister Family Papers, HSP. Gamble, *City Government of Savannah,* pp. 289, 300–304. Kemble, *Further Records,* pp. 198, 361.

23. *Darien Timber Gazette,* March 31, 1876.

24. J. W. Leigh, *Other Days,* pp. 180, 187. Kemble, *Further Records,* pp. 201, 210–13, 220. Gamble, *City Government of Savannah,* pp. 300–301.

25. Kemble, *Further Records,* pp. 151, 201. Hilton, *High Water on the Bar,* pp. 18–19. In 1915 Amelia M. Watson was told by Darien blacks that the Butler boatmen wore red shirts and black pants, and the boats flew red and white flags (Watson's "Kemble Collection," Lenox Library).

Chapter 24.
Milestones and Gravestones

1. Fanny Kemble Wister, *That I May Tell You,* p. 75.

2. Ibid., pp. 76, 69–123.

3. Wainwright, ed., *A Philadelphia Perspective,* p. 560. In the "Letterbook of the Estate of G. M. Butler," Peter C. Hollis noted on September 16, 1871, that "Mrs. Butler departed this life on 7th inst." On September 21 he wrote Henry Morris on the wines, and on September 27, Colonel McAllister. The names and

ages of the heirs are from the letterbook. In 1871 PB had not been dead for "many years." Perhaps Hollis refers to wines belonging to Major Butler (Wister Family Papers, HSP).

4. Woodward, *Meet General Grant*, p. 437. Kemble, *Further Records*, p. 155. As did his mother, Algernon Sartoris had a fine singing voice.

5. Fanny Kemble Wister, *That I May Tell You*, p. 79. Wright, *Fanny Kemble and the Lovely Land*, pp. 179–80.

6. Lee, "Frances Anne Kemble," p. 669. The twenty-seven stanzas of Sarah Wister's "Boat of Grass" first appeared in a wartime issue of the *Pennsylvania Freedman's Bulletin*, and later in an anthology (Elliott, ed., *Poetry for Children*, pp. 313–18). See also Wright, *Fanny Kemble and the Lovely Land*, p. 182.

7. Wright, *Fanny Kemble and the Lovely Land*, p. 180

8. Fanny Kemble Wister, *That I May Tell You*, p. 79.

9. Ibid., p. 80.

10. Sarah Wister was a haphazard diarist. The Wister Family Papers contain her Civil War diary, the "Early Years of a Child of Promise," and in addition several small volumes covering short stretches of time. The Sartoris entry follows a travel bit dated "June 1870."

11. Fanny Kemble Wister, *That I May Tell You*, pp. 81–84. The Hofwyl School gave its name to a portion of the old Troup plantation Broadfield when it was partitioned by inheritors. Ophelia Troup Dent called her share "Hofwyl" for the school her husband, George C. Dent, had attended in the 1830s. Hofwyl is a mainland plantation on the Glynn County side of the Altamaha, and is now a state-owned historic site. See Vanstory, *Georgia's Land of the Golden Isles*, pp. 103–4. Cate, *Our Todays and Yesterdays*, p. 198.

12. Fanny Kemble Wister, *That I May Tell You*, p. 86.

13. Ibid., p. 87.

14. Ibid., pp. 89, 91.

15. Ibid., pp. 93–95.

16. Edel, ed., *The Letters of Henry James*, 1:318. Edel, *Henry James: The Conquest of London*, pp. 84–86.

17. Edel, ed., *The Letters of Henry James*, 1:318, 328, 400, 460. Edel, *Henry James: The Conquest of London*, pp. 114–17, 120, 170, 178–80, 320. James's "uneasiness" is noted by his able biographer on p. 115. "H" was the artist Ernest Hebert, director of the French Academy at the Villa Medici. Fanny Kemble Wister, *That I May Tell You*, p. 95.

18. Kemble, *Records of a Girlhood*, p. 543. Kemble, *Further Records*, pp. 3, 13, 28.

19. Kemble, *Further Records*, p. 127. James, "Frances Anne Kemble," *Essays in London and Elsewhere*, p. 83. Kemble, *Records of a Girlhood*, p. 590.

20. Wright, *Fanny Kemble and the Lovely Land*, p. 192. Kemble, *Further Rec-*

ords, p. 121. FK to Owen Wister, probably late 1875 or early 1876, a typewritten letter on her "poor machine." She could not imagine "its ever being a pleasant means of intercourse with ones friends" (Owen Wister Papers, Library of Congress).

21. Kemble, *Further Records*, pp. 111, 107, 207.

22. Ibid., p. 214. Leigh, *Ten Years on a Georgia Plantation*, p. 193. The 1870 census of McIntosh County, Savannah Public Library.

23. Kemble, *Further Records*, p. 233. Edel, *Henry James: The Conquest of London*, pp. 289–90. Edel, ed., *The Letters of Henry James*, 2:147–48.

24. A letter from Frances Leigh to FK, May 1, 1881, in Furnas, *Fanny Kemble*, p. 413. Wright, *Fanny Kemble and the Lovely Land*, p. 206.

25. Anne B. Procter to FK, August 17, 1879, telling of the death of Adelaide Sartoris on August 6, 1879, Folger Library, EE 596-599. Edel, ed., *The Letters of Henry James*, 1:70. James, *Essays in London and Elsewhere*, pp. 112, 114. Count Alfred Guillaume Gabriel D'Orsay (1801–1852), a French dandy, arbiter, and *elegantarium* of English society; Maria Edgeworth (1767–1849), an Irish novelist; Charles Greville, see chapter 17, "Butler vs. Butler," and chapter 21, "Inevitable Sambo."

Chapter 25. *Straight Up to God*

1. Carson, *The History of the Celebration*, 1:70–71.

2. Kemble, *Further Records*, p. 350. Wylly, *Memories*, p. 34. James M. Couper to Caroline Couper Lovell, August 12, 1912, Cate Collection, GHS. James M. Couper's plantation work records, Butler Family Papers, HSP.

3. Kemble, *Records of a Later Life*, pp. 156, 172, 174.

4. Ibid., p. 160 n. 141.

5. The inscription from Ezekiel 25:9, in Frances Butler Leigh, *Ten Years on a Georgia Plantation*, p. xi.

6. Frances Butler Leigh, *Ten Years on a Georgia Plantation*, pp. 239–40. J. W. Leigh, *Other Days*, appendix.

7. Quotation from a letter in the manuscript section, HSP, no date or source shown, in Wright, *Fanny Kemble and the Lovely Land*, pp. 208–9.

8. James, *Essays in London and Elsewhere*, p. 113. Edel, ed., *Henry James: The Conquest of London*, p. 351.

9. HJ to Grace Norton, July 27, 1887, in Lubbock, ed., *The Letters of Henry James*, 1:128.

10. HJ to Grace Norton, October 17, 1882, ibid., 1:95. Sarah Wister's diaries, London, August 24, 1889, Wister Family Papers, HSP. Edel, ed., *Henry James: The Middle Years*, p. 53, and *Henry James: The Conquest of London*, pp. 121–22.

Sarah Wister was eight years older than HJ. "The Solution" was written in 1889, after her London visit. FK also gave HJ the plot of his *Washington Square*.

11. Fanny Kemble Wister, *That I May Tell You*, pp. 102–23. See the biographical sketch introducing the Owen Wister Papers, Library of Congress.

12. Fanny Kemble Wister, *That I May Tell You*, pp. 16–17, 19. Owen Jones Wister to Sarah Wister, February 3, 1883, Wister Family Papers, HSP.

13. Earnest, S. *Weir Mitchell*, pp. 73, 237.

14. The deed of partition for Butler's Island is not on file in McIntosh County and was probably destroyed in the 1933 fire. The Glynn County partition, book LL, May 3, 1894, pp. 475–80, Glynn County, Brunswick.

15. Anne Thackeray Ritchie, "Chapters from Some Unwritten Memories," pp. 549–55.

16. Sarah Wister to Owen Jones Wister, March 10, 1889; Sarah Wister's diaries, London, 1889; both in the Wister Family Papers, HSP. Ransome, ed., *The Terrific Kemble*, p. 259.

17. Sarah Wister to Owen Jones Wister, May 17, 1889, Wister Family Papers, HSP.

18. Entries for March 30, 1883, and September 1, 1889, Sarah Wister's diaries, Wister Family Papers, HSP. The quotation on the miniatures is from Sarah Wister's letter to Dr. Emmet, January 31, 1887, quoted by Victor Hugo Paltsits in "Notes on the Portraits," a chapter in Farrand, *The Fathers of the Constitution*, pp. 236–37. A similar letter from Sarah Wister to Clarence W. Bowen, November 18, 1890, in Bowen's *History of the Centennial*, p. 482, tells of Sarah Wister's father, Pierce Butler, having seen the portrait of Major Butler "with a broom handle through it" in the lumber room of the Chestnut Street house.

19. Copies of the letters from James Dent, July 29, 1912, and from Mrs. Wilder, August 28, 1912, are in the Cate Collection, GHS, and the emphasis may have been added by Mrs. Cate. They were published in part in Lovell, *The Golden Isles of Georgia*, pp. 209–13. James T. Dent married Miriam Cohen, the daughter of Miriam Gratz Moses Cohen; see chapter 17, "Butler vs. Butler." Caroline Couper Lovell was a great-granddaughter of John Couper of Cannon's Point. It is surprising that FK was strong enough to escort Mrs. Wilder to Westminster Abbey and to go in with "the crowd."

20. The words are from Eleanor Brianzoni (Ellen) to Frances Cobbe, in the Frances Anne Kemble Letters to Various People, Folger Library. The other two who loved FK were Owen Wister and his father, Owen Jones Wister. Edel, ed., *The Letters of Henry James*, 3:399–400.

21. James, *Essays in London and Elsewhere*, p. 107.

22. *Darien Timber Gazette*, January 21, 1893.

23. Julia King died on November 25, 1892 (Myers, ed., *Children of Pride*, p. 1583). Julia King Papers, Midway Museum.

Chapter 26. *Lady Baltimore*

1. Lord Rosebery became prime minister in 1894 and resigned in 1895. His first official appointment was that of James Leigh as the dean of Hereford. J. W. Leigh, *Other Days,* pp. 145, 222.

2. Aleck and Daphne were among the slaves retained in the 1859 division; see chapter 18, "The Weeping Time." Aleck's letter to Sarah Wister, January 10, 1896, Wister Family Papers, HSP. More on the Alexanders is given in the 1915 interviews with former Butler slaves Celia Davis, Mary Mann, and Dora Jeanette Alexander by Amelia M. Watson, in her "Kemble Collection," Lenox Library. For RK, Jr.'s fiddles, see chapter 14, "The Mease Boys Change Their Names." Kemble, *Georgian Journal,* pp. 282, 273.

3. Fanny Kemble Wister, *That I May Tell You,* pp. 6, 12.

4. J. W. Leigh, *Other Days,* pp. 226–27.

5. The Delegal case was given broad coverage in Georgia newspapers. Eight months after the alleged attack, Matilda Ann Hope charged Henry Delegal with rape. The *Savannah Morning News,* August 24, 1899, said, "Delegal is of the big black type, with slouching gait and an altogether disreputable appearance which however may have been enhanced by his stay in jail and the probable fear he has for his life." On September 9, 1899, the *News* reported that there were "many in Darien who would like to see the negro legally executed just for the wholesome effect it would have." The newspaper added, "Fortunately for justice and the negro, those so inclined, if there really are any, were not able to have their wish realized." The paper reported that it was "commonly stated" by white people of Darien that Delegal was not guilty as accused. F. M. Mann to Sarah Wister, August 31, 1899, Wister Family Papers, HSP.

6. Sarah Wister's letter to the benefactors, March 20, 1900, was written from Aiken, South Carolina (Wister Family Papers, HSP).

7. Wright, *Fanny Kemble and the Lovely Land,* p. 213. Sarah Wister to Owen Jones Wister, March 10, 1899, Wister Family Papers, HSP. Wylly, *Memories,* p. 36. "Mrs. Couper" was the widow of James Hamilton Couper.

8. Sarah Wister to George Owens, undated, Wister Family Papers, HSP.

9. The Strain contract is recorded in McIntosh County, Darien, book H, pp. 52–54, April 17, 1901, and pp. 259–60, July 8, 1903; book I, pp. 121–22, December 28, 1906. The General's Island and Darien property, book I, pp. 160–61, 163–69, January 7, 1907; the 434-1/4 acres, book H, p. 505, August 6, 1905. Major Butler's purchase from the McCalls, Butler Family Papers, HSP.

10. Sarah Wister and Frances Leigh to C. Downing, Jr., February 18, 1888, deed book EE, pp. 463–65; Sarah Wister and Frances Leigh to C. Downing, February 7, 1889, deed book JJ; both in Glynn County, Brunswick.

11. Deeds of partition between Sarah Wister and Frances Leigh, May 3, 1894, deed book LL, pp. 475–77, 478–80, Glynn County, Brunswick.

12. The Frances Leigh sales piece is undated (Wister Family Papers, HSP).

13. Frances Leigh to O. F. Chichester, January 16, 1908, deed book 3-A, p. 50; Frances Leigh to F. D. M. Strachan, St. Clair tract, June 15, 1908, p. 330; Frances Leigh to F. D. M. Strachan, Cannon's Point, August 17, 1908, p. 334; all in Glynn County, Brunswick. The St. Clair tract, exchanged in 1828, was evidently reacquired by the Butlers.

14. Fanny Kemble Wister, *That I May Tell You*, pp. 127–28, 133, 161. Owen Wister, *Lady Baltimore*, 1925 edition, p. 9.

15. Owen Wister, *Lady Baltimore*, p. 17. Owen Wister, "Letters Between President Theodore Roosevelt and Owen Wister."

16. Owen Wister, *Lady Baltimore*, 1925 edition, p. ix.

17. Ibid., pp. 171, 175–77.

18. Ibid., p. 201.

19. Ibid., pp. 216–17.

20. Owen Wister, *Lady Baltimore*, 1928 edition, pp. xvi–xvii, xviii. Owen Wister, *Roosevelt: The Story of a Friendship*, pp. 247–65, a retelling of the Wister-Roosevelt differences that arose from *Lady Baltimore*.

21. Owen Wister, *Lady Baltimore*, 1925 edition, p. 167.

22. Owen Wister, *Lady Baltimore*, 1928 edition, pp. xix, xxii, xxiv. Theodore Roosevelt's political career was marked by moves into and out of the good graces of the country's black citizens.

23. Owen Wister, "Letters Between President Theodore Roosevelt and Owen Wister."

24. Owen Wister, *Lady Baltimore*, 1928 edition, OW's preface. James, *The American Scene*, pp. 416, 418.

25. For more on the Miles Brewton house, see chapter 2, "Pierce Butler, Patriot." Owen Wister, *Lady Baltimore*, 1928 edition, OW's preface. Miss Susan Pringle lived in the Brewton house at the time of the Wisters' stay in Charleston. Owen Wister, *Roosevelt: The Story of a Friendship*, pp. 100, 247.

26. Payne, *Owen Wister*, pp. 236–37, 308.

27. Owen Wister, *Roosevelt: The Story of a Friendship*, p. 101. Major Pierce Butler to John Leckey, February 11, 1791, PB Letterbook, 1790–1794, SCL. Owen Wister, *Lady Baltimore*, 1925 edition, p. ix.

Epilogue

1. Fanny Kemble Wister, *That I May Tell You*, pp. 171–75, 205. Thomas Butler, "The Butlers of South Carolina and County Carlow," p. 57. Burke, ed., *Genealogical and Heraldic History*, pp. 427–29. Watson "Kemble Collection," Lenox Library.

2. HJ to Owen Wister, December 26, 1909, in Lubbock, ed., *The Letters of*

Henry James, 2:148. HJ to James Leigh, February 9, 1911, in Leigh, *Other Days*, p. 220. Watson "Kemble Collection," Lenox Library.

3. J. W. Leigh, *Other Days*, p. 219.

4. Fanny Kemble Wister, *That I May Tell You*, pp. 152, 153, 179, 221, 225, 222. Florence Bayard Kane said the child born in 1913 was called Sarah Siddons Wister, for Fanny Kemble's aunt.

5. Ibid., pp. 22, 267, an entry of June 6, 1915 in Owen Wister's diary.

6. Owen Wister to St. Simons Island Development Company, December 7, 1920, deed book 3-N, pp. 326–27; Sheriff of Glynn County to Owen Wister, July 19, 1922, deed books 3-O, p. 798, and 3-P, p. 21; Owen Wister to John A. Metcalf, September 27, 1923, deed book 3-Q, p. 794; all in Glynn County, Brunswick.

7. *Philadelphia Bulletin*, August 22, 1922. "Chestnut Street, 6th to 9th," Campbell Collection, HSP.

8. See chapter 14, "The Mease Boys Change Their Names," and chapter 18, "The Weeping Time."

9. Sarah Wister's memorandum on Butler Place, Butler Family Papers, HSP. Fanny Kemble Wister, *That I May Tell You*, pp. 205, 209–10, 266. Owen Wister to Amelia M. Watson, June 19, 1916, in her "Kemble Collection," Lenox Library. See chapter 4, "Private Life."

10. An undated memorandum by Florence Bayard Kane, Wister Family Papers, HSP. Fanny Kemble Wister (Mrs. Walter Stokes) could cast no light on Miss Kane's "Archives." Fanny Kemble Wister, *That I May Tell You*, p. 3.

11. Biographical sketch of Owen Wister introducing the Owen Wister Papers, Library of Congress.

12. Inglesby, "The Return of the Native," pp. 28, 32–33.

13. At present the development at Hampton has not kept pace with other similar projects on St. Simons and nearby Sea Island.

14. In 1908 Little St. Simons Island was purchased by O. F. Chichester, who was acting as an agent for a New York pencil manufacturing company. Abundant red cedar trees were harvested, converted to "slats," and used to make pencils. When all the cedar that could be used was cut, Philip Berolzheimer, an owner of the company, purchased the island for his private use, and it remains in the possession of that family. Many cedars, turned and twisted by the constant ocean winds, remain much a part of the island landscape. From notes of Burnette Vanstory, St. Simons Island.

15. Colonel Huston died in 1938, WPA's *Georgia: A Guide*, pp. 285–86.

16. Singleton, "The Archaeology of Afro-American Slavery in Coastal Georgia."

17. Smith, "Boom Town in the Horsefields," pp. 50–52.

18. Burke, ed., *Genealogical and Heraldic History*, pp. 427–29.

19. The McLanahan genealogical compilation, Cate Collections, GHS.

20. Report of the births in Chatham County, first week of August 1979, *Savannah Morning News*, August 12, 1979.

21. Price, *The Royal Tour*.

22. Roswell King to Major Pierce Butler, March 30, 1804, Butler Family Papers, HSP. See chapter 9, "The Slaves."

23. Christ Church records show that Frances Butler was buried in the Pierce Butler tomb, yet her name does not show with the others carved on the stone. The Thomas Butler tomb has no names to indicate who is buried there.

24. "Great gittin up morning" is from the spiritual "Fare Thee Well." The other line is from "Face the Rising Sun," in *The Carolina Low Country*, p. 270.

25. Morison, *The Oxford History of the American People*, p. 316. See chapter 5, "Pierce Butler's Public Life, 1776–1789."

 Bibliography

Collections, Official Records, and Other Documents

BOSTON ATHENAEUM
Pierce Butler–Alleyne Otis Letter, 1851.

BRITISH LIBRARY
Weeden Butler–Pierce Butler Correspondence, Add Mss 16.603.

CHATHAM COUNTY COURT HOUSE, SAVANNAH
Probate and Superior Court Records.

CHRIST CHURCH, PHILADELPHIA
Minutes of the Vestry.

FOLGER SHAKESPEARE LIBRARY
Frances Anne Kemble Letters to Various People.
Letters to and from Fanny Kemble.

GEORGIA DEPARTMENT OF ARCHIVES AND HISTORY
James Ladson–Pierce Butler Indentures.

GEORGIA HISTORICAL SOCIETY
Graham Deeds to Pierce Butler.
Margaret Davis Cate Collection.
William Jones Papers.
Julia King Papers.

GLYNN COUNTY COURT HOUSE, BRUNSWICK
County Deed Books.

HISTORICAL SOCIETY OF PENNSYLVANIA
Butler Family Papers.

Pierce Butler–Library Company Manuscripts.
Pierce Butler Letterbooks, 1787–1822 and 1794–1822.
Wister Family Papers.
H. E. Drayton Papers.
James Rush–Library Company Papers.
Gratz Collection.
Sidney George Fisher Collection.
Joshua Francis Fisher Collection.
Cadwalader Collection, J. F. Fisher Correspondence.
Deborah Norris Logan Diaries.
Charlotte Wilcocks Diary.
David J. Kennedy Watercolors: *Butler House at Chestnut and Eighth Streets* and *Butler Place.*
Helen C. Perkins Collection.
Jane Campbell Collection.
Genealogical Society of Pennsylvania.
Thompson Wescott Scrapbooks: Biographies of Philadelphia.

MISS CLERMONT LEE, SAVANNAH
Frances Motte Middleton–Pierce Butler Marmalade Memorandum, circa 1792.

LENOX LIBRARY ASSOCIATES
Amelia M. Watson "Kemble Collection."

LIBRARY OF CONGRESS
Pierce Butler Papers.
Pierce Butler Collection.
Owen Wister Papers.
Frances Anne Kemble Papers.
Margaret Hall Collection.
George Cockburn Papers.

ARCHIVES DEPARTMENTALES DE LA MARTINIQUE, FORT DE FRANCE
Vauclin Parish Records, Butler–de Mallevault Marriage, 1812.

MIDWAY MUSEUM
Julia King Papers.

MUSEUM OF COASTAL HISTORY, ST. SIMONS ISLAND
Couper Collection.

NATIONAL ARCHIVES
Records of the Mixed Claims Commission, War of 1812.

PUBLIC ARCHIVES OF NOVA SCOTIA, HALIFAX

NOVA SCOTIA LEGISLATIVE LIBRARY, HALIFAX

NEWPORT HISTORICAL SOCIETY, NEWPORT, RHODE ISLAND
Newport County Records, Will of Thomas Butler, 1838.

CITY HALL, PHILADELPHIA
Wills and Deeds.

SAVANNAH PUBLIC LIBRARY
Thomas Gamble Collection.

SOUTH CAROLINA DEPARTMENT OF ARCHIVES AND HISTORY
Wills and Land Grants.

SOUTH CAROLINA HISTORICAL SOCIETY
Petition of Ralph Izard and Edward Rutledge, 1795.
Pinckney Family Collection.

SOUTH CAROLINIANA LIBRARY
Pierce Butler Letterbook, 1790–1794.
Pierce Butler Papers.
Francois Didier Petit de Villers Letter, 1807.

UNIVERSITY OF NORTH CAROLINA, SOUTHERN HISTORICAL COLLECTION
William Page Papers.
W. A. Couper Papers.
Miriam Gratz Moses Papers.
Thomas Butler King Collection.
Mackay Stiles Papers.
John Berkley Grimball Diary.

Books, Articles, Pamphlets, and Miscellaneous Writings

Abstract of Wills, 1707–1745. Dublin, Ireland.

Ackerman, Robert K. *South Carolina Colonial Land Policies.* Columbia, 1977.

Adams, John. *Novangulus.* Boston, 1819.

Anderson, Major General W. H., C.B. *The History of the Twenty-Second Cheshire Regiment, 1689–1849.* London, 1920.

Andrews, Eliza Frances. *War-Time Journal of a Georgia Girl, 1864–1865.* New York, 1908.

Annals of Congress, the Debates and Proceedings. Eighth Congress. Washington, D.C., 1852.

Aptheker, Herbert, ed. *A Documentary History of the Negro People in the United States.* 2 vols. 1951. Reprint. New York, 1968.

Archibald, Adams. "Story of the Deportation of Negroes to Sierra Leone." *Nova Scotia Historical Collections,* vol. 7, *1889–1891,* Halifax.

Armstrong, Margaret. *Fanny Kemble, A Passionate Victorian.* New York, 1938.

Ashby, Clifford. "Fanny Kemble's Vulgar Journal." *Pennsylvania Magazine of History and Biography* 98 (1974).

Atherton, Gertrude, ed. *A Few of Hamilton's Letters.* New York, 1903.

Baker, William S. "Washington After the Revolution, 1784–1789." *Pennsylvania Magazine of History and Biography* 20 (1896).

Ballard, Allen B. *One More Day's Journey.* New York, 1984.

Bancroft, Frederic. *Slave Trading in the Old South.* New York, 1959.

Barnwell, Joseph W., ed. "Correspondence of Arthur Middleton, Signer of the Declaration of Independence." *South Carolina Historical Magazine* 26 (1925), 27 (1926).

Barnwell, Robert W., Jr. "Loyalism in South Carolina, 1765–1785." Ph.D. dissertation, Duke University, 1941.

Barry, Richard. *Mr. Rutledge of South Carolina.* New York, 1942.

Beard, Charles A., and Mary R. Beard. *The Rise of American Civilization.* Rev. ed., vols. 1 and 2 included. New York, 1939.

Beatty, Joseph M., Jr., ed. "Letters of Judge Henry Wynkoop," *Pennsylvania Magazine of History and Biography* 38 (1914).

Becker, Robert A., and Merrill Jensen, eds. *Documentary History of the First Federal Elections, 1789–1790.* Madison, Wis., 1976.

Bell, Malcolm, Jr. "We Shall Overcome?" Madeira Club paper, Georgia Historical Society, Savannah, 1963.

Benét, William Rose. *The Reader's Encyclopedia.* New York, 1948.

Berquist, Harold E., Jr. "Henry Middleton and the Arbitrament of the Anglo-American Slave Controversy by Tsar Alexander I." *South Carolina Historical Magazine* 82 (1981).

Biographical Directory of the South Carolina House of Representatives. Vol. 2, *The Commons House of Assembly, 1692–1775.*

Bobbe, Dorothea. *Fanny Kemble.* New York, 1931.

Boswell, James. *The Life of Samuel Johnson, LL.D.* Oxford ed. 2 vols. London, 1904.

Bowen, Catherine Drinker. *Miracle at Philadelphia.* Boston, 1966.

Bowen, Clarence Winthrop, ed. *The History of the Centennial Celebration of the Inauguration of George Washington as First President of the United States.* New York, 1892.

Brady, Patrick S. "The Slave Trade and Sectionalism in South Carolina, 1787–1808." *Journal of Southern History* 38 (1972).

Bremer, Fredrika. *The Homes of the New World.* New York, 1853.

Brydges, Sir Egerton, K.J. *Collins Peerage of England.* London, 1812.

Buck, Charles N. *Memoirs, 1791–1841.* Philadelphia, 1941.

Bull, Elias B. "Storm Towers on the Santee Delta." *South Carolina Historical Magazine* 81 (1980).

Bull, Henry DeSaussure. "Ashley Hall‚ Plantation." *South Carolina Historical Magazine* 53 (1952).

Bullard, Mary R. *Black Liberation on Cumberland Island in 1815.* De Leon Springs, Fla., 1983.

Burchard, Peter. *One Gallant Rush.* New York, 1965.

Burgess, Eleanor. "Saint Josephine, 1826–1906." *Journal of the Butler Society* (1980–81).

Burke, J. B., ed. *Burke's Genealogical and Heraldic History of the Peerage, Baronetage, and Knightage.* London, 1970.

Burnand, Sir Francis. *Records and Reminiscences.* 2 vols. London, 1904.

Burns, James MacGregor. *The Vineyard of Liberty.* New York, 1982.

Burr, Anna Robeson. *Weir Mitchell: His Life and Letters.* New York, 1929.

Burt, Nathaniel. *The Perennial Philadelphians.* Boston, 1963.

Butler, Annie R. *Nearly a Hundred Years Ago.* London, 1907.

Butler, Pierce. *Mr. Butler's Statement.* Philadelphia, 1850.

Butler, Pierce, vs. Frances Anne Butler, Narrative of the Proceedings. Philadelphia, 1848.

Butler, Colonel Sir Thomas. "The Butlers of South Carolina, U.S.A., and the Butlers of County Carlow, Ireland." *Journal of the Butler Society,* Kilkenny (1980–1981).

Butterfield, L. H., ed. *Letters of Benjamin Rush.* 2 vols. Princeton, 1951.

Campbell, Colin, ed. *The Journal of Colonel Archibald Campbell.* Darien, Ga., 1981.

Candler, Allen D., ed. *The Revolutionary Records of the State of Georgia.* Atlanta, 1908.

Candler, Allen D., and Lucian Lamar Knight, eds. *The Colonial Records of Georgia.* Vols. 3 and 7. Atlanta, 1904–1916.

Cantwell, Robert. *Alexander Wilson, Naturalist and Pioneer.* Philadelphia, 1961.

Carney, James, ed. *Poems of the Butlers of Ormonde, Cahir and Dunboyne.* Dublin, 1945.

The Carolina Low Country. Society for the Preservation of Spirituals, New York, 1961.

Carson, Hampton L. *The History of the Celebration of the One Hundredth Anniversary of the Promulgation of the Constitution of the United States.* 2 vols. Philadelphia, 1889.

Carter, Clarence Edwin, ed. *The Correspondence of General Thomas Gage with the Secretaries of State, 1763–1775.* 2 vols. New Haven, 1931.

Carter, Hodding. *The Angry Scar.* New York, 1959.

Cate, Margaret Davis. "Mistakes in Fanny Kemble's Georgia Journal." *Georgia Historical Quarterly* 44 (March 1960).

_____. *Our Todays and Yesterdays.* Brunswick, 1930.

Channing, William Ellery. *Slavery.* 4th ed., revised. Boston, 1836.

Chesnut, Mary Boykin. *A Diary from Dixie.* Boston, 1949.

Cheves, Langdon. "Blake of South Carolina." *South Carolina Historical Magazine* 1 (1900).

_____. "Izard of South Carolina." *South Carolina Historical Magazine* 2 (1901).

_____. "Middleton of South Carolina." *South Carolina Historical Magazine* 2 (1901).

Cheves, Langdon, and A. S. Salley, Jr. "The Bull Family of South Carolina." *South Carolina Historical Magazine* 1 (1900).

Chiasson, Paulette M. "As Others Saw Us: Nova Scotia Travel Literature from the 1770s to the 1860s." *Nova Scotia Historical Review* (1982).

Chichester, Henry Manners, and Burges-Short, George. *The Records and Badges of Every Regiment and Corps in the British Army.* London, 1900.

Child, L. Maria. *Isaac T. Hopper: A True Life.* New York, 1881.

Clairmont, Donald H., and Dennis W. Magill. *Nova Scotia Blacks: An Historical and Structural Overview.* Halifax, 1970.

Clifton, James M. "Hopeton, Model Plantation of the Antebellum South." *Georgia Historical Quarterly* 66 (1982).

_____. "The Rice Driver: His Role in Slave Management." *South Carolina Historical Magazine* 82 (1981).

Coffin, Charles C. *Building the Nation.* New York, 1882.

Coghlan, Francis. "Pierce Butler, 1744–1822: First Senator from South Carolina." *South Carolina Historical Magazine* 78 (1977).

_____. "Senator Pierce Butler: The Aristocrat as Revolutionary." *Journal of the Butler Society,* Kilkenny (1976).

Collections of the Genealogical Society of Pennsylvania. 2 vols. Philadelphia.

Conrad, Georgia Bryan. "Reminiscences of a Southern Woman." *Southern Workman* (1901).

Corner, George W., ed. *The Autobiography of Benjamin Rush.* Princeton, 1948.

Cornish, Dudley Taylor. *The Sable Arm: Negro Troops in the Union Army, 1861–1865.* New York, 1956.

Coulter, E. Merton. *Georgia's Disputed Ruins.* Chapel Hill, 1937.

_____. *A Short History of Georgia.* Chapel Hill, 1933.

_____. *Thomas Spalding of Sapelo.* Baton Rouge, 1940.

_____. "Tunis G. Campbell: Negro Reconstructionist in Georgia." *Georgia Historical Quarterly* 51 (1967), 52 (March 1968).

Courlander, Harold. *A Treasury of African American Folklore.* New York, 1976.

Cox, Jacob D. *March to the Sea.* New York, 1882.

Crouse, Maurice A., ed. "The Letterbook of Peter Manigault, 1763–1773." *South Carolina Historical Magazine* 70 (1969).

Curtis, George William. Review of Frances Anne Kemble's *Journal of a Residence on a Georgian Plantation in 1838–1839. Atlantic Monthly*, August 1863.

Curtis, John. "A Century of Grand Opera in Philadelphia." *Pennsylvania Magazine of History and Biography* 44 (1920).

Davis, John. *Travels of Four Years and a Half in the United States of America During 1798, 1799, 1800, 1801 and 1802.* New York, 1909.

Dewey, Mary E. *Life and Letters of Catharine M. Sedgwick.* New York, 1871.

"Diary of John Berkley Grimball." *South Carolina Historical Magazine* 56 (1955).

Dictionary of American Biography. New York, 1964.

Dictionary of National Biography. London, 1909.

Dodson, W. C., ed. *Campaigns of Wheeler and His Cavalry.* Atlanta, 1899.

Donnan, Elizabeth, ed. *Documents Illustrative of the History of the Slave Trade to America.* 4 vols. New York, 1935.

Doughty, Arthur G., ed. *Historical Journal of the Campaigns in North America by Captain John Knox.* 3 vols. Toronto, 1916.

Drayton, John, LL.D. *Memoirs of the American Revolution.* 2 vols. Charleston, 1821.

Drescher, Seymour. *Econocide.* Pittsburgh, 1977.

Driver, Leota S. *Fanny Kemble.* Chapel Hill, 1933.

Duncan, Russell. *Freedom's Shore: Tunis Campbell and the Georgia Freedmen.* Athens, 1986.

Earnest, Ernest Penney. *S. Weir Mitchell.* Philadelphia, 1950.

Eaton, Clement. *A History of the Old South.* New York, 1949.

Edel, Leon. *Henry James: The Conquest of London, 1870–1881.* Philadelphia, 1962.

———. *Henry James: The Middle Years, 1882–1895.* Philadelphia, 1962.

———, ed. *The Letters of Henry James.* 3 vols. Cambridge, Mass., 1974.

Elliott, Maud Howe. *This Was My Newport.* Cambridge, Mass., 1944.

Elliott, Samuel, ed. *Poetry for Children.* New York, 1879.

Emilio, Luis Fenollosa. *The Assault on Fort Wagner.* Boston, 1887.

Erskine, Mrs. Steuart, ed. *Letters and Friendships: Anna Jameson.* London, 1915.

Ettinger, Amos Aschbach. *James Edward Oglethorpe, Imperial Idealist.* Oxford, 1936.

Everard, Major H. *History of Thomas Farrington's Regiment, Subsequently Designated the Twenty-ninth (Worcestershire) Foot, 1694–1891.* Worcester, 1891.

Farley, M. Foster. "The South Carolina Negro in the American Revolution, 1775–1783." *South Carolina Historical Magazine* 79 (1978).

Farrand, Max. *The Fathers of the Constitution.* New York, 1921.

———. *The Framing of the Constitution of the United States.* 3 vols. New Haven, 1913.

———. *The Records of the Federal Convention of 1787.* 4 vols. New Haven, 1911.

Faulkner, Thomas. *An Historical and Topographical Description of Chelsea and Its Environs.* London, 1810.

Federal Cases, Circuit and District Courts, 1789–1880. Book 4, case no. 2241, *Butler v. Hopper.*

Fergusson, C. B., and D. C. Harvey. *A Documentary Study of the Establishment of the Negroes in Nova Scotia Between the War of 1812 and the Winning of Responsible Government.* Public Archives of Nova Scotia, Publication no. 8. Halifax, 1948.

Fermor, Patrick Leigh. *The Traveller's Tree.* London, 1950.

Fisher, Joshua Francis. *Recollections.* Philadelphia, 1929.

Fisher, Sydney George. *Men, Women and Manners in Colonial Times.* Philadelphia, 1900

Fleetwood, Rusty. *Tidecraft.* Savannah, 1982.

Fogel, Robert William, and Stanley L. Engerman. *Time on the Cross.* Boston, 1974.

Ford, Worthington Chauncey. *British Officers Serving in America, 1754–1774.* Boston, 1894.

Franklin, Benjamin. *Historicus.* Broadside published anonymously in Boston, March 23, 1790.

Furnas, J. C. *Fanny Kemble.* New York, 1982.

Gamble, Thomas. *A History of City Government of Savannah, Georgia, 1790 to 1901.* Savannah, 1900.

———. *Thomas Gamble Scrapbooks.* Savannah Public Library.

Geffen, Elizabeth M. "William Henry Furness, Philadelphia Antislavery Preacher." *Pennsylvania Magazine of History and Biography* 82 (1958).

Genovese, Eugene D. *From Rebellion to Revolution.* New York, 1981.

———. *Roll, Jordan, Roll.* New York, 1974.

Gibbs, Henry. *Affectionately Yours, Fanny.* London, 1945.

Gilpin, Henry D., ed. *The Papers of James Madison.* 3 vols. Mobile, 1842.

Glenn, Robert S., Jr. "The Colonization of Sierra Leone, 1787–1807." Typescript, Georgia Historical Society, Savannah.

Gordon, Robert W. "The Negro Spiritual." In *The Carolina Low Country.* pp. 191–222. New York, 1961.

Granger, Mary, ed. *Drums and Shadows.* Work Projects Administration, Athens, 1940.

———. *Savannah River Plantations.* Work Projects Administration, Savannah, 1947.

Grant, John N. "Black Immigrants into Nova Scotia, 1776–1815." *Journal of Negro History* (1973).

Gray, Tom S., Jr. "The March to the Sea." *Georgia Historical Quarterly* 14 (June 1930).

Hall, Captain Basil. *Travels in North America.* 2 vols. Philadelphia, 1829.

Handlin, Oscar. *Race and Nationality in American Life.* New York, 1957.

Harden, William. *A History of Savannah and South Georgia.* 2 vols. Chicago, 1913.

Harper, Francis, ed. *The Travels of William Bartram.* Naturalist's ed. New Haven, 1958.

Harris, Thadeus Mason, D.D. *Biographical Memorials of James Oglethorpe.* Boston, 1846.

Harrison, Eliza Cope, ed. *Philadelphia Merchant: The Diary of Thomas P. Cope, 1800–1851.* South Bend, Ind., 1978.

Hart, Charles Henry. "Thomas Sully, Register of Portraits." *Pennsylvania Magazine of History and Biography* 32 (1908).

Hartridge, Walter Charlton, ed. *The Letters of Don Juan McQueen to His Family.* Columbia, 1943.

————. *The Letters of Robert Mackay to His Wife, 1795–1816.* Athens, 1949.

Hawes, Lilla M., ed. "A Letterbook of Lachlan McIntosh." *Georgia Historical Quarterly* 38 (1954).

Hayes, J. D., ed. *Samuel Francis DuPont: A Selection from His Civil War Letters.* 3 vols. Ithaca, 1969.

Heard, George Alexander. "St. Simons Island During the War Between the States." *Georgia Historical Quarterly* 22 (1938).

Hearn, Lafcadio. *Youma.* 1900. Reprint. New York, 1969.

Henderson, Lillian, ed. *Roster of the Confederate Soldiers of Georgia, 1861–1865.* Atlanta, 1955–1958.

Herskovits, Melville J. *The Myth of the Negro Past.* Boston 1958.

Heyward, DuBose. "The Negro in the Low Country." In *The Carolina Low Country,* pp. 171–87. New York, 1961.

Heyward, Duncan Clinch. *Seed from Madagascar.* Chapel Hill, 1937.

Hicks Beach, Lady Victoria. *Life of Sir Michael Hicks Beach.* 2 vols. London, 1932.

Higginbothan, Don, ed. *The Papers of James Iredell.* 2 vols. Raleigh, 1976.

Higgins, W. Robert. "Factors Dealing in the External Negro Trade." *South Carolina Historical Magazine* 65 (1964).

Higginson, Thomas Wentworth. *Army Life in a Black Regiment.* 1870. Reprint. East Lansing, Mich., 1960.

Hill, Peter P. "A Masked Acquisition: French Designs on Cumberland Island, 1794–1795." *Georgia Historical Quarterly* 64 (1980).

Hilton, Thomas. *High Water on the Bar.* Savannah, 1951.

Holmgren, Virginia C. *Hilton Head: A Sea Island Chronicle.* Hilton Head, 1959.

Hotchkin, The Reverend S. F. *The York Road, Old and New.* Philadelphia, 1892.

House, Albert Virgil. *Planter Management and Capitalism in Ante Bellum Georgia.* New York, 1954.

Inglesby, Edith. "The Return of the Native." *Islander,* Hilton Head, S.C., July 1971.

Izard, Ralph. *Correspondence of Mr. Ralph Izard of South Carolina from the Year 1774 to 1804.* Vol. 1. New York, 1844.

Jackson, Harvey H. "The Darien Anti-Slavery Petition of 1739 and the Georgia Plan." *William and Mary Quarterly* (October 1977).

James, Henry. *The American Scene.* New York, 1967.

––––––. *Essays in London and Elsewhere.* New York, 1893.

James, William. *A Full and Correct Account of the Military Occurrences of the Late War Between Great Britain and the United States of America.* 2 vols. London, 1818.

Jervey, Elizabeth Heyward. "Death Notices." *South Carolina Historical Magazine* 51 (1950).

Johnson, Joseph, M.D. *Traditions and Reminiscences.* Charleston, 1851.

Jones, Charles C. *A Catechism of Scripture, Doctrine and Practice for Families and Sabbath Schools. Designed Also for the Oral Instruction of Colored Persons.* 1837. Reprint, 3d ed. Savannah and New York, 1844.

Jones, Charles C., Jr. *The History of Georgia.* 2 vols. Boston, 1883.

––––––. *Negro Myths from the Georgia Coast.* Augusta, 1888.

Jones, E. Alfred. *American Members of the Inns of Courts.* London, 1924.

Jones, George Fenwick. "The Black Hessians: Negroes Recruited by the Hessians in South Carolina and Other Colonies." *South Carolina Historical Magazine* 83 (1982).

Kemble, Frances Anne. *Further Records.* New York, 1891.

––––––. *Journal.* 2 vols. London, 1835.

––––––. *Journal of a Residence on a Georgian Plantation in 1838–1839.* 1863, 1961. Reprint, ed., with an introduction, John A. Scott. Athens, 1984.

––––––. *Poems.* Philadelphia, 1844.

––––––. *Records of a Girlhood.* New York, 1884.

––––––. *Records of a Later Life.* New York, 1882.

––––––. *A Year of Consolation.* London and New York, 1847.

Kerkhoff, Johnson D. *Aaron Burr: A Romantic Biography.* New York, 1931.

King, Roswell, Jr. "A Letter to the Editor." *Southern Agriculturist* 1 (1828).

King, Spencer B., Jr. *Darien: The Death and Rebirth of a Southern Town.* Macon, 1981.

Kline, Mary Jo, and Joanne Wood Ryan, eds. *Political Correspondence and Public Papers of Aaron Burr.* 2 vols. Princeton, 1983.

Laurens, Henry. *The Papers of Henry Laurens.* A continuing series of volumes, the first of which was published in Columbia, 1968. Ed. Philip Hamer et al. 10 vols.

––––––. *A South Carolina Protest Against Slavery.* New York, 1882.

Lawrence, Alexander A. *James Moore Wayne: Southern Unionist.* Chapel Hill, 1943.

Lee, Henry. "Frances Anne Kemble." *Atlantic Monthly,* May 1893.

Lee, Richard H. *Memoir of Richard Henry Lee.* 2 vols. Philadelphia, 1825.

Legare, John D. "An Account of an Agricultural Excursion into Southern Georgia." *Southern Agriculturist* 6 (1833).

Leigh, Frances Butler. *Ten Years on a Georgia Plantation Since the War.* London, 1883.

Leigh, J. W., D.D. *Other Days.* London, 1921.

LeRoy, J. Rutgers, Esq. "Americans Buried in Pere LaChaise, Paris." *Pennsylvania Magazine of History and Biography* 43 (1919).

Letters from Nova Scotia and New Brunswick. Edinburgh, 1829.

Lewis, Bessie. *Hampton Plantation.* St. Simons Island, 1978.

―――. *Patriarchial Plantations of St. Simons Island.* St. Simons Island, 1974.

―――. *They Called Their Town Darien.* Darien, 1975.

A List of the General and Field Officers . . . on the British and Irish Establishments. (The Army Lists.) London, 1761, 1764, 1765, and 1767.

Littlefield, Daniel C. *Rice and Slaves.* Baton Rouge, 1981.

Litwack, Leon F. *Been in the Storm So Long.* New York, 1979.

Livermore, Thomas L. *Numbers and Losses in the Civil War in America, 1861–1865.* Boston, 1901.

Lomansk, Milton. *Aaron Burr: The Years from Princeton to Vice President, 1756–1805.* New York, 1979.

Lombard, Mildred E. "Contemporary Opinions of Mrs. Kemble's *Journal of a Residence on a Georgian Plantation in 1838–1839.*" *Georgia Historical Quarterly* 14 (December 1930).

London County Council. *The Survey of London.* Part 1, *The Parish of Chelsea.* London, 1900.

Looney, Robert F. *Old Philadelphia in Early Photographs, 1839–1914.* New York, 1976.

Lovell, Caroline Couper. *The Golden Isles of Georgia.* Boston, 1933.

Lubbock, Percy, ed. *The Letters of Henry James.* 2 vols. New York, 1920.

Luck, Surgeon John T. *Robert Gould Shaw: Memorial.* Cambridge, Mass., 1864.

Lumpkin, Katharine DuPre. *The Emancipation of Angelina Grimké.* Chapel Hill, 1974.

Lusk, William Crittendon. *War Letters of William Thompson Lusk.* New York, 1911.

Lyell, Sir Charles. *A Second Visit to the United States of North America.* 2 vols. New York, 1849.

McAllister, Ward. *Society As I Have Found It.* New York, 1891.

McCowen, George Smith, Jr. *The British Occupation of Charleston, 1780–1782.* Columbia, 1972.

McCrady, Edward. *The History of South Carolina in the Revolution.* 2 vols. New York, 1901–1902.

Maclay, Edgar S., ed. *Journal of William Maclay, U.S. Senator from Pennsylvania, 1789–1791.* New York, 1890.

McLendon, S. G. *History of Public Domain in Georgia.* Atlanta, 1924.

McRee, Griffith J. *Life and Correspondence of James Iredell.* 2 vols. New York, 1857–1858.

Mahon, John K. *The War of 1812.* Gainesville, Fla., 1972.

Malone, Dumas. *Jefferson: The Virginian.* Boston, 1948.

Mannix, Daniel P., and Malcolm Cowley. *Black Cargoes.* New York, 1976.

Marshall, John. *Royal Naval Biography.* London, 1823.

Martell, J. S. *Immigration to and Emigration from Nova Scotia, 1815–1838.* Public Archives of Nova Scotia, Publication no. 6. Halifax, 1942.

Martin, Clarece. *A History of the Presbyterian Church of Roswell.* Dallas, 1984.

Mayo, Mark. *Encyclopedia of the American Revolution.* New York, 1966.

Mease, James, M.D. *The Picture of Philadelphia.* Philadelphia, 1811.

Meltzer, Milton, and Patricia G. Holland, eds. *Lydia Maria Child: Selected Correspondence, 1817–1880.* Amherst, 1982.

Meroney, Geraldine M. "William Bull's First Exile from South Carolina, 1777–1781." *South Carolina Historical Magazine* 80 (1979).

Miller, Stephen F. *Memoir of General Blackshear.* Philadelphia, 1858.

Mitchell, S. Weir. *A Madeira Party.* New York, 1895.

———. *The Red City.* New York, 1908.

Moore, Caroline T. *Abstracts of Wills of the State of South Carolina, 1783–1800.* Columbia, 1974.

Moorsom, Captain W. *Letters from Nova Scotia.* London, 1830.

Morison, Samuel Eliot. *The Oxford History of the American People.* New York, 1965.

Moultrie, William. *Memoirs of the American Revolution.* 2 vols. New York, 1802.

Murdoch, Richard K. "Correspondence of French Consuls in Charleston, South Carolina, 1793–1797." *South Carolina Historical Magazine* 74 (1973).

Murray, Amelia Matilda. *Letters from the United States, Cuba, and Canada.* New York, 1856.

Myers, Robert Manson, ed. *Children of Pride.* New Haven, 1972.

Nason, D. *A Journal of a Tour from Boston to Savannah.* Cambridge, Mass., 1849.

Nevins, Allan, ed. *The Diary of Philip Hone.* New York, 1927.

Official Records of the Union and Confederate Armies. Washington, D.C., 1880–1901.

Official Records of the Union and Confederate Navies. Washington, D.C., 1894–1927.

Olsberg, Nicholas R. "Ship Registers in the South Carolina Archives." *South Carolina Historical Magazine* 74 (1973).

Parrish, Lydia. *Slave Songs of the Georgia Sea Islands*. New York, 1942.

Payne, Darwin. *Owen Wister*. Dallas, 1985.

Pennington, Patience. *A Woman Rice Planter*. Introduction by Owen Wister. New York, 1928.

Philadelphia *City Directories*.

The Philadelphia Club. Philadelphia, 1934.

Philipson, Rabbi David, D.D., ed. *Letters of Rebecca Gratz*. Philadelphia, 1929.

Phillips, Ulrich B. *Life and Labor in the Old South*. Boston, 1929.

Pidgin, Charles Felton. *Theodosia*. Boston, 1907.

Playfair, William. *British Family Antiquity*. London, 1811.

Pope-Hennesy, Una, ed. *The Aristocratic Journey*. New York, 1931.

Premo, Terri L. "Like a Being Who Does Not Belong: The Old Age of Deborah Norris Logan." *Pennsylvania Magazine of History and Biography* 107 (1983).

Prescott, Arthur Taylor, D.C.L. *Drafting the Federal Constitution*. Baton Rouge, 1941.

Presley, Delma Eugene, ed. *Dr. Bullie's Notes: James Holmes, M.D.* Atlanta, 1976.

Price, Harry. *The Royal Tour: or, The Cruise of the H.M.S. Ophir*. New York and Exeter, 1980.

Quarles, Benjamin. *The Negro in the American Revolution*. 1961. Reprint. New York, 1973.

———. *The Negro in the Civil War*. 1953. Reprint. Boston, 1969.

Quincy, Josiah, Jr. "Journal, 1773." In the *Proceedings, 1916* of the Massachusetts Historical Society.

Raddall, Thomas H. *Halifax, Warden of the North*. Toronto, 1948.

Ramsay, David. *The History of the Revolution of South Carolina*. 2 vols. Trenton, 1785.

Ransome, Eleanor, ed. *The Terrific Kemble*. London, 1978.

Ravenel, Mrs. St. Julien. *Charleston: The Place and the People*. New York, 1929.

A Refutation of the Calumnies. By a South Carolinian. A pamphlet.

Register, Jeannie Heyward. "Marriage and Death Notices." *South Carolina Historical Magazine* 26 (1925).

Rhode Island General Assembly. *The Remains of General Nathanel Greene*. Providence, 1903.

Rice, Howard C., Jr., ed. *Travels in North America in the Years 1780, 1781, and 1782 by the Marquis de Chastellux*. 2 vols. Chapel Hill, 1963.

Richards, Audrey. "A Talk on the Family of the Reverend Weeden Butler." *Journal of the Butler Society* (1980–81).

Richardson, Emma B. "Letters of William Richardson." *South Carolina Historical Magazine* 47 (1946).

Richardson, Joanna. "The Kemble Dynasty." *History Today* (May 1974).

Riddell, William Renwick. "The Slave in Canada." *Journal of Negro History* (July 1920).

Ritchie, Anne (Lady Anne Thackeray Ritchie). "Chapters from Some Unwritten Memories." *Living Age*, September 2, 1893.

Rogers, George C., Jr. *Charleston in the Age of the Pinckneys.* 1969. Reprint. Columbia, 1980.

———. *Evolution of a Federalist.* Columbia, 1962.

———. "The Letters of William Loughton Smith to Edward Rutledge." *South Carolina Historical Magazine* 69 (1968).

———. "The Papers of James Grant of Ballindalloch Castle, Scotland." *South Carolina Historical Magazine* 77 (1976).

Rogers, Seth (surgeon, First South Carolina Volunteers). "Letters to His Daughter." In the *Proceedings, 1909–1910* of the Massachusetts Historical Society.

Roper, Laura Wood. *FLO: A Biography of Frederick Law Olmsted.* Johns Hopkins, 1973.

Rose, Lisle K. *Prelude to Democracy: The Federalists in the South, 1789–1800.* Lexington, 1968.

Salley, A. S., ed. "Papers of the First Council of Safety." *South Carolina Historical Magazine* 1 (1900).

Schachner, Nathan. *Aaron Burr: A Biography.* New York, 1937.

Scharf, J. Thomas, and Thompson Westcott. *History of Philadelphia.* 3 vols. Philadelphia, 1844.

Scott, John Anthony. "On the Authenticity of Fanny Kemble's *Journal of a Residence on a Georgian Plantation in 1838–1839.*" *Journal of Negro History* 46, no. 4 (October 1961).

Sedgwick, Henry Dwight. "The Sedgwicks of Berkshire." *Collections of the Berkshire Historical and Scientific Society,* 1900.

Sellers, Charles Coleman. *Mr. Peale's Museum.* New York, 1980.

1776: The British Story of the American Revolution. The Catalogue of the "1776" exhibition at the National Maritime Museum. London, 1976.

Sherman, William T. *Memoirs.* 2 vols. New York, 1875.

Shryock, Richard H., ed. *Letters of Richard D. Arnold, M.D.* Durham, 1929.

Sideman, Belle Becker, and Lillian Friedman, eds. *Europe Looks at the Civil War.* New York, 1960.

Sikes, Lewright B. *The Public Life of Pierce Butler, South Carolina Statesman.* Washington, D.C., 1979.

Simpson, Henry. *Lives of Eminent Philadelphians.* Philadelphia, 1859.

Singleton, Theresa Ann. "The Archaeology of Afro-American Slavery in Coastal Georgia: A Regional Perception of Slave Household and Community Patterns." Ph.D. dissertation, University of Florida, 1980.

Smith, Alice R. Huger, and D. E. Huger Smith. *The Dwelling Houses of Charleston, South Carolina.* Philadelphia, 1917.

Smith, Deborah B. "Boom Town in the Horsefields." *Atlanta Magazine,* January 1983.

Smith, Henry A. M. "The Ashley River: Its Seats and Settlements." *South Carolina Historical Magazine* 20 (1919).

———. "Goose Creek." *South Carolina Historical Magazine* 29 (1928).

Smith, Julia Floyd. *Slavery and Rice Culture in Low Country Georgia, 1750–1860.* Knoxville, 1985.

Smith, Page. *John Adams.* 2 vols. New York, 1962.

Some Early Epitaphs in Georgia. Georgia Society of Colonial Dames, Savannah, 1924.

Spalding, Thomas. "Brief Notes." *Southern Agriculturist* 1 (1828) and 3 (1830).

Steed, Hal. *Georgia, Unfinished State.* New York, 1942.

Stegeman, John F., and Janet A. Stegeman. *Caty: A Biography of Catharine Littlefield Greene.* Athens, 1985.

Steinbeck, John. *Travels with Charley.* New York, 1962.

Stevens, Hazard. *The Life of Isaac Ingalls Stevens.* Boston, 1900.

Supreme Court of Georgia. Savannah, January term 1862, *Butler v. James and Butler.*

Swartz, Sally. "Pauline Stoney's Story." *Savannah Magazine,* June 1977.

Tansill, Charles C., ed. *Documents Illustrative of the Formation of the American States.* Washington, D.C., 1927.

Temple, Sarah Blackwell Gober. *The First Hundred Years: A Short History of Cobb County, Georgia.* Atlanta, 1935.

Thomas, E. S. *Reminiscences of the Last Sixty-five Years.* 2 vols. Hartford, 1840.

Thompson, C. Mildred. *Reconstruction in Georgia.* 1915. Reprint. Savannah, 1972.

Thomson, Mortimer Neal. *What Became of the Slaves on a Georgian Plantation?* A pamphlet, 1863. The article first appeared in the *New York Daily Tribune,* March 9, 1859.

Townsend, Sara Bertha. *An American Soldier: The Life of John Laurens.* Raleigh, 1958.

Turner, Edward Raymond. *The Negro in Pennsylvania: Slavery, Servitude, Freedom, 1639–1861.* New York, 1969.

Turner, Lorenzo Dow. *Africanisms in the Gullah Dialect.* Chicago, 1949.

Tyng, Dudley A. *Our Country's Troubles.* Boston, 1856.

———. *A Statement to the Congregation of the Church of the Epiphany, Philadelphia.* Philadelphia, 1856.

Updyke, Francis A. *The Diplomacy of the War of 1812.* Baltimore, 1915.

Van Doren, Mark, ed. *The Correspondence of Aaron Burr and His Daughter Theodosia.* New York, 1929.

Vanstory, Burnette. *Georgia's Land of the Golden Isles.* Athens, 1970.

Wainwright, Nicholas B. *"Butler v. Butler:* A Divorce Case Incident." *Pennsylvania Magazine of History and Biography* 79 (1955).

_____, ed. *A Philadelphia Perspective: The Diary of Sidney George Fisher Covering the Years 1834–1871.* Philadelphia, 1967.

Walker, James W. St.G. *The Black Loyalists.* New York, 1976.

Wallace, David Duncan. *The History of South Carolina.* 3 vols. New York, 1934.

_____. *Life of Henry Laurens.* New York, 1915.

Wallace, Henry Edward, Jr. "Sketch of John Innskeep." *Pennsylvania Magazine of History and Biography* 28 (1904).

Walsh, Richard, ed. *The Writings of Christopher Gadsden, 1746–1805.* Columbia, 1966.

Washington, William. "Queries on the Culture of Rice." *Southern Agriculturist* 1 (1828).

Webber, Mabel L. "Historical Notes." *South Carolina Historical Magazine* 12 (1911).

_____. "Josiah Smith's Diary." *South Carolina Historical Magazine* 34 (1933).

_____. "The Thomas Pinckney Family of South Carolina." *South Carolina Historical Magazine* 39 (1938).

Welch, Richard E., Jr. *Theodore Sedgwick, Federalist: A Political Portrait.* Middletown, Conn., 1965.

Wells, Tom Henderson. "Charles Augustus Lafayette Lamar: Gentleman Slave Trader." *Georgia Historical Quarterly* 47 (1963).

Westwood, Howard C. "Sherman Marched—And Proclaimed Land for the Landless." *South Carolina Historical Magazine* 85 (January 1984).

White, George. *Historical Collections of Georgia.* New York, 1854.

_____. *Statistics of the State of Georgia.* Savannah, 1849.

White, Leonard D. *The Federalists.* New York, 1956.

Wildes, Harry Emerson. *Anthony Wayne.* New York, 1941.

Williams, George W. "Eighteenth-Century Organists of St. Michael's." *South Carolina Historical Magazine* 53 (1952).

Williamson, Joel. *After Slavery: The Negro in South Carolina During Reconstruction, 1861–1877.* 1965. Reprint. New York, 1975.

Wilson, Philip Whitwell, ed. *The Greville Diary: Charles Cavendish Fulke Greville.* 2 vols. New York, 1927.

Windley, Lathan A., comp. *Runaway Slave Advertisements.* 4 vols. Westport, Conn., 1983.

Winks, Robin W. *The Blacks in Canada.* New Haven, 1971.

Winther, Oscar Osburn, ed. *Theodore Upson: With Sherman to the Sea.* Baton Rouge, 1943.

Wister, Fanny Kemble. *Fanny: The American Kemble.* Tallahassee, 1972.

_____. *Owen Wister Out West.* Chicago, 1958.

————. "Sarah Butler Wister's Civil War Diary." *Pennsylvania Magazine of History and Biography* 52 (1978).

————. *That I May Tell You.* Wayne, Penn., 1979.

Wister, Owen. *Lady Baltimore.* New York, 1906, 1925, and the revised "Uniform Edition" of 1928.

————. "Letters Between President Theodore Roosevelt and Owen Wister." *Saturday Evening Post,* April 19, 1930.

————. *Roosevelt: The Story of a Friendship.* New York, 1930.

Wood, Betty. "A Note on the Georgia Malcontents." *Georgia Historical Quarterly* 63 (1979).

Wood, Peter H. *Black Majority.* New York, 1974.

Woodward, C. Vann, ed. *Mary Chesnut's Civil War.* New Haven, 1981.

Woodward, W. E. *Meet General Grant.* New York, 1928.

Work Projects Administration. *Drums and Shadows.* Ed. Mary Granger. Athens, 1940.

————. *Georgia: A Guide to Its Towns and Countryside.* Athens, 1940.

————. *Savannah River Plantations.* Ed. Mary Granger. Savannah, 1947.

Wright, Constance. *Fanny Kemble and the Lovely Land.* New York, 1972.

Wright, Esmond. "Red, White and Black Loyalists." In *1776: The British Story of the American Revolution.* London, 1976.

Wylly, Charles Spalding. *Memories.* Brunswick, 1916.

————. *The Seed That Was Sown in the Colony of Georgia.* New York, 1910.

Zahniser, Marvin A. *Charles Cotesworth Pinckney, Founding Father.* Chapel Hill, 1967.

Newspapers and Periodicals

American Daily Advertiser, Philadelphia
Argus, Philadelphia
Atlanta Constitution
Atlanta Journal
Atlanta Magazine
Atlantic Monthly
Charleston Mercury
Charlestown Gazette
Coastlines Georgia
Columbian Magazine
Columbian Museum and Savannah Advertiser
Columbian Museum and Savannah Daily Gazette
Darien Gazette
Darien Timber Gazette
Gazette of the State of Georgia, Savannah

Georgia Gazette, Savannah
Georgia Historical Quarterly
The Georgian, Savannah
Harper's Weekly
Islander, Hilton Head, South Carolina
Journal of the Butler Society
Journal of Negro History
Journal of Southern History
Living Age
London Chronicle or Universal Evening Post
McIntosh County News, Darien
Massachusetts Historical Society Proceedings
National Intelligencer
New York Daily Tribune
New York Evening Post
New York Mirror
New York Semi-Weekly Tribune
New York Times
Niles Weekly Register
Nova Scotia Historical Review
Nova Scotia Historical Society Collections
Pennsylvania Correspondent, Newsletter of the Historical Society of Pennsylvania
Pennsylvania Gazette
Pennsylvania Magazine of History and Biography
Philadelphia Bulletin
Philadelphia Sunday Dispatch
Review of Politics
Saturday Evening Post
Savannah Daily Morning News
Savannah Daily News Herald
Savannah Magazine
Savannah Morning News
Savannah Republican
South Carolina and American General Gazette, Charleston
South Carolina Gazette, Charleston
South Carolina Gazette and Country Journal, Charleston
South Carolina Historical Magazine
Southern Agriculturist
Southern Literary Messenger
Southern Workman
Times, London
William and Mary Quarterly

Index